DALÍ IN 400 IMAGES

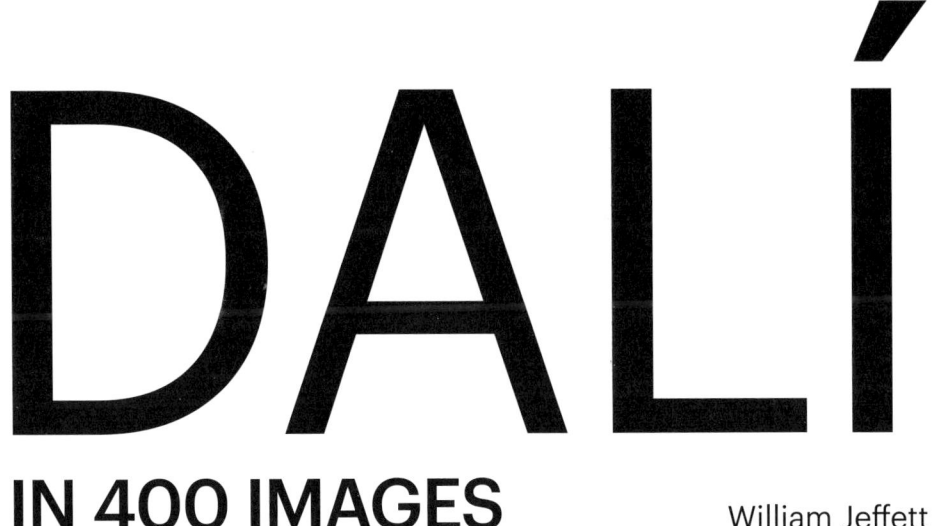

DALÍ

IN 400 IMAGES

William Jeffett

Ludion

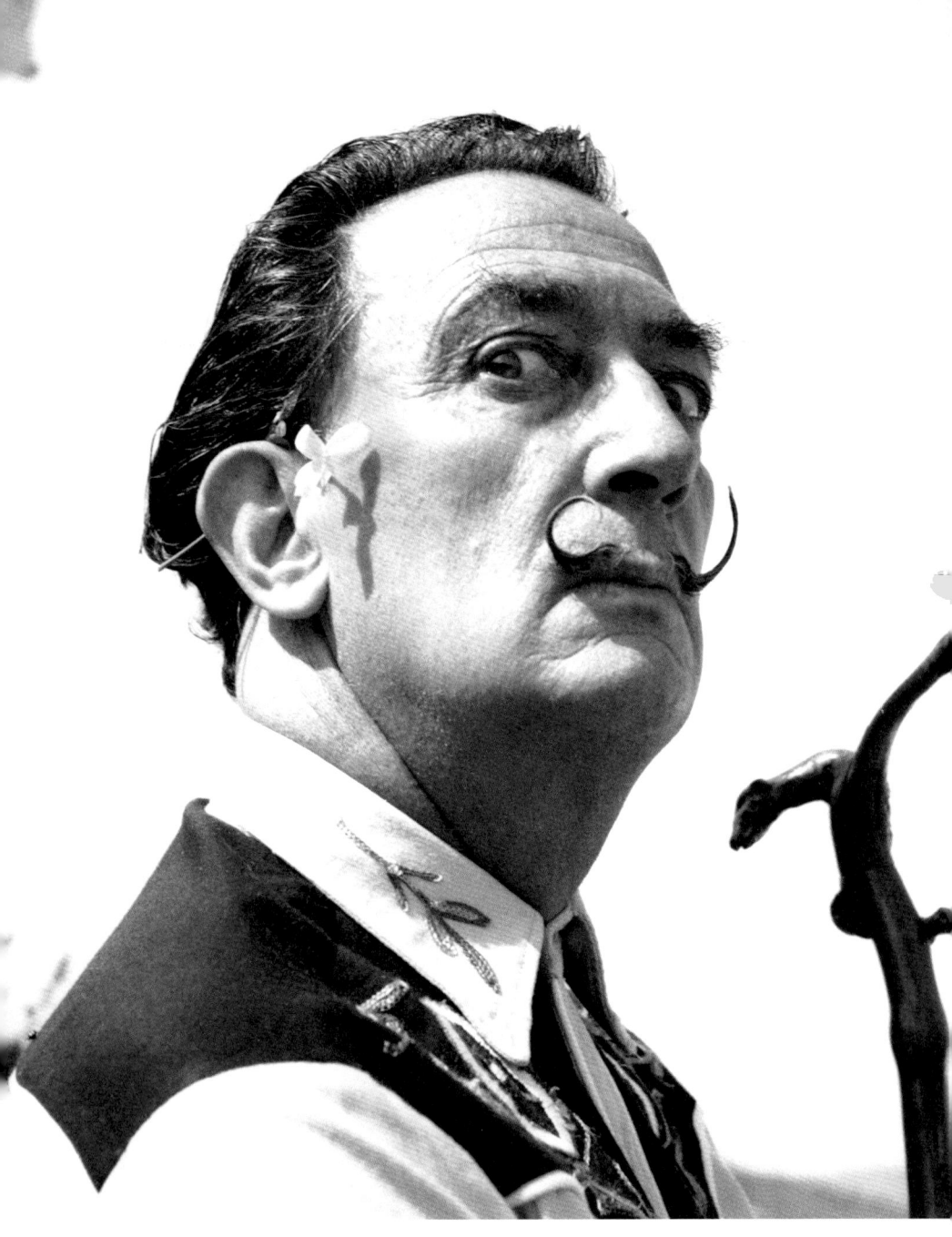

Lies Wiegman (photographer), Dalí, 1961. Collection of The Dalí Museum.

Introduction

The Catalan artist Salvador Dalí is one of the most famous artists of the twentieth century. Considered an eccentric figure and undoubtedly one of the most significant painters of the Surrealist movement, Dalí often gave the impression of forging a provocative personality around a personal myth informed by psychoanalysis and literary and philosophical references. While his personality is now well established and his major works widely reproduced, the scope and richness of his art remain little known.

Dalí was active in many areas of cultural activity, including set designs for film, ballet and opera, highly visible activities that helped contribute to his colourful public persona. He was also a prodigious writer, of essays, an autobiography and a novel, and of texts that he often wrote to accompany the work he presented in exhibitions.

From the mid-1920s, the young Dalí's paintings were exhibited and reproduced in numerous publications. As strange as some of his images may have seemed at first glance, his talent as a painter was recognised very early on, and by 1928, at the age of twenty-four, he was participating in international exhibitions. He therefore never worked in isolation or obscurity. During his first visit to Paris in 1926, he visited Picasso's studio and was integrated three years later into the Surrealist group and recognised with a solo exhibition. For the next decade, Dalí would remain a key figure of the movement.

The focus of this publication is on Dalí's painting and his writings on the subject. In particular, this book highlights Dalí's work through his exhibitions and public appearances at each stage of his career, with the aim of offering the reader a subtle understanding of the complexity and sophistication of his art.

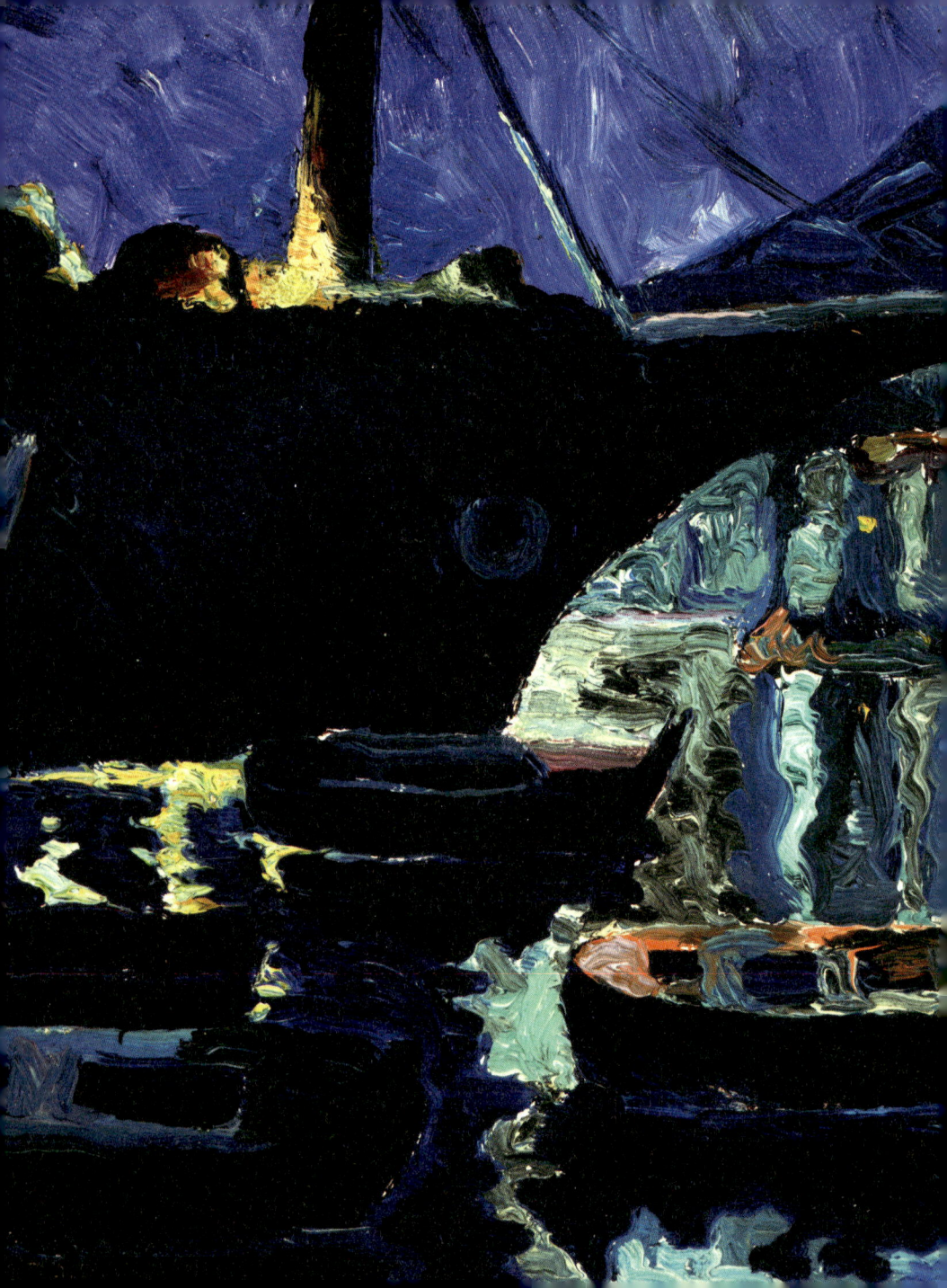

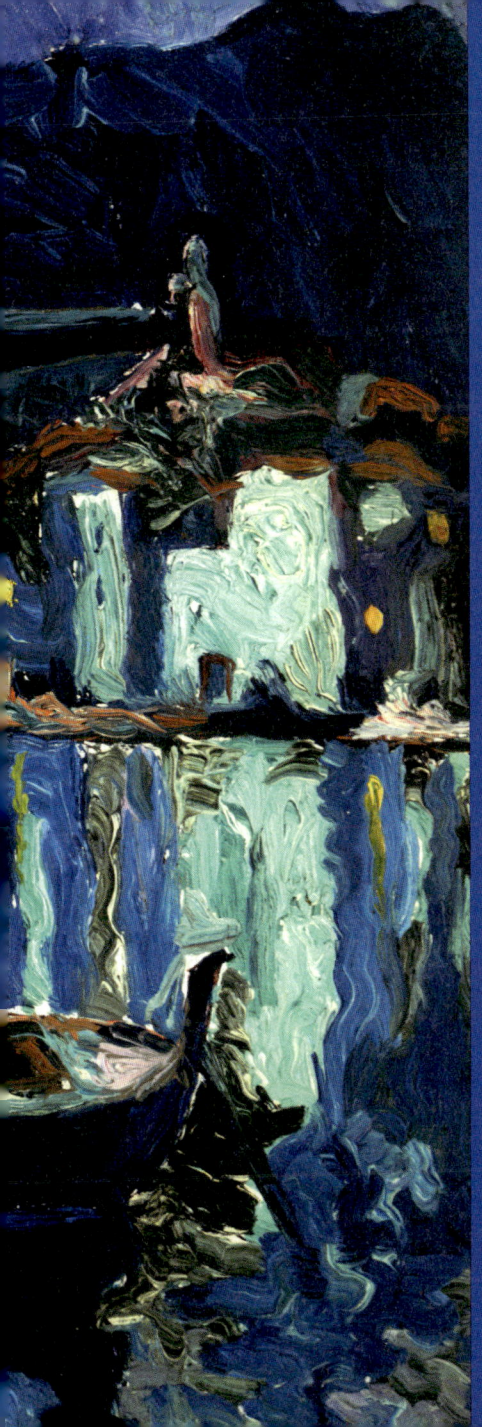

Dalí's Beginnings and Post-impressionism

1916–1924

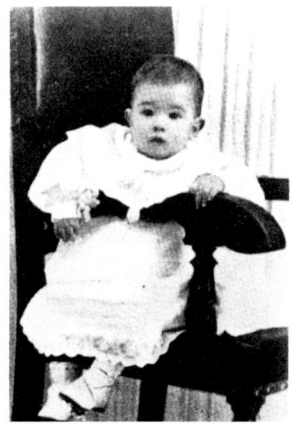

Dalí as a baby, c. 1905.

Salvador Dalí was born on 11 May 1904 in Figueres, a small, thriving city located in the Ampurdán plane in Catalonia, Spain, not far from the coastal fishing village of Cadaqués, to a prosperous and cultivated family where he grew up in comfort by the day's standards. His father was a prominent notary, a liberal Federalist who was not particularly interested in religion, while his mother was a practising Catholic. Dalí was a 'replacement' child – a child conceived to replace a missing sibling – his name, Salvador, belonged to both his father and the brother who had died the year before Dalí was born. During his adolescence, Dalí's mother also died, and his father married his aunt. Dalí would later make much of this early experience, along with his status as a replacement child, in his tell-all autobiography *The Secret Life of Salvador Dalí* (1942).

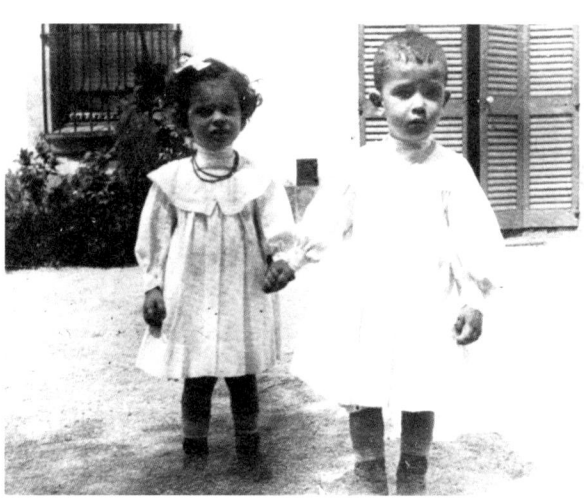

The young Dalí with his cousin Montserrat Dalí Pascual in Cabrils, Spain, c. 1907.

Dalí's Beginnings and Post-impressionism

His parents made sure the young Dalí received a fine education, and on the whole, the young student received good marks. He began studying art early in life and became active in his local artistic and cultural world in his teens.

Dalí showed a talent for art from an early age. He began to paint from around 1910 to 1914 before he was ten, though it is difficult to pinpoint an exact date on the execution of his first painting. His early works reveal an awareness of the traditional Catalan school of landscape painting, which dominated the art world in the first two decades of the century. In 1916, while a student in Figueres, Dalí was exposed to an important teacher, Juan Núñez Fernández (1877–1963), who was an expert in drawing and printmaking.

From around 1910 the Dalí family was also in touch with the Pichot family, all of whom were engaged in the various arts. During this time the Dalís began to spend their summers in Cadaqués, the coastal village nearby, where the already well-known Spanish artist Pablo Picasso (1881–1973) had visited and worked in the summer of 1910. In 1916, Ramon Pichot (1871–1925), a painter and friend of Picasso's, invited Dalí to use his summer home, an impressive Catalan farmhouse located near Figueres named Molí de la Torre (The Tower Mill). While he was there, Dalí was impressed by Pichot's canvases, which could best be described as a form of Post-impressionism, and Dalí later wrote of, 'My discovery of French Impressionism...'. Dalí was immediately converted to an exploration of this style, which marked his work for a considerable period, well into the mid-1920s. As Dalí ran out of domestic space, the Pichots also made Ramon's studio in Cadaqués available to him.

Though the young Dalí had not yet travelled abroad, he was well informed about the arts through publications often supplied to him by his uncle Anselm Domènech Ferrés, who owned Barcelona's Librería Verdaguer. Dalí also owned a set of Gowans & Gray's art books, monographs devoted to the Old Masters, and was aware of, or attended, a series of international and national exhibitions staged in the Palau de les Belles Arts in Barcelona. Notable ones that included works of French Impressionism included those of 1907 and 1917, while we know from his diaries that Dalí attended the 1920 Spring Exhibition, a national exhibition full of examples of Catalan painting marked by French influences. In the same year, also in Barcelona, the Galeries Dalmau presented the Exposició d'Art francès d'avantguarda, with an accompanying catalogue that included both Post-impressionists and artists of the emerging avant-garde, including Henri Matisse (1869–1954). While Dalí may not have seen this exhibition, it is likely that he knew of its illustrated catalogue from his art historian friend Joan Subias Galter (1897–1984). In his diaries from 1920, Dalí extolled the French Impressionists and revealed a wide knowledge gleaned from his extensive reading of texts on their work. Other sources for his thinking at this time derive from unpublished manuscripts by Dalí now in the Museu Abelló in Mollet del Vallès near Barcelona. From these sources it is clear that Dalí greatly admired Pierre-Auguste Renoir (1841–1919), Claude Monet (1840–1926), Paul Cézanne (1839–1906) and Matisse, among other French painters.

The Galeries Dalmau would prove to be important for Dalí; he first exhibited there in a group show of students in early 1922 and they would later represent his work. Also in 1922, Dalmau presented an exhibition of work by the French painter Francis Picabia (1879–1953) with an introduction by the French writer and poet André Breton (1896–1966) and a lecture staged by Breton at the cultural association the Ateneu, entitled 'Caractères de l'évolution moderne et ce qui en participe'. Dalí did not see this exhibition as he had just begun his studies at the Academy of Fine Arts in Madrid, however it is likely that he would have heard of it while at the Residencia de Estudiantes, where he lived while studying in Madrid, and would have become familiar with the many new ideas related to the avant-garde. These ranged from his interest in Cézanne to the post-war return to order represented in part by the review *L'Esprit Nouveau*, which Dalí subscribed to.

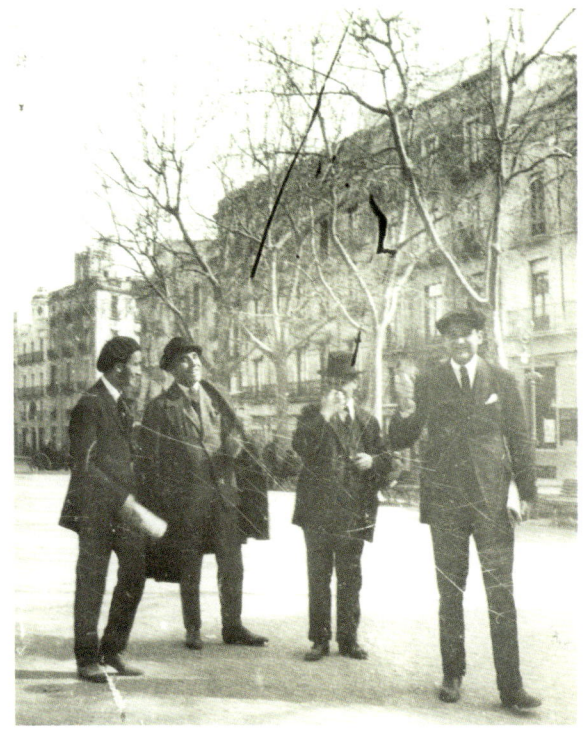

Dalí with three other men, *c.* 1920.

1916–1924

Before he left for Madrid, probably in around 1921, Dalí's uncle Anselm sent him a book on behalf of Ramon Pichot, who was living in Paris at the time. The book was the Italian painter and sculptor Umberto Boccioni's (1882–1916) *Pittura scultura futuriste (dinamismo plastico)* (1914), a work that exposed Dalí to a host of new positions ranging from Futurism to Cubism. At this point Dalí abruptly rejected Cézanne and Impressionism. After arriving in Madrid, the young artist's style changed rapidly as he explored a wide variety of avant-garde positions. These styles ranged from Expressionism to the Purism related to *L'Esprit Nouveau* and eventually, especially by 1924, to Cubism. Dalí's earlier representations of Cadaqués in painterly terms had become increasingly structured, first under the influence of Cézanne and later on in positions related to Cubism, with his increasingly geometrical representation of the village's buildings. A host of factors contributed to this development, ranging from the French post-war tendency 'Return to Order' – a term coined by the French poet, artist and future film director Jean Cocteau (1889–1963) that proposed a return to Classicism – and the Catalan Noucentisme, which were both conservative twists on avant-garde styles. For some time, Dalí's main subject remained his beloved Cadaqués.

While in Madrid, Dalí and his peers at the Academy of Fine Arts and the Residencia were impressed by the more progressive faculty, especially the painter Daniel Vázquez Díaz (1882–1969), who had lived in Paris and known both the Spanish painter Juan Gris (1887–1927) and Picasso and had worked with the language of Cubism. When Vázquez Díaz was passed over for the Chair of Painting position in the autumn of 1923, Dalí and other students took the side of the Andalucian painter. While Dalí was not the instigator of the ensuing protest, he was blamed and suspended for the remainder of the academic year. On his return to Figueres, Dalí took advantage of this time to learn printmaking from his former teacher Núñez. During this period Dalí's father also acquired a printing press for his son and Dalí continued to explore the language of Cubism in painting.

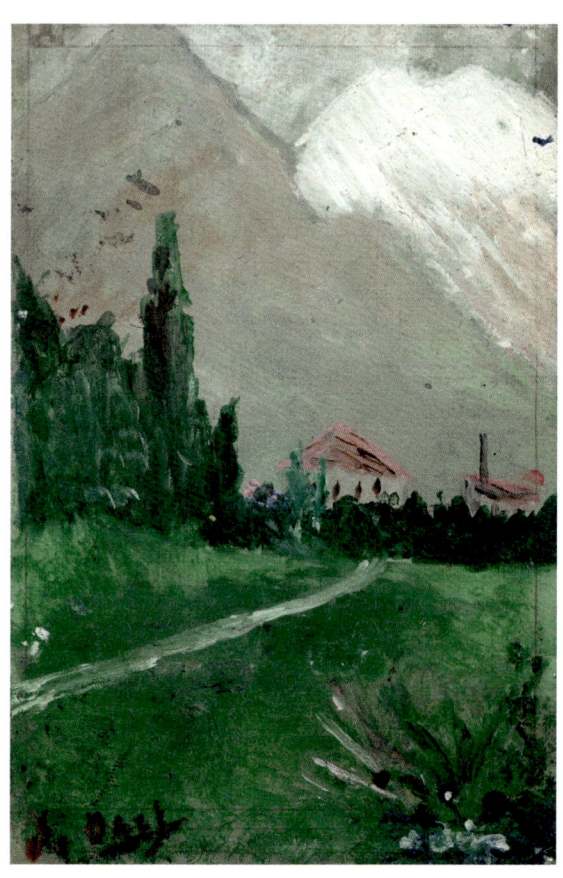

1
Landscape
1910–1914
Oil on cardboard, 14 × 9 cm
The Dalí Museum, St. Petersburg, Florida

Dalí's Beginnings and Post-impressionism

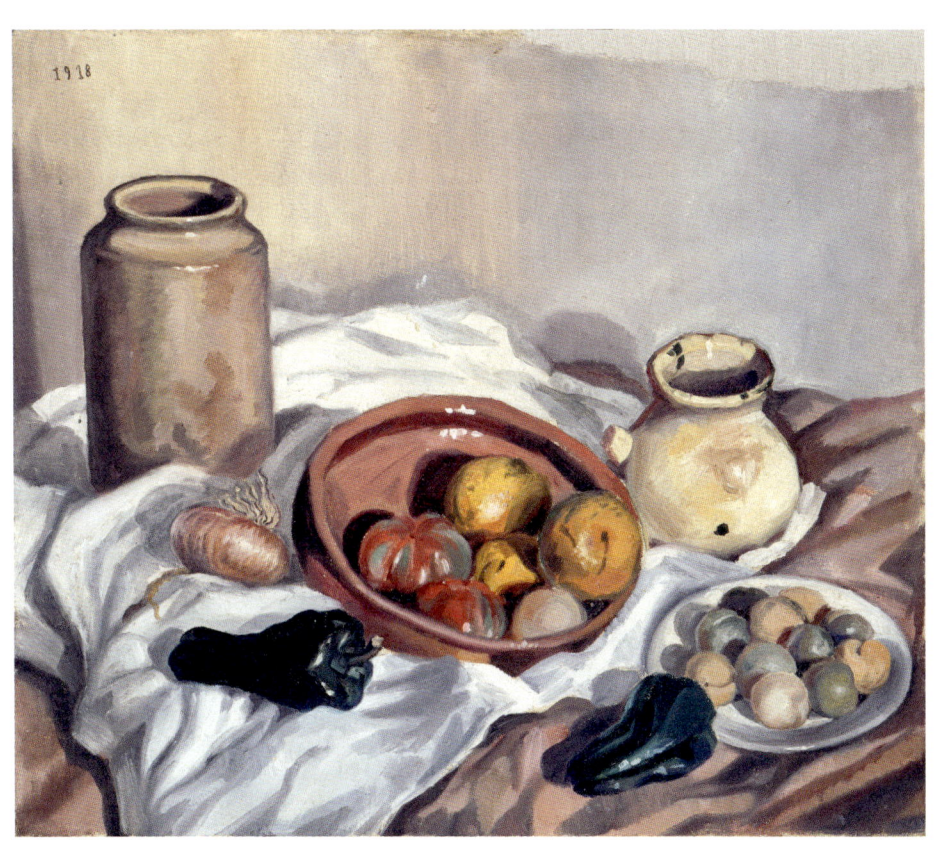

2
Still Life
1918
Oil on canvas, 60 × 70 cm
Museo Nacional Centro de Arte Reina Sofía, Madrid. Dalí bequest

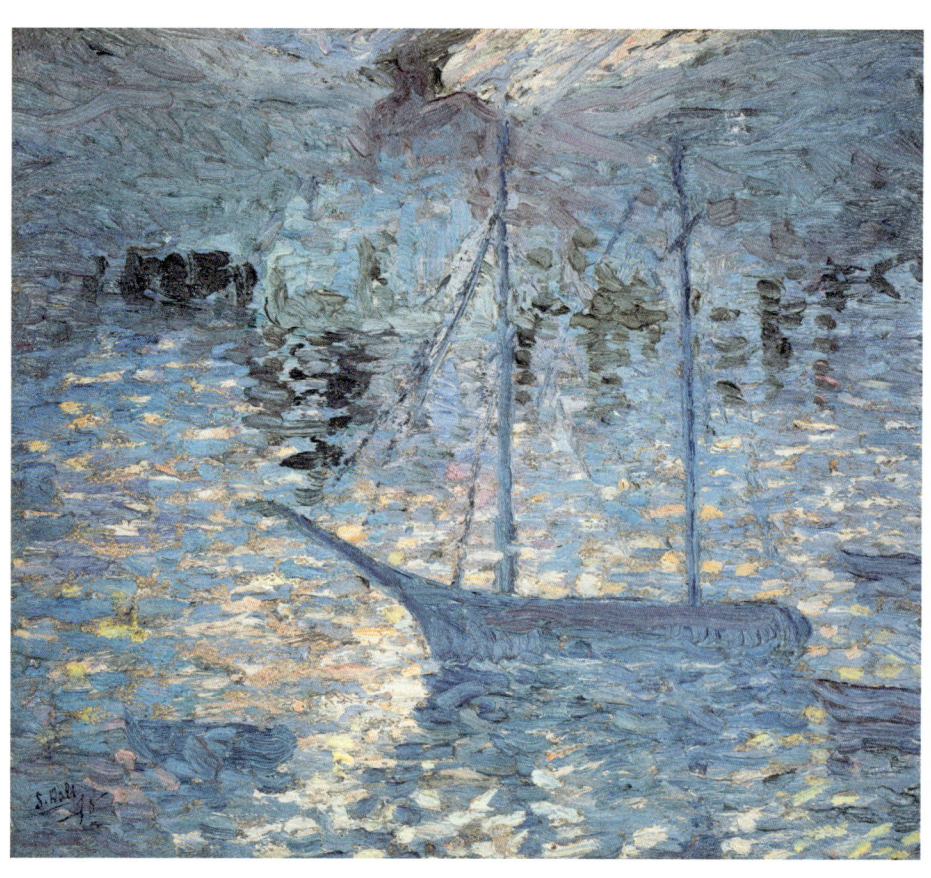

3
Moonlit Night
1918
Oil on canvas, 26 × 31 cm
The Dalí Museum, St. Petersburg, Florida

Dalí's Beginnings and Post-impressionism

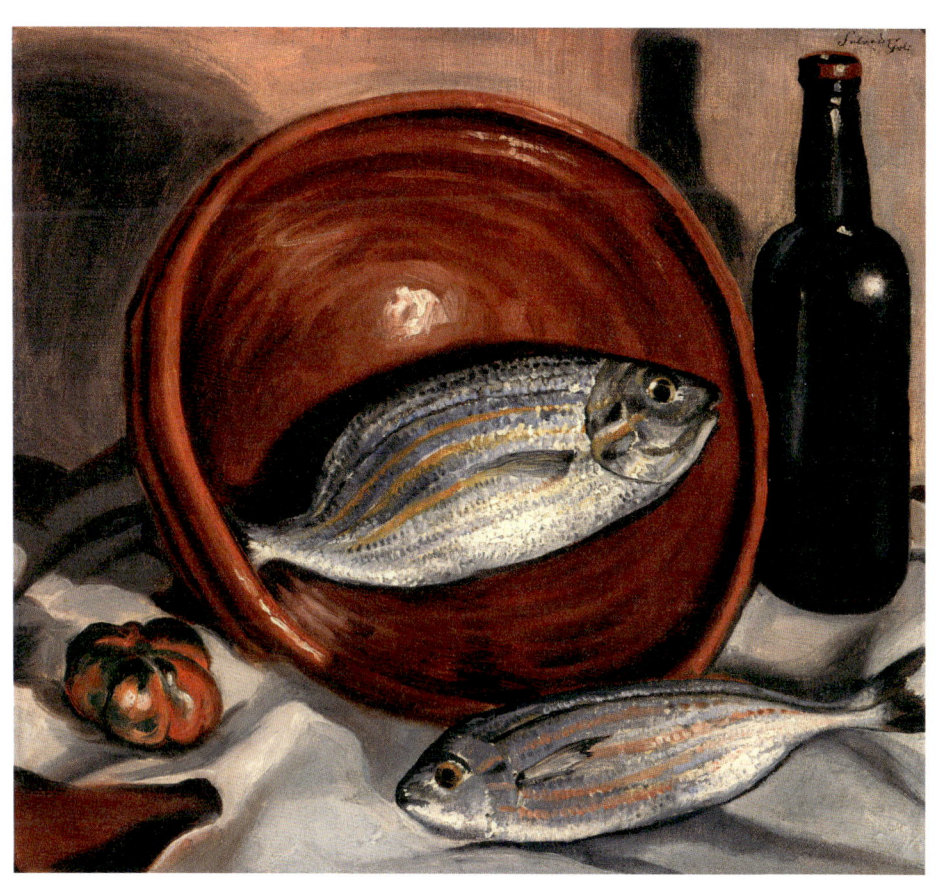

4
Still Life. Fish with Red Bowl
c. 1918
Oil on canvas, 50.2 × 55.3 cm
The Dalí Museum, St. Petersburg, Florida

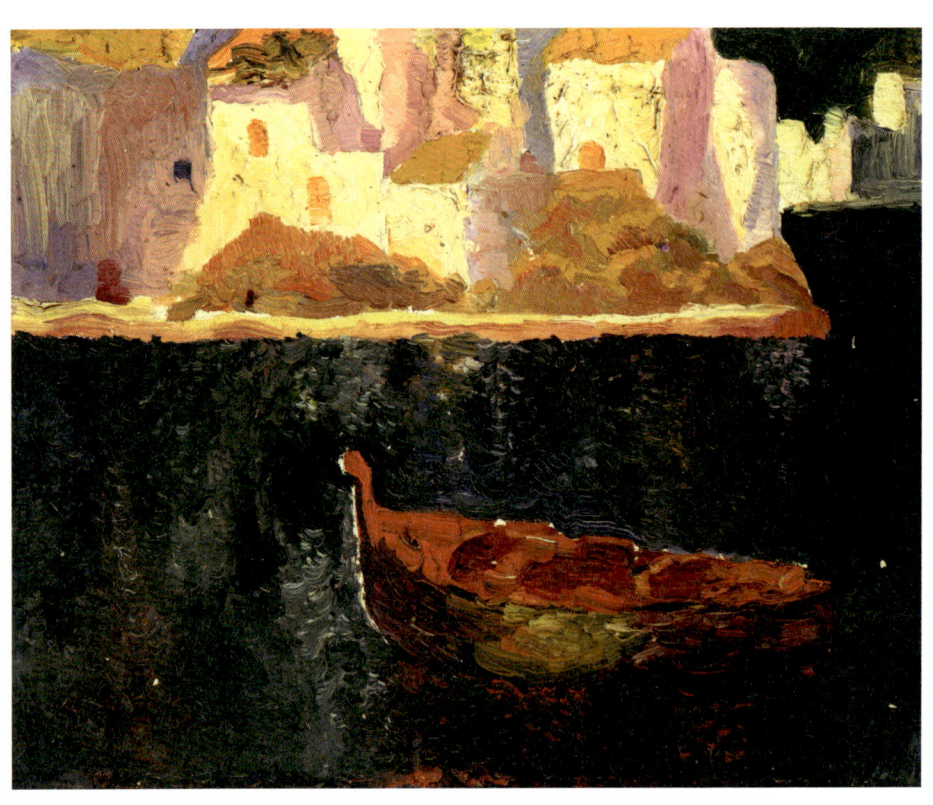

5
Punta Es Baluard in the Riba d'en Pichot, Cadaqués
c. 1918
Oil on canvas, 21 × 28 cm
The Dalí Museum, St. Petersburg, Florida

Dalí's Beginnings and Post-impressionism

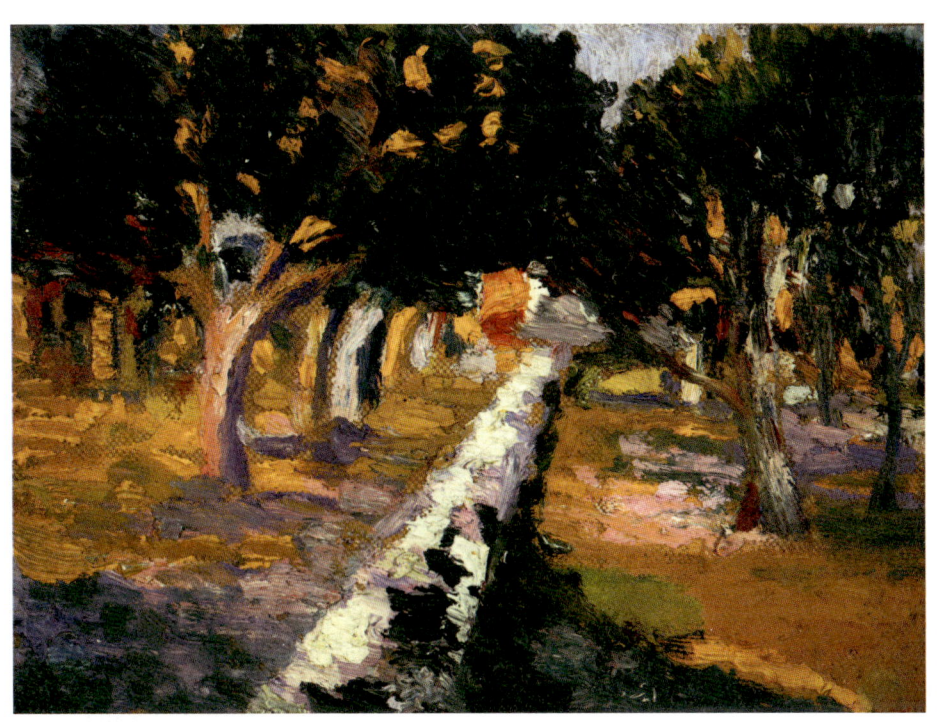

6
Vegetable Garden at Es Llaner, Cadaqués
c. 1918
Oil on canvas, 20 × 27.5 cm
The Dalí Museum, St. Petersburg, Florida

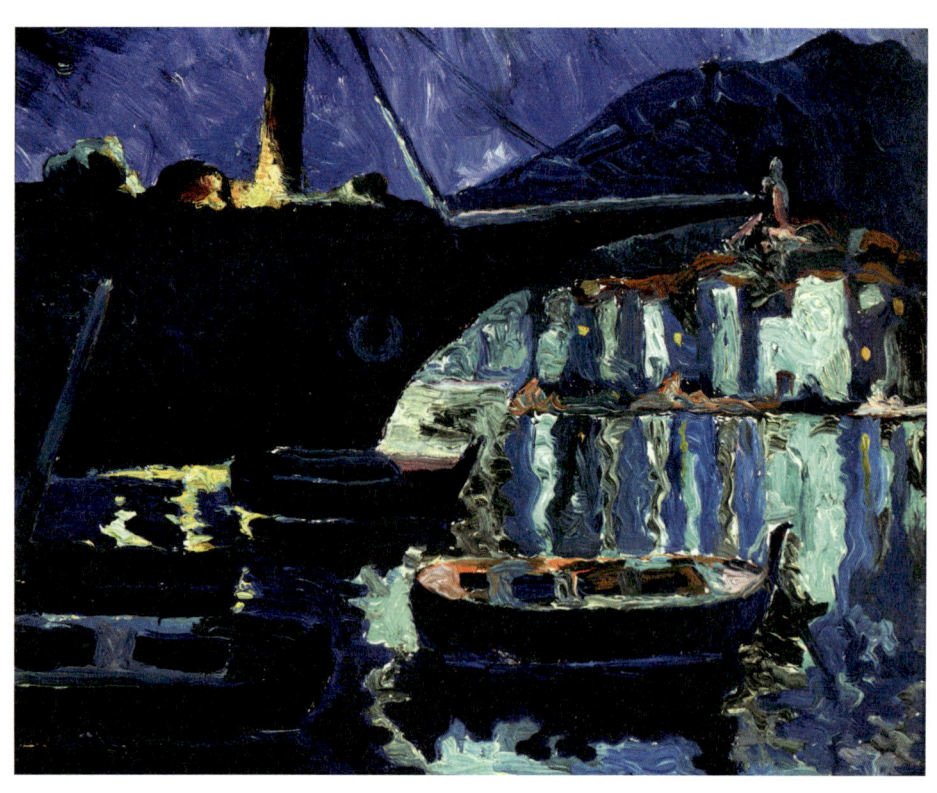

7
Port of Cadaqués (Night)
c. 1918
Oil on canvas, 18.8 × 26.4 cm
The Dalí Museum, St. Petersburg, Florida

Dalí's Beginnings and Post-impressionism

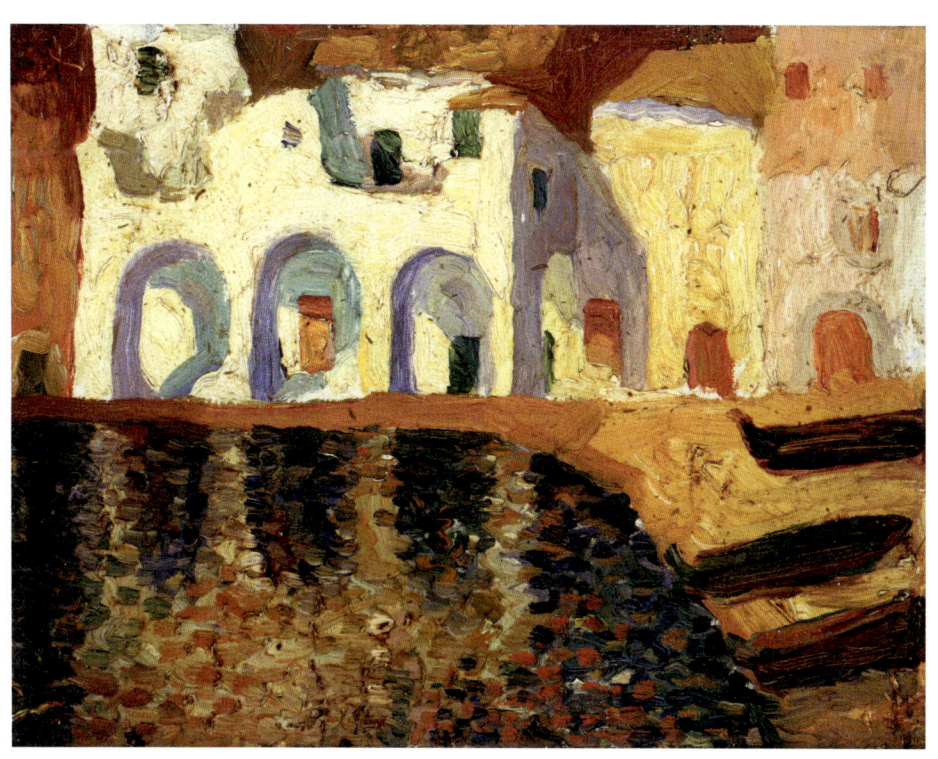

8
Port Alguer, Cadaqués
c. 1918
Oil on canvas, 21.5 × 28 cm
The Dalí Museum, St. Petersburg, Florida

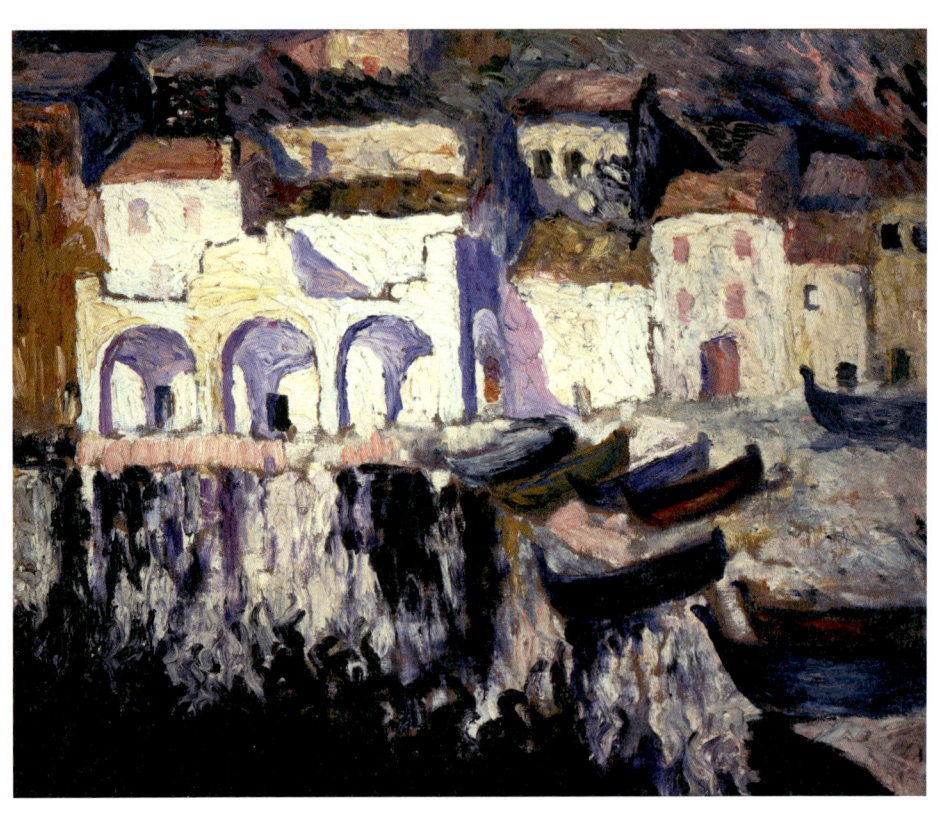

9
View of Port Alguer, Cadaqués
c. 1918
Oil on canvas, 44 × 55.3 cm
The Dalí Museum, St. Petersburg, Florida

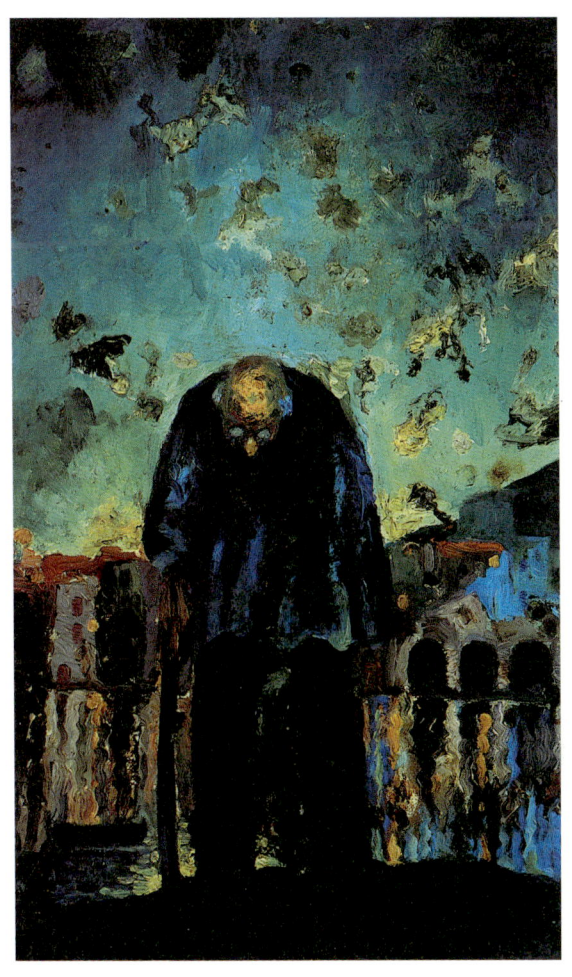

10
Old Man at the Twilight Hour
c. 1918
Oil on canvas, 50 × 30 cm
Fundació Gala-Salvador Dalí, Figueres

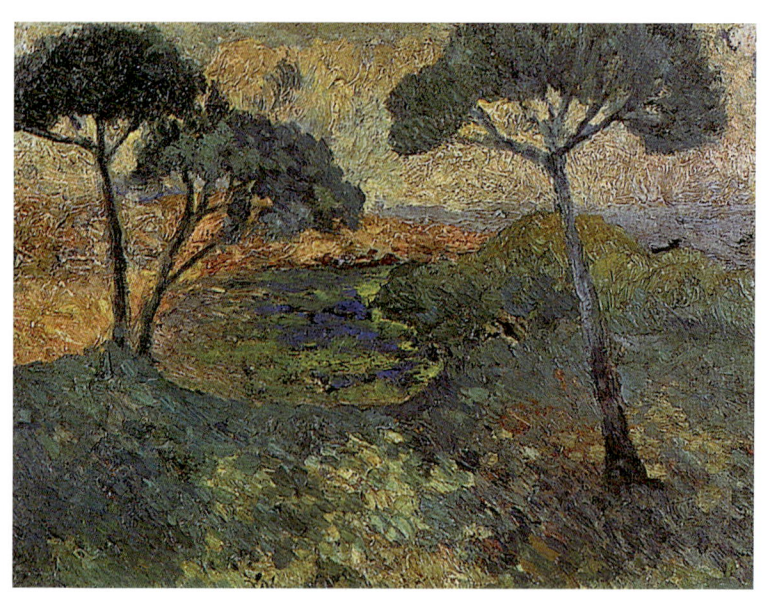

11
The Three Pines
c. 1918
Oil on canvas, 28 × 38 cm
Fundació Gala-Salvador Dalí, Figueres

Dalí's Beginnings and Post-impressionism

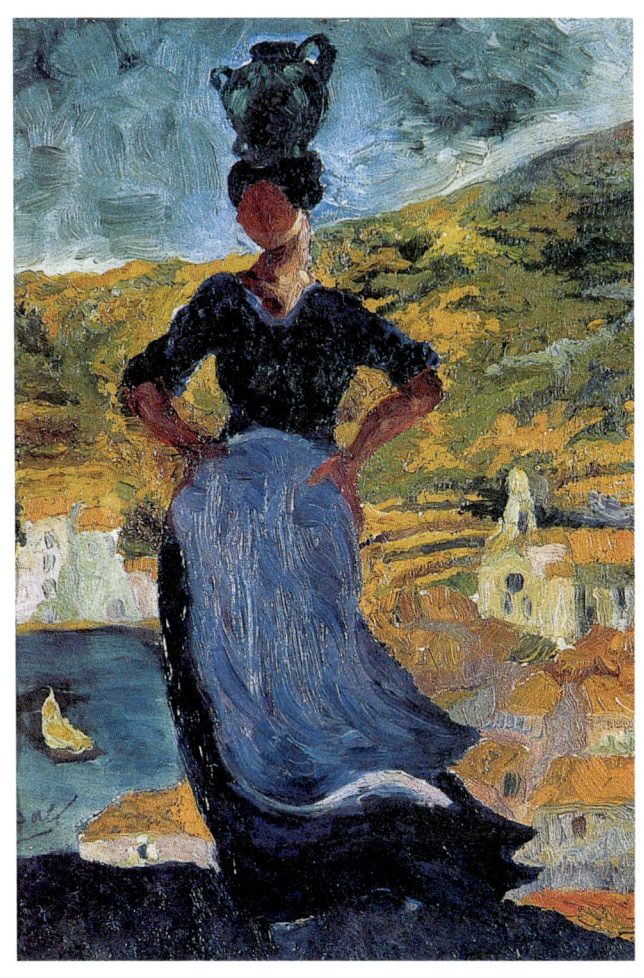

12
The Woman with the Pitcher
c. 1918
Oil on canvas, 34.6 × 26 cm (measurements framed)
Private collection

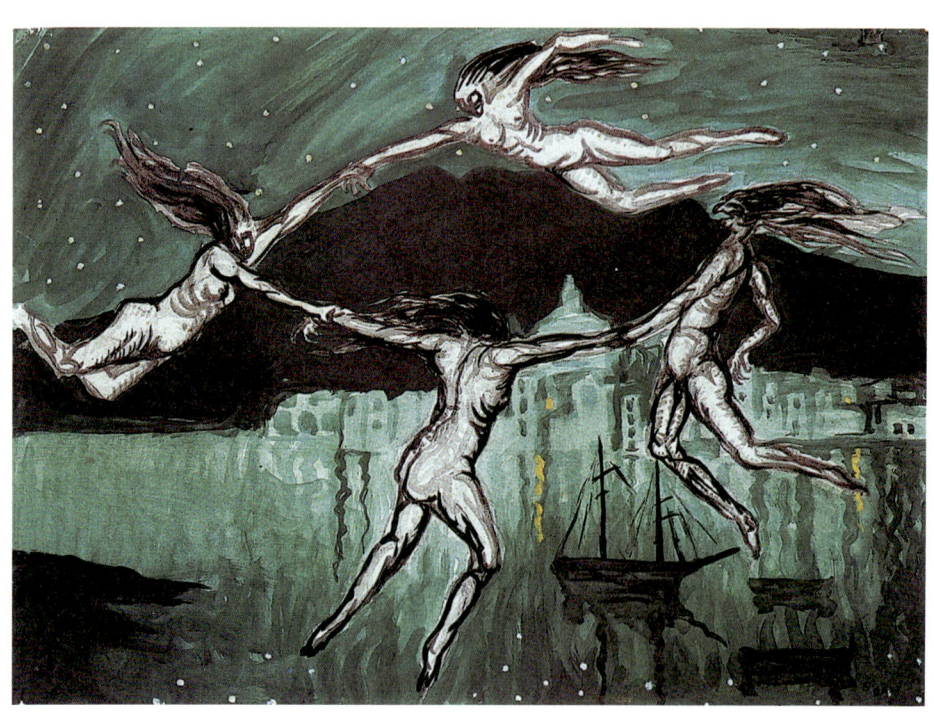

13
The Sardana of the Witches
c. 1918
Watercolour, oil and ink wash on paper, 42 × 59.5 cm
The Dalí Museum, St. Petersburg, Florida

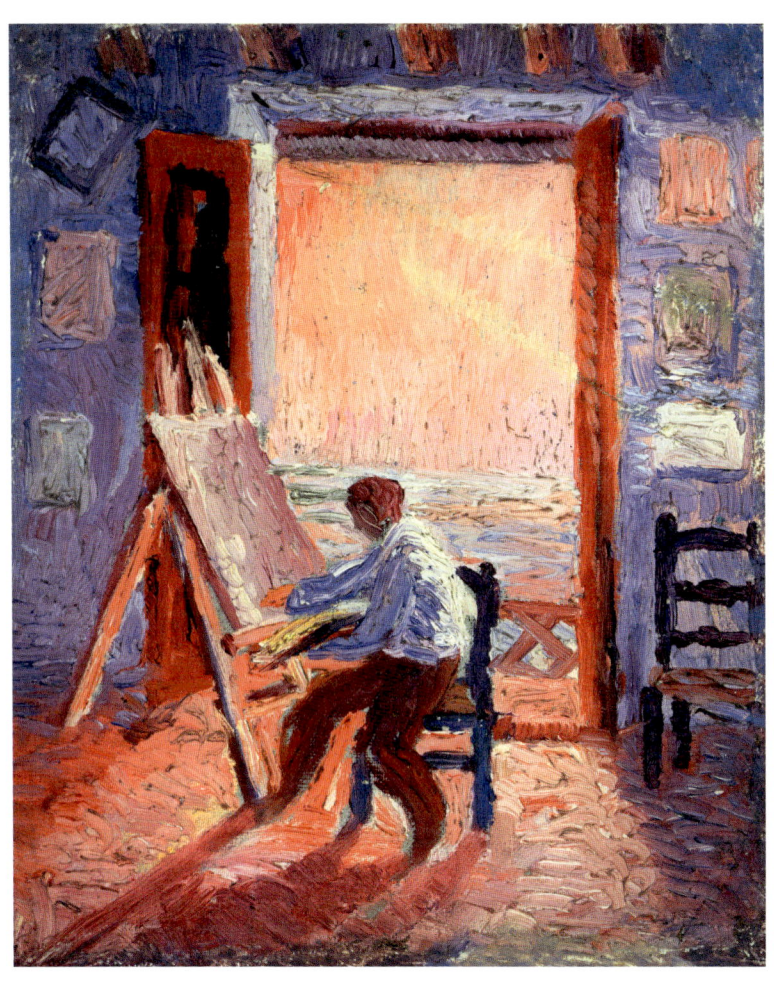

14
Self-Portrait in the Studio
c. 1919
Oil on canvas, 26.7 × 21 cm
The Dalí Museum, St. Petersburg, Florida

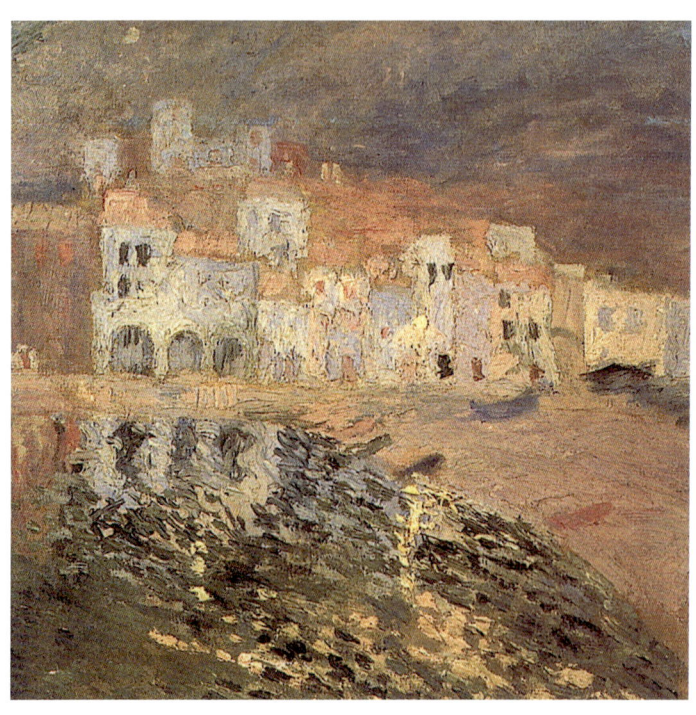

15

Landscape of Cadaqués. Port Alguer

c. 1919

Oil on canvas, 36 × 38.5 cm

Fundació Gala-Salvador Dalí, Figueres. Dalí bequest

Dalí's Beginnings and Post-impressionism

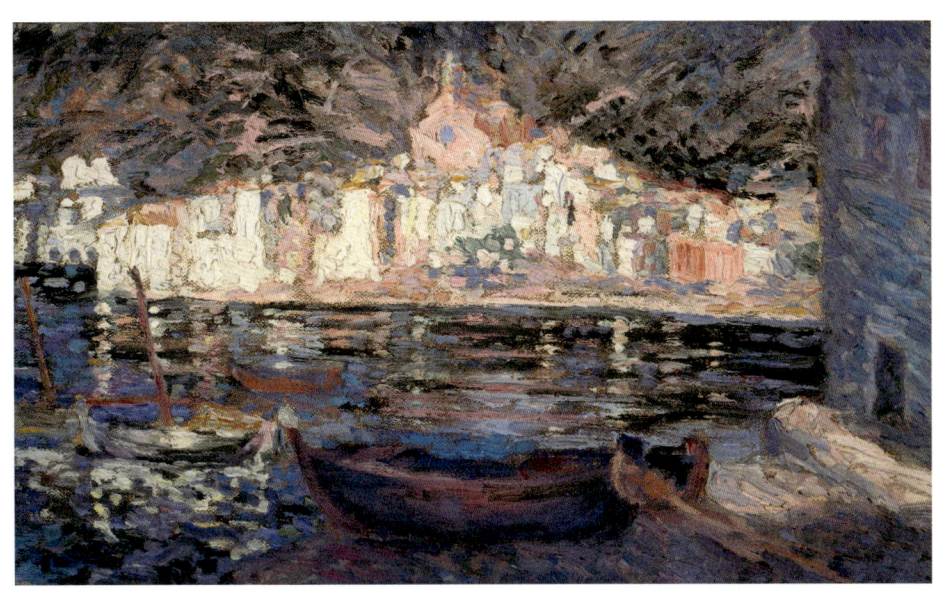

16
View of Cadaqués from Es Pianc
c. 1919
Oil on canvas, 29.2 × 48.3 cm
The Dalí Museum, St. Petersburg, Florida

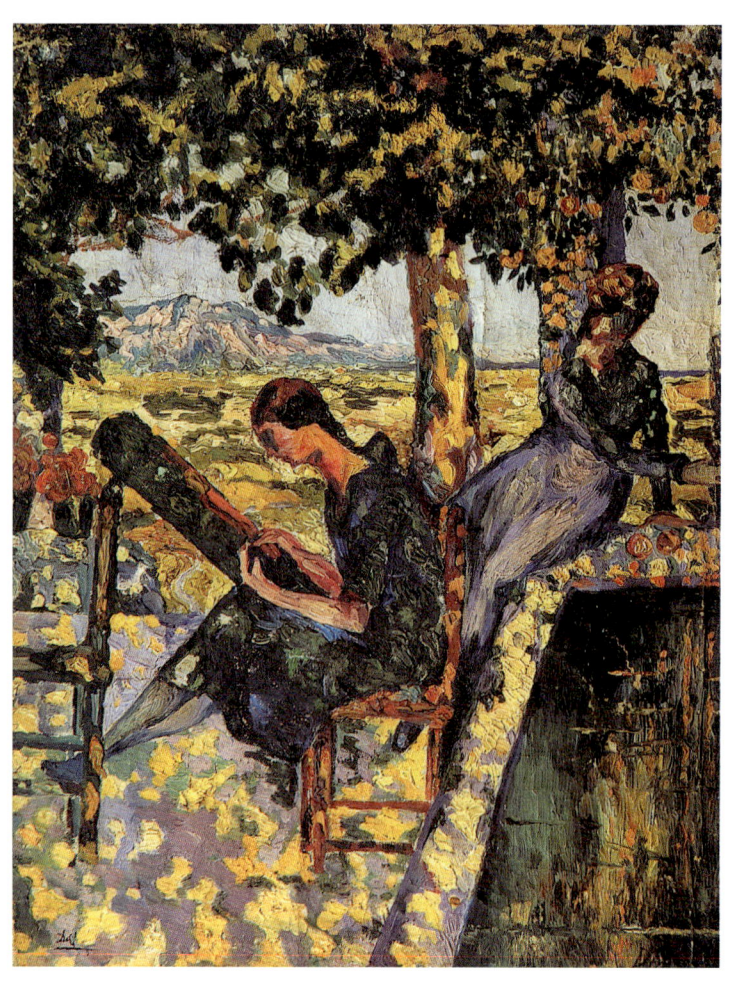

17

Girls in a Garden. The Cousins

c. 1919

Oil on canvas, 53 × 41 cm

Morohashi Museum of Modern Art, Fukushima Prefecture, Japan

Dalí's Beginnings and Post-impressionism

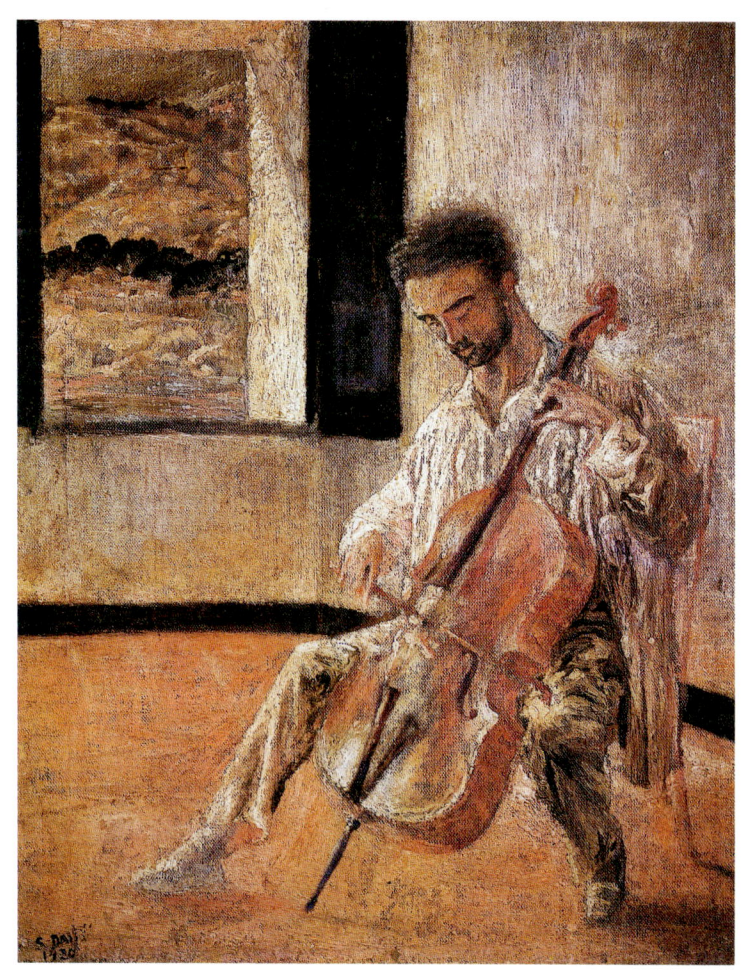

18
Portrait of the Cellist Ricard Pichot
1920
Oil on canvas, 61.5 × 50 cm
Fundació Gala-Salvador Dalí, Figueres

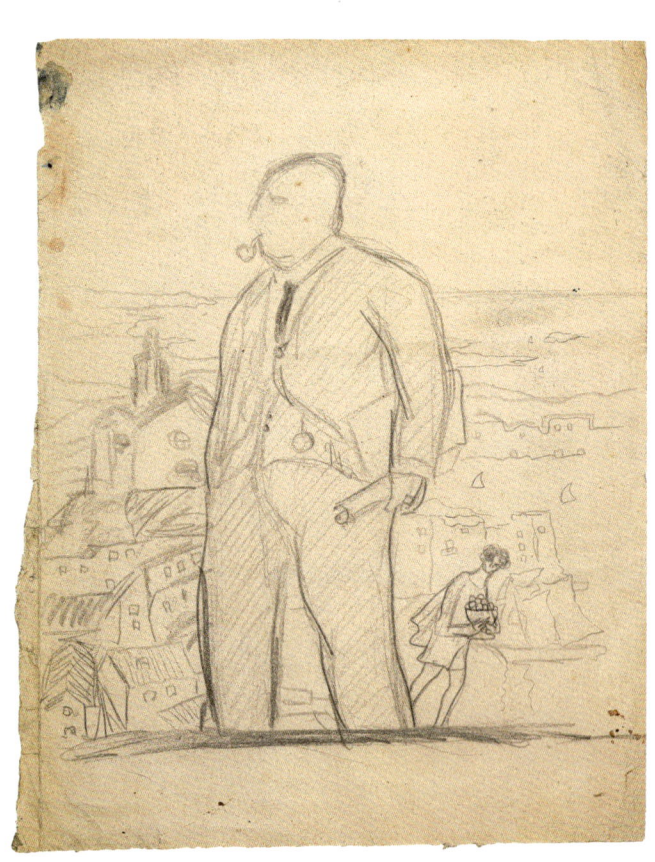

19
Study for "Portrait of My Father"
1920
Pencil on paper, 32.5 × 26 cm
Fundació Gala-Salvador Dalí, Figueres. Dalí bequest

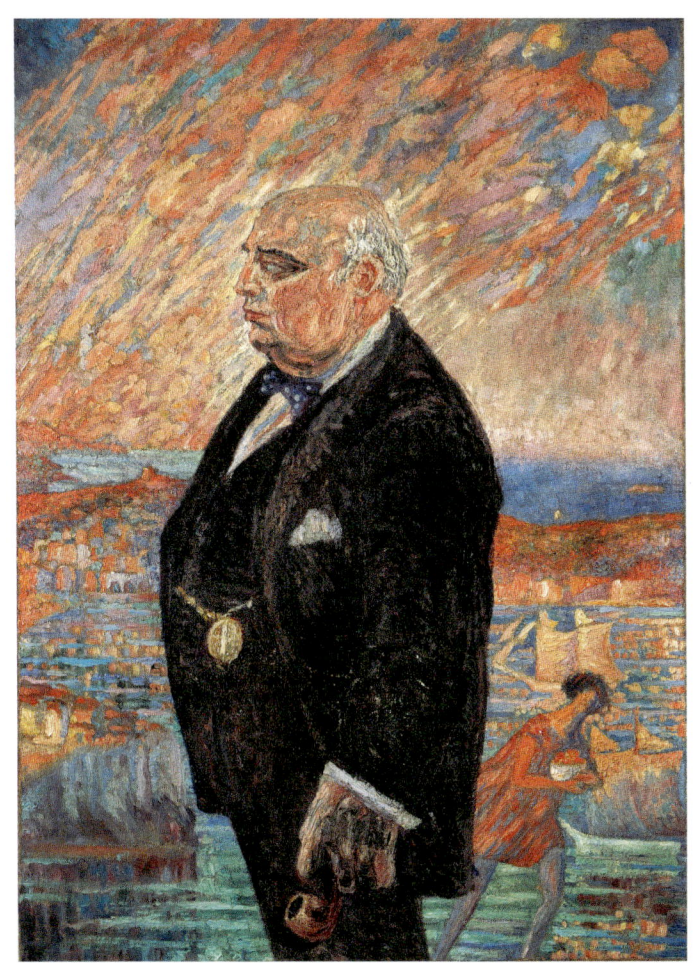

20
Portrait of My Father
1920
Oil on canvas, 91 × 66.5 cm
Fundació Gala-Salvador Dalí, Figueres. Dalí bequest

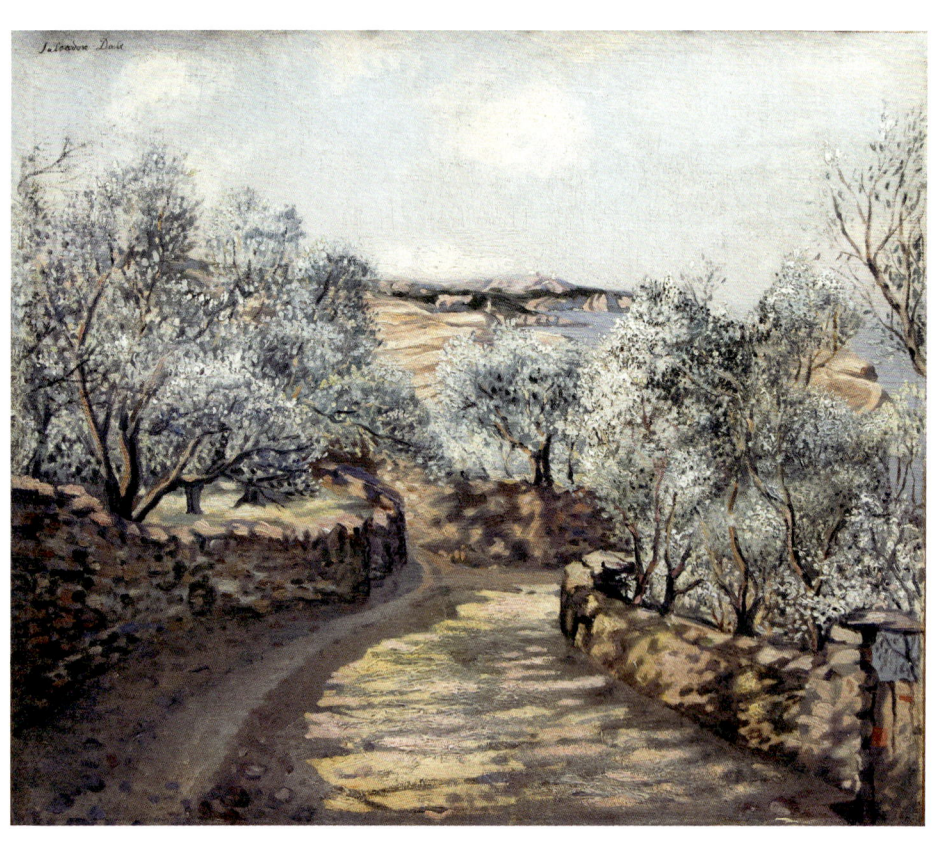

21
Camí de Portlligat. Cadaqués (The Lane to Portlligat. Cadaqués)
c. 1921
Oil on canvas, 57.8 × 68 cm
The Dalí Museum, St. Petersburg, Florida

Dalí's Beginnings and Post-impressionism

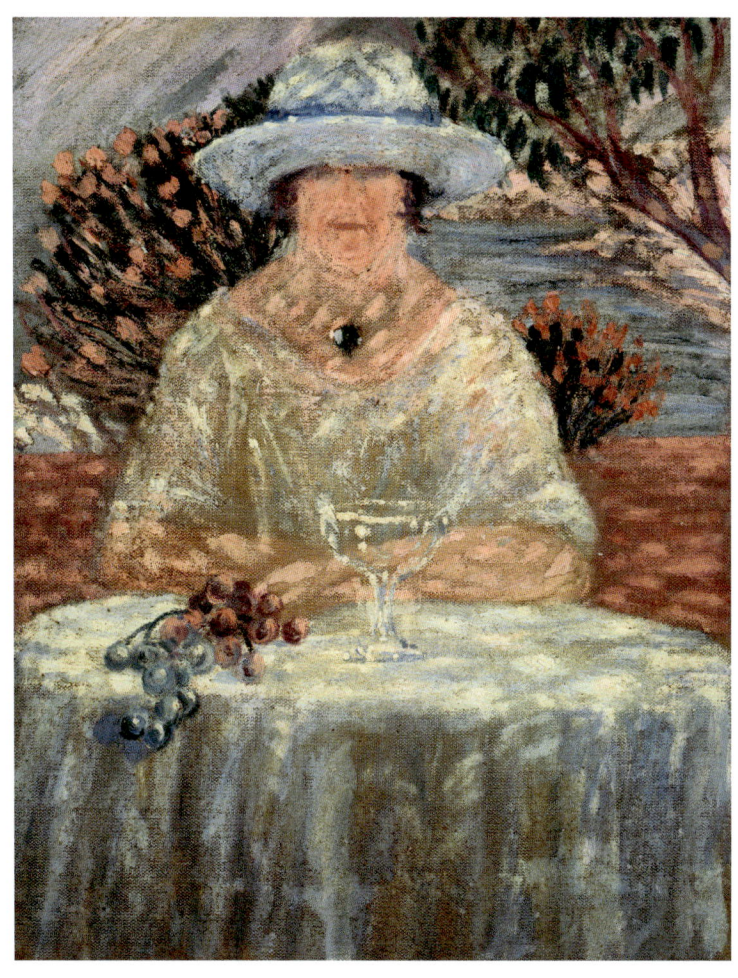

22
Portrait of "la Tieta" (Catalina Domènech Ferrer)
c. 1920
Oil on canvas, 52.7 × 41.3 cm
The Dalí Museum, St. Petersburg, Florida

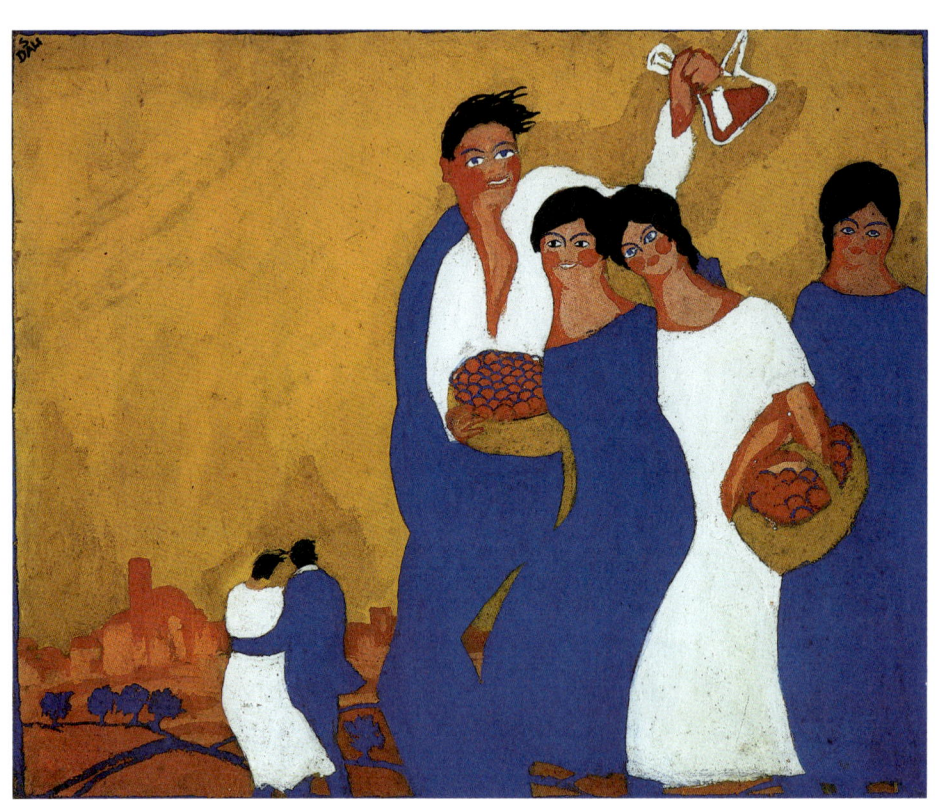

23
Poster for the Fair of the Holy Cross
1921
Gouache on paper, 52 × 64 cm
The Dalí Museum, St. Petersburg, Florida

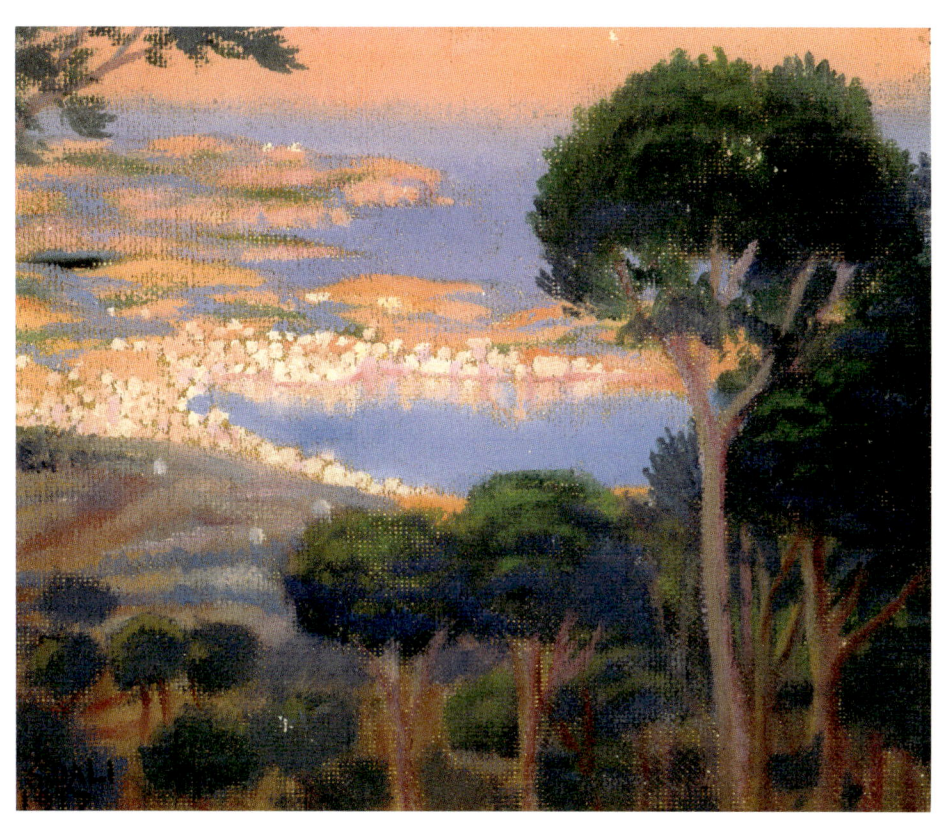

24
Paisatge de Cadaqués (Landscape of Cadaqués)
c. 1921
Oil on canvas, 39.4 × 48.3 cm
The Dalí Museum, St. Petersburg, Florida

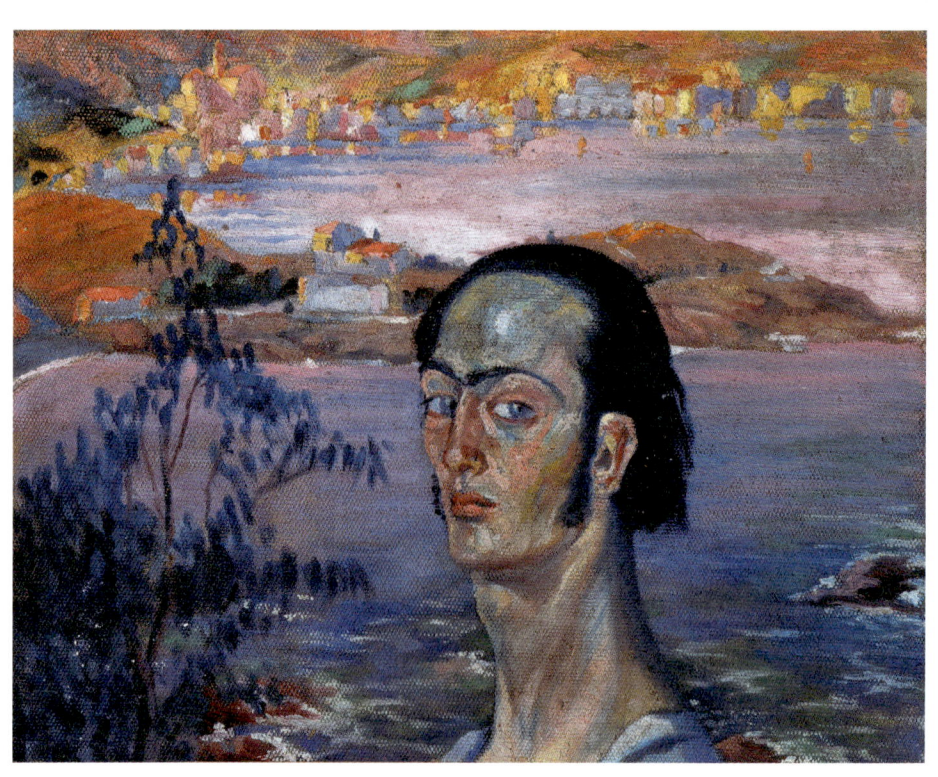

25

Self-Portrait with Raphaelesque Neck

c. 1921

Oil on canvas, 40.5 × 53 cm

Fundació Gala-Salvador Dalí, Figueres. Dalí bequest

Dalí's Beginnings and Post-impressionism

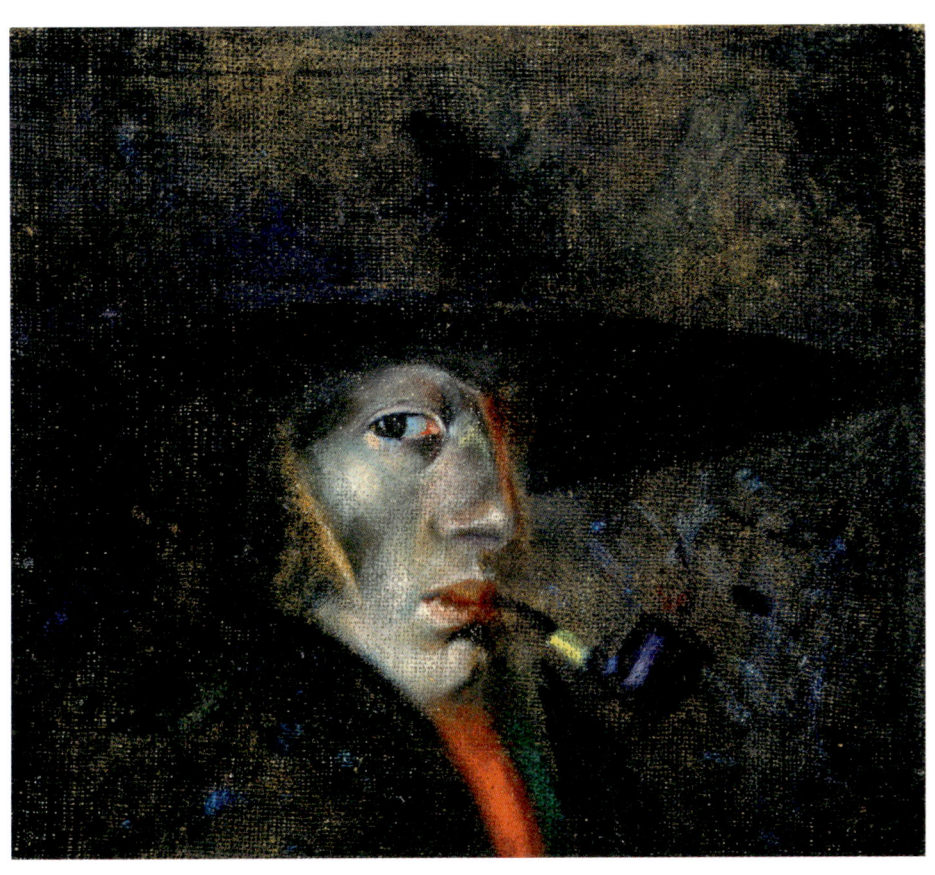

26
Self-Portrait
c. 1921
Oil on canvas, 36.8 × 41.9 cm
The Dalí Museum, St. Petersburg, Florida

1916–1924

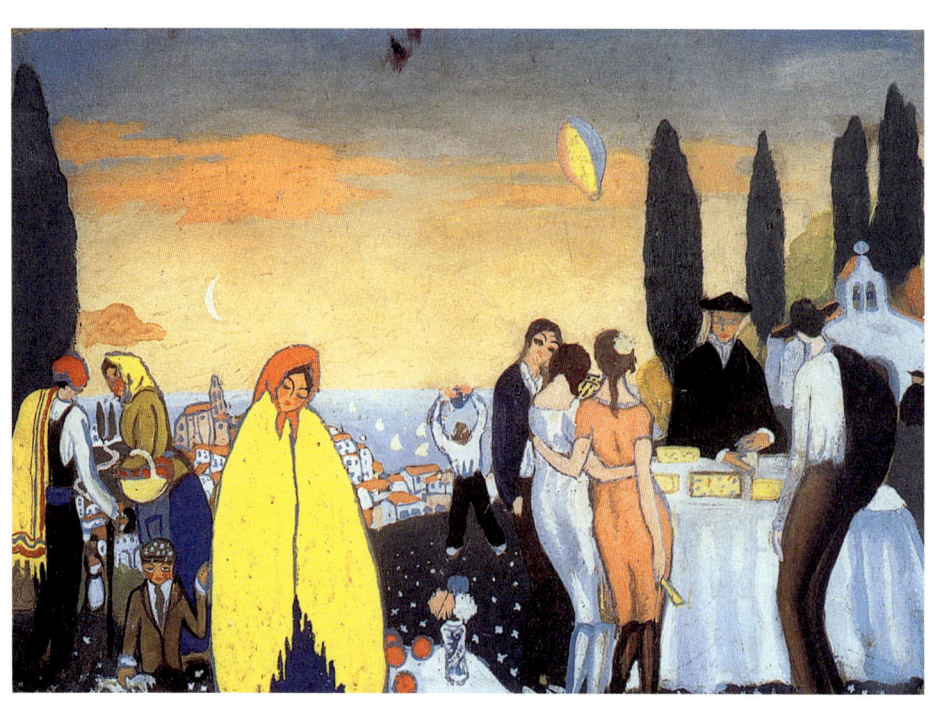

27
La festa a l'ermita (Fiesta at the Hermitage)
c. 1921
Tempera on cardboard, 52 × 75 cm
Town Hall of Figueres, on permanent deposit at the Fundació Gala-Salvador Dalí, Figueres

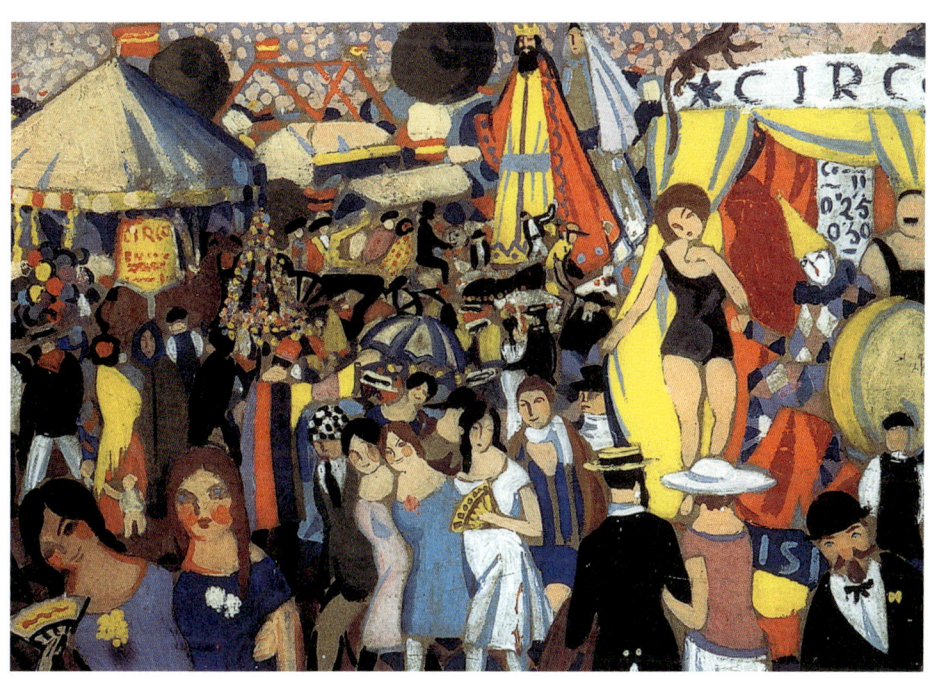

28
The Fair of the Holy Cross at Figueres
c. 1922
Tempera on cardboard, 52 × 75 cm
Town Hall of Figueres, on permanent deposit at the Fundació Gala-Salvador Dalí, Figueres

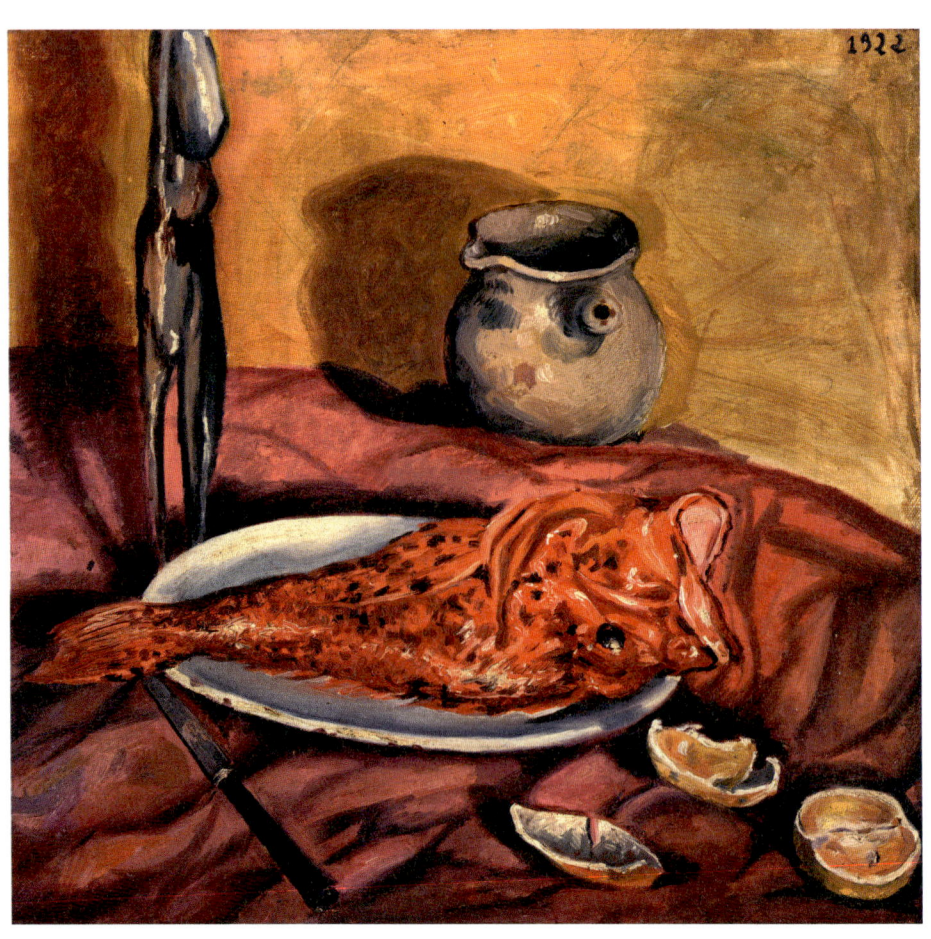

29
Still Life with Scorpion-Fish
1922
Oil on canvas, 54.3 × 57.2 cm
The Dalí Museum, St. Petersburg, Florida

Dalí's Beginnings and Post-impressionism

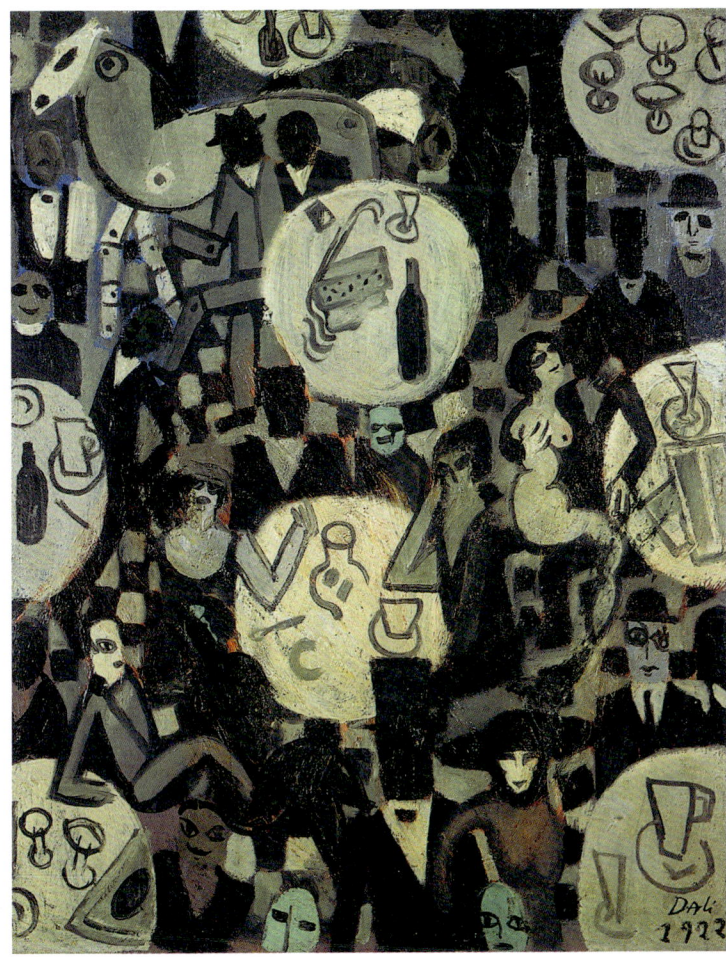

30
Cabaret Scene
1922
Oil on canvas, 52 × 41 cm
Morohashi Museum of Modern Art, Fukushima Prefecture, Japan

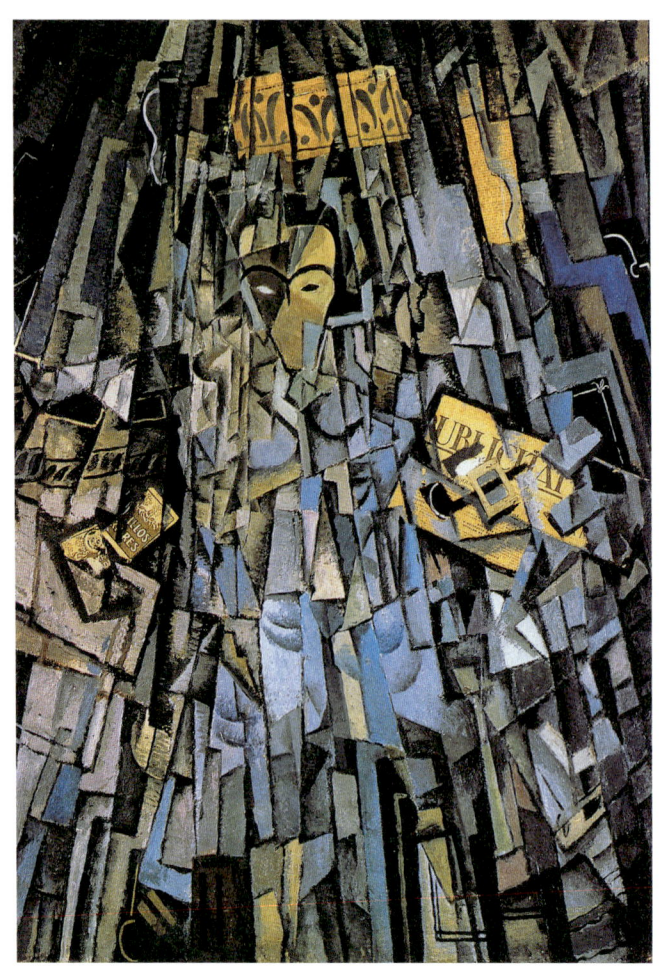

31
Cubist Self-Portrait
1923
Oil and collage on cardboard on wood panel, 104 × 75 cm
Museo Nacional Centro de Arte Reina Sofía, Madrid. Dalí bequest

Dalí's Beginnings and Post-impressionism

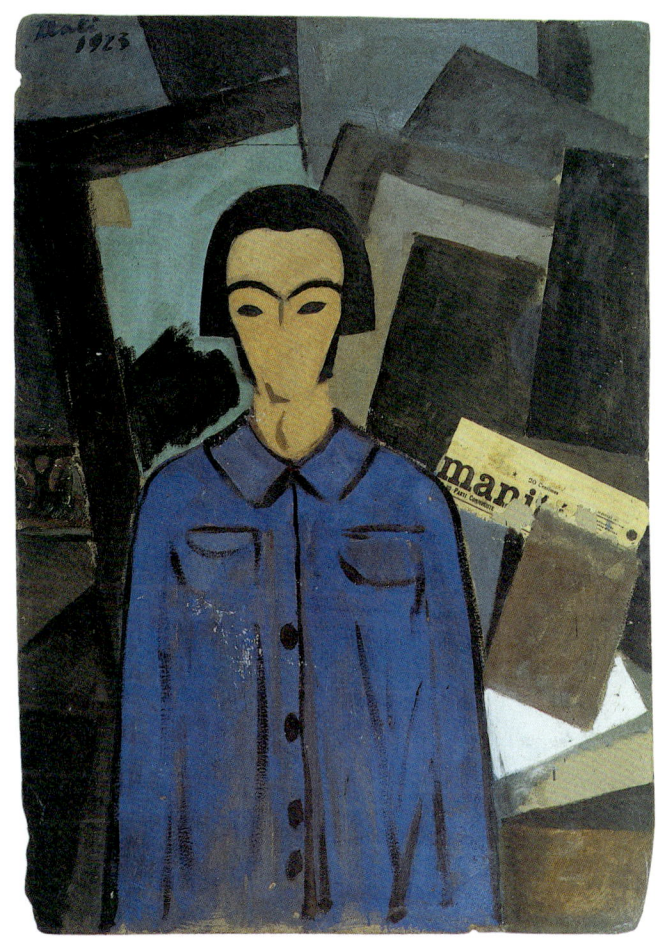

32
Self-Portrait with "L'Humanité"
1923
Tempera, oil and collage on cardboard, 105 × 75 cm
Town Hall of Figueres, on permanent deposit at the Fundació Gala-Salvador Dalí, Figueres

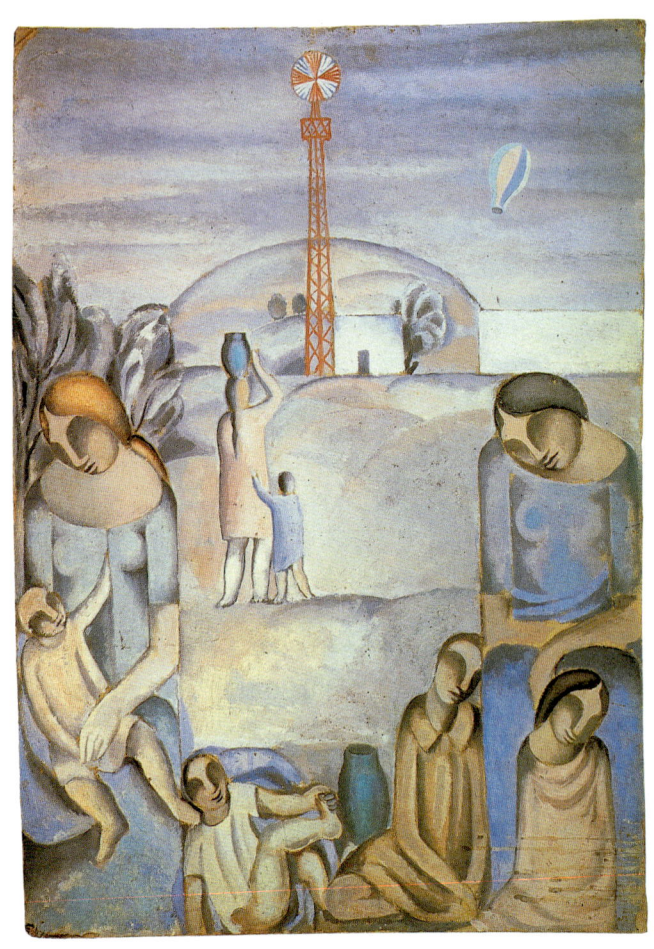

33
Empordà Landscape with Figures
c. 1923
Tempera on cardboard, 115 × 95 cm
Fundació Gala-Salvador Dalí, Figueres. Dalí bequest

Dalí's Beginnings and Post-impressionism

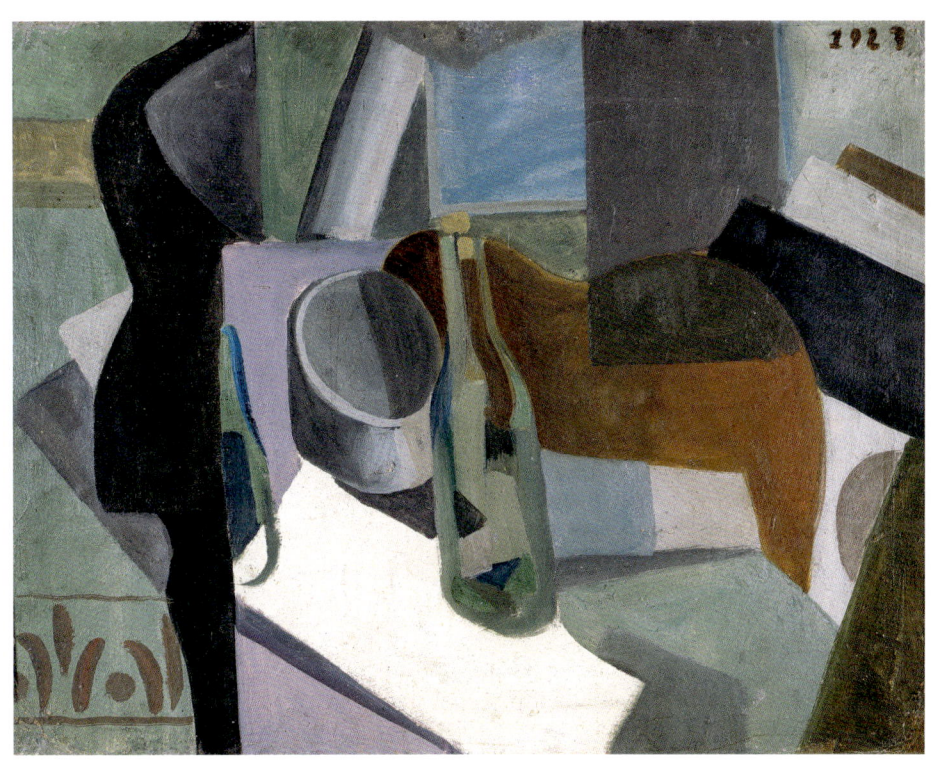

34
Still Life
1923
Oil on cardboard, 50 × 65 cm
Museo Nacional Centro de Arte Reina Sofía, Madrid. Dalí bequest

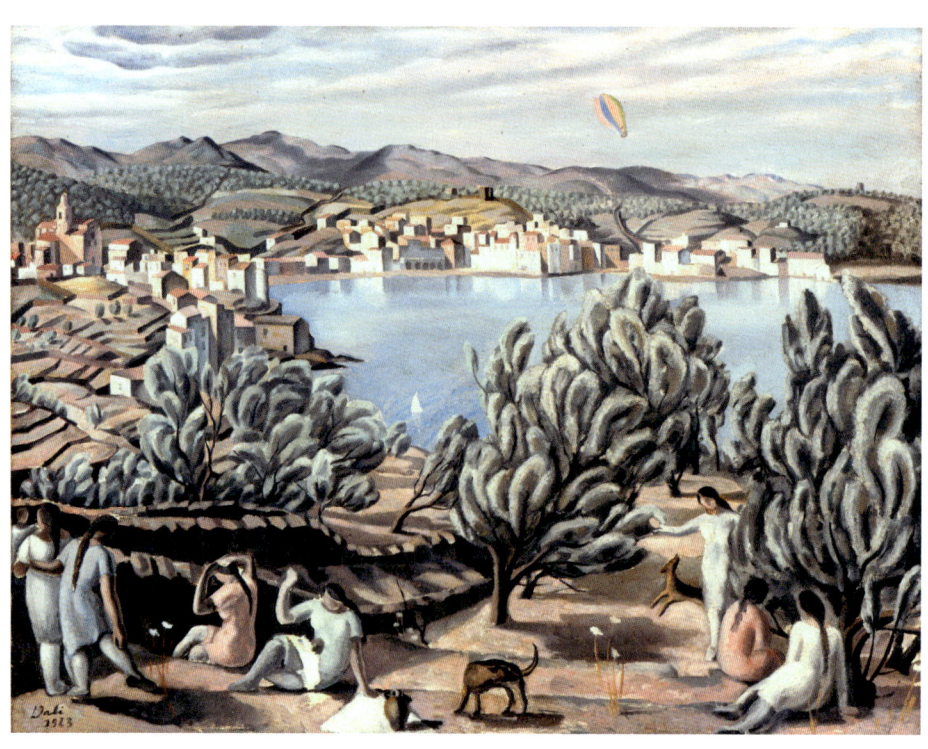

35
Cadaqués
1923
Oil on canvas, 96.5 × 127 cm
The Dalí Museum, St. Petersburg, Florida

Dalí's Beginnings and Post-impressionism

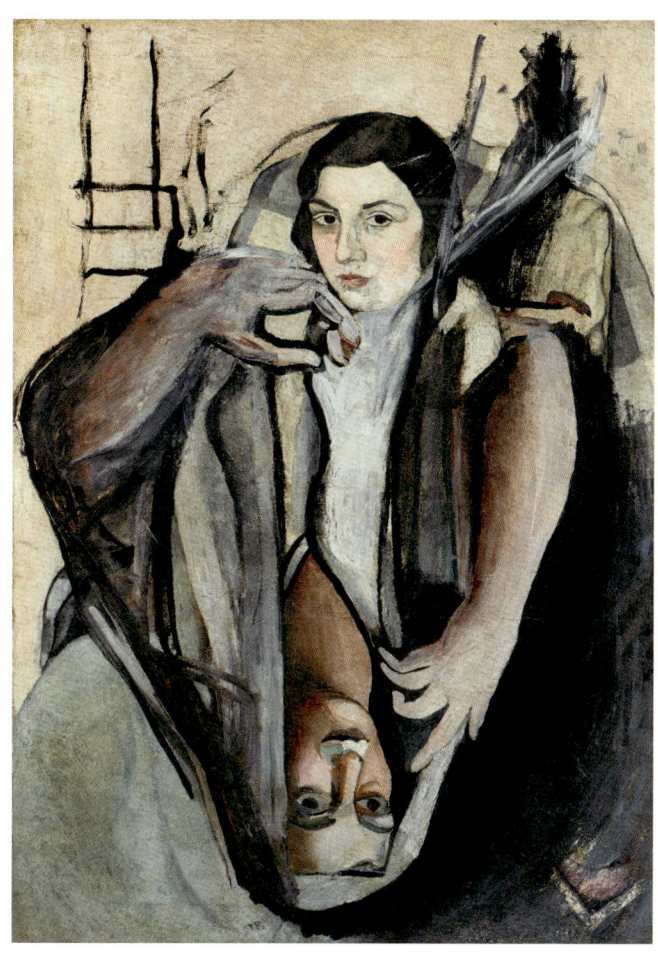

36
Portrait of My Sister (present state)
c. 1923
Oil on canvas, 104 × 75.3 cm
The Dalí Museum, St. Petersburg, Florida

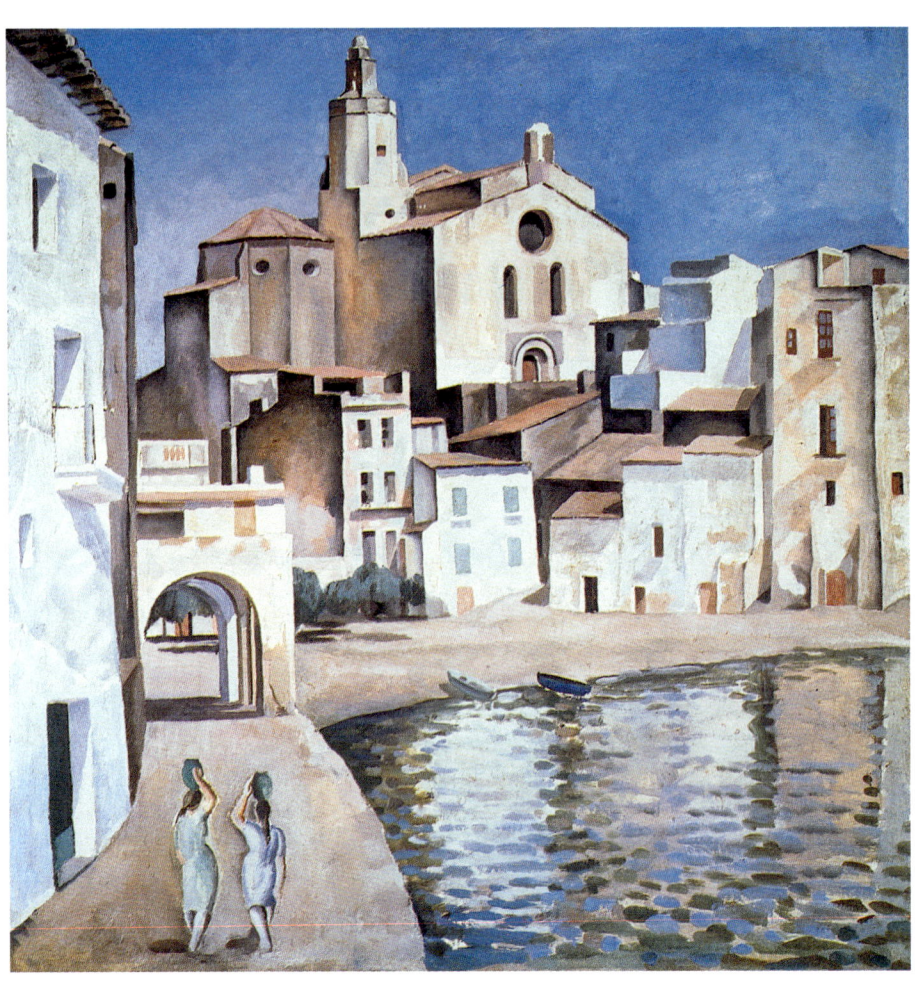

37
Port Alguer
c. 1923
Oil on canvas, 100.5 × 100.5 cm
The Dalí Museum, St. Petersburg, Florida

Dalí's Beginnings and Post-impressionism

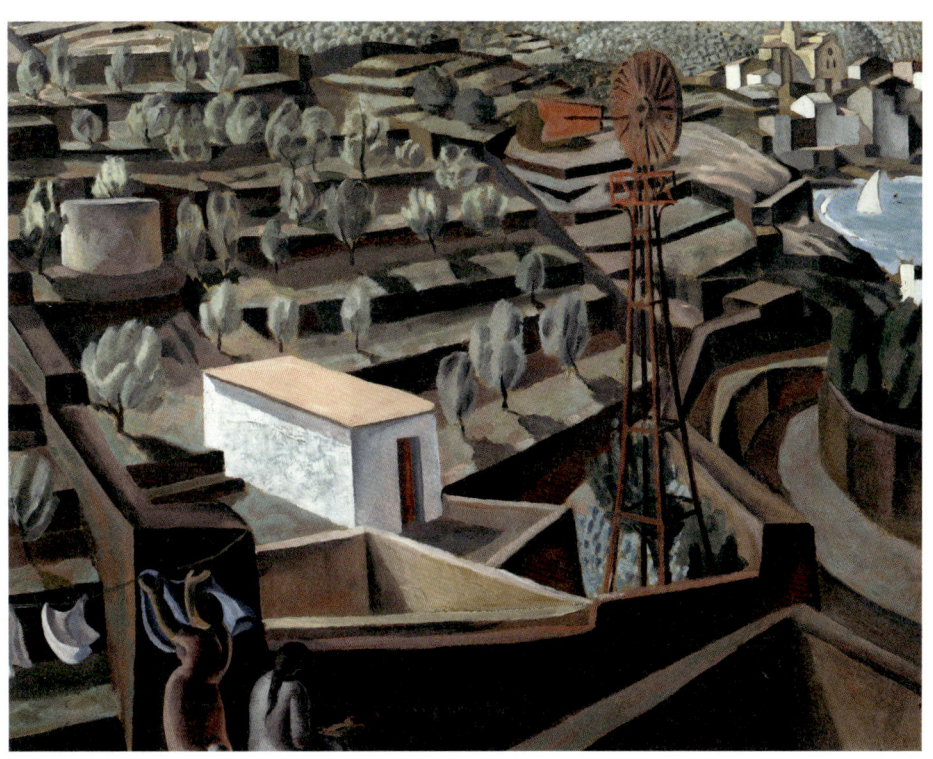

38
The Mill. Cadaqués Landscape
c. 1923
Tempera and oil on cardboard, 75 × 97 cm
Fundació Gala-Salvador Dalí, Figueres

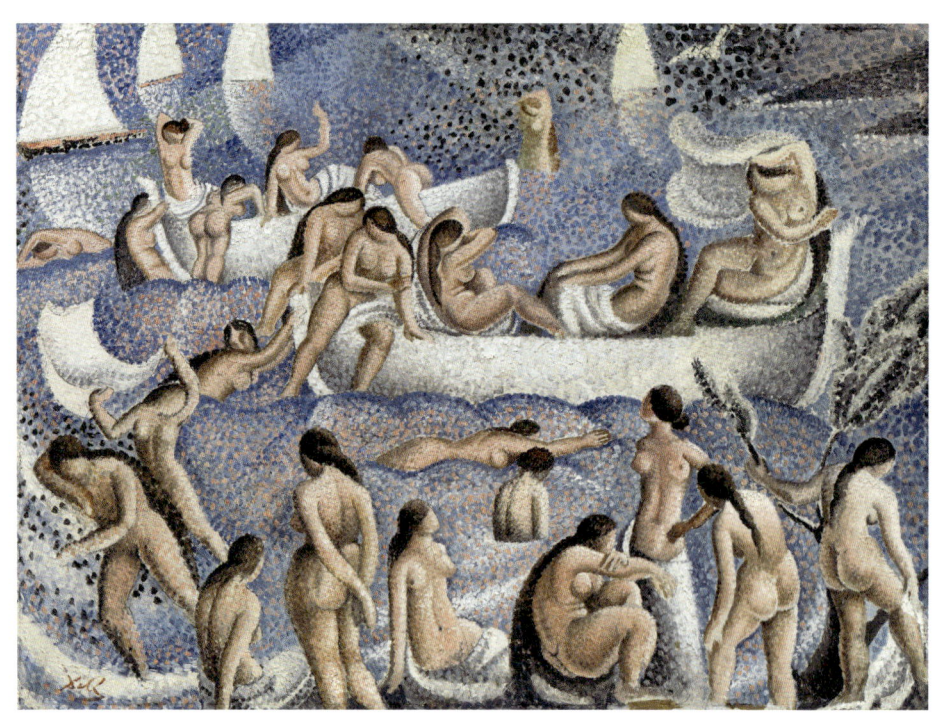

39
Bathers of Es Llaner
1923
Oil on cardboard on plywood panel, 73.8 × 101.5 cm
Fundació Gala-Salvador Dalí, Figueres

Dalí's Beginnings and Post-impressionism

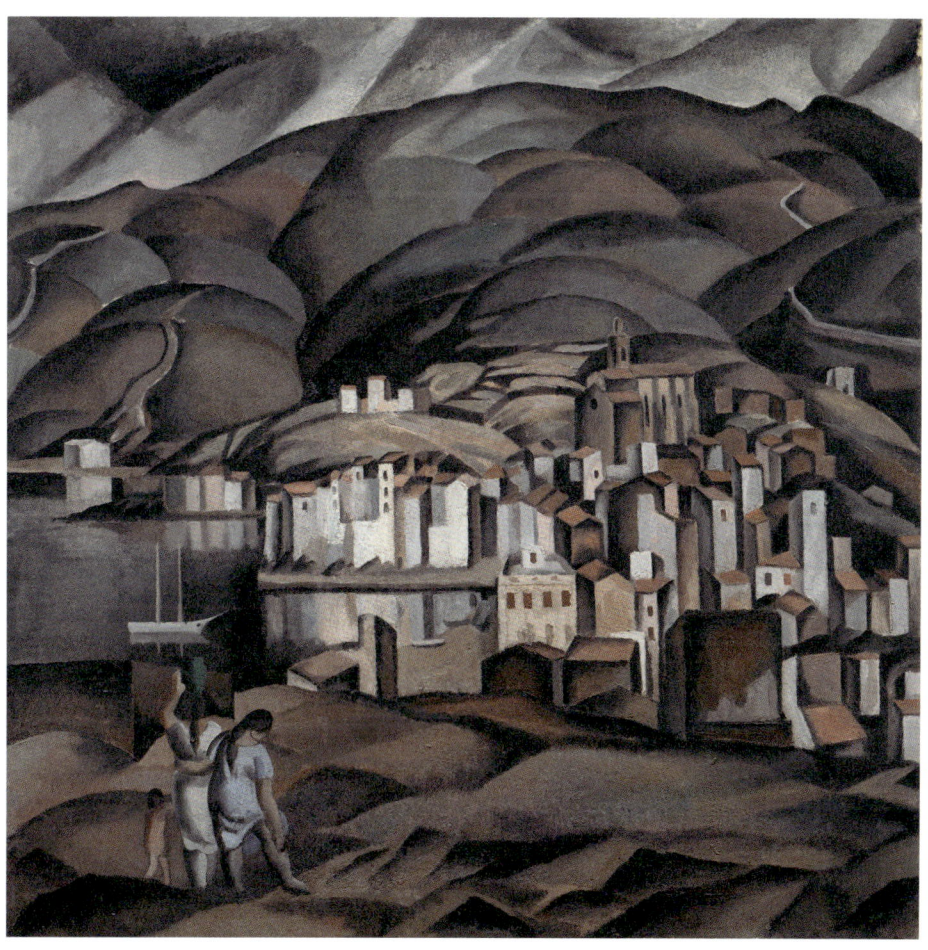

40
Cadaqués
c. 1923
Oil on canvas, 98 × 100 cm
Fundació Gala-Salvador Dalí, Figueres. Dalí bequest

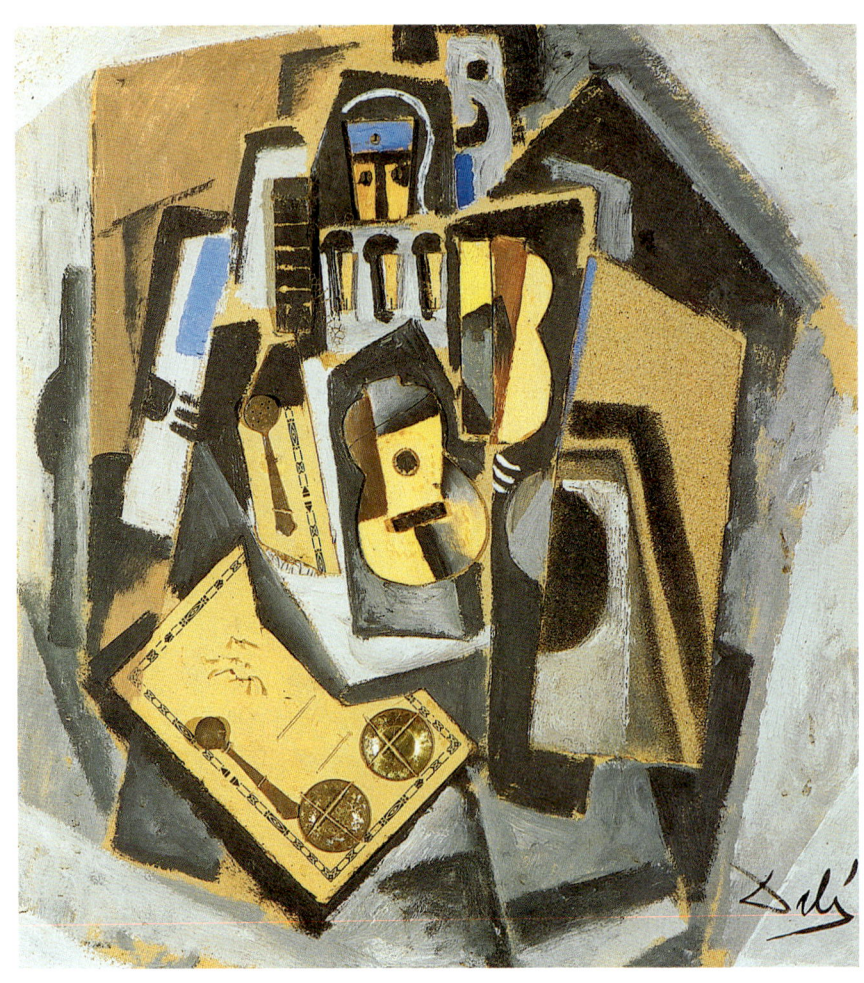

41

Pierrot with Guitar

c. 1923

Oil and collage on cardboard, 54.5 × 52.3 cm

Museo Nacional Thyssen-Bornemisza, Madrid

Dalí's Beginnings and Post-impressionism

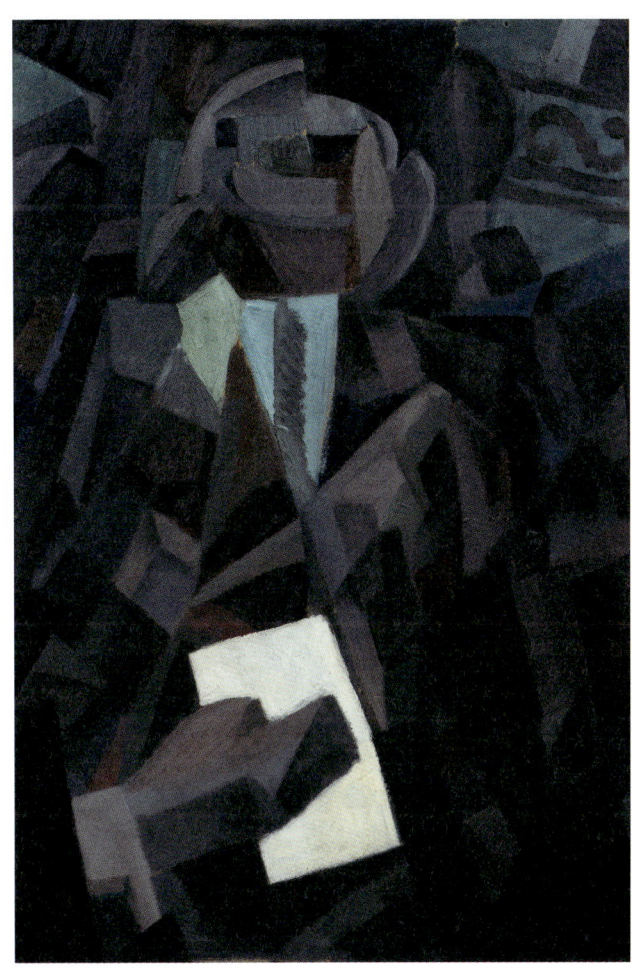

42
Cubist Composition
c. 1923
Tempera and oil on cardboard, 74.8 × 52 cm
Fundació Gala-Salvador Dalí, Figueres. Dalí bequest

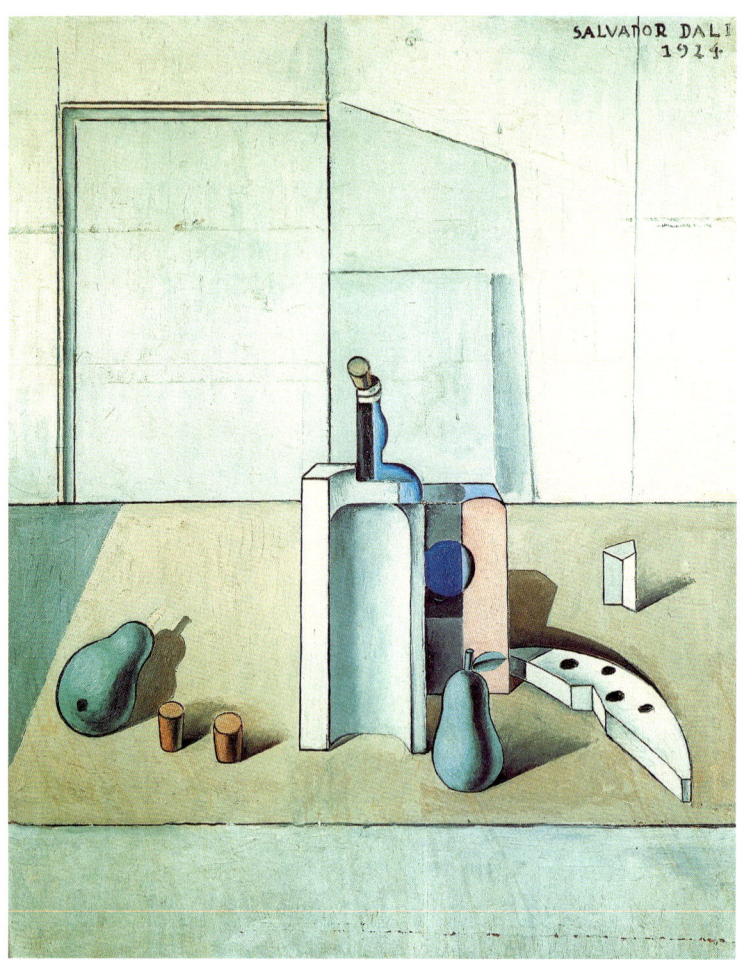

43
Naturaleza muerta (Still Life)
1924
Oil on canvas, 125 × 99 cm
Museo Nacional Centro de Arte Reina Sofía, Madrid

Dalí's Beginnings and Post-impressionism

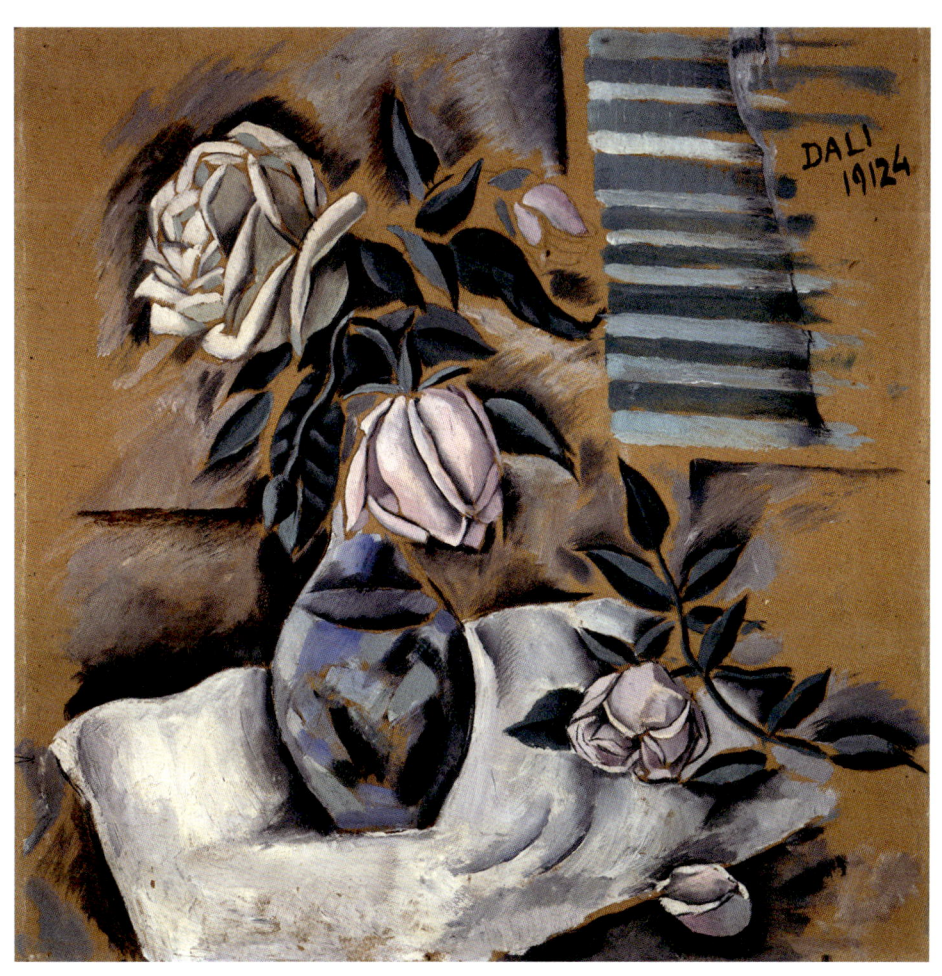

44
Bunch of Flowers
1924
Oil on cardboard, 50 × 52 cm
The Dalí Museum, St. Petersburg, Florida

Dalí's Beginnings and Post-impressionism

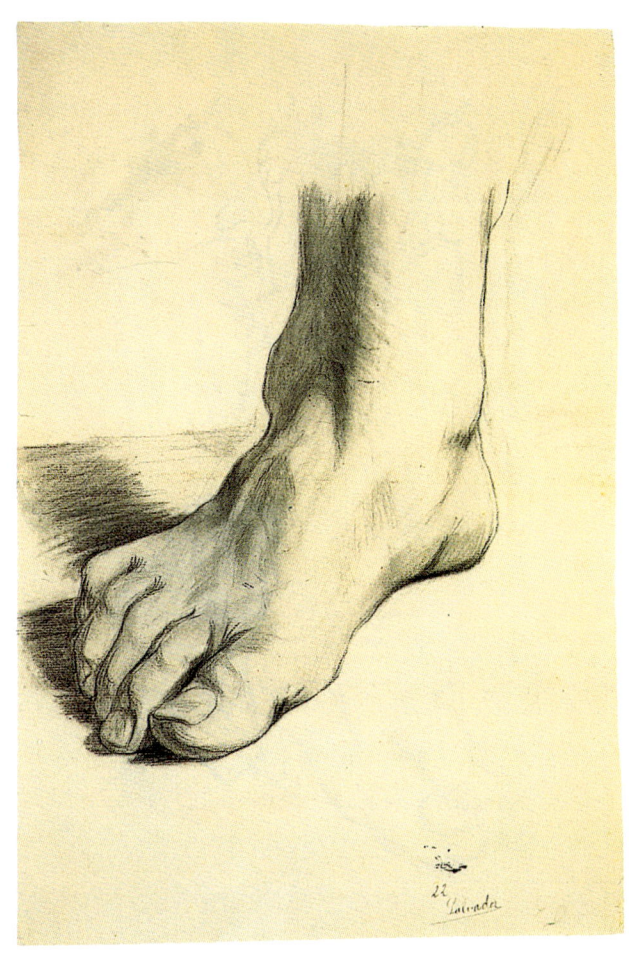

45
Study of a foot
1922
Pencil on paper, 47 × 31.5 cm
Fundació Gala-Salvador Dalí, Figueres. Dalí bequest

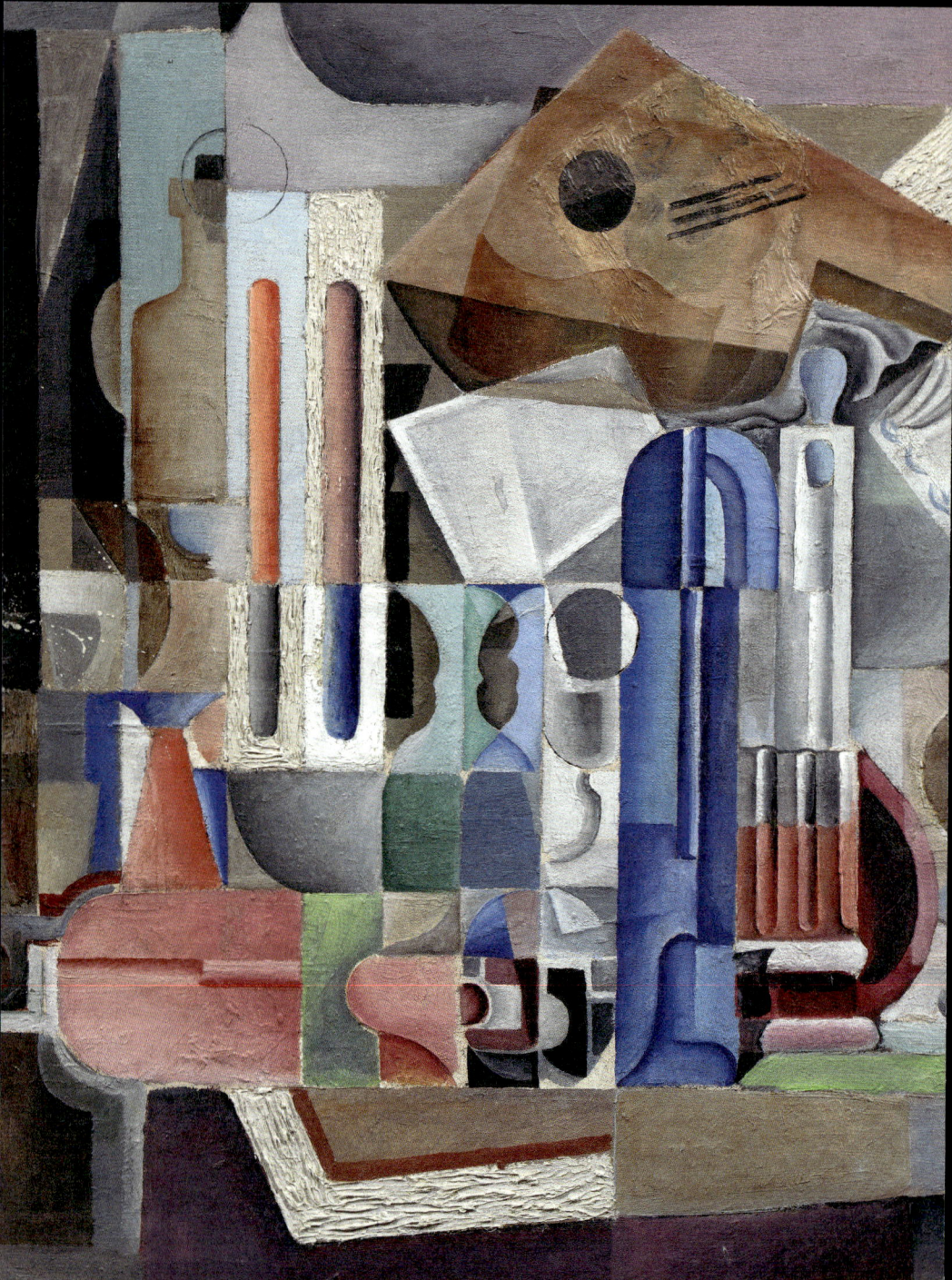

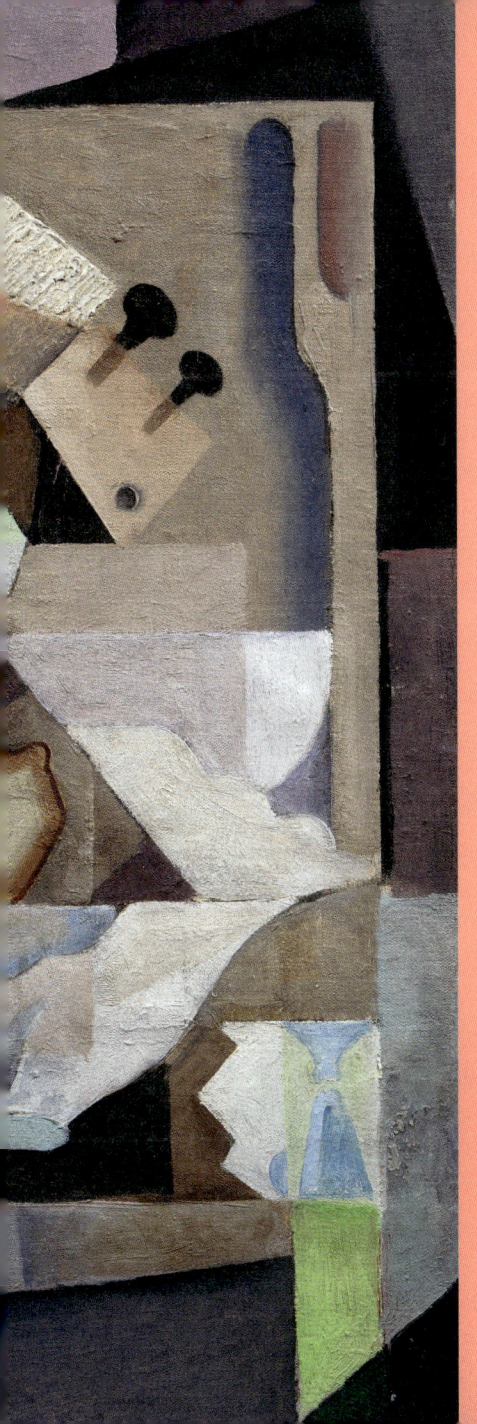

Cubism
and Beyond

1924–1926

In the autumn of 1922, Dalí left Figueres to take up his studies at the Academy of Fine Arts in Madrid. Though his entrance into the Academy was facilitated by his father, Dalí would later play down his father's role in his enrolment. While the art school in Madrid was dominated by conservative artists, the students were very aware of the new and more progressive movements that were arriving in the Spanish capital. These included a whole host of literary movements influenced by both the French and the Spanish-speaking world. Beyond Surrealism, the pan-Spanish literary and artistic movement Ultraism was very visible in Madrid. During this period, Dalí's work retained a sense of increasingly linear figuration, a form of sharply-focused realism mediated by photography. Works like *Portrait of My Sister* (1925) [61] and *Girl from Figueres* (1926) [75] can be related to other painterly movements such as the German style known as The New Objectivity. At the same time, Dalí's interest in geometric composition led him to explore variations on Cubism. Picasso of course was already the most important Spaniard working in Paris and was increasingly becoming a celebrity in the French capital.

An interesting feature of Dalí's work during this period is the coexistence of his linear figurative works alongside cubist experimentation. Indeed, Picasso too had explored Classicism and post-cubist experimentation in the years following the conclusion of World War I (a direction characteristic of Cocteau's 'Return to Order'). Dalí's first successful Cubist paintings date from 1923. 1924 was the first official year of Surrealism, as it was the year in which Breton published his *Manifeste du surréalisme*. Exactly when Dalí read this work is not clear, though its publication was reviewed almost immediately in the Spanish philosopher José Ortega y Gasset's (1883–1955) magazine *Revista de Occidente* published in Madrid.

Recall that Dalí's painting professor Vázquez Díaz had painted in a Cubist style. In 1924, Dalí's canvases reveal a sophisticated awareness of the Cubist composition, not only drawing on that of Vázquez Díaz, but also demonstrating an awareness of Picasso and Georges Braque (1882–1963). Specifically, Dalí's painting *Still Life* (1924) [48] can be compared with Picasso's paintings of 1909. Dalí's work at this time was by no means mere student work, and he soon came to have a public presence through exhibitions and publications in Madrid.

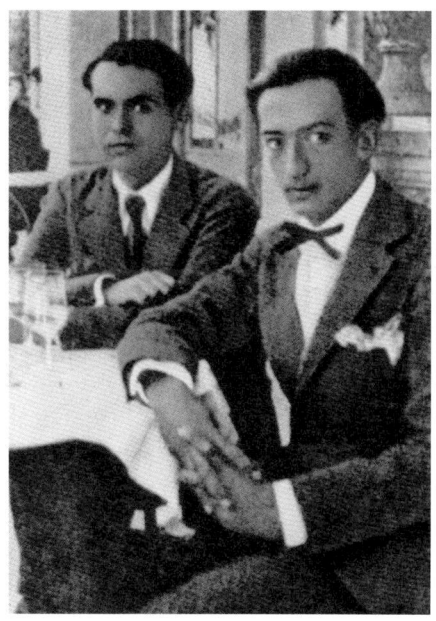

Dalí with the poet Federico García Lorca, c. 1925.

In 1925, Dalí was one of several young artists included in the Primera Exposición de la Sociedad de Artistas Ibéricos held in Madrid from May to June 1925. While most of his contributions represented variations on Cubism, Dalí also presented more realistic works, once again demonstrating his capacity to simultaneously create works in multiple styles. These works were also noted in the press. The literary review *Alfar*, founded in La Coruña in northwest Spain, published a manifesto, signed by numerous contemporary writers, including the poet Federico García Lorca (1898–1936) and Vázquez Díaz, in which a work by Dalí was reproduced. His works were also reproduced in the illustrated magazine *Nuevo Mundo* published in Madrid. This exhibition very much marked the beginning of Dalí's public presence in the Spanish capital. Meanwhile, back in Barcelona, Dalí was promoted by Galeries Dalmau with his first solo exhibitions in the Catalan capital in 1925 and again in 1926.

In the spring of 1926, Dalí made his first journey to Paris, where he visited Picasso and went to view the collection of paintings at the Musée du Louvre.

At that time Picasso was preparing a solo exhibition planned for June 1926 at the Galerie Rosenberg in Paris, directed by the French art dealer Paul Rosenberg (1881–1959). This would comprise a new body of Picasso's paintings, which retained some elements of Cubism, but introduced motifs that could be related to both Classicism and Surrealism, such as a plaster head prop that was often depicted with an accompanying shadow, as in *Studio with Plaster Head* (1925): this was a shadow that metaphorically split the head in two, as if it were divided between light and dark, between the outer and inner realms. These works made a tremendous impact on Dalí, whose work following the trip was noticeably influenced by these motifs derived from Picasso. These include the geometric fragmentation of figures, as well as a form of realism derived from Picasso's return to Classicism, but most importantly the split-figure motif with the plaster head became one of central importance to Dalí for some time. A number of the works that Dalí created during this period were exhibited in his second solo exhibition with Galeries Dalmau, which took place at the end of 1926.

Yet Dalí also continued with his exploration of a realism mediated through photography and meticulously painted. This exploration resembled Picasso's return to Classicism as well as the Spanish Old Masters of the seventeenth century, such as Francisco de Zurbarán (1598–1664). Perhaps the most spectacular of these paintings, *The Basket of Bread* (1926) [70], was also seen in Dalí's 1926 show at Galeries Dalmau, and in 1928 became his first work to be exhibited internationally, when it featured in the *Twenty-Seventh International Exhibition of Paintings* at the Carnegie Institute, Pittsburgh, in the United States.

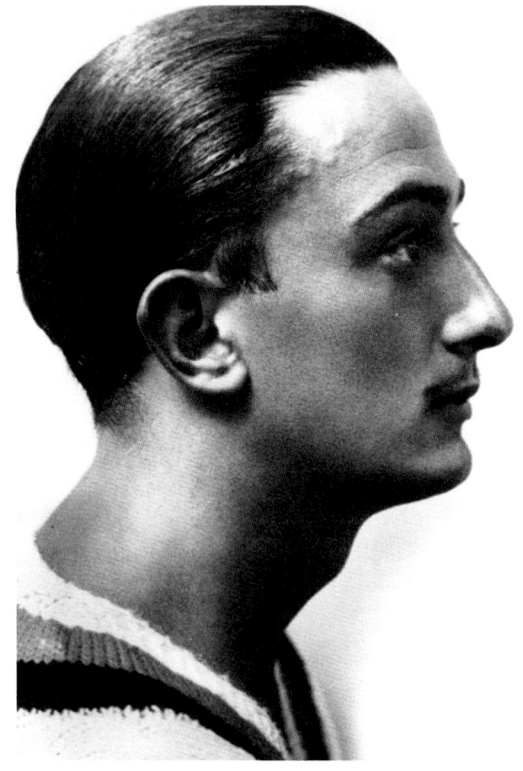

Dalí, 1926. Collection of The Dalí Museum.

1924–1926

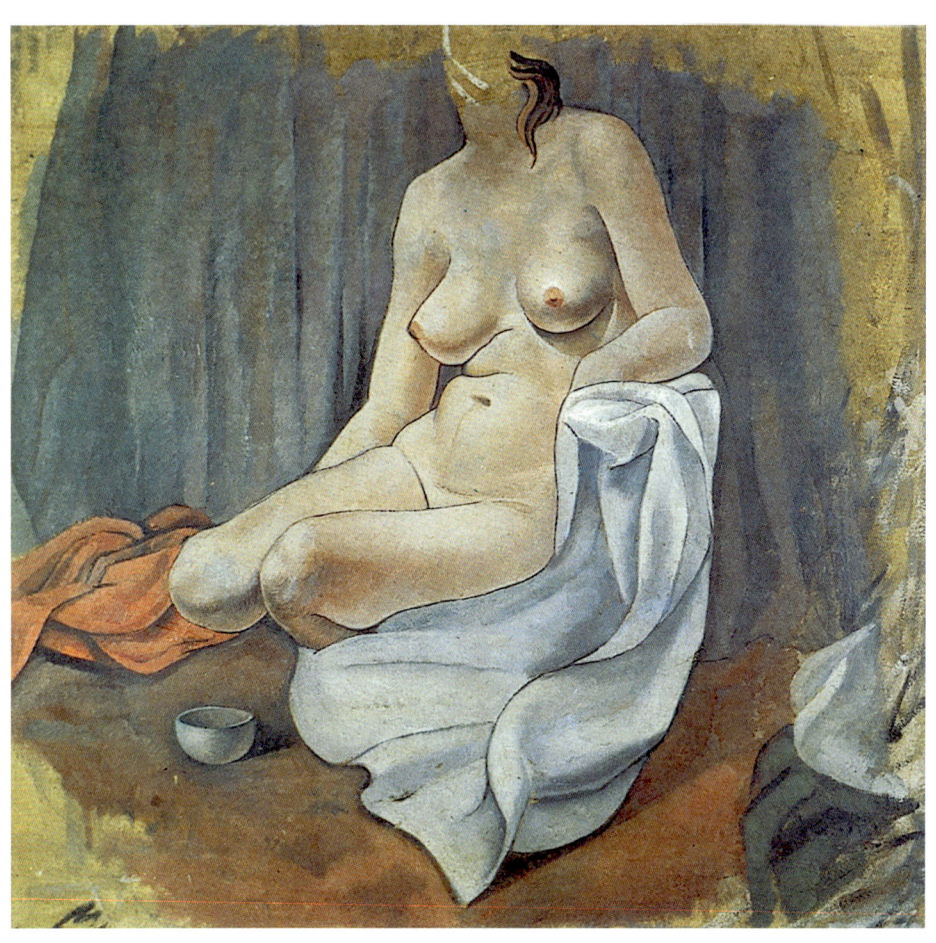

46
Desnudo (Nude)
c. 1924
Oil on thin cardboard, 46 × 48.5 cm
Museo Nacional Centro de Arte Reina Sofía, Madrid

　　　　　　　　Cubism and Beyond

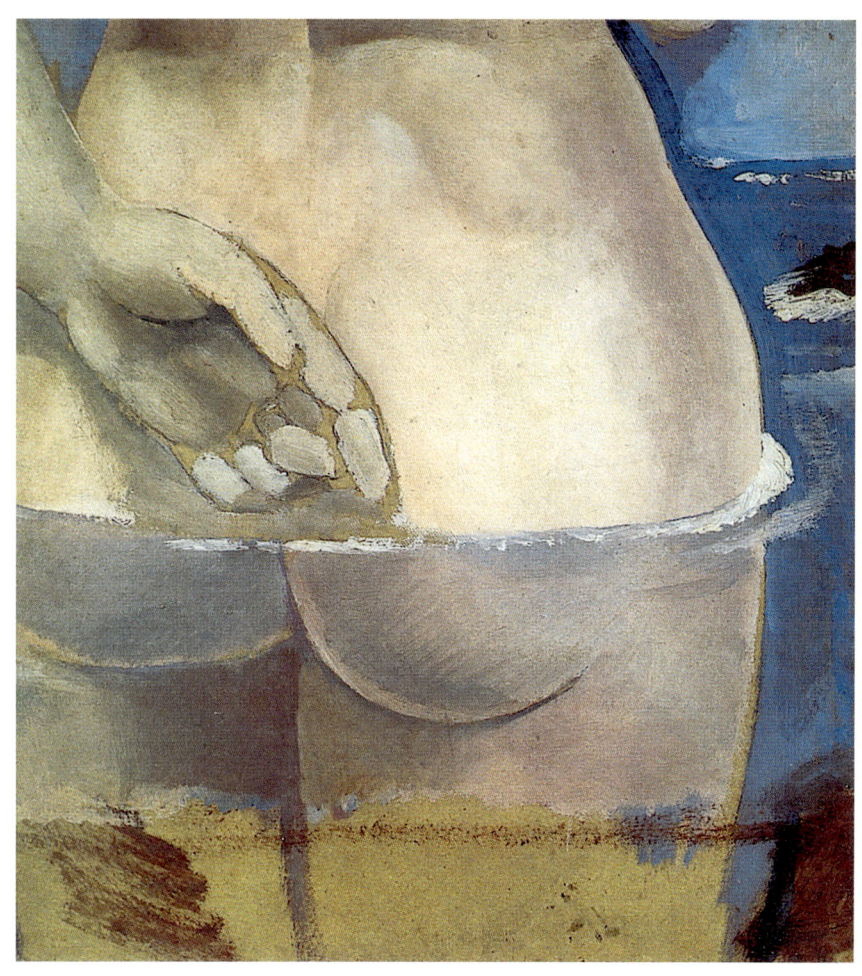

47
Nude in the Water
c. 1924
Oil on thin cardboard, 50.5 × 47 cm
Museo Nacional Centro de Arte Reina Sofía, Madrid

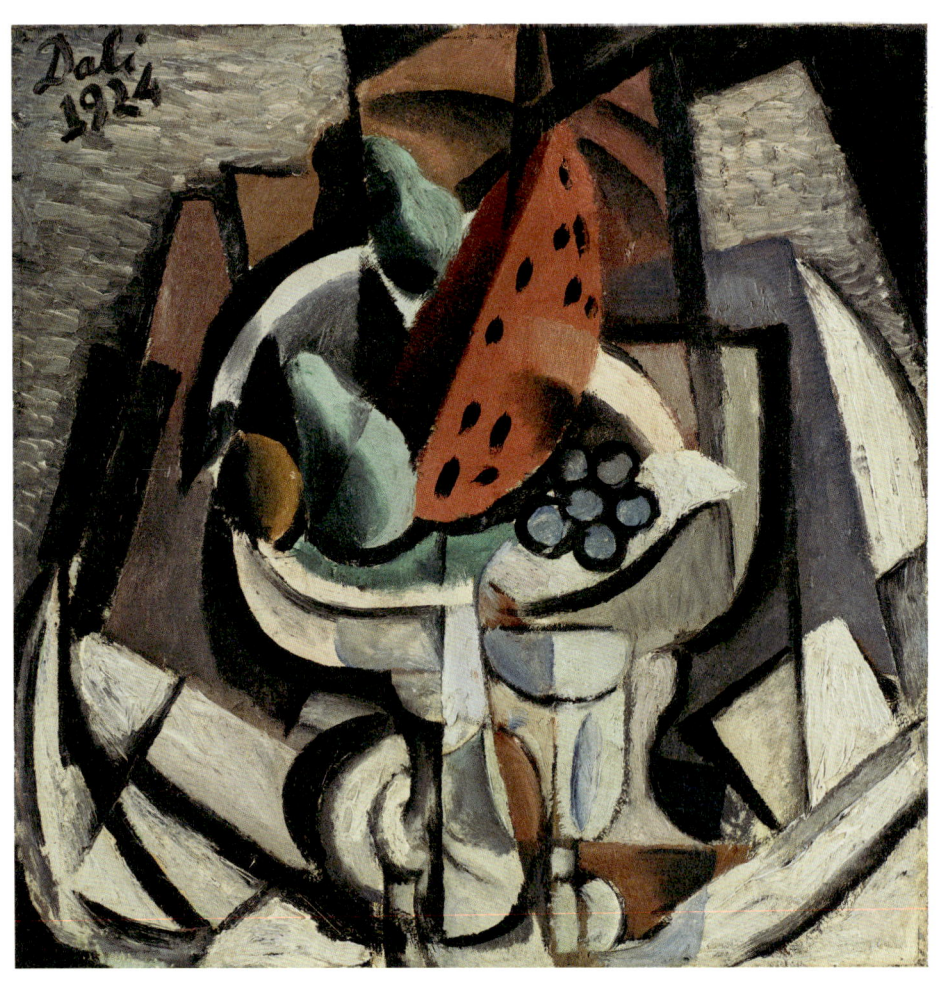

48
Naturaleza muerta (Still Life)
1924
Oil on canvas, 49.5 × 49.5 cm
The Dalí Museum, St. Petersburg, Florida

Cubism and Beyond

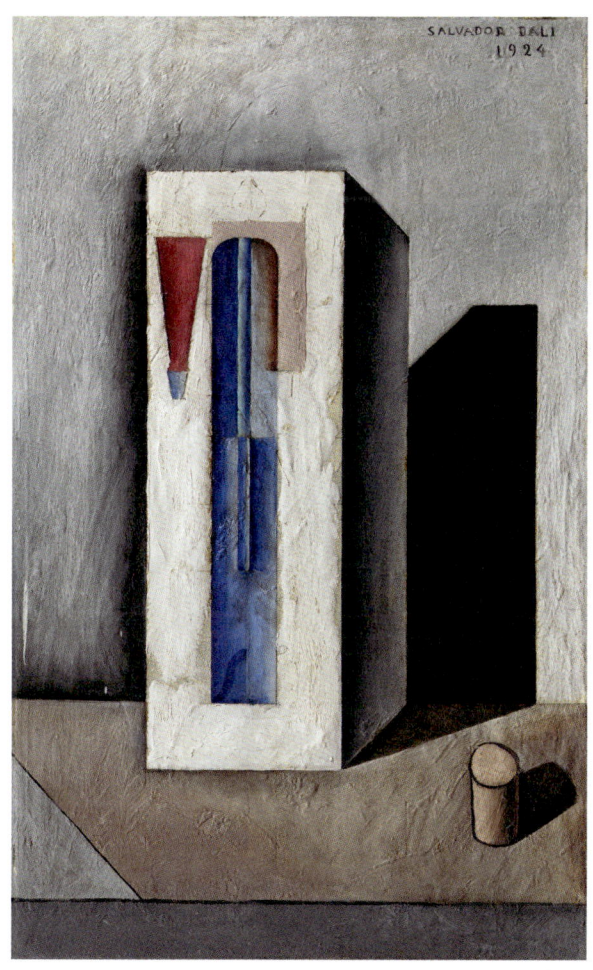

49
Naturaleza muerta (Still Life)
1924
Oil on canvas, 80.5 × 50 cm
Town Hall of Figueres, on permanent deposit at the Fundació Gala-Salvador Dalí, Figueres

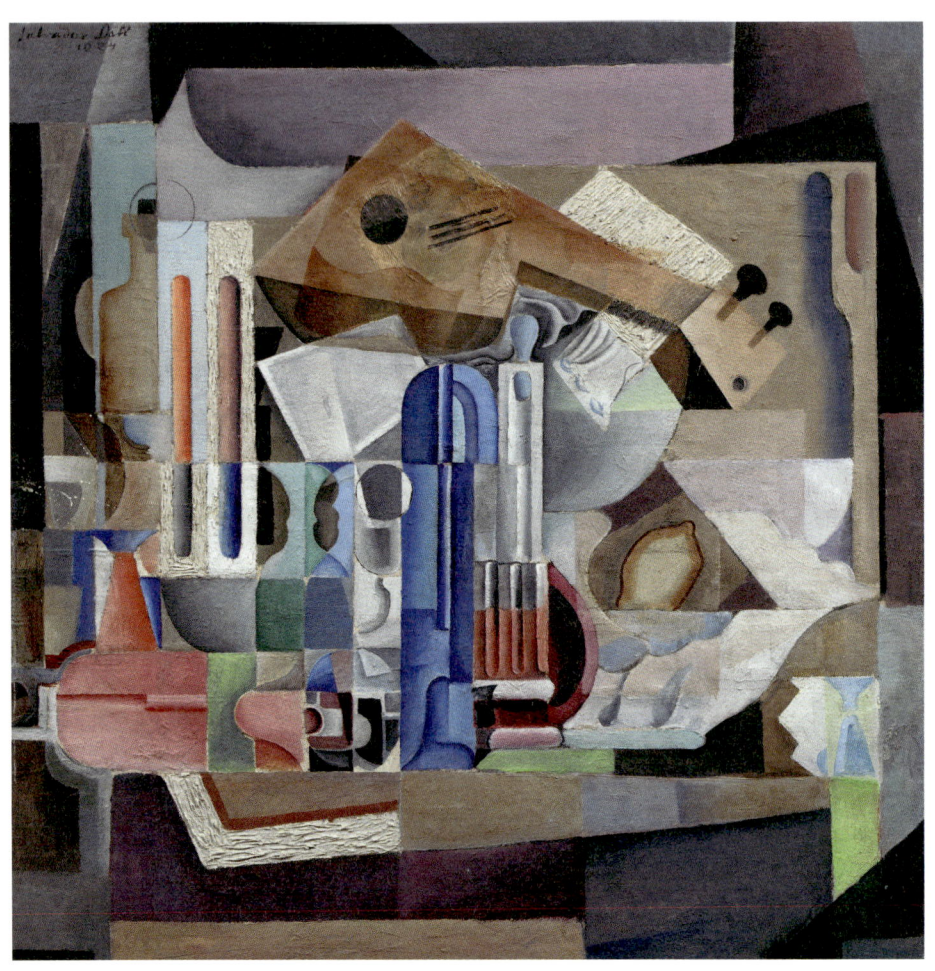

50

Still Life

1924

Oil on canvas, 99.5 × 99 cm

Fundació Gala-Salvador Dalí, Figueres

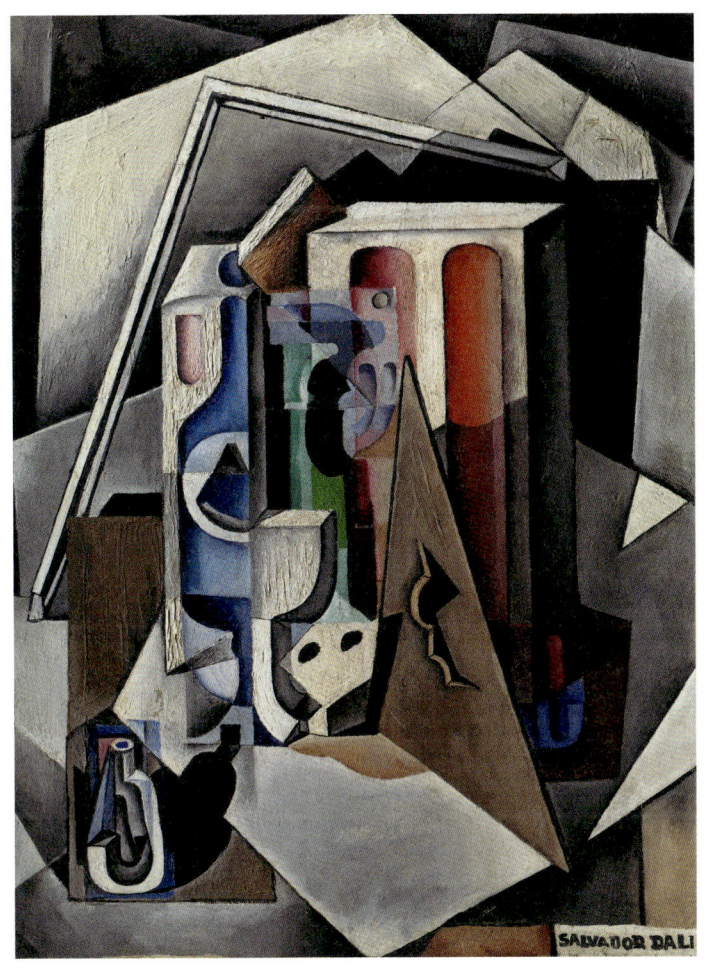

51
Naturaleza muerta (Still Life)
c. 1924
Oil on canvas, 83.5 × 62 cm
Fundació Gala-Salvador Dalí, Figueres. Dalí bequest

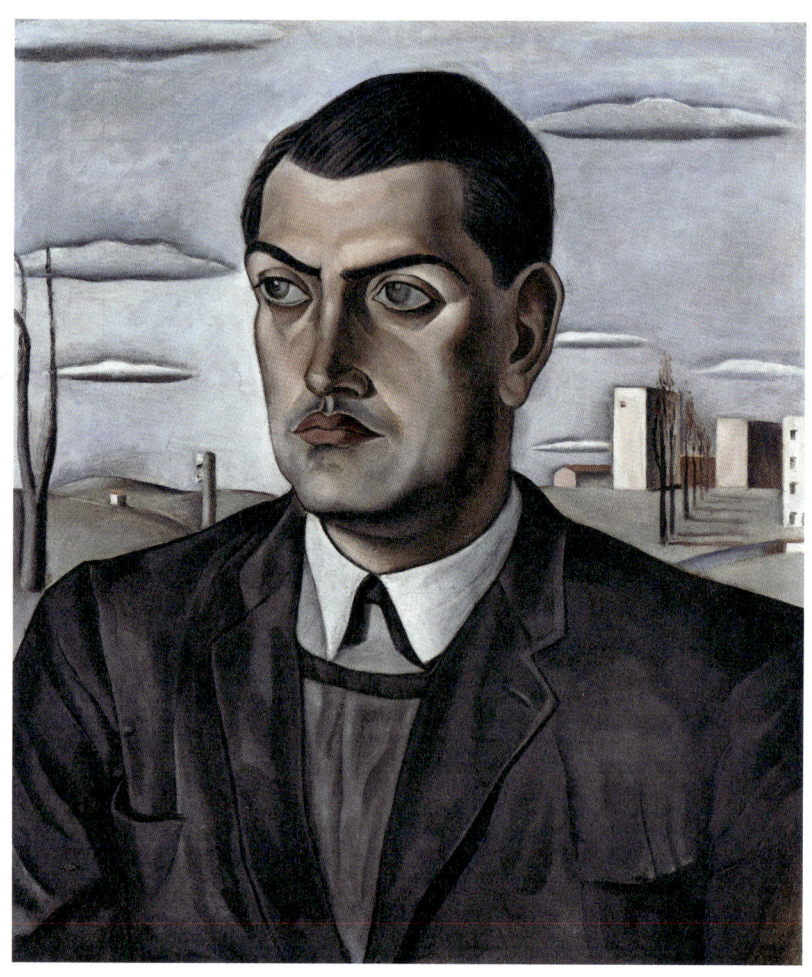

52
Retrato de Luis Buñuel (Portrait of Luis Buñuel)
1924
Oil on canvas, 70 × 60 cm
Museo Nacional Centro de Arte Reina Sofía, Madrid

Cubism and Beyond

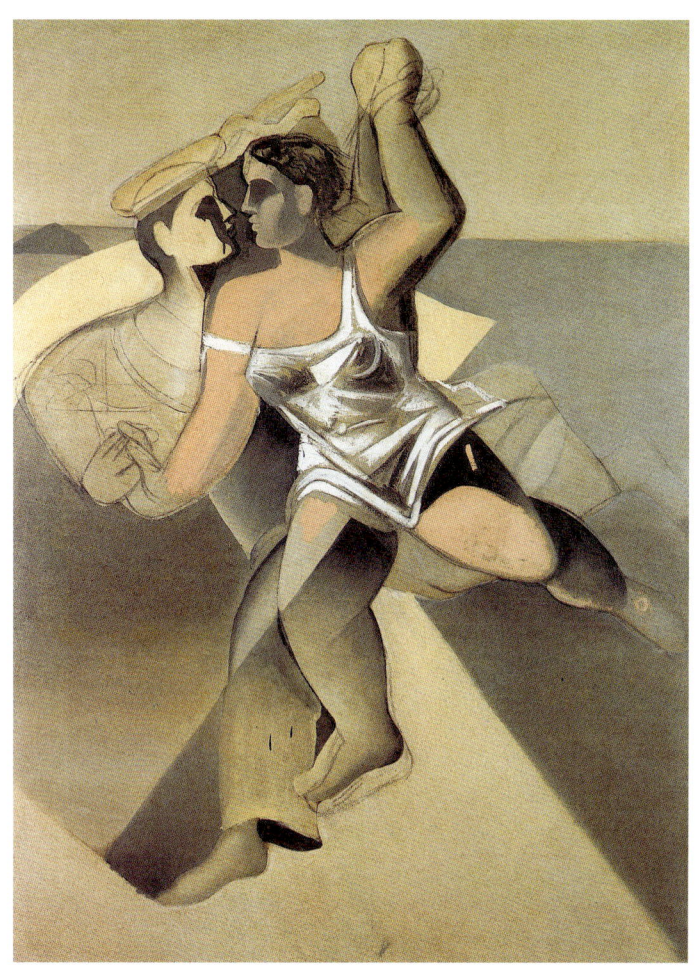

53
Venus and Sailor
c. 1925
Oil on canvas on wood panel, 198 × 149 cm
Fundació Gala-Salvador Dalí, Figueres

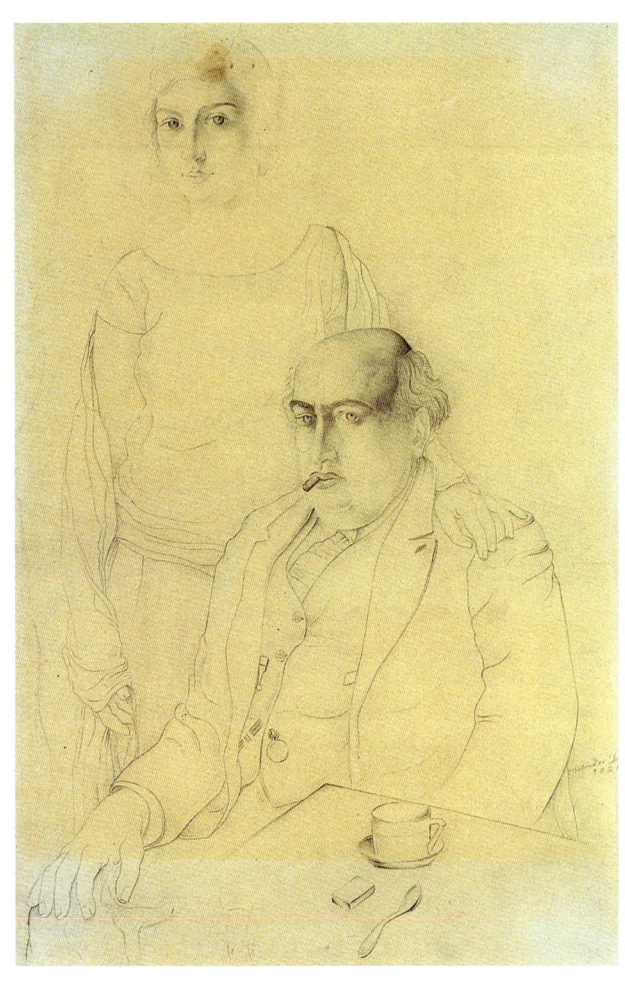

54
Don Salvador and Ana María Dalí (Portrait of the Artist's Father and Sister)
1925
Graphite pencil on cardboard, 49 × 32.8 cm
Museu Nacional d'Art de Catalunya, Barcelona

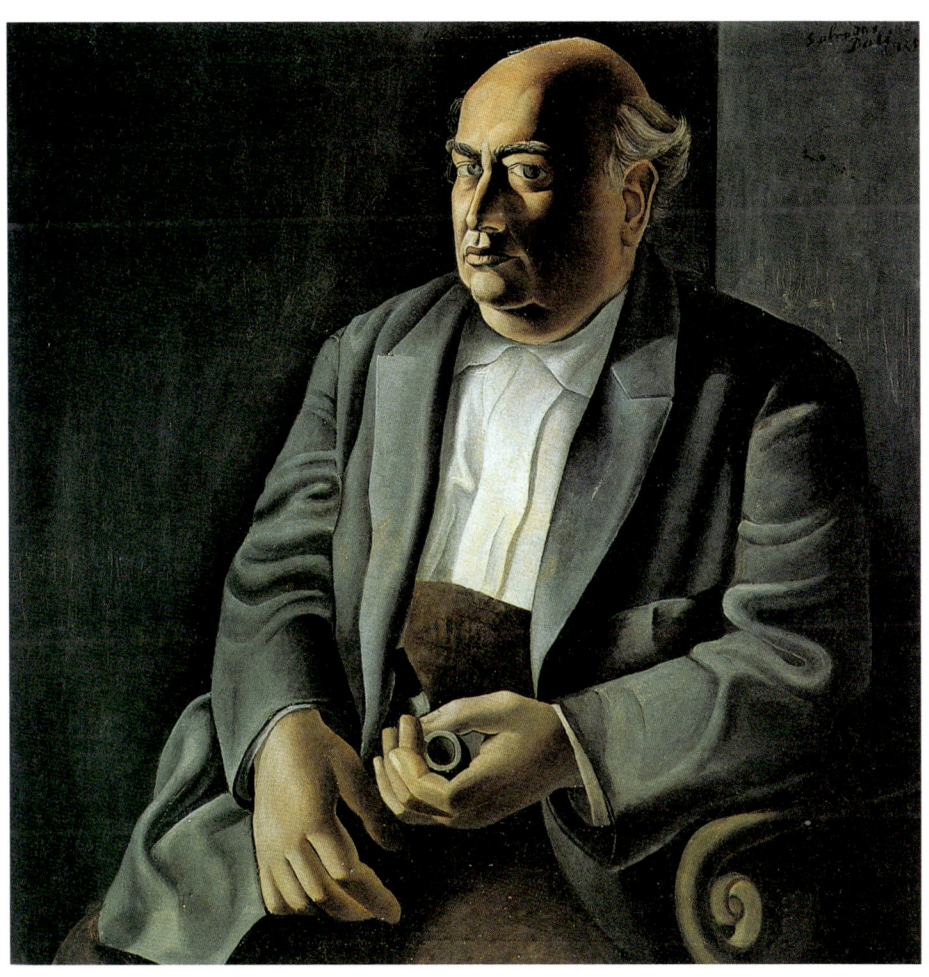

55
Retrat del meu pare (Portrait of My Father)
1925
Oil on canvas, 104.5 × 104.5 cm
Museu Nacional d'Art de Catalunya, Barcelona

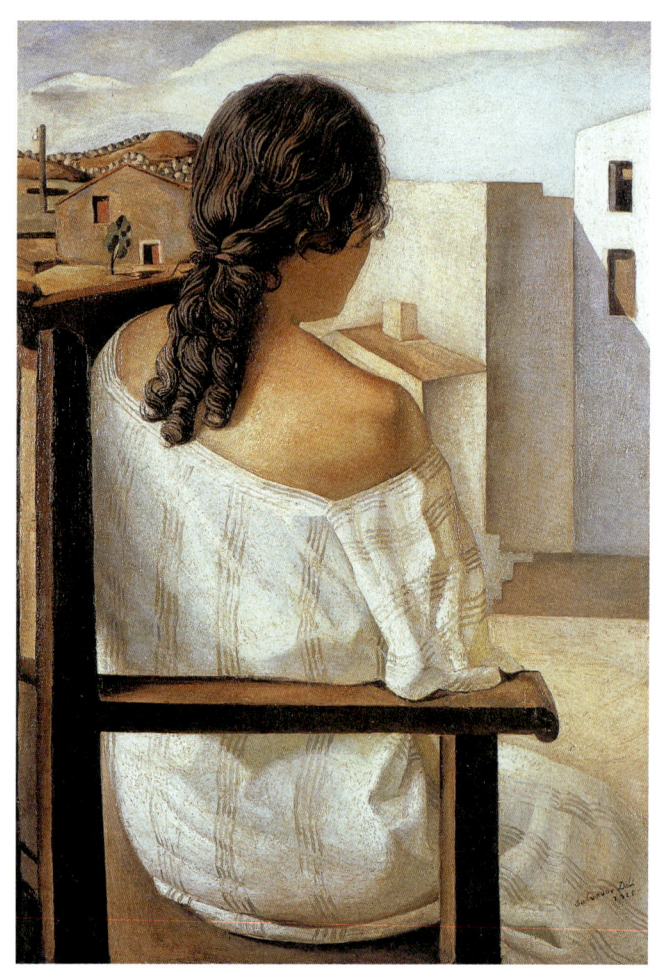

56
Retrato (Portrait)
1925
Oil on canvas, 104 × 74 cm
Museo Nacional Centro de Arte Reina Sofía, Madrid

Cubism and Beyond

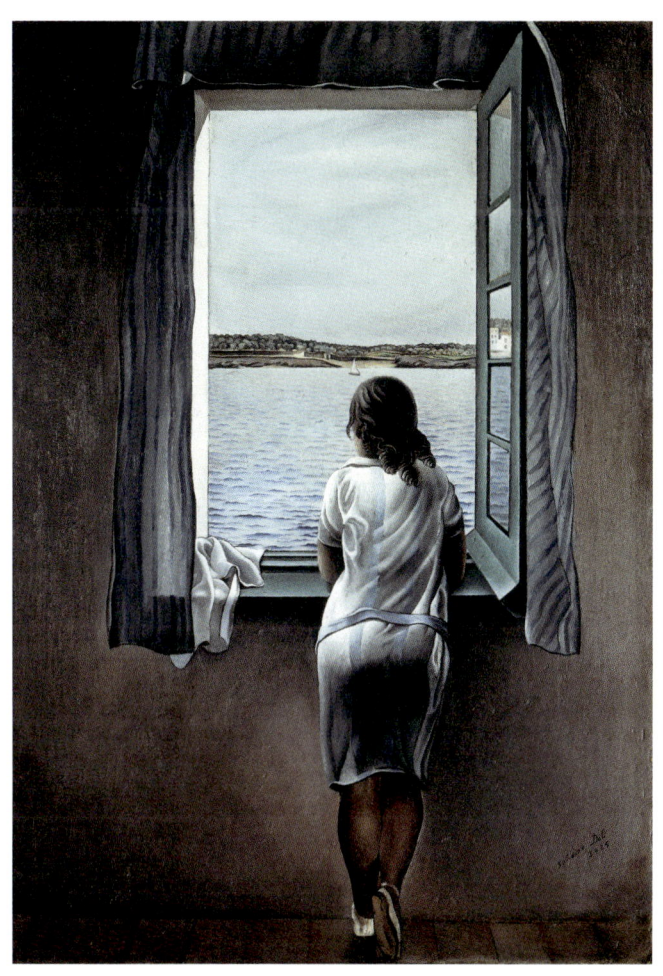

57
Figura en una finestra (Figure at a Window)
1925
Oil on cardboard, 105 × 74.5 cm
Museo Nacional Centro de Arte Reina Sofía, Madrid

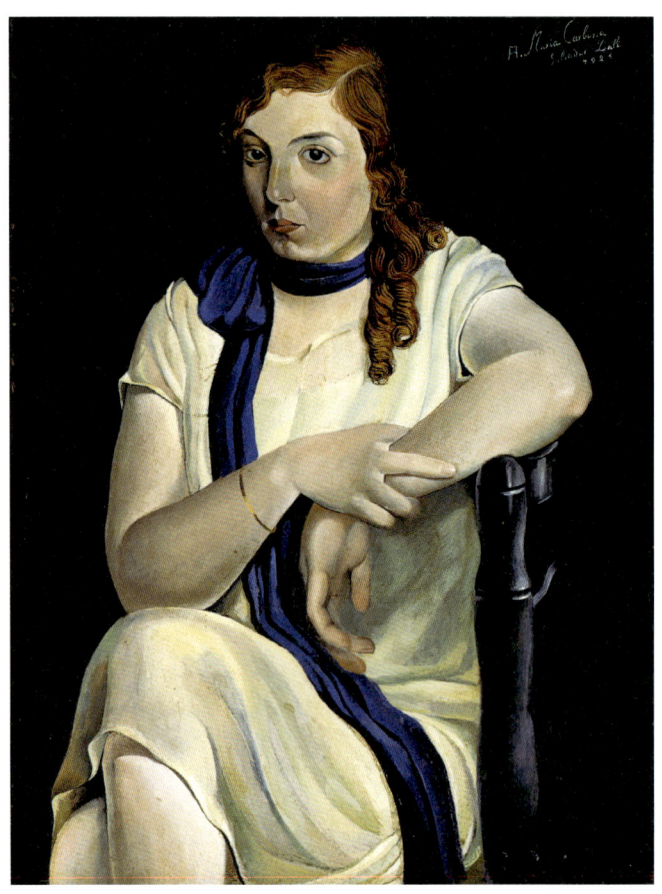

58–59
Retrat de Maria Carbona (Portrait of Maria Carbona [front]*)*
and *Naturaleza Muerta (Still Life* [back]*)*
1925
Oil on cardboard, 52 × 39.2 cm
Musée des beaux-arts de Montréal, Montréal
(Gift of Association des bénévoles du Musée des beaux-arts de Montréal)

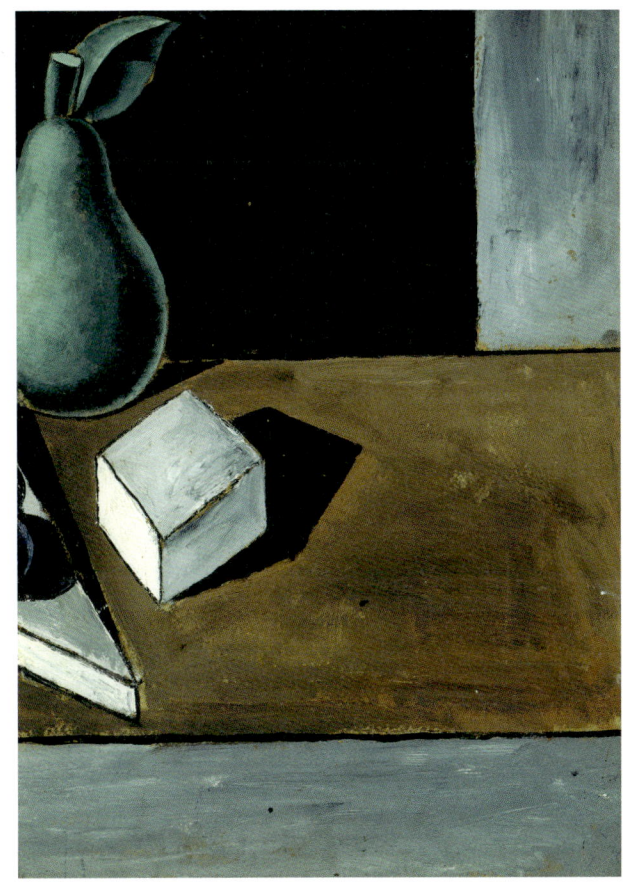

1924–1926

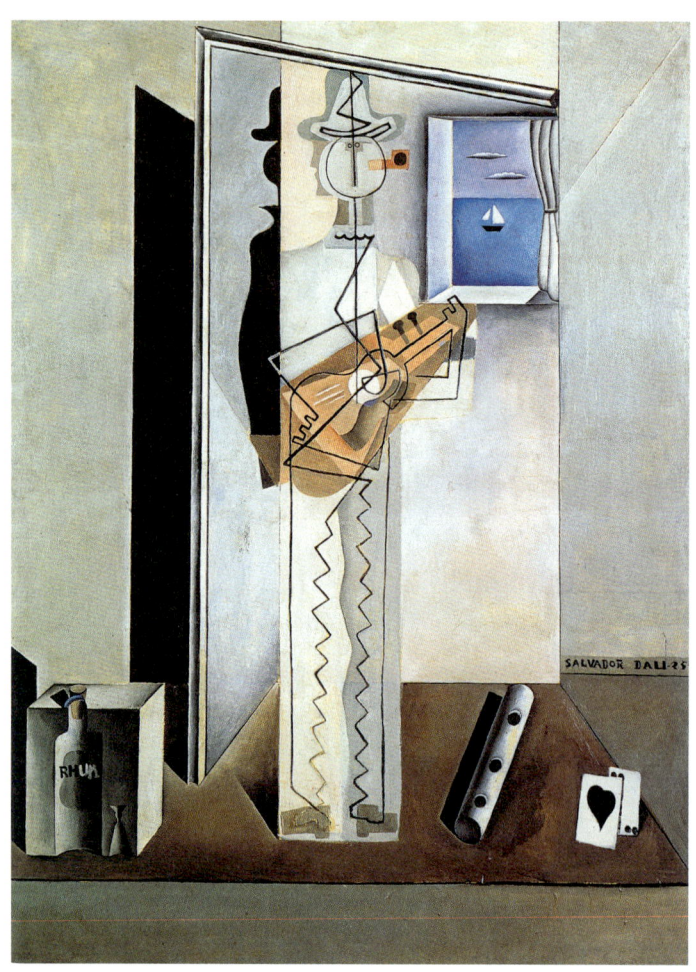

60
Pierrot tocant la guitarra (Pintura cubista)
(Pierrot Playing the Guitar [Cubist Painting])
1925
Oil on canvas, 198 × 149 cm
Museo Nacional Centro de Arte Reina Sofía, Madrid. Dalí bequest

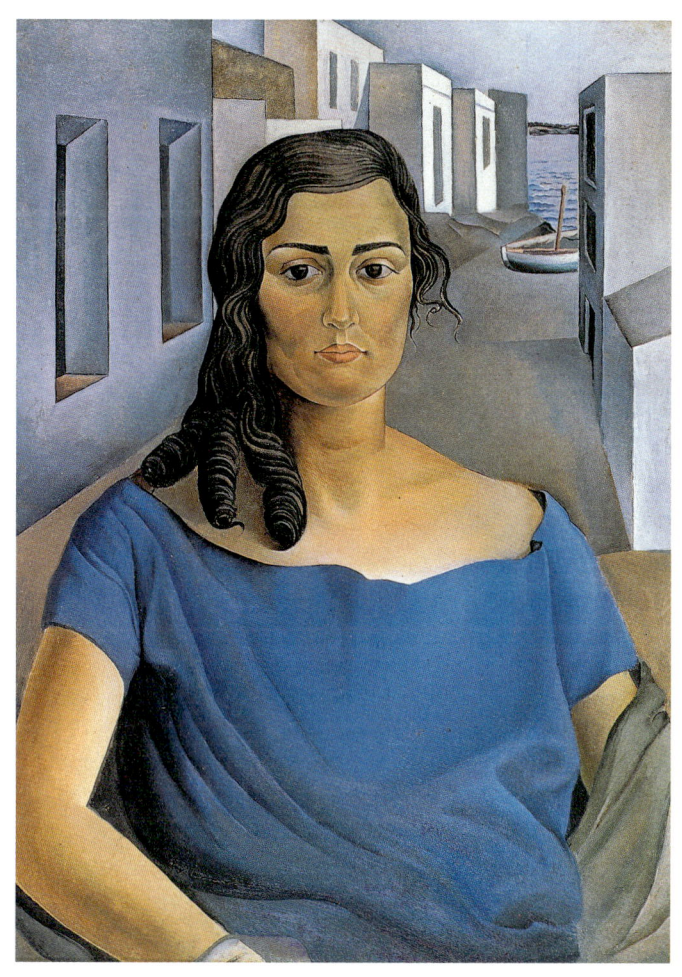

61
Retrat de la meva germana (Portrait of My Sister)
1925
Oil on canvas, 92 × 65 cm
Fundació Gala-Salvador Dalí, Figueres. Dalí bequest

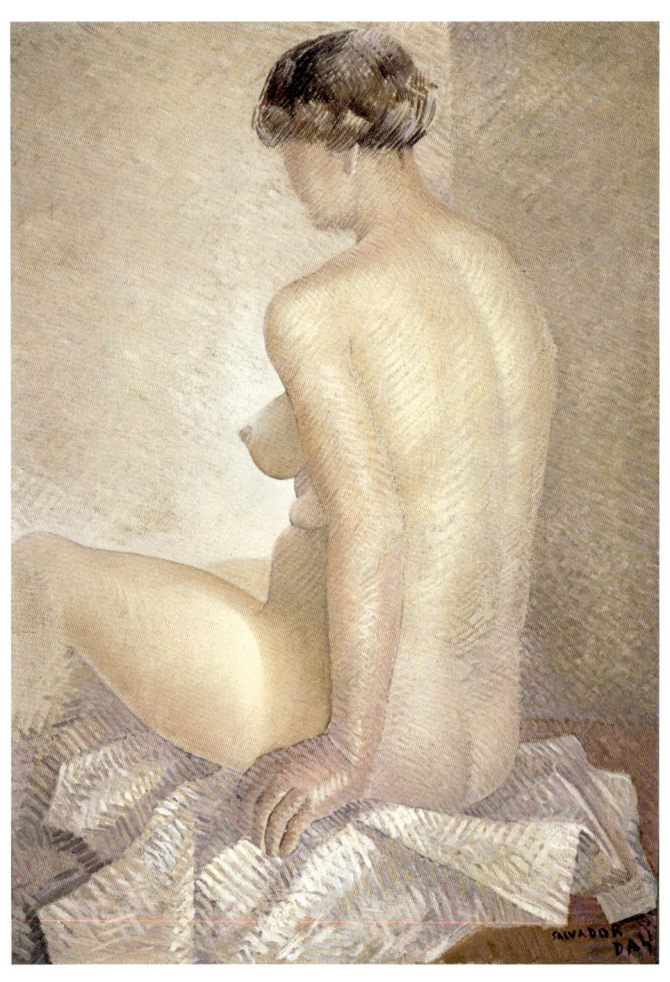

62
Study of a Nude
1925
Oil on canvas, 99.1 × 71.2 cm
The Dalí Museum, St. Petersburg, Florida

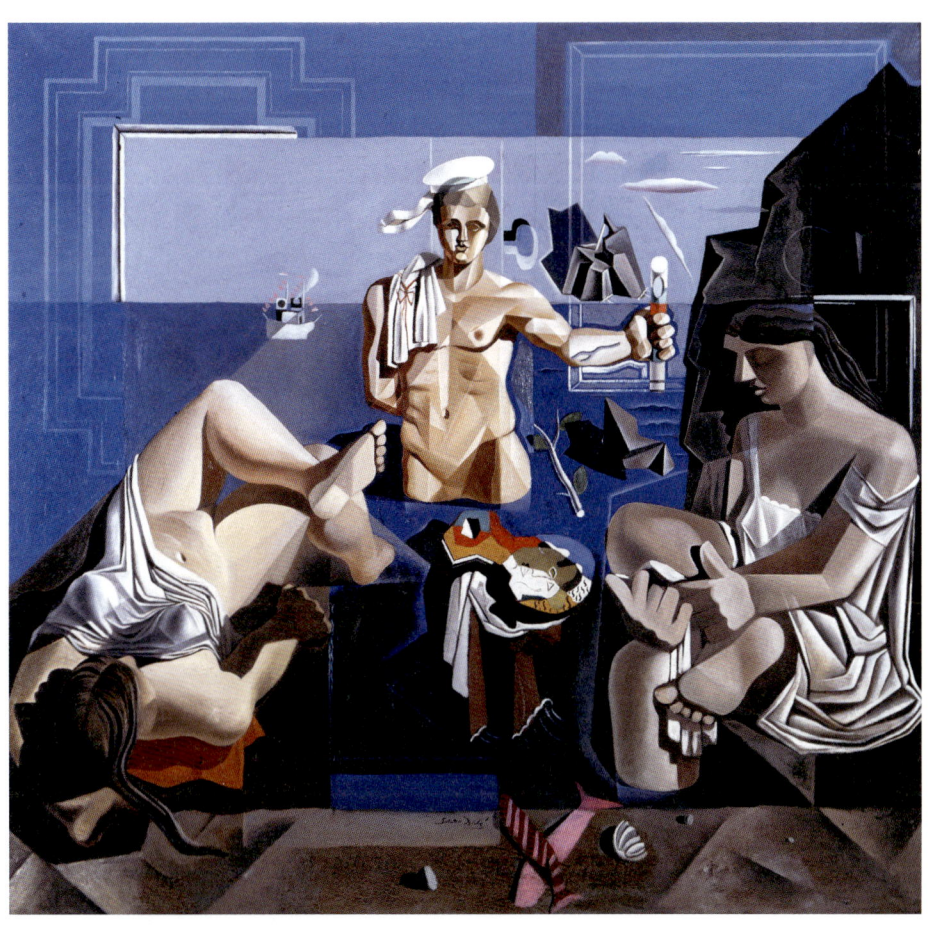

63
Composició amb tres figures. "Acadèmia neocubista"
(Composition with Three Figures. "Neo-cubist Academy")
1926
Oil on canvas, 190 × 200 cm
Museu de Montserrat, Montserrat, Barcelona

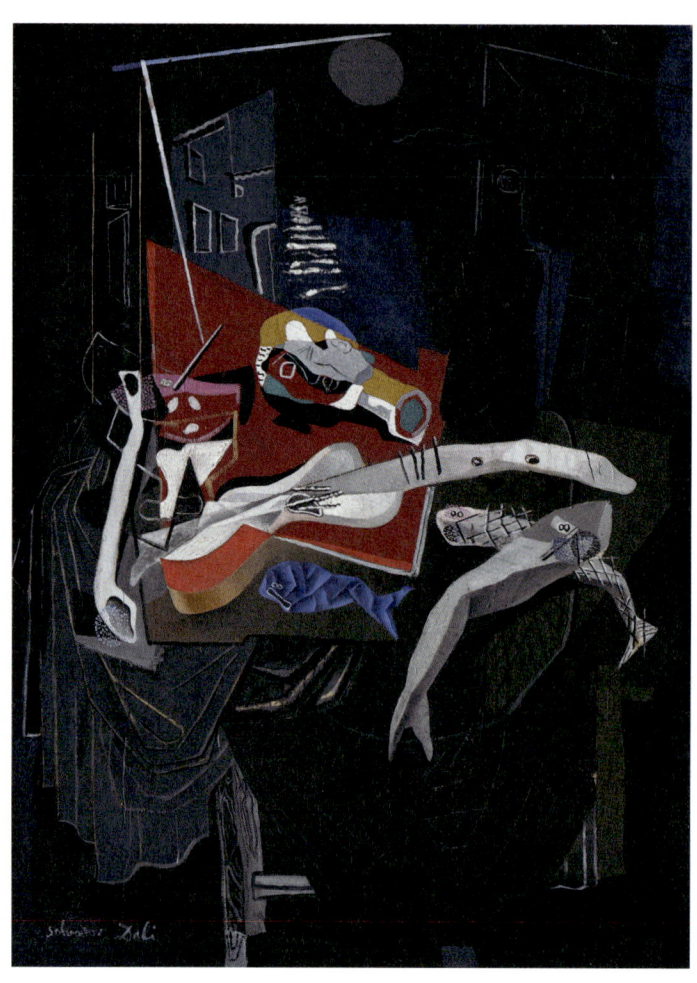

64

Natura morta (Still Life)

1926

Oil on canvas, 199 × 150 cm

Museo Nacional Centro de Arte Reina Sofía, Madrid. Dalí bequest

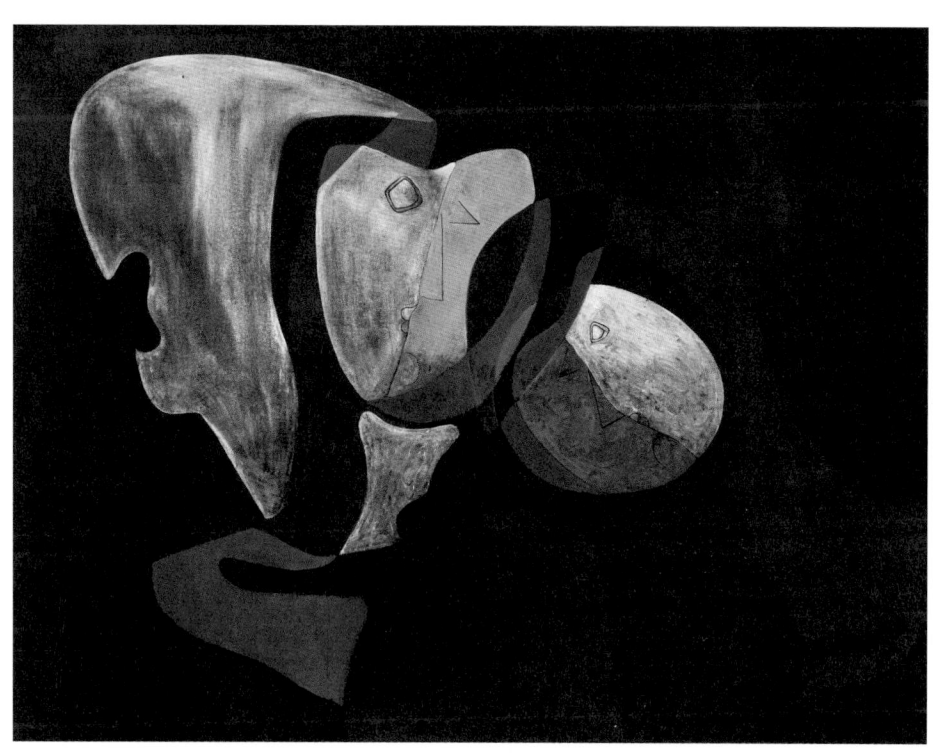

65
Dues figures (Two Figures)
1926
Oil on canvas, 149 × 198 cm
Museo Nacional Centro de Arte Reina Sofía, Madrid. Dalí bequest

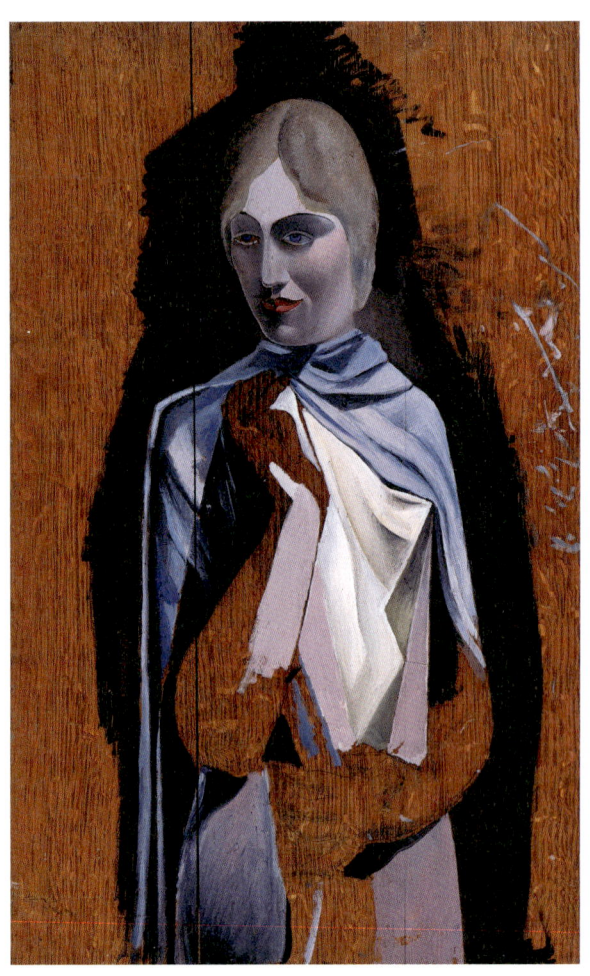

66
Retrat de la Ramoneta Montsalvatge (Portrait of Ramoneta Montsalvatge)
1925
Oil on wood panel, 61 × 38 cm
Town Hall of Figueres, on permanent deposit at the Fundació Gala-Salvador Dalí, Figueres

Cubism and Beyond

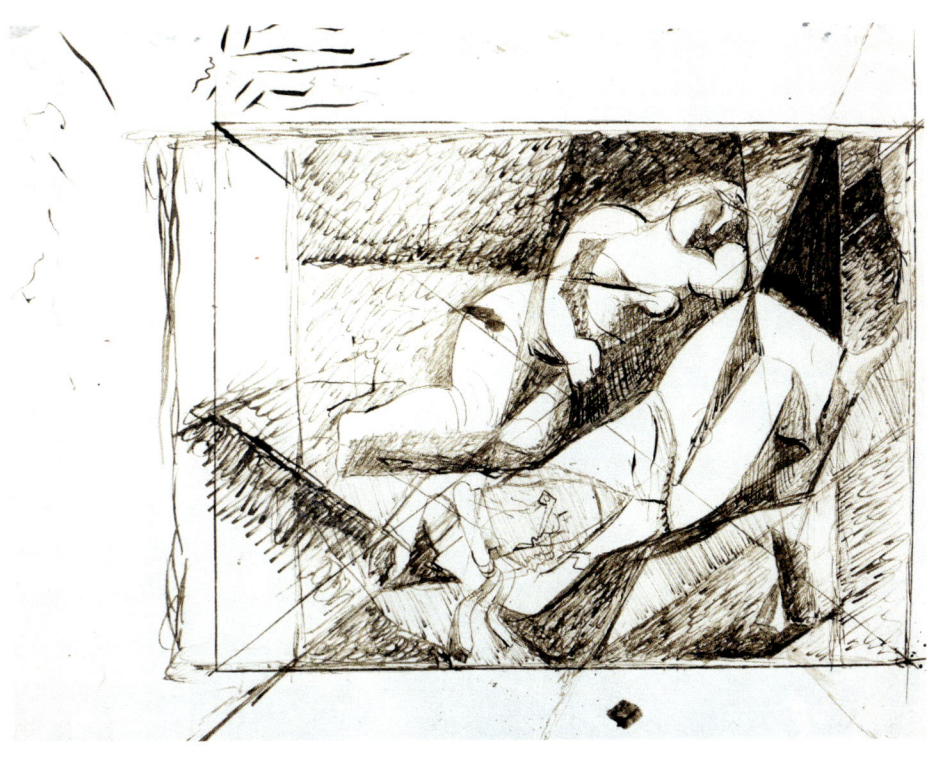

67
Cubist Study of Figures on a Beach
c. 1925–1926
Ink on paper, 19.7 × 25.4 cm
The Dalí Museum, St. Petersburg, Florida

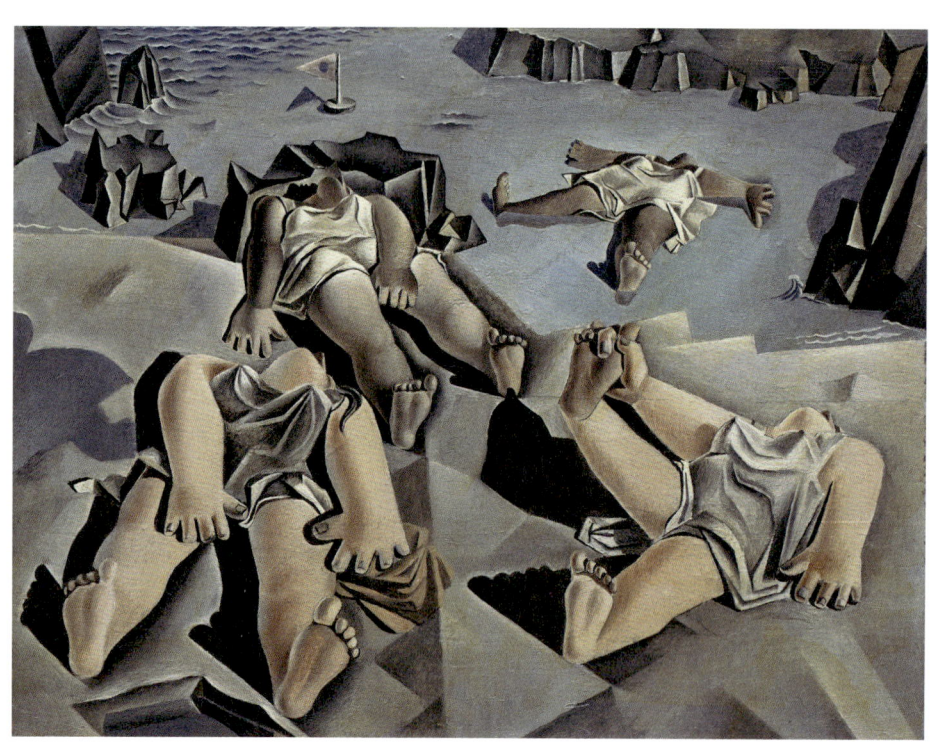

68
Figures ajagudes a la sorra (Figures Lying on the Sand)
1926
Oil on wood panel, 20.7 × 27.3 cm
Fundació Gala-Salvador Dalí, Figueres

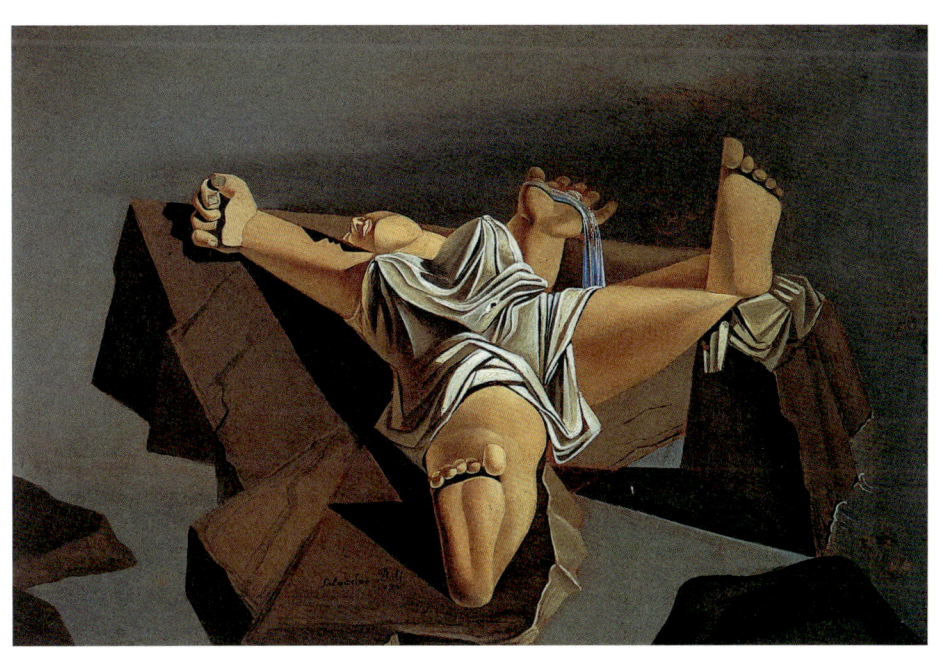

69
Figura damunt les roques (Figure on the Rocks)
1926
Oil on board, 27 × 41 cm
The Dalí Museum, St. Petersburg, Florida

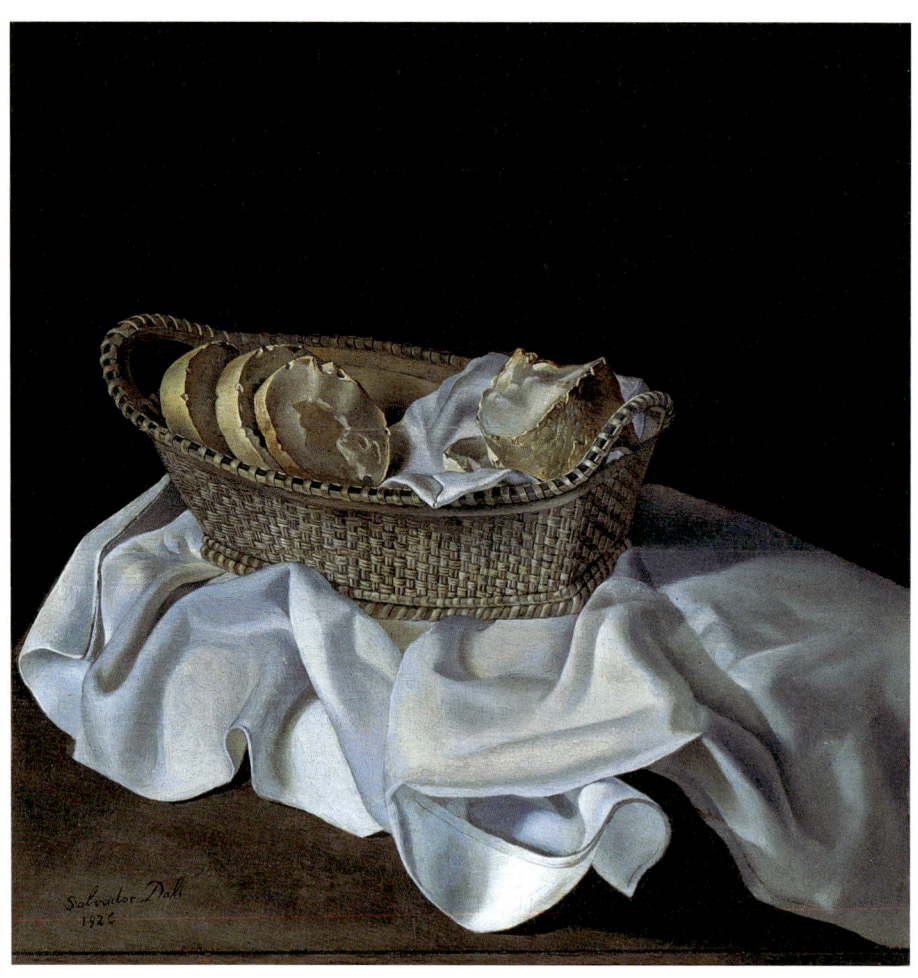

70
Panera del pa (The Basket of Bread)
1926
Varnish paint on wood panel, 31.5 × 31.5 cm
The Dalí Museum, St. Petersburg, Florida

Cubism and Beyond

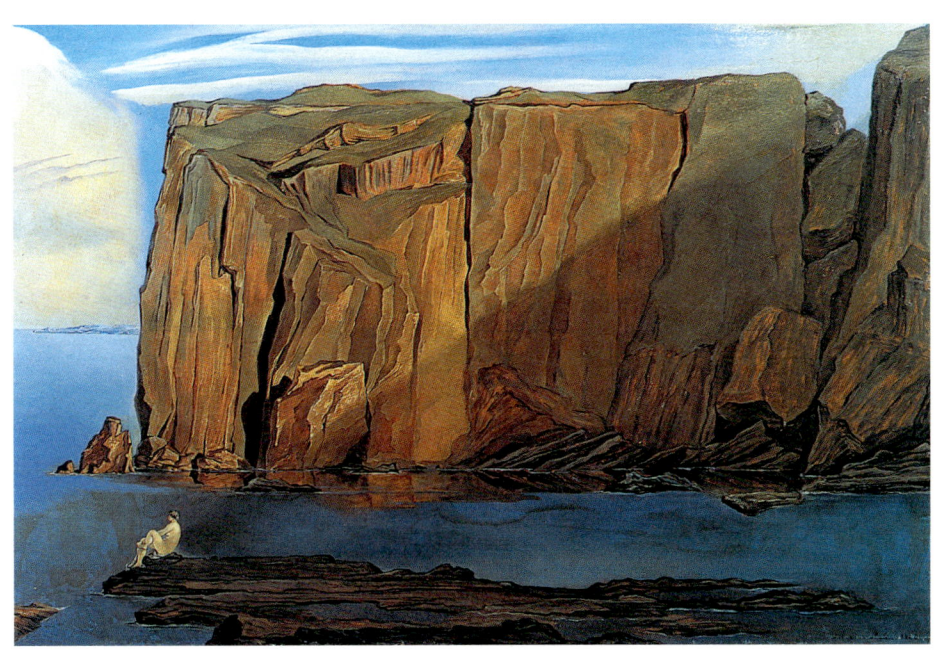

71
Penya-segats (Cliffs)
1926
Oil on wood panel, 27 × 41 cm
Private collection

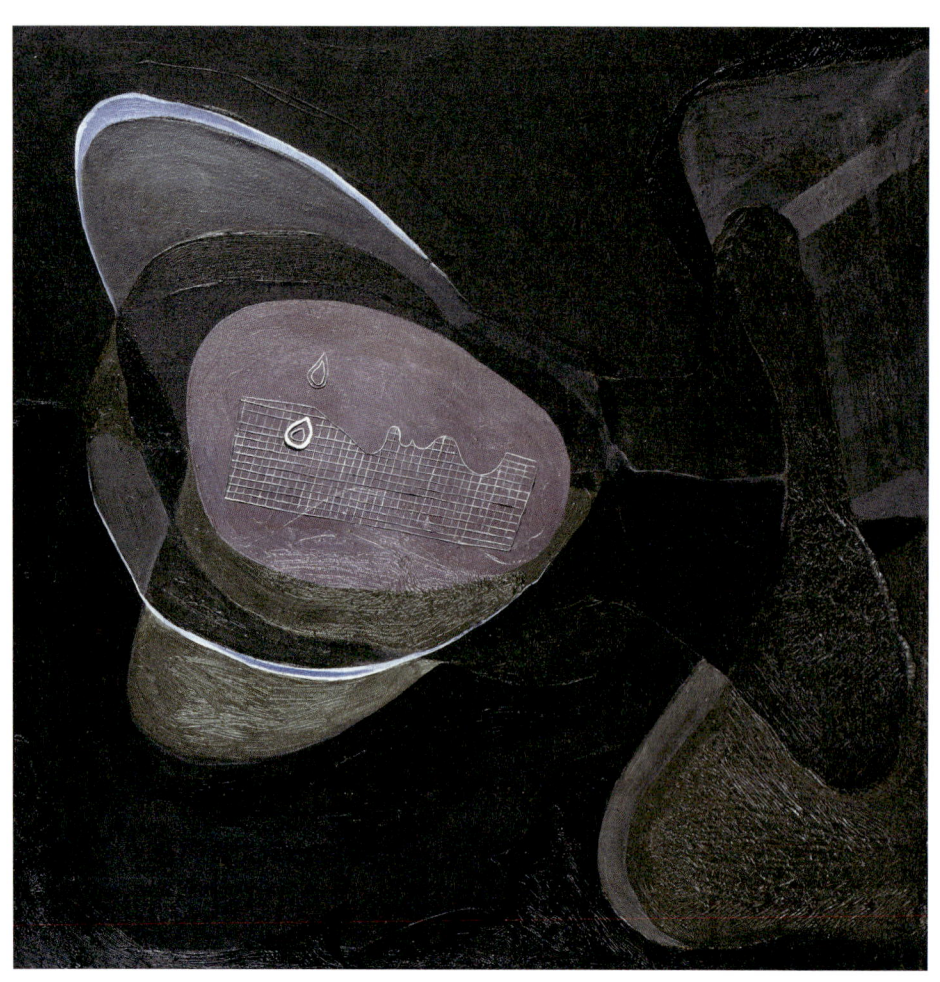

72

Cap (Head)

1926

Oil on canvas, 100 × 100 cm

Town Hall of Figueres, on permanent deposit at the Fundació Gala-Salvador Dalí, Figueres

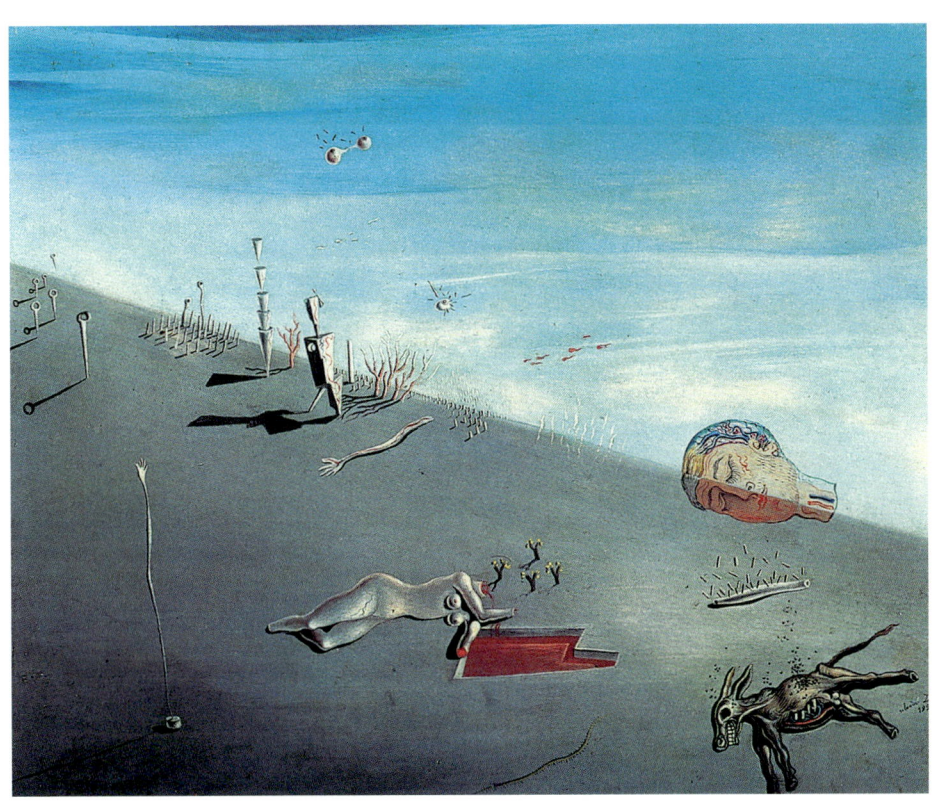

73
Étude pour « Le miel est plus doux que le sang »
(Study for "Honey is Sweeter than Blood")
1926
Oil on wood panel, 37.8 × 46.2 cm
Fundació Gala-Salvador Dalí, Figueres

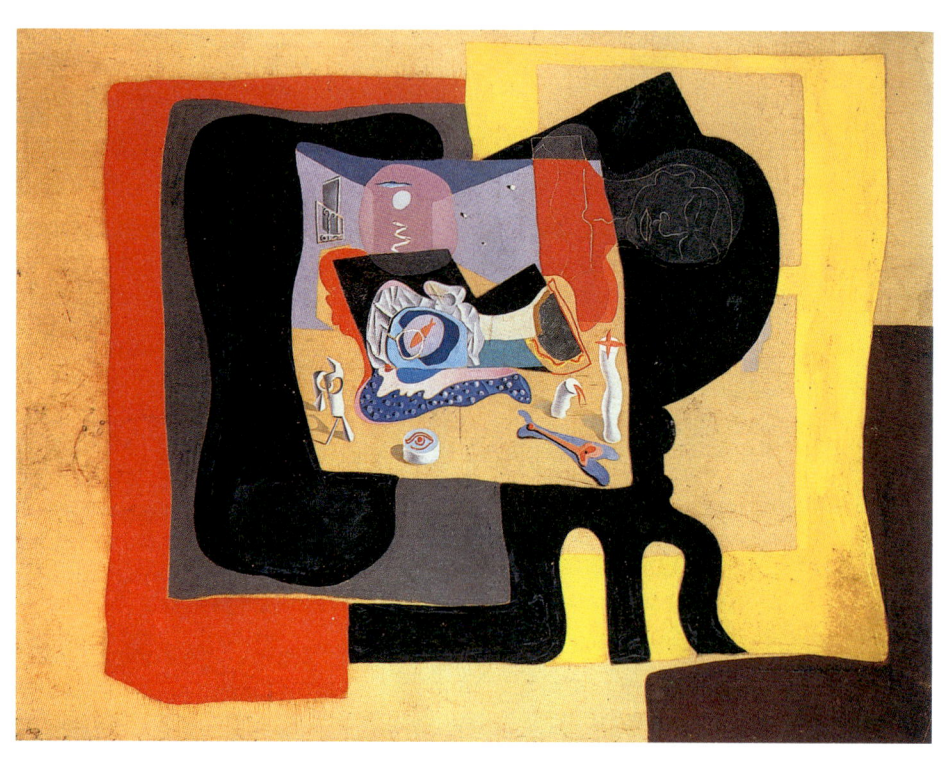

74
Natura morta (Still Life)
1926
Oil on canvas, 148 × 199 cm
Fundació Gala-Salvador Dalí, Figueres. Dalí bequest

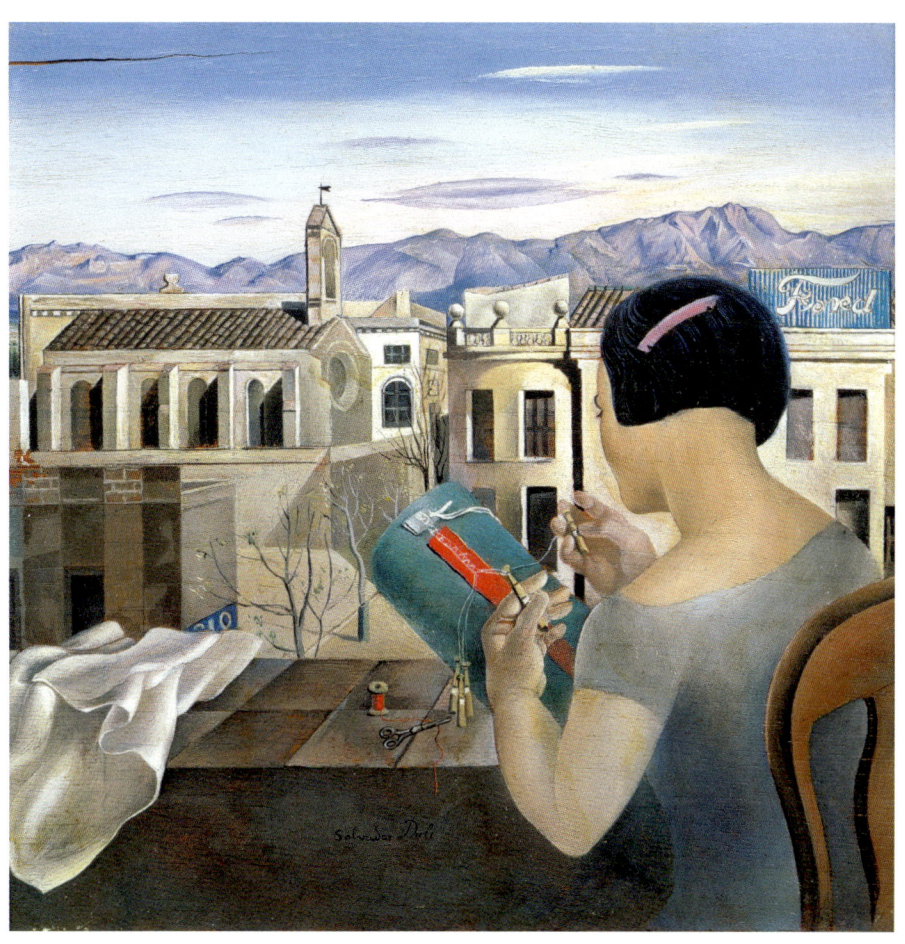

75
Noia de Figueres (Girl from Figueres)
1926
Oil on wood panel, 20.8 × 21.5 cm
Fundació Gala-Salvador Dalí, Figueres

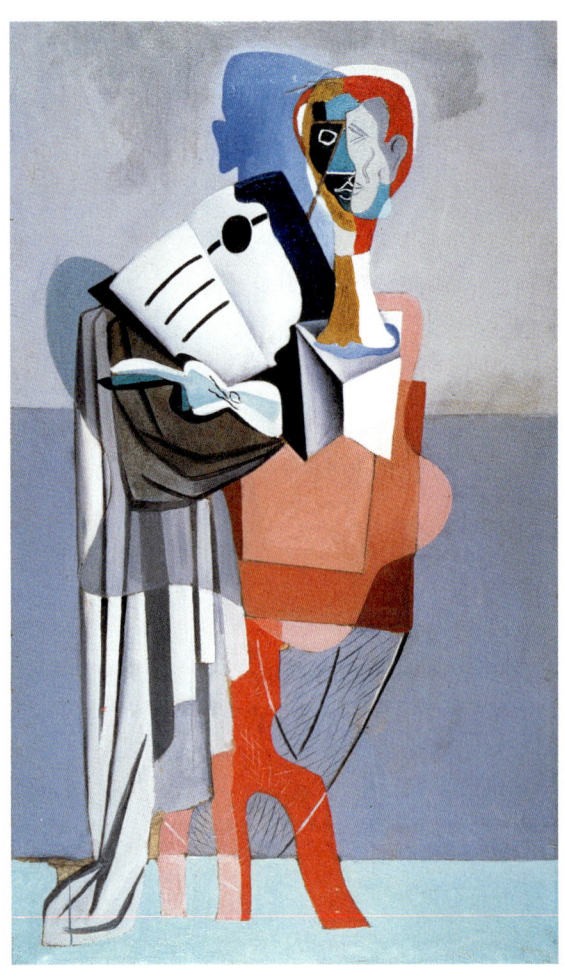

76
Taula davant el mar (Table in front of the Sea)
1926
Oil on canvas, 149.5 × 90 cm
Town Hall of Figueres, on permanent deposit at the Fundació Gala-Salvador Dalí, Figueres

Cubism and Beyond

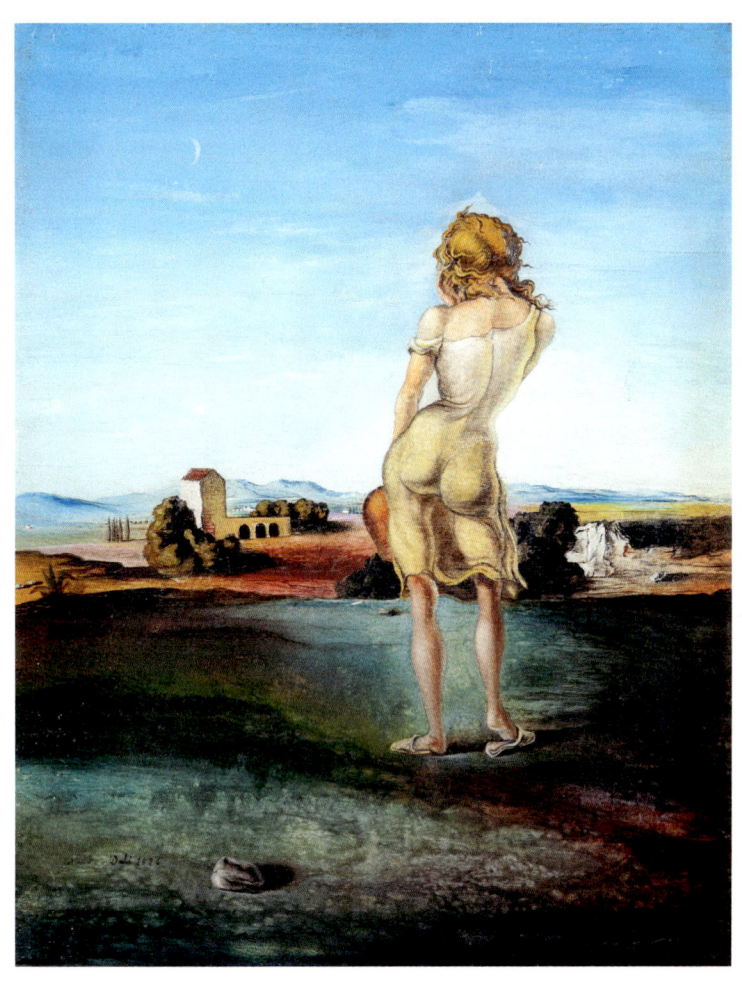

77
La noia dels rulls (Girl with Curls)
1926
Oil on wood panel, 51 × 40 cm
The Dalí Museum, St. Petersburg, Florida

1924–1926

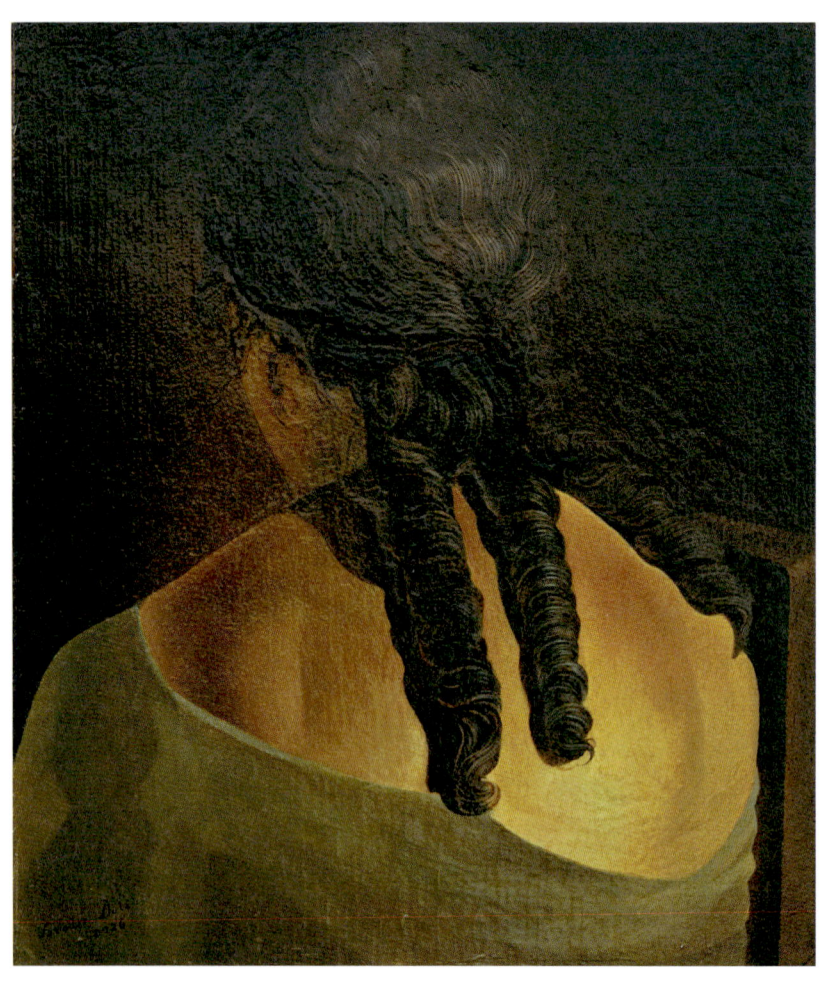

78
Girl's Back
1926
Oil on wood panel, 32 × 27 cm
The Dalí Museum, St. Petersburg, Florida

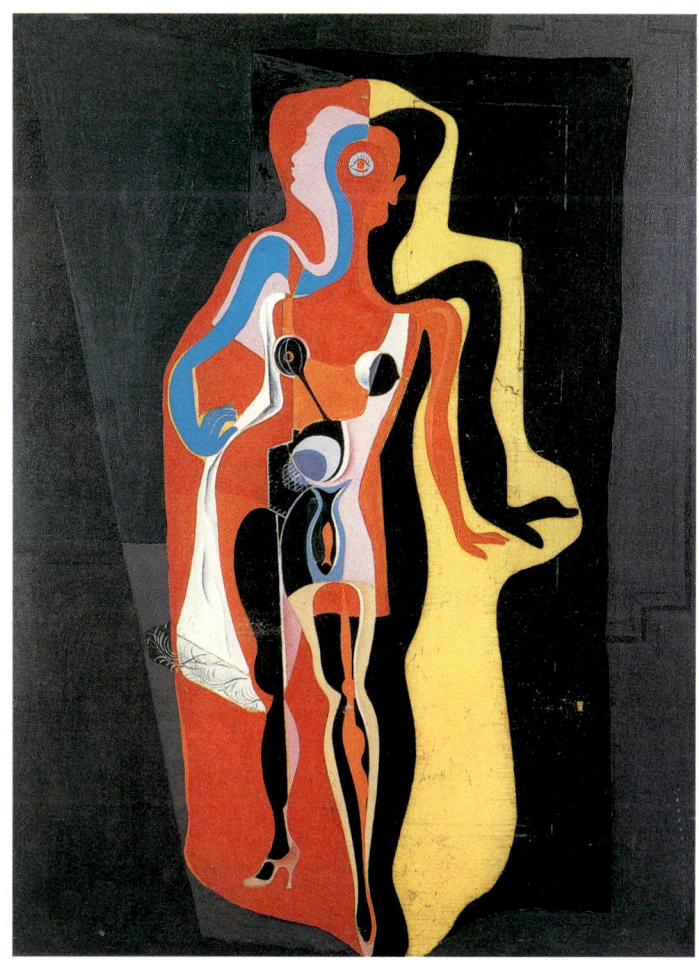

79
Figura (Figure)
1926
Oil on canvas, 198 × 148 cm
Fundació Gala-Salvador Dalí, Figueres. Dalí bequest

1924–1926

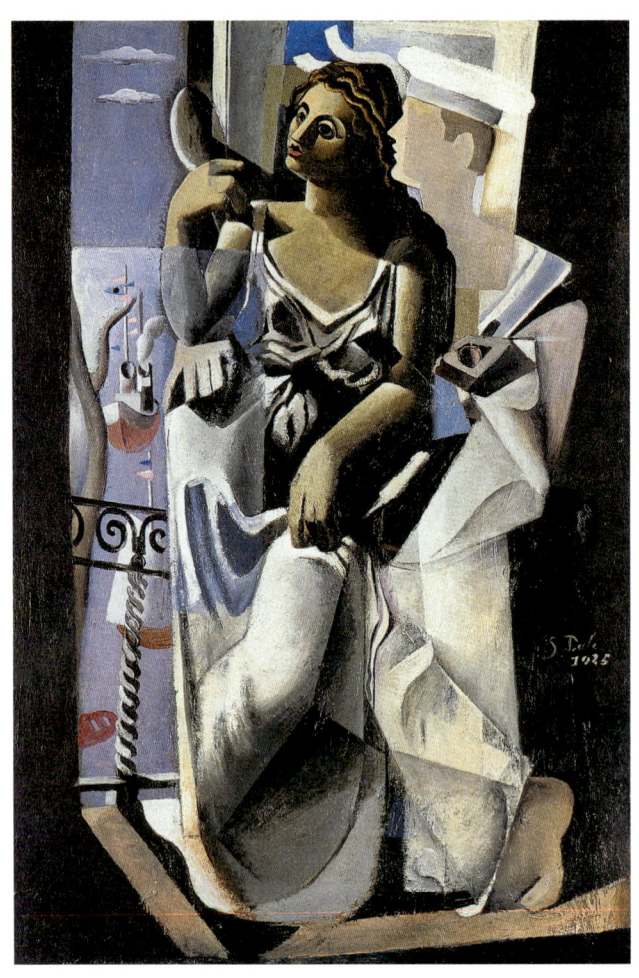

80
Venus i un mariner (Homenatge a Salvat-Papasseit)
(Venus and Sailor [Homage to Salvat-Papasseit])
1925
Oil on canvas, 215 × 147.5 cm (measurements framed)
Ikeda Museum of 20th Century Art, Itō, Shizuoka Prefecture, Japan

Cubism and Beyond

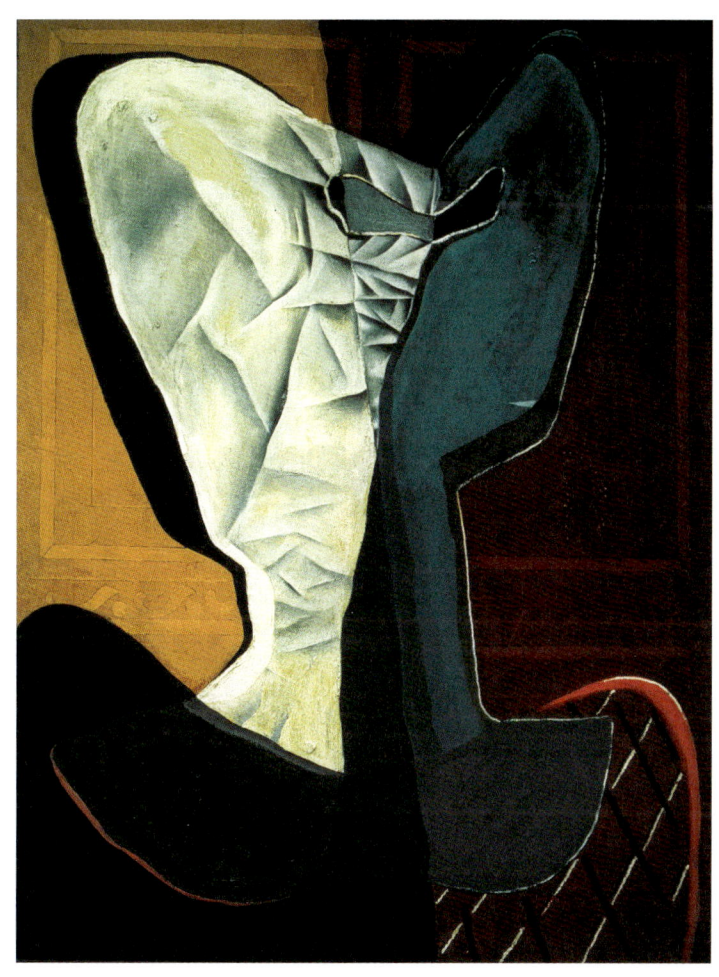

81
Arlequí (Harlequin)
1926
Oil on canvas, 196.5 × 150 cm
Museo Nacional Centro de Arte Reina Sofía, Madrid

1924–1926

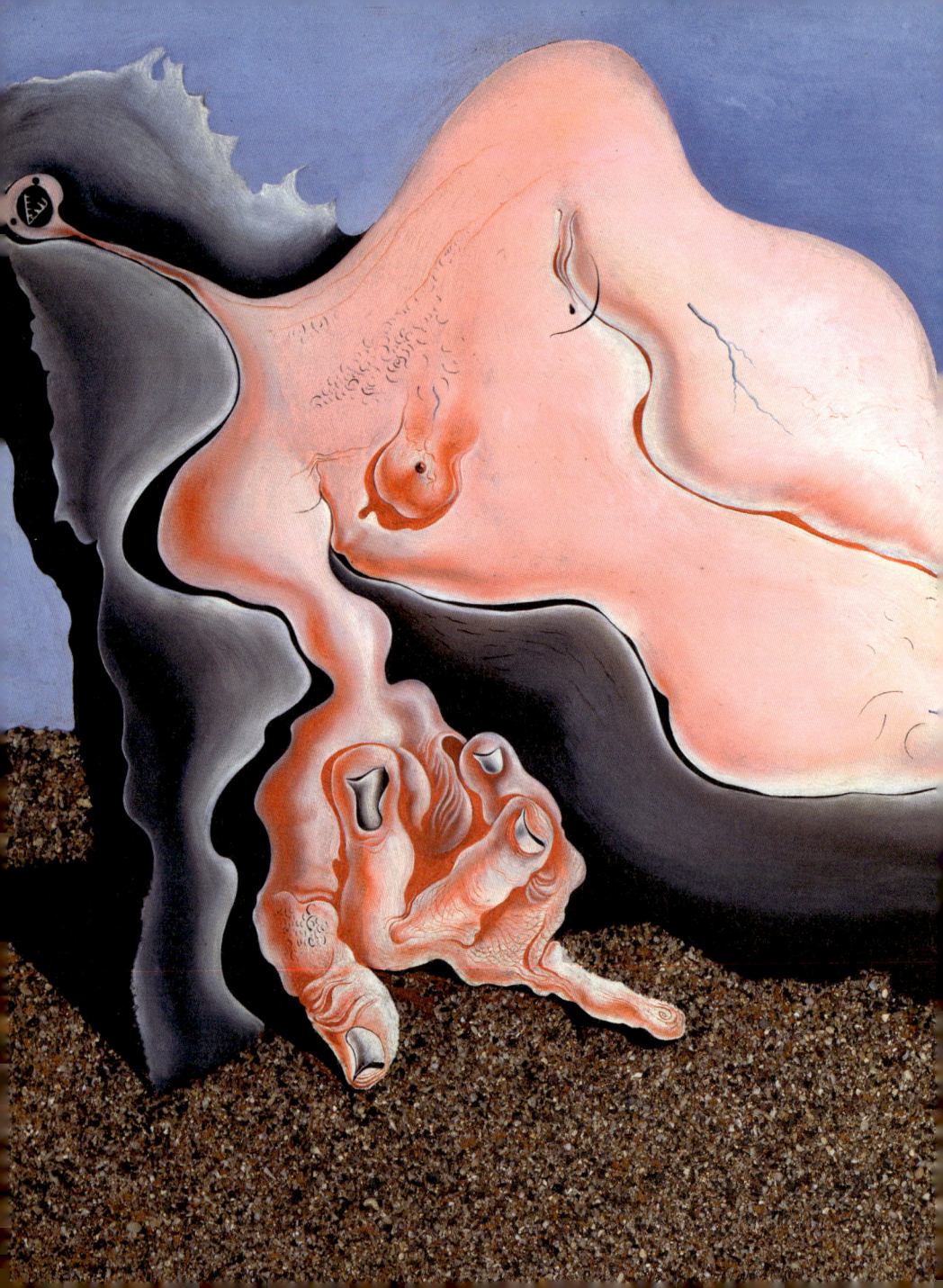

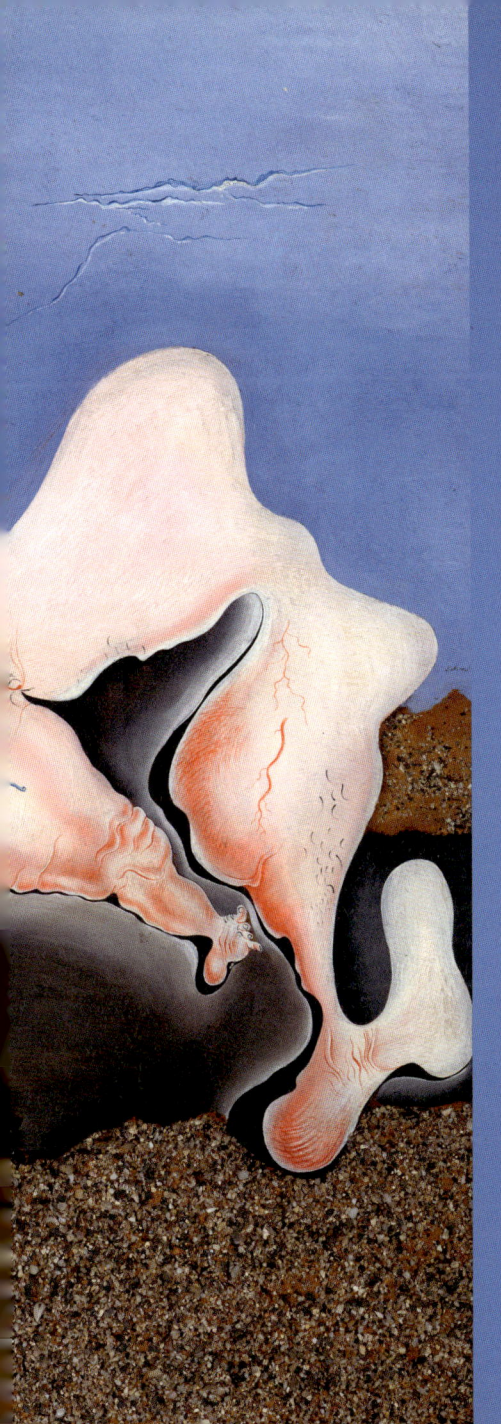

From Cubism
to Anti-Art

1927–1928

In 1927, as reported by the French critic Maurice Raynal (1884–1954) in his *Anthologie de la peinture en France de 1906 à nos jours* (1927) and repeated in the French and Spanish press, the Catalan painter Joan Miró (1893–1983) proclaimed, 'I want to assassinate painting'. This attack on painting was a challenge to the concept of painting understood as the preeminent Fine Art and proposed instead that art should be fused with lived experience. At the same time, Miró's proclamation opened up the problem of 'anti-art,' a provocation that was immediately taken up by the younger Dalí and many of his art critic peers working in Catalonia.

For Dalí, anti-art and 'anti-painting' were stepping stones towards Surrealism, yet it is important to clarify that they were not the same thing. Anti-art engaged with aspects of mass culture not associated with the Fine Arts, including the objectivity of photography, while anti-painting sought to incorporate non-artistic materials into painting. Catalan critics like Sebastià Gasch (1897–1980), a supporter of both Miró and Dalí, was ambiguous about Surrealism. Miró however was already very much engaged with the movement, having participated in the group's events, most notably the 1925 exhibition of Surrealist painting held at the Galerie Pierre, Paris, and Breton had already bought one of the artist's paintings. Anti-artistic ideas were played out in the Catalan press in newspapers like Barcelona's *La Publicitat* and in the literary review *L'Amic de les arts*, published in nearby Sitges. Eventually Dalí, Gasch and the writer Lluís Montanyà (1903–1985) set out this position in their stridently worded and collectively signed *Yellow Manifesto*, published in March 1928, which denounced conventional Catalan artistic modes.

Some of Dalí's paintings from 1926 to 1927 drew on the motif from Picasso's plaster heads, seemingly split in two, and suggesting a metaphorical division, to which Dalí introduced the suggestion of a second, doubled figure. This was for him a more private and subjective evocation of his close friend the poet Lorca, and this compositional device points to their artistic complicity. An example of this was his *Harlequin* (1926) [81], which figured in his second solo exhibition at Galeries Dalmau in 1926.

In 1927, another group of paintings, that may be called 'anti-paintings', were clearly designed to shock and provoke the regional Catalan audience, given that they too had a public presence in exhibitions and publications. For example, Dalí's *Apparatus and Hand* (1927) [83], presents a bizarre geometric construction, whose head is composed of a throbbing red hand. This figure occupies a kind of terrace set between a Mediterranean seaside scene that throws sharp shadows and is accompanied by a female bather to the right, and to the left a rotting donkey and a floating female torso. While notionally a simple bathing scene, Dalí stretches the possibilities of this subject to its limit.

Similarly, *Futile Efforts* (1927–28) [85], also known as *Little Ashes,* shows a torso of a female figure giving birth to a bird emerging from her womb. This disturbing figure is accompanied by a disembodied thumb, rotting donkeys, fragments of nude female bathers, a detached male head and a host of other disturbing details. Various writers have suggested Dalí's imagery in 1927 derived from a fascination with masturbation. Indeed, these works may also reveal his reading of psychoanalyst Sigmund Freud's (1856–1939) works in Spanish translation.

The public life of these works is worth noting. *Apparatus and Hand* [83] was exhibited in Barcelona's Autumn Salon, held at the Sala Parés in 1927. It was then exhibited in Figueres in 1928, Madrid in 1929 and Paris in 1929, as well as being reproduced in the international art press in Belgium and Mexico in 1930. Similarly, *Futile Efforts* was also exhibited in Madrid and Paris in 1929 and reproduced in the Madrid newspaper supplement *Blanco y Negro* in 1929. The remarkable public visibility of Dalí's anti-painting demonstrates how Dalí was preparing to launch himself in Paris.

Dalí was aided in this by Miró who brought his dealer, Pierre Loeb, of the Galerie Pierre, where the first group exhibition of Surrealist painting had taken place in 1925, from Paris to visit Dalí in Figueres in mid-September 1927. The subject of Dalí's painting during this anti-art phase was bathers on the beach. Dali had brought to bear specific reference to his experience of Cadaqués, while retaining an awareness of Picasso's distortions of the bather subject (as seen in his 1927 Dinard bathers series), filtered through Dalí's own, peculiar self-mythology. In 1928, Dalí continued in this direction, often provoking public controversy, and once again, these works were destined to have a public life.

Now Dalí began including sand and small rocks from real beaches to represent bathers on the beach. While the incorporation of sand in painting was not entirely new – both Braque and Picasso had used sand, and, more recently in 1927, the French artist André Masson (1896–1987) had mixed sand into pigment, as well as using sand and glue to extend automatic drawing into automatic painting – Dalí retained a more disturbing and overtly sexual figuration that gestured towards Surrealism. His figures were sometimes aggressively erotic, as in *Two Figures on a Beach* (1928) [98], which was under consideration for inclusion in the Autumn Salon at Sala Parés. The painting showed a nude female torso and to the left, a small male figure represented by an erect phallus. Both were set on sand and gravel representing the beach. But the work went too far for Joan Maragall (1860–1911), Director of the Sala Parés, who infuriated Dalí by rejecting it. Finally, Galeries Dalmau decided to show the piece in its Inaugural Exhibition of the 1928 to 1929 season, but with a piece of cork hiding the offending parts, a compromise that did not please the young painter. A similar painting using a fisherman's cork net float affixed to the surface was also exhibited as *Female Nude* (1928) [102], giving some idea of the effect, though the cork does not remain on *Two Figures on a Beach*. Nevertheless, *Female Nude* was exhibited again in Madrid in 1928 and reproduced in the press in Madrid and Brussels. The other painting proposed for exhibition in 1928 at Sala

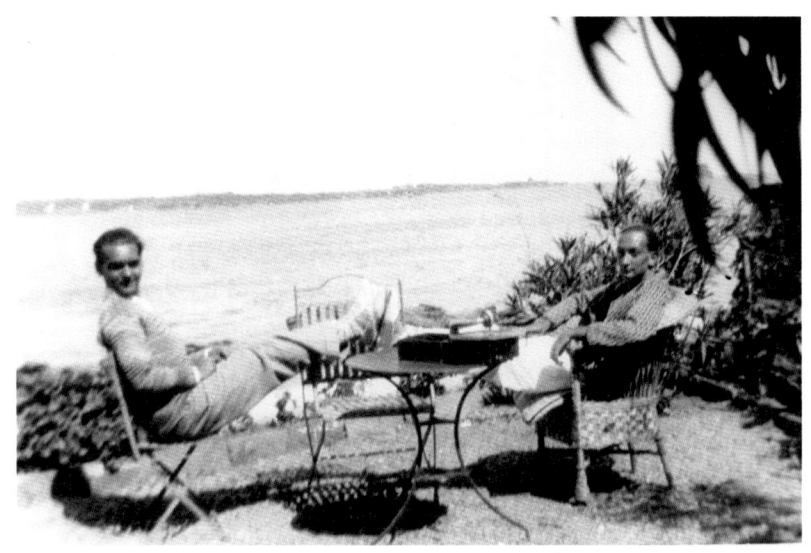

Dalí and Lorca in Cadaqués, Spain, 1927. Collection of The Dalí Museum.

Parés was *Thumb, Beach, Moon and Decaying Bird* (1928) [87]. Though less overtly shocking, it was still an odd, nocturnal landscape painting compared to the other works on display. Once again, Dali deployed sand and gravel to represent a beach setting, in which he sets a disembodied thumb and dead bird, bathed in moonlight. This painting also had a public life – it was reproduced in a 1928 newspaper review of the exhibition by writer Carles Capdevila (1879–1937), who found little of a shocking nature – and again on the cover of the literary newspaper *La Gaceta literaria* alongside a poem by the Spanish poet Jorge Guillén (1893–1984) titled *Festividad*.

Dalí's use of the unconventional materials of sand and small rocks also featured in two other bather pictures from 1928: *Female Nude* [99] and *Bathers* [100]. In the former, the head of the figure is greatly diminished and endowed with sharp, monstrous teeth. Its body is distorted, which emphasises the figure's breasts and sex. An outstretched hand is greatly enlarged, its little finger suggestive of an erect phallus. In the second figure, the bather is reduced to a lump-like torso, presented almost as an enormous thumb or a big toe perhaps. In the background more ethereal and transparent bathers appear to float above the sea. Dalí's rising international presence was evidenced by the inclusion of both these panels in an important group exhibition held at the Kunsthaus, Zürich, titled *Abstrakte und surrealistische Malerei und Plastik* (1929). Moreover, as a result of this exhibition, both works were reproduced in the French review *Documents*, first published in 1929 and edited by the French writer Georges Bataille (1897–1962), who represented a group of dissident Surrealists who rejected Breton's more mainstream Surrealism and who used *Documents* as his main instrument in challenging the opposing faction. Dalí would briefly associate with Bataille and the other members of his group, but rapidly the Catalan artist would choose Breton's Surrealism.

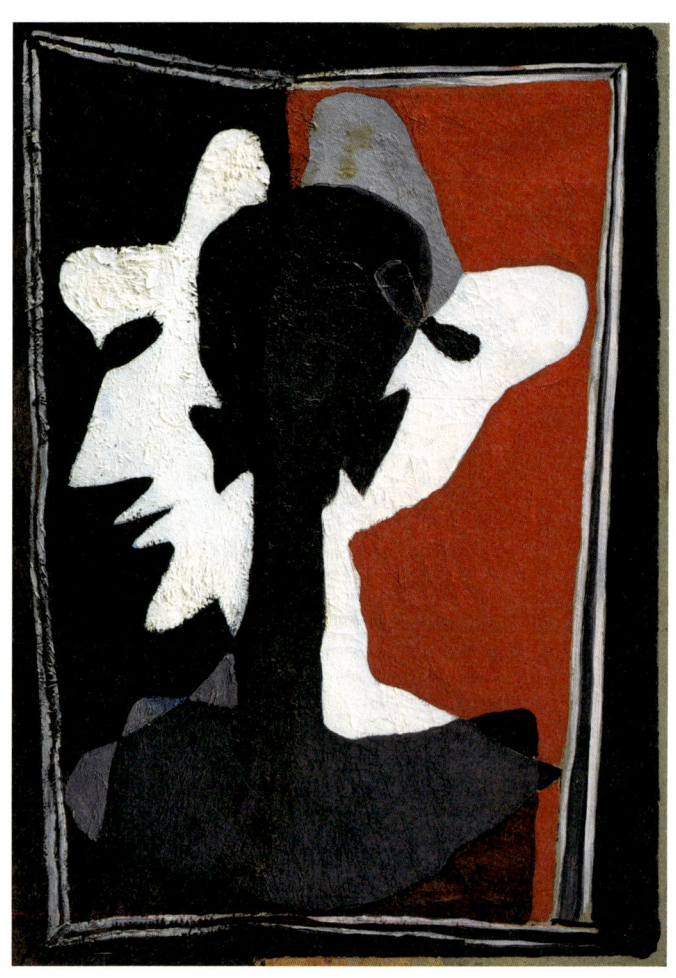

82
Self-Portrait Splitting into Three
1926–1927
Oil on canvas, 71.5 × 51.5 cm
Town Hall of Figueres, on permanent deposit at the Fundació Gala-Salvador Dalí, Figueres

From Cubism to Anti-Art

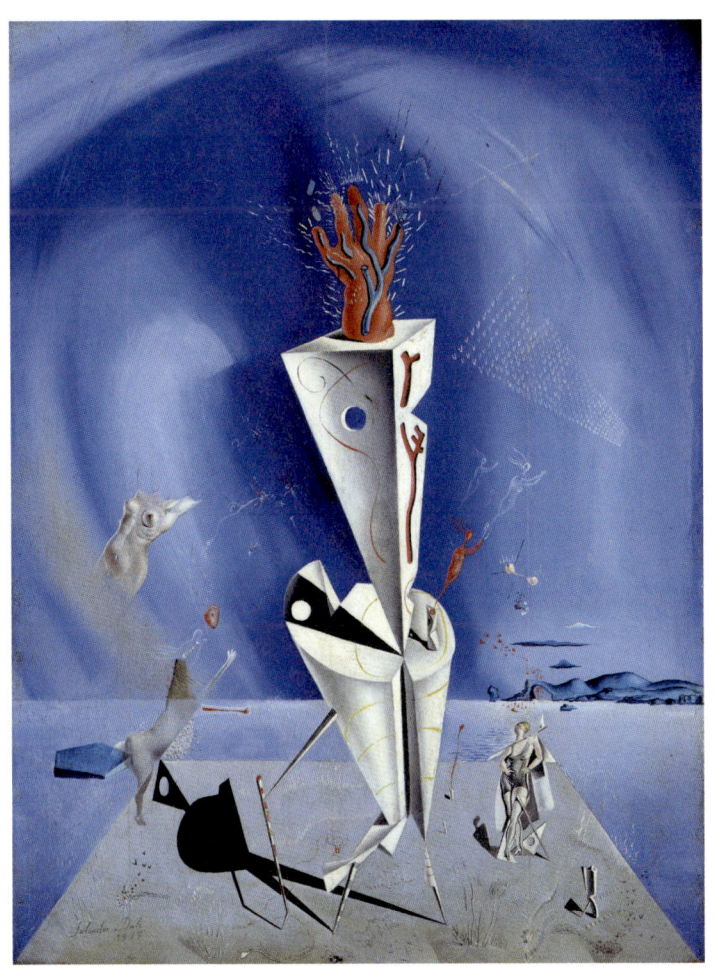

83
Aparell i mà (Apparatus and Hand)
1927
Oil on wood panel, 62.2 × 46.6 cm
The Dalí Museum, St. Petersburg, Florida

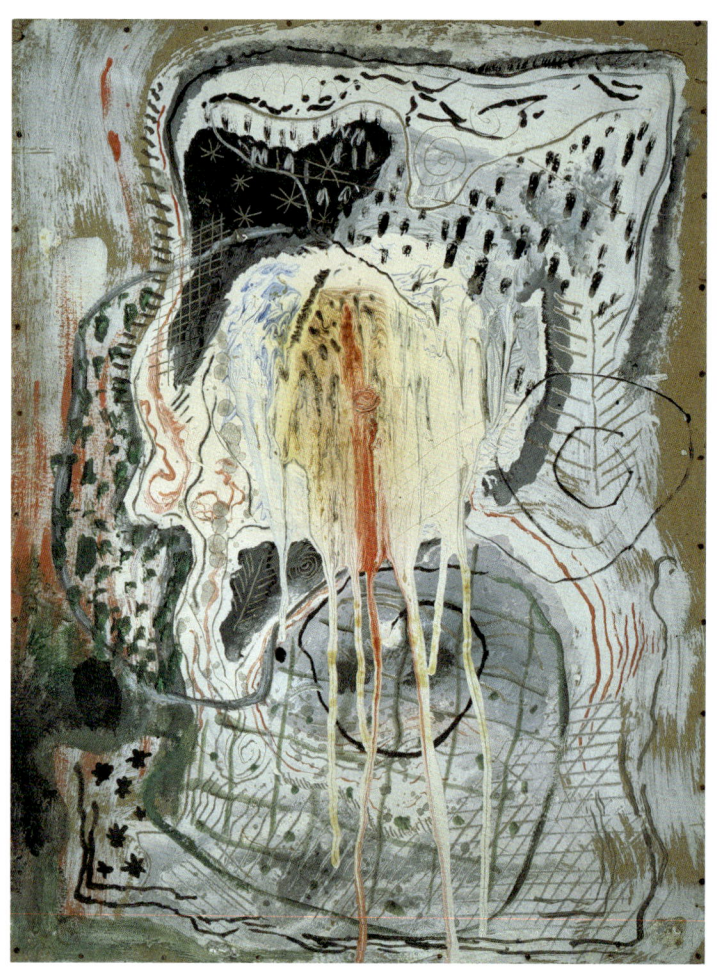

84
Female Nude Seated in an Armchair
1927–1928
Mixed media on cardboard, 68.8 × 52.5 cm
Town Hall of Figueres, on permanent deposit at the Fundació Gala-Salvador Dalí, Figueres

From Cubism to Anti-Art

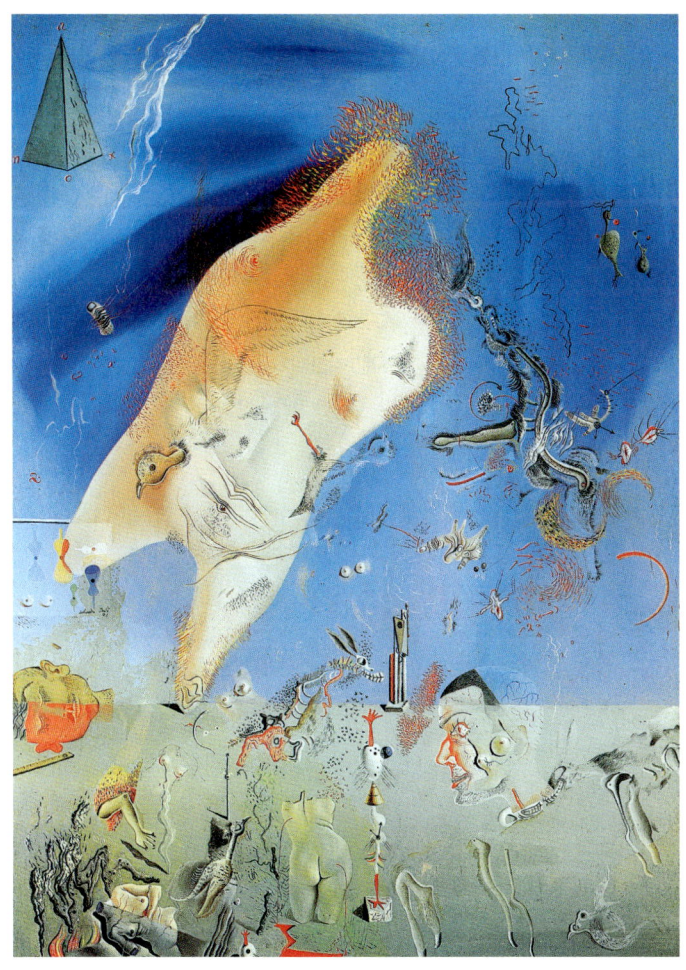

85
Los esfuerzos estériles (Futile Efforts)
1927–1928
Oil on plywood panel, 64 × 48 cm
Museo Nacional Centro de Arte Reina Sofía, Madrid

1927–1928

From Cubism to Anti-Art

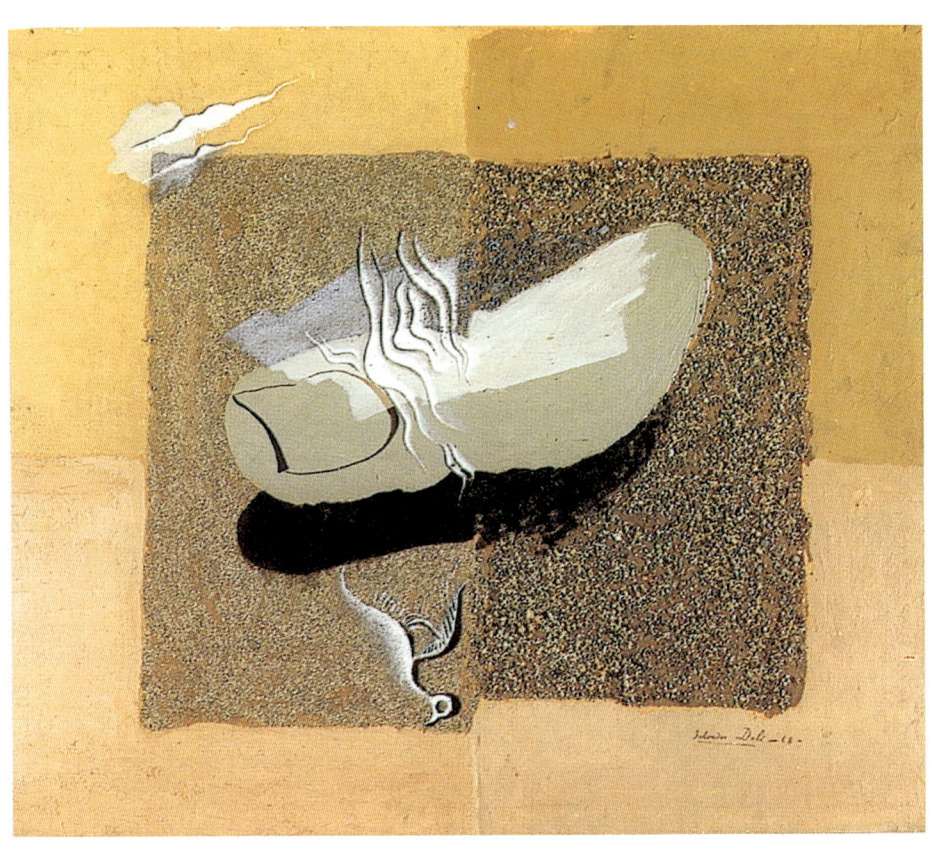

86
The Wounded Bird
1928
Oil, sand and gravel on cardboard, 55 × 65.5 cm
The Mizne-Blumental Collection. Tel Aviv Museum of Art, Tel Aviv, Israel

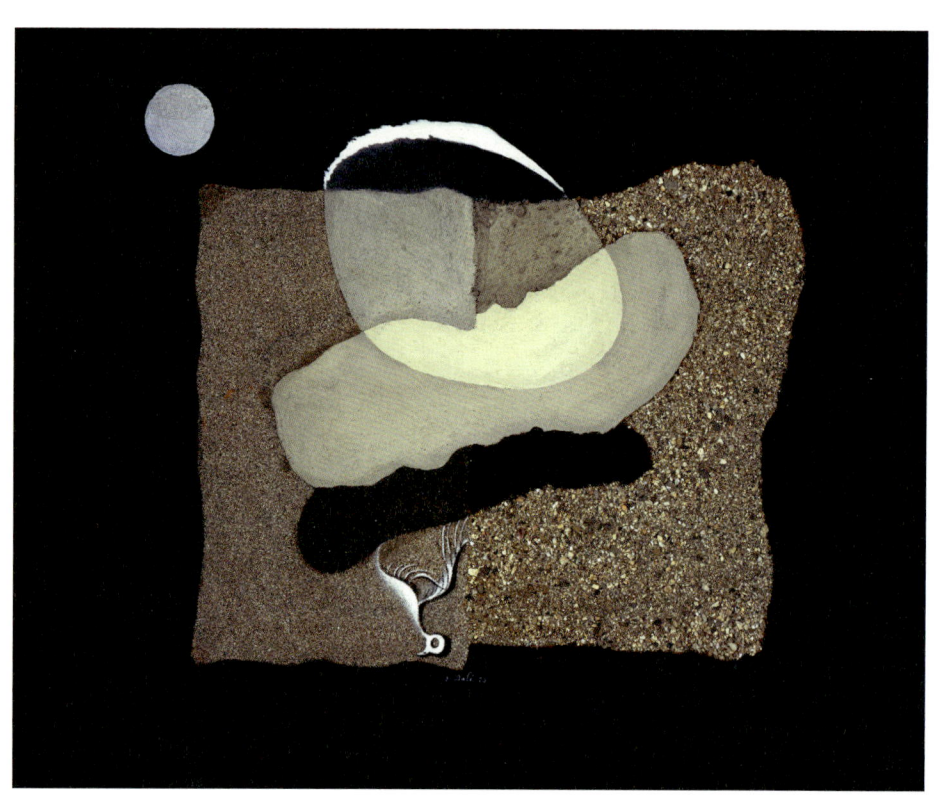

87
Dit gros, platja, lluna i ocell podrit (Thumb, Beach, Moon and Decaying Bird)
1928
Oil and collage on wood panel, 50 × 61 cm
The Dalí Museum, St. Petersburg, Florida

From Cubism to Anti-Art

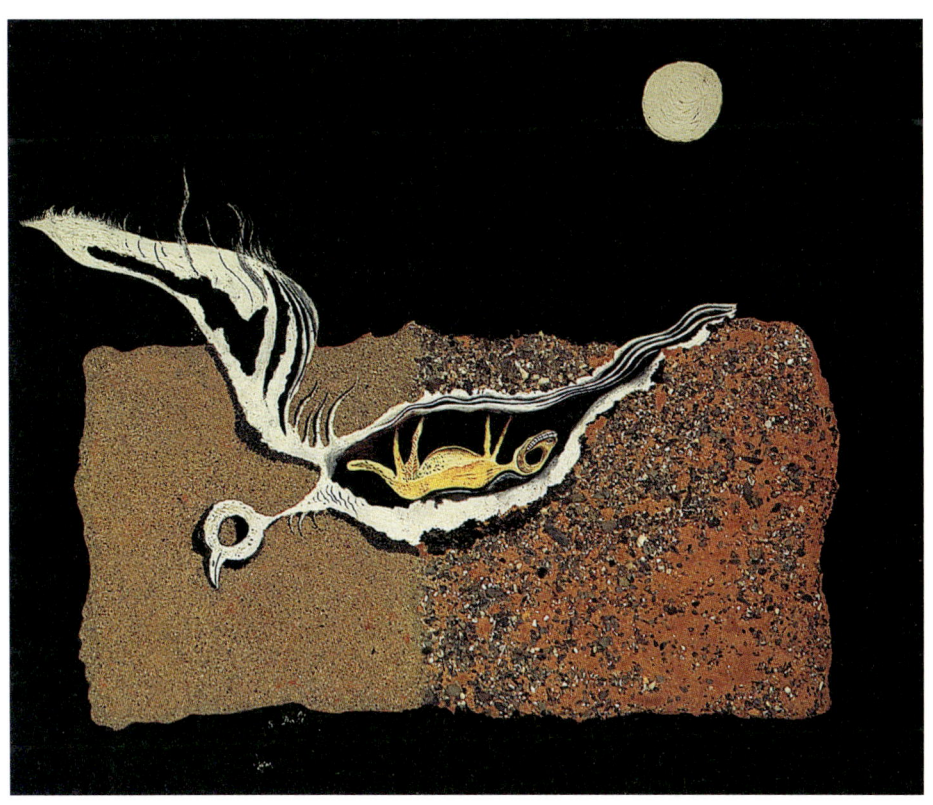

88
Bird
c. 1928
Oil, sand, pebbles and gravel on board, 49.7 × 61 cm
Scottish National Gallery of Modern Art, Edinburgh

1927–1928

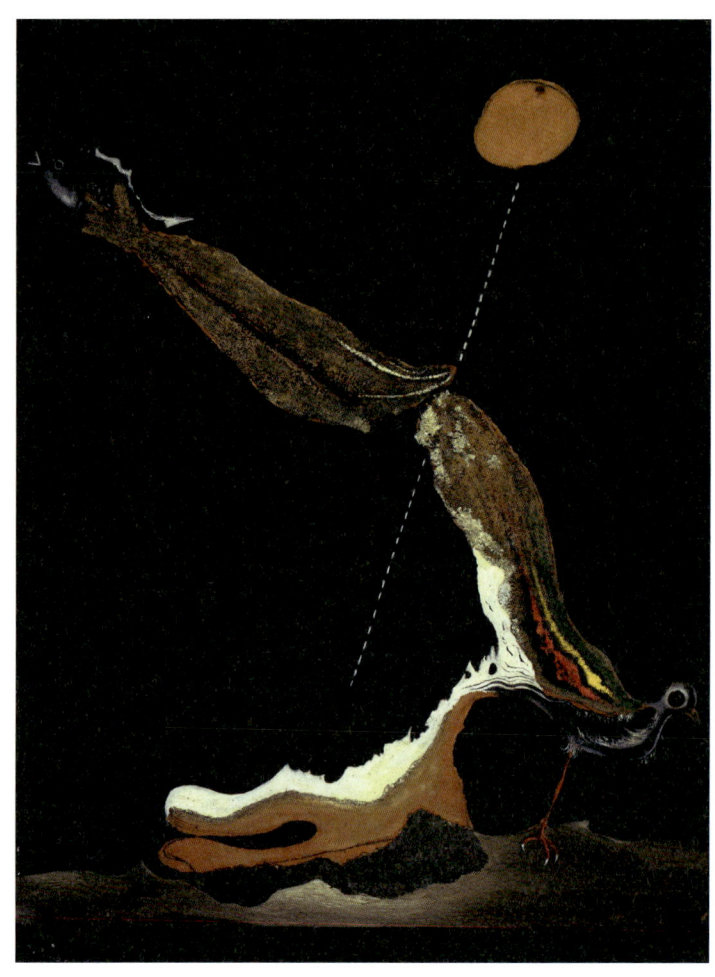

89
Bird...Fish
c. 1928
Oil and collage on wood panel, 61 × 49 cm
The Dalí Museum, St. Petersburg, Florida

From Cubism to Anti-Art

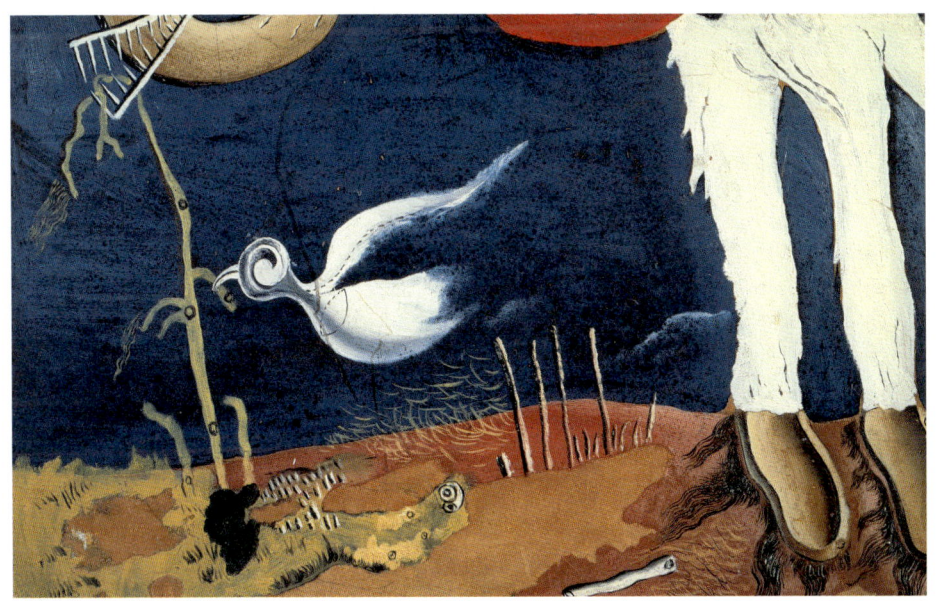

90
Rotting bird
c. 1928
Oil and sand on cardboard, 35 × 57 cm
Town Hall of Figueres, on permanent deposit at the Fundació Gala-Salvador Dalí, Figueres

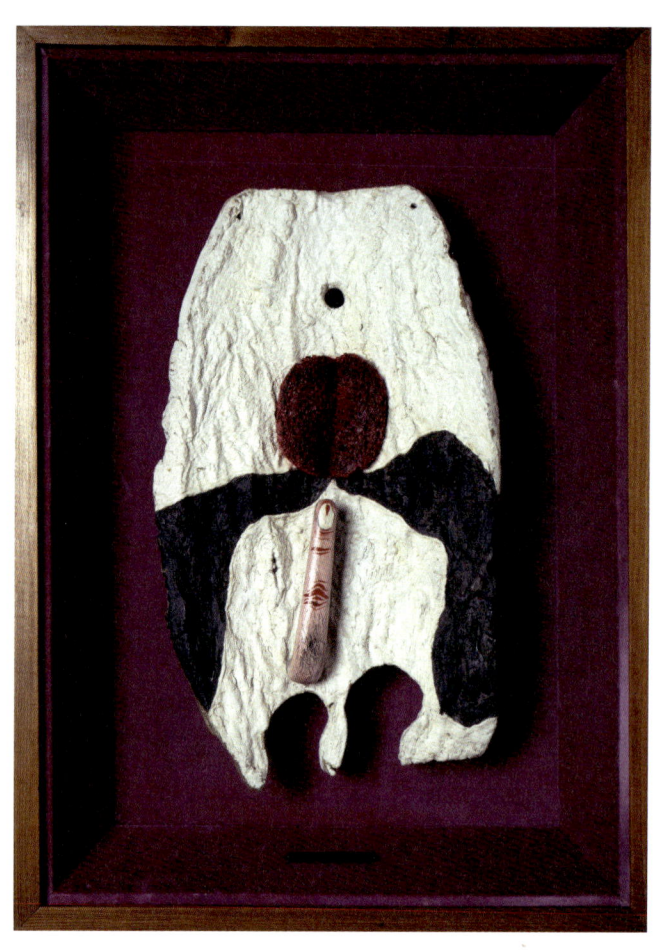

91
Anthropomorphic Beach (present state)
1928
Painted cork, sponge and wood, 48 × 28 cm
The Dalí Museum, St. Petersburg, Florida

From Cubism to Anti-Art

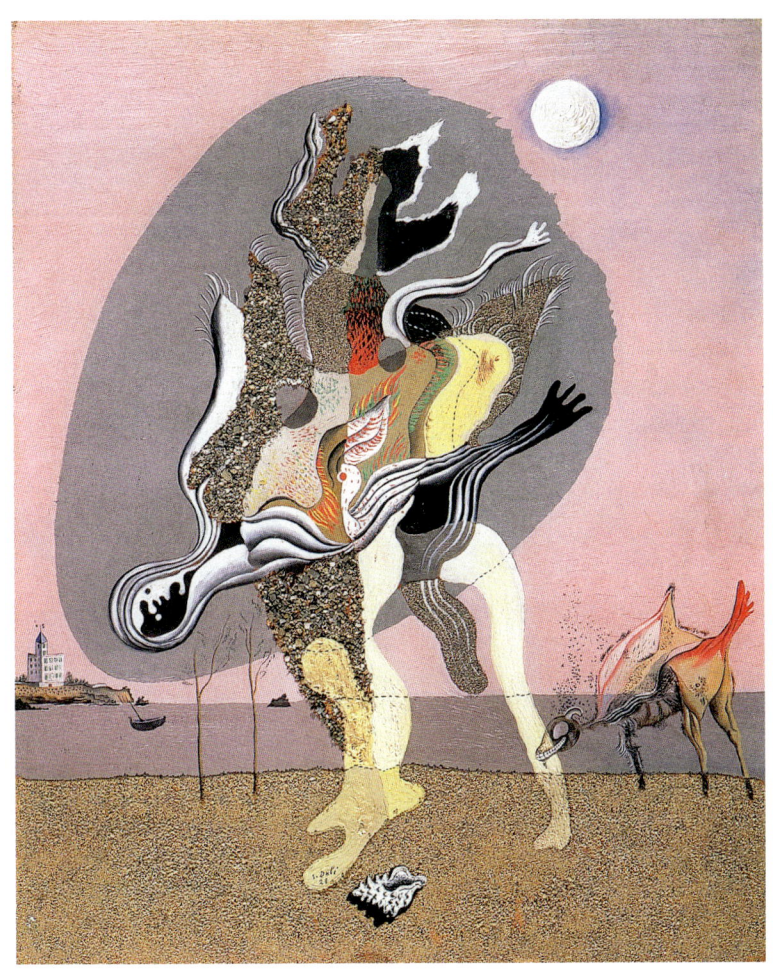

92
The Stinking Ass
1928
Oil, sand and gravel on wood panel, 61 × 50 cm
Musée National d'Art Moderne, Centre Pompidou, Paris

1927–1928

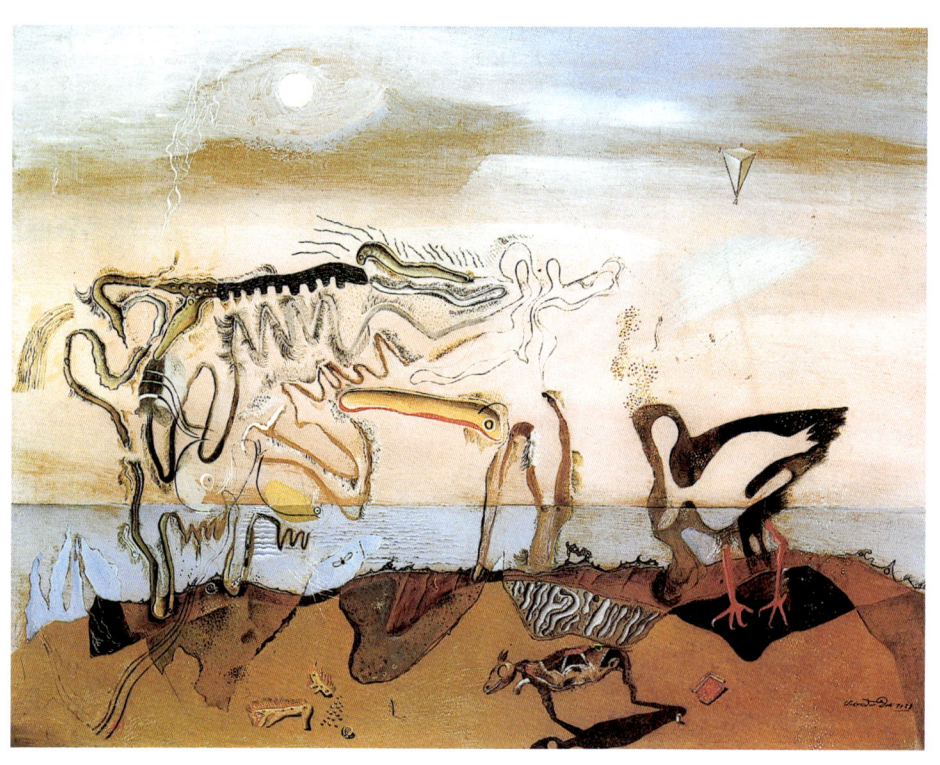

93
The Spectral Cow
1928
Oil on plywood panel, 50.2 × 64.5 cm
Musée National d'Art Moderne, Centre Pompidou, Paris

From Cubism to Anti-Art

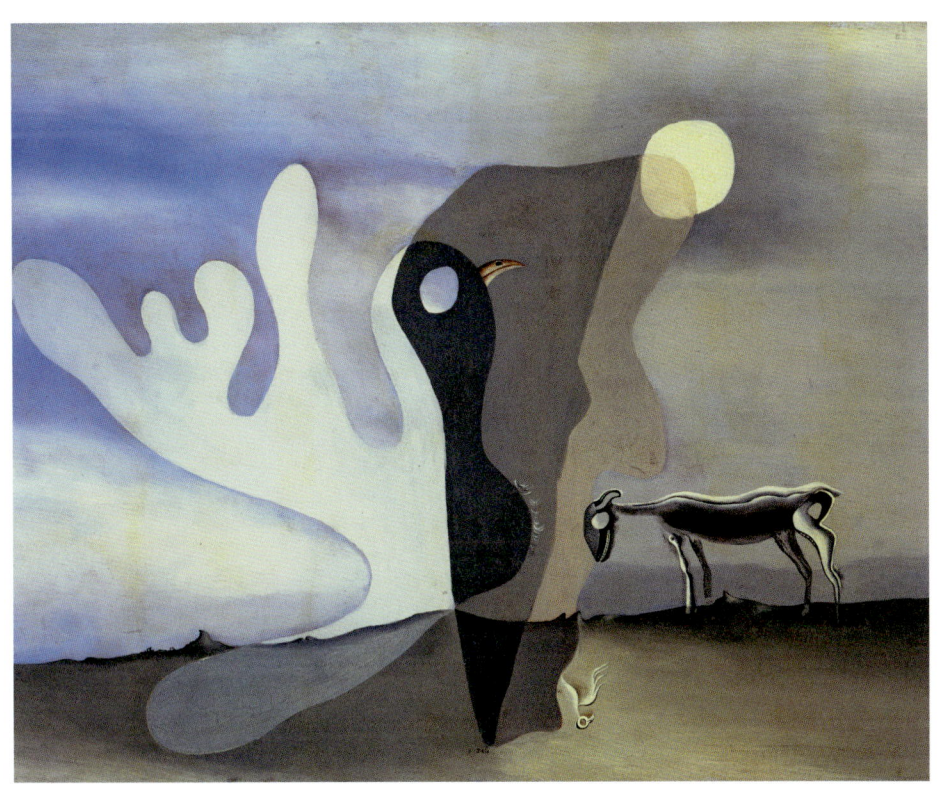

94
The Spectral Cow or *The Ram*
c. 1928
Oil on wood panel, 50.2 × 61.7 cm
The Dalí Museum, St. Petersburg, Florida

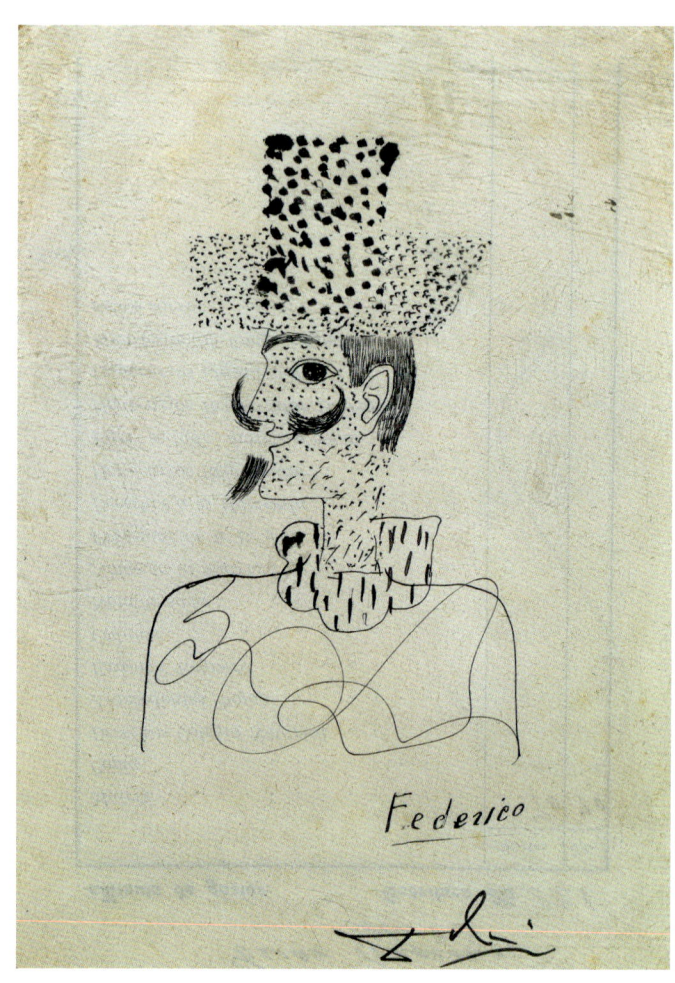

95
Self-Portrait (dedicated to Federico García Lorca)
1928
Pen and ink on paper, 22 × 16 cm
Collection Juan Abello Prat, Mollet del Vallès

From Cubism to Anti-Art

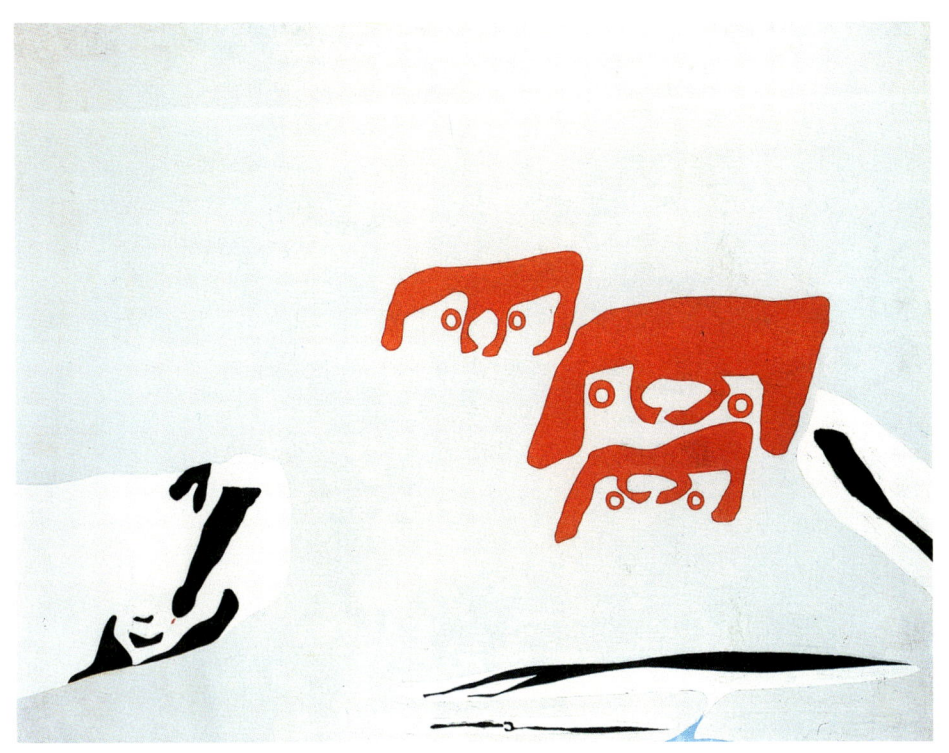

96
Four Fishermen's Wives in Cadaqués
c. 1928
Oil on canvas, 148 × 196 cm
Museo Nacional Centro de Arte Reina Sofía, Madrid. Dalí bequest

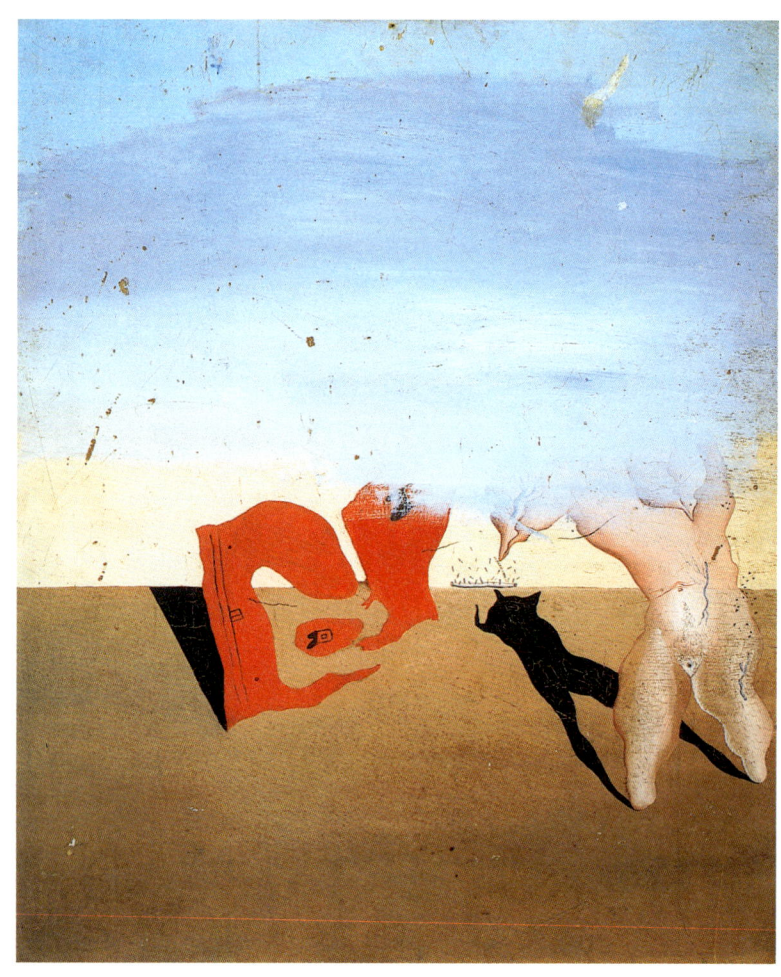

97
Surrealist Composition
c. 1928
Oil on cardboard, 75.5 × 63 cm
Town Hall of Figueres, on permanent deposit at the Fundació Gala-Salvador Dalí, Figueres

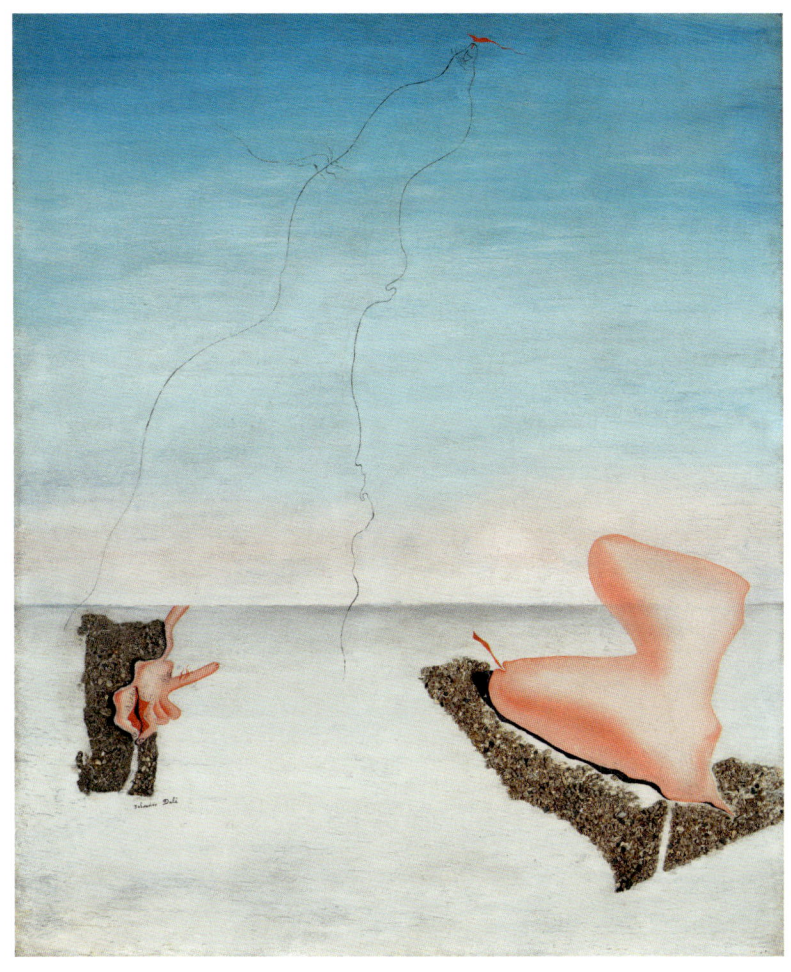

98
Dues figures en una platja (Two Figures on a Beach)
1928
Oil, shells and sand on cardboard, 76.2 × 62.2 cm
San Francisco Museum of Modern Art, San Francisco, California
Fractional gift of Jan and Mitsuko Shrem, Clos Pegase Winery Collection

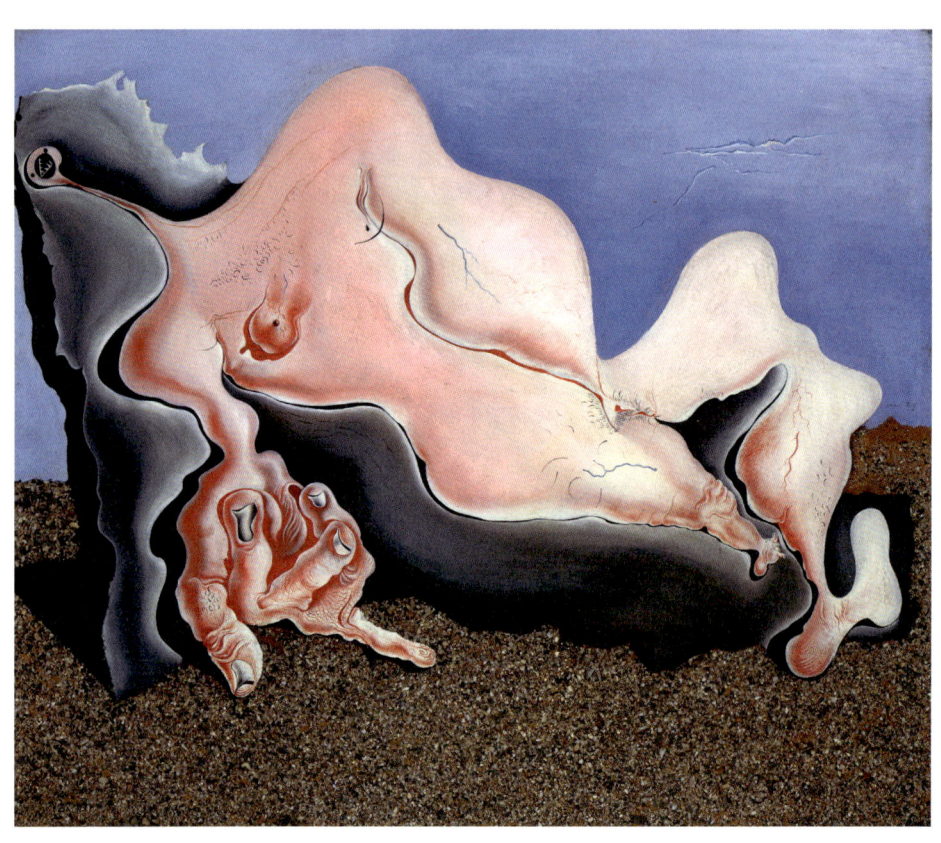

99
Nu féminin (Female Nude)
1928
Oil and collage on wood panel, 63.5 × 75 cm
The Dalí Museum, St. Petersburg, Florida

From Cubism to Anti-Art

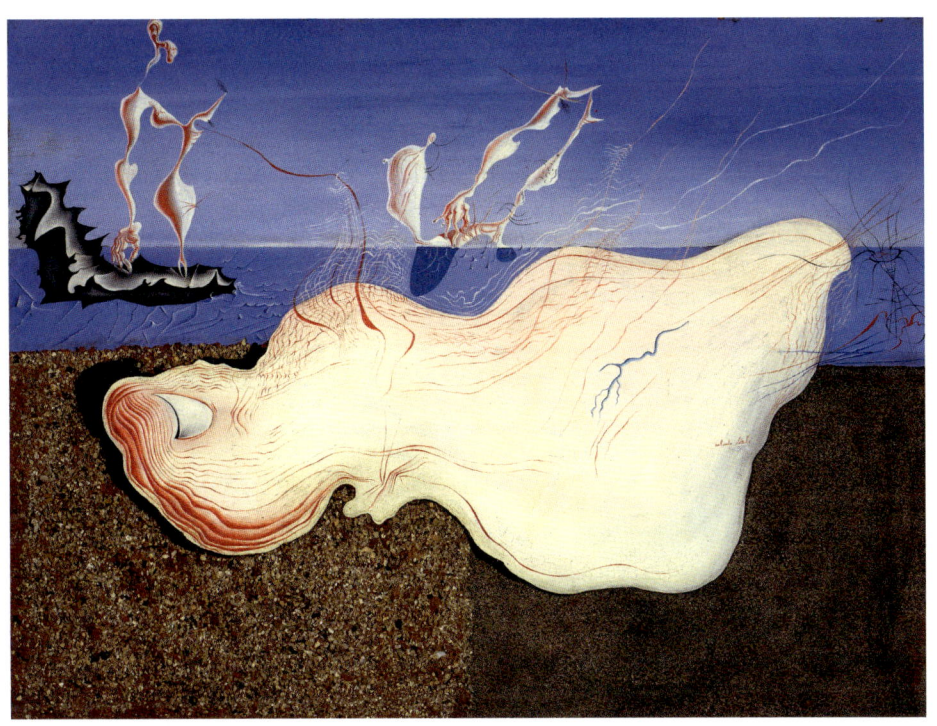

100
Baigneuses (Bathers)
c. 1928
Oil and collage on wood panel, 52 × 71.7 cm
The Dalí Museum, St. Petersburg, Florida

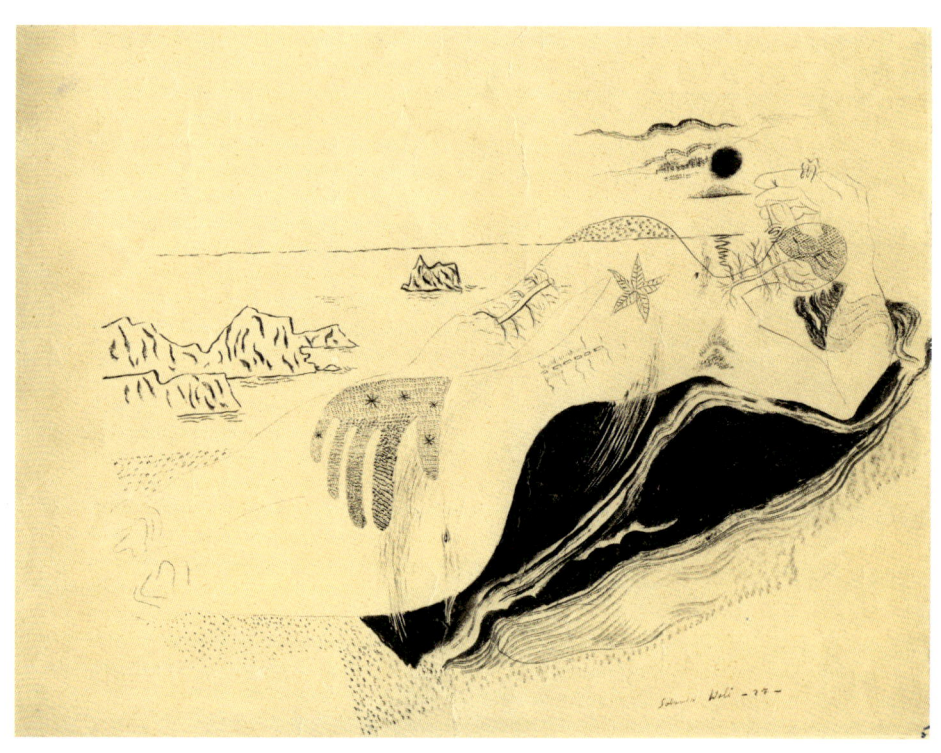

101
The Bather
1927
Ink on paper, 24.1 × 30.5 cm
The Dalí Museum, St. Petersburg, Florida

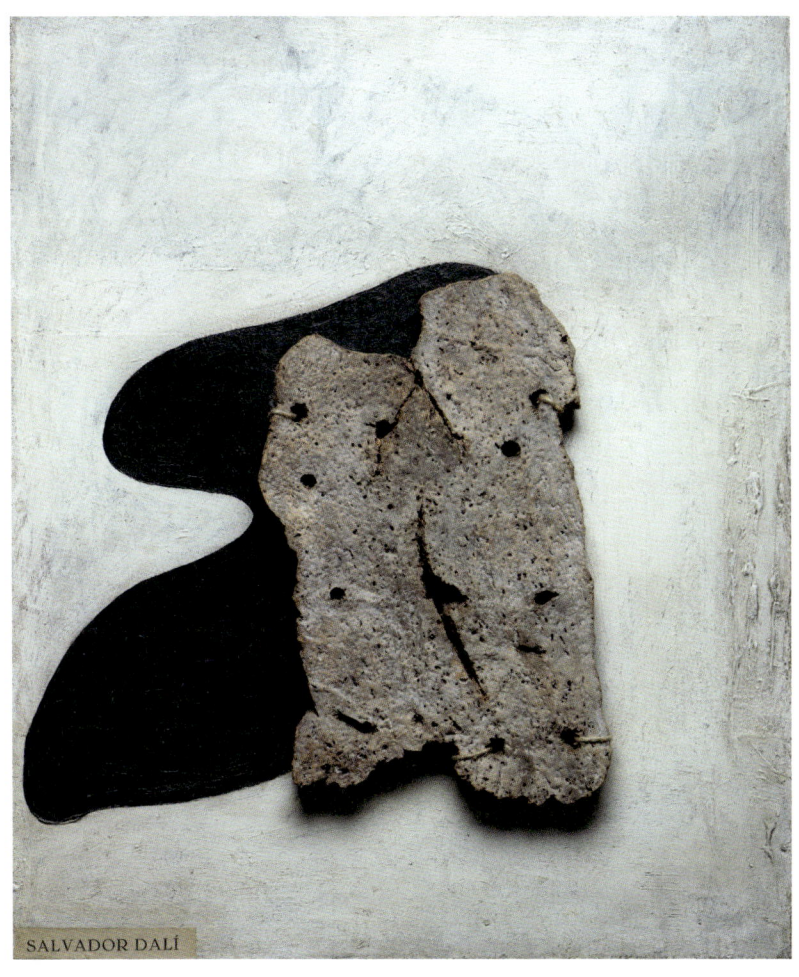

SALVADOR DALÍ

102
Nu femení (Female Nude)
1928
Oil with cork attached with string and collage on canvas, 70.5 × 60 cm
Collection William B. Jordan

103
Untitled
c. 1928
Oil on canvas, 148 × 198 cm
Museo Nacional Centro de Arte Reina Sofía, Madrid. Dalí bequest

From Cubism to Anti-Art

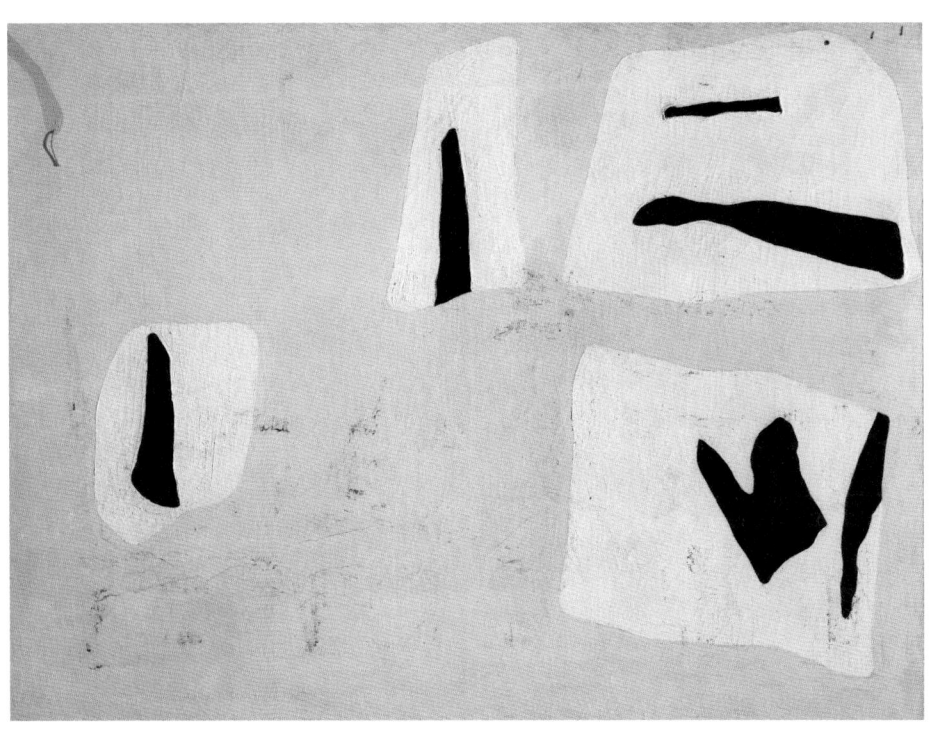

104
Abstract Composition
c. 1928
Oil and collage (string) on canvas, 148 × 198 cm
Museo Nacional Centro de Arte Reina Sofía, Madrid. Dalí bequest

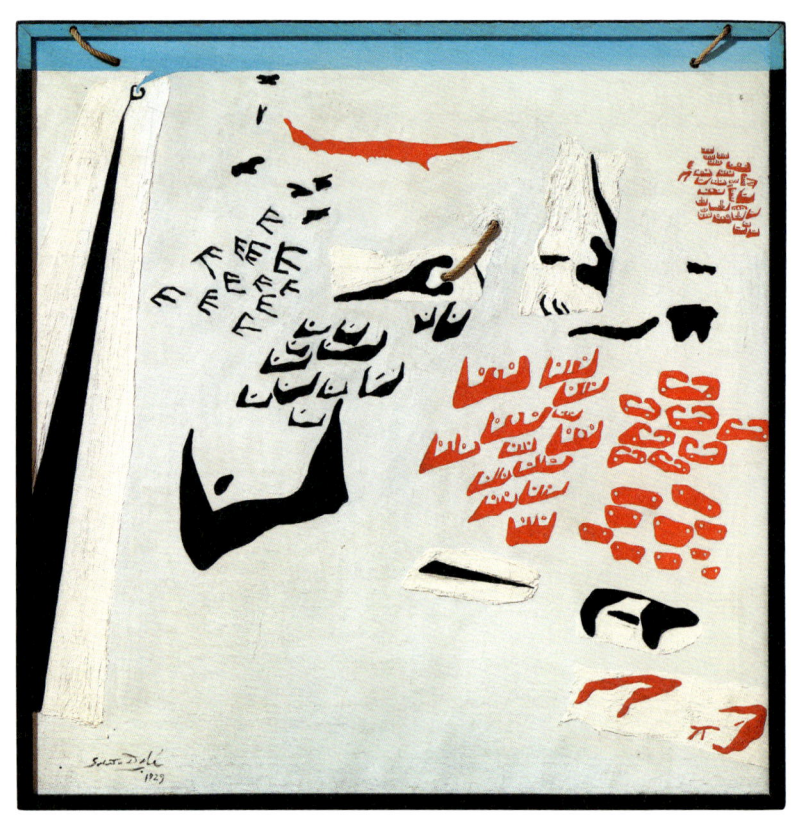

105
Fishermen in the sun
1928
Oil and rope on canvas, 100 × 100 cm
Private collection

From Cubism to Anti-Art

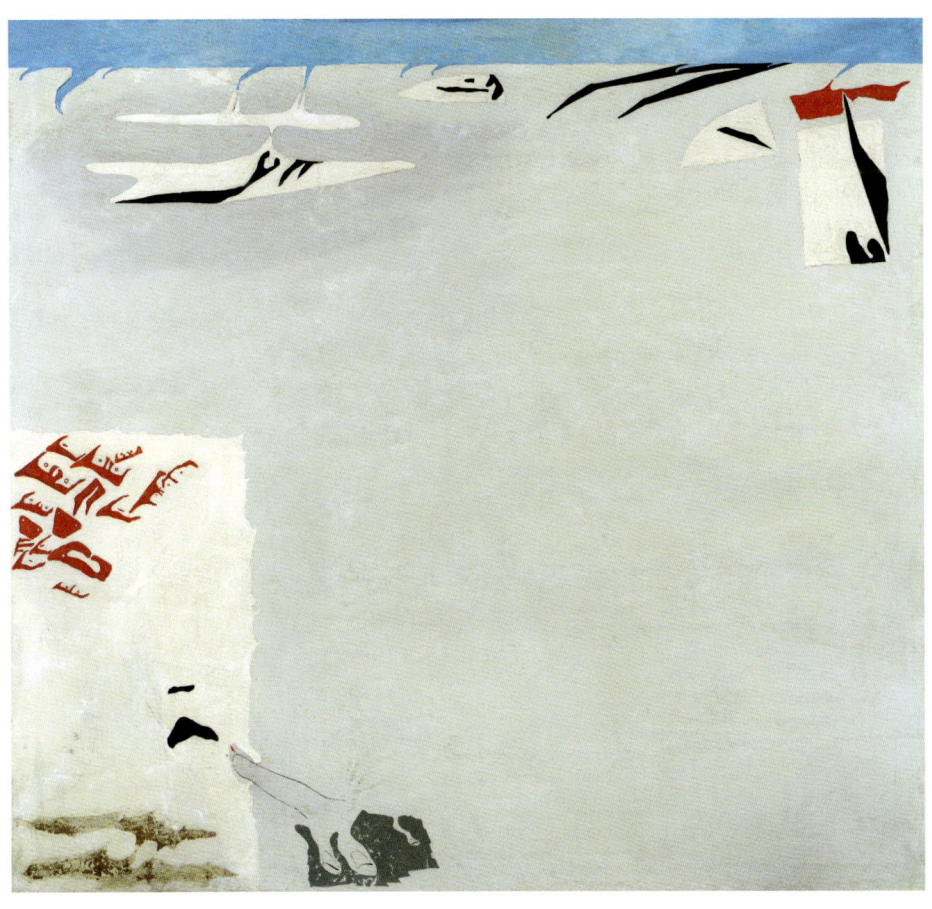

106
Fishermen's Wives
c. 1928
Oil and sand on canvas, 185.5 × 199 cm
Fundació Gala-Salvador Dalí, Figueres

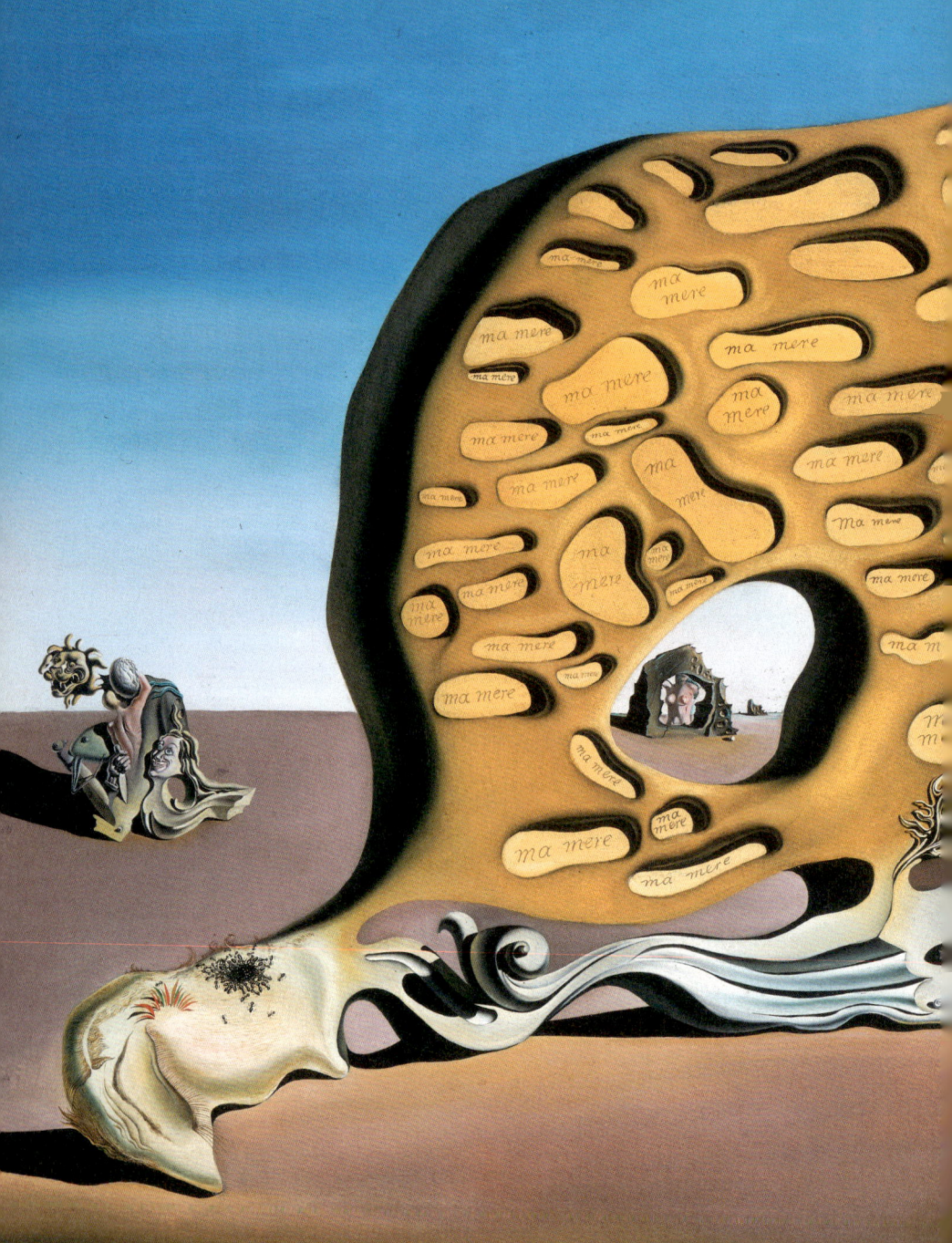

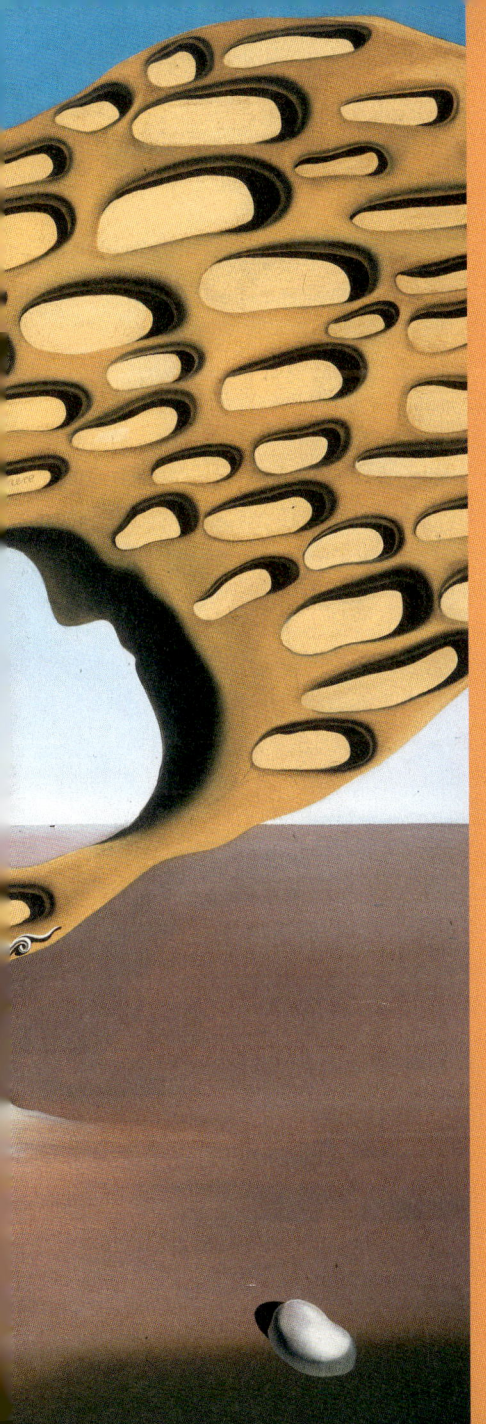

Surrealism

1929–1939

Dalí finally went to Paris in the spring of 1929, primarily to work on the production for the film *Un Chien Andalou (The Andalusian Dog)*, which he was working on with his colleague from the Residencia de Estudiantes, the Aragonese filmmaker Luis Buñuel (1900–1983); but while there, he also sought to launch an assault on the artistic world of the French capital. Dalí arrived in late March in anticipation of the early-April beginning of the production. Just before leaving Spain, Buñuel asked Dalí to bring Spanish ants with him, as the insects figured as protagonists in one of the most famous scenes in the film.

Shortly after arriving in Paris, Dalí began painting *The First Days of Spring* (1929) [114], a work that combined collage and painting seamlessly and included small vignettes of a highly personal nature drawing on Freudian subject matter. Dalí showed the painting to the French Surrealist poet Robert Desnos (1900–1945) at the brasserie La Coupole, later recalling the encounter in his autobiography, 'He certainly understood the originality of my painting, which was called *The First Days of Spring*, and in which libidinous pleasure was described in symbols of a surprising objectivity.' During this time Dalí wrote a series of articles for the Barcelona newspaper *La Publicitat* documenting the cultural scene of Paris. During his relatively short stay, Dalí was very busy. Miró presented him to Breton, the leader of Surrealism, and to the other members of the Surrealist group, as well as to dealers including the Belgian Camille Goemans (1900–1960), with whom Dalí would sign a contract in mid-May 1929, promising all of his work until the exhibition planned to open in November 1929 in Paris. With the intention of setting to work on preparing paintings for the exhibition, Dalí returned to Spain shortly before the premiere of the film on 6 June 1929.

Over the late summer holiday, Dalí invited the Belgian artist René Magritte (1898–1967), along with Goemans, the French poet Paul Éluard (1895–1952) and their romantic partners, as well as Éluard's daughter Cécile (1918–2016) and Buñuel to visit Cadaqués. During this stay Dalí was magnetically

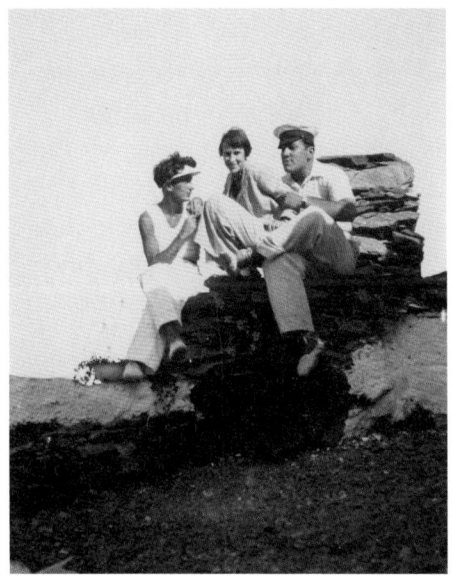

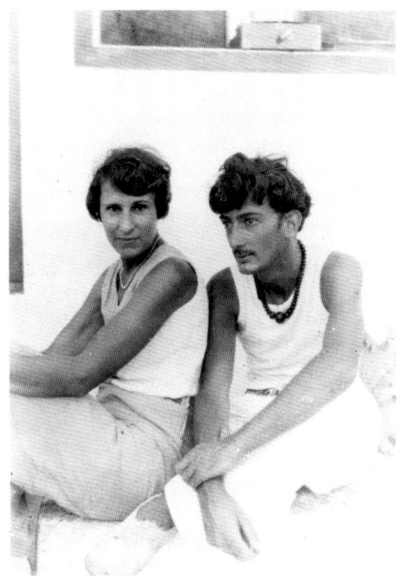

Stefano Bianchetti (photographer), Dalí, Gala and René Char in Cadaqués, Spain, c. 1930. Collection of The Dalí Museum.

Dalí and Gala, c. 1930.

attracted to Gala Éluard (née Elena Ivanovna Diakonova) (1894–1982) who was Russian and married to Paul Éluard. When Éluard returned before the others to take care of some business in Paris, Gala and Cécile stayed on with Dalí for several more weeks. This was the beginning of the most important romantic relationship in Dalí's life and the couple would never separate.

After Gala departed Cadaqués, Dalí returned to painting in preparation for his exhibition. Some of his greatest paintings were painted over this summer and the autumn of 1929, including *Accommodations of Desire* [107], *Illuminated Pleasures* [108], *Face of the Great Masturbator* [113], *The Lugubrious Game* [115] and *Portrait of Paul Éluard* [118]. These, together with *The First Days of Spring* (1929) [114] and the earlier *Apparatus and Hand* (1927) [83] and *Futile Efforts* (1927–28) [85], made the exhibition shocking to say the least. Goemans produced a catalogue for the exhibition with an introduction by Breton. As if this were not enough to launch Dalí, in December 1929 the Surrealist publication *La Révolution surréaliste*, which was published from 1924 to 1929, featured the screenplay of *Un Chien Andalou* as well as Breton's *Second Manifeste du surréalisme*, to which Dalí was a signatory. Breton's new manifesto purged a number of key artists and writers from the early phase of the movement and launched a new group, including the rising young artistic star Dalí. From that point onwards, and throughout the 1930s, Dalí would spend most of his time in Paris, with summer trips to Spain.

The success of *Un Chien Andalou* was followed in October 1930 with the première of the even more scandalous film that Dalí also made with Buñuel, *L'Âge d'Or*, which all the Surrealists attended. For the rest of the decade Dalí participated in all the group's exhibition activities. In December 1931, he contributed to the new Surrealist review *Le Surréalisme au service de la révolution*, published from 1930 to 1933, with texts and related works proposing what he called 'Objects Functioning Symbolically'. These enigmatic constructions were meant to have partially originated in dreams, a means of inspiration that Breton had already proposed in his earlier 1925 essay *Introduction au discours sur le peu de la réalité*. Dalí's idea was also a response to the Swiss sculptor Alberto Giacometti's (1901–1966) *Suspended Ball* (1930), which, with its mobile and tactile elements was also included in Dalí's category. With his 'Objects Functioning Symbolically', Dalí introduced a whole new area of practice to Surrealism.

Such 'Objects Functioning Symbolically' were central to Galerie Pierre Colle's *Surrealist Exhibition* held in June 1933, which featured both Dalí and Giacometti's objects, not to mention important paintings by Dalí including *Meditation on the Harp* (c. 1933) [166]. Dalí appeared once more with the group in their contribution to the *Salon des surindépendants* held in Paris in October and November 1933. Dalí presented his striking symbolic object, *Retrospective Bust of a Woman* (1933) [170] in both of these exhibitions,

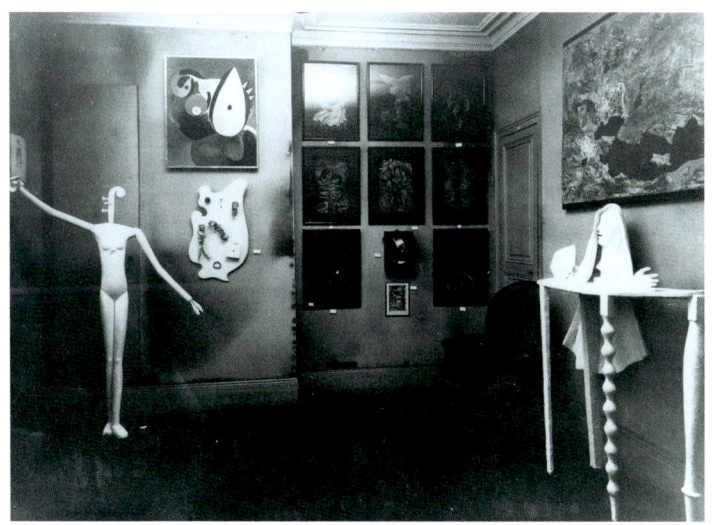

Man Ray (photographer), installation shot of the Surrealist Exhibition, Galerie Pierre Colle, Paris, France, June 1933. Collection of The Dalí Museum.

an assemblage comprised of a painted bust wearing a loaf of bread and a corn necklace and crowned with a decorative inkwell based on the figures from the nineteenth-century French artist Jean-François Millet's (1814–1875) painting *The Angelus* (1857–59).

In May 1936 the group staged the *Exhibition of Surrealist Objects* in Paris at the Galerie Charles Ratton, where Dalí's contribution included his *Aphrodisiac Jacket* (1936), consisting of a man's dinner jacket and a woman's brassière hung on the wall. The object was also displayed, alongside a number of important paintings lent by Dalí's patrons – the French nobleman Vicomte de Noailles (1891–1981), the British poet and collector Edward James (1907–1984) and Éluard himself – at the *International Surrealist Exhibition* in London in June, where Dalí gave his famous inaudible lecture in a diving suit. In 1937, Dalí lent his canvas *The Spectre of Sex-Appeal* (c. 1934) [198] to the Paris exhibition *L'Art Cruel*,

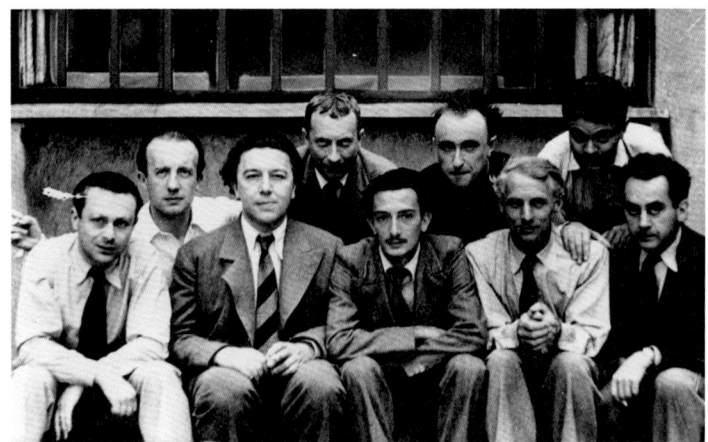

Man Ray (photographer), The Surrealists at Tristan Tzara's House, Montmartre, Paris. Front row, left to right: Tristan Tzara, André Breton, Salvador Dalí, Max Ernst, Man Ray; Back row: left to right: Paul Éluard, Hans Arp, Yves Tanguy, René Crevel, 1931. Collection of The Dalí Museum.

a group exhibition organised to protest the violence of the Spanish Civil War and presented at the Galerie Billiet-Pierre Vorms from 1937 to 1938. While this exhibition, curated by the Franco-Spanish future director of the Musée national d'art moderne in Paris, Jean Cassou (1897–1986), was by no means an official Surrealist exhibition, in that it included numerous artists who leaned towards either Expressionism or politically-engaged positions distant from Surrealism, Dalí found himself in the company of Masson (represented by four caricature drawings challenging the military brutality of Franco's uprising), Picasso (represented by the two etchings *The Dream and Lie of Franco* [1937]) and finally a group of photographs by the German photographer Erwin Blumenfeld, whose *Minotaure* (1937) (also known as *The Dictator*) photomontage depicted a figure with a cow's head to represent the bestiality of Fascism. All three of these artists had participated in or were fellow travellers with Surrealism; and while they explored images of extreme cruelty, they did so in protest and as a statement of solidarity with the Spanish Republic. In the mid-1930s, Dalí also made a small

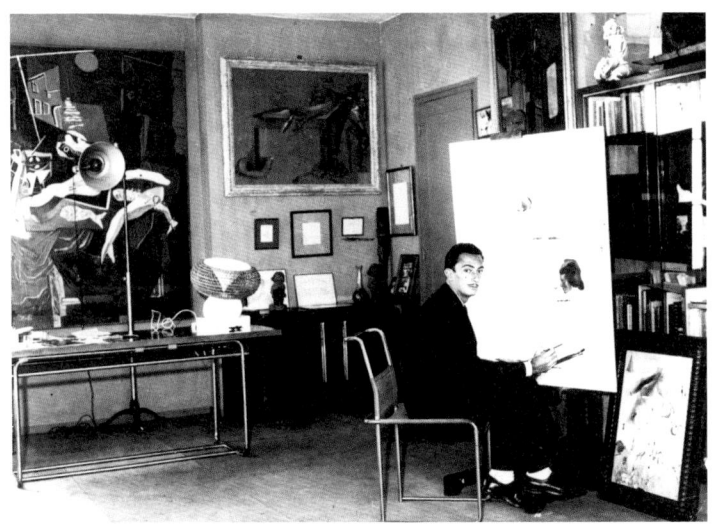

Dalí at an easel in his Paris apartment, c. 1934–1936. Collection of The Dalí Museum, Bettmann Archive/Corbis.

group of prominent pictures referencing the Spanish Civil War, including *Soft construction with boiled apricots* (1936) [235], *Autumnal Cannibalism* (c. 1936) [228] and *Spain* (1938) [271], in which he applied his psychoanalytic preoccupations to the representation of current historical events in each painting, though in this way and from an explicitly political point of view, all three images remain highly subjective and ambiguous.

The 1938 *International Exhibition of Surrealism* was staged at the Galerie Beaux-Arts in Paris from January to February and was followed by a modified presentation at the Galerie Robert in Amsterdam that spring. Not only did Dalí dress one of the Surrealist mannequins for the alley of mannequins installation made by various artists, he also made perhaps his best known Surrealist object in the form of *Rainy Taxi*, which greeted the viewer just before the entrance to the exhibition, and featured an actual taxi. The interior of the exhibition was dark and specially lit by a coal brazier set in a coalsack-lined ceiling, creating a highly theatrical mode of display. Due to the spectacular nature of his contributions, the 1938 exhibition represented a high point in Dalí's engagement with the movement.

However, by 1934, Dalí had already fallen afoul of the political infighting in the group. His initial transgression was to have exhibited *The Enigma of William Tell* (c. 1933) [178], whose face seemed remarkably like that of the Russian revolutionary Vladimir Lenin (1870–1924), in the February 1934 *Salon des Indépendants*. Not only was this venue not sanctioned by the group, as the exhibition had not been organised by them, but the painting was also seen as disrespectful of the father of the Russian Revolution, which many of the group held enormous respect for. To make matters worse, many members of the group, even those closest to him, like Éluard and the Romanian poet Tristan Tzara (1896–1963), were perturbed by Dalí's unhealthy fascination with what he referred to as the 'hitlerian phenomenon.' Letters were sent to all the members calling for their position on the matter, and Dalí was summoned on the fifth of February to a meeting to explain himself to the group. Dalí's attitude at the meeting was playful and clown-like; he was ill at the time and decided to present himself all bundled up, with a thermometer in his mouth, clearly not appearing to take the matter seriously. But the Surrealists certainly did. Dalí's 'trial' took place on the eve of the tumultuous Fascist riots of the sixth of February in Paris, where a number of people were killed when the police fired on the crowd. After coming close to expulsion, Dalí eventually accepted the criticism of the group and committed to support their 'revolutionary' activities. Having narrowly avoided this crisis, he then carried on his engagement with the group, though Breton never completely set aside his concerns about Dalí's politics. And neither did Dalí, who devoted more and more energy to international exhibitions.

By the spring of 1939, Surrealism had undergone a new set of internal crises in response to the worsening political situation, and estranged figures like Masson had come back into Breton's favour. Dalí, once more, was planning

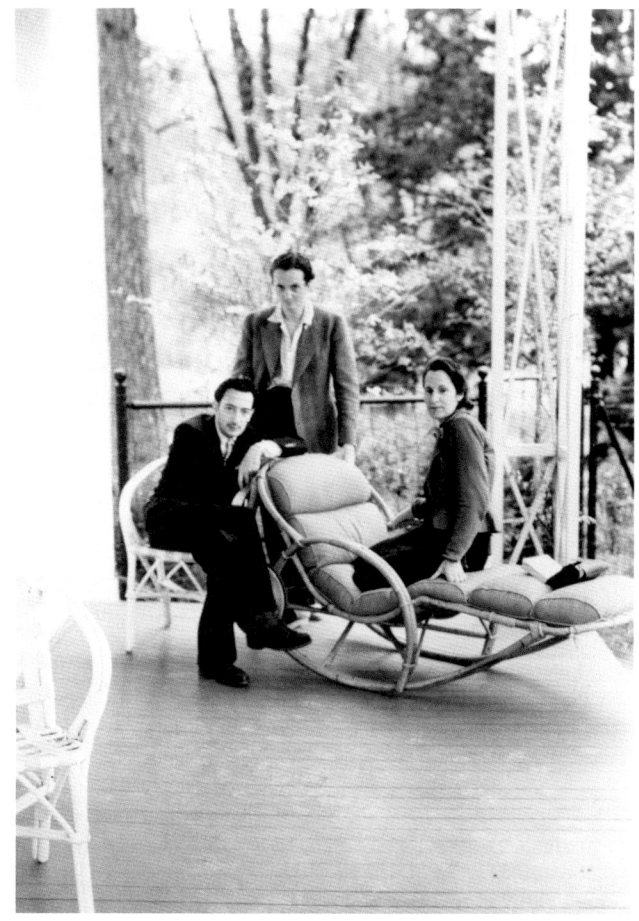

James Thrall Soby (photographer), Dalí and Gala at the home of the collector and curator James Thrall Soby in Farmington, Connecticut, US, 1939. Collection of The Dalí Museum.

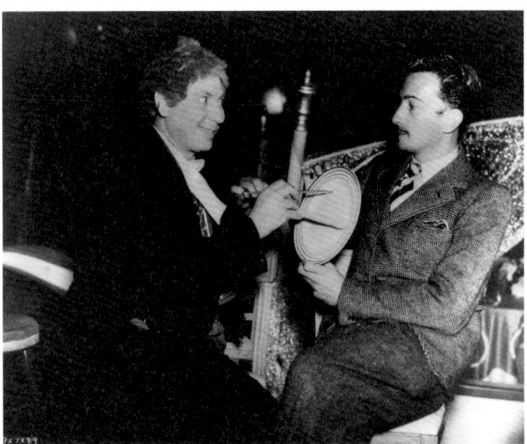

Meliton Casals (photographer), Dalí and comedian Harpo Marx
face each other holding instruments and a plate between filming
scenes of the comedy film *A Day at the Races*, collection of
The Dalí Museum, February 1937.

an important exhibition in New York, this time with the Julien Levy Gallery.
The exhibition included the painting *The Enigma of Hitler* (1939) [275],
one of several incorporating telephones that Dalí painted in 1938 and
1939 responding to the diplomatic crisis known as the Munich Agreement
between the Prime Minister of the United Kingdom Neville Chamberlain
(1869–1940) and Adolf Hitler (1889–1945). Like the above paintings related
to the Spanish Civil War, this series is representative of Dalí's ambiguous
and highly subjective response to the political crisis and to the failed
negotiations that inevitably led to World War. Whether it was the exhibition
of the controversial *The Enigma of Hitler* or other mostly political issues, by
the spring of 1939 Breton publicly stated his rupture with Dalí in the pages
of the Surrealist review *Minotaure*, and this time, the break would prove to
be definitive.

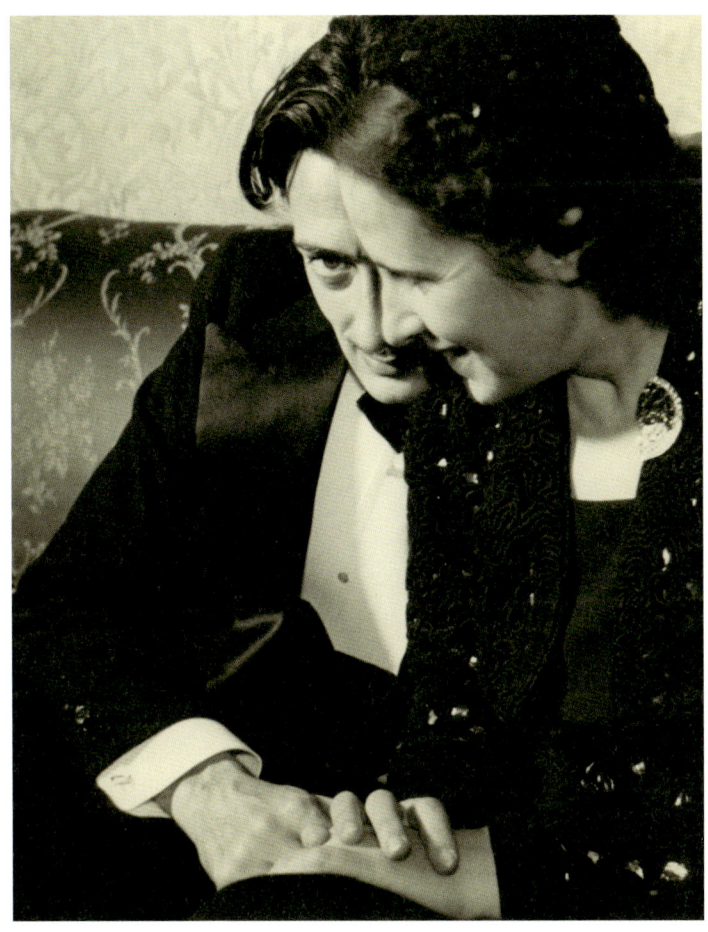

Eric Schaal (photographer), Dalí and Gala, c. 1930s. Collection of The Dalí Museum.

1929–1939

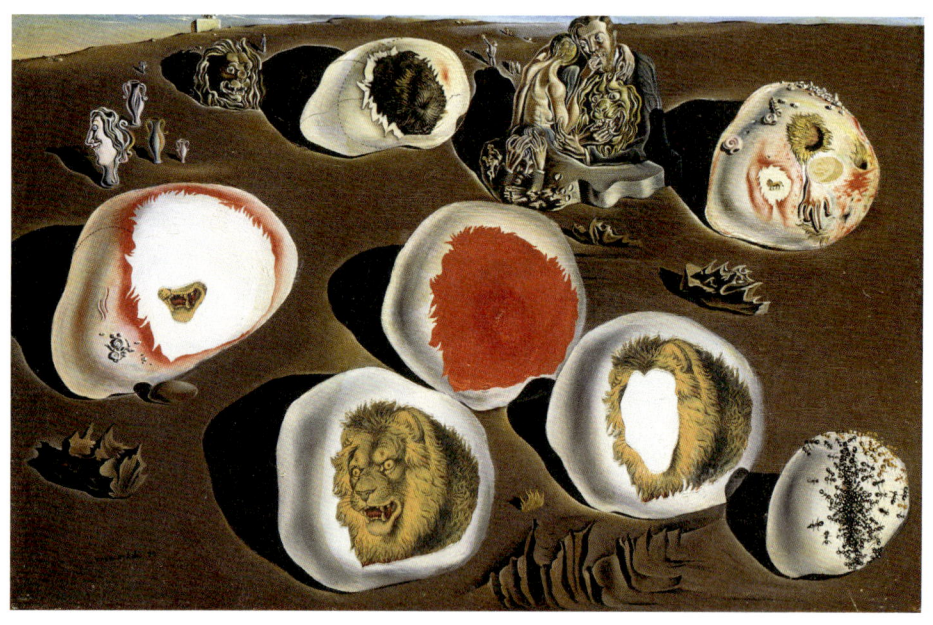

107
Les accommodations des désirs (The Accommodations of Desire)
1929
Oil and collage on cardboard, 22.5 × 35 cm
The Metropolitan Museum of Art, New York. Jacques and Nastasha Gelman Collection, 1998

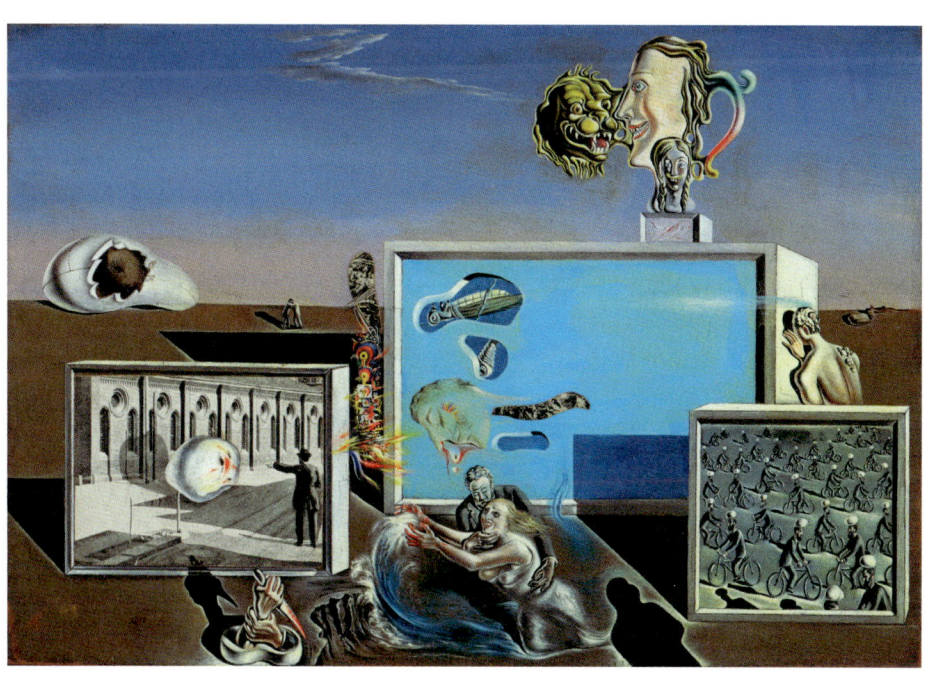

108
Les plaisirs illuminés (Illuminated Pleasures)
1929
Oil and collage on chipboard panel, 23.8 × 34.7 cm
The Museum of Modern Art, New York. The Sidney and Harriet Janis Collection, 1967

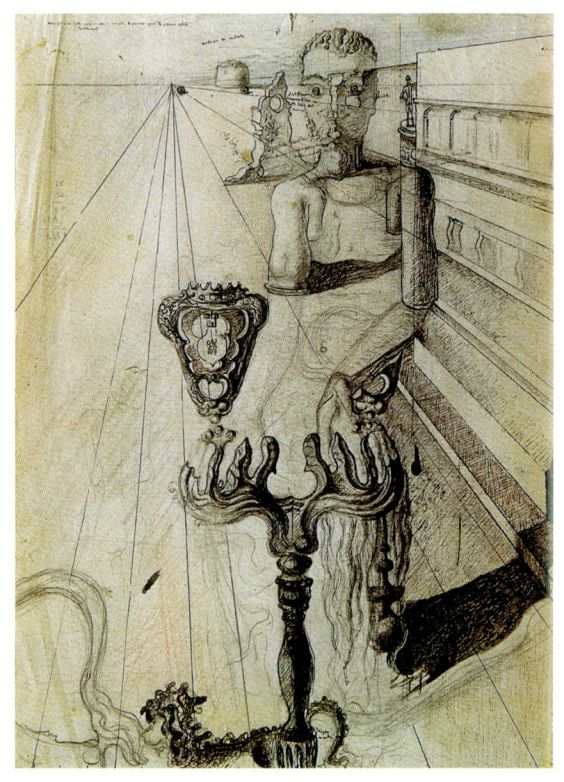

109
Study for "The Invisible Man"
1929
Pencil on paper, 28 × 20 cm
Private collection

Surrealism

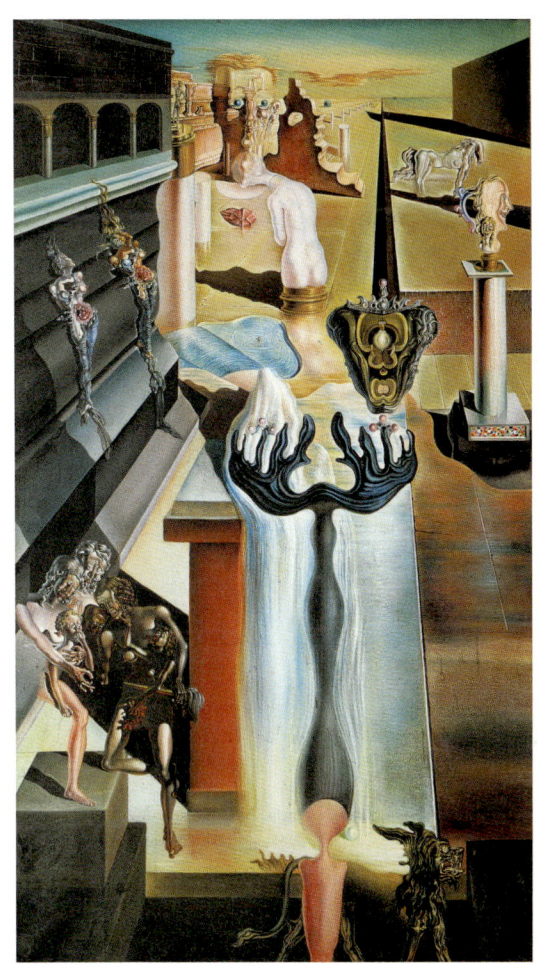

110
L'homme invisible (The Invisible Man)
1929–1932
Oil on canvas, 140 × 81 cm
Museo Nacional Centro de Arte Reina Sofía, Madrid. Dalí bequest

1929–1939

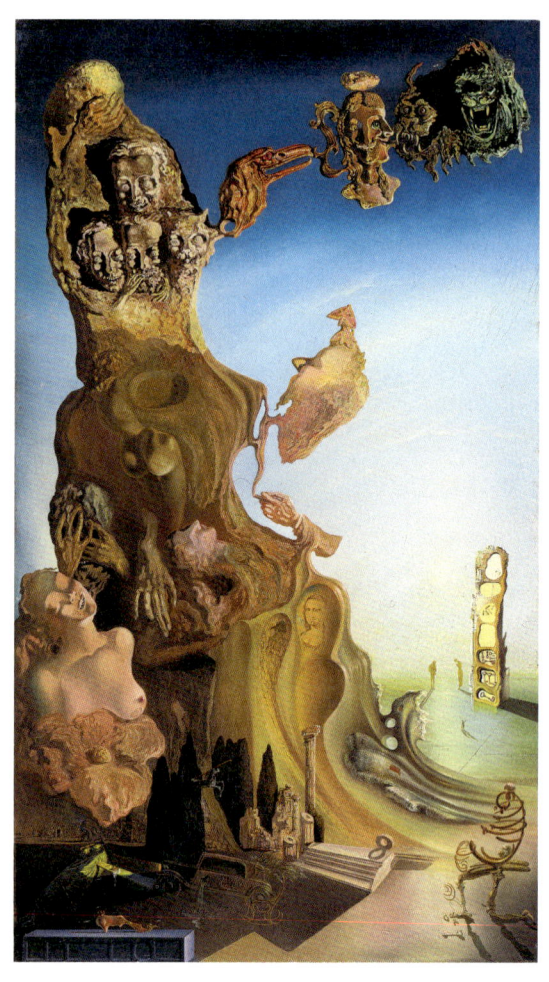

111
La mémoire de la femme-enfant (The Memory of the Woman-Child)
1929
Oil and collage on canvas, 140 × 81 cm
Museo Nacional Centro de Arte Reina Sofía, Madrid. Dalí bequest

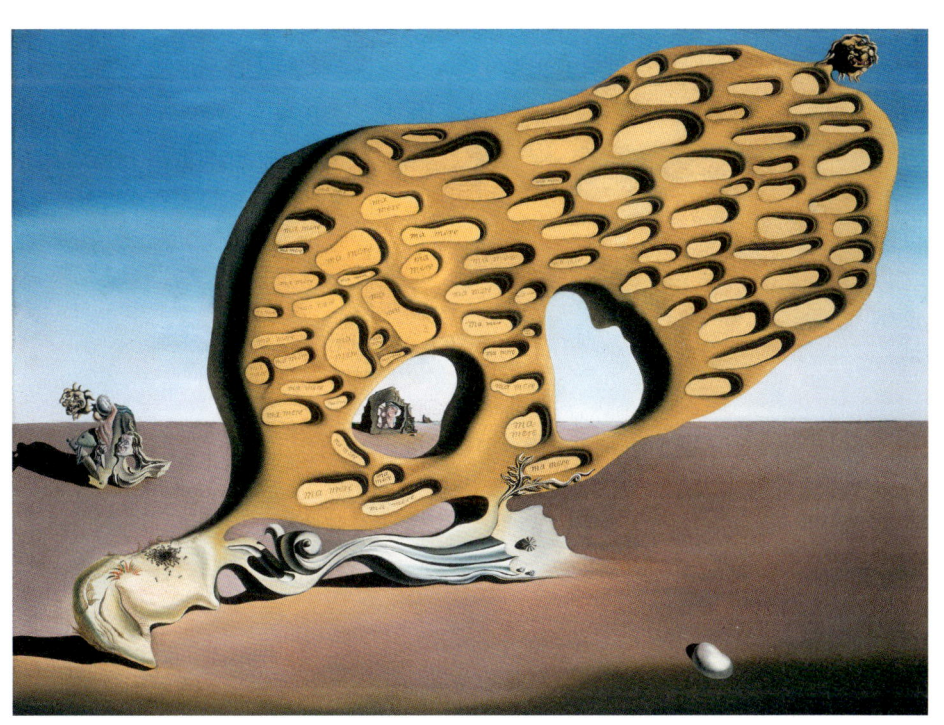

112
The Enigma of Desire or *Ma mère, ma mère, ma mère*
1929
Oil on canvas, 110.5 × 150.5 cm
Bayerische Staatsgemäldesammlungen, Sammlung Moderne Kunst, Pinakothek der Moderne, Munich

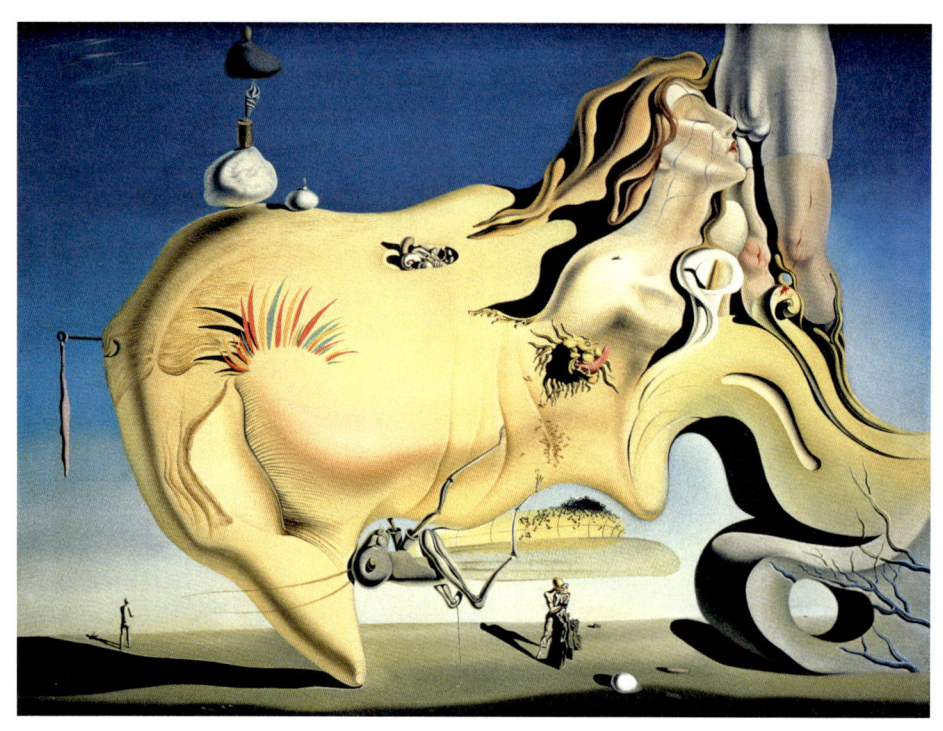

113
Visage du Grand Masturbateur (Face of the Great Masturbator)
1929
Oil on canvas, 110 × 150 cm
Museo Nacional Centro de Arte Reina Sofía, Madrid. Dalí bequest

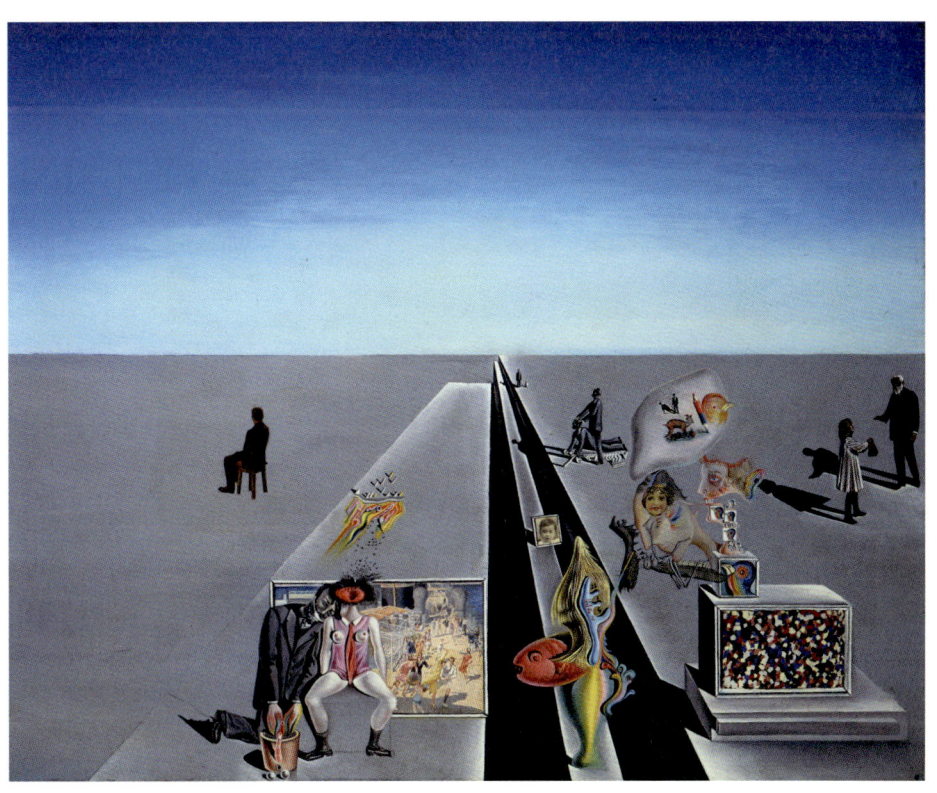

114
Les premiers jours du printemps (The First Days of Spring)
1929
Oil and collage on wood panel, 49.5 × 64 cm
The Dalí Museum, St. Petersburg, Florida

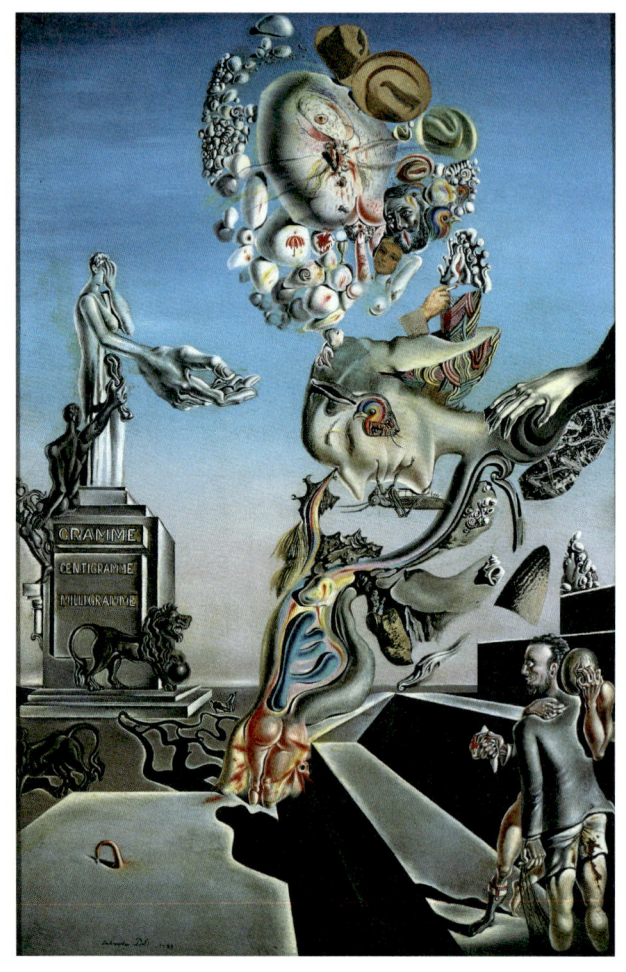

115
Le jeu lugubre (The Lugubrious Game)
1929
Oil and collage on cardboard, 44.4 × 30.3 cm
Private collection

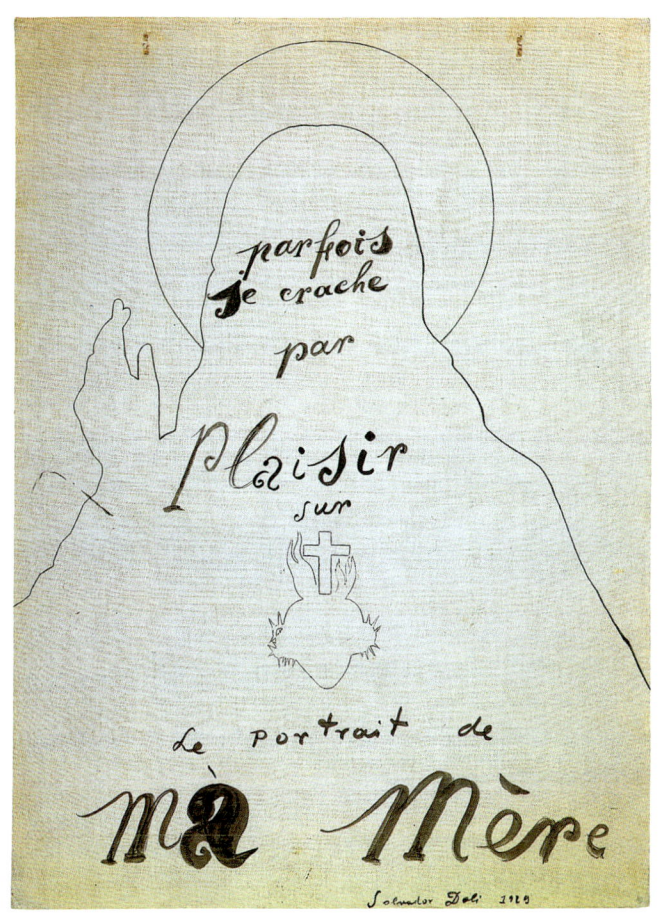

116
The Sacred Heart
1929
Ink on canvas, 68.5 × 50.1 cm
Musée National d'Art Moderne, Centre Georges Pompidou, Paris

1929–1939

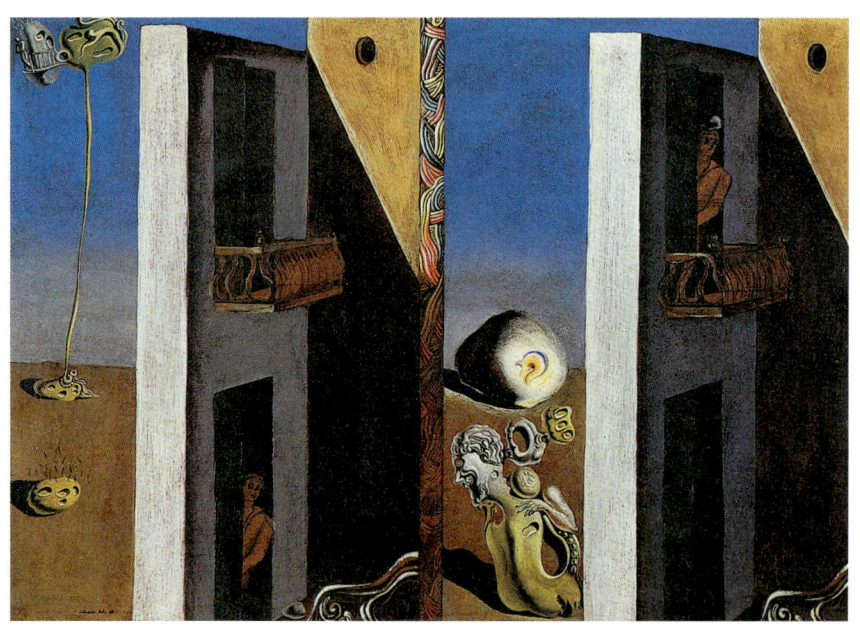

117
Homme d'une complexion malsaine écoutant le bruit de la mer
(A Man of Unhealthy Complexion Listening to the Sound of the Sea)
1929
Oil on wood panel, 23.5 × 34.5 cm
Museu da Chácara do Céu, Fundação Raymundo Ottoni de Castro Maya, Rio de Janeiro

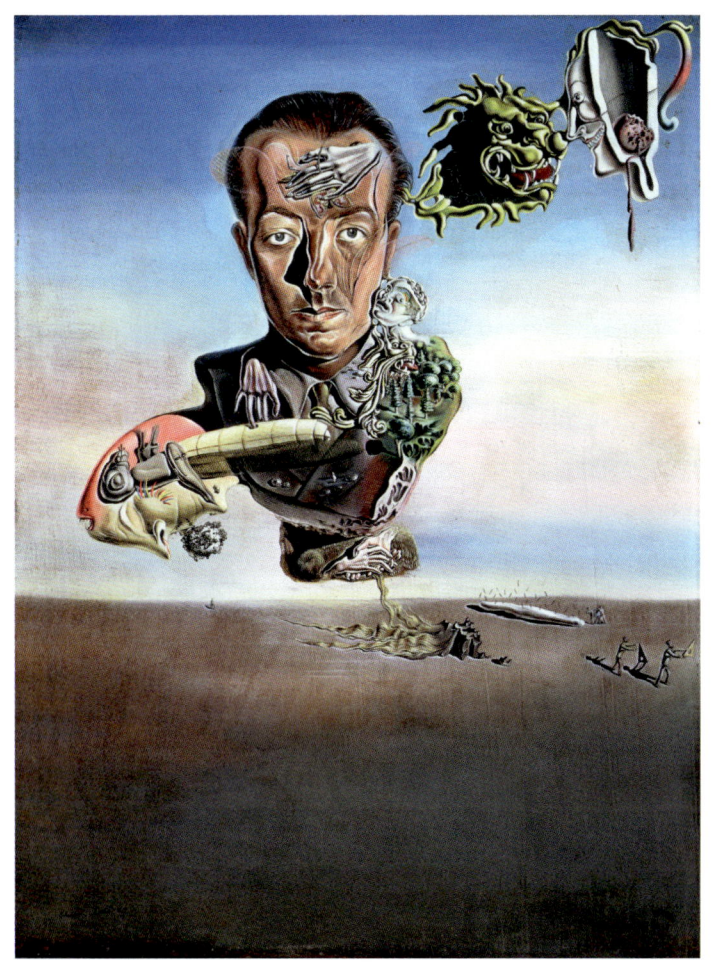

118
Portrait de Paul Éluard (Portrait of Paul Éluard)
1929
Oil on cardboard, 33 × 25 cm
Private collection

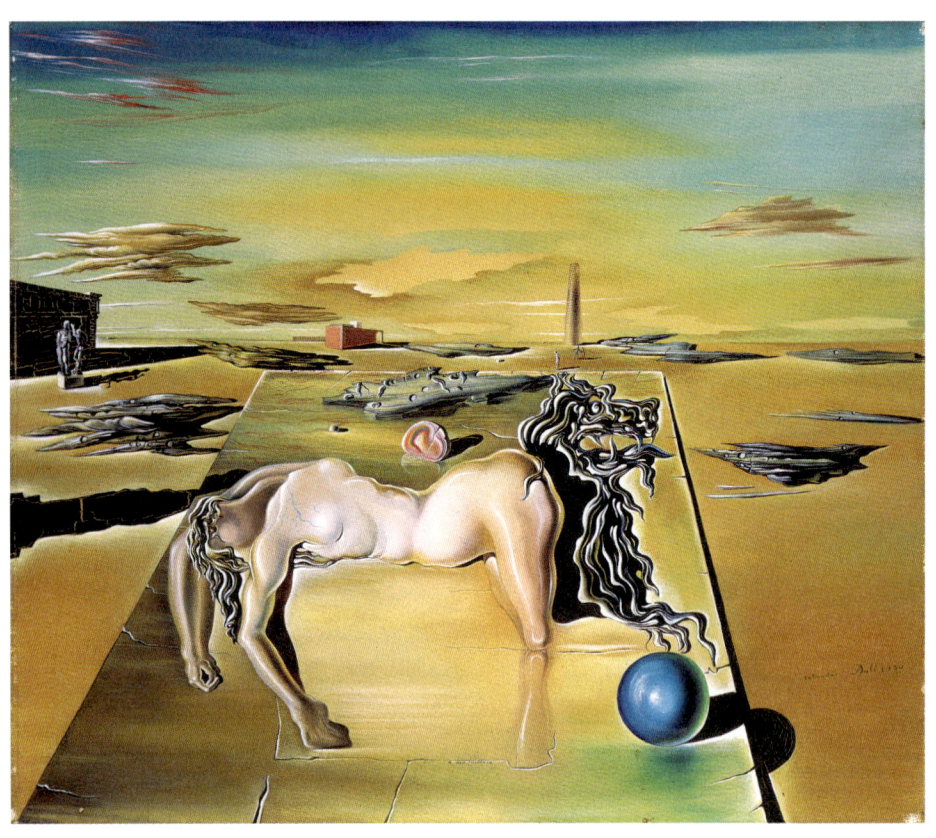

119

Dormeuse, cheval, lion (Sleeping Woman, Horse, Lion)

1930

Oil on canvas, 60.6 × 70.4 cm

Pola Museum of Art, Pola Art Foundation, Hakone, Kanagawa Prefecture, Japan

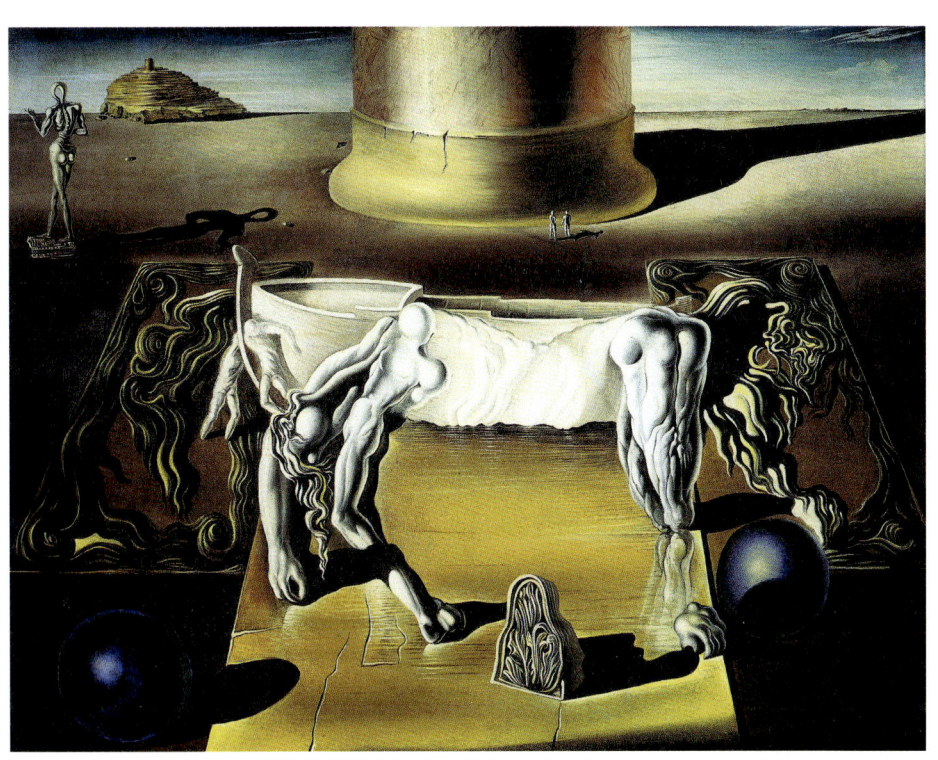

120
Dormeuse cheval lion invisibles (Invisible Sleeping Woman Horse Lion)
1930
Oil on canvas, 50.2 × 65.2 cm
Musée National d'Art Moderne, Centre Pompidou, Paris. Gift of Association Bourdon, Paris, 1993

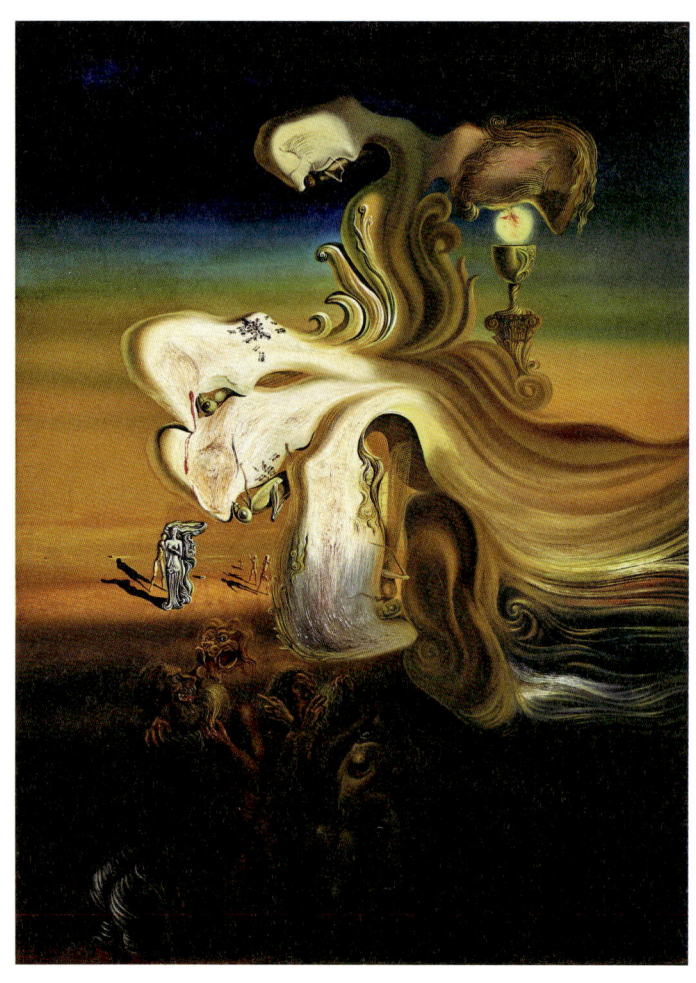

121
La profanation de l'hostie (Profanation of the Host)
c. 1930
Oil on canvas, 100 × 73 cm
The Dalí Museum, St. Petersburg, Florida

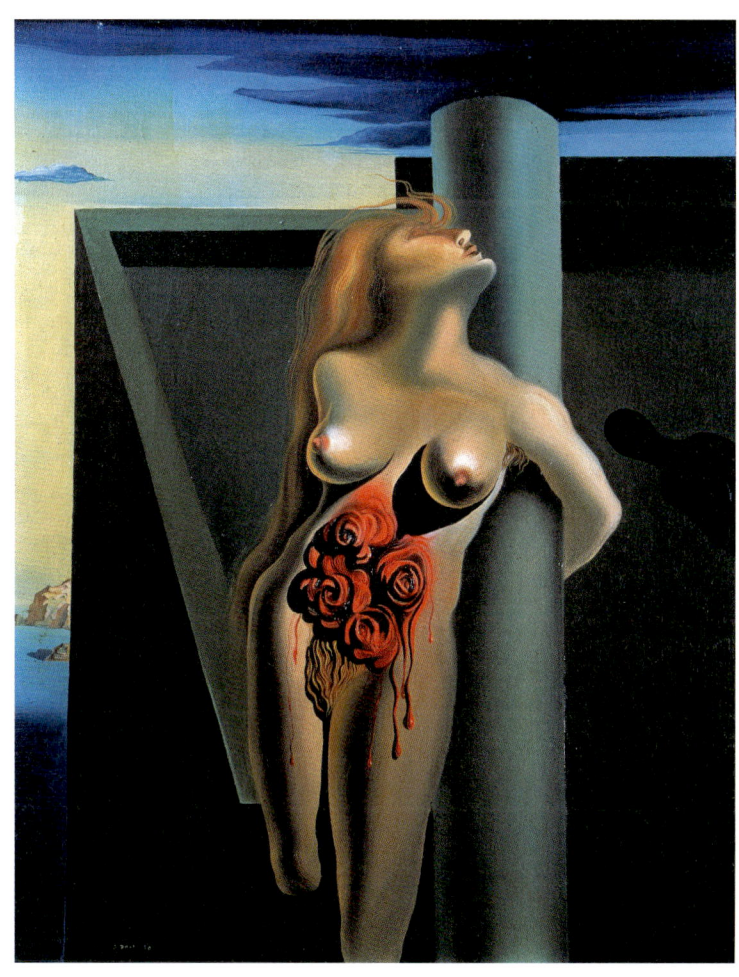

122
The Bleeding Roses
1930
Oil on canvas, 61 × 50 cm
ABANCA Art Collection, A Coruña

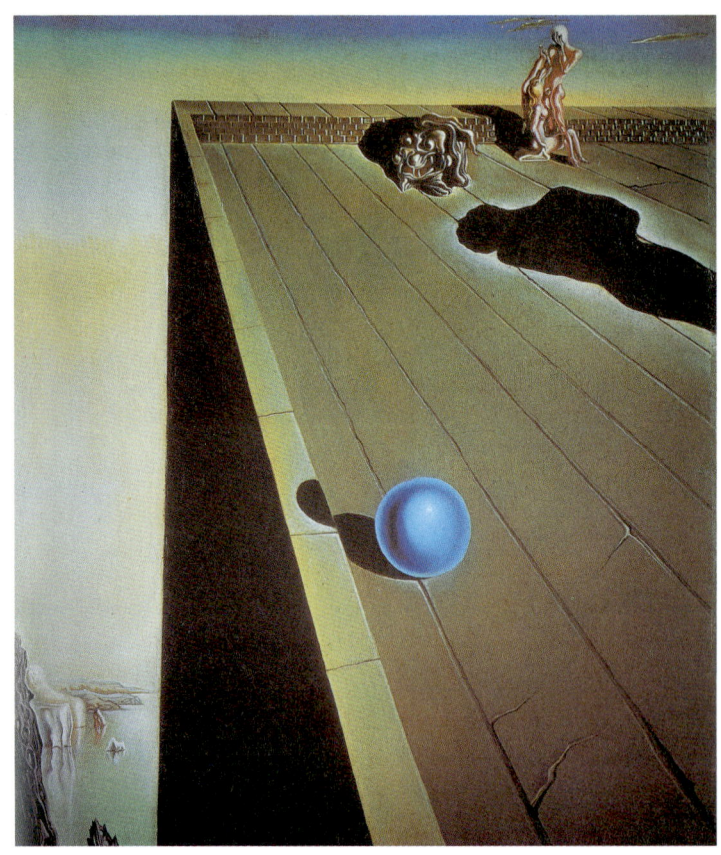

123
Vertigo or the Tower of Pleasure
1930
Oil on canvas, 60 × 50 cm
Private collection

Surrealism

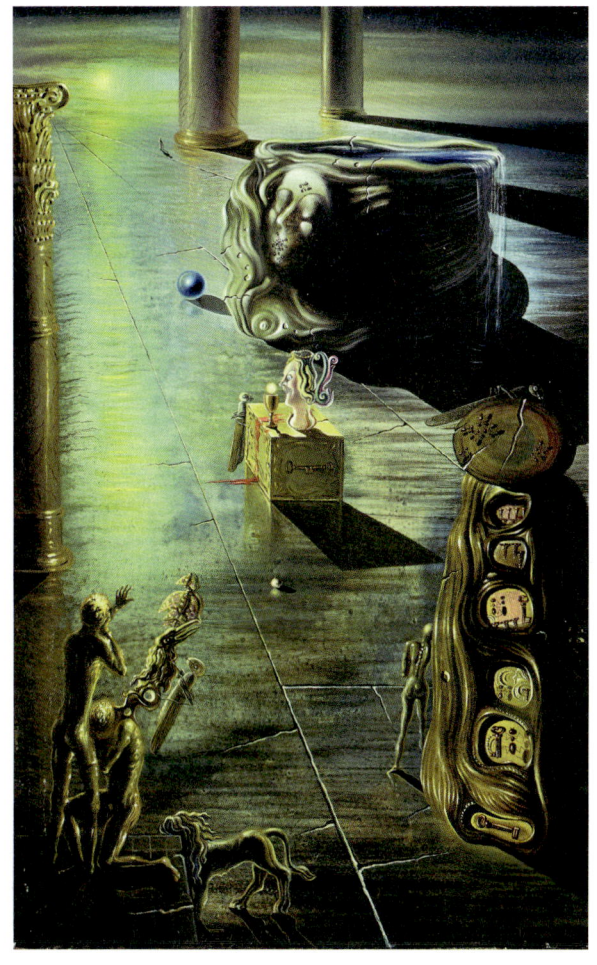

124
The Font
1930
Oil and collage on board, 66 × 41 cm
The Dalí Museum, St. Petersburg, Florida

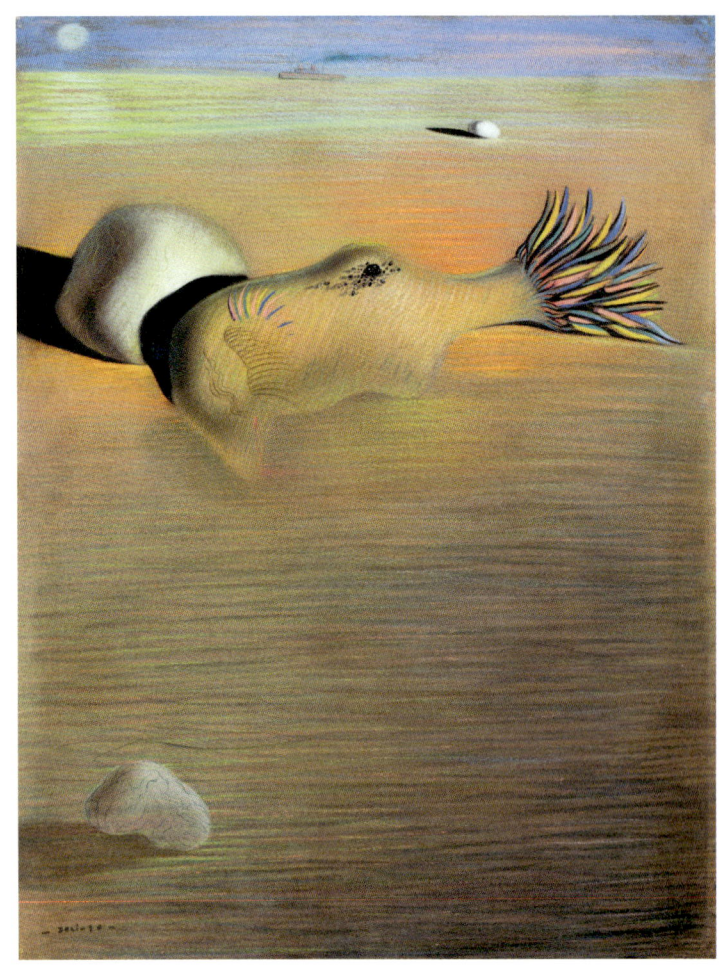

125
The Lost Face – The Giant Masturbator
1930
Pastel on paper, 64.8 × 48.9 cm
The Dalí Museum, St. Petersburg, Florida

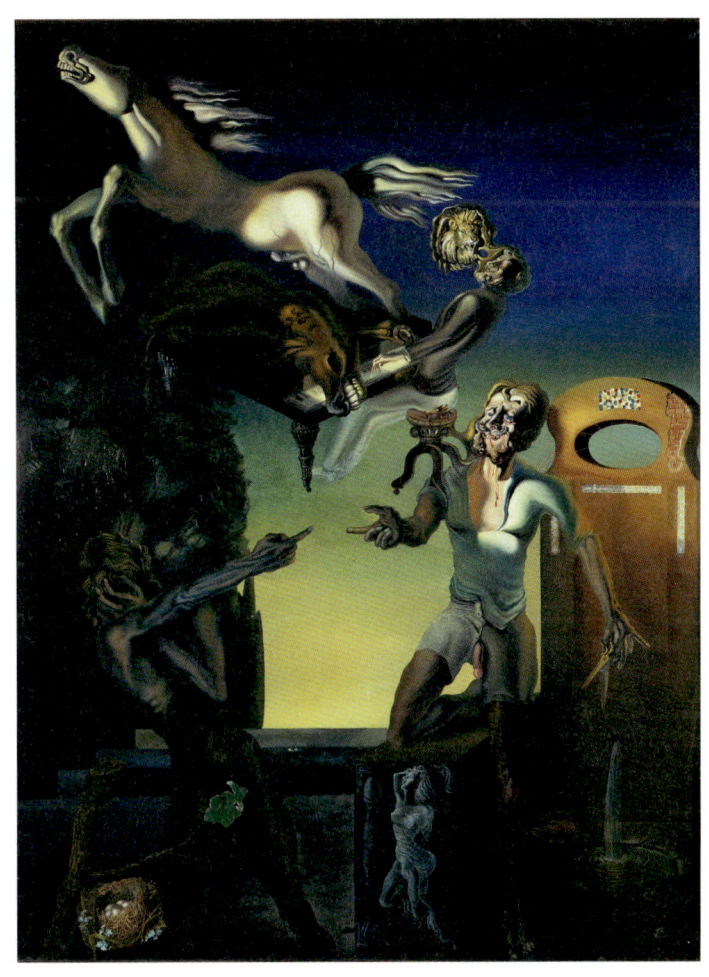

126
William Tell
1930
Oil and collage on canvas, 113 × 87 cm
Musée National d'Art Moderne, Centre Georges Pompidou, Paris

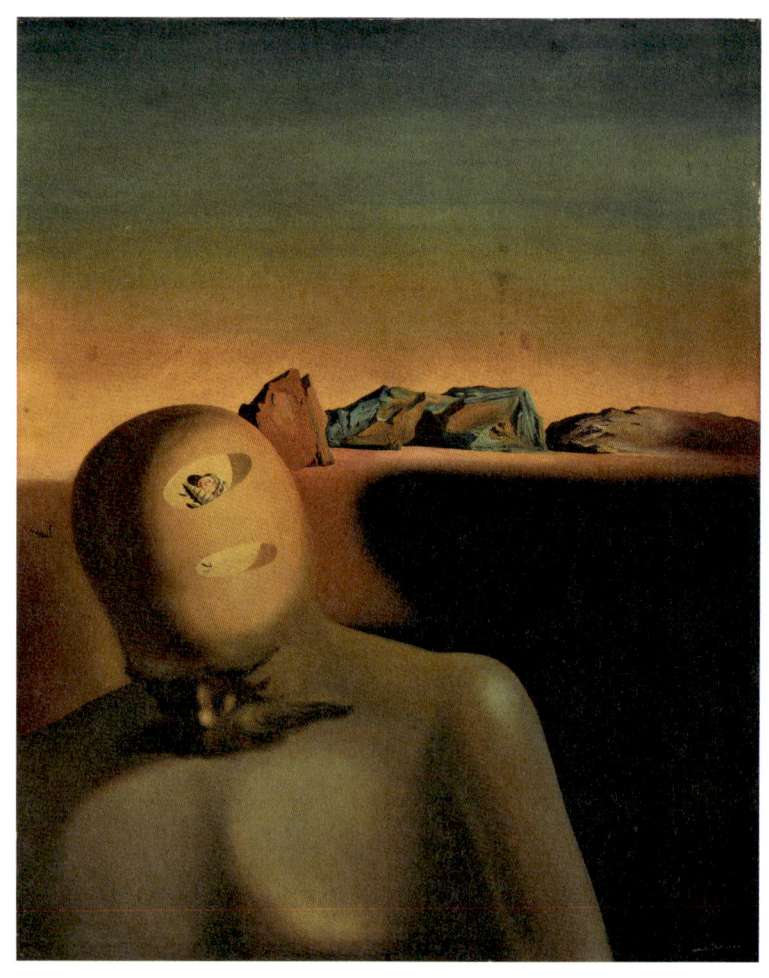

127
The Average Bureaucrat
1930
Oil on canvas, 81 × 64.8 cm
The Dalí Museum, St. Petersburg, Florida

Surrealism

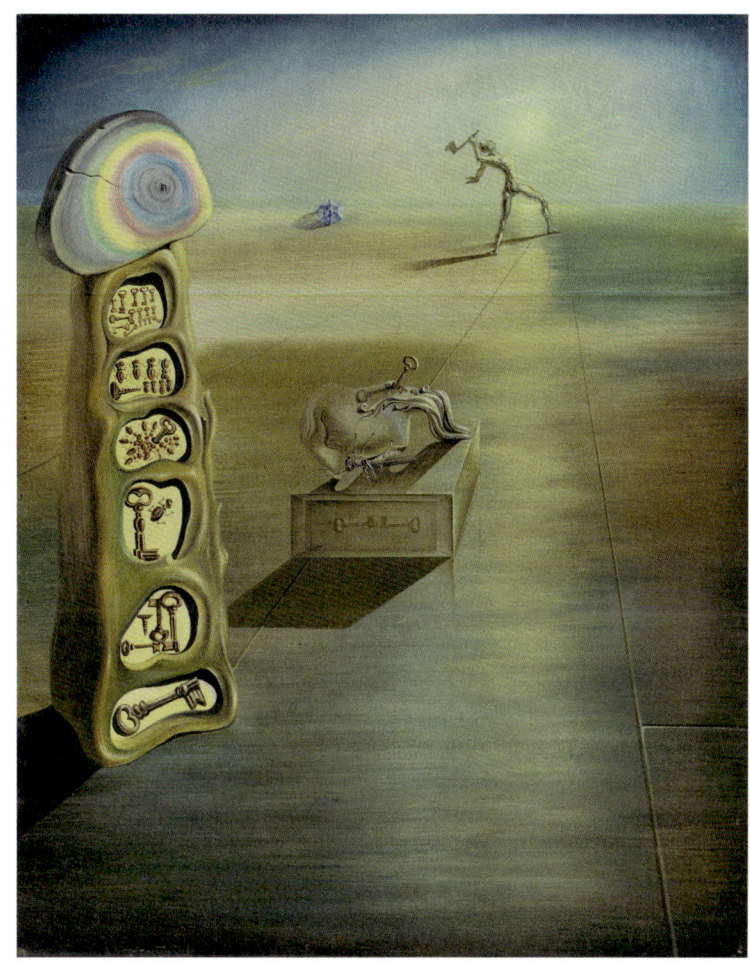

128
La libre inclinación del deseo (The Free Inclination of Desire)
1930
Oil on board, 39.4 × 30.4 cm
Yale University Art Gallery, Charles B. Benenson, B.A. 1933, Collection, New Haven, Connecticut

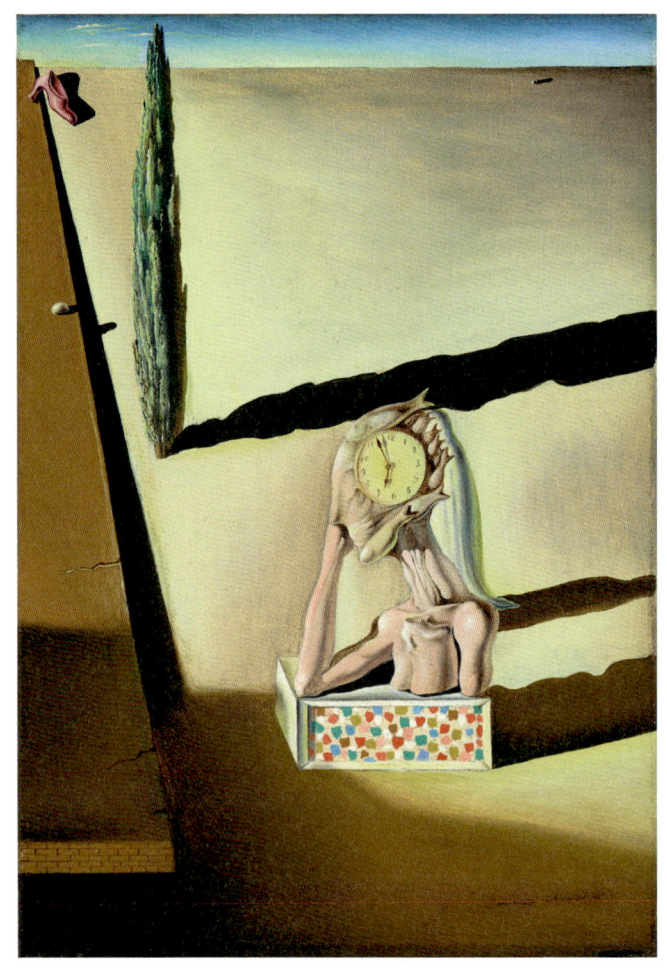

129
Homme poisson (Fish Man)
1930
Oil on canvas, 26.2 × 18.5 cm
Meadows Museum, Southern Methodist University, Dallas, Texas

Surrealism

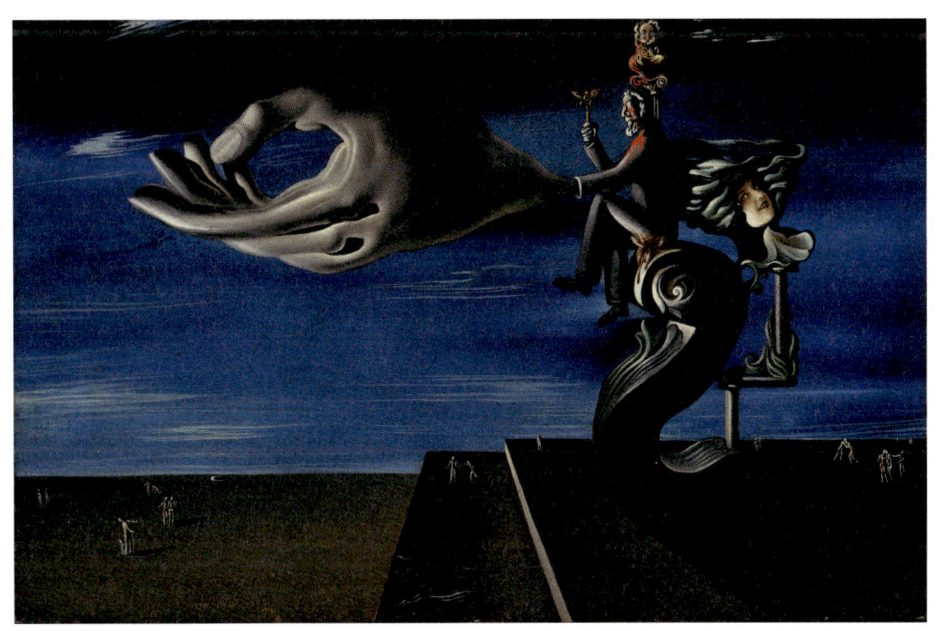

130
The Hand (The Remorse of Conscience)
1930
Oil and collage on canvas, 41 × 66 cm
The Dalí Museum, St. Petersburg, Florida

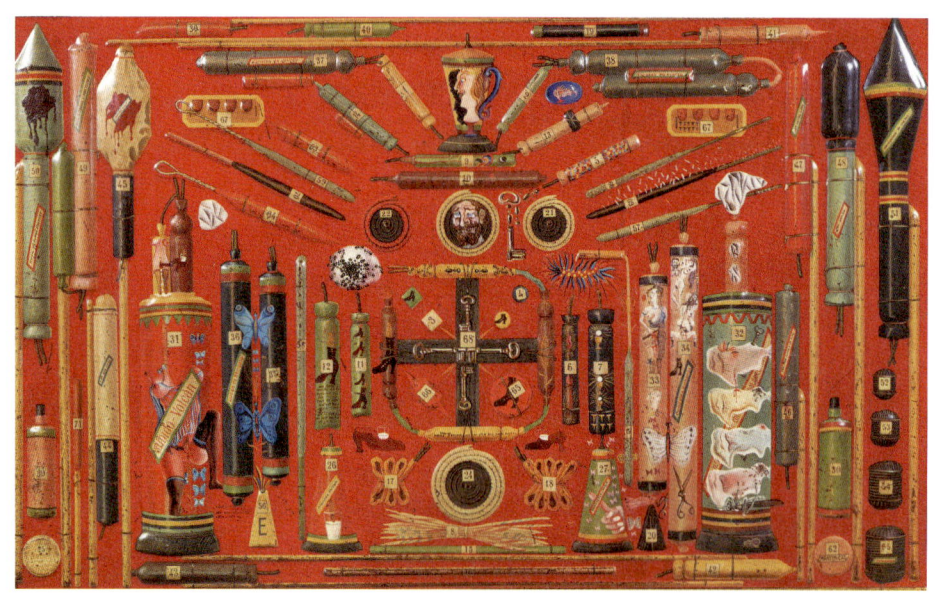

131
Planche d'associations démentielles (Board of Demented Associations)
1930–1931
Oil on metal, 40 × 65.5 cm
Private collection

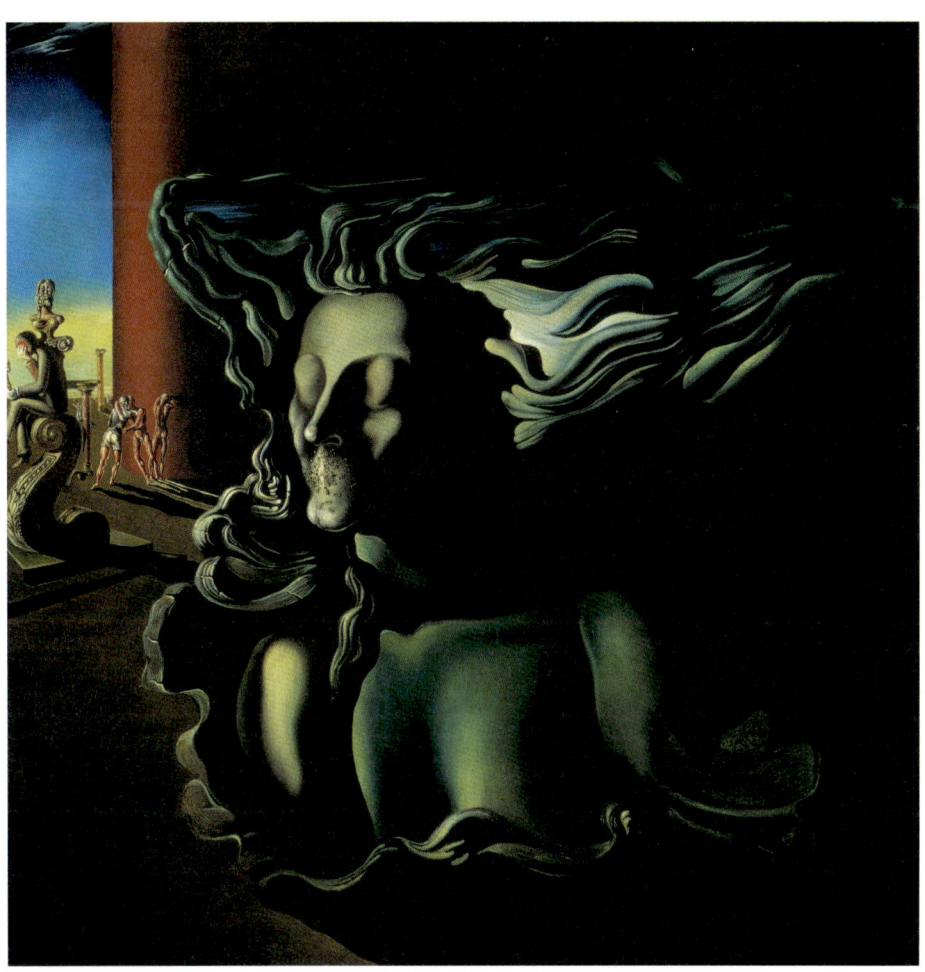

132
The Dream
c. 1930
Oil on canvas, 96 × 96 cm
The Cleveland Museum of Art, Ohio

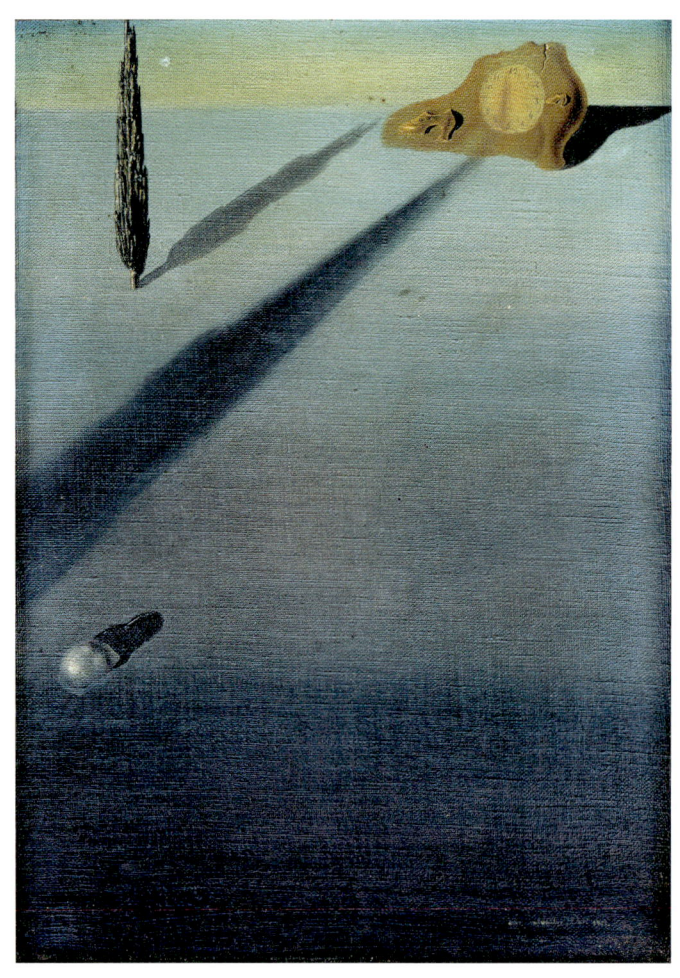

133
The Sense of Speed
1931
Oil on canvas, 33 × 24 cm
Fundació Gala-Salvador Dalí, Figueres

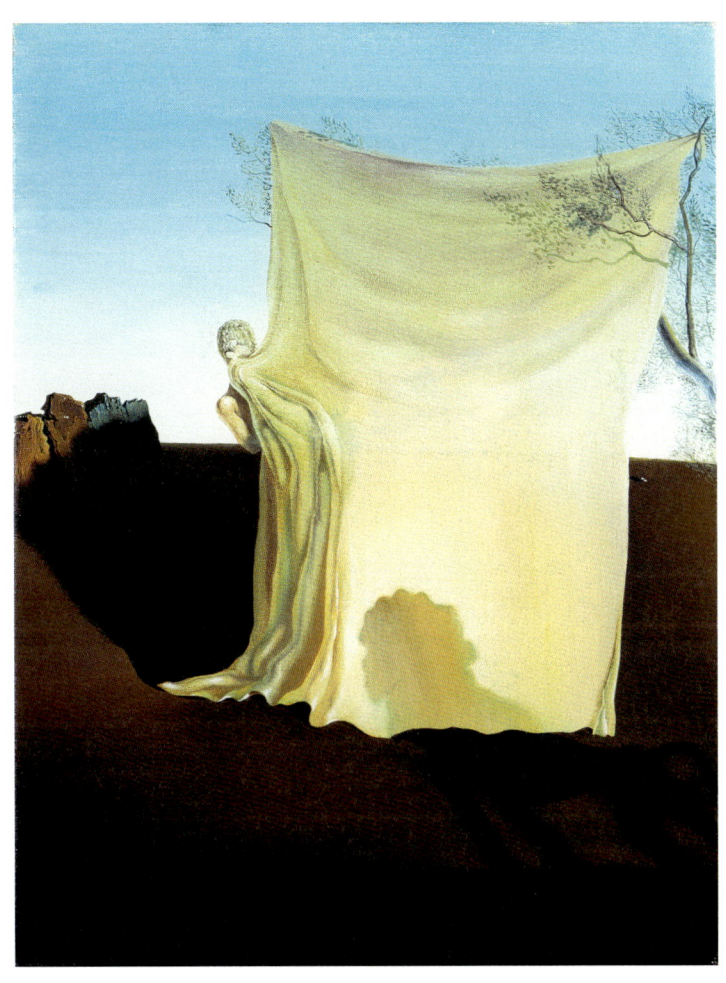

134
Le sentiment du devenir (The Feeling of Becoming)
1931
Oil on canvas, 35.2 × 27.3 cm
Private collection

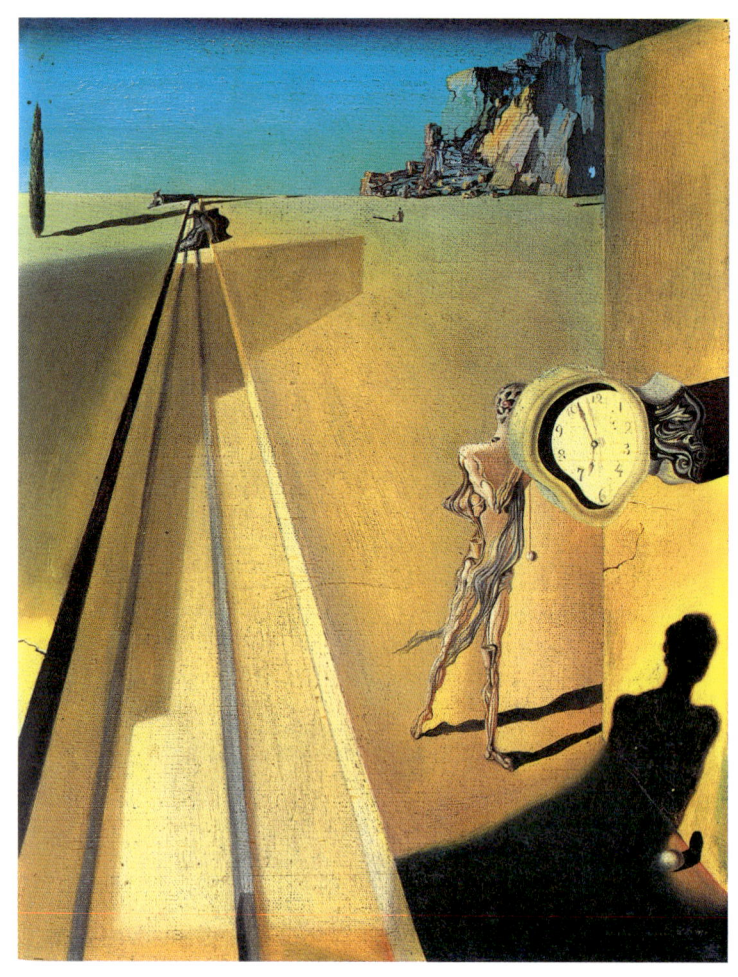

135
Premature Ossification of a Railway Station
1931
Oil on canvas, 31.5 × 27 cm
Private collection

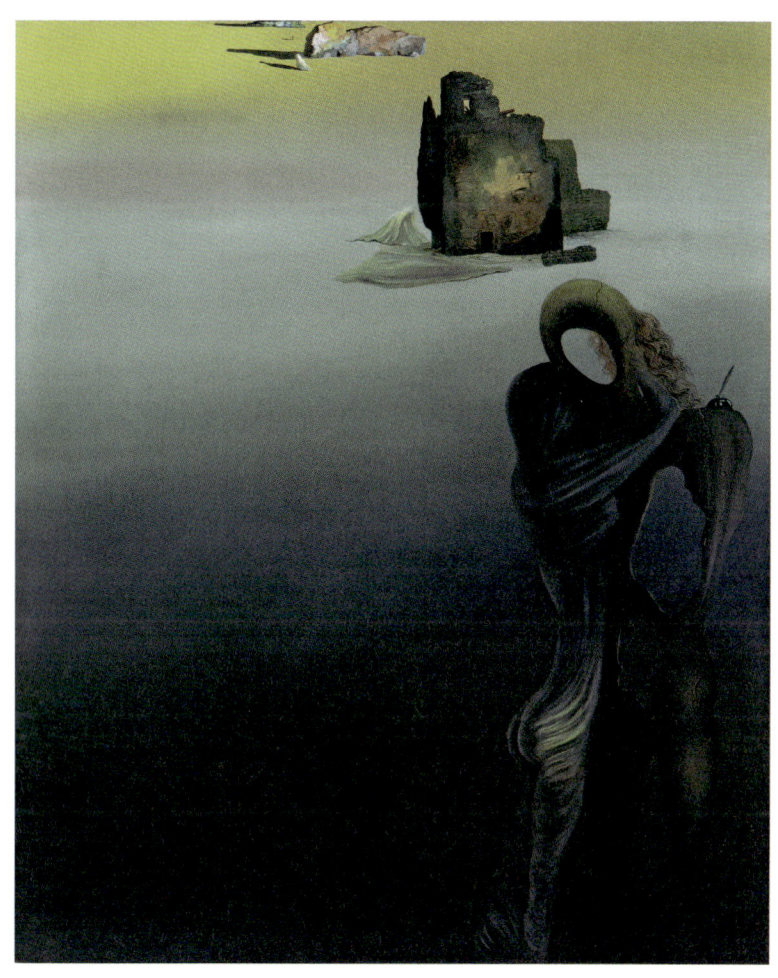

136
Gradiva Rediscovers the Anthropomorphic Ruins (Retrospective Fantasy)
c. 1931–1932
Oil on canvas, 65 × 54 cm
Museo Nacional Thyssen-Bornemisza, Madrid

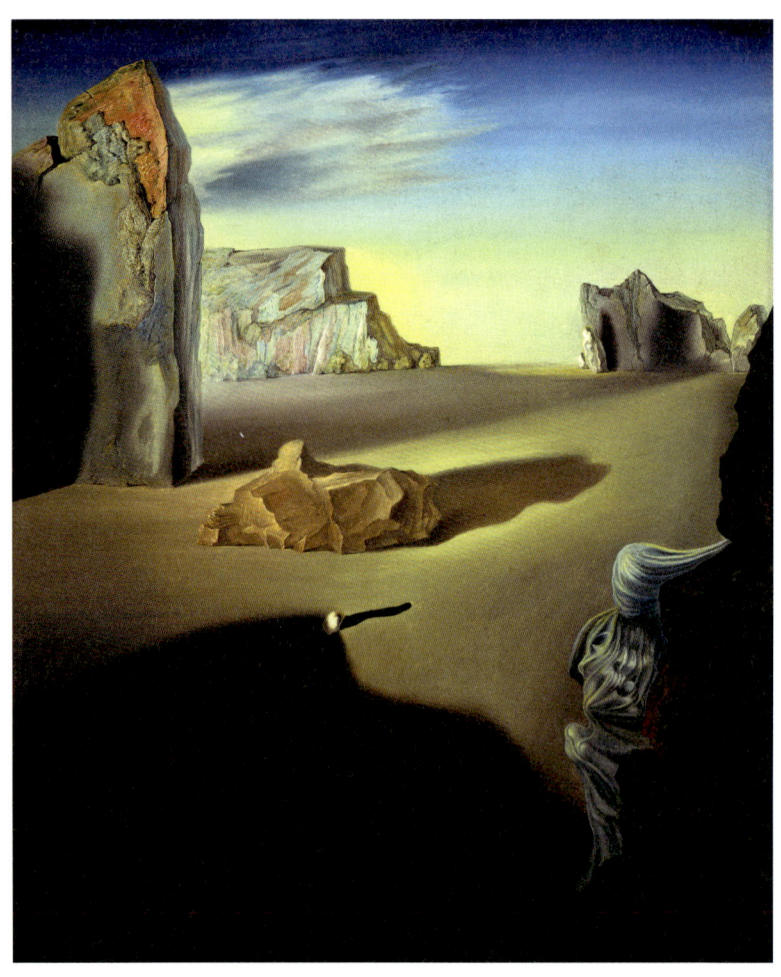

137
The Shades of Night Descending
1931
Oil on canvas, 61 × 50 cm
The Dalí Museum, St. Petersburg, Florida

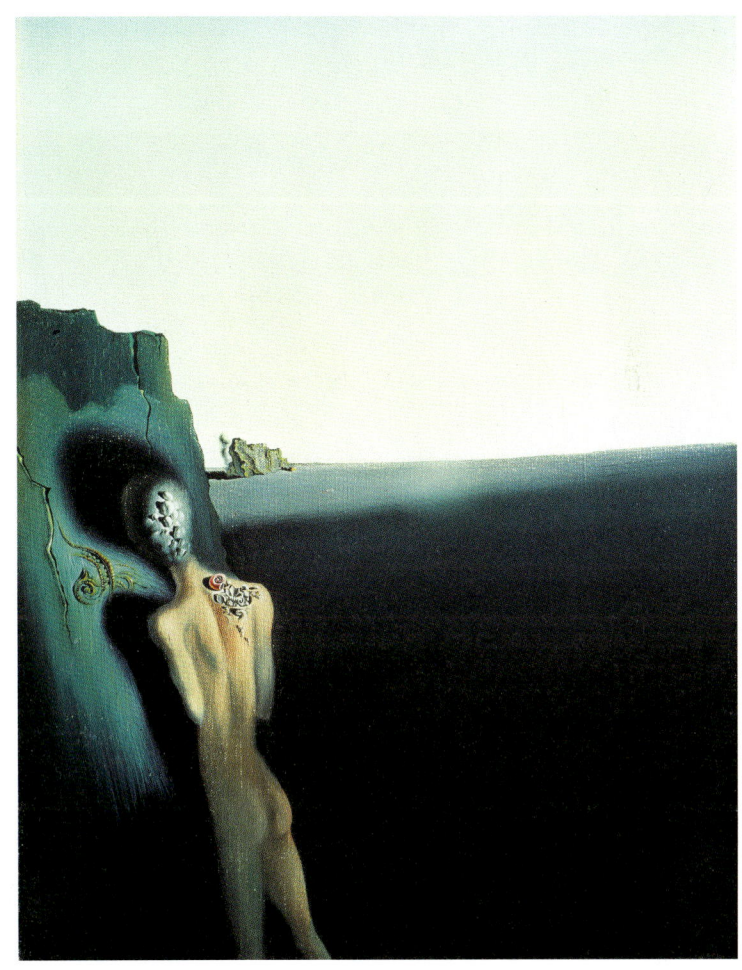

138
The Anthropomorphous Echo
1931
Oil on canvas, 36 × 26 cm
Private collection

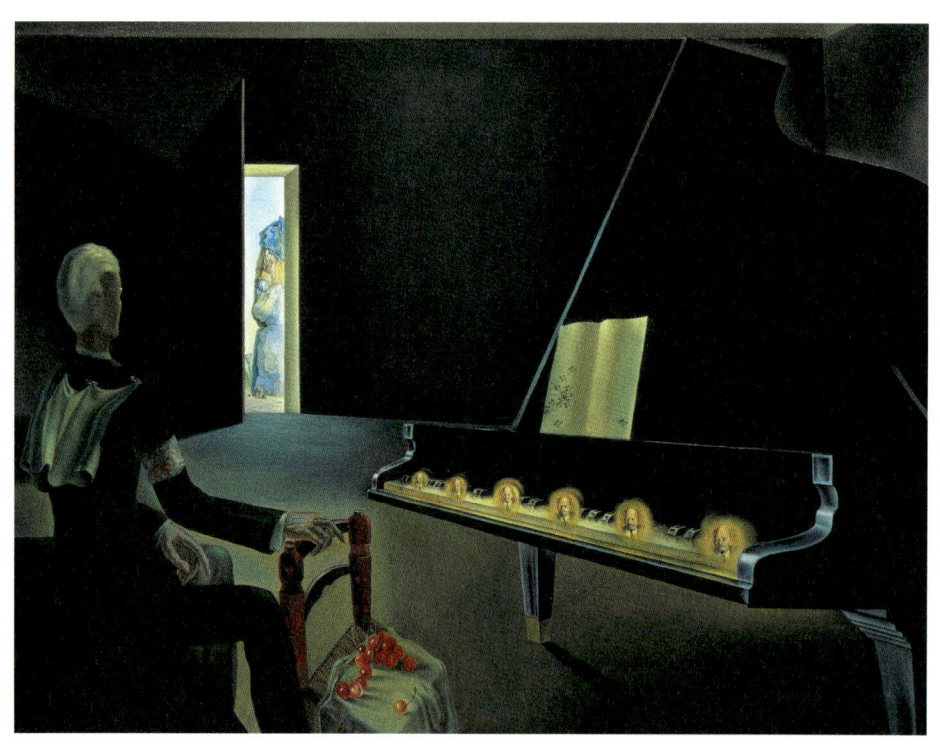

139
Partial Hallucination. Six Images of Lenin on a Grand Piano
1931
Oil on canvas, 114 × 146 cm
Musée National d'Art Moderne, Centre Pompidou, Paris

Surrealism

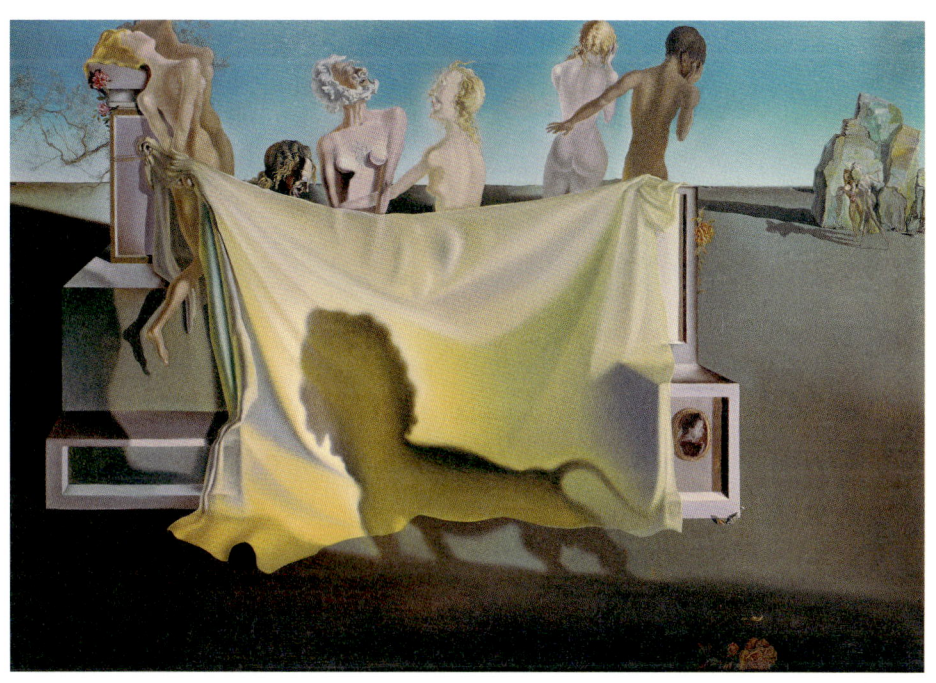

140
La vieillesse de Guillaume Tell (The Old Age of William Tell)
1931
Oil on canvas, 98 × 140 cm
Private collection

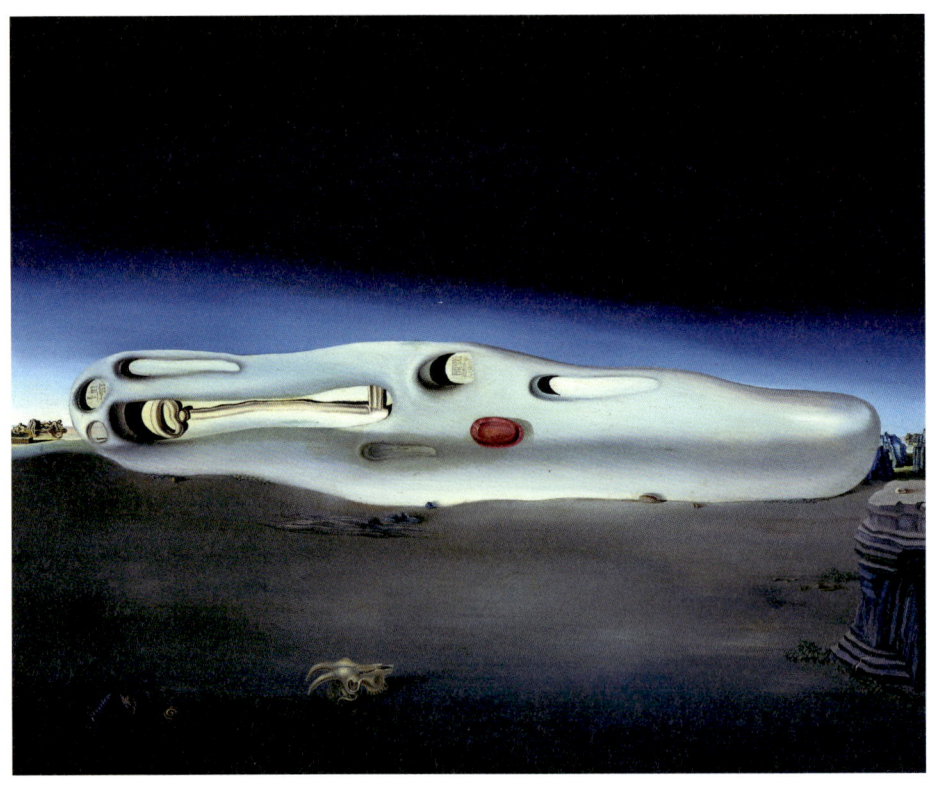

141
Diurnal Fantasies
1931
Oil on canvas, 81.3 × 100.3 cm
The Dalí Museum, St. Petersburg, Florida

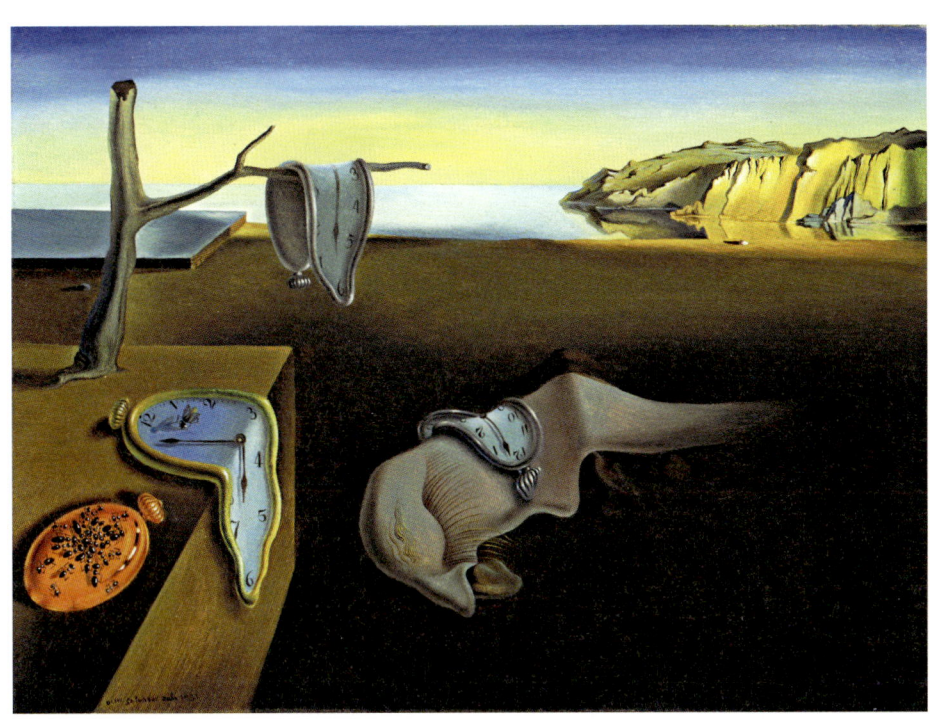

142
The Persistence of Memory
1931
Oil on canvas, 24.1 × 33 cm
The Museum of Modern Art, New York

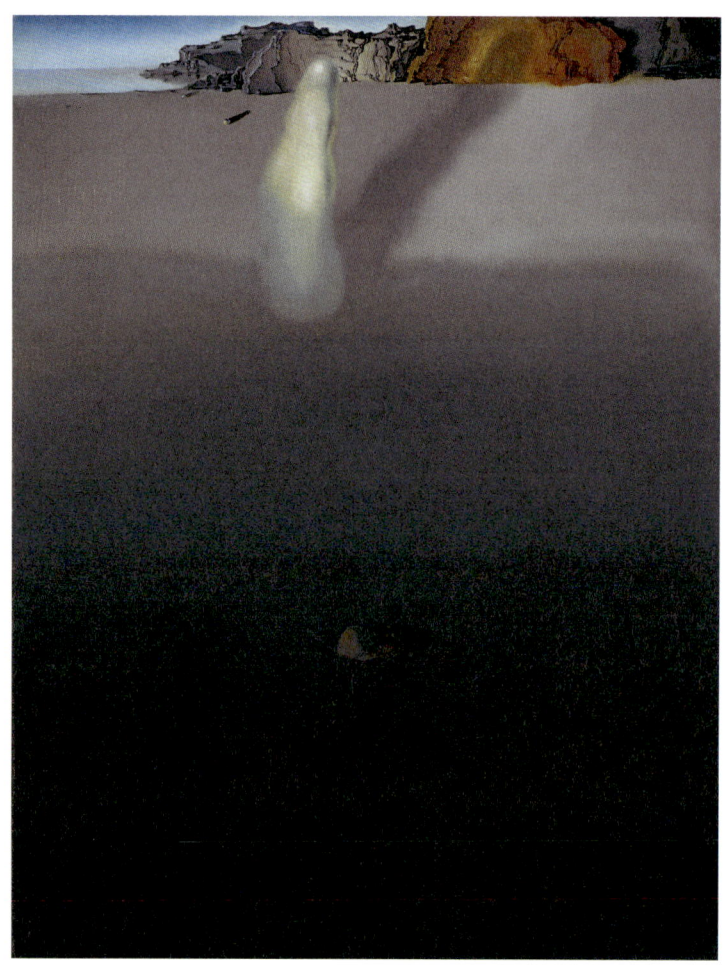

143
At the Seaside
1931
Oil on canvas, 33.7 × 26.4 cm
The Dalí Museum, St. Petersburg, Florida

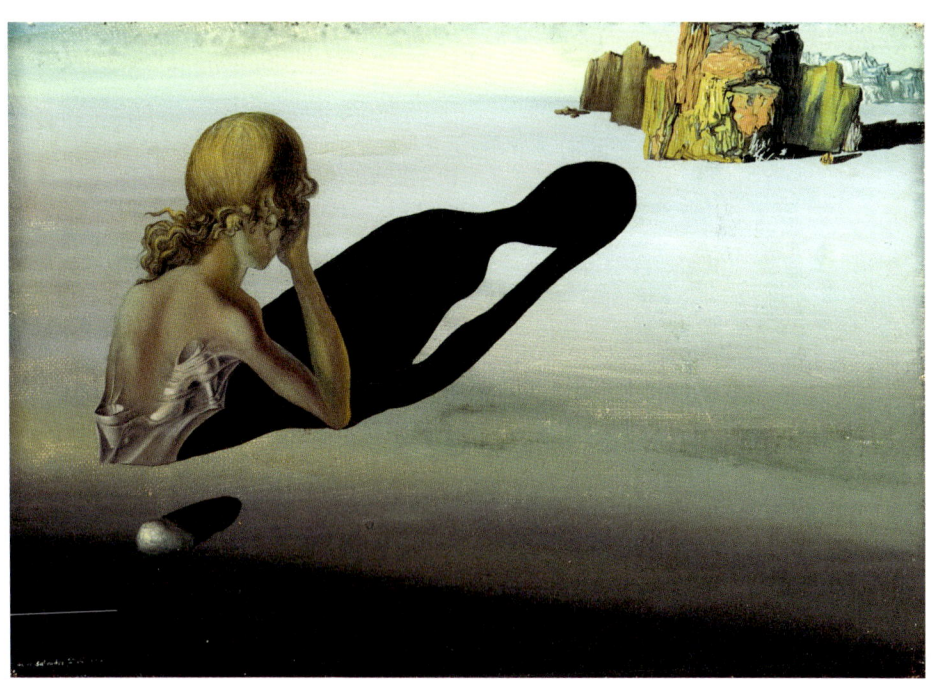

144
Remorse
1931
Oil on canvas, 19.1 × 26.7 cm
Eli and Edythe Broad Art Museum (formerly Kresge Art Museum),
Michigan State University, East Lansing, Michigan

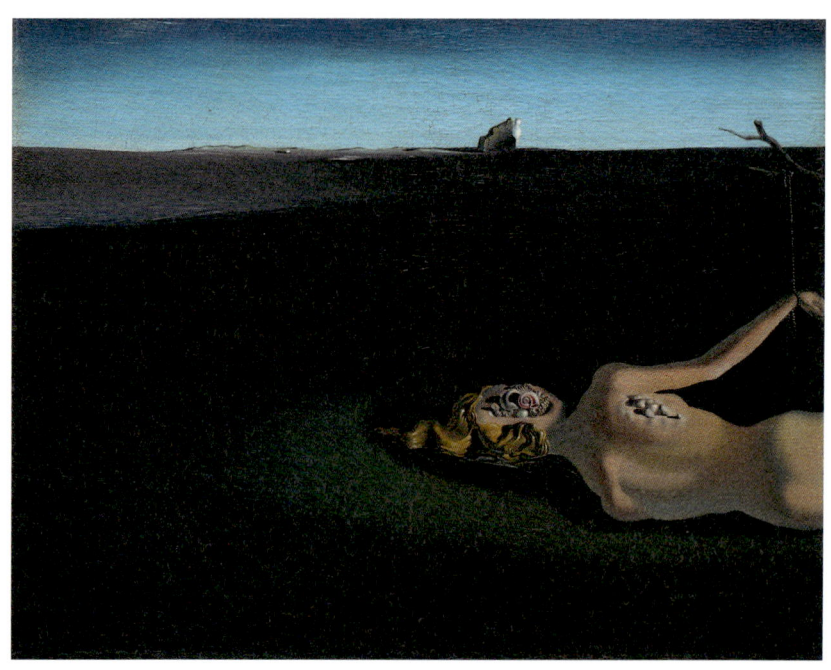

145
Untitled (Woman Sleeping in a Landscape)
1931
Oil on canvas, 27.2 × 35 cm
Peggy Guggenheim Collection, Venice

Surrealism

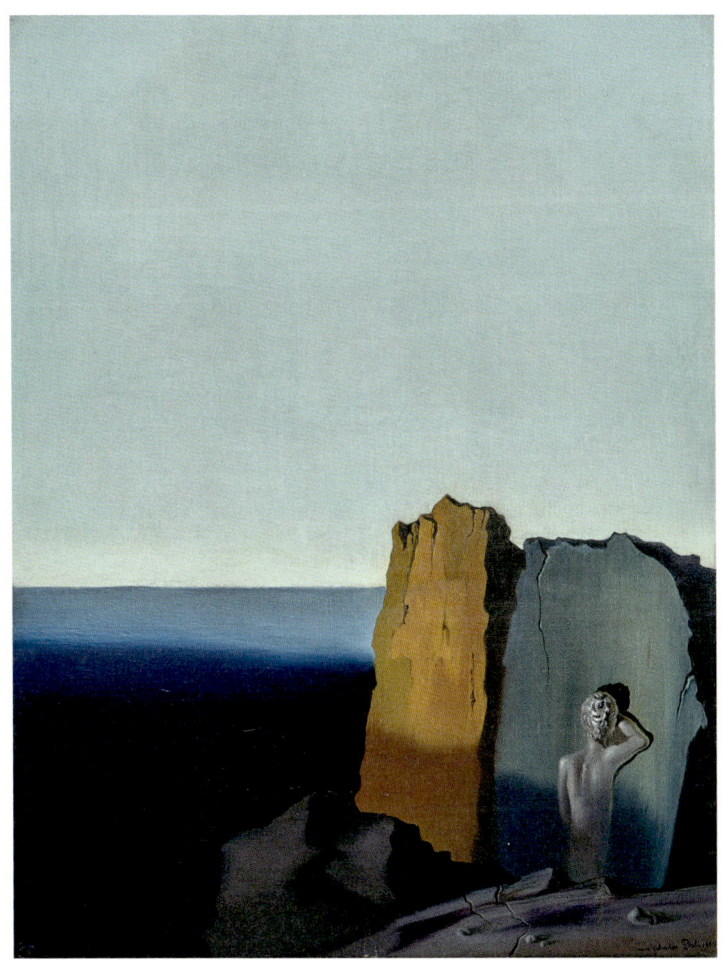

146
La solitude (Solitude)
1931
Oil on canvas, 35.3 × 27.2 cm
Wadsworth Atheneum, Hartford, Connecticut. Purchased through the gift of Henry and Walter Keney

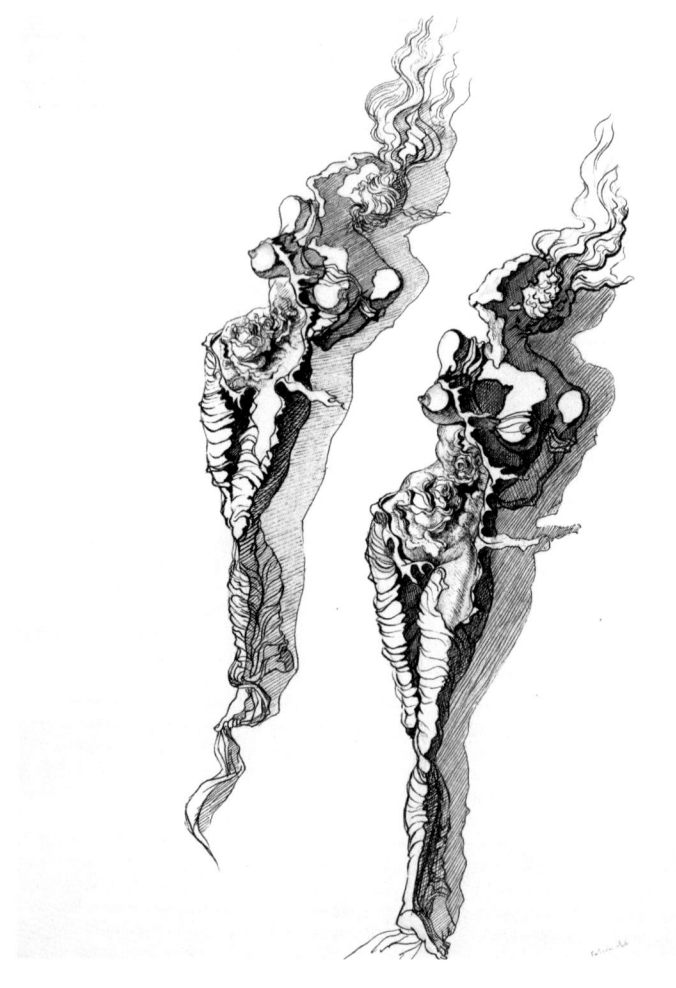

147
Gradiva
c. 1930
Ink and pencil on paper, 31.1 × 22.9 cm
The Dalí Museum, St. Petersburg, Florida

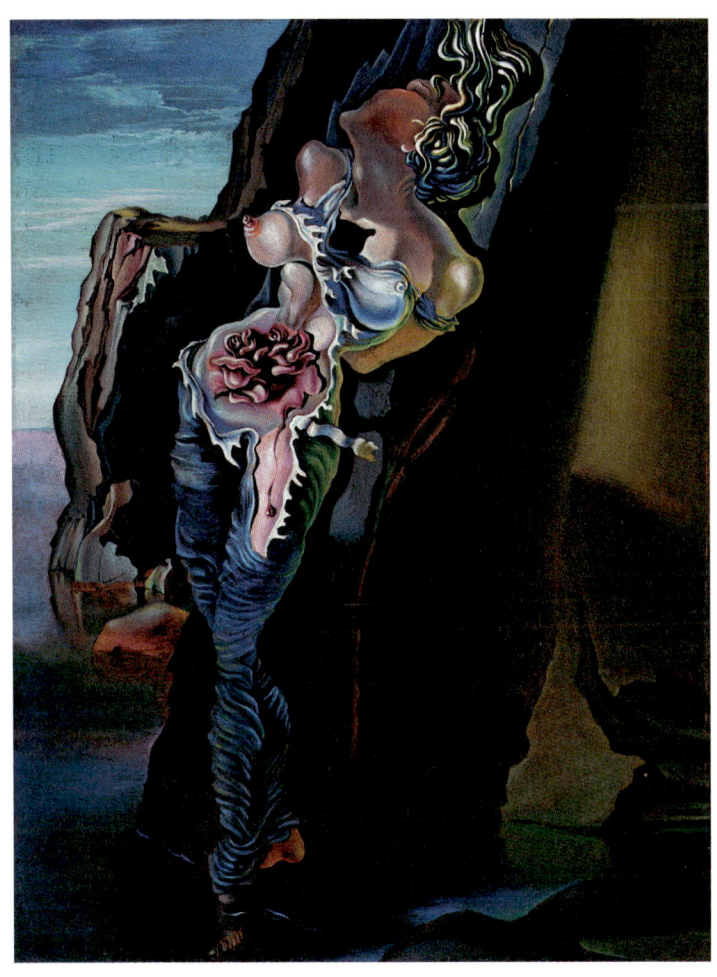

148
Gradiva
1931
Oil on copper, 26.6 × 15.5 cm
Private collection

1929–1939

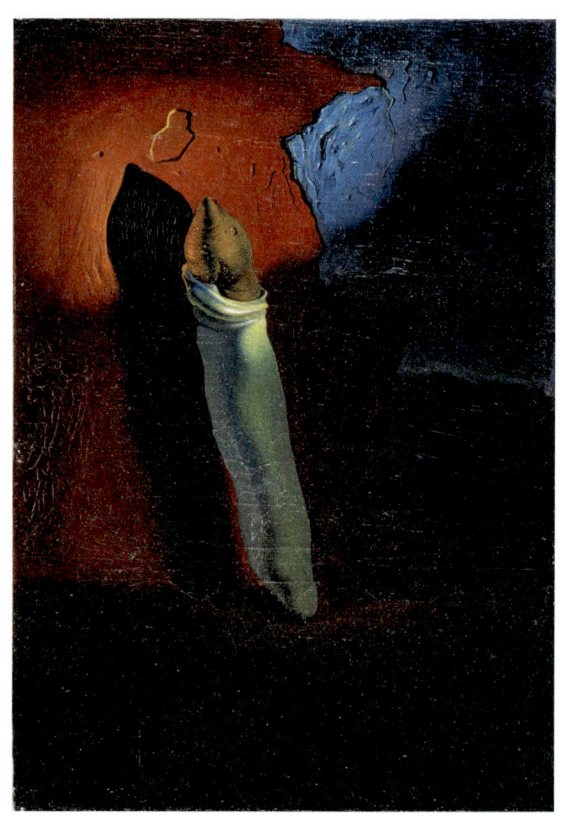

149
Anthropomorphic Bread
1932
Oil on canvas, 24 × 16.5 cm
Town Hall of Figueres, on permanent deposit at the Fundació Gala-Salvador Dalí, Figueres

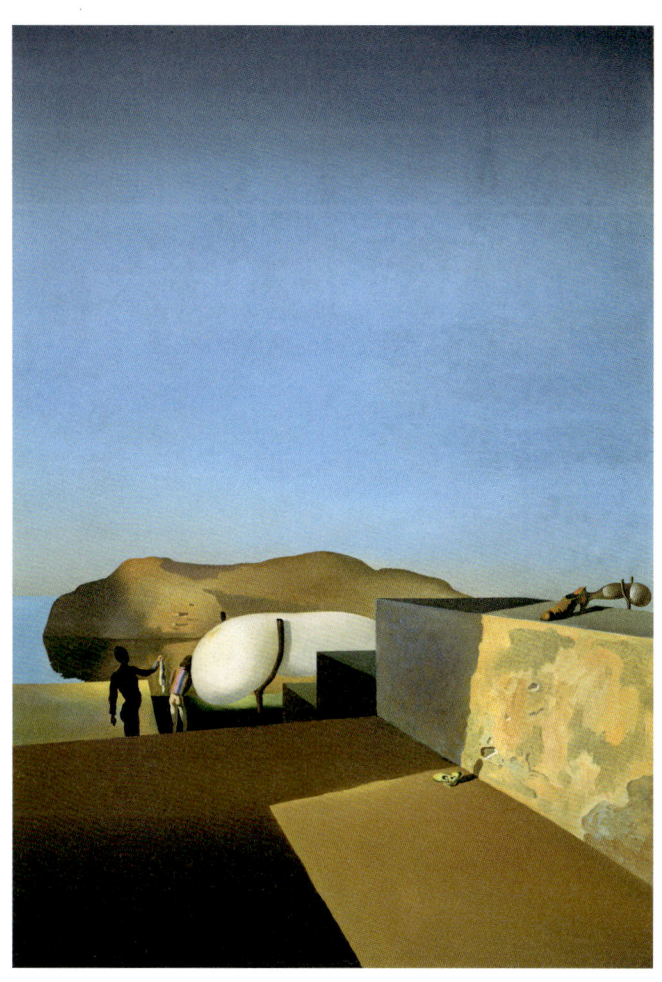

150
Persistence of Fair Weather
c. 1932
Oil on canvas, 66.7 × 47 cm
The Dalí Museum, St. Petersburg, Florida

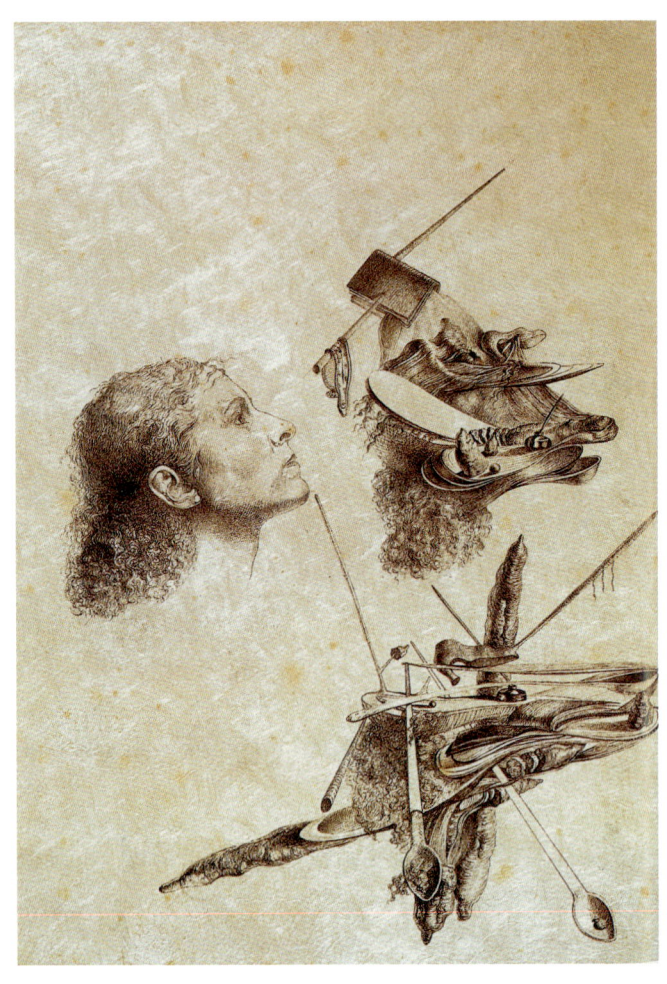

151
Paranoiac Metamorphosis of Gala's Face
1932
India ink on Japan paper, 29 × 21 cm
Fundació Gala-Salvador Dalí, Figueres

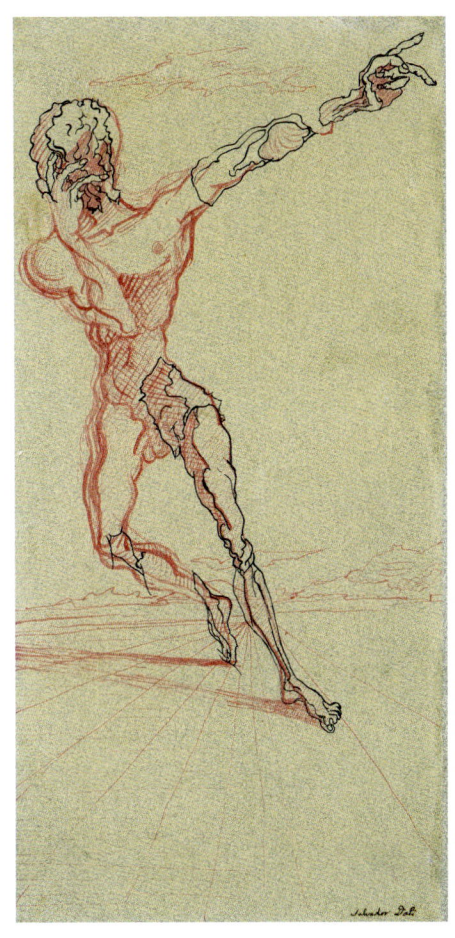

152
Figure after "William Tell"
1932
Red and black ink, 25 × 14 cm
The Dalí Museum, St. Petersburg, Florida

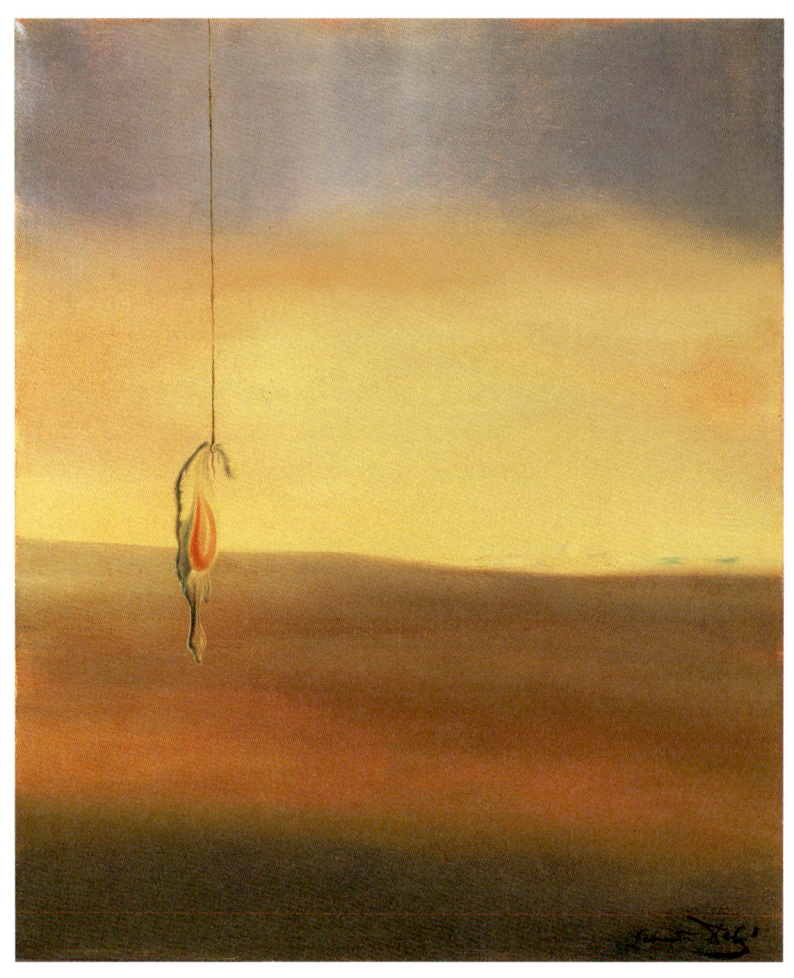

153
Egg on the Plate without the Plate
c. 1932
Oil on canvas, 55 × 46 cm
Private collection

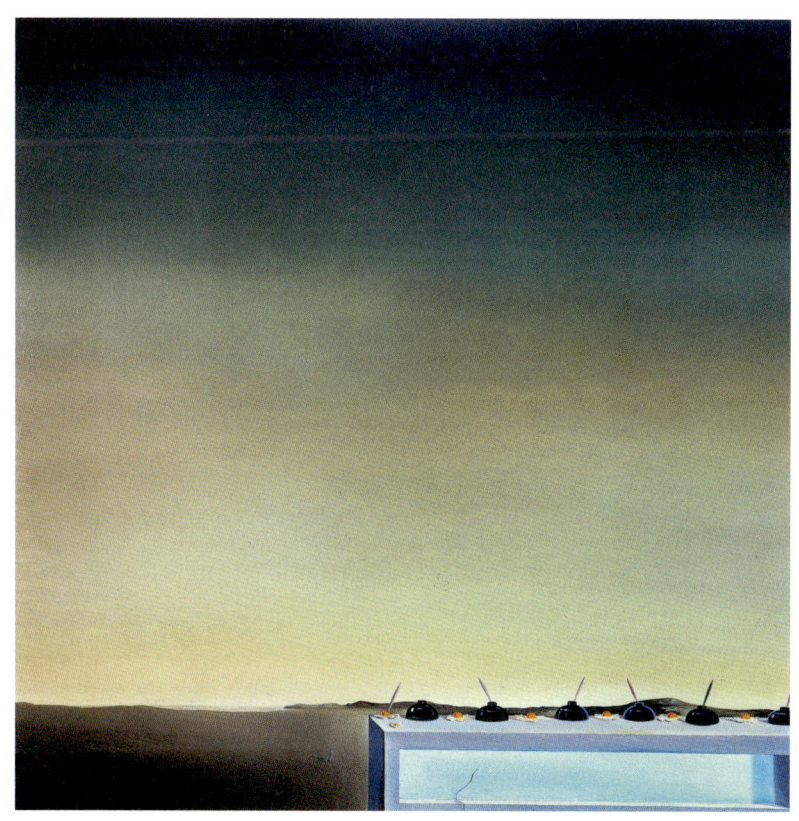

154
The Nostalgia of the Cannibal
1932
Oil on canvas, 47.2 × 47.2 cm
Sprengel Museum, Hanover

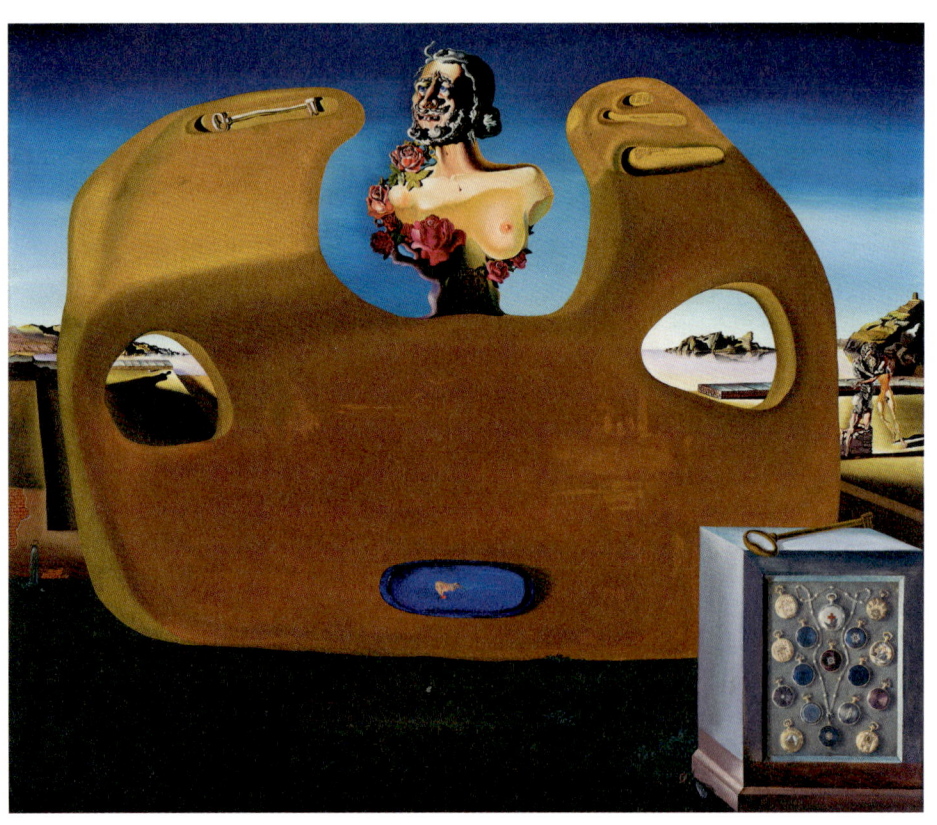

155
Memory of the Child-Woman
1932
Oil on canvas, 99 × 120.7 cm
The Dalí Museum, St. Petersburg, Florida

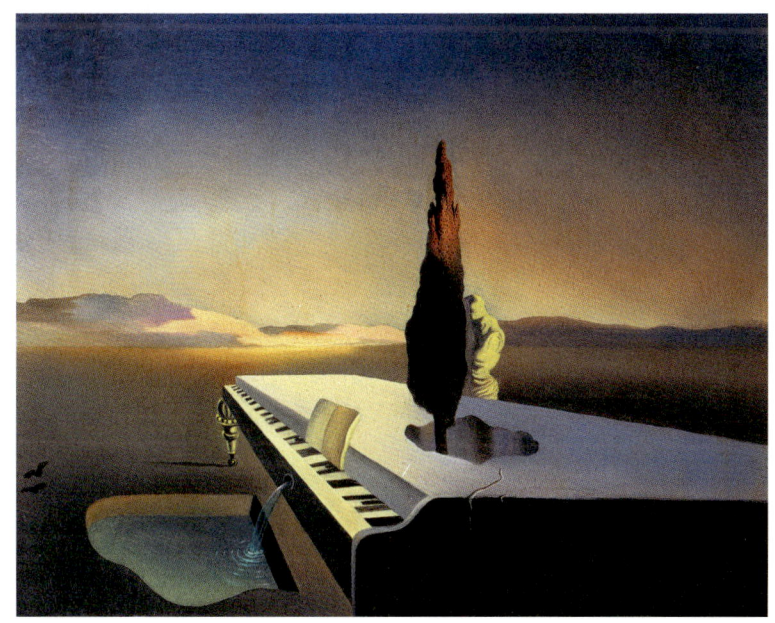

156
Necrophilic Fountain Flowing from a Grand Piano
c. 1932
Oil on canvas, 22 × 27 cm
Private collection

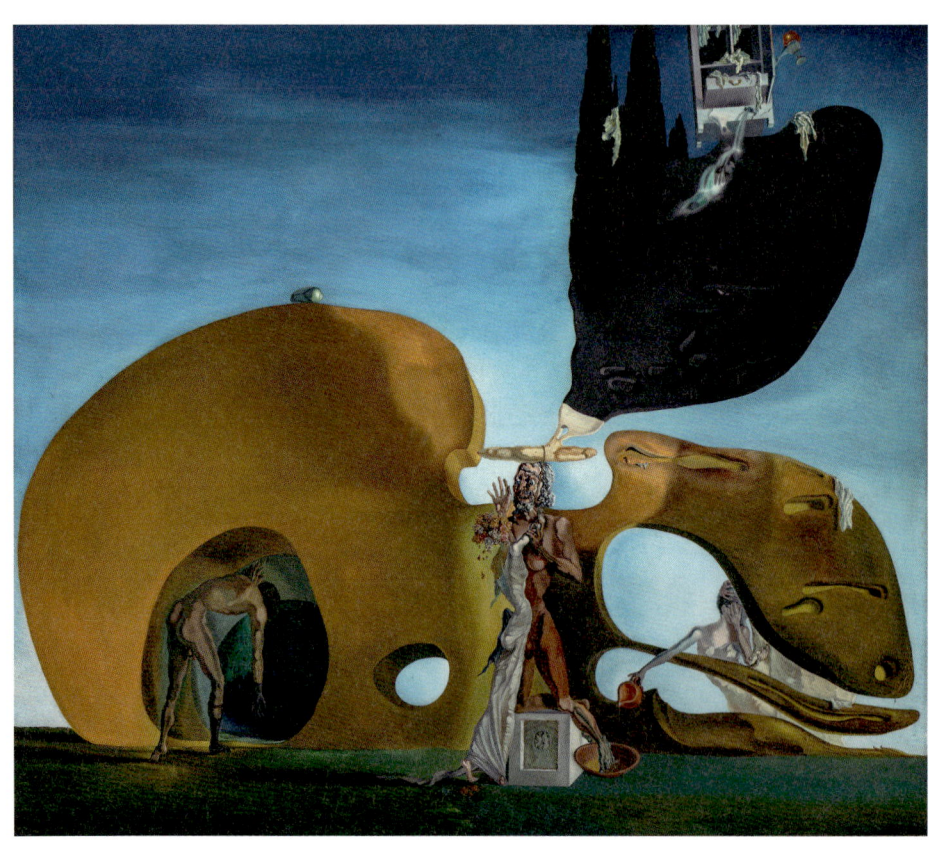

157
Birth of Liquid Desires
1932
Oil and collage on canvas, 96.1 × 112.3 cm
Peggy Guggenheim Collection, Venice

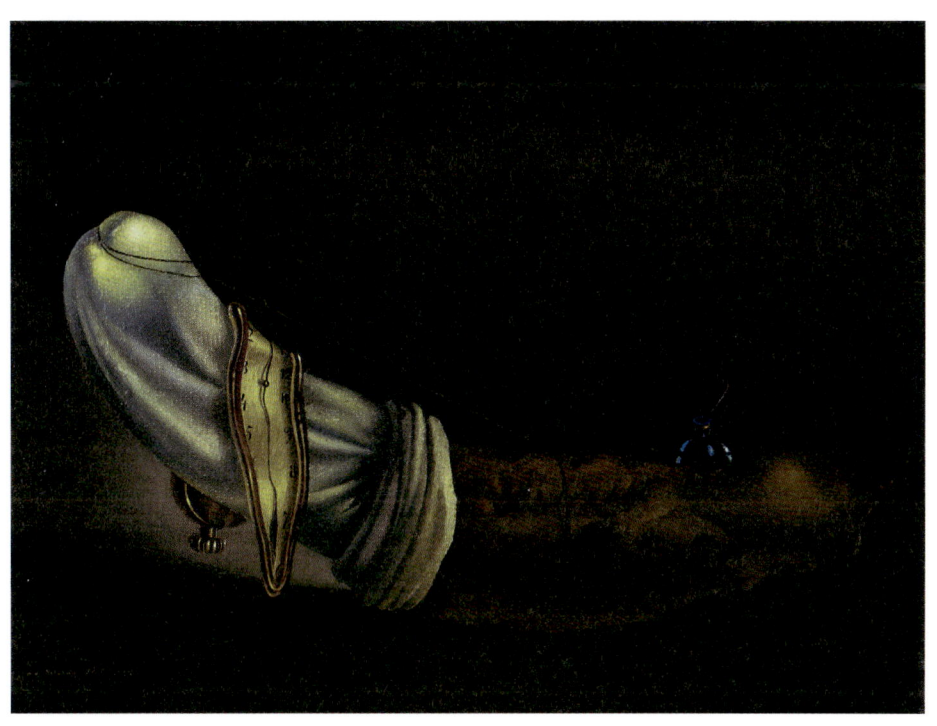

158
Catalan bread
1932
Oil on canvas, 24 × 33 cm
The Dalí Museum, St. Petersburg, Florida

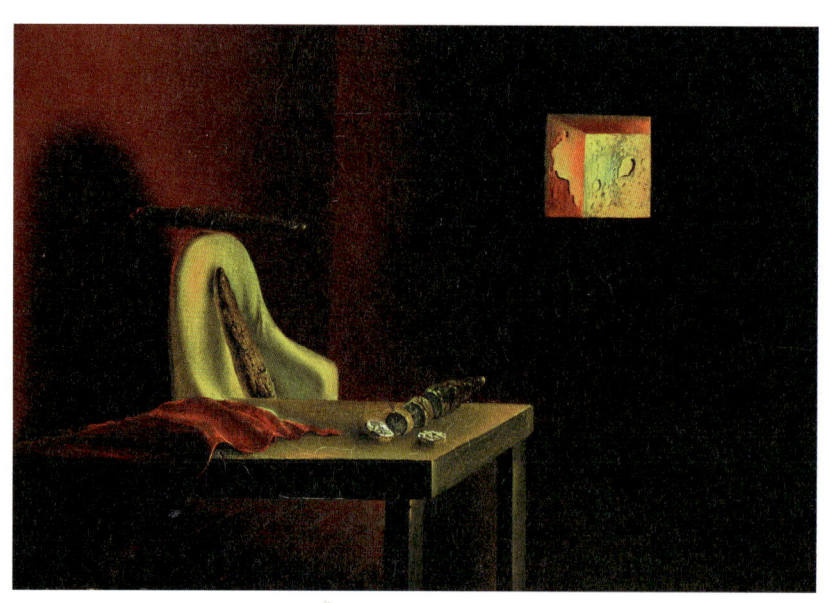

159
The Invisible Man
1932
Oil on canvas, 16.5 × 23.8 cm
The Dalí Museum, St. Petersburg, Florida

Surrealism

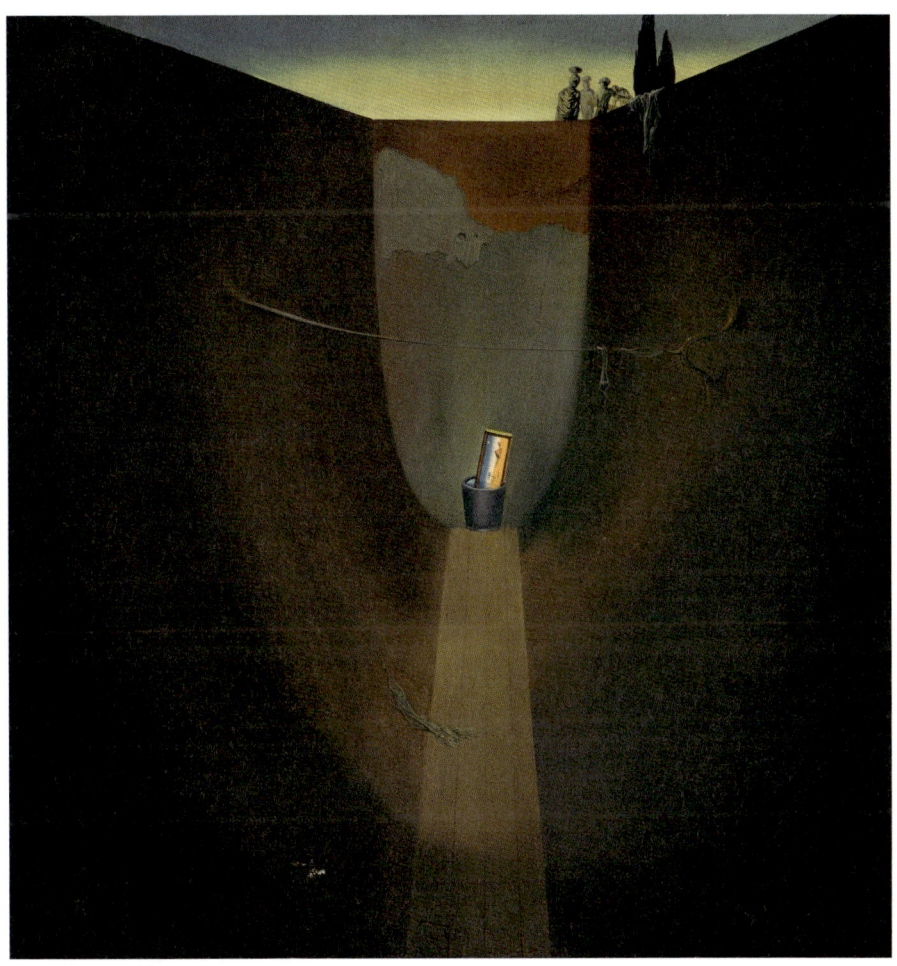

160
Suez
c. 1932
Oil on canvas, 47 × 47 cm
The Dalí Museum, St. Petersburg, Florida

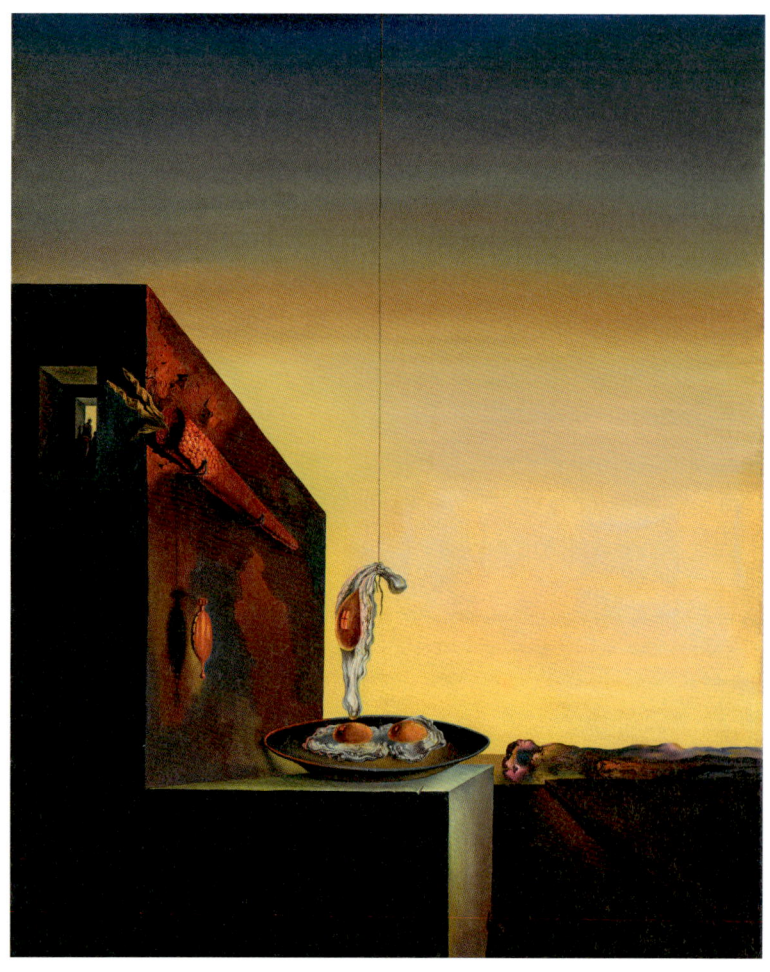

161
Eggs on the plate (without the plate)
1932
Oil on canvas, 60 × 41.9 cm
The Dalí Museum, St. Petersburg, Florida

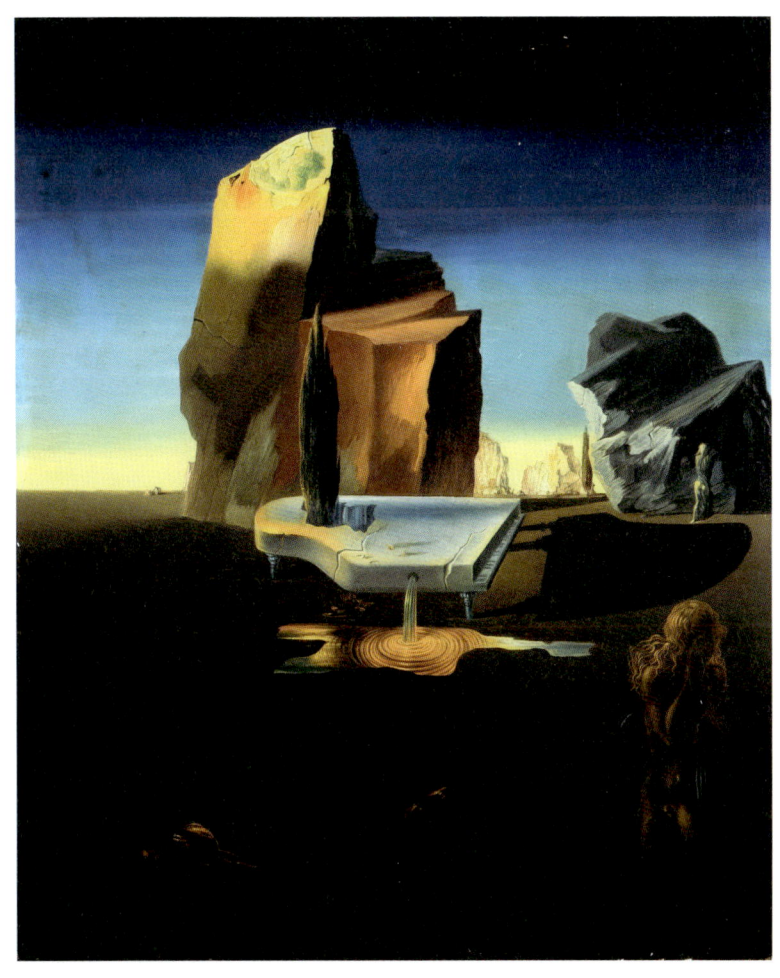

162
The Mysterious Sources of Harmony
c. 1932
Oil on canvas, 54.6 × 45.7 cm
Private collection

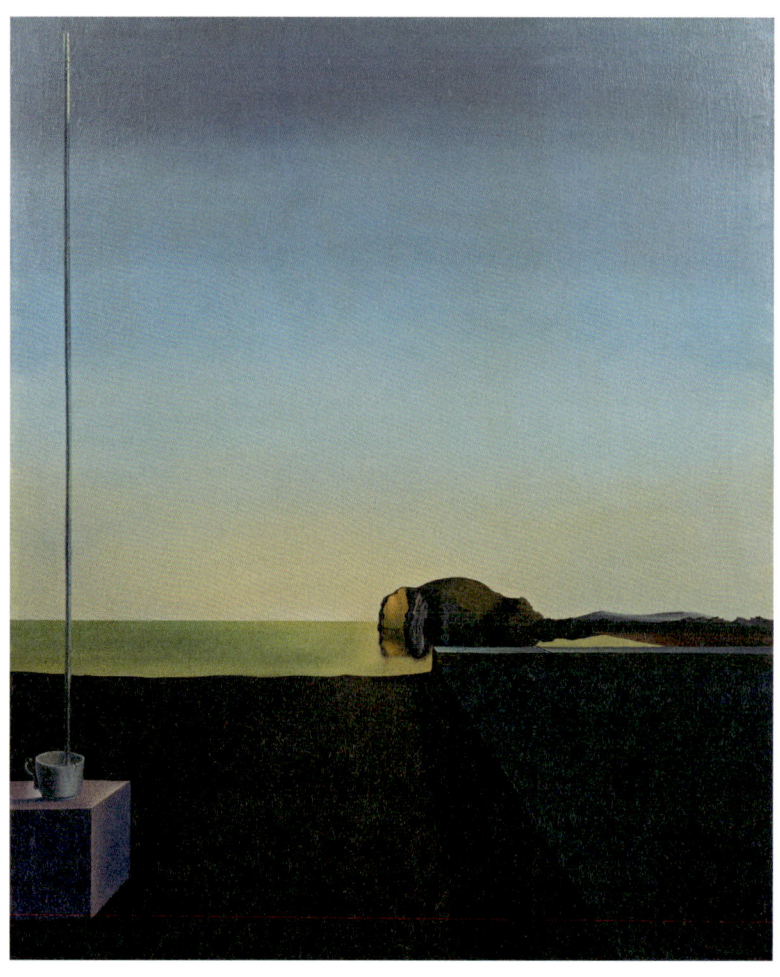

163
The Real Painting of "The Isle of the Death"
by Arnold Böcklin at the Angelus Time
1932
Oil on canvas, 77.5 × 64.5 cm
Von der Heydt-Museum, Wuppertal

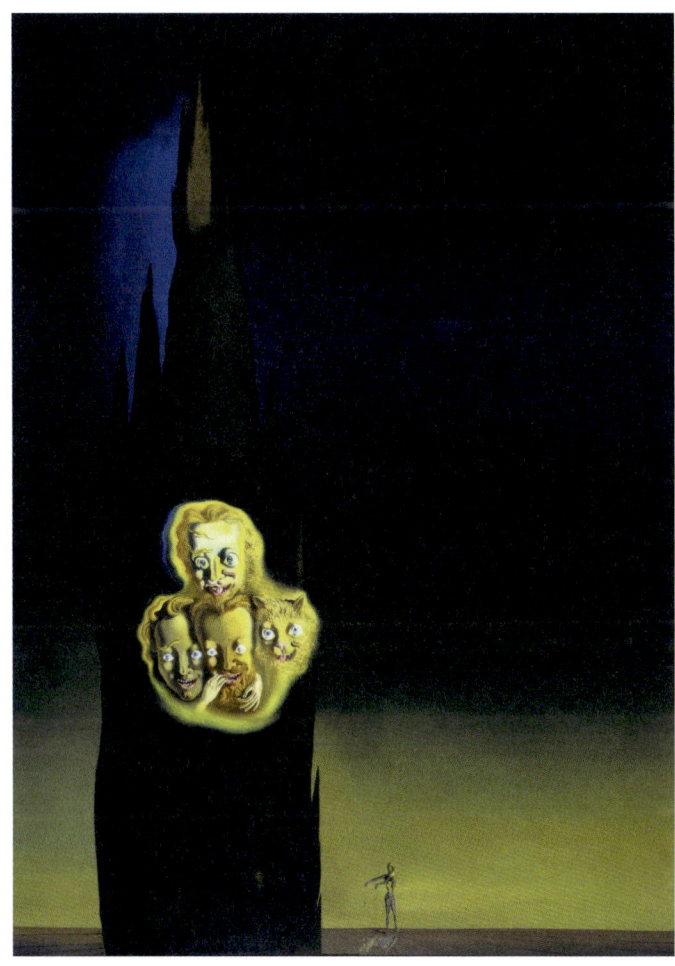

164
Phosphene of Della Porta
c. 1932
Oil on canvas, 109 × 80 cm
Private collection

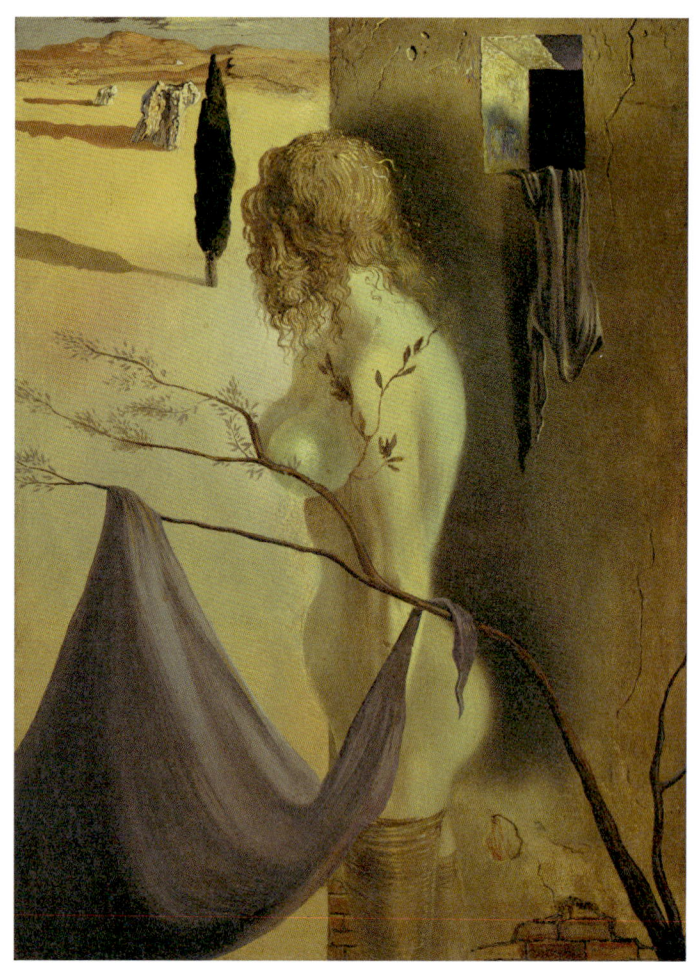

165
Le signal de l'angoisse (The Signal of Anguish)
c. 1932–1936
Oil on wood panel, 21.8 × 16.2 cm
Scottish National Gallery of Modern Art, Edinburgh

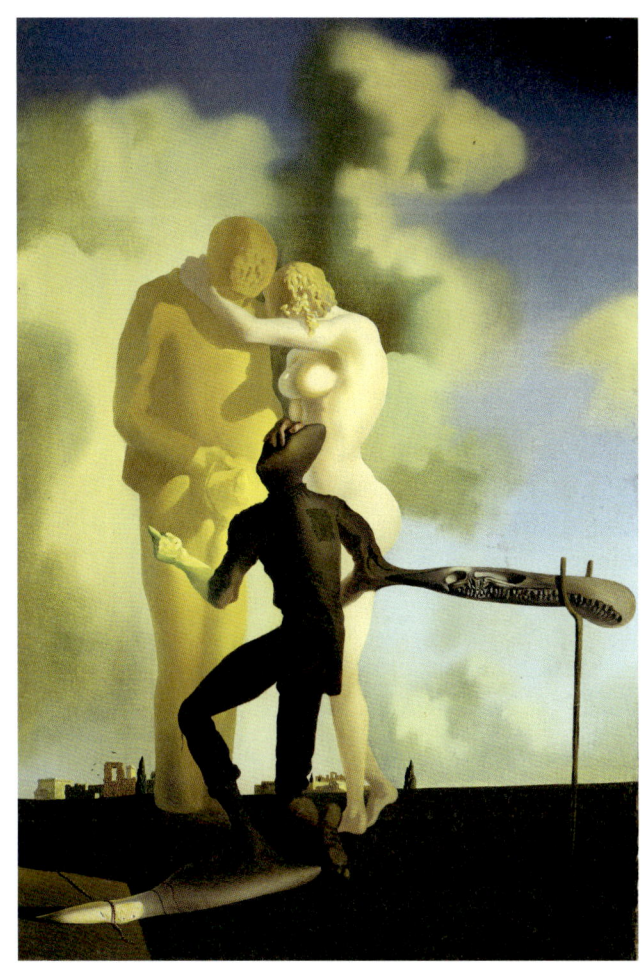

166
Meditation on the Harp
c. 1933
Oil on canvas, 67 × 47 cm
The Dalí Museum, St. Petersburg, Florida

1929–1939

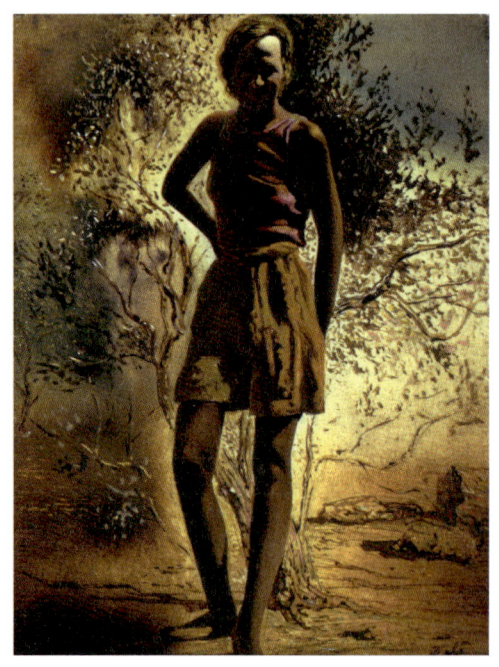

167
Portrait of Gala
c. 1933
Oil on wood panel, 8.5 × 5.6 cm
The Dalí Museum, St. Petersburg, Florida

Surrealism

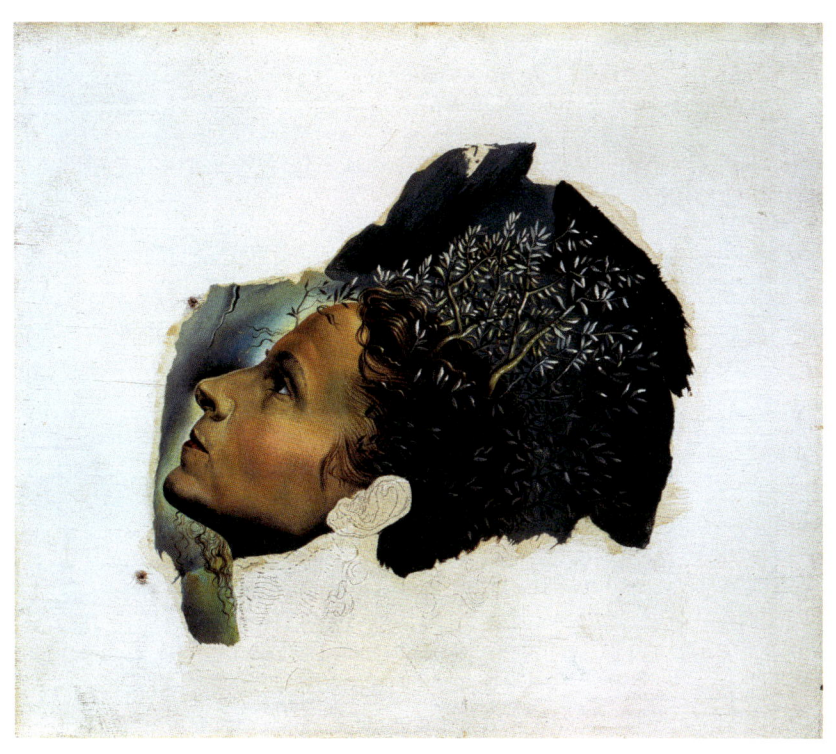

168
Automatic beginning of a Portrait of Gala
c. 1933
Oil on plywood panel, 14 × 16.2 cm
Fundació Gala-Salvador Dalí, Figueres

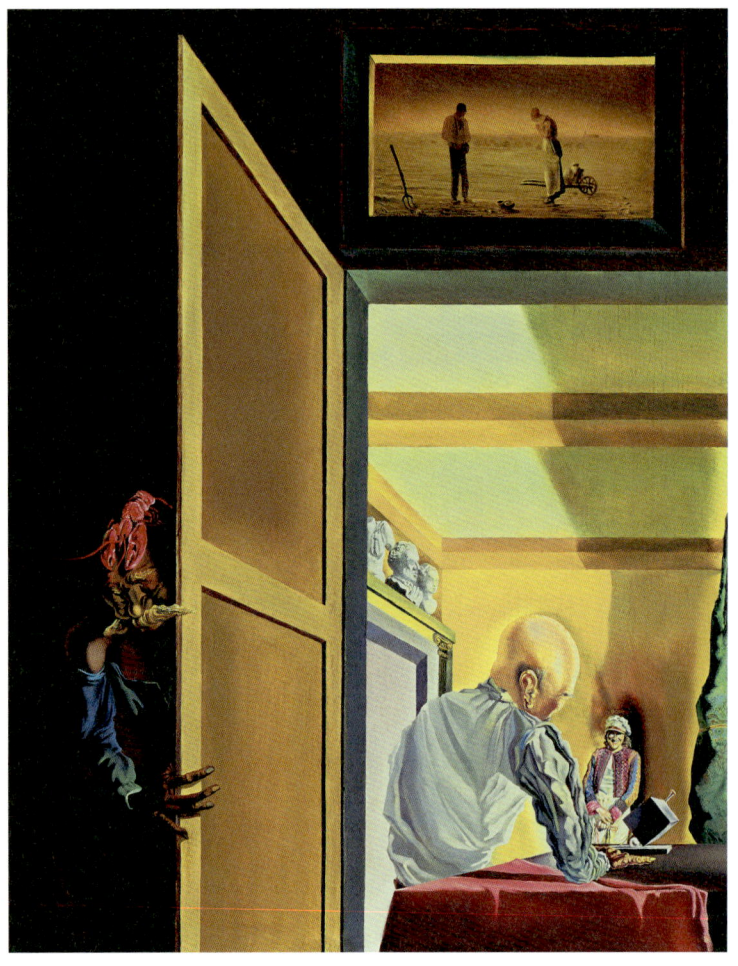

169
Gala and the Angelus of Millet Preceding the Imminent Arrival of the Conical Anamorphoses
c. 1933
Oil on wood panel, 24.2 × 19.2 cm
National Gallery of Canada, Ottawa

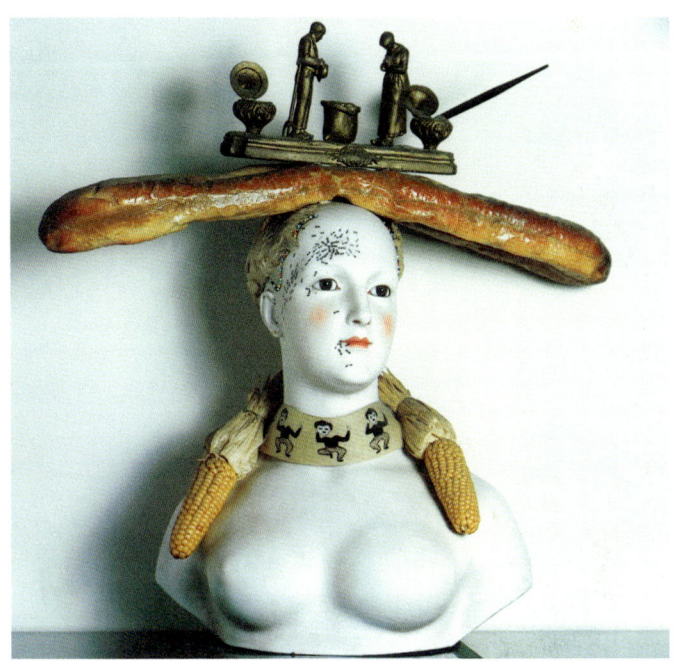

170
Retrospective Bust of a Woman
1933
Assemblage. Painted porcelain, bread, corn, feathers, paint on paper, beads, sand and ink stand,
73.9 × 69.2 × 32 cm
The Museum of Modern Art, New York
Acquired through the Lillie P. Bliss Bequest and gift of Philip Johnson (both by exchange)

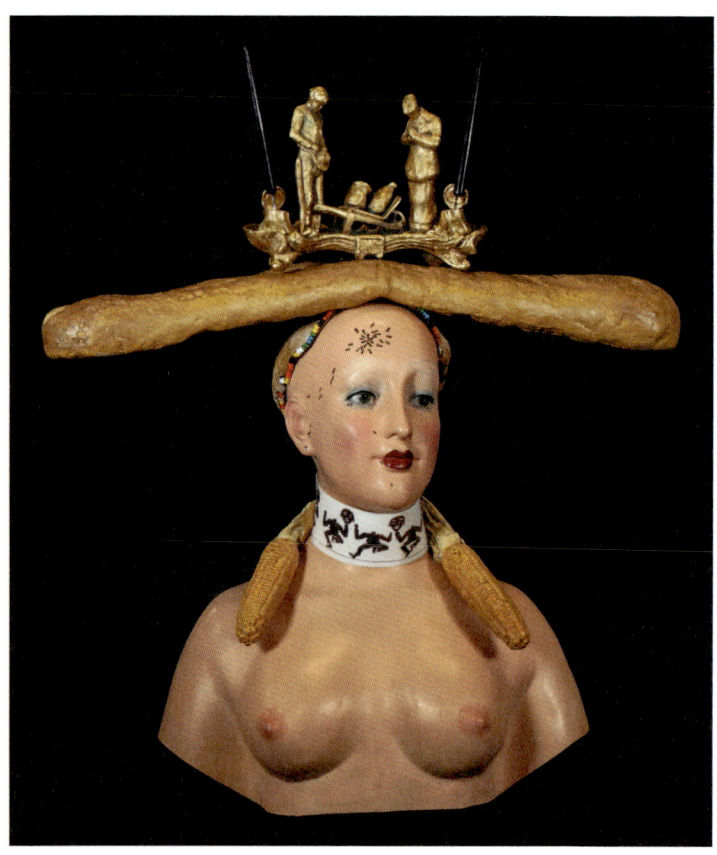

171

Retrospective Bust of a Woman

Original 1933; cast *c.* 1976–1977

Hand-painted and gilded bronze, feathered cap, beads, plastic strip and two wooden ink pens,
69.9 × 54 × 34.9 cm

The Dalí Museum, St. Petersburg, Florida

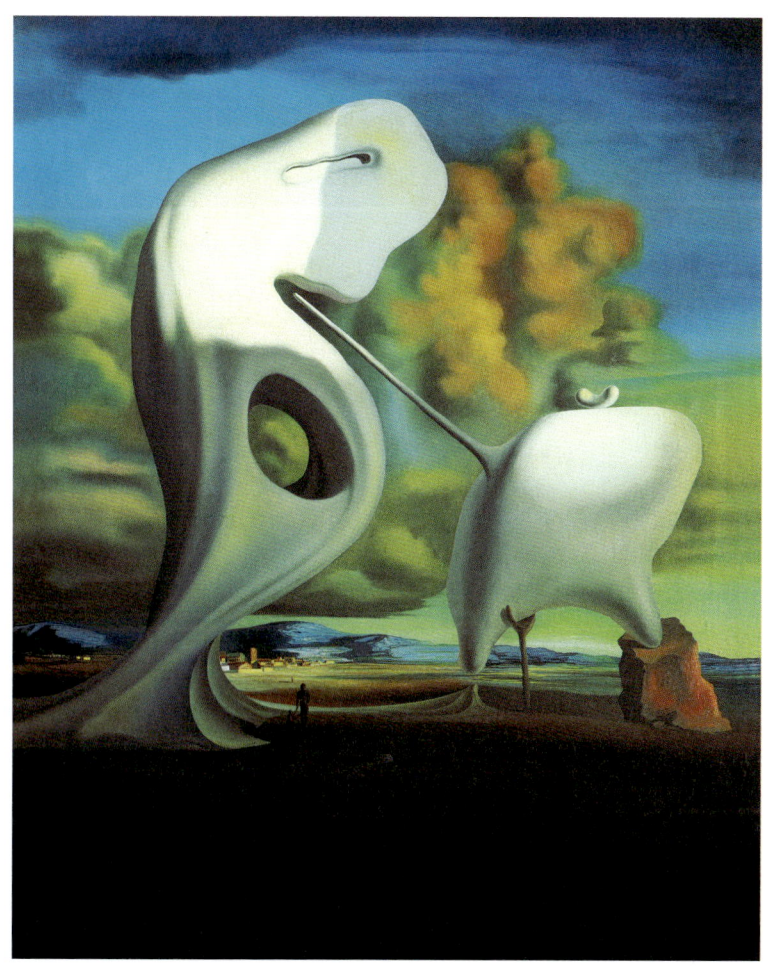

172
The Architectural Angelus of Millet
1933
Oil on canvas, 73 × 60 cm
Museo Nacional Centro de Arte Reina Sofía, Madrid

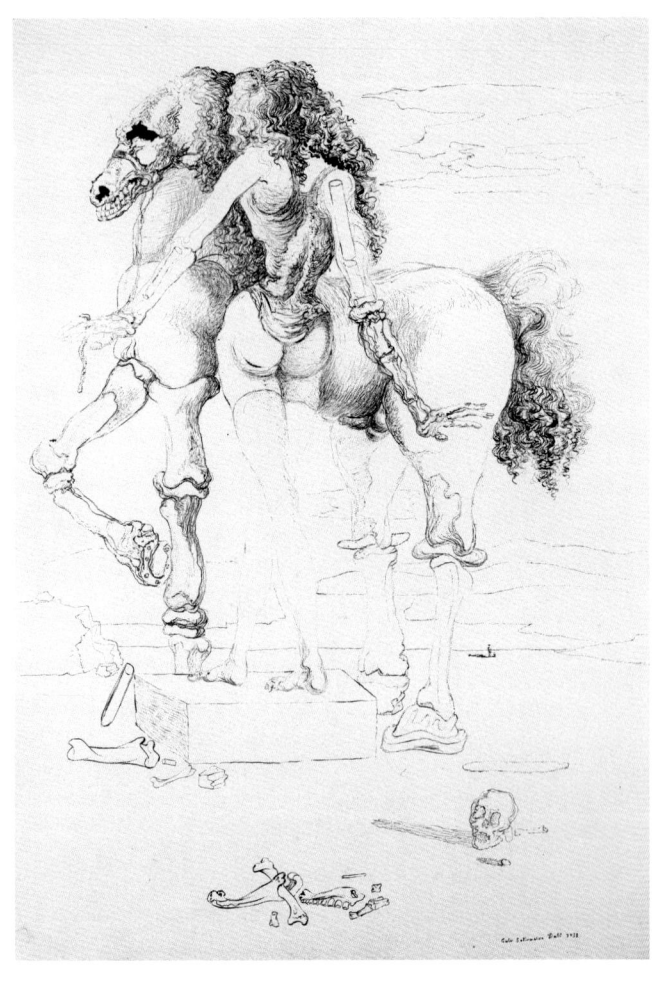

173
Surrealist Horse – Woman-Horse
1933
Pencil and pen on paper, 52.6 × 25 cm
The Dalí Museum, St. Petersburg, Florida

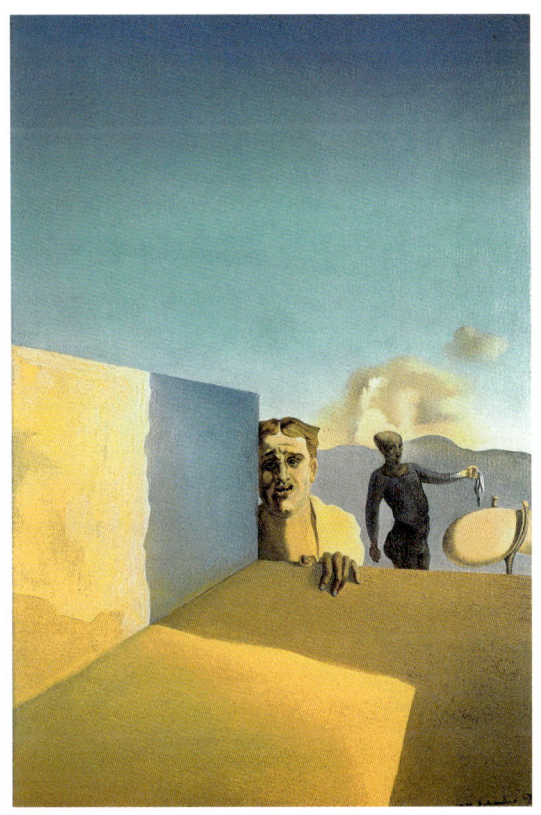

174
The Anguished Barber by the Persistency of Good Weather
c. 1933
Oil on canvas, 24 × 15.5 cm
Perls Galleries, New York

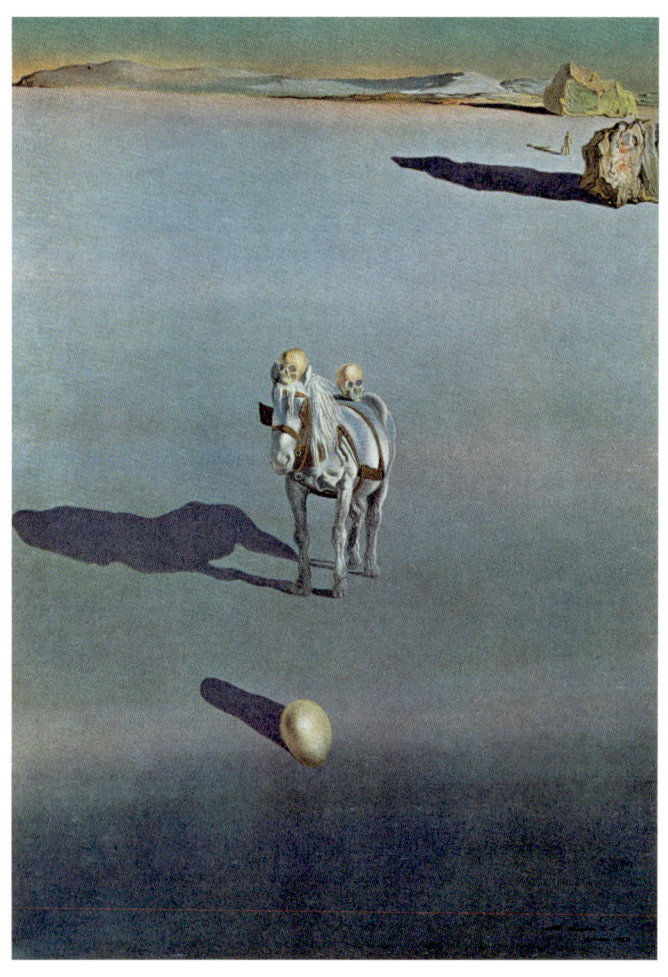

175
Geological Destiny
1933
Oil on wood panel, 21 × 16 cm
Private collection

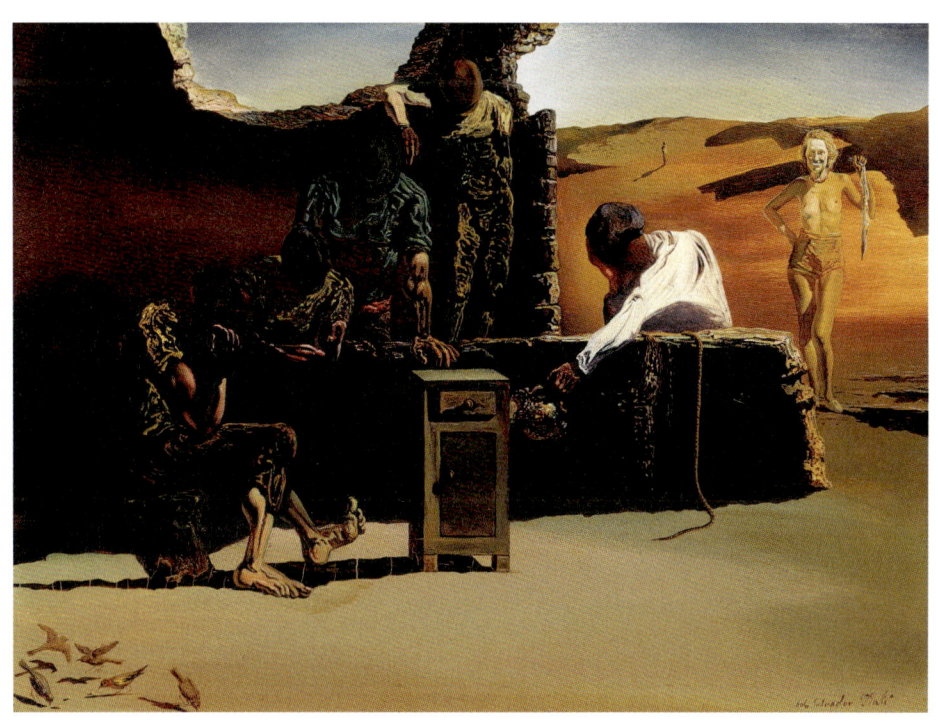

176
Cadernera – cadernera (Goldfinch – goldfinch)
c. 1934
Oil and tempera on wood panel, 15.9 × 21.7 cm
Munson-Williams-Proctor Institute, Utica, New York

1929–1939

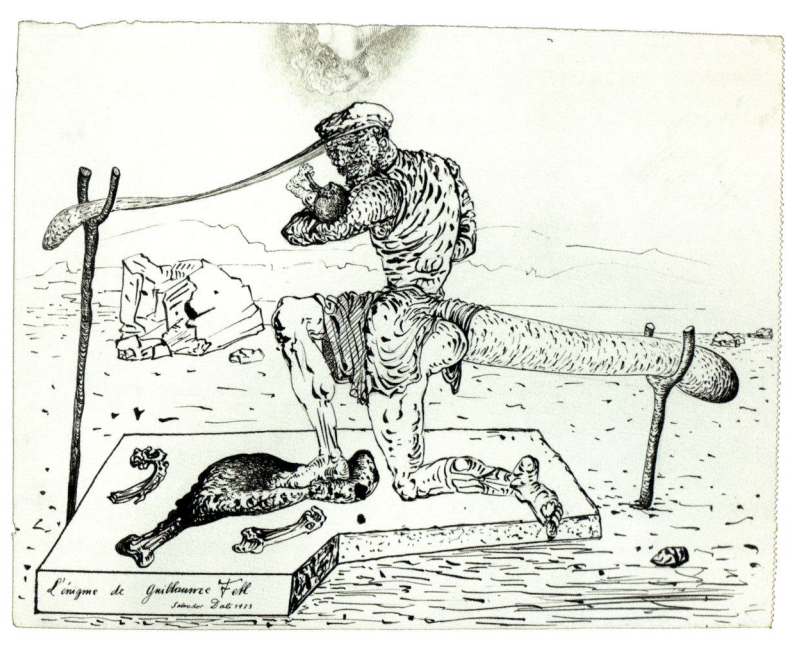

177
The Enigma of William Tell with the Apparition of a Celestial Gala
1933
Ink and pencil on paper, 16.8 × 21.9 cm
The Dalí Museum, St. Petersburg, Florida

Surrealism

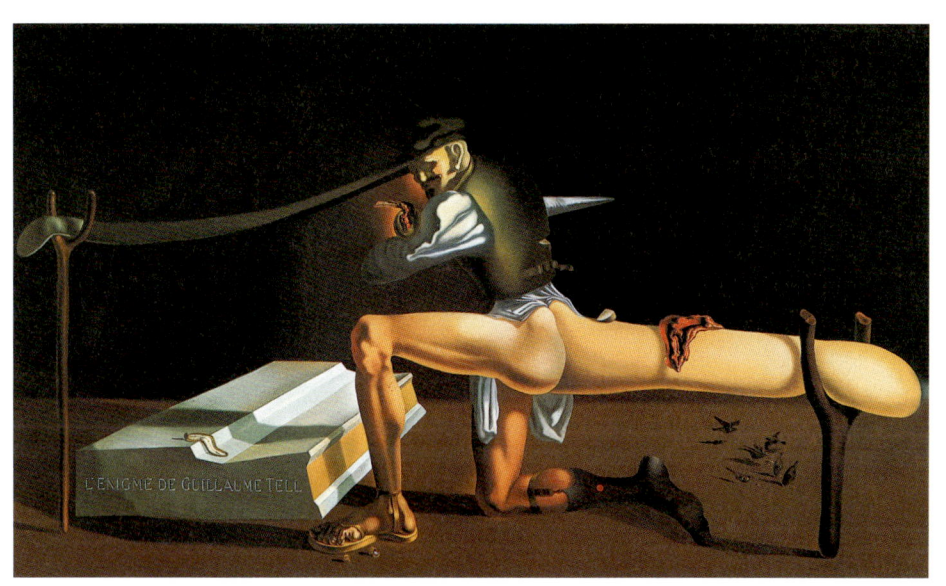

178
The Enigma of William Tell
c. 1933
Oil on canvas, 201.3 × 346.5 cm
Moderna Museet, Stockholm

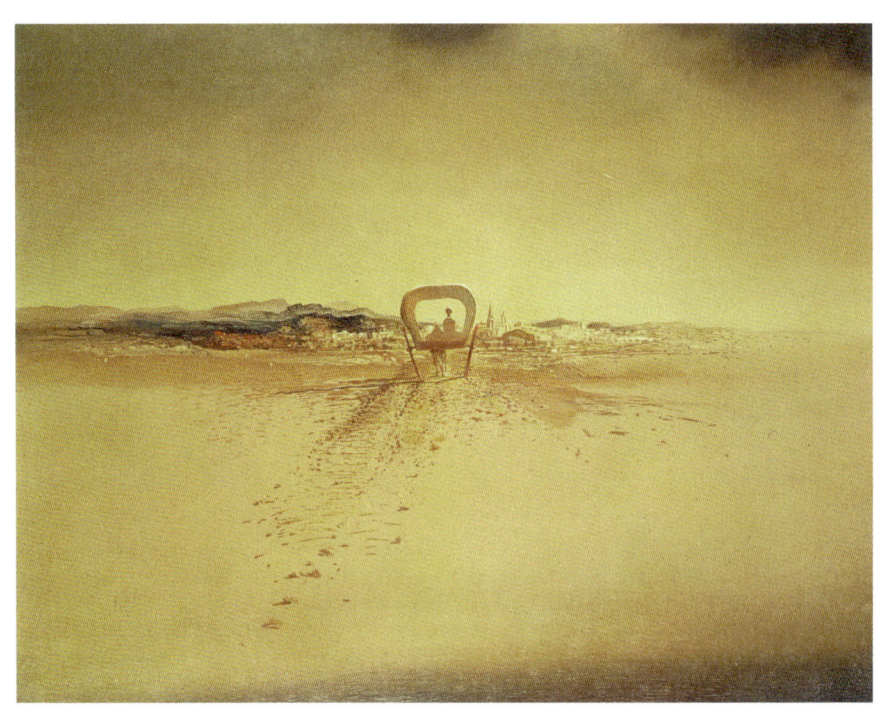

179

The Phantom Cart

1933

Oil on wood panel, 15.9 × 21.9 cm

Yale University Art Gallery, New Haven, Connecticut

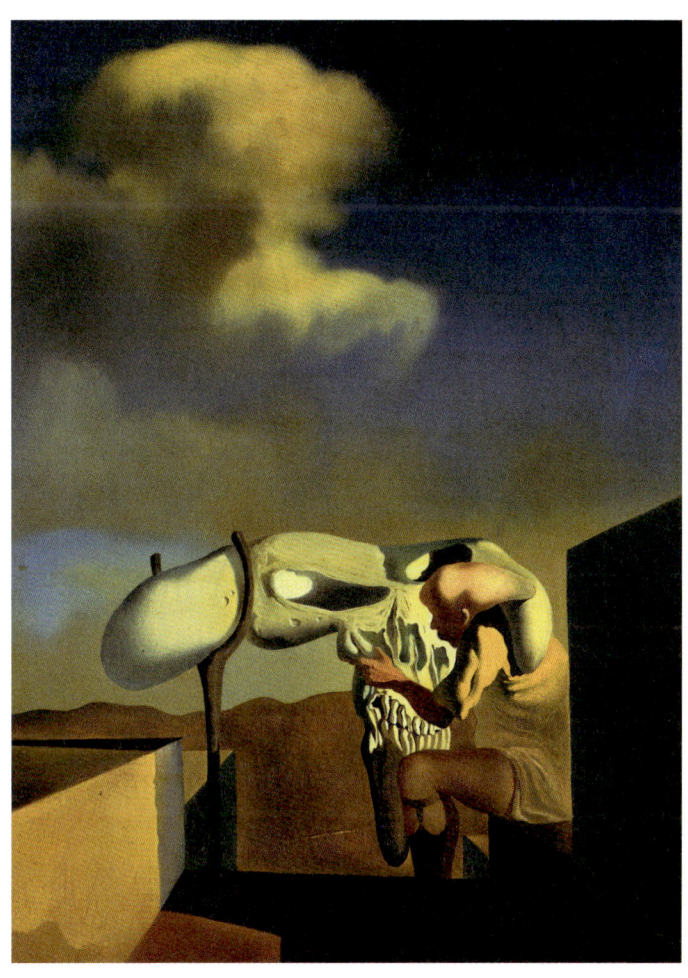

180
Average Atmospherocephalic Bureaucrat in the Act of Milking a Cranial Harp
c. 1933
Oil on canvas, 22.2 × 16.5 cm
The Dalí Museum, St. Petersburg, Florida

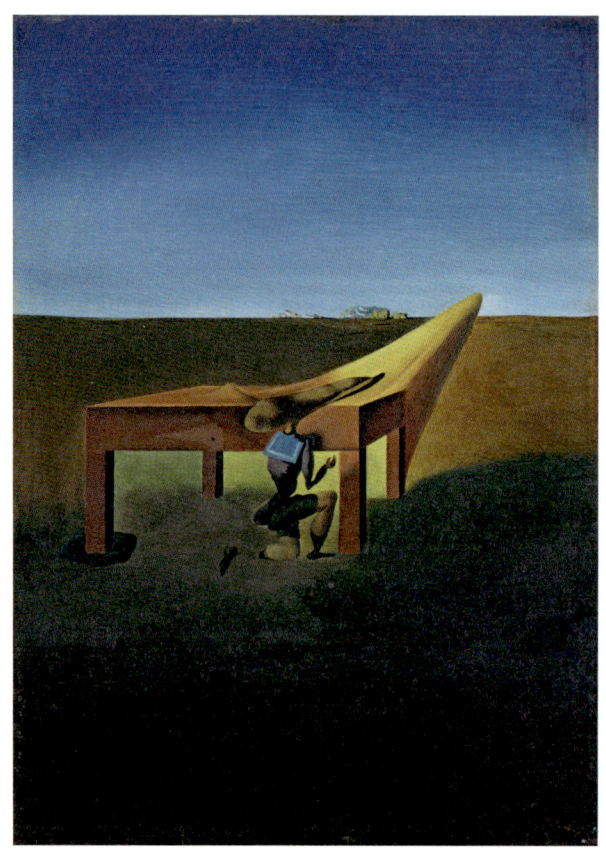

181

Myself at the Age of Ten When I was a Grasshopper Child (Castration Complex)

c. 1933

Oil on wood panel, 21.9 × 16.2 cm

The Dalí Museum, St. Petersburg, Florida

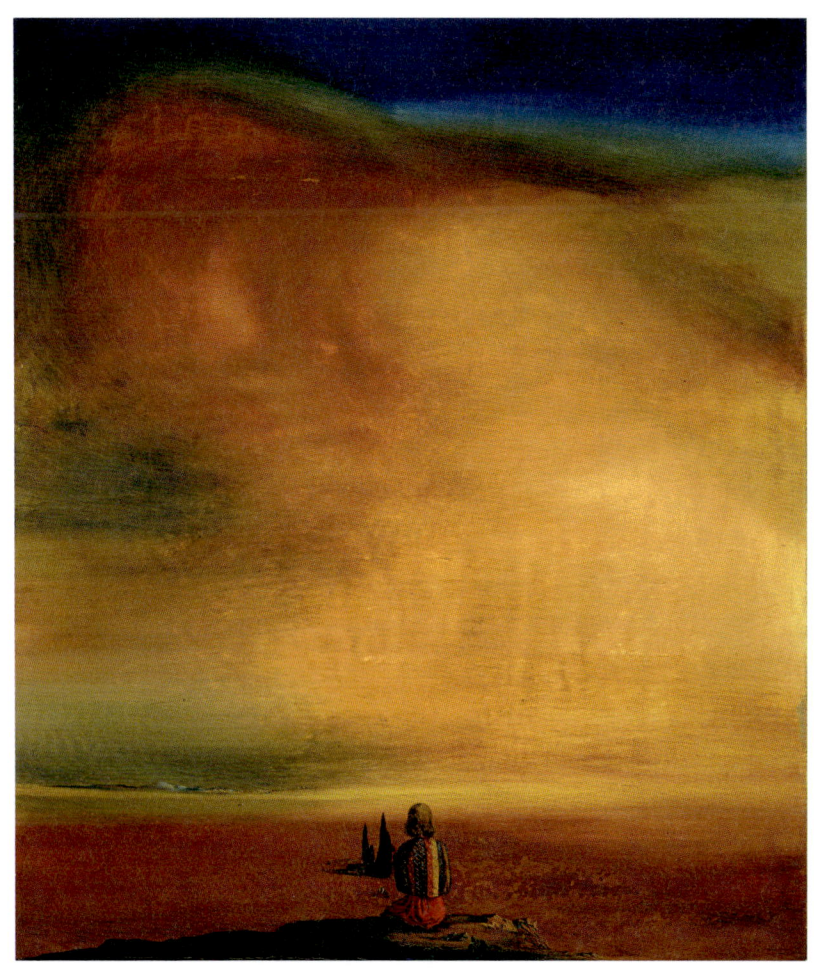

182
The Sugar Sphinx
1933
Oil on canvas, 72.7 × 59.7 cm
The Dalí Museum, St. Petersburg, Florida

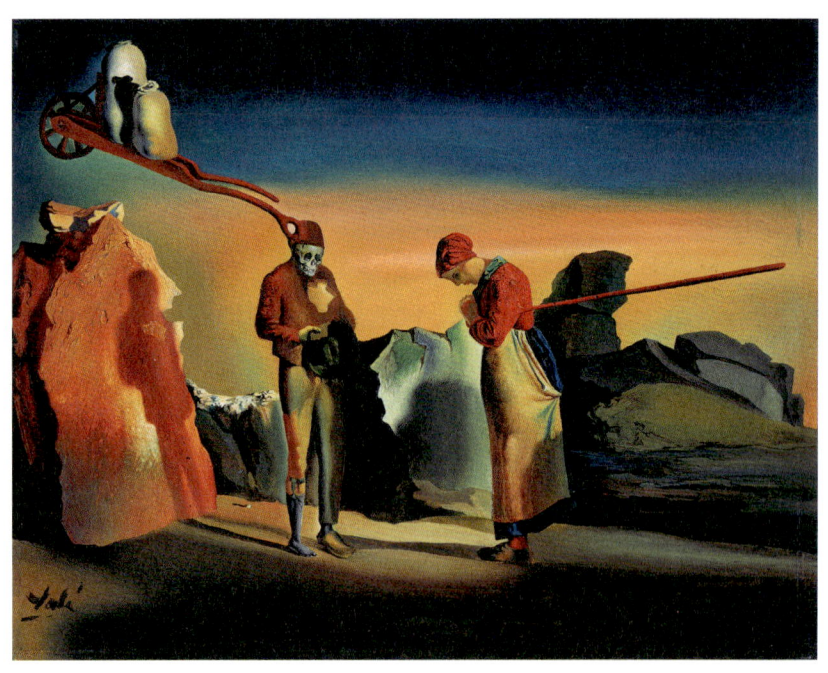

183
Atavism at twilight
c. 1933
Oil on wood panel, 13.3 × 17.9 cm
Kunstmuseum Bern, Bern

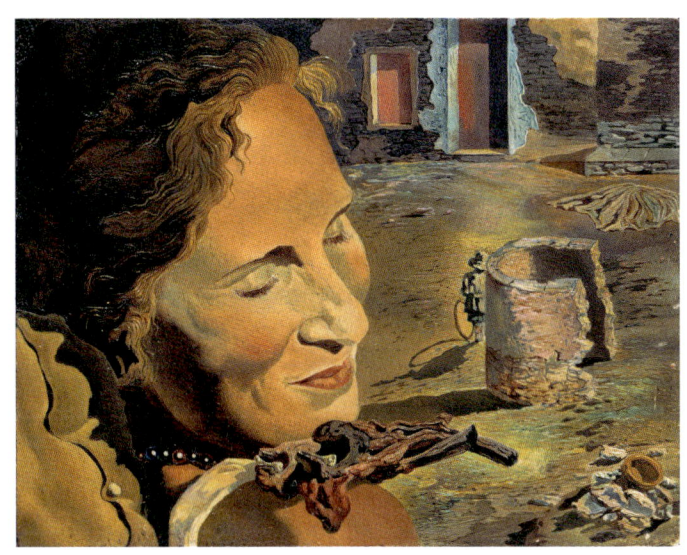

184
Portrait of Gala with Two Chops Balanced on Her Shoulder
c. 1934
Oil on wood panel, 6.8 × 8.8 cm
Fundació Gala-Salvador Dalí, Figueres

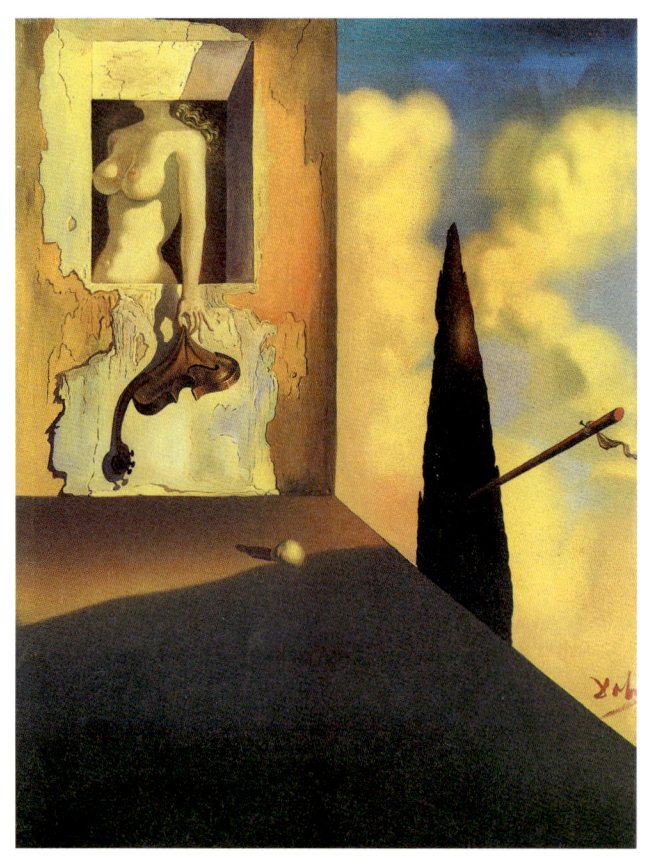

185
Masochistic instrument
c. 1934
Oil on canvas, 62 × 47 cm
Julian & Josie Robertson Collection, New York.
Promised future gift to Auckland Art Gallery Toi o Tāmaki, New Zealand

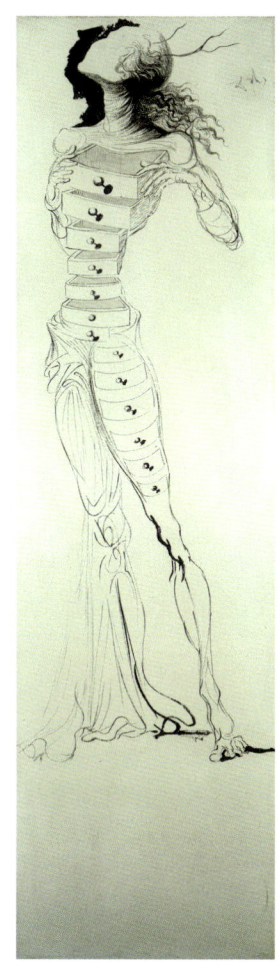

186
Figure with Drawers. For a Four-part Screen
c. 1934
Pencil and pen on paper, 52 × 15 cm
Collection Italcambio

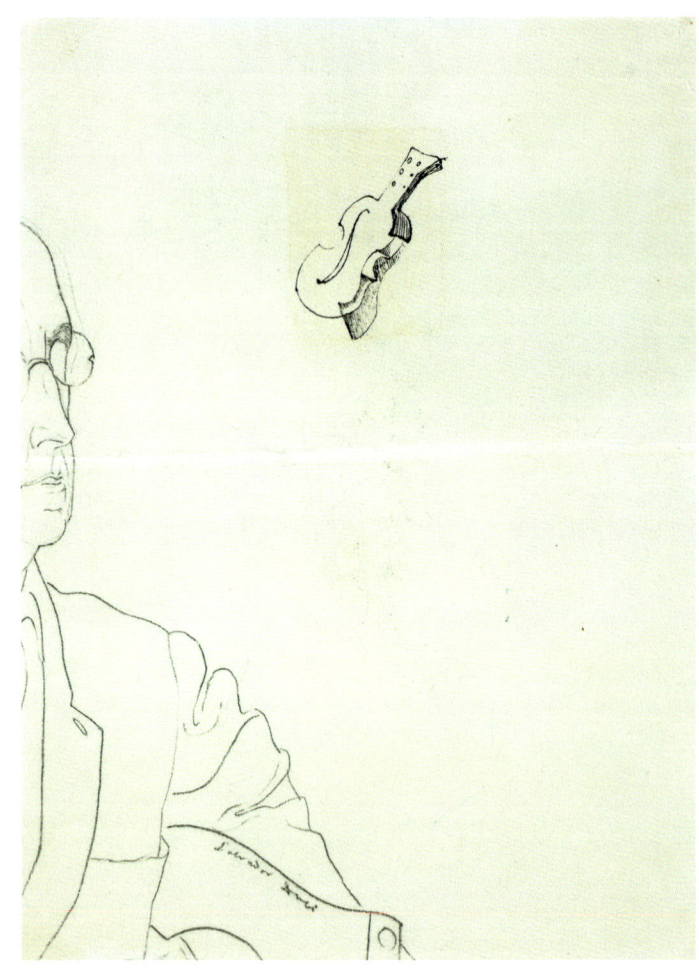

187
Sketch of Manuel de Falla
c. 1926–1927
Pencil on paper, 28.3 × 20.6 cm
The Dalí Museum, St. Petersburg, Florida

Surrealism

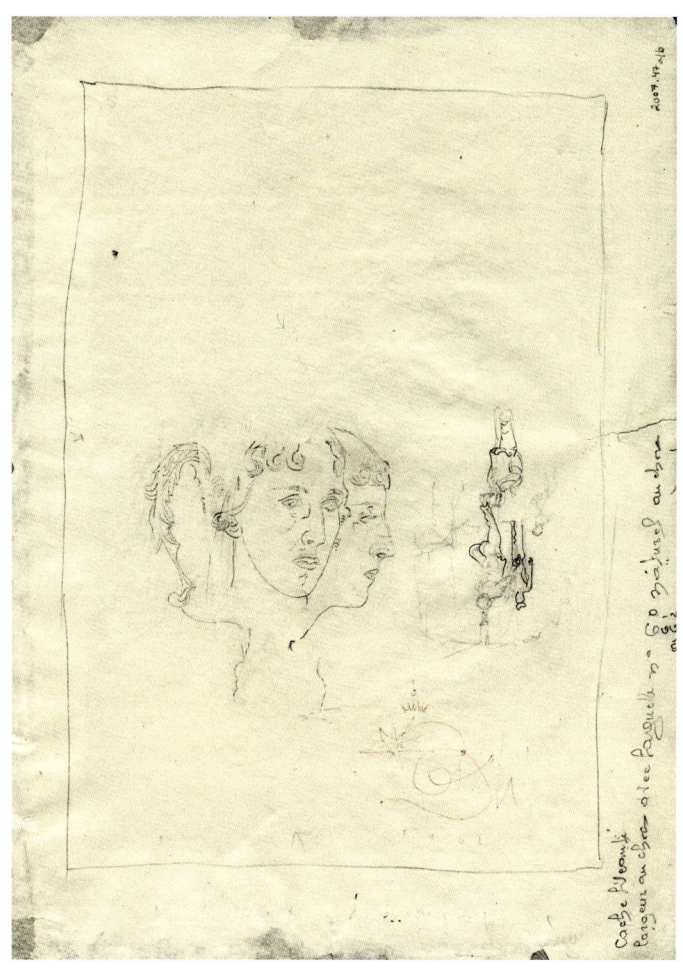

188
Study for the "Portrait of Vicomtesse de Noailles"
c. 1933
Pencil on paper, 24 × 16.5 cm
The Dalí Museum, St. Petersburg, Florida

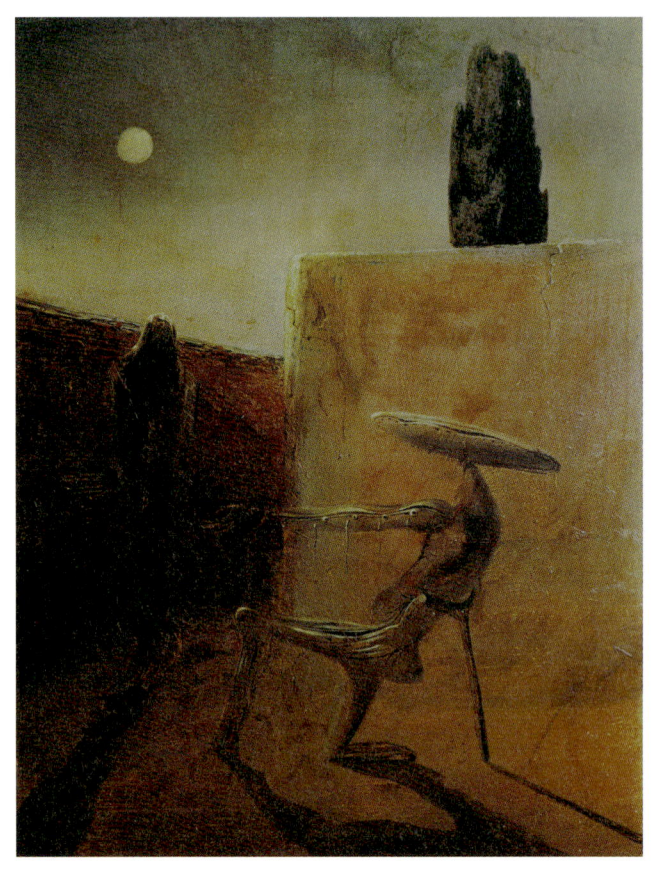

189
The Ghost of Vermeer of Delft
c. 1934
Oil on canvas, 23 × 19 cm
Private collection, Switzerland

Surrealism

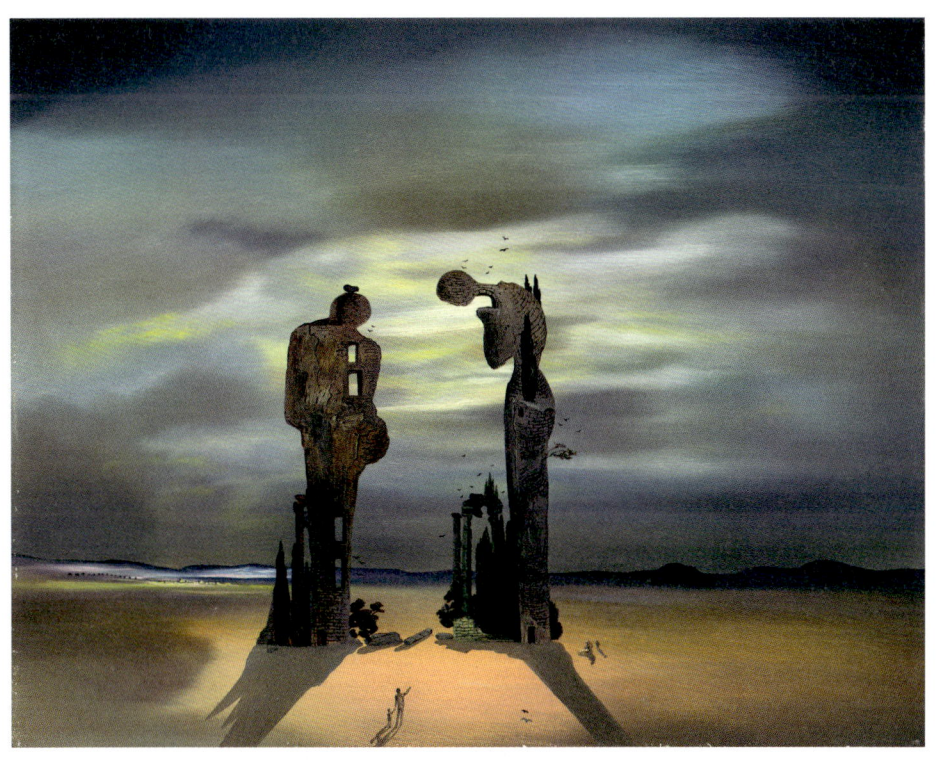

190
Archaeological Reminiscence of Millet's "Angelus"
c. 1934
Oil on wood panel, 31.5 × 39.4 cm
The Dalí Museum, St. Petersburg, Florida

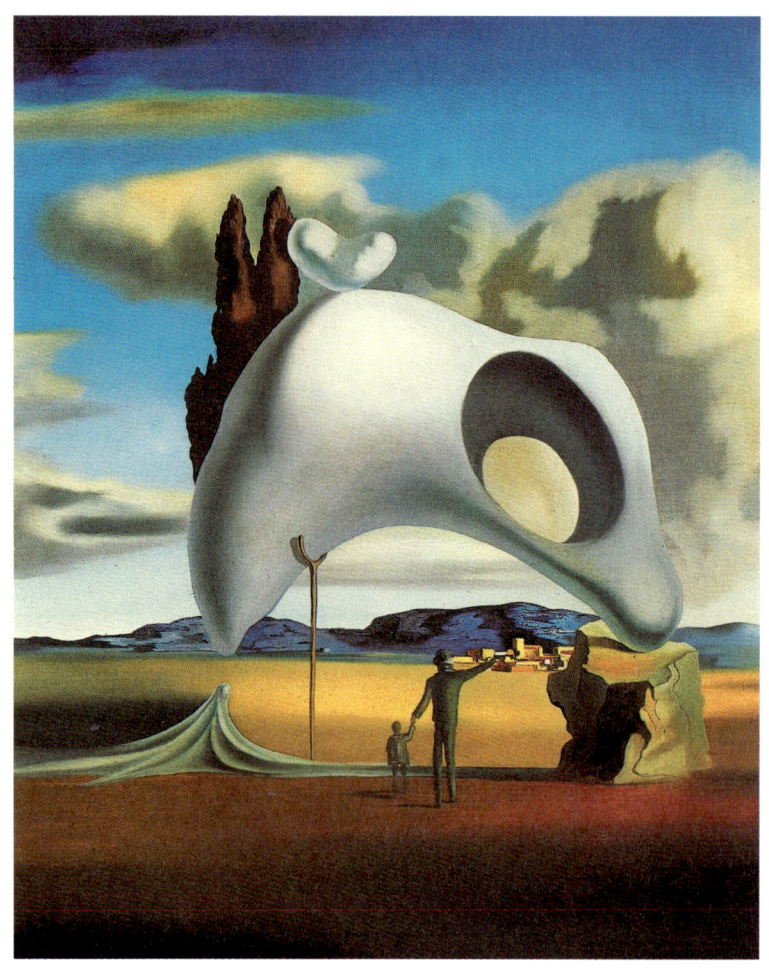

191
Atavistic Vestiges after the Rain
c. 1934
Oil on canvas, 65 × 54 cm
Private collection

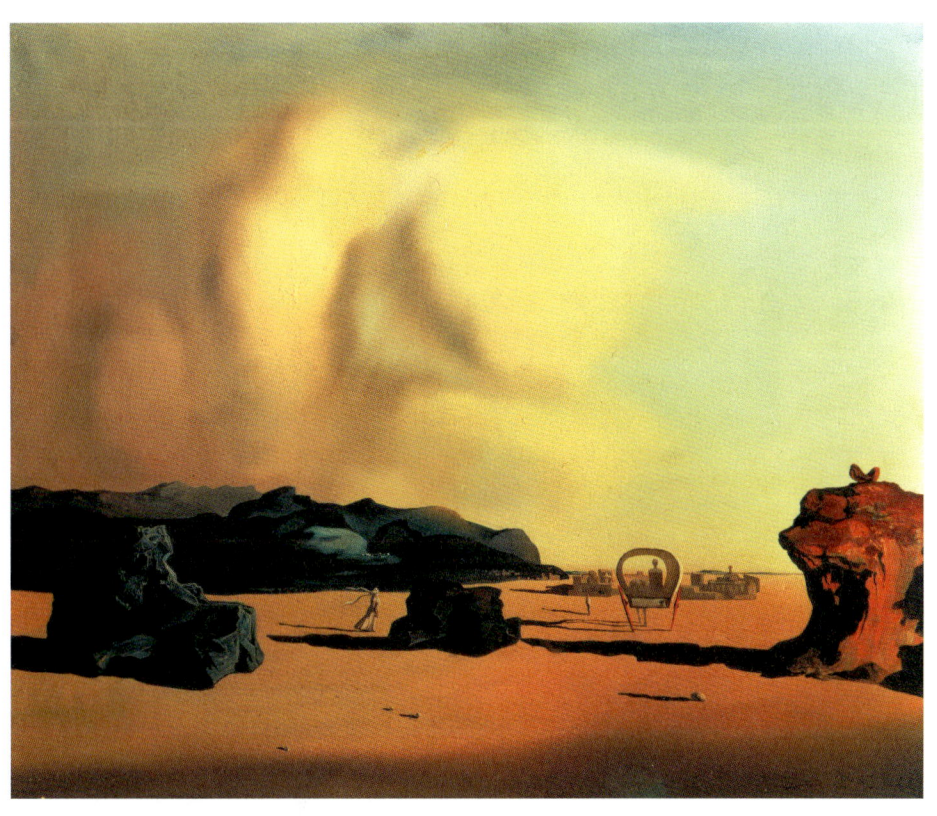

192
Moment of Transition
1934
Oil on canvas, 54 × 64.5 cm
Private collection

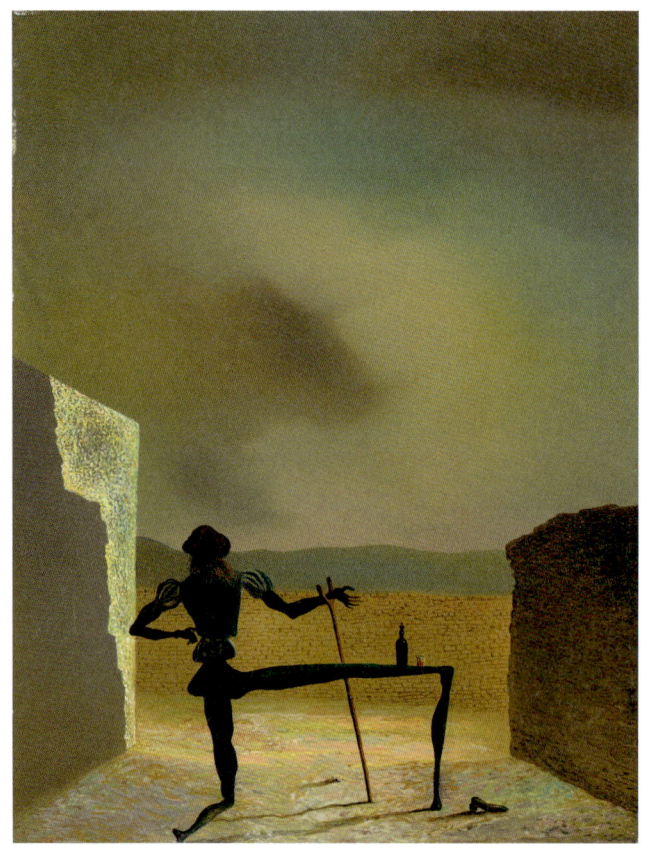

193

The Ghost of Vermeer of Delft Which Can Be Used as a Table (Phenomenologic Theory of Furniture-Nutrition)

c. 1934

Oil on wood panel, 18.1 × 14 cm

The Dalí Museum, St. Petersburg, Florida

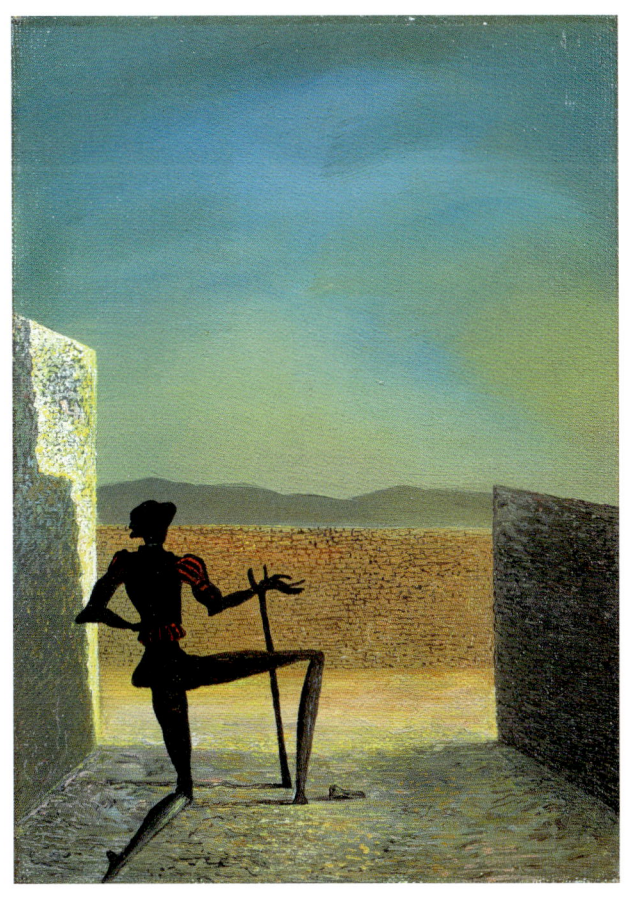

194
Masquerader, intoxicated by the limpid atmosphere
c. 1934
Oil on canvas, 21.5 × 15.5 cm
Private collection

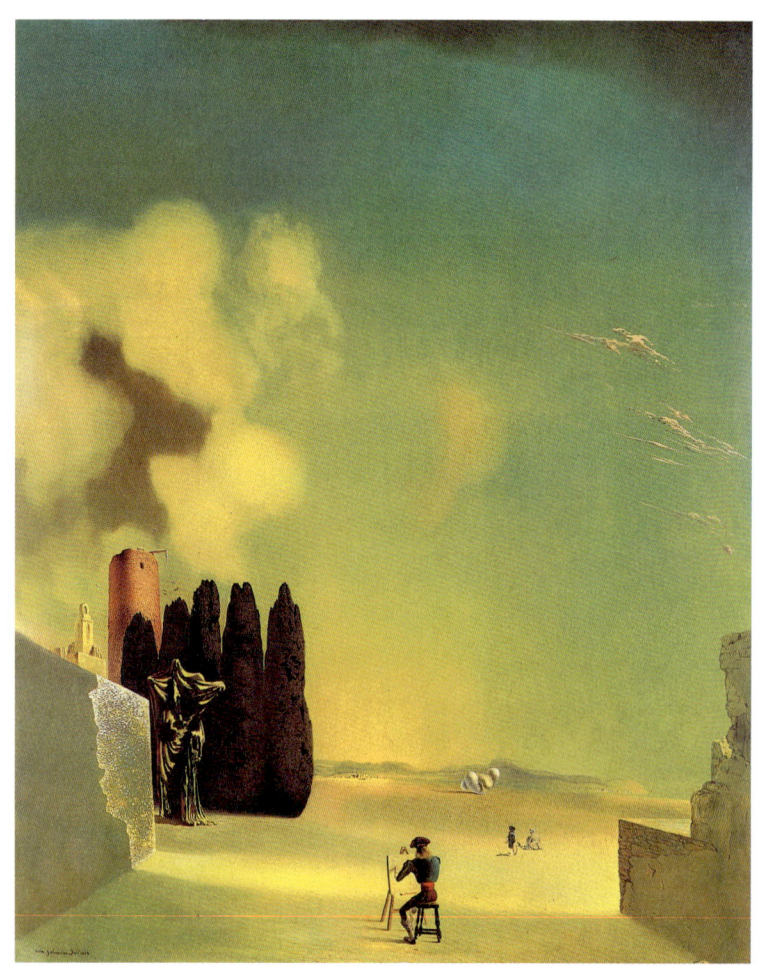

195
Enigmatic Elements in a Landscape
1934
Oil on wood panel, 72.8 × 59.5 cm
Fundació Gala-Salvador Dalí, Figueres

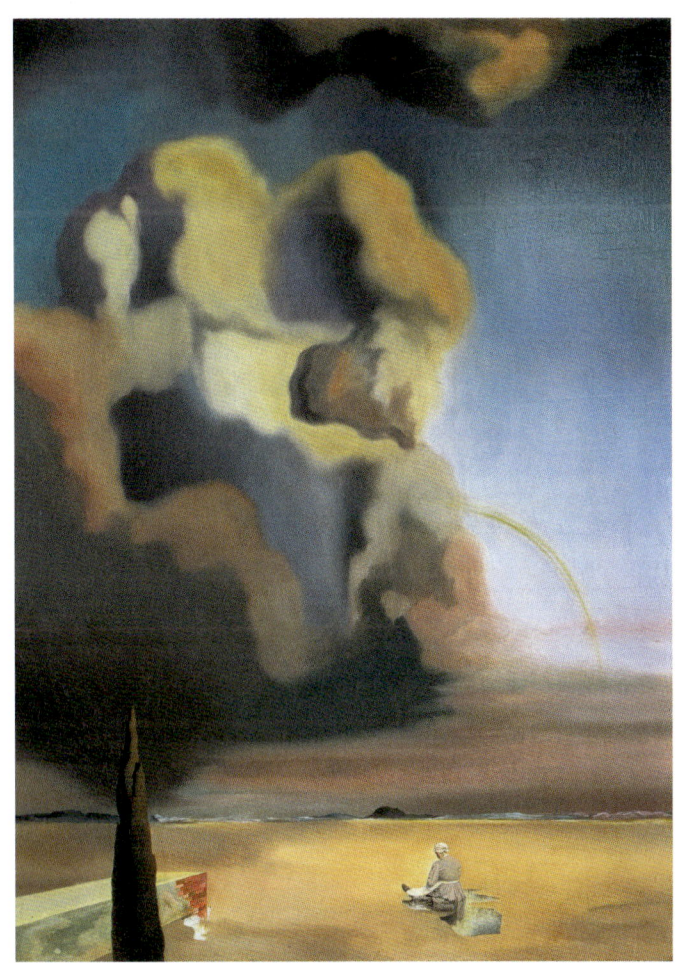

196
The Spectre and the Phantom
1934
Oil on canvas, 100 × 73 cm
Osaka City Museum of Modern Art, Osaka Prefecture, Japan

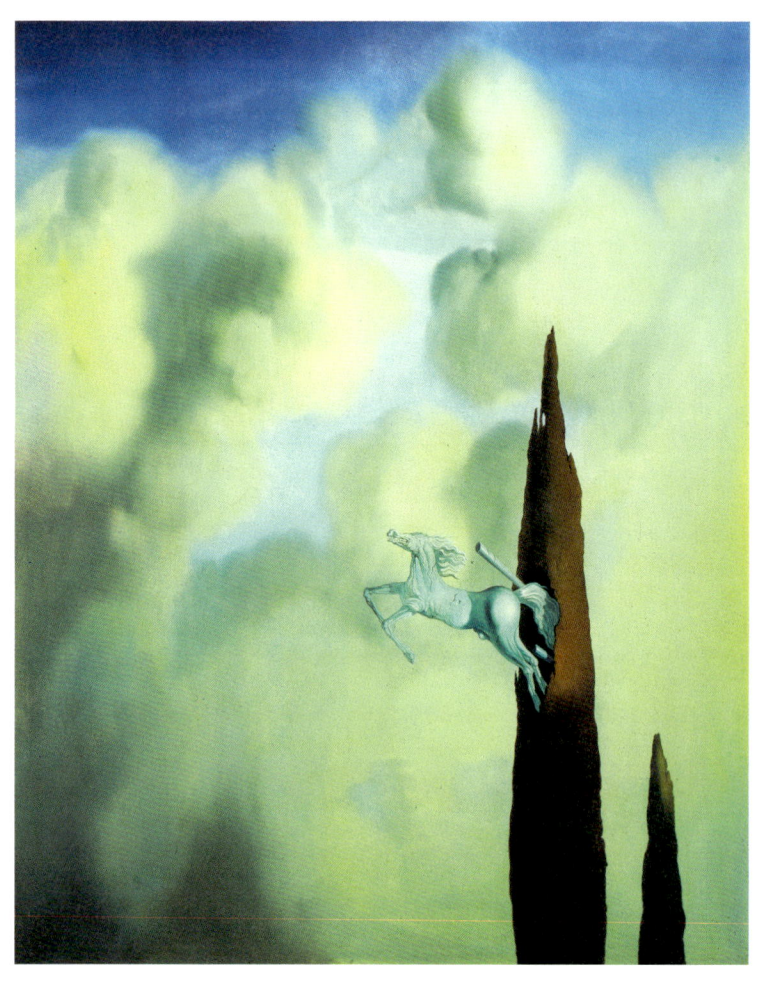

197
Morning Ossification of the Cypress
c. 1934
Oil on canvas, 82 × 66 cm
Private collection

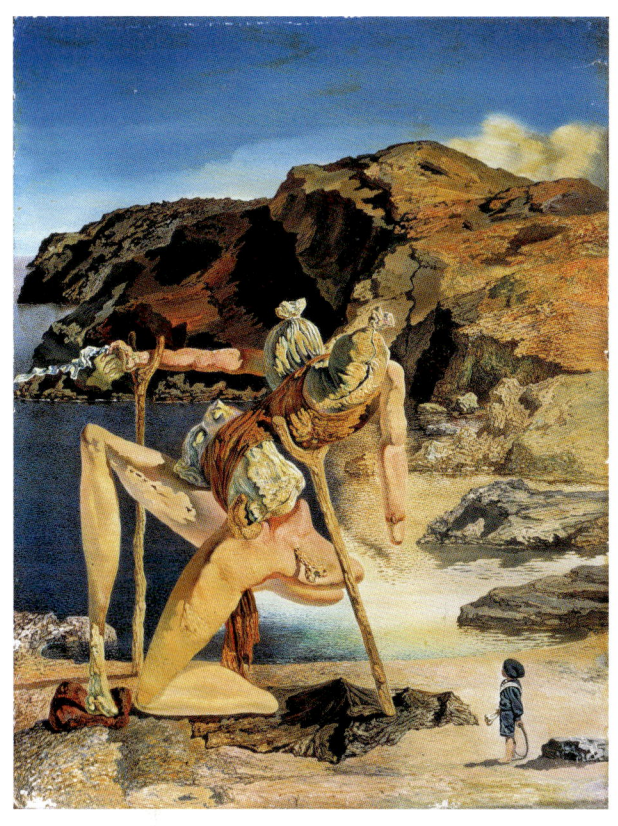

198
The Spectre of Sex-Appeal
c. 1934
Oil on wood panel, 17.9 × 13.9 cm
Fundació Gala-Salvador Dalí, Figueres

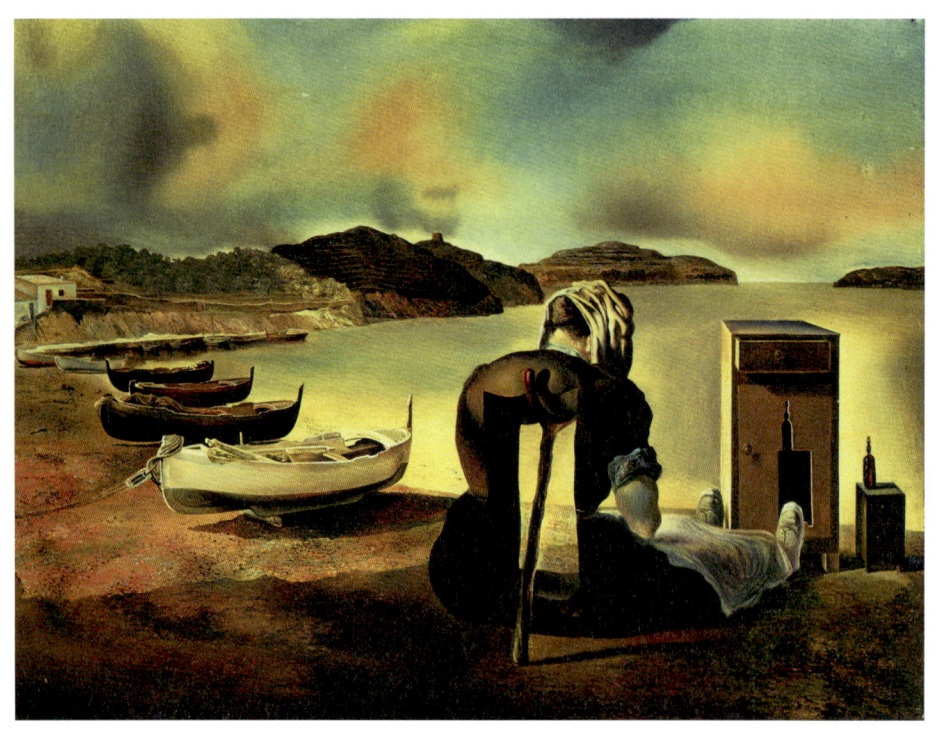

199
The Weaning of Furniture-Nutrition
1934
Oil on wood panel, 17.8 × 24.1 cm
The Dalí Museum, St. Petersburg, Florida

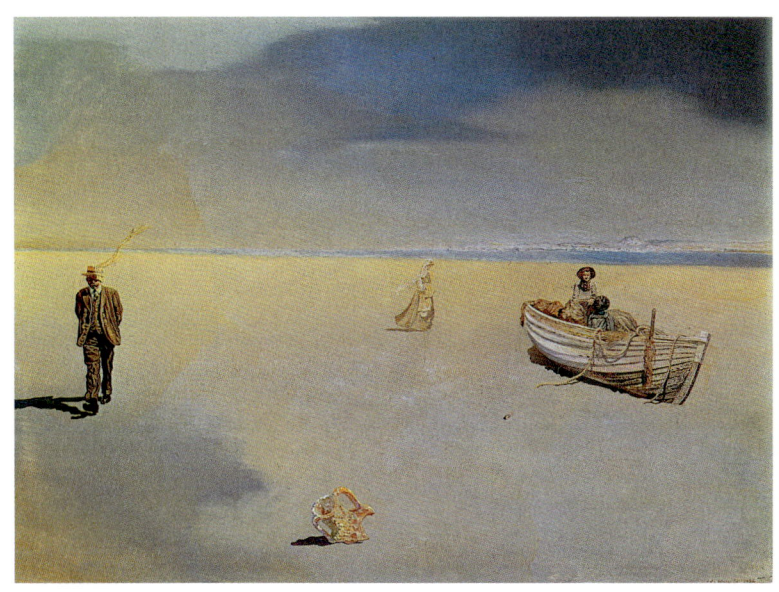

200
Paranoiac-astral image
1934
Oil on wood panel, 15.6 × 22.1 cm
Wadsworth Atheneum, Hartford, Connecticut
The Ella Gallup Sumner and Mary Catlin Sumner Collection Fund

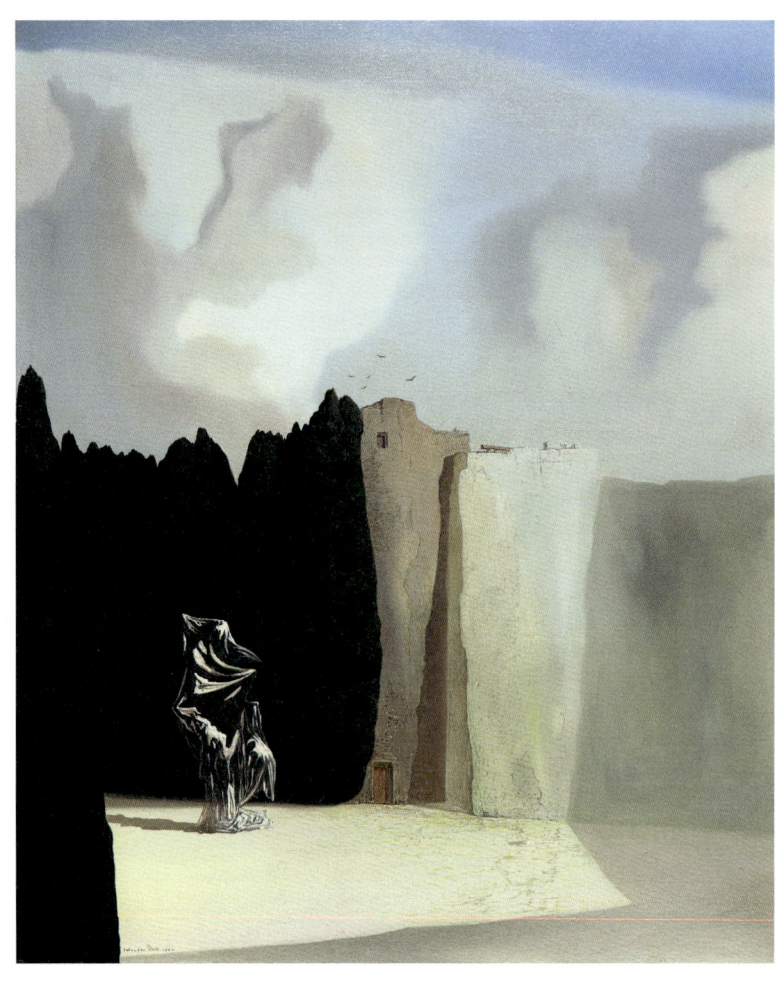

201
West Side of the Isle of the Death
(Reconstructed Compulsive Image After Böcklin)
1934
Oil on canvas, 66 × 54.5 cm
Abanca Art Collection, A Coruña

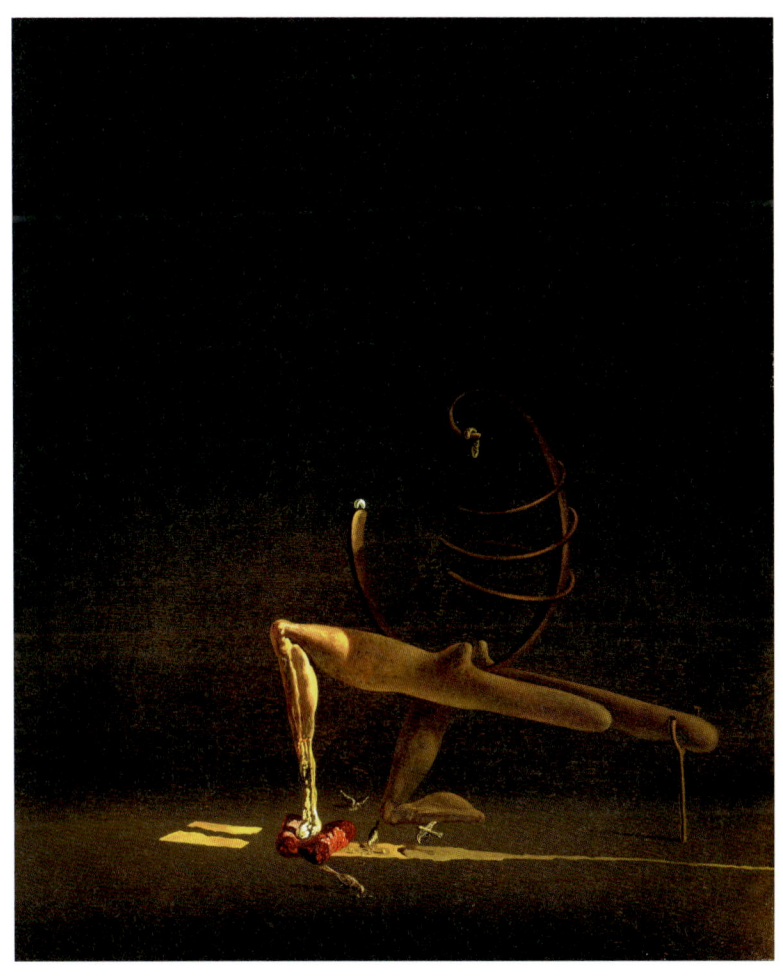

202
The Javanese Mannequin
c. 1934
Oil on canvas, 64.8 × 54 cm
The Dalí Museum, St. Petersburg, Florida

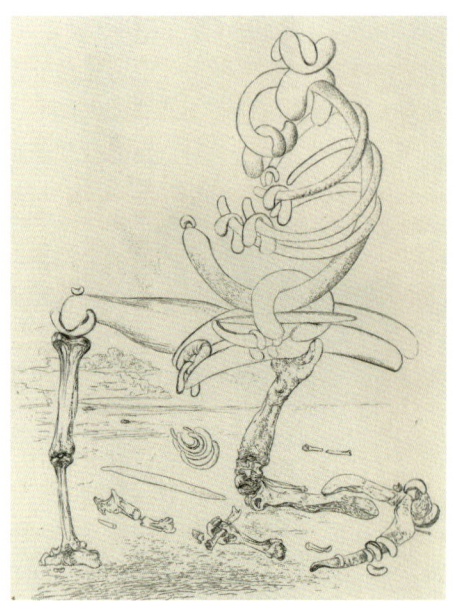
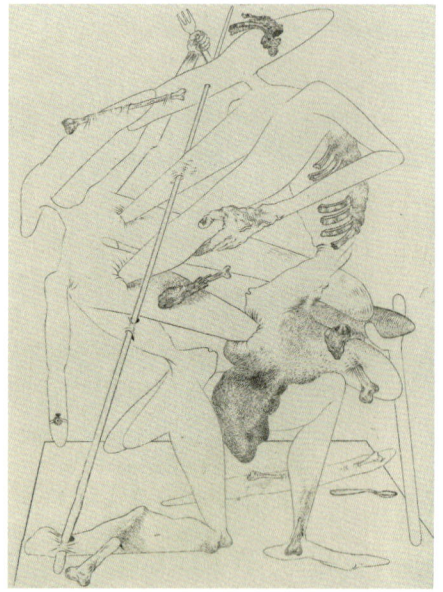

203–206
From *Les Chants de Maldoror*
1934
Etching and drypoint on paper, 22 × 16.5 cm
The Dalí Museum, St. Petersburg, Florida

Surrealism

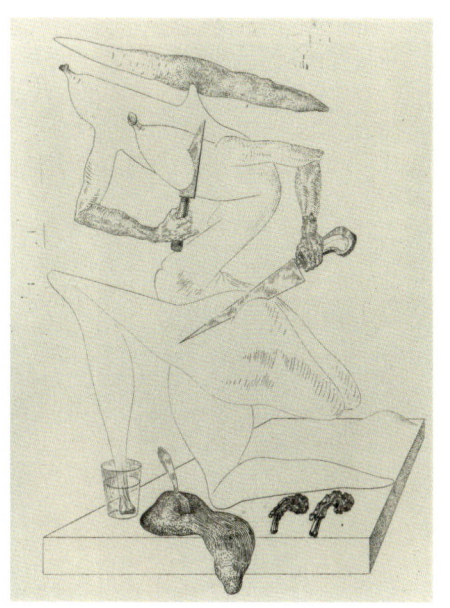

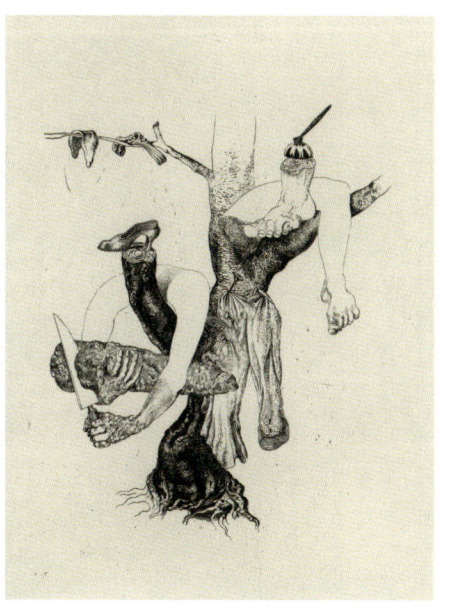

1929–1939

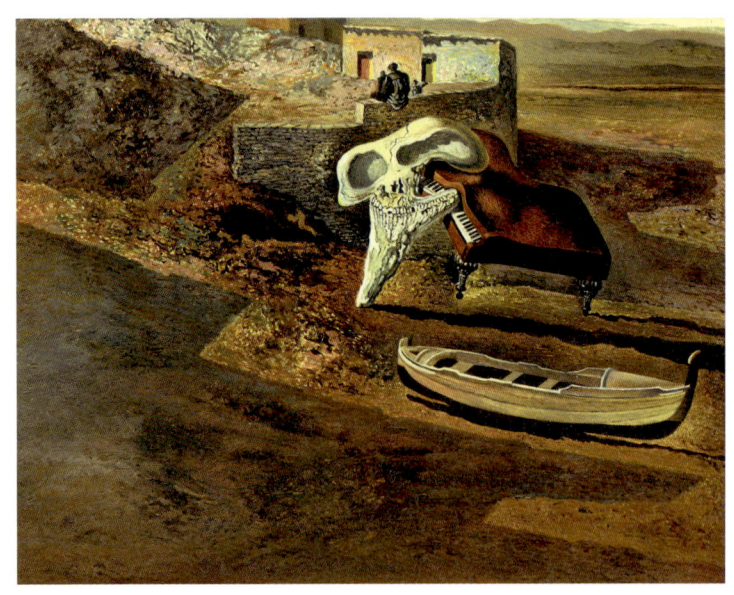

207
Atmospheric Skull Sodomizing a Grand Piano
1934
Oil on wood panel, 14 × 17.8 cm
The Dalí Museum, St. Petersburg, Florida

Surrealism

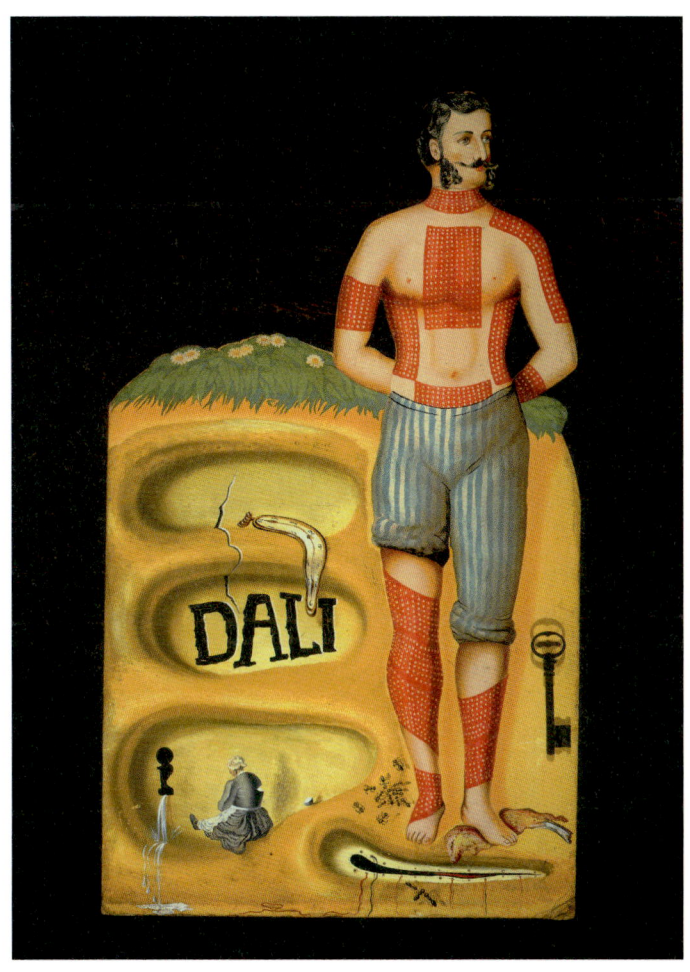

208
Surrealist Poster
c. 1934
Oil, lithography and key on plywood panel, 68.6 × 45.7 cm
The Dalí Museum, St. Petersburg, Florida

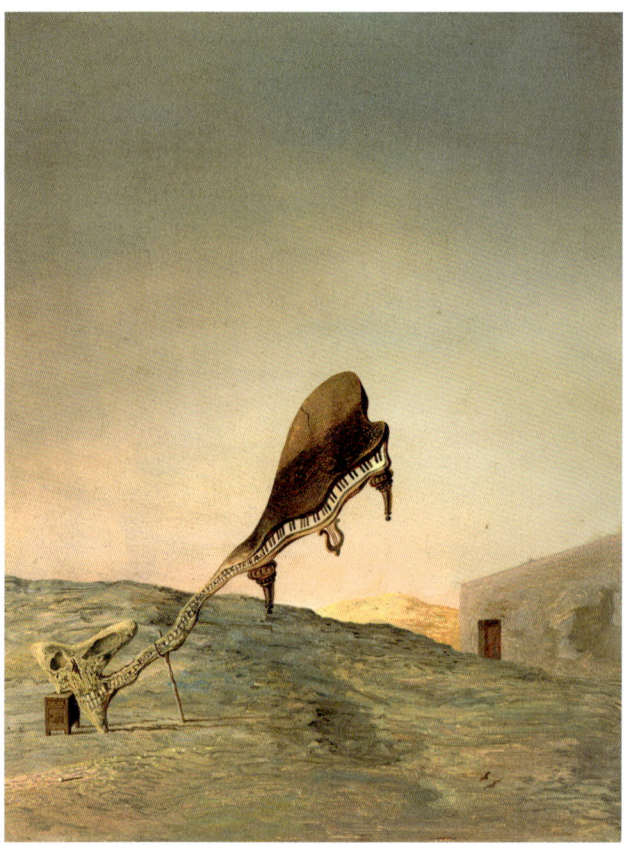

209
Skull and Its Lyric Appendage Leaning on a Bedside Table which Should Have the Temperature of a Cardinal Nest
c. 1934
Oil on wood panel, 24.1 × 19.1 cm
The Dalí Museum, St. Petersburg, Florida

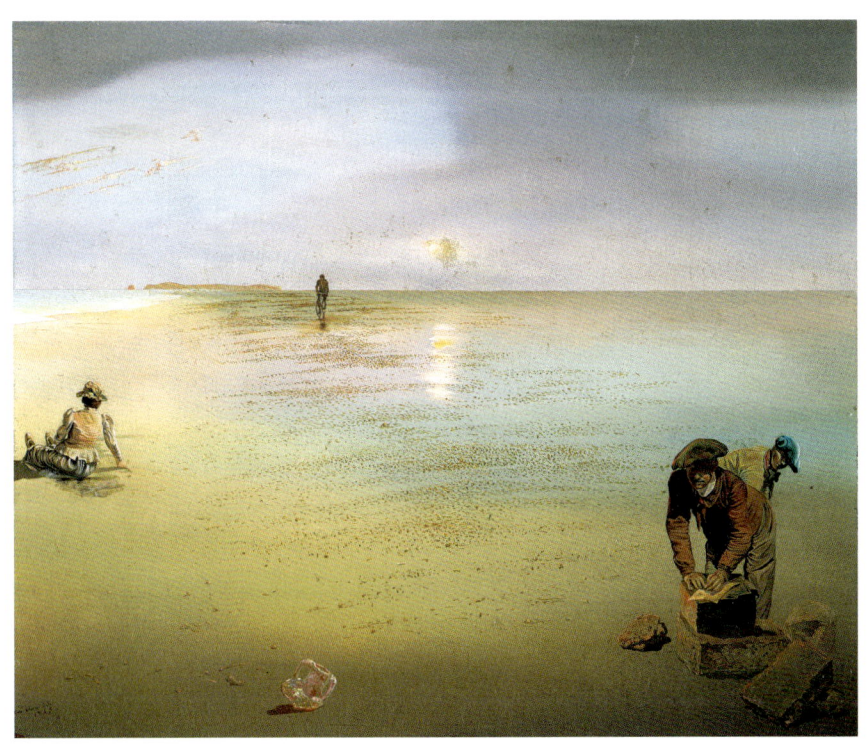

210
Mediumnistic-Paranoiac Image
c. 1934
Oil on wood panel, 19 × 22.8 cm
Private collection

1929–1939

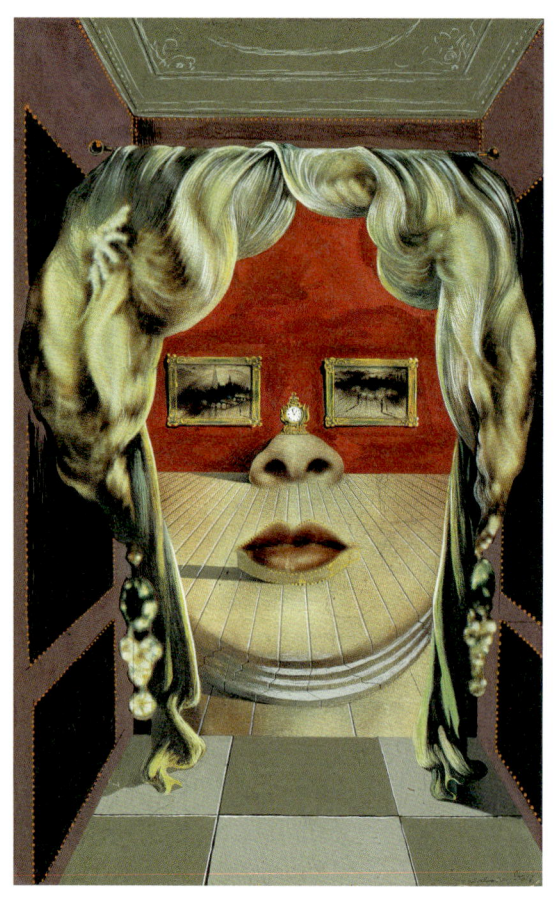

211

Mae West's Face Which May Be Used as a Surrealist Apartment
1934–1935
Gouache on newspaper, 31 × 17 cm
The Art Institute of Chicago

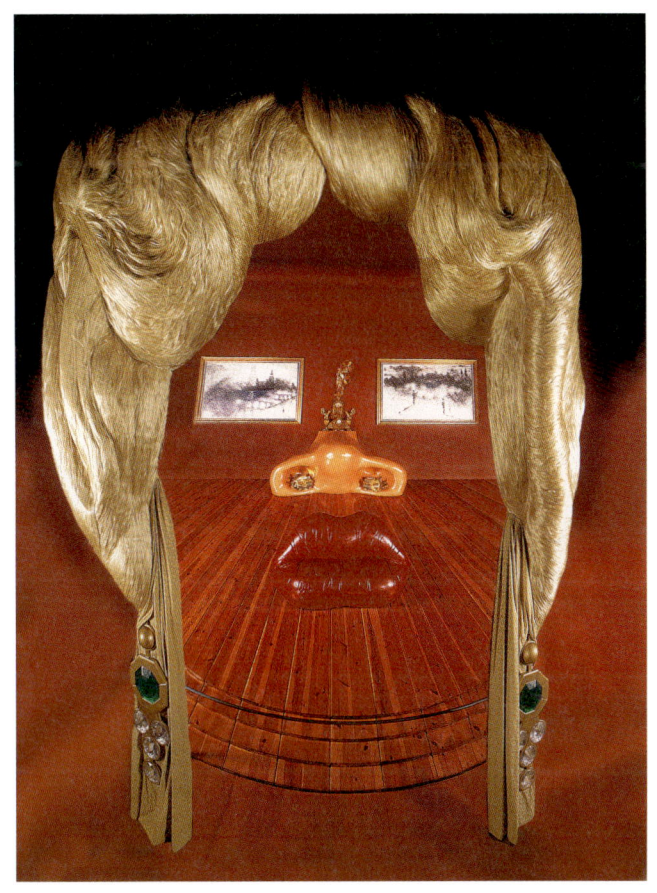

212
The Face of Mae West
1934–1935
Mixed media
Fundació Gala-Salvador Dalí, Figueres

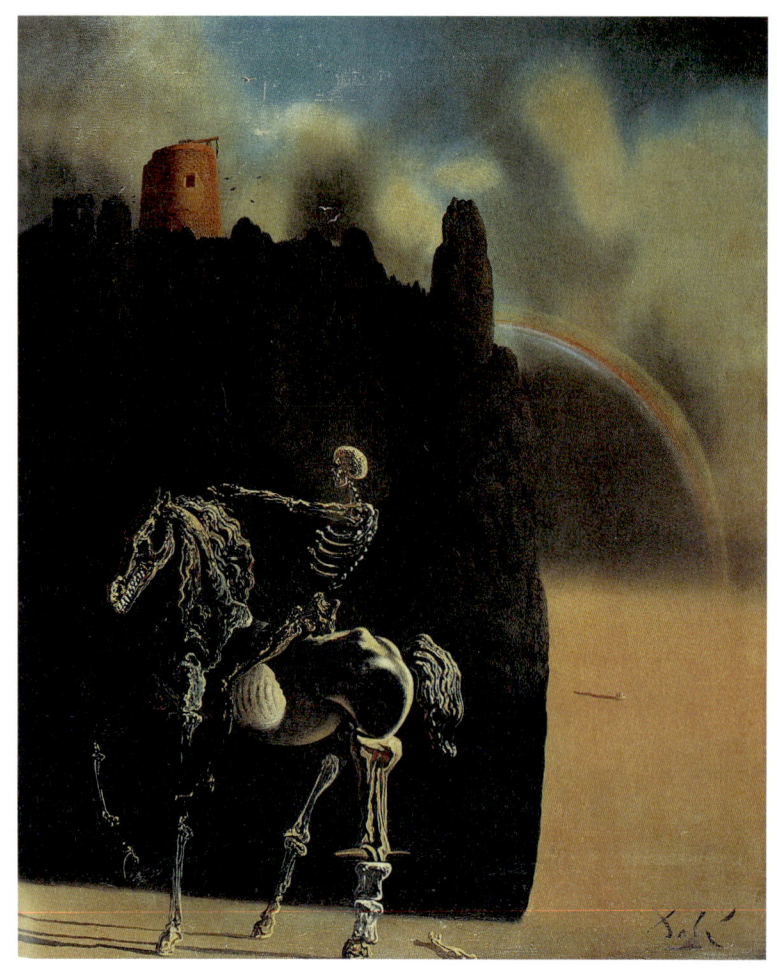

213
The Knight of Death
c. 1934
Oil on canvas, 65 × 54 cm
Private collection

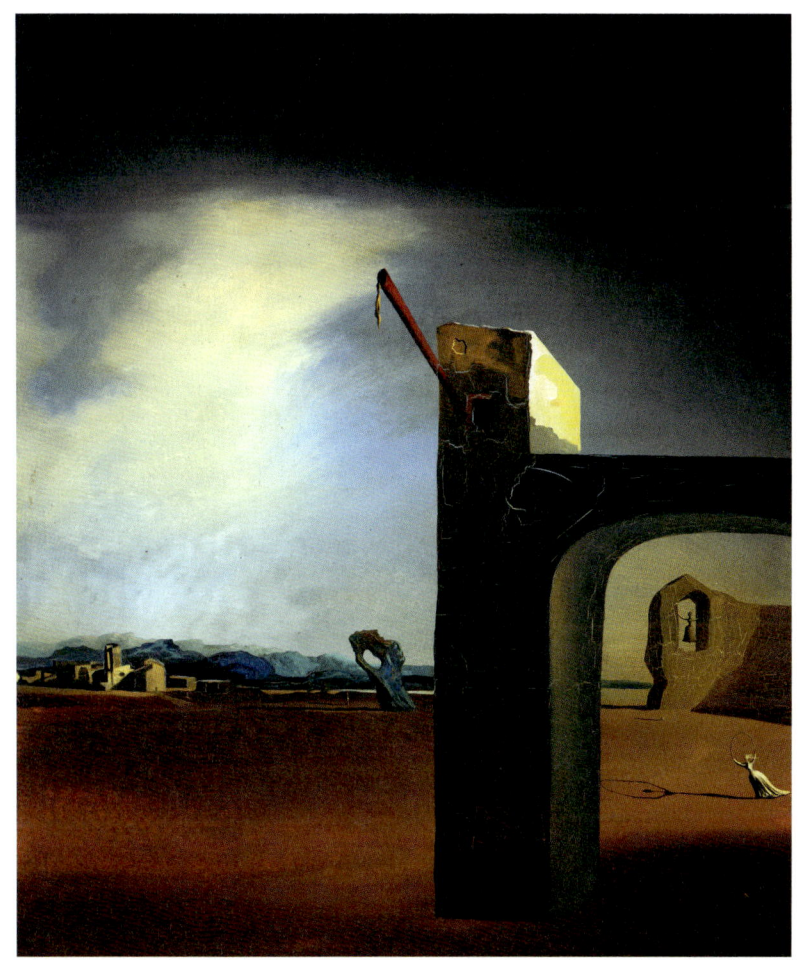

214
Morphological Echo
c. 1935
Oil on canvas, 64.8 × 61.6 cm
The Dalí Museum, St. Petersburg, Florida

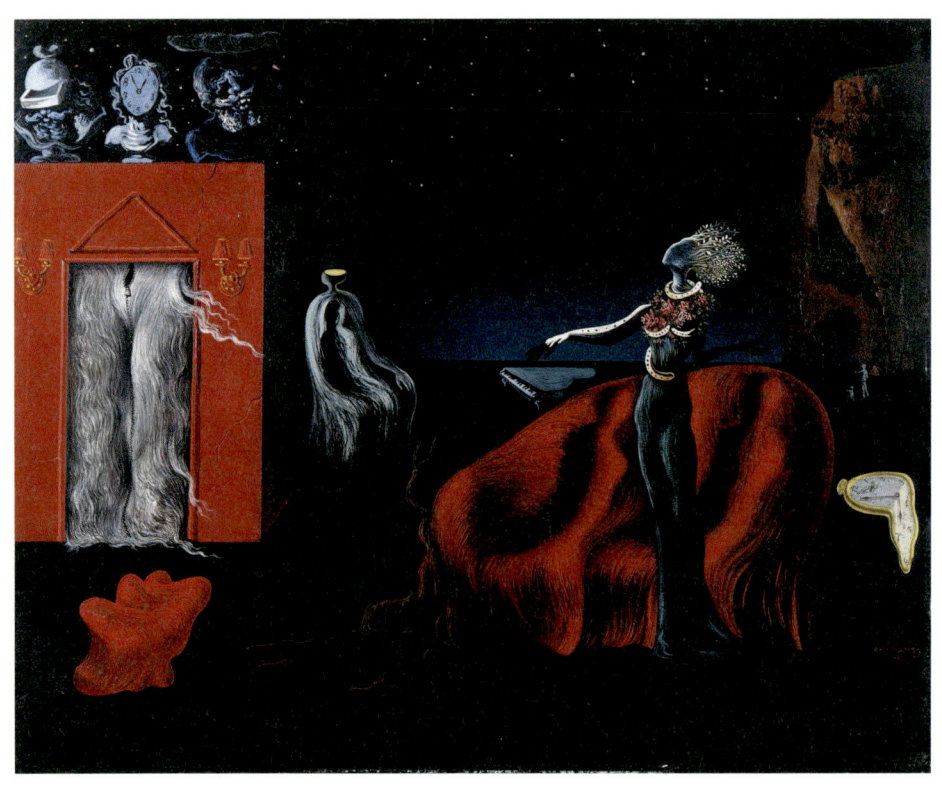

215
Singularities
c. 1935
Oil and collage on board, 40.5 × 50 cm
Fundació Gala-Salvador Dalí, Figueres

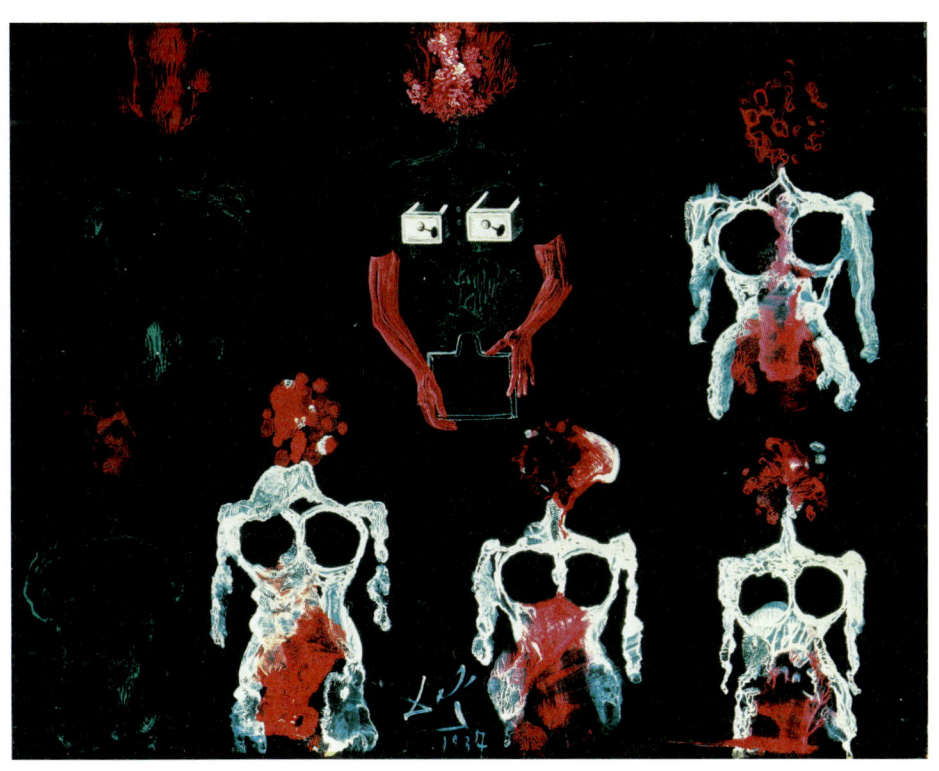

216
Anatomical Studies – Transfer series
1937
Oil on cardboard on panel, 50 × 64 cm
Private collection

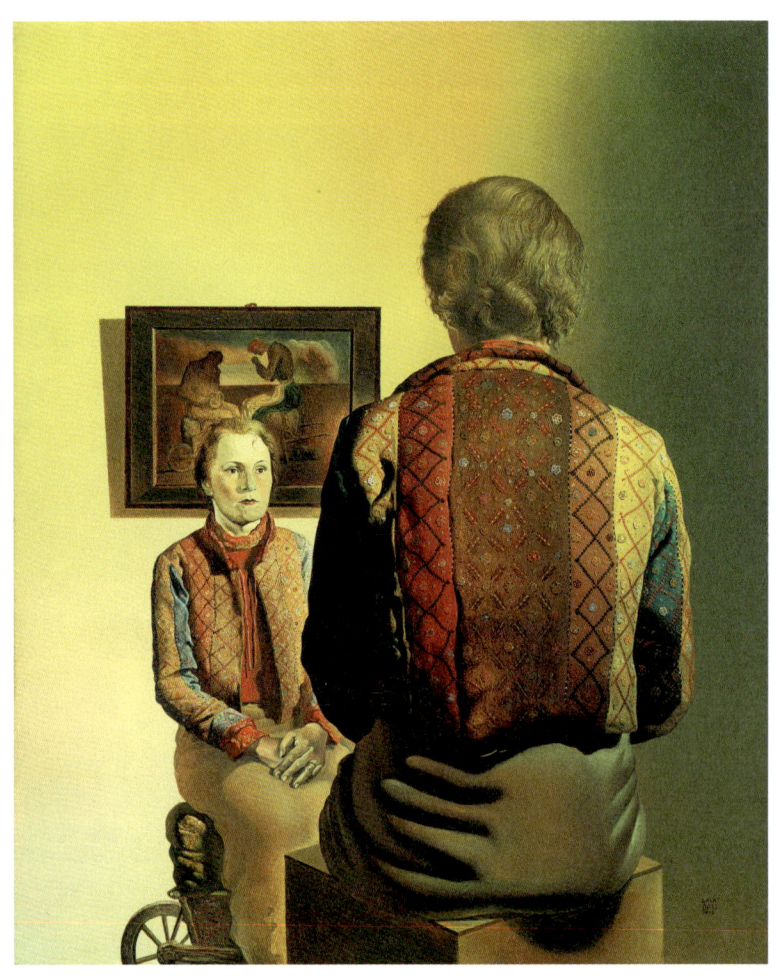

217
The Angelus of Gala
1935
Oil on wood panel, 32.4 × 26.7 cm
The Museum of Modern Art, New York

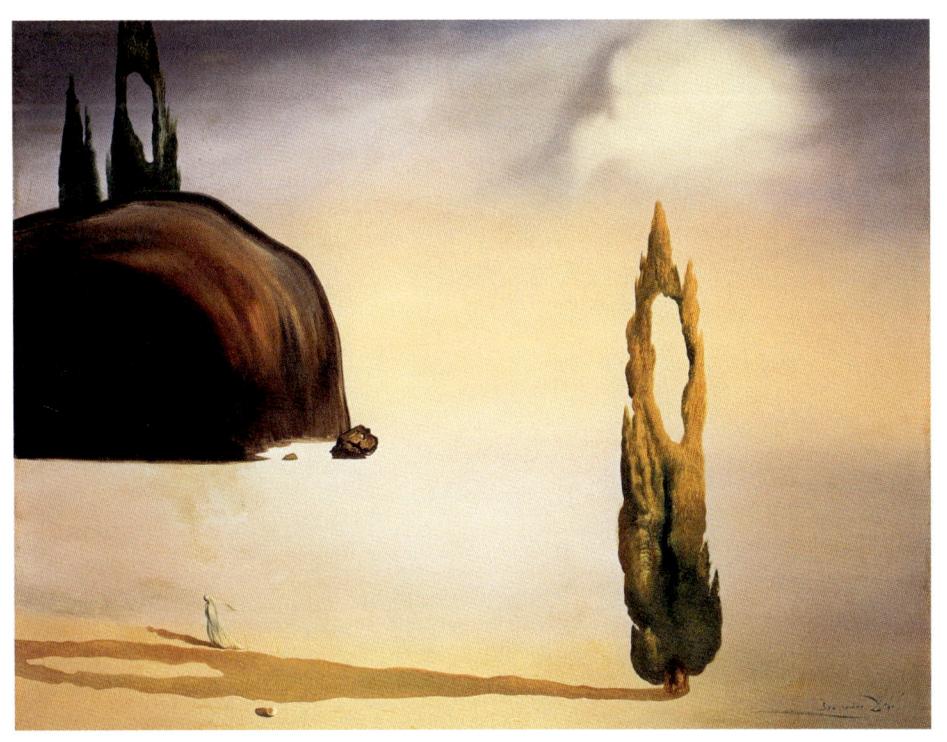

218
The Echo of the Void
c. 1935
Oil on canvas, 73 × 92 cm
Private collection

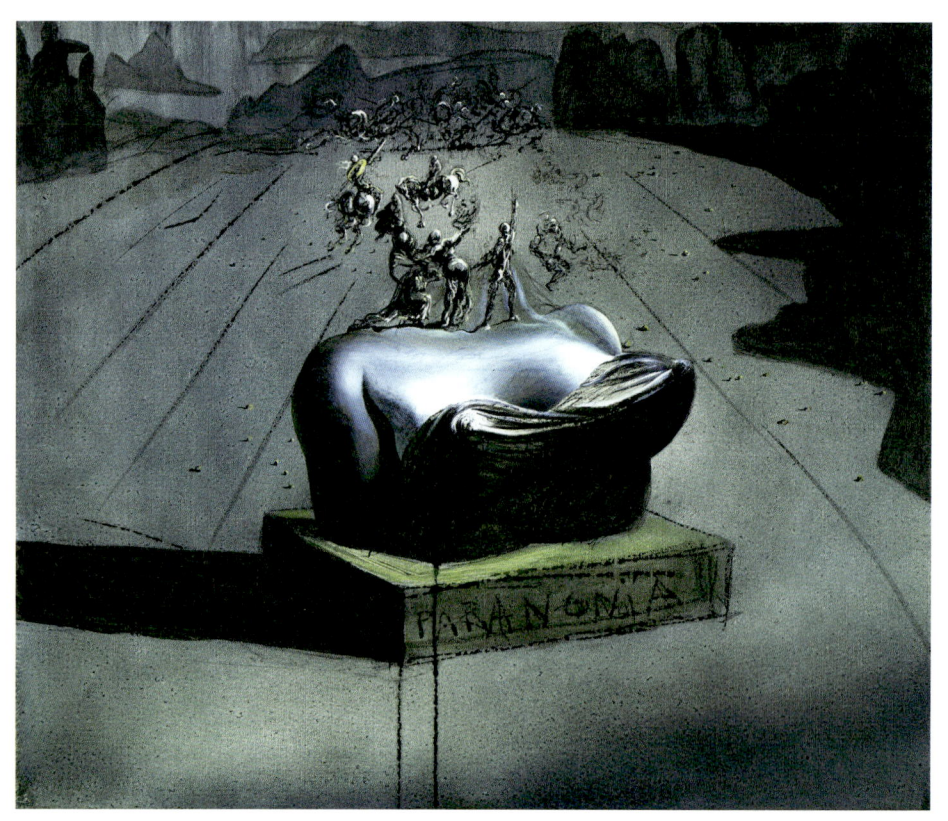

219
Paranoia
c. 1935
Oil on canvas, 38.1 × 46 cm
The Dalí Museum, St. Petersburg, Florida

Surrealism

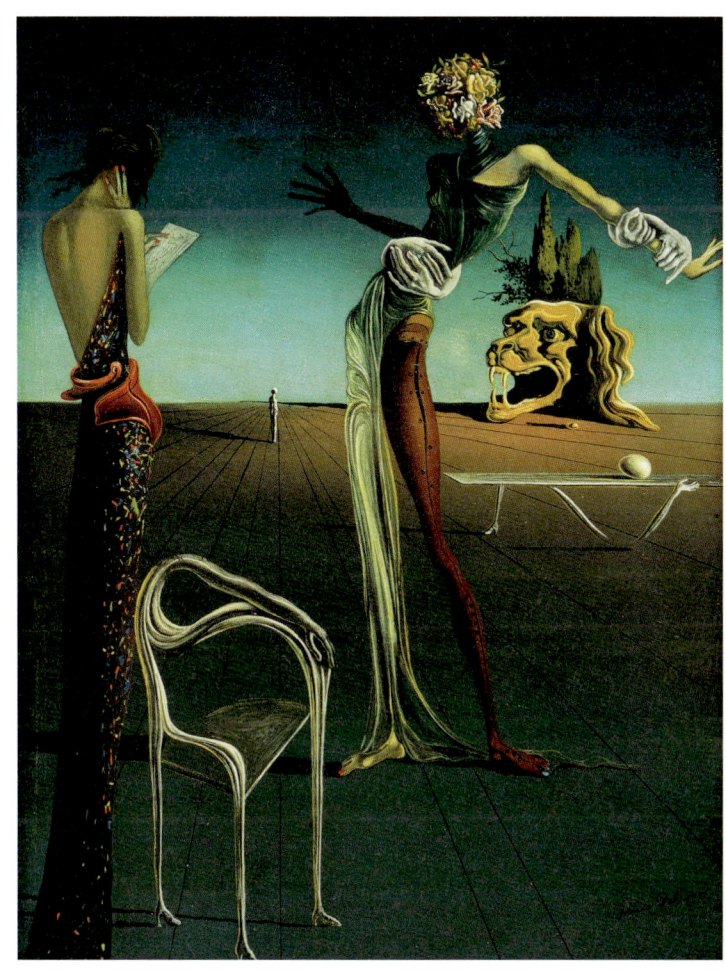

220
Woman with Head of Roses
1935
Oil on wood panel, 35 × 27 cm
Kunsthaus Zürich, Zurich

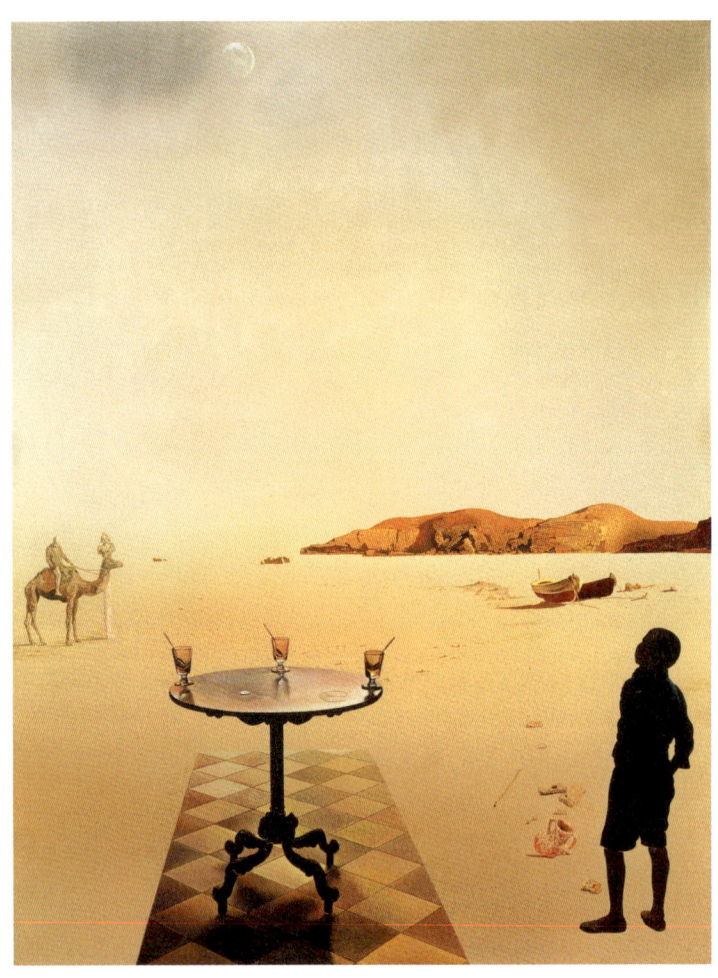

221
Sun-table
1935
Oil on wood panel, 60 × 46 cm
Museum Boijmans Van Beuningen, Rotterdam

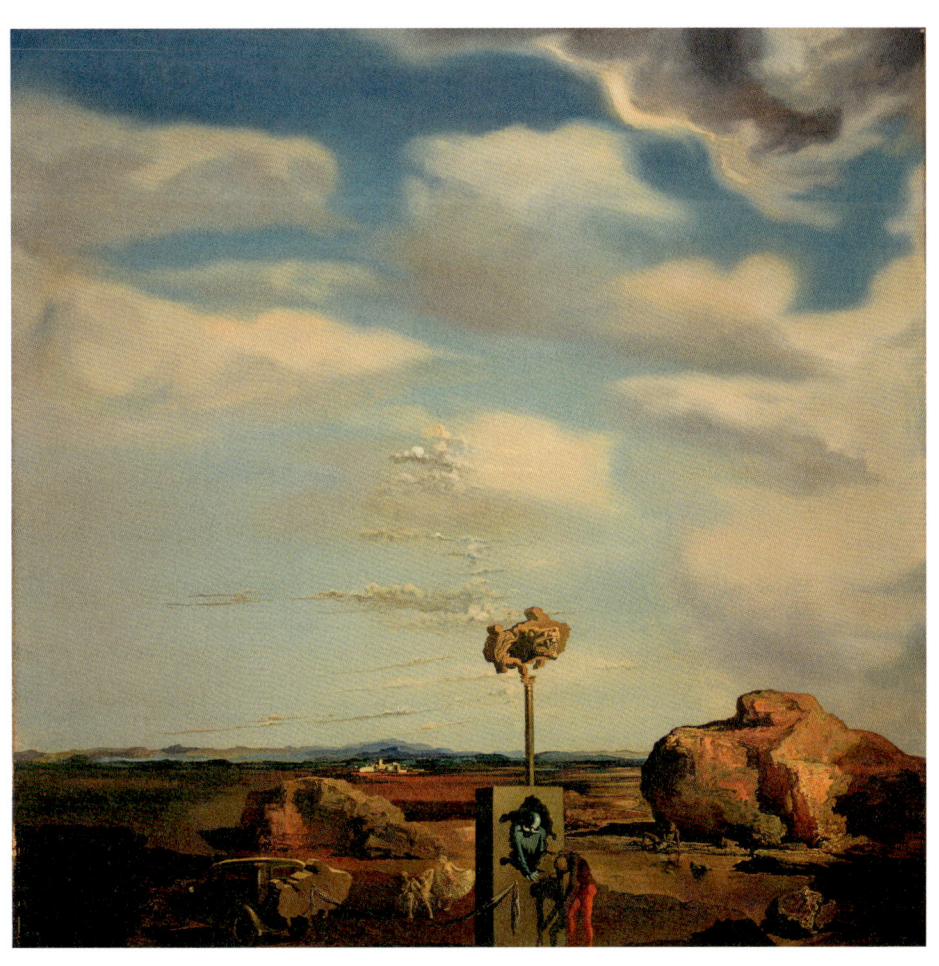

222
Puzzle of Autumn
c. 1935
Oil on canvas, 97.9 × 97.9 cm
The Dalí Museum, St. Petersburg, Florida

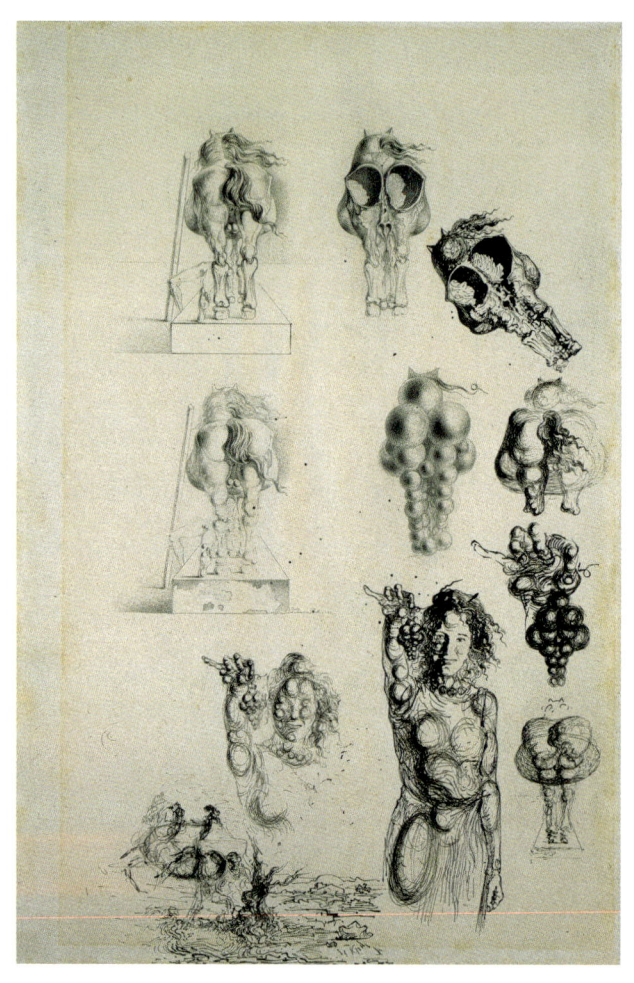

223
Study for "Suburbs of a Paranoiac-Critical Town"
1935
Ink and pencil on paper, 32.5 × 20.3 cm
Private collection

Surrealism

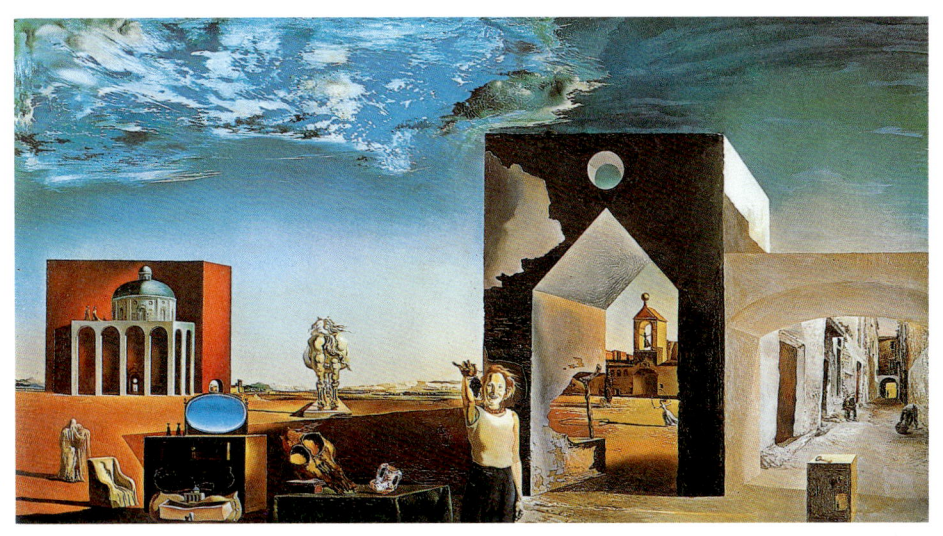

224
Suburbs of the "paranoiac-critical" afternoon (on the outskirts of European history)
1935
Oil on wood panel, 46 × 66 cm
Private collection

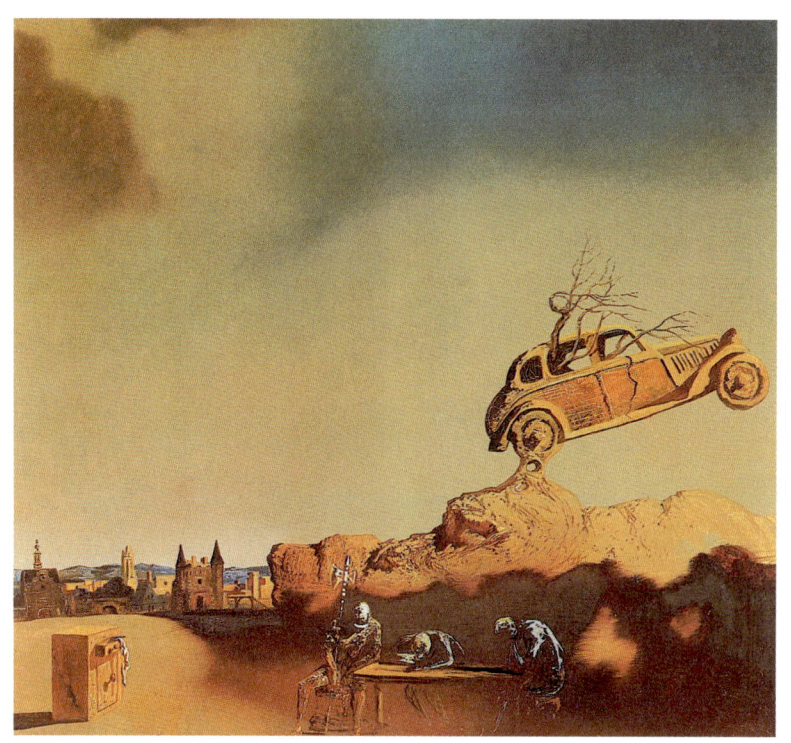

225
Apparition of the town of Delft
c. 1936
Oil on wood panel, 30 × 35 cm
Private collection

Surrealism

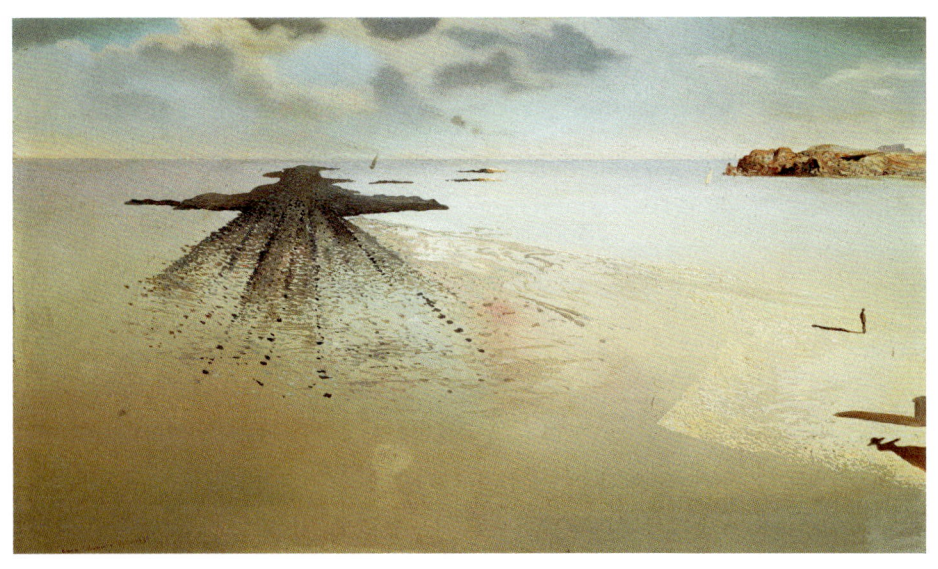

226
Geological Justice
1936
Oil on wood panel, 11 × 19 cm
Private collection

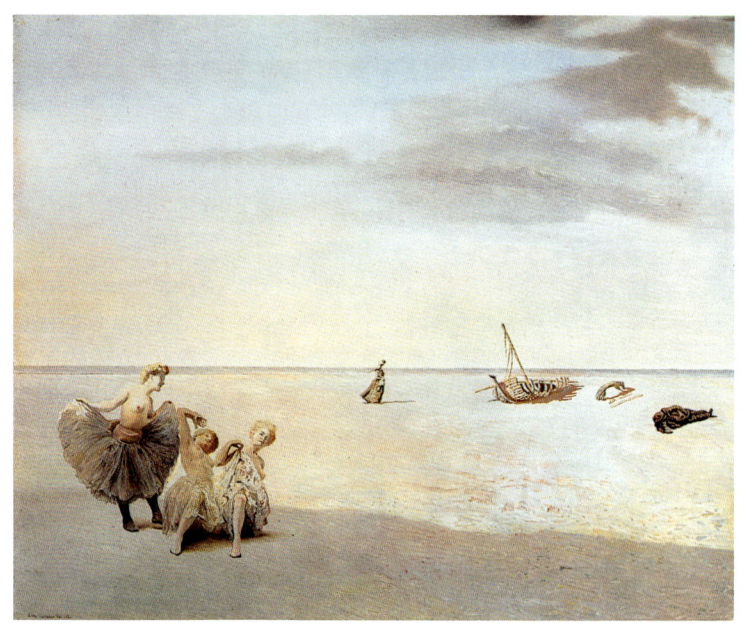

227
The Forgotten Horizon
1936
Oil on wood panel, 22.2 × 26.7 cm
Tate Modern, London

Surrealism

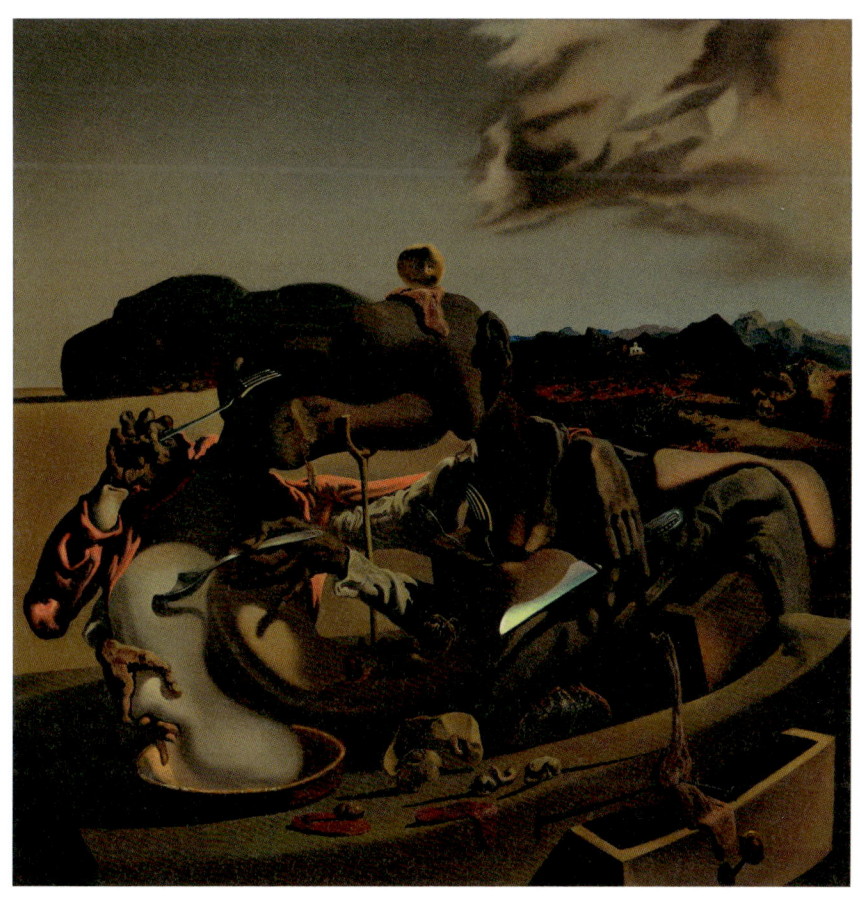

228
Autumnal cannibalism
c. 1936
Oil on canvas, 65.1 × 65.1 cm
Tate Modern, London

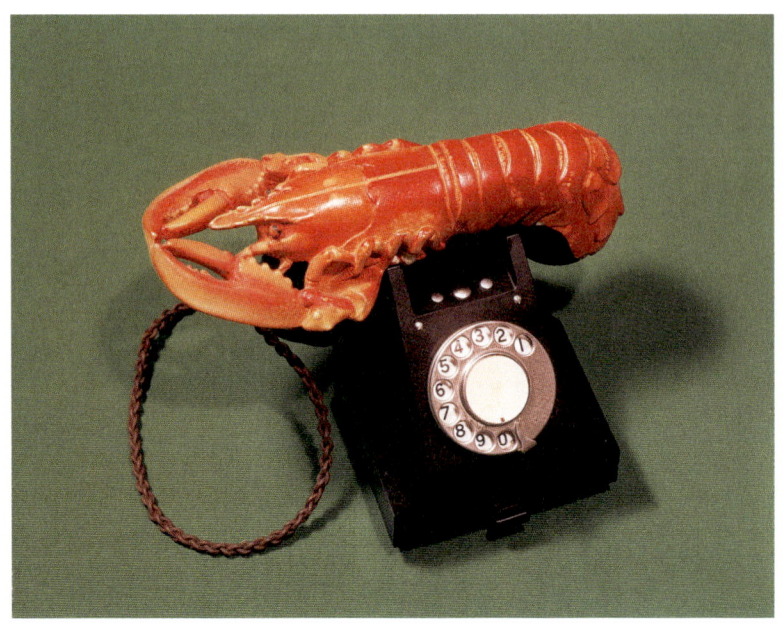

229
Lobster Telephone
1936
Telephone with painted plaster lobster, 15 × 30 x 17 cm
Museum Boijmans Van Beuningen, Rotterdam

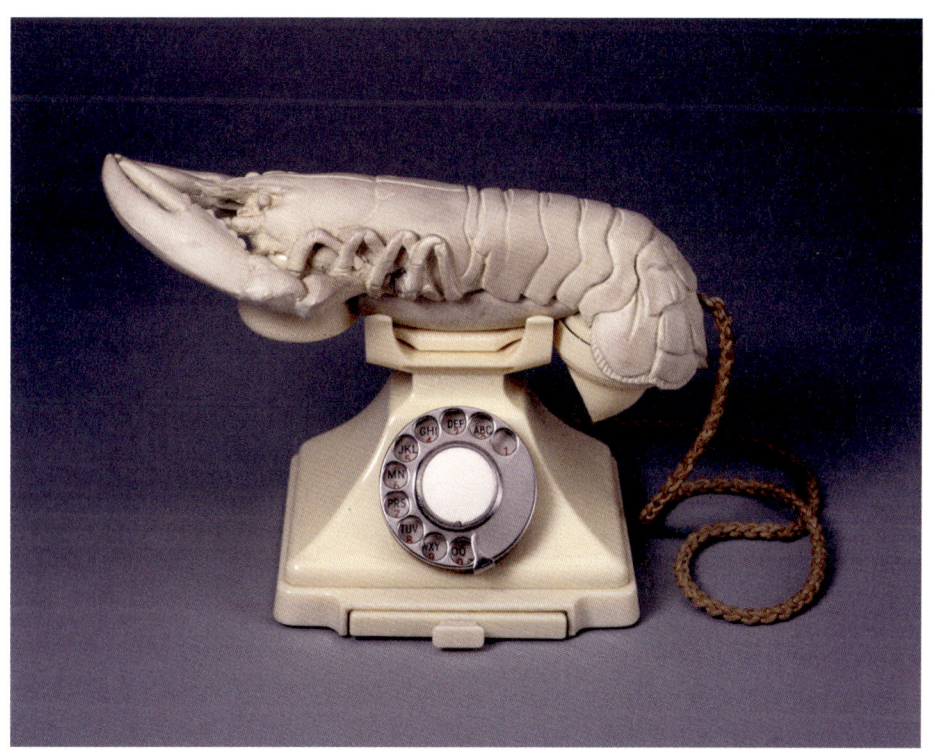

230
Lobster Telephone
c. 1936–1938
Plastic (Bakelite) and painted plaster lobster, 17.8 × 30.5 × 11.4 cm
The Dalí Museum, St. Petersburg, Florida

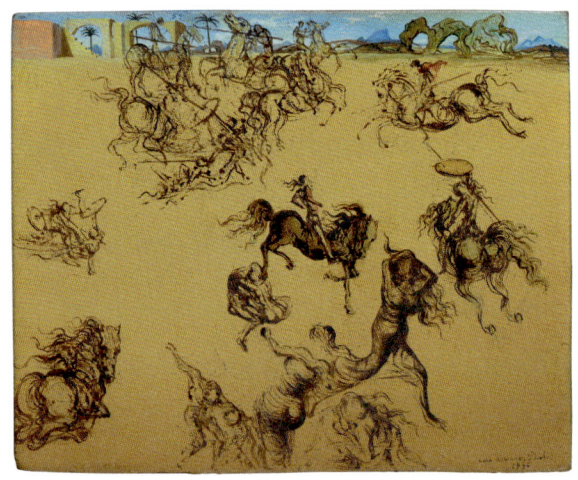

231
Feminine head which has the form of a battle
1936
Oil on wood panel, 10.2 × 12.7 cm
Private collection

Surrealism

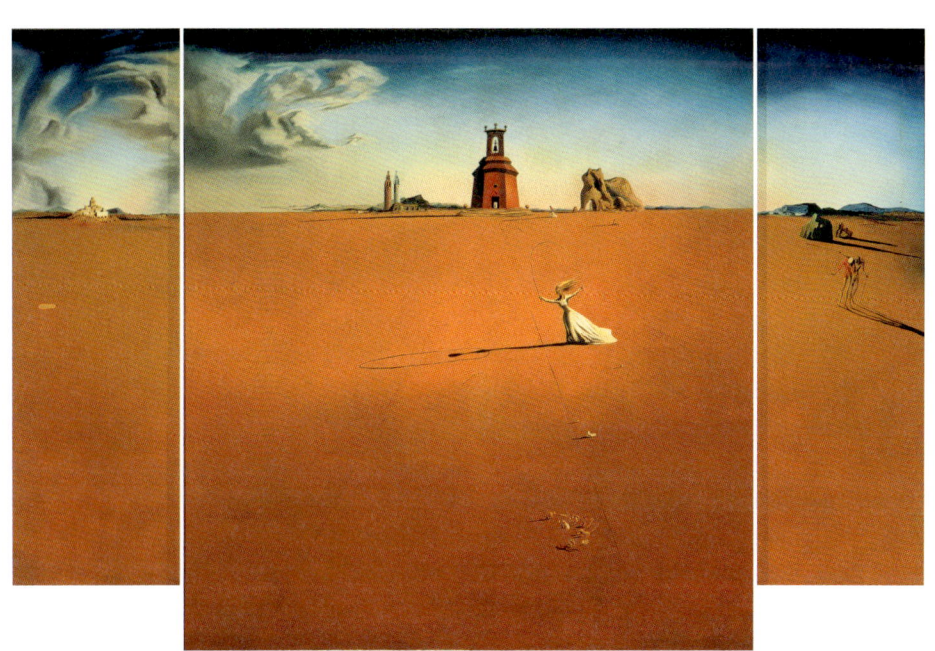

232
Landscape with Girl Skipping
1936
Oil on canvas, 293 × 280 cm (central painting), 261 × 84 cm (each lateral painting)
Museum Boijmans Van Beuningen, Rotterdam

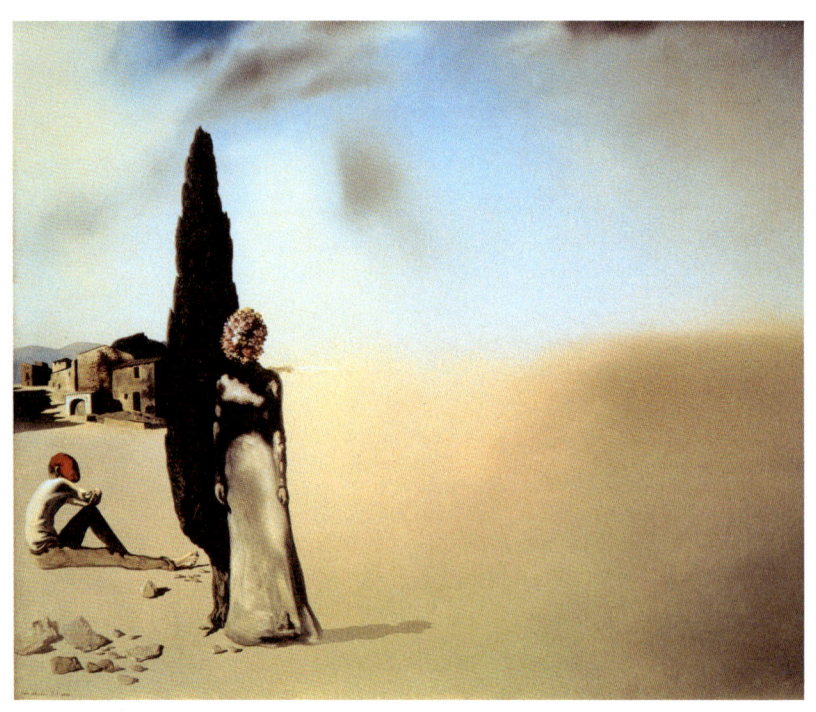

233
Necrophilic Spring
1936
Oil on canvas, 54 × 65 cm
Private collection

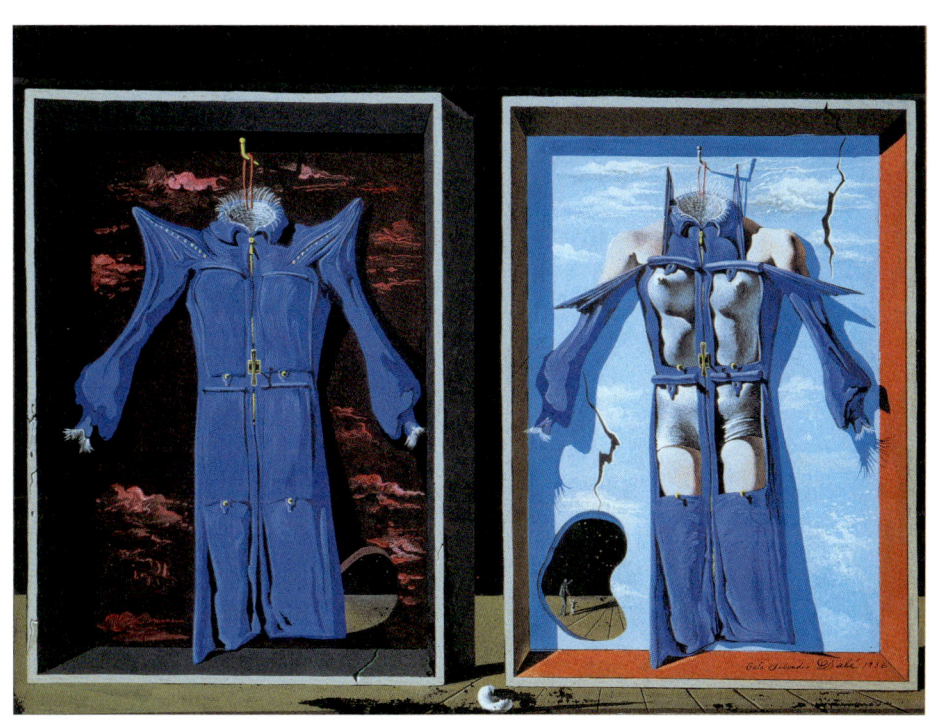

234
Night and Day Clothes of the Body
1936
Gouache on paper, 30 × 40 cm
Private collection

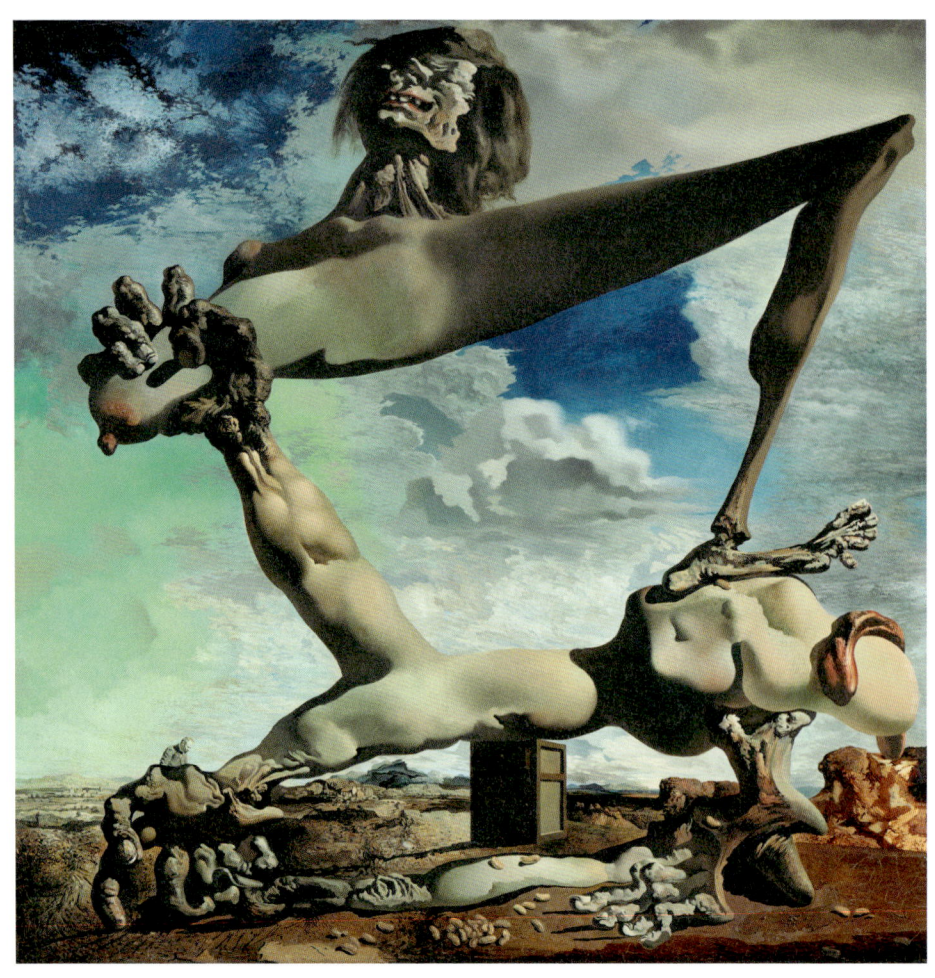

235
Soft construction with boiled apricots
(Soft Construction with Boiled Beans [Premonition of Civil War])
1936
Oil on canvas, 99.9 × 100 cm
Philadelphia Museum of Art, Philadelphia, Pennsylvania

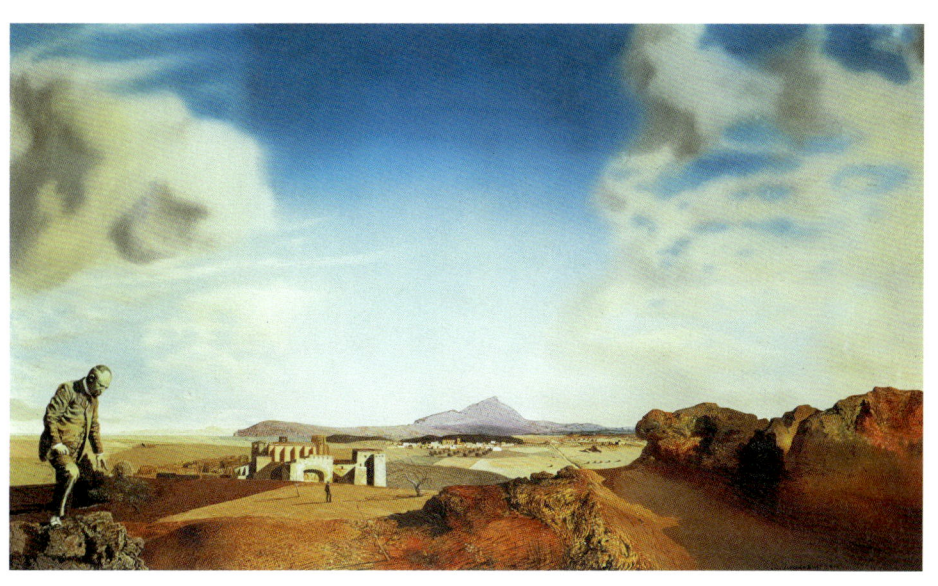

236
Diurnal Melancholy (The Chemist of the Empordà in Search of the Void)
1936
Oil and collage on wood panel, 30 × 52 cm
Museum Folkwang, Essen

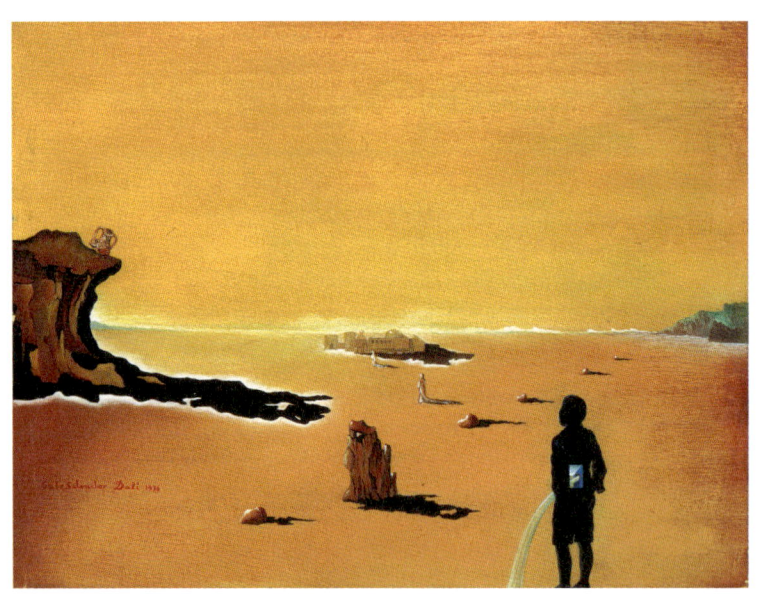

237
Surrealist landscape
1936
Oil on canvas, dimensions unknown
Galerie Malingue, Paris

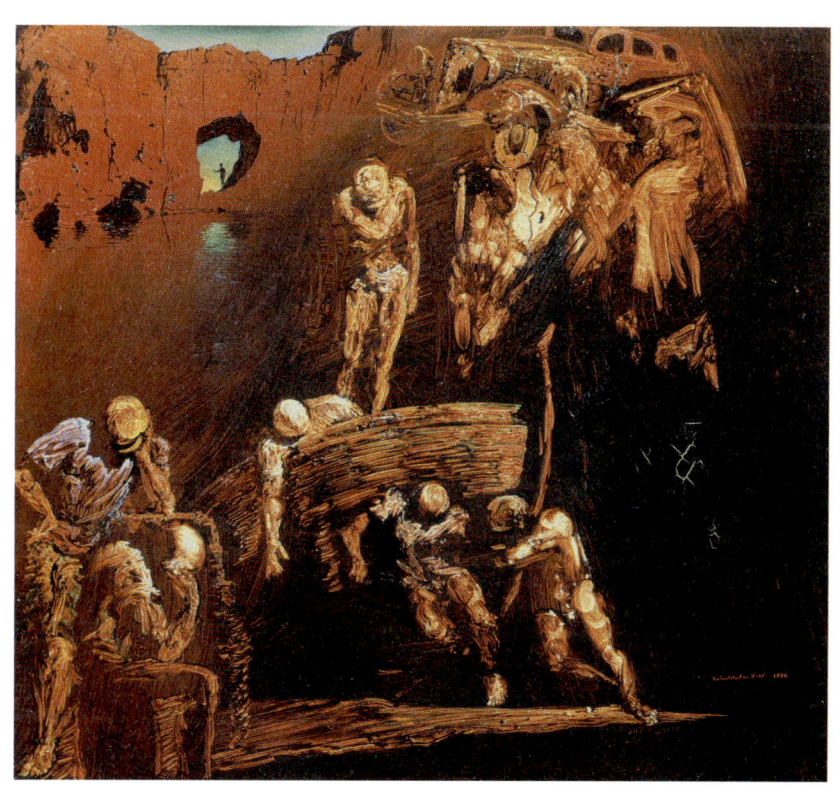

238
The fossil automobile of Cape Creus
1936
Oil on wood panel, 31 × 37 cm
Nahmad collection, Switzerland

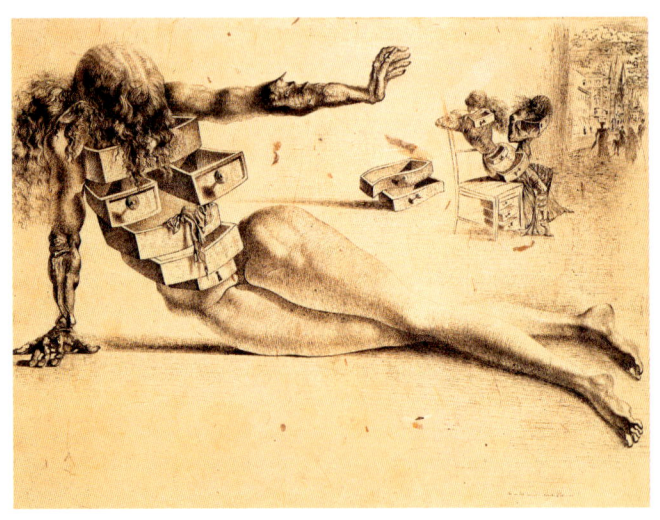

239
City of drawers. Study for the "Anthropomorphic Cabinet"
1936
Pen and ink on paper, 32 × 41.5 cm
Collection Paul L. Herring, New York

Surrealism

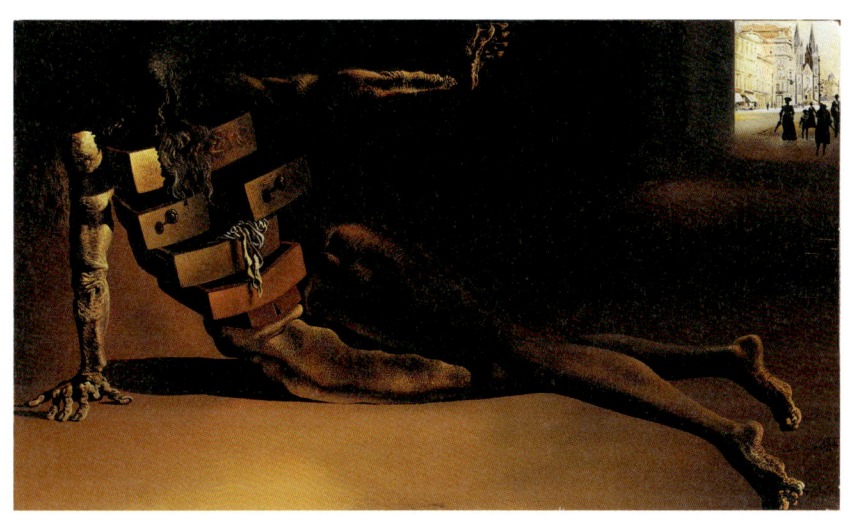

240
The Anthropomorphic Cabinet
1936
Oil on wood panel, 25.4 × 44.2 cm
Kunstsammlung Nordrhein-Westfalen, Düsseldorf

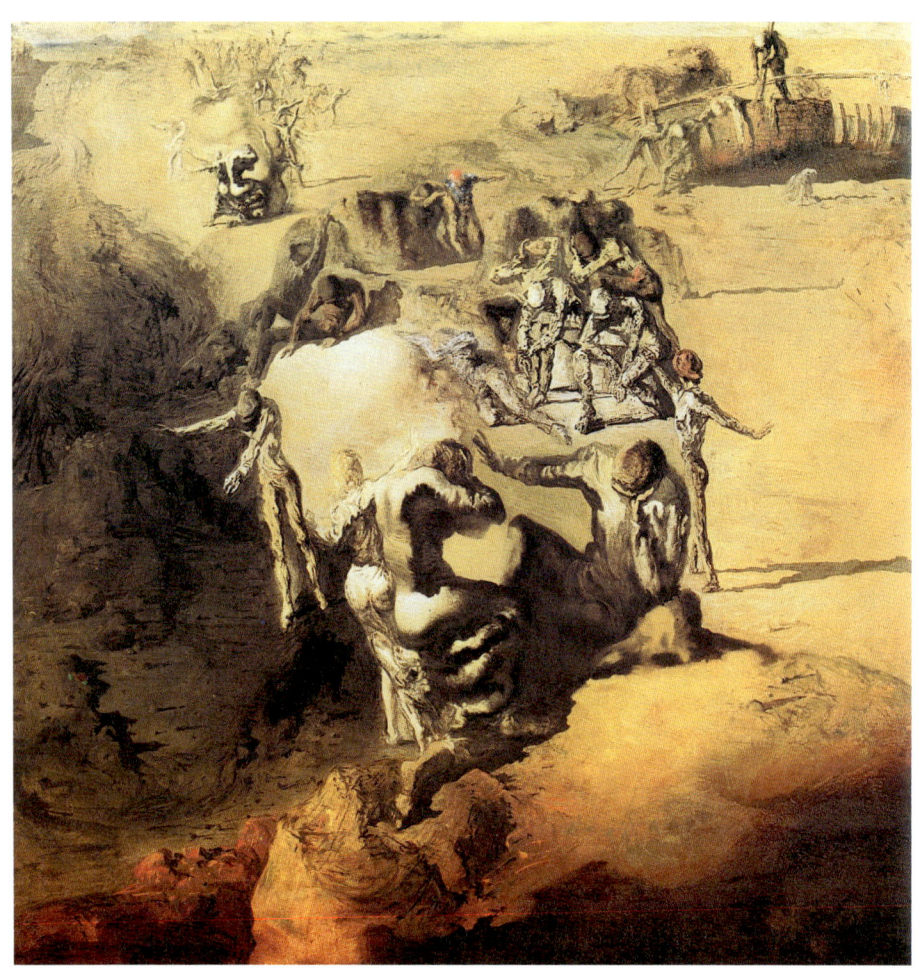

241
The Great Paranoic
1936
Oil on canvas, 62 × 62 cm
Museum Boijmans Van Beuningen, Rotterdam

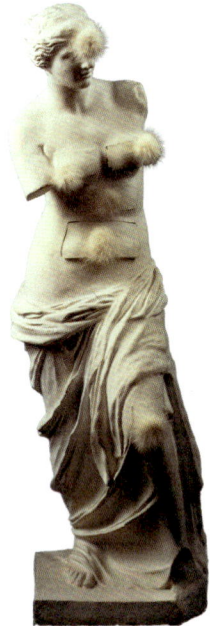

242
Venus de Milo with Drawers
1936
Bronze with plaster-like mount and fur tassels, 98 × 32.5 × 34 cm
Museum Boijmans Van Beuningen, Rotterdam

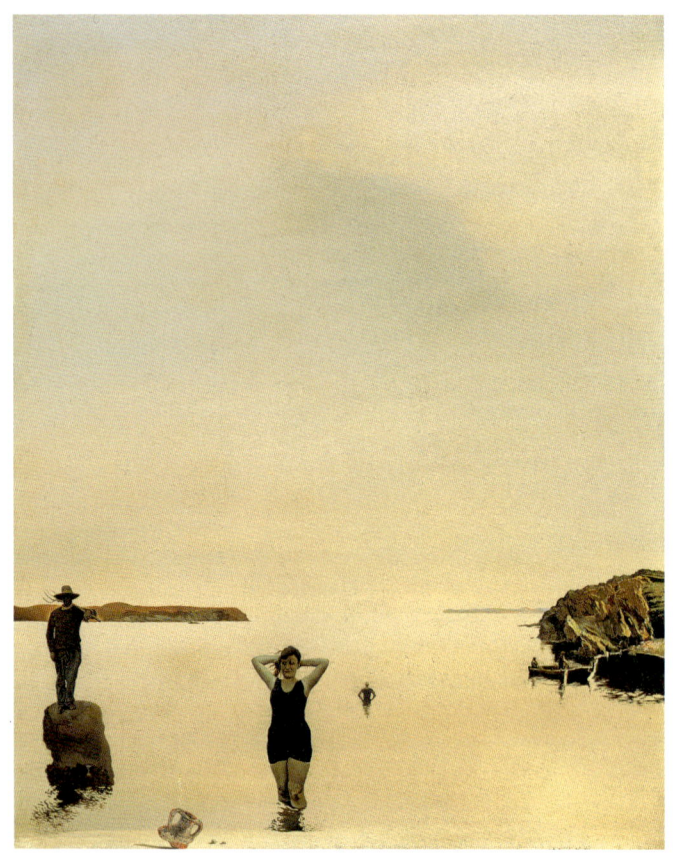

243
White calm
1935
Oil on wood panel, 41 × 33 cm
Private collection

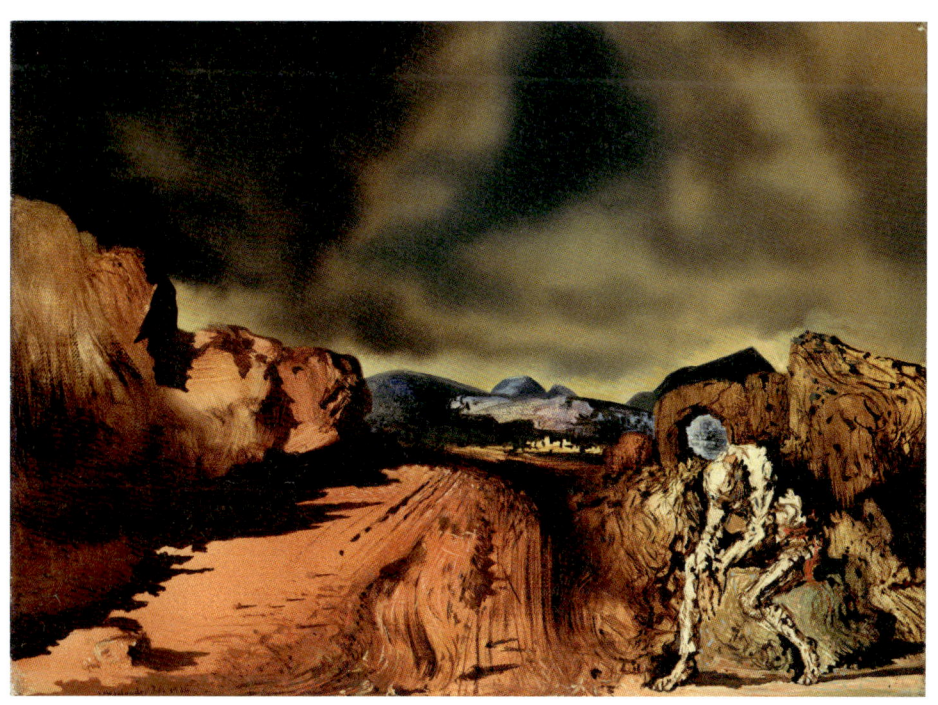

244
The man with the head of blue hortensias
1936
Oil on canvas, 16.2 × 22 cm
The Dalí Museum, St. Petersburg, Florida

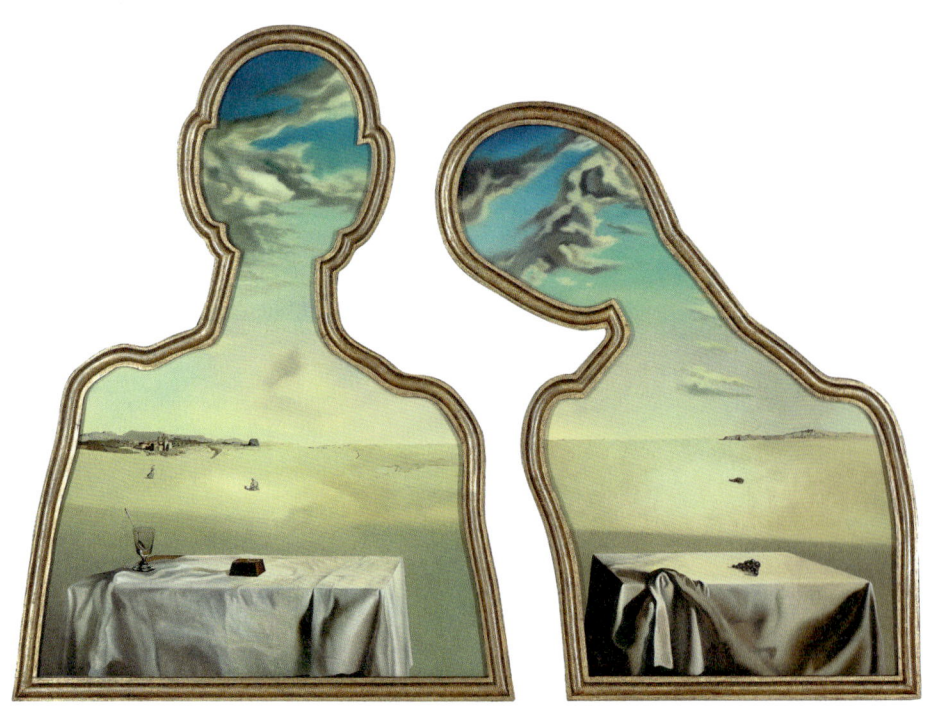

245
A Couple with Their Heads Full of Clouds
1936
Oil on plywood, 92.5 × 69.5 cm (left figure), 82.5 × 62.5 cm (right figure)
Museum Boijmans Van Beuningen, Rotterdam

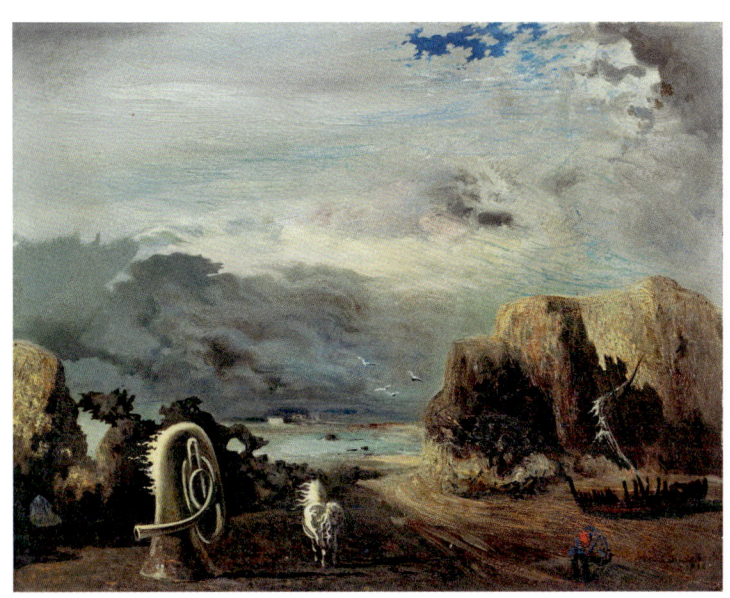

246
A Trombone and a Sofa Fashioned out of Saliva
1936
Oil on wood panel, 19 × 24 cm
Private collection

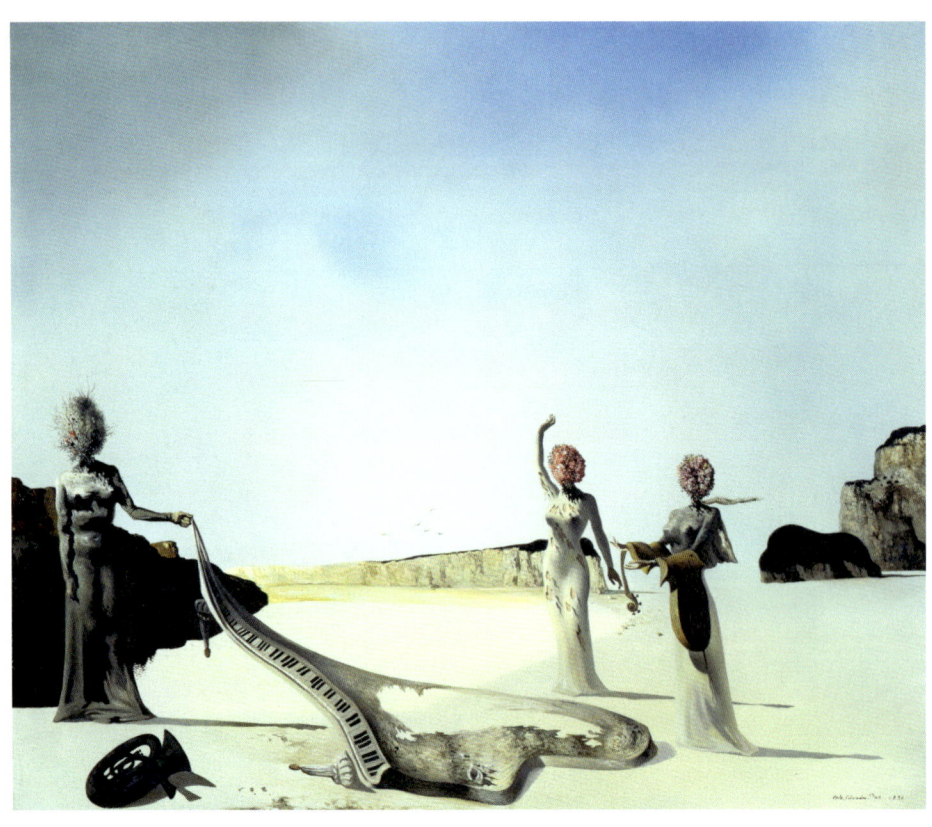

247
Three young surrealist women holding in their arms the skins of an orchestra
1936
Oil on canvas, 53 × 65 cm
The Dalí Museum, St. Petersburg, Florida

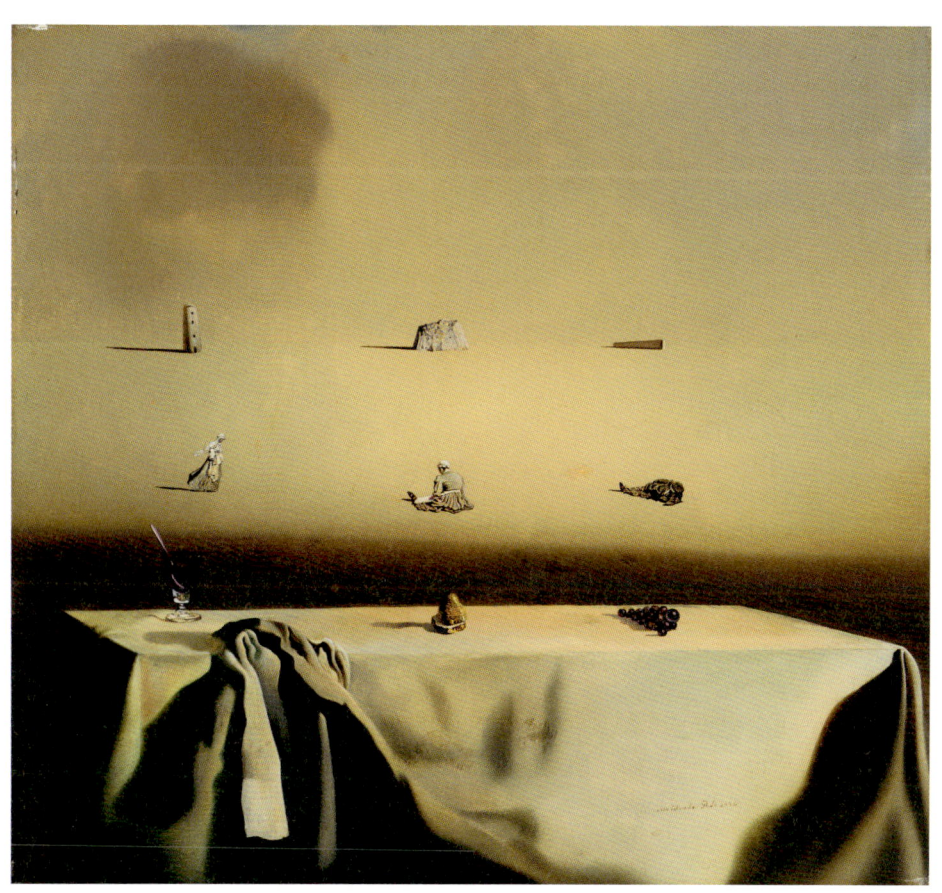

248
Morphological echo
1936
Oil on wood panel, 30.5 × 33 cm
The Dalí Museum, St. Petersburg, Florida

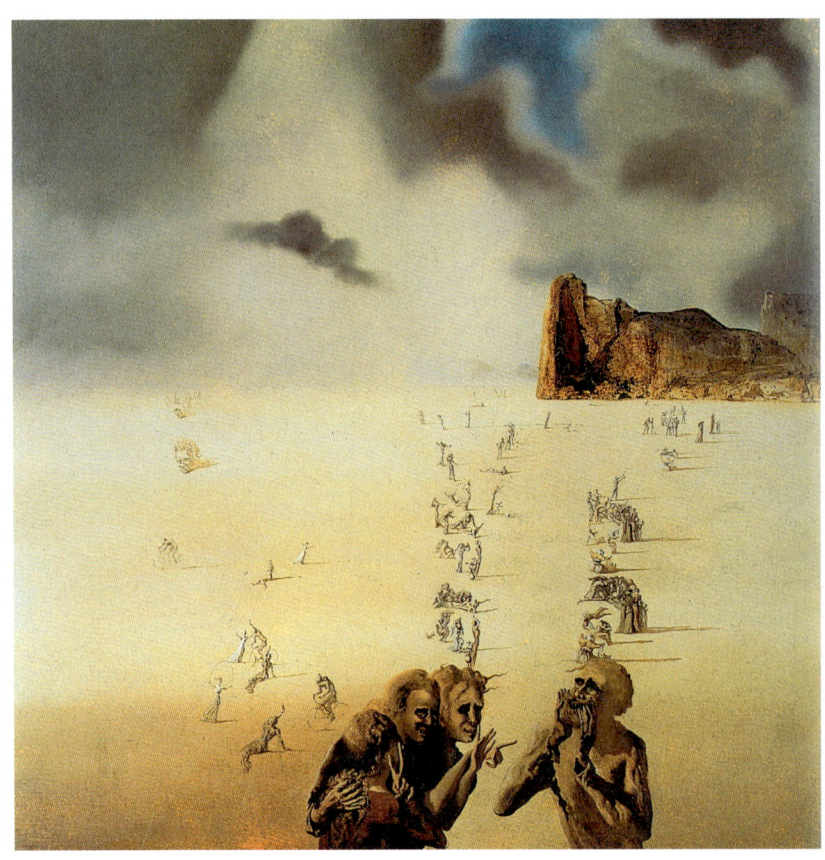

249
Perspectives (Premonition of the paranoiac perspectives for the soft structures)
c. 1936
Oil on canvas, 65 × 65.5 cm
Emanuel Hoffmann Foundation, on permanent loan to the Öffentliche Kunstsammlung, Basel

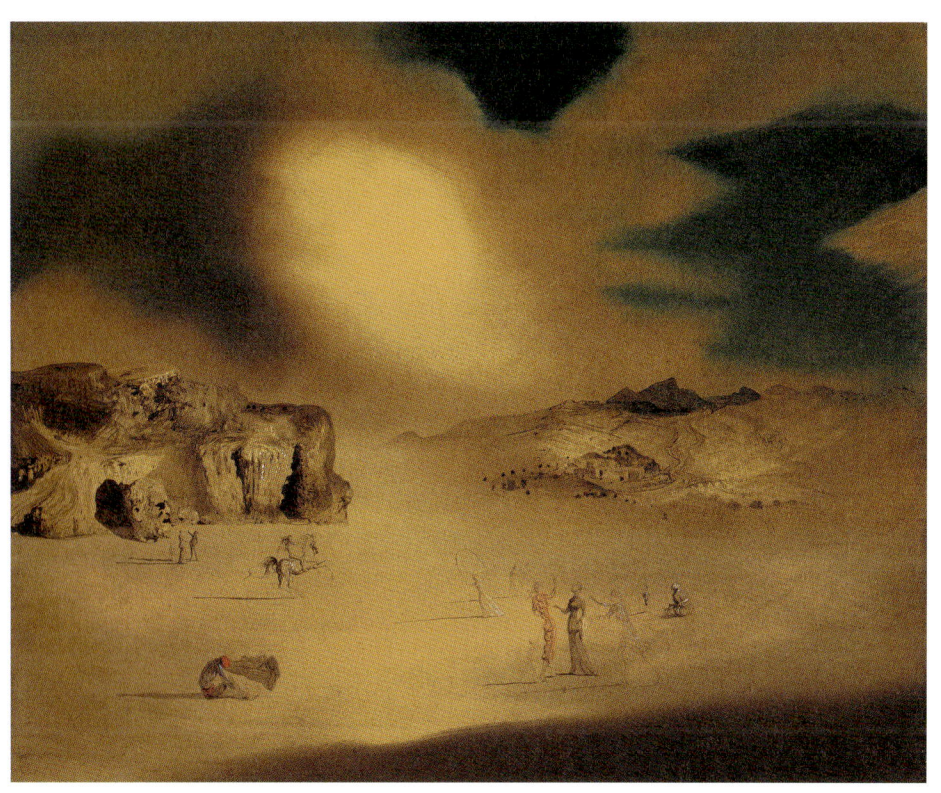

250
Average Pagan Landscape
1937
Oil on canvas, 38.5 × 46.5 cm
Fundació Gala-Salvador Dalí, Figueres

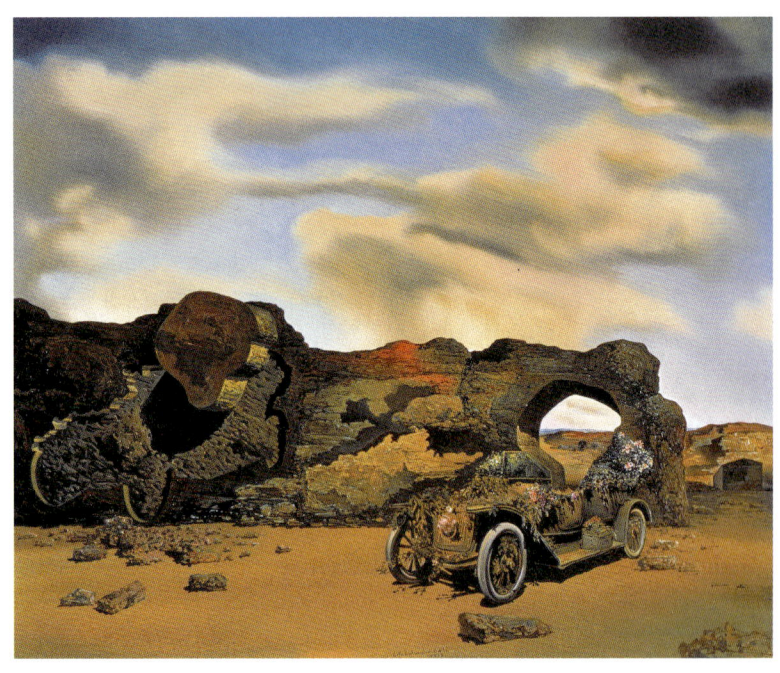

251
Paranoiac-Critical Solitude
1935
Oil on wood panel, 19 × 23 cm
Private collection

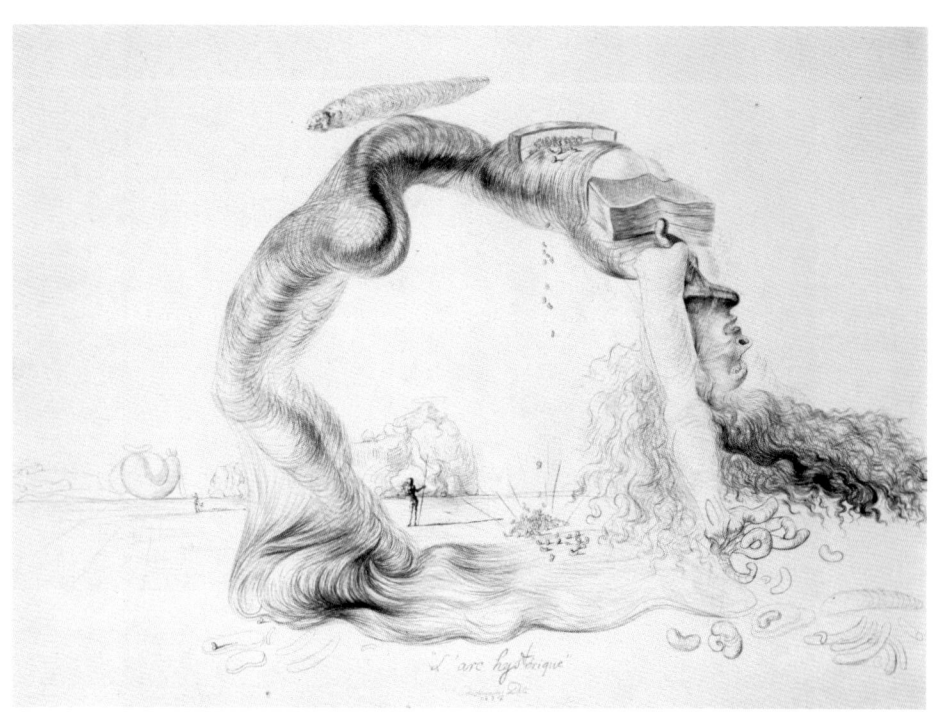

252
L'Arc hystérique (The Hysterical Arch)
1937
Ink on paper, 55.9 × 76.2 cm
The Dalí Museum, St. Petersburg, Florida

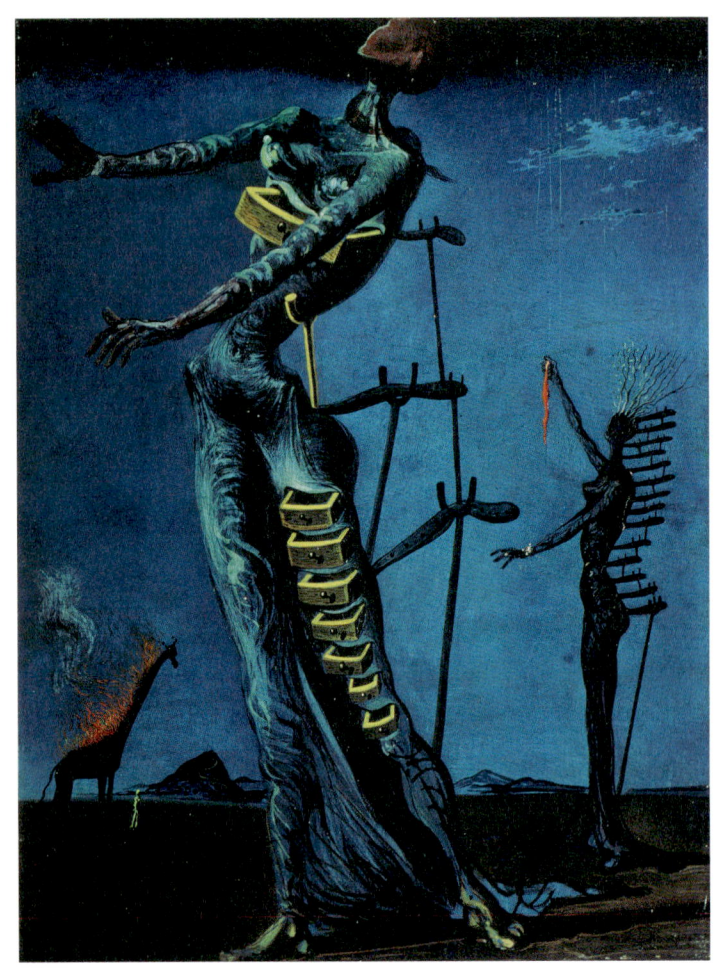

253
Burning Giraffe
c. 1937
Oil on wood panel, 35 × 27 cm
Emanuel Hoffmann Foundation

Surrealism

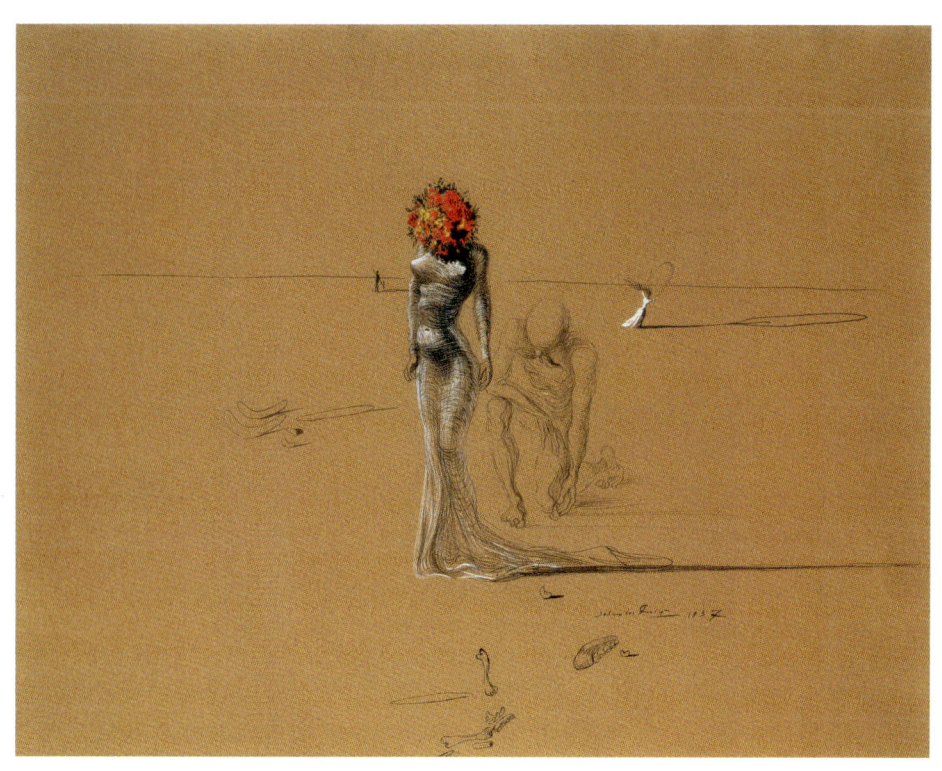

254
Untitled (Female Figure with Head of Flowers)
1937
Technique and dimensions unknown
Private collection

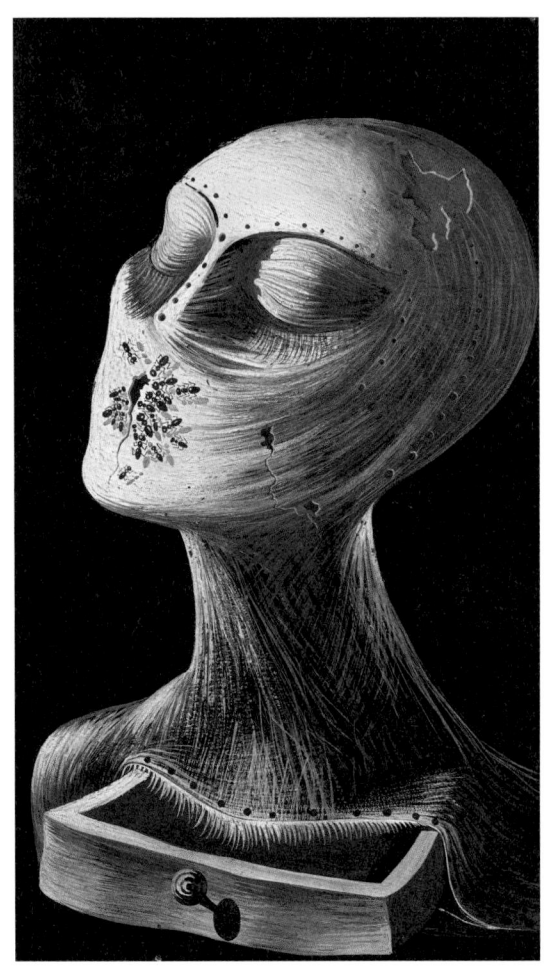

255
Face with Ants
1936
Gouache and black ink on paper, 24 × 13.5 cm
Private collection

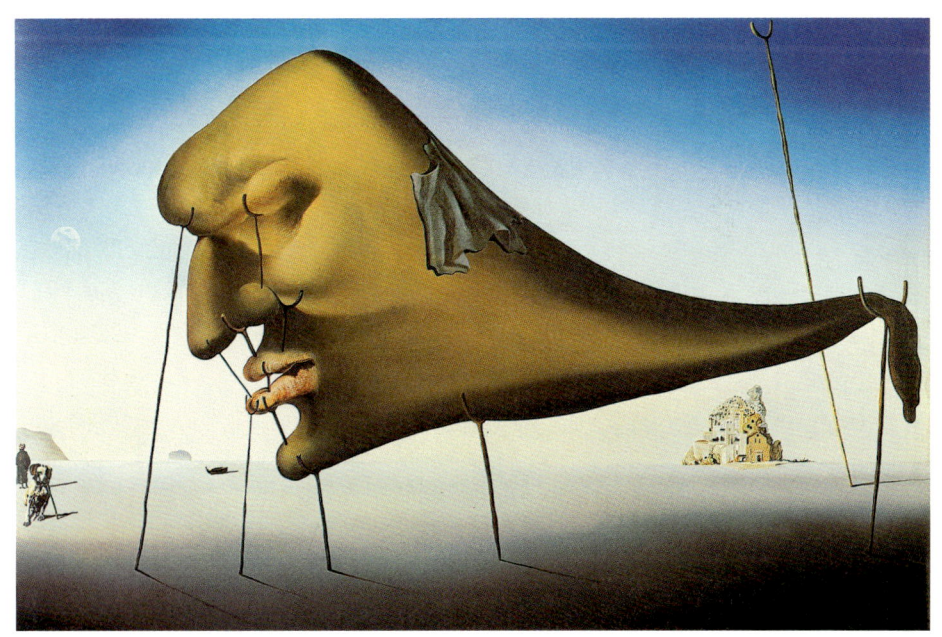

256
Sleep
c. 1937
Oil on canvas, 51 × 78 cm
Private collection

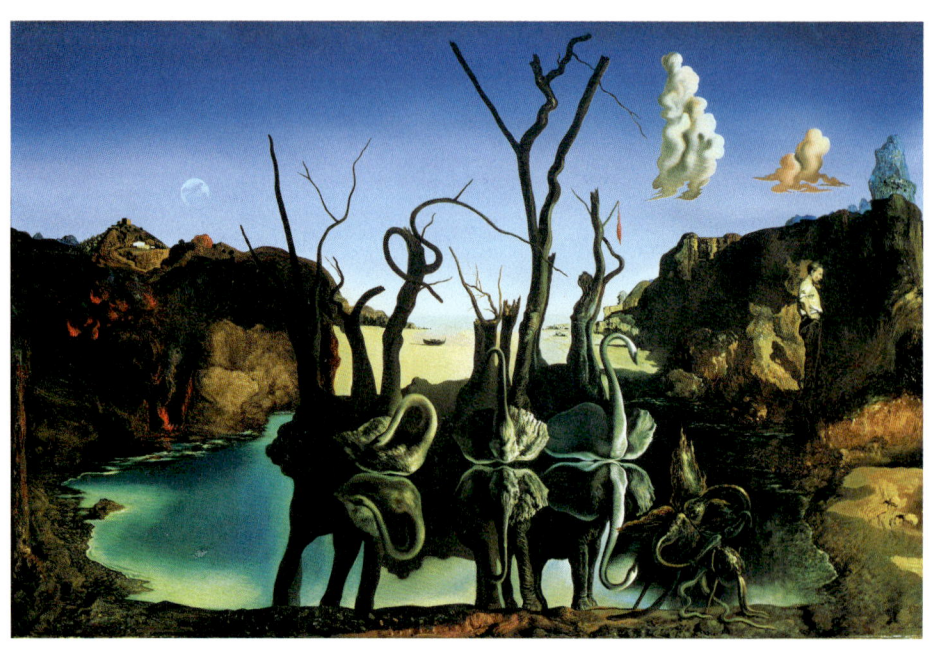

257
Swan Reflecting Elephants
1937
Oil on canvas, 51 × 77 cm
Private collection

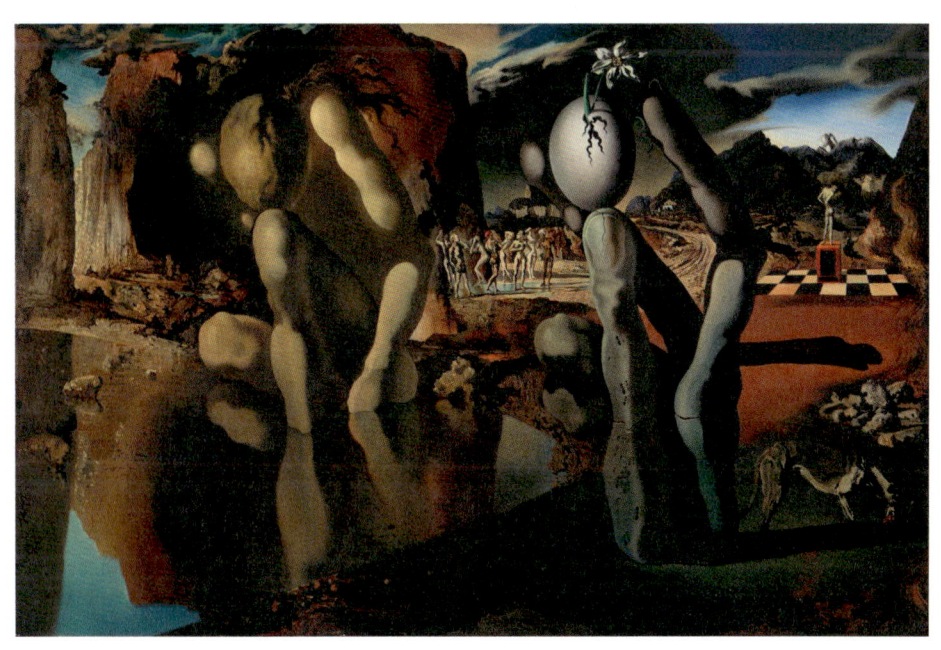

258
Metamorphosis of Narcissus
1937
Oil on canvas, 51.1 × 78.1 cm
Tate Modern, London

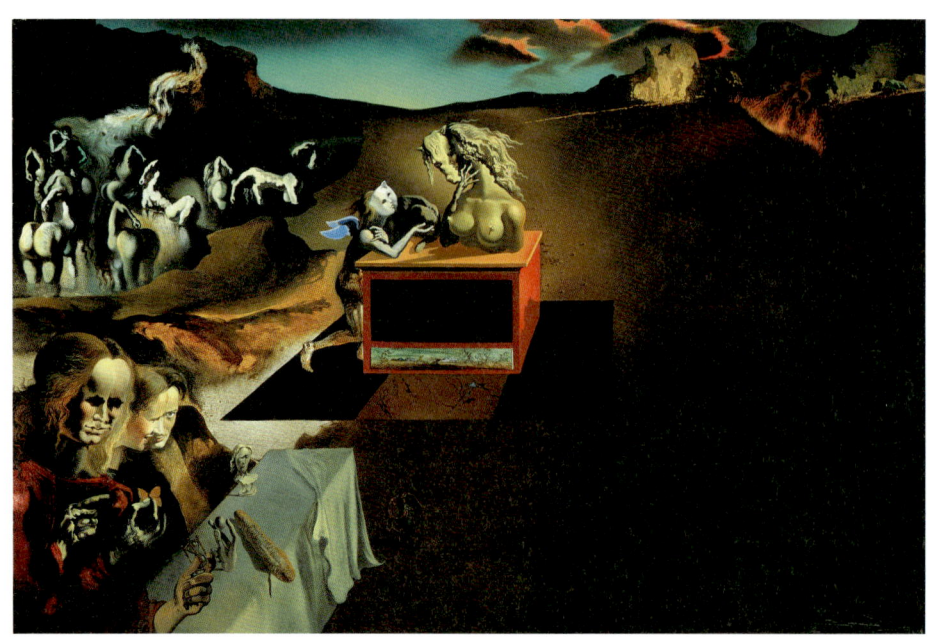

259
Invention of the Monster
c. 1937
Oil on canvas, 51.4 × 78.1 cm
The Art Institute of Chicago, Illinois

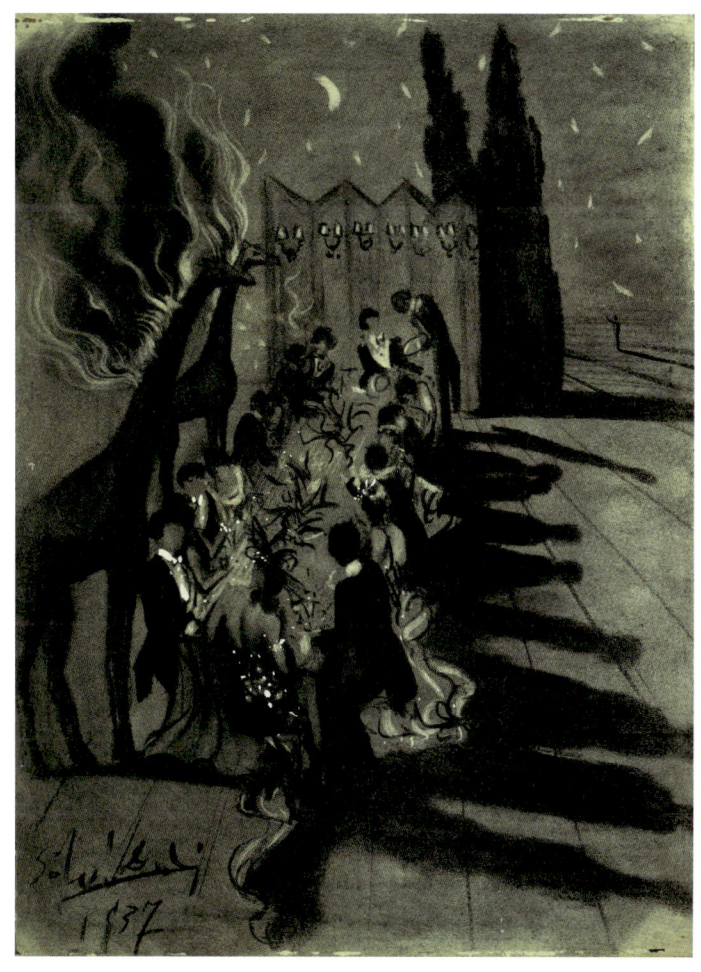

260
Dinner in the Desert Lit by Burning Giraffes
1937
Charcoal and gouache on paper, 61.6 × 45.7 cm
The Dalí Museum, St. Petersburg, Florida

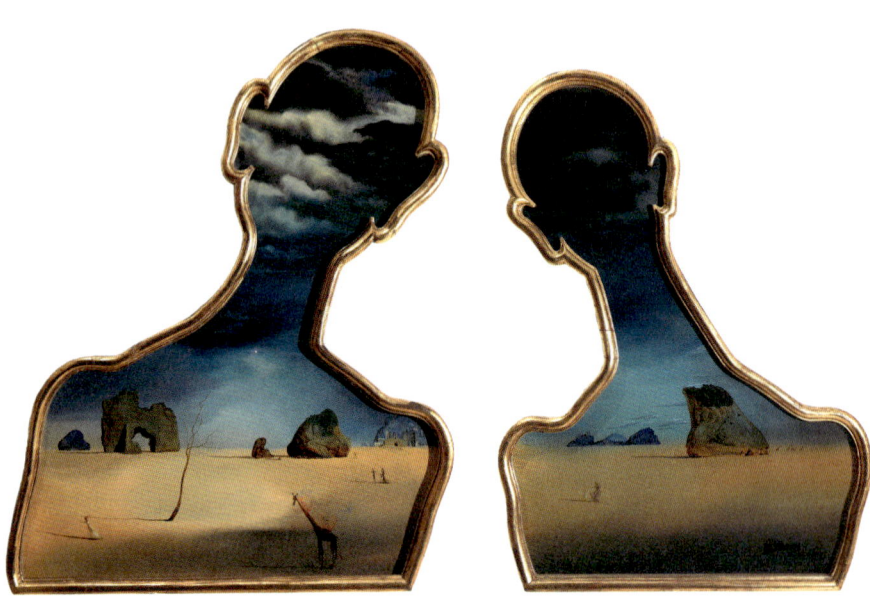

261
A Couple with Their Heads Full of Clouds
1937
Oil on wood panel, 94.5 × 74.5 cm (left figure), 87.7 × 65.8 cm (right figure)
Private collection

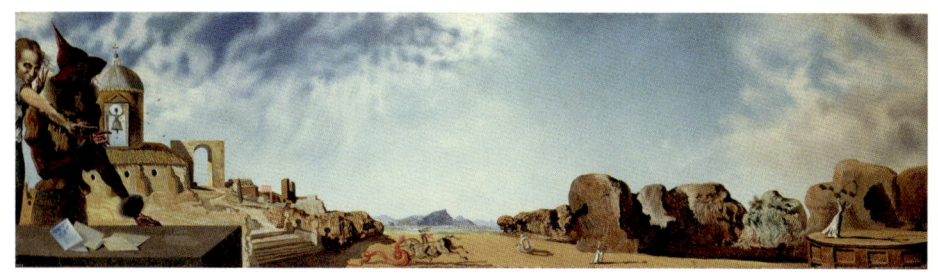

262
Anthropomorphic Echo
1937
Oil on board, 14.3 × 51.8 cm
The Dalí Museum, St. Petersburg, Florida

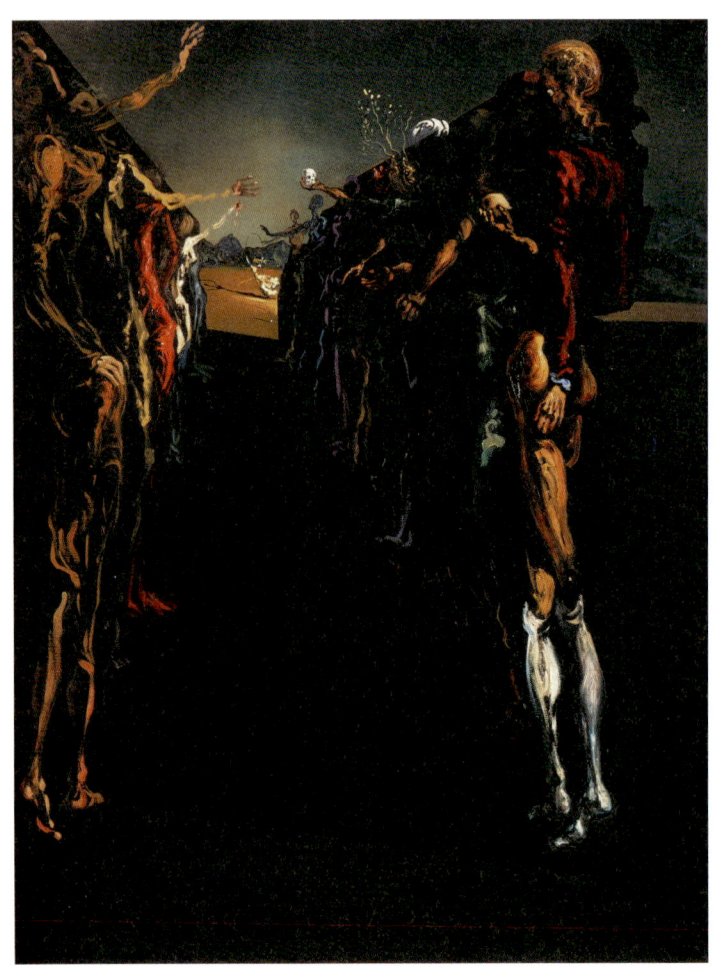

263
Palladio's Corridor of Thalia
c. 1938
Oil on canvas, 116 × 88.5 cm
Mie Prefectural Art Museum, Tsu, Mie Prefecture, Japan

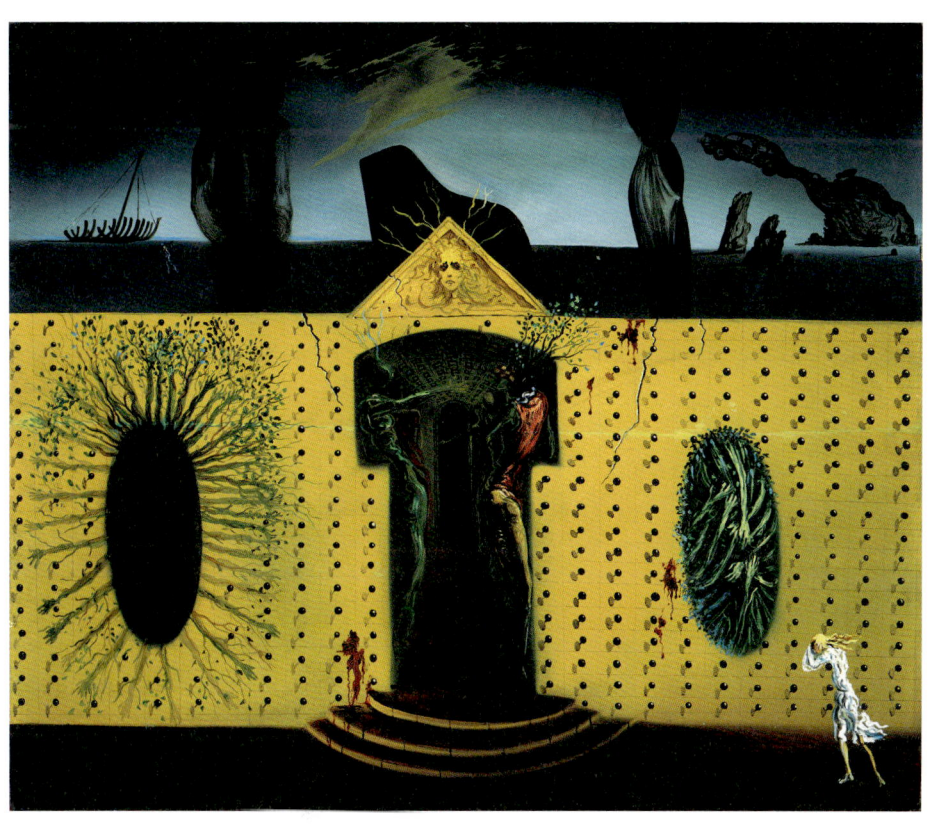

264
Mad Tristan
1938
Oil on wood panel, 45.7 × 54.9 cm
The Dalí Museum, St. Petersburg, Florida

1929–1939

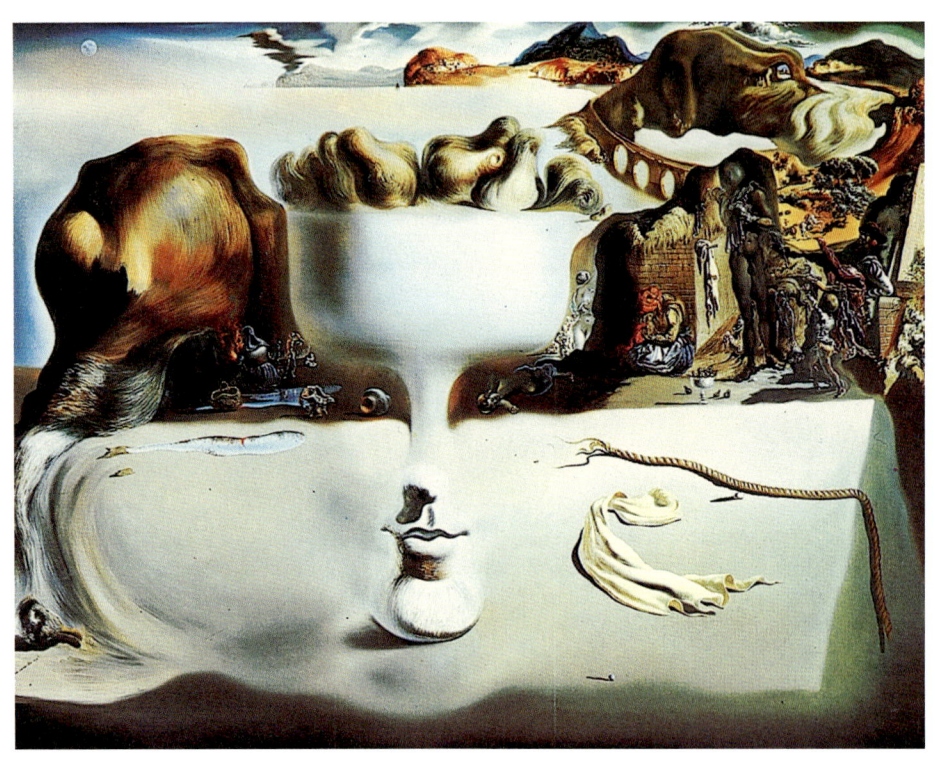

265
Apparition of Face and Fruit Dish on a Beach
1938
Oil on canvas, 114.3 × 143.8 cm
Wadsworth Atheneum, Hartford, Connecticut
The Ella Gallup Sumner and Mary Catlin Sumner Collection Fund

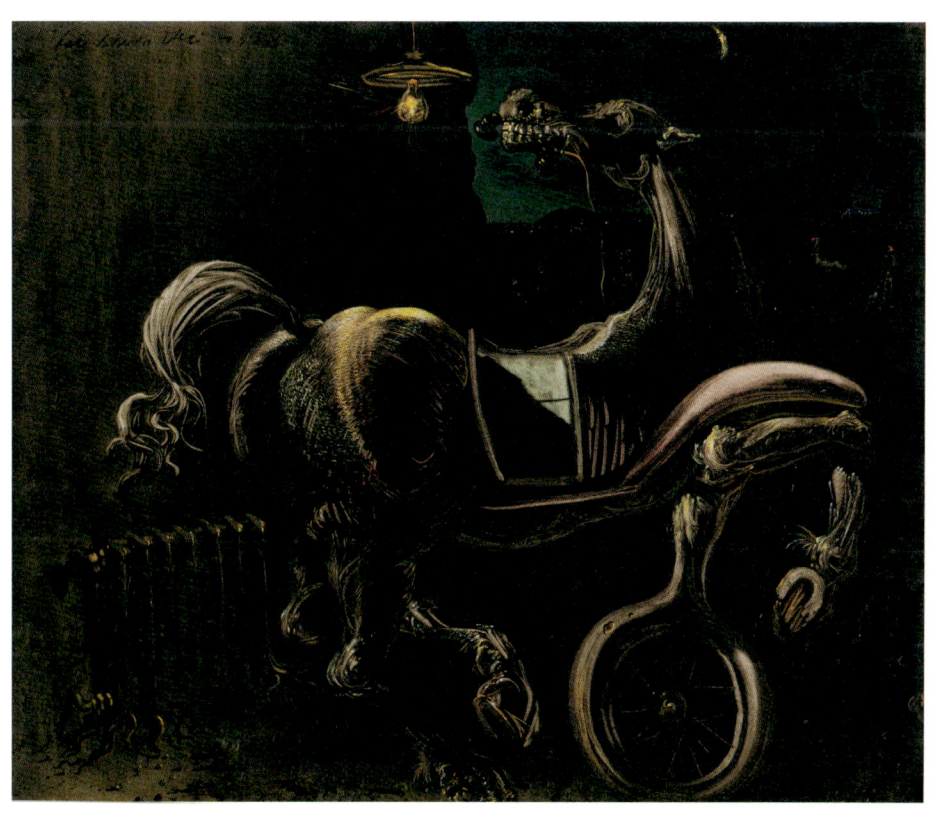

266
Debris of an automobile giving birth to a blind horse biting a telephone
1938
Oil on canvas, 54.5 × 65.1 cm
The Museum of Modern Art, New York

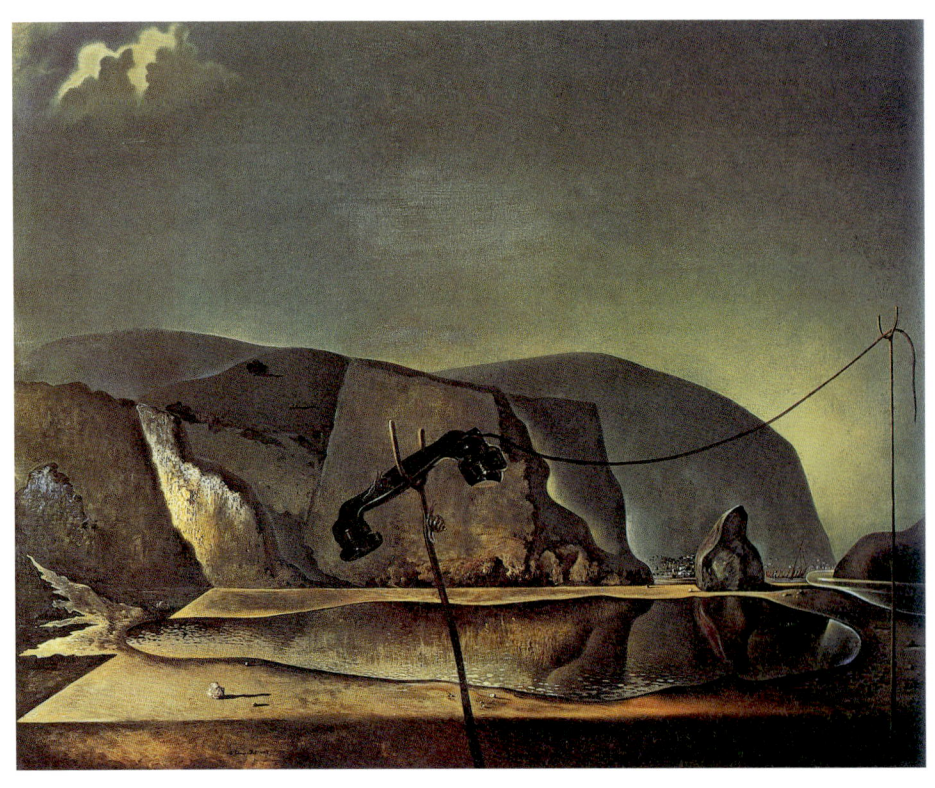

267
Melancholic eccentricity
1938
Oil on canvas, 73 × 92.1 cm
Tate Modern, London

Surrealism

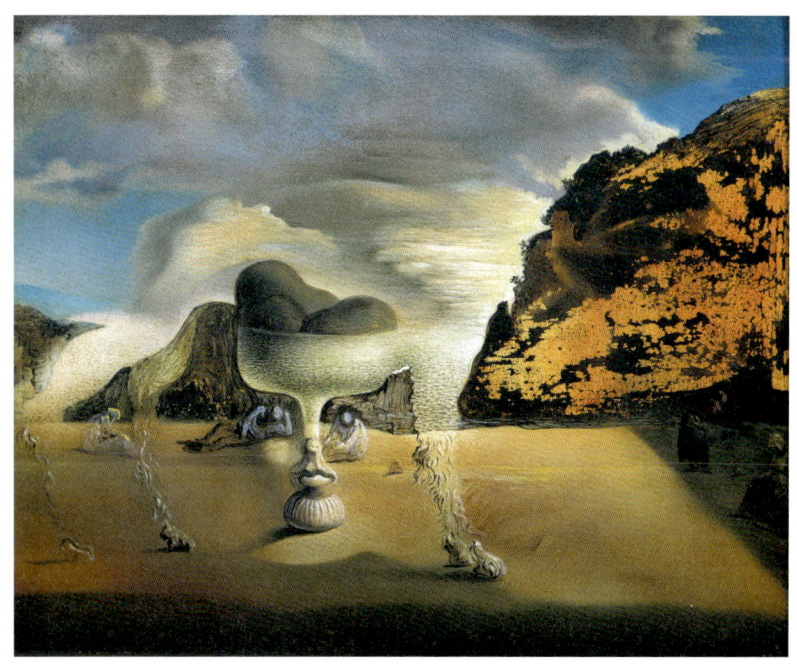

268
Invisible Afghan with Apparition, on the Beach, of the Face of García Lorca,
in the Form of a Fruit Dish with Three Figs
c. 1938
Oil on wood panel, 19.2 × 24.1 cm
Private collection

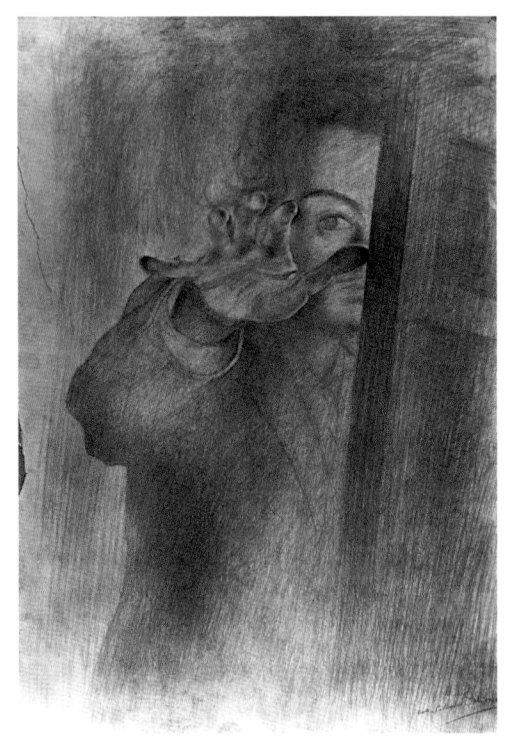

269
Study for the self-portrait in "Impressions of Africa"
1938
Pencil on paper, 52 × 33 cm
Museum Boijmans Van Beuningen, Rotterdam

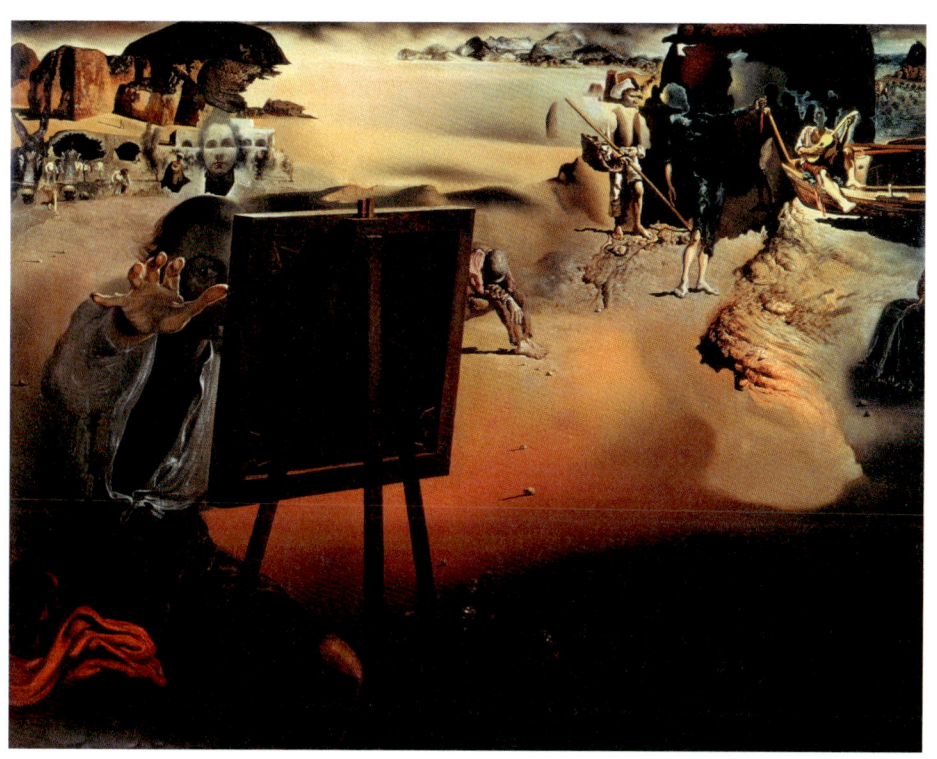

270
Impressions of Africa
c. 1938
Oil on canvas, 91.5 × 117.5 cm
Museum Boijmans Van Beuningen, Rotterdam

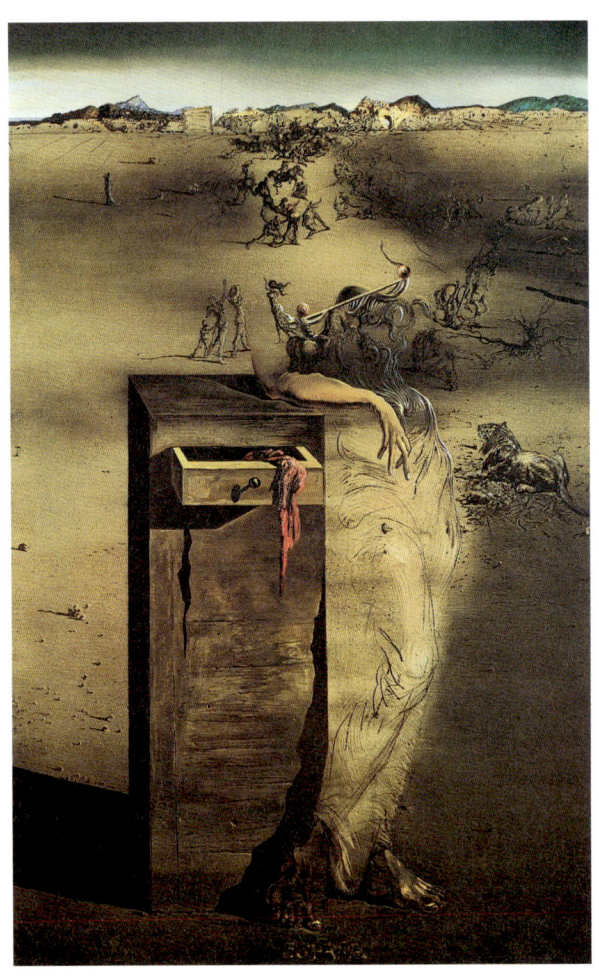

271
Spain
1938
Oil on canvas, 92 × 60 cm
Museum Boijmans Van Beuningen, Rotterdam

Surrealism

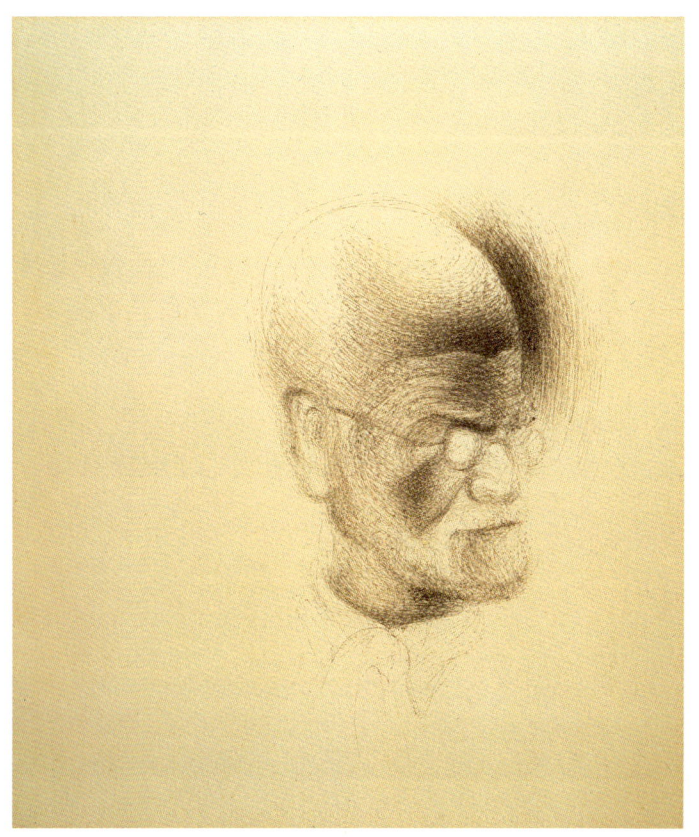

272
Portrait of Freud
1938
Ink on paper, 29.5 × 26.5 cm
Freud Museum, London

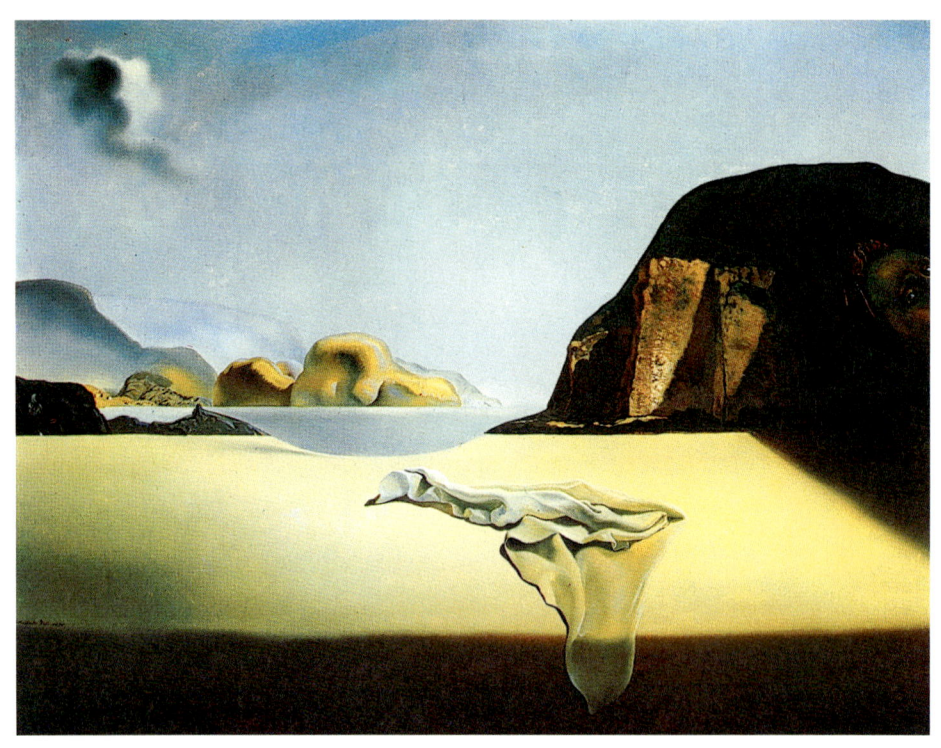

273
The Transparent Simulacrum of the Feigned Image
1938
Oil on canvas, 72.4 × 92.1 cm
Albright Knox Art Gallery, Buffalo, New York

Surrealism

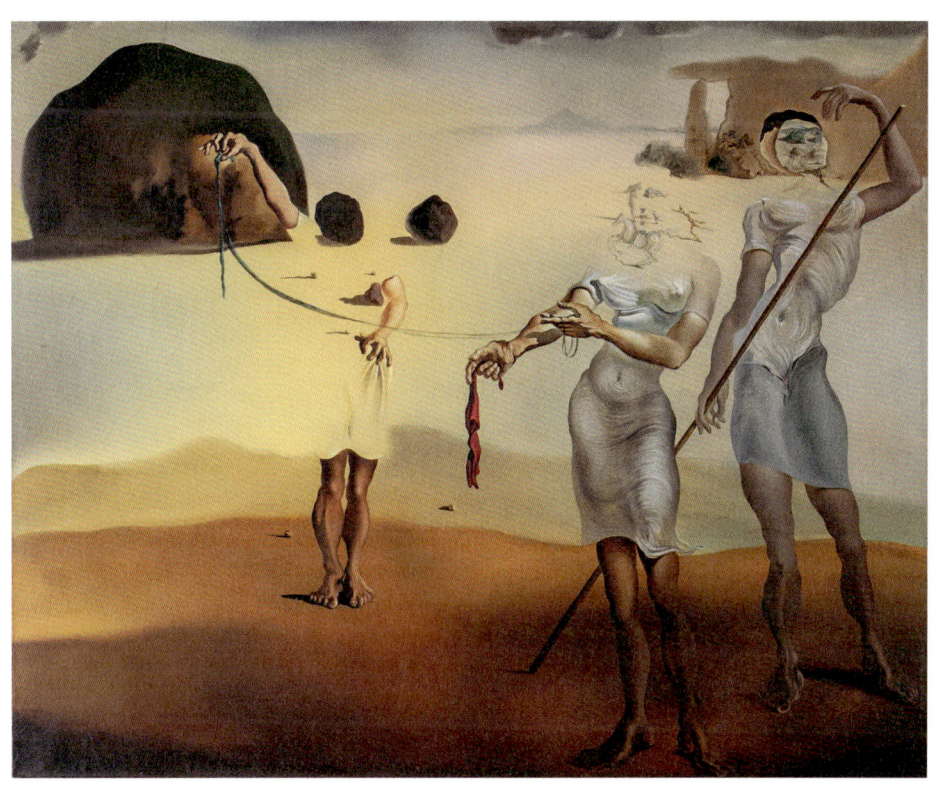

274
Enchanted beach with three fluid graces
c. 1938
Oil on canvas, 65 × 81.3 cm
The Dalí Museum, St. Petersburg, Florida

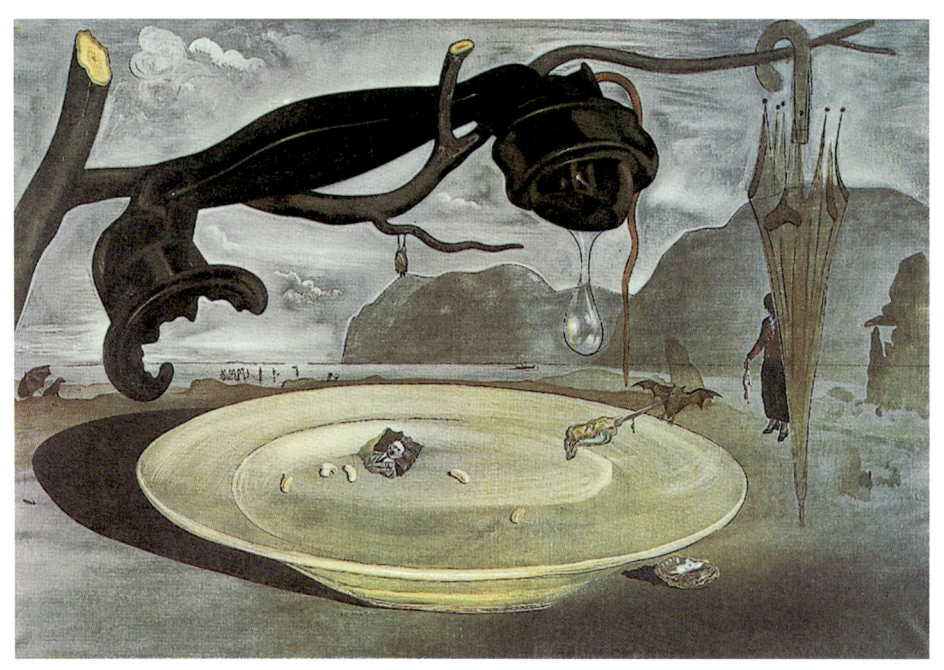

275
The Enigma of Hitler
1939
Oil on canvas, 95 × 141 cm
Museo Nacional Centro de Arte Reina Sofía, Madrid

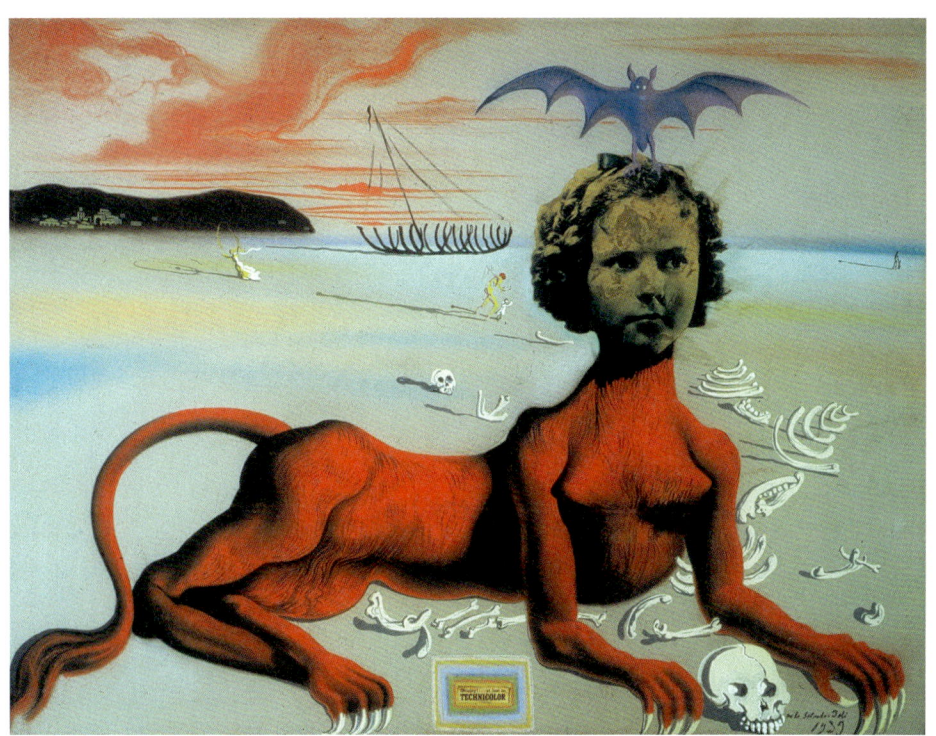

276
Shirley Temple, the Youngest, Most Sacred Monster of the Cinema in Her Time
1939
Gouache, pastel and collage on cardboard, 75 × 100 cm
Museum Boijmans Van Beuningen, Rotterdam

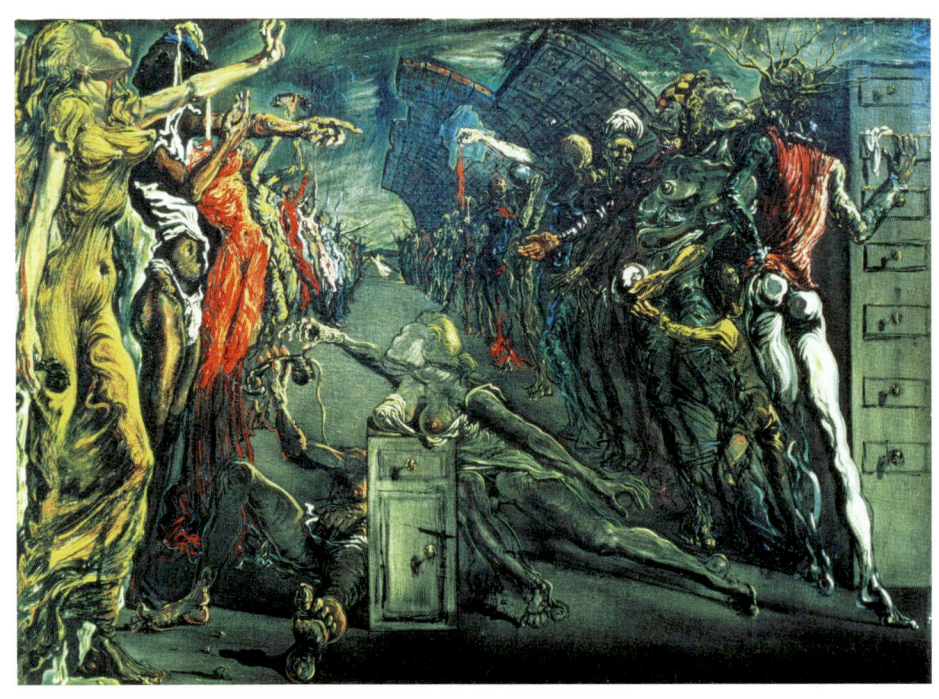

277
Palladio's corridor of dramatic disguise
1938
Oil on canvas, 73 × 104 cm
Private collection

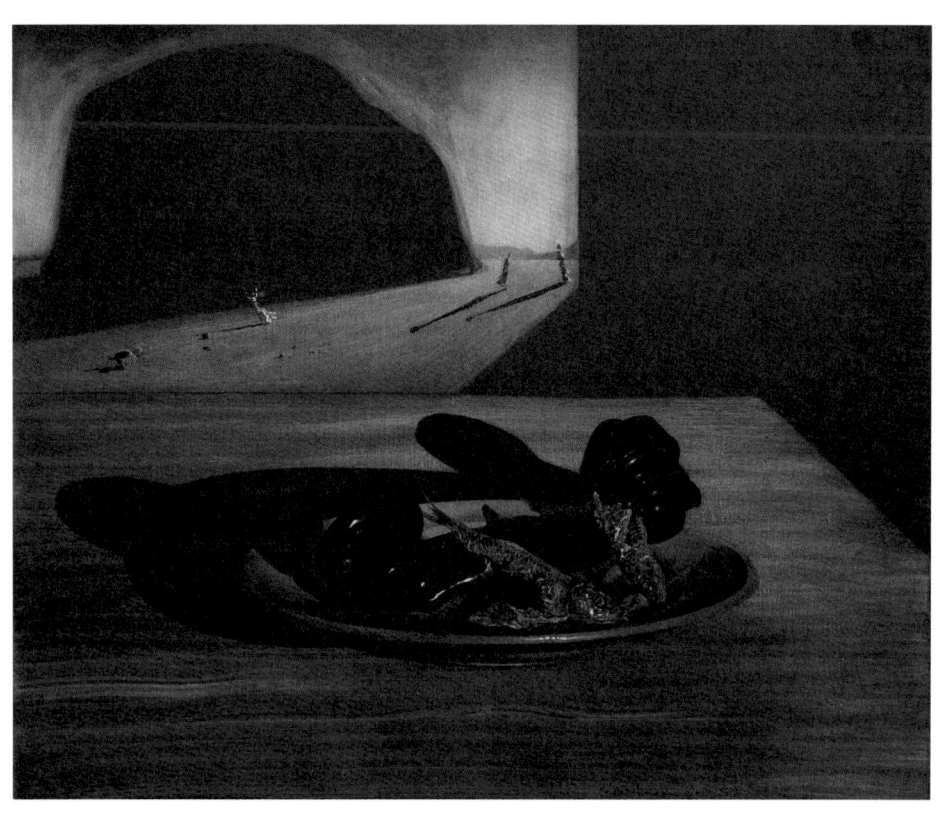

278
Telephone in a Dish with Three Grilled Sardines
1939
Oil on canvas, 45.7 × 54.9 cm
The Dalí Museum, St. Petersburg, Florida

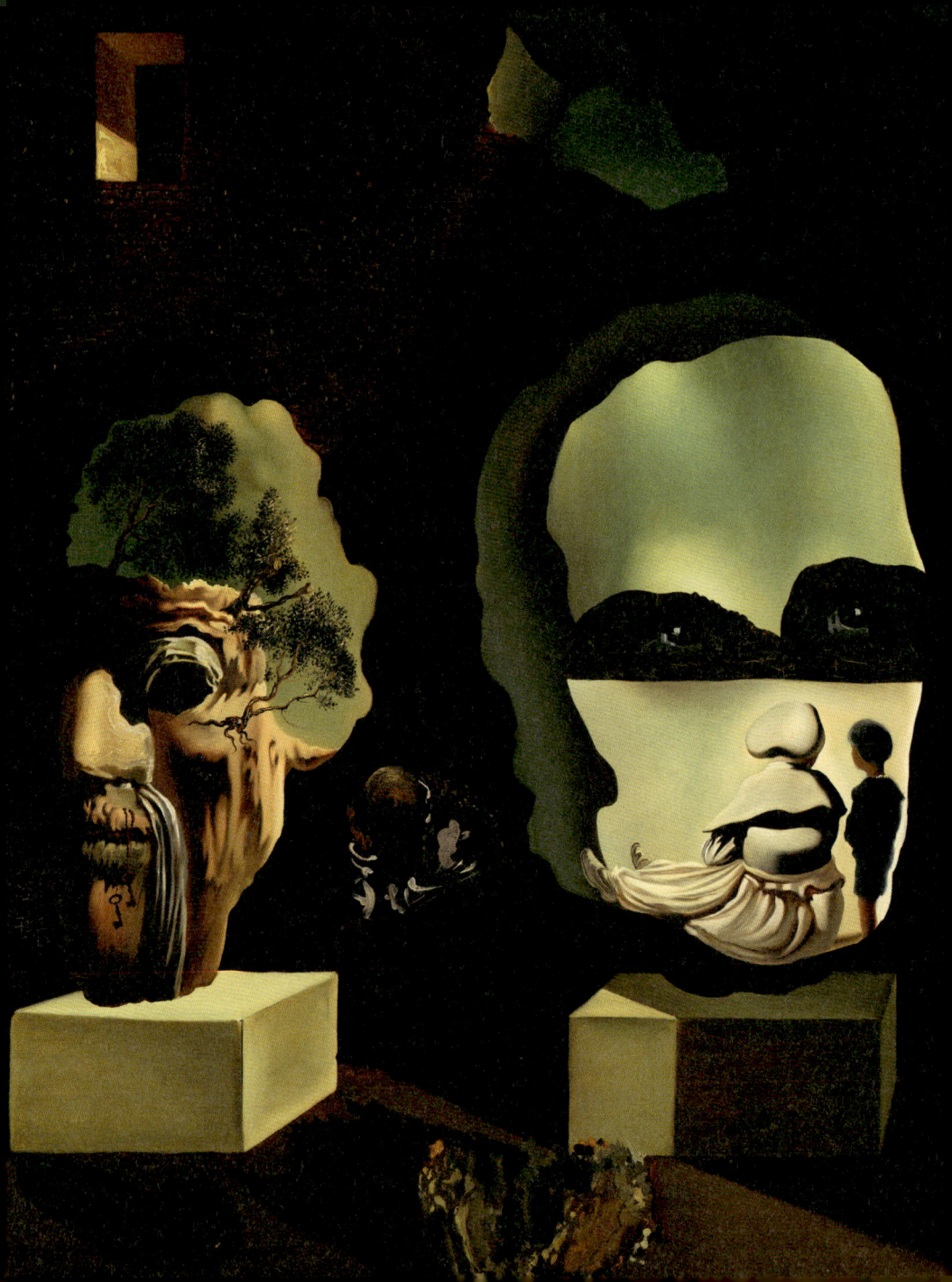

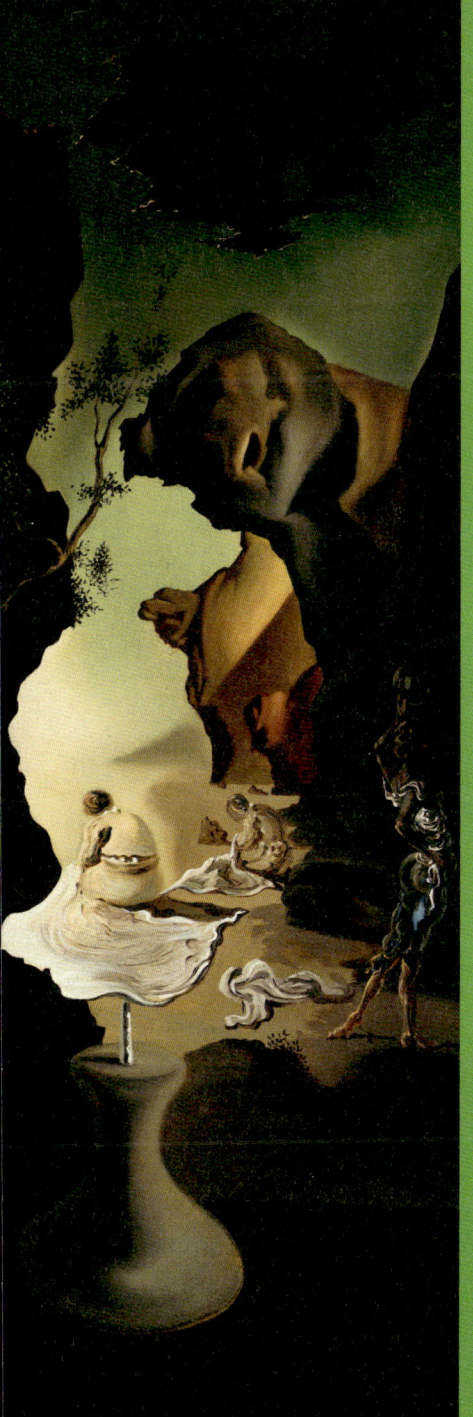

Dalí in America

1940–1948

Due to the German invasion of France in May 1940, Dalí arrived in the United States of America in August, where he would stay until 1948. His principal base in the US was New York, though he also spent time in California. This period in Dalí's life and work would prove decisive in that it consolidated his image in the public eye, which due to his exhibitions and public antics during the 1930s was already significantly visible. It also positioned him as a key figure in European art, despite his earlier ruptures with Breton and the Surrealist group. Indeed, in presenting himself to the American audience as the embodiment of Surrealism, Dalí effectively upstaged the official members of the group. Many of them were also in exile in America, but their lack of English meant they were less visible to the American public.

Soon after his arrival, Dalí was invited to join the American writer Caresse Crosby (1892–1970) in her estate in Hampton Manor in Virginia. Once there, he set to work painting, as well as writing his autobiography. His first painting executed in the US was titled *Daddy Longlegs of the Evening – Hope!* (1940) [279], a translation from the more poetic French expression: 'araignée du soir – espoir', which translates as 'spider in the evening, hope' and denotes the superstition that to see a spider in the evening is a sign of good luck. The painting is a complex allegory, using recognisable images represented in a combination of both hard and soft forms. The cannon and the horse, both symbols of war, are clearly defined, while the lower part of the statue of *The Winged Victory of Samothrace*, the Ancient Greek sculpture representing the goddess Niké, and the female nude that is draped around the barren tree are rendered as though made of soft, pliable materials. Furthermore, the lower body of the female figure blends into an amorphous, amoeba-like head that can be identified as a self-portrait of the artist, as he had also included this detail in paintings from the 1930s, including *The Persistence of Memory* (1931) [142]. In the foreground, a winged cupid, covering its eyes, is witness to this bizarre scene – a painting that is a highly subjective and ambiguous reaction to the War, in that it is far from sociological or descriptive and full of symbolism that points to Dalí's personal mythology.

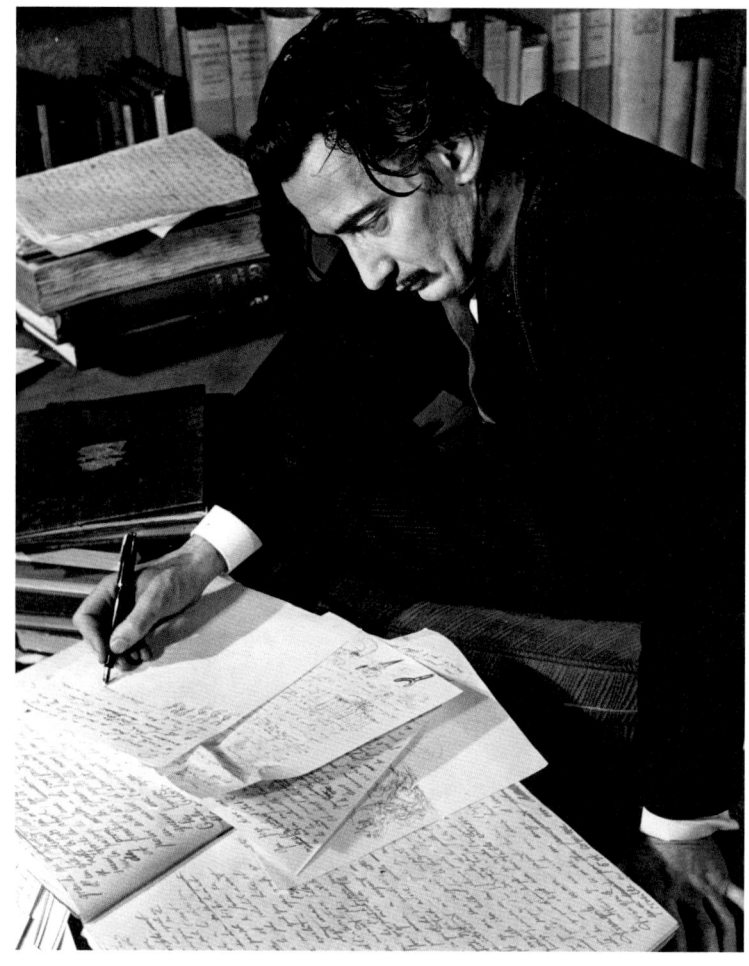

Eric Schaal (photographer), Dalí writing his autobiography *The Secret Life of Salvador Dalí* in Hampton Manor, Virginia, 1941.

In 1941, the art dealer Julien Levy (1906–1981) gave Dalí another important solo exhibition at his gallery in New York, which later travelled to Chicago and Los Angeles, and included *Daddy Longlegs of the Evening – Hope!* as well as the more controversial and partially finished *Sketch for the Portrait of His Excellency Don Juan Cardenas, Spanish Ambassador* (c. 1943). In the catalogue to the exhibition Dalí proclaimed his desire 'TO BECOME CLASSIC.' This work and Dalí's new discourse provoked a strong reaction from the exiled group of Surrealists, including Breton and the Greek-American poet Nicolas Calas (1907–1988), the latter of whom denounced Dalí in a text entitled *Anti-Surrealist Dalí*. Dalí was particularly visible in 1941, as the Museum of Modern Art in New York gave him a monographic retrospective, which included many important works from the 1930s to 1941, and thus offered the viewer a complete picture of Dalí as an artist. Extraordinarily, the exhibition was presented alongside a parallel retrospective of Miró. The Dalí exhibition attracted much attention, and in some ways the parallel exhibitions presented two alternate interpretations of Surrealism. It is likely that younger American artists, including Jackson Pollock (1912–1956), saw both exhibitions. Surrealists in exile, such as Masson, found Dalí's constant public visibility irritating, an attitude that the French painter expressed in his personal correspondence.

The publication of Dalí's *The Secret Life of Salvador Dalí* (1942) continued to position Dalí in the public eye. The book was a sort of tell-all autobiography presented in a highly exaggerated manner with an extravagant use of language. It revealed much to a fascinated public and prompted numerous reviews in the press. Moreover, it was within this written work that Dalí reinforced his new direction as simultaneously representing Surrealism and as embodying a return to tradition, by which he meant the tradition of the Old Masters. 'Surrealism' he wrote, 'was to be more and more identified with me, and with me only,' and, 'I believed only in the supreme reality of tradition.' In conclusion, he proposed the idea of what he called 'RENAISSANCE' as a solution to the conflict between tradition and revolution.

Dalí in America

Dalí's next important solo show was at Knoedler Gallery in New York, from April to May 1943. In this exhibition he showcased his new Classical approach to both drawing and painting. To reinforce this return to Classicism, he made a series of new, highly-finished presentation drawings, which were reproduced in the first section of the Knoedler catalogue, preceding images of the paintings themselves, an editorial choice that asserted his idea that drawing was the foundation of painting. In the catalogue essay, 'Dalí to the Reader,' he wrote, 'In the domain of drawing, my whole ambition is to rediscover the tradition of the old masters.' His text, as well as the images in the exhibition, evoked both the Renaissance and what he called the 'poetry of America.' While the paintings were mostly portraits, *"Geopoliticus" child watching the birth of the new man* (1943) [303] can be read as a representation of the growing importance of American culture prophesied by Dalí. The exhibition also included the finished version of Dalí's portrait *His Excellency Don Juan Cardenas, Spanish Ambassador* (c. 1943) [301], Spain's official diplomatic representative in the US. Breton, irritated by both Dalí's intense public presence and specifically with this painting, which he considered a statement of support for the Spanish dictator Francisco Franco (1892–1975), denounced Dalí in a lecture that he gave at Yale University, which was published in the Surrealist review *VVV*: 'La Situation du Surréalisme entre Les Deux Guerres.' It was in this lecture that Breton labelled Dalí 'Avida Dollars' – an anagrammatic nickname that suggested love of money. Breton's comments about Dalí seem to have been timed to anticipate the Knoedler exhibition, as Breton was already aware of the earlier unfinished version of the painting, however the text's impact remained inconsequential to the American audience. Quite why Dalí painted this portrait remains unclear, yet, as the Collection Manager, Librarian and Archivist of The Dalí Museum, Florida, Shaina Harkness has suggested in an article on 'Dalí in Virginia', his motive may have been more mundane, as it is likely that the Spanish Ambassador had helped Dalí in obtaining a visa and had possibly known Dalí for several years. From this point onwards, Dalí embraced

Breton's monicker, and the nickname did nothing more than contribute to Dalí's ever-growing and carefully constructed public persona.

In 1944 Dalí published his novel *Hidden Faces*, a work set in the period ranging from 1934 and projecting into the future to the closing days of World War II, which at the time of publication was ongoing. The novel recounts a group of decadent aristocrats removed from the tumult of the world and preoccupied with their rural estate and cork groves, and concludes, after a reflection on the Dutch painter Johannes Vermeer's (1632–1675) work *The Art of Painting* (c. 1666–68), with a highly speculative account of Hitler's death, which had not occurred at the time of writing. Though Dalí's narrative could be considered presumptuous, given that the war still raged on, the book was received with consternation. Most critics did not understand the work. One critic labelled its characters 'decadent' and called for it to be 'censored' and described it as 'an aborted novel.' Another critic seemed to reject the content, but saw merit in the writing as well as a kind of literary fascination, even describing it as 'remarkably interesting.' In the 1943 catalogue for his exhibition at Knoedler Gallery, Dalí suggested that he paid homage to 'the literary tradition of Balzac' in the novel. However, given that American newspaper reviewers were less than familiar with French literature, it appears that any stylistic evocations to French literary tradition were lost on them.

While Dalí devoted great effort to other forms of cultural activity in the 1940s, including opera and film set design, he continued to paint. His 1945 solo exhibition at Bignou Gallery in New York focused on his new Classical direction. In the foreword to the exhibition catalogue Dalí declared: 'One day it will be discovered that painting was already discovered by Raphael and Vermeer.' The exhibition included paintings, both on canvas and panel, of a highly finished and almost academic quality at odds with avant-garde experimentation. Dalí also included works like *The Apotheosis of Homer (Diurnal Dream of Gala)* (c. 1945) [315]; *My Wife, Nude, Contemplating*

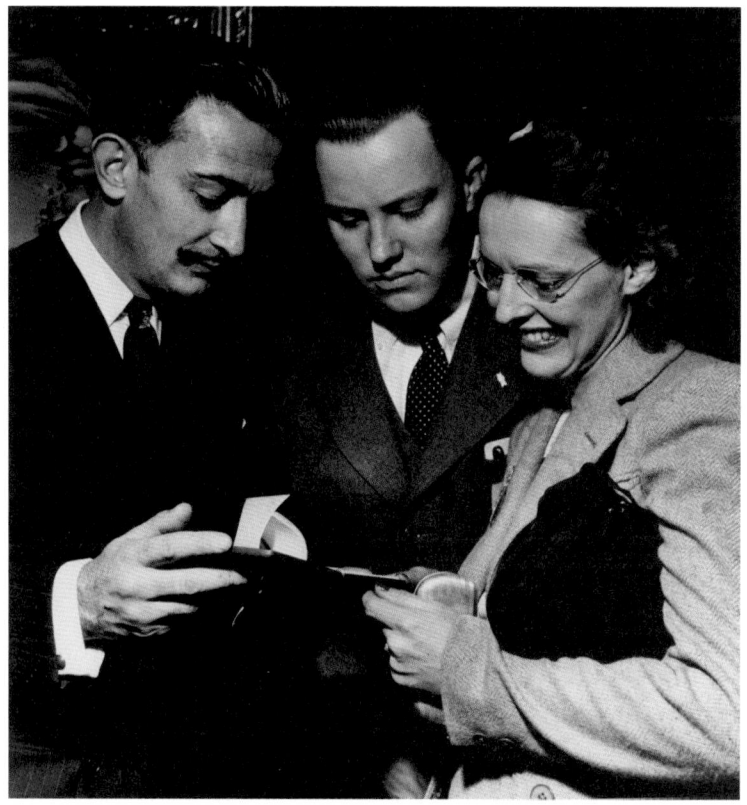

Dalí with philanthropists Albert Reynolds Morse and Eleanor Reese Morse, who would later found the Salvador Dalí Museum in St. Petersburg, Florida, US, at the Knoedler Gallery, New York, 1943. Collection of The Dalí Museum.

Her Own Flesh Becoming Stairs, Three Vertebrae of a Column, Sky and Architecture (1945) [320]; *Galarina* (1945) [314] and *The Resurrection of the Flesh* (c. 1940) in the catalogue, where the reproductions were accompanied by detailed explanations, which emphasised how long Dalí had worked on each piece and explained their symbolism.

Dalí was shifting to a radical affirmation of painting and the traditions of the past. This move represented a turn away from the developments of modern art understood in terms of formalism, abstraction and pure experimentation. When, in 1948, Dalí published *50 Secrets of Magic Craftsmanship*, a book based on the model of classical painting treatises, presented ostensibly as an instruction manual on painting, though full of extravagant remarks, he explained, 'Since this book is to be the book of the justice of painting, it will inevitably be cruel to modern painting.' In this book, Dalí seemed to be defending the tradition of Old Master painting understood as a form of thought, and was, as a consequence, expressing an implicit denunciation of modern art, which he presented as merely an empty and decorative formalism.

In the wake of World War II, Dalí was especially affected by the atomic bombing of Japan in August 1945. To his return to classicism, he added a fascination with modern physics in what he came to term 'Nuclear Mysticism.' His exhibition *New Paintings by Salvador Dalí*, which opened in November 1947 at Bignou Gallery in New York included works with titles such as *Leda Atomica* (1947–49) [334]; *One Second Before the Awakening from a Dream Provoked by the Flight of a Bee Around a Pomegranate* (c. 1944) [310]; *Portrait of Pablo Picasso in the Twenty-first Century* (1947) [330]; and *Three Sphinxes of Bikini* (1947); the latter referring to the controlled Atomic test explosions held from 1946 into the 1950s on Bikini Atoll in the Marshall Islands in the Northwestern Pacific Ocean. During this period, Dalí was also carefully planning his imminent return to Spain. As he explained in the catalogue to accompany his exhibition at Bignou Gallery, he needed four months to complete the still-unfinished *Leda Atomica,* after which he planned to depart immediately from New York carrying the painting 'in extremely light but adroitly constructed cases,' to be opened only on his arrival in Europe.

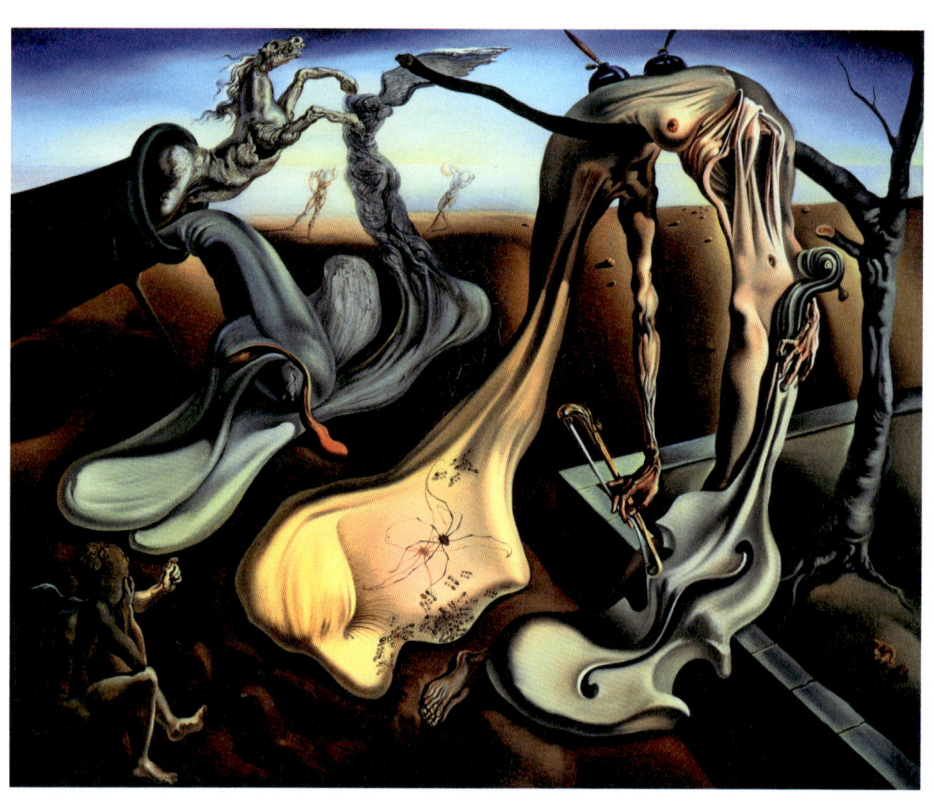

279
Daddy Longlegs of the Evening – Hope!
1940
Oil on canvas, 40.5 × 50.8 cm
The Dalí Museum, St. Petersburg, Florida

Dalí in America

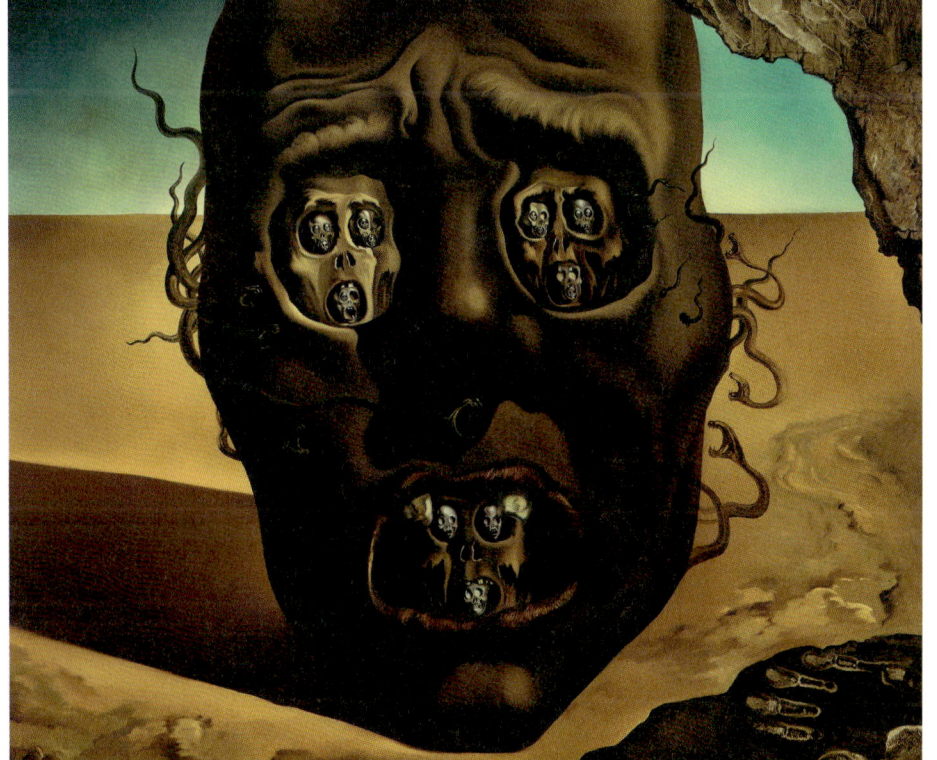

280
Visage of the War
1940
Oil on canvas, 64 × 79 cm
Museum Boijmans Van Beuningen, Rotterdam

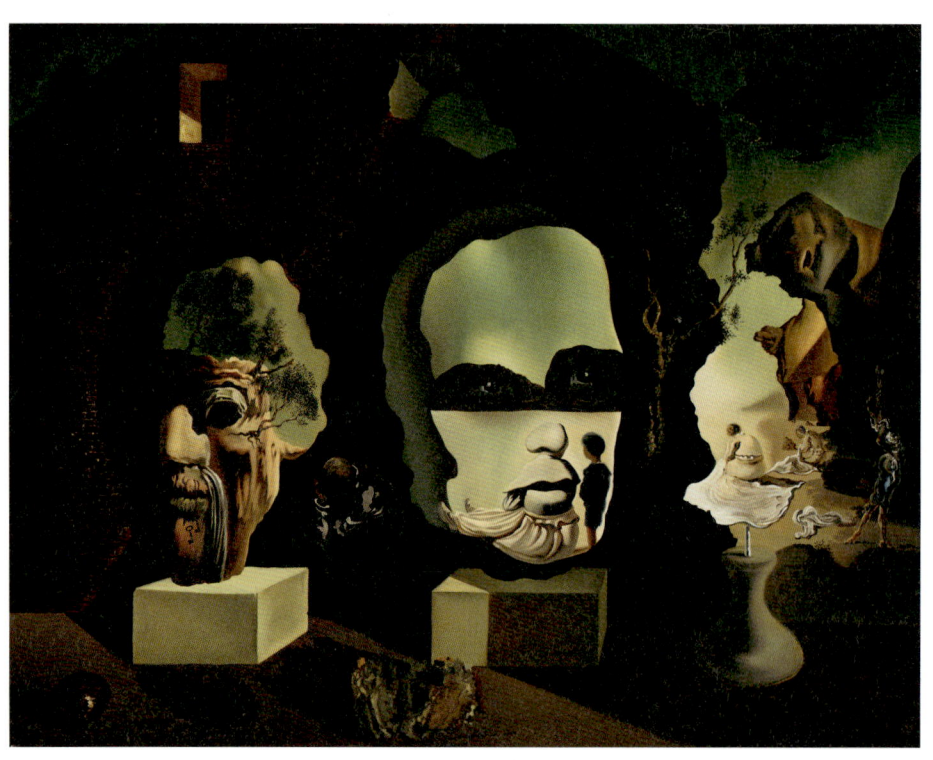

281
Old age, adolescence, infancy
1940
Oil on canvas, 50 × 65 cm
The Dalí Museum, St. Petersburg, Florida

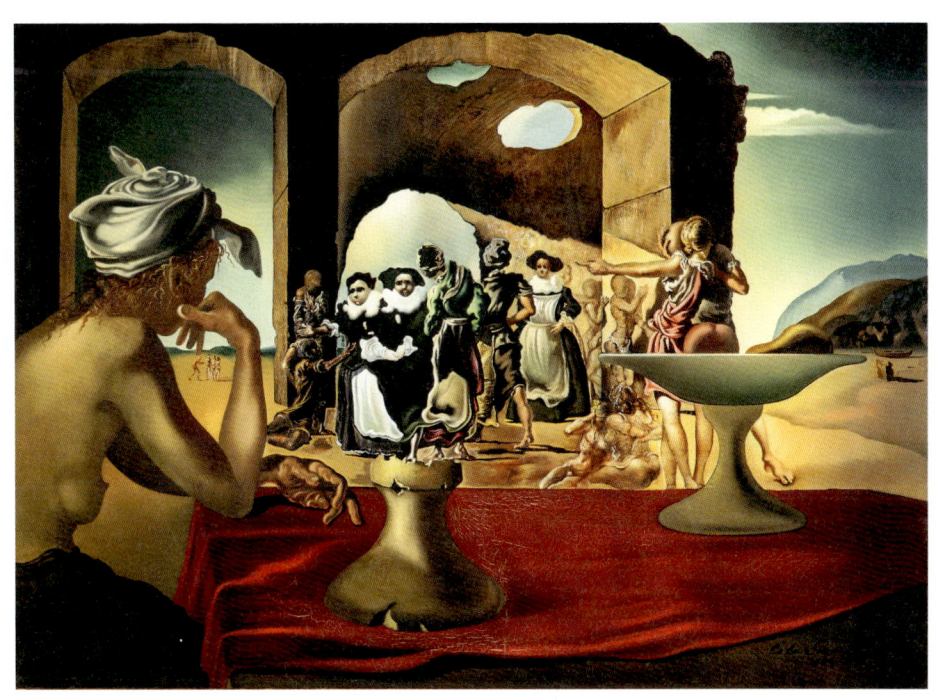

282
Slave market (with apparition of the invisible bust of Voltaire)
1940
Oil on canvas, 46.2 × 65.2 cm
The Dalí Museum, St. Petersburg, Florida

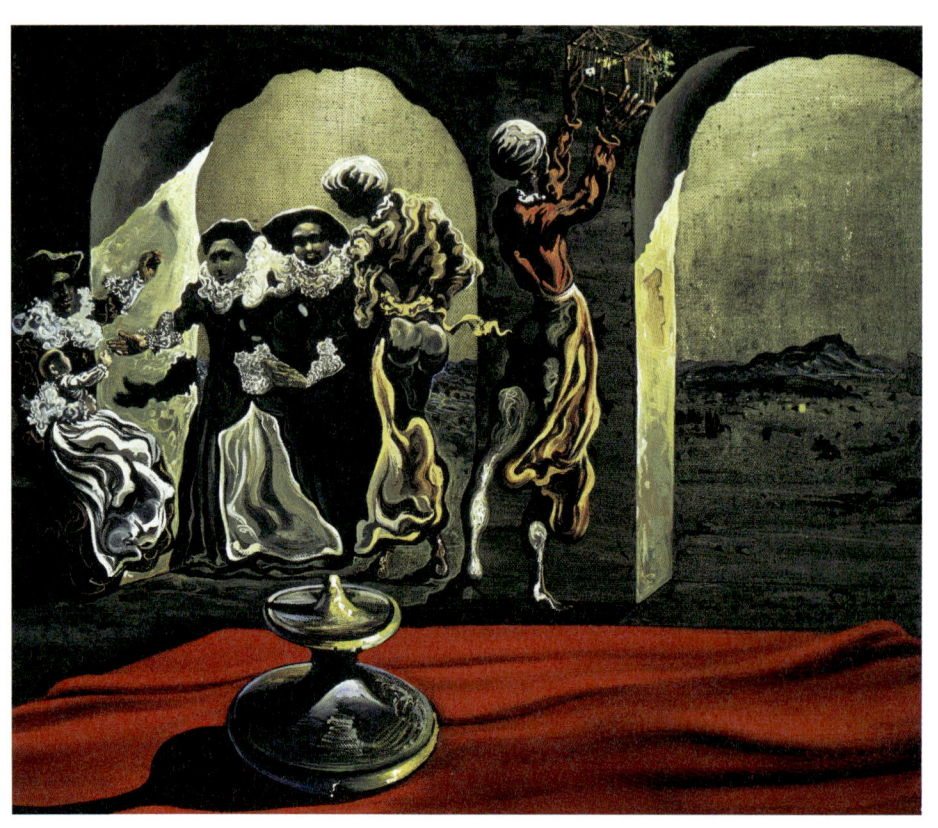

283
Bust of Voltaire
1941
Oil on canvas, 46.3 × 55.3 cm
The Dalí Museum, St. Petersburg, Florida

Dalí in America

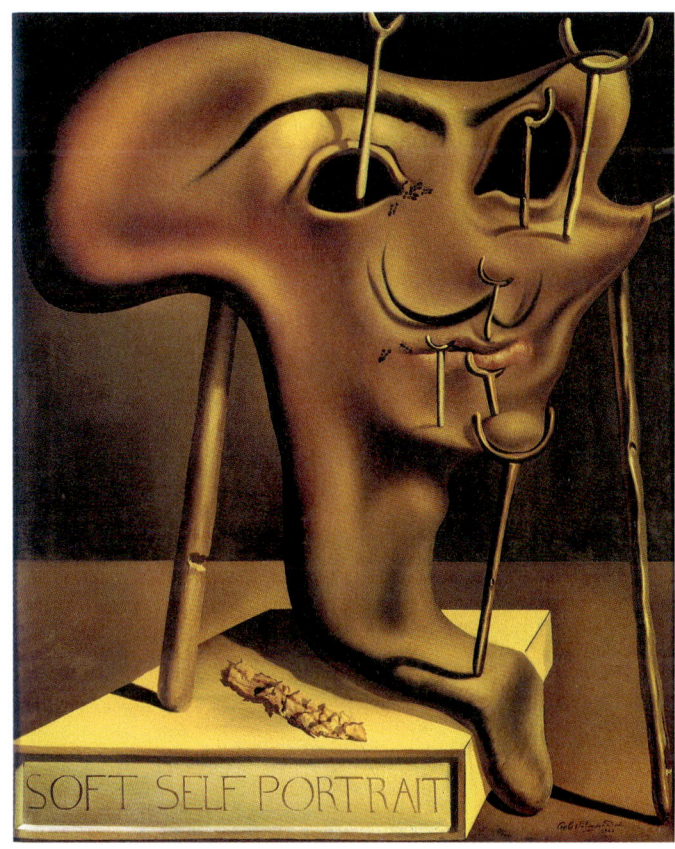

284
Soft self-portrait with grilled bacon
1941
Oil on canvas, 61 × 51 cm
Town Hall of Figueres, on permanent deposit at the Fundació Gala-Salvador Dalí, Figueres

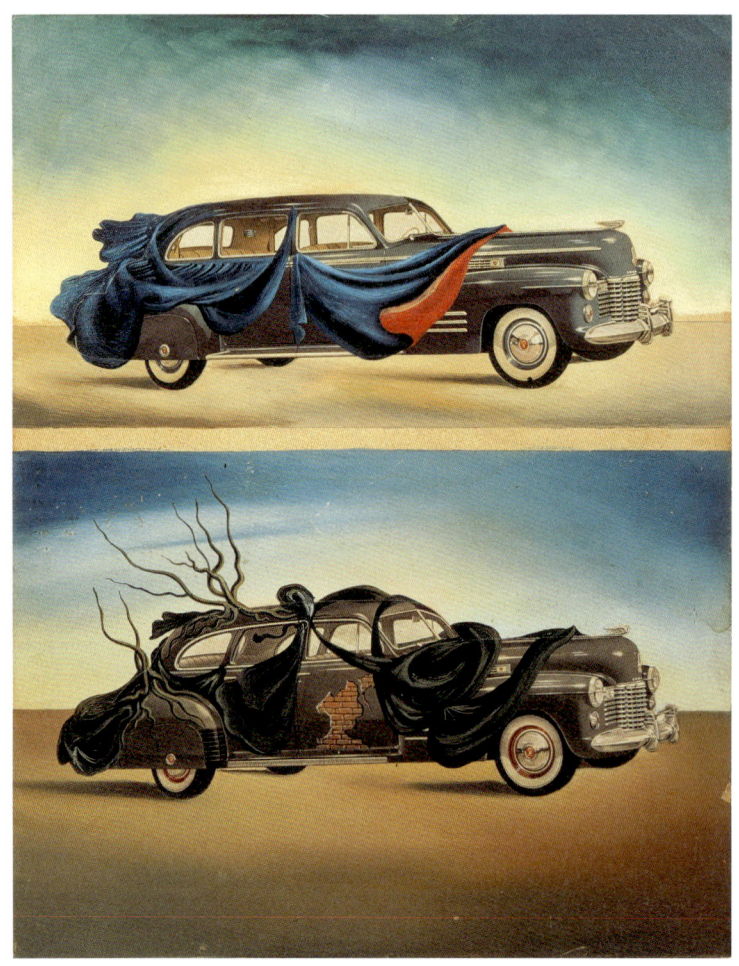

285
Untitled (Dressed Automobiles)
c. 1941
Oil and collage on cardboard, 49.9 × 39.4 cm
Town Hall of Figueres, on permanent deposit at the Fundació Gala-Salvador Dalí, Figueres

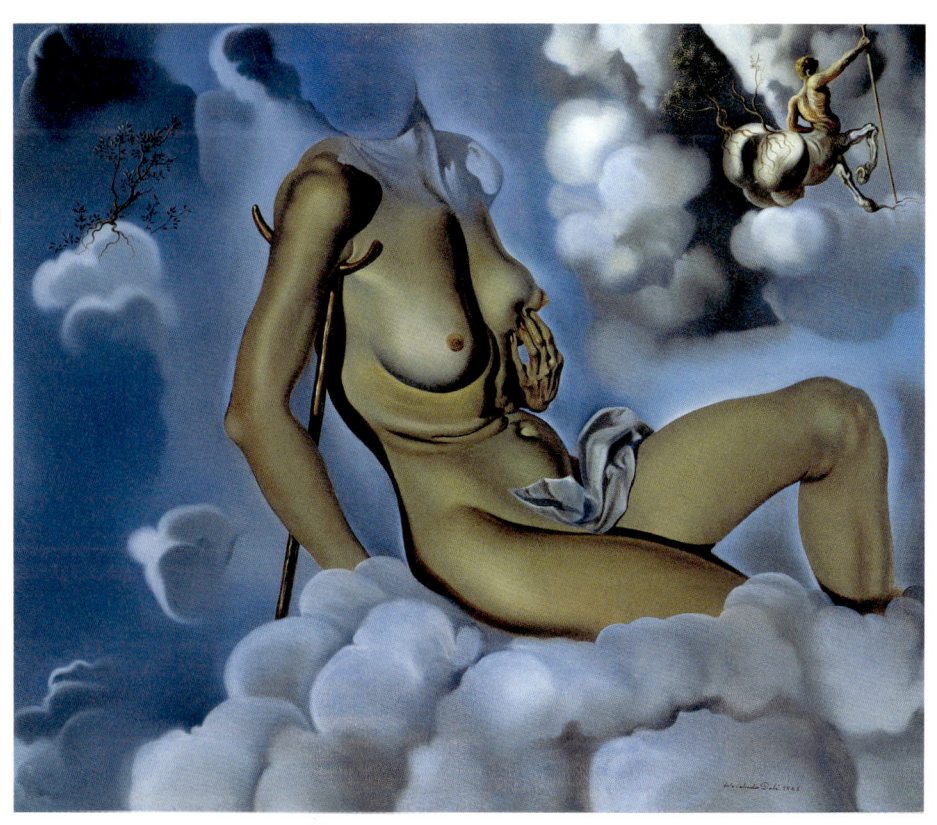

286
Honey is sweeter than blood
1941
Oil on canvas, 49.5 × 60 cm
The Santa Barbara Museum of Art, California

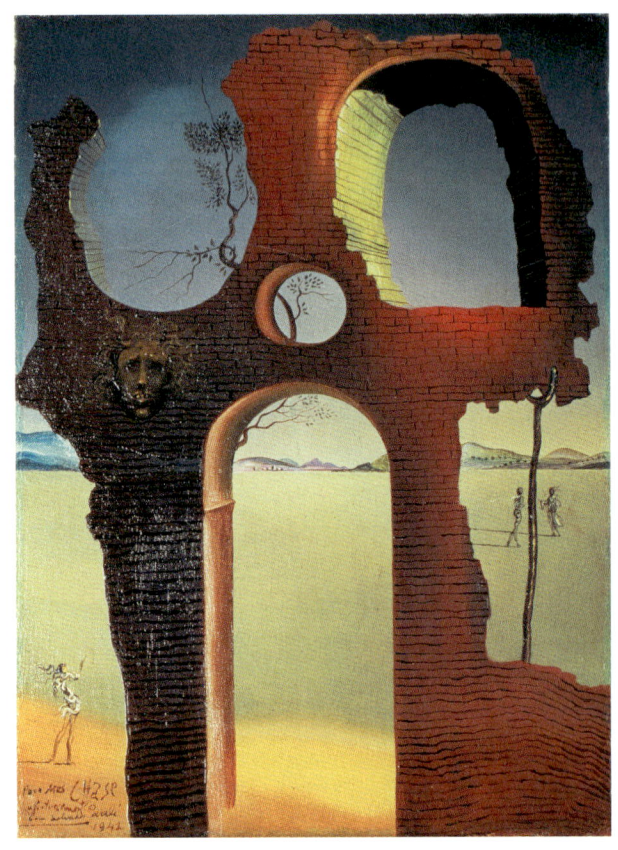

287
Untitled (Ruin with Head of Medusa and Landscape)
1941
Oil on canvas, 38 × 24.5 cm
Juan Abelló Gallo collection, Madrid

Dalí in America

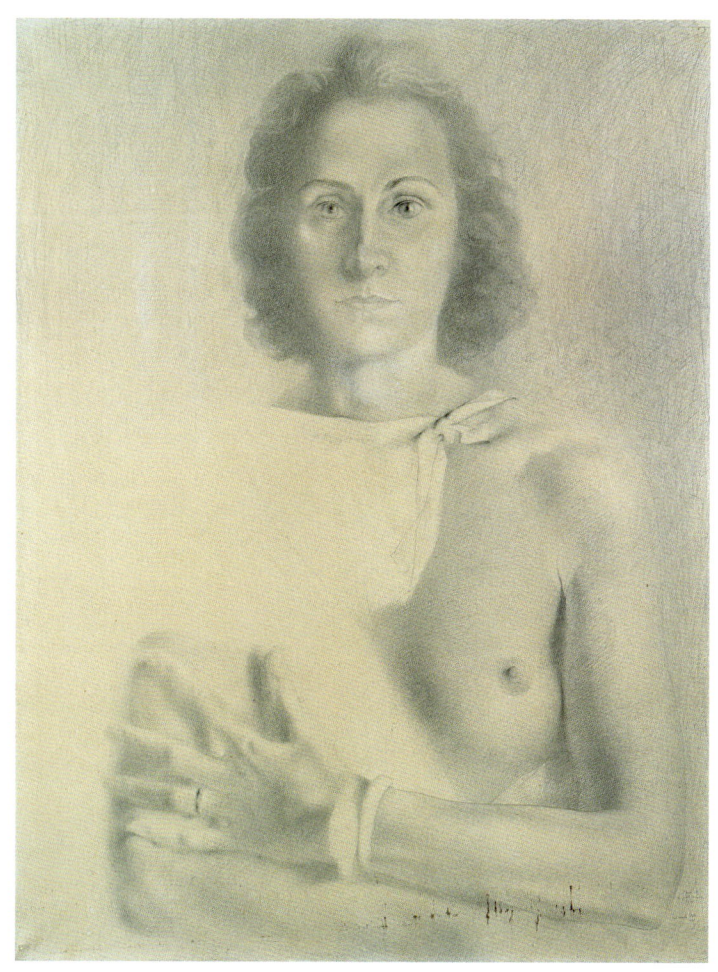

288
Portrait of Gala
1941
Pencil on paper, 63.9 × 49 cm
Museum Boijmans Van Beuningen, Rotterdam

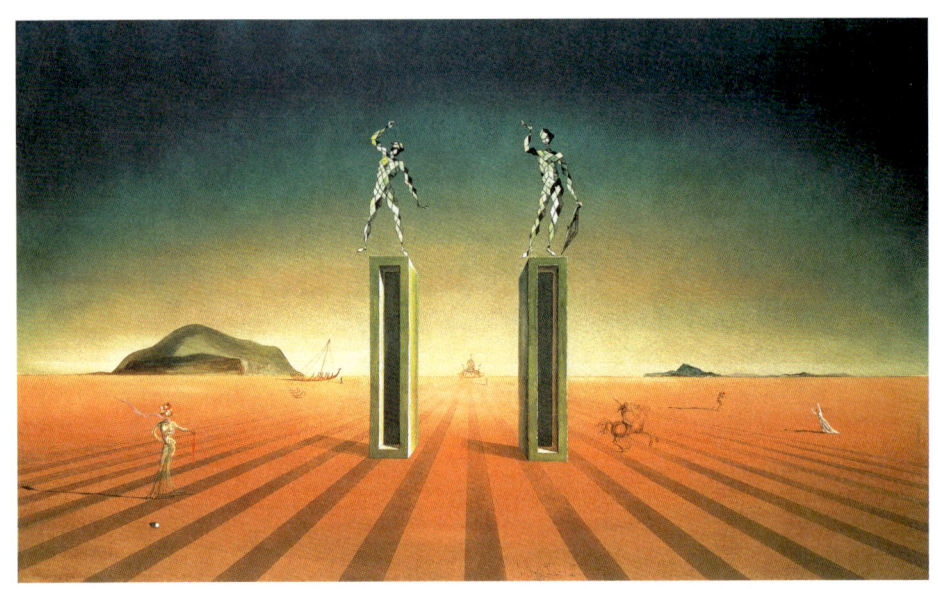

289
Untitled (Two Harlequins)
1942
Oil on canvas, 217 × 358 cm
Private collection

Dalí in America

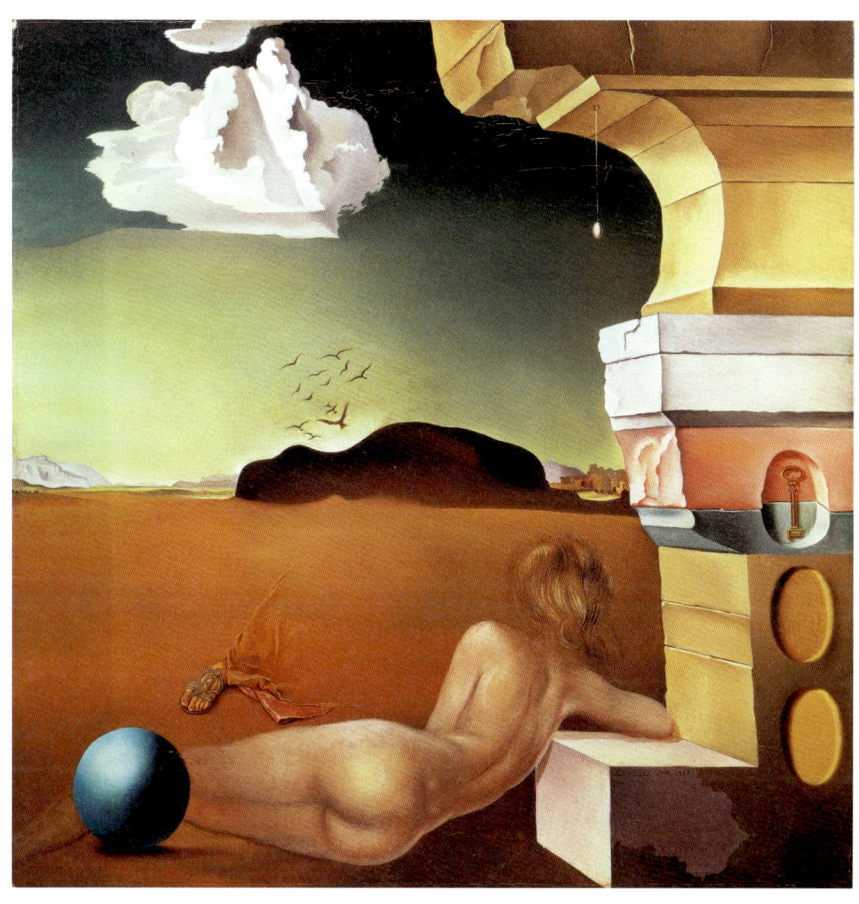

290
Nude on the Plain of Roses
1942
Oil on canvas, 50 × 50 cm
Private collection

Dalí in America

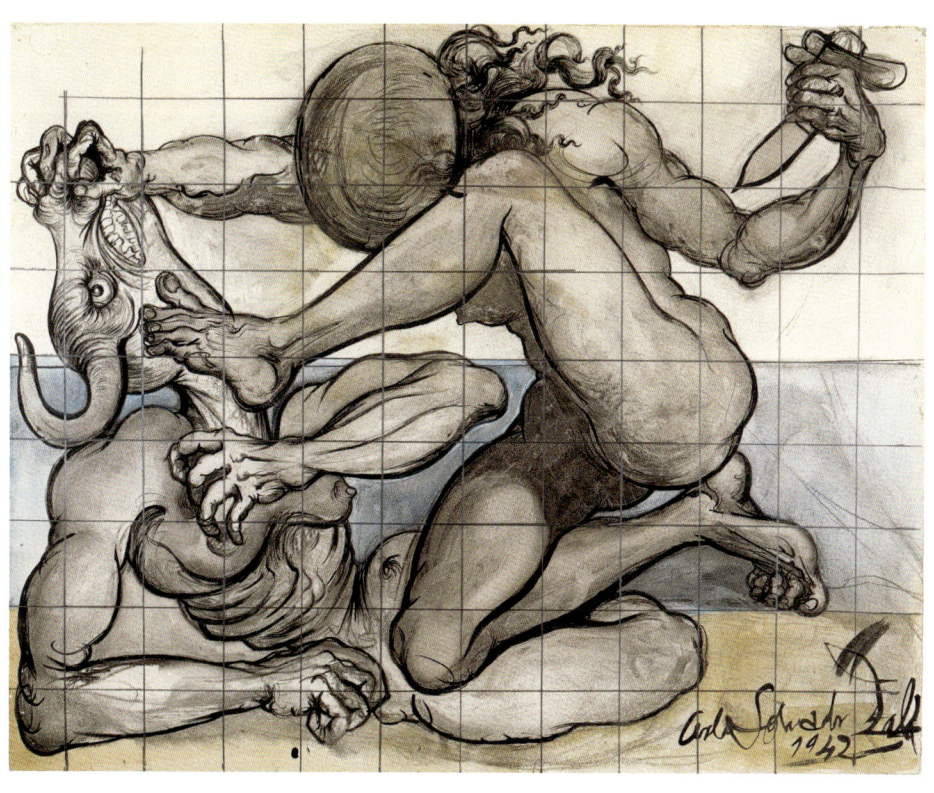

291
Study for the set of "Labyrinth" – Fighting the Minotaur
1942
Pencil, India ink, watercolour and gouache, 58.6 × 73.8 cm
Fundació Gala-Salvador Dalí, Figueres

1940–1948

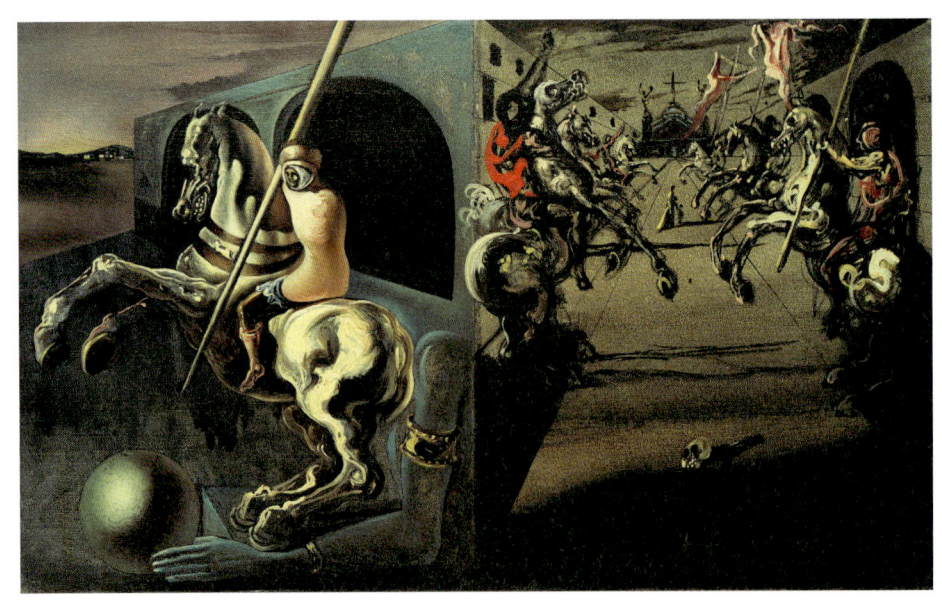

292
Project for "Romeo and Juliet"
1942
Oil on canvas, 31 × 51 cm
Private collection

Dalí in America

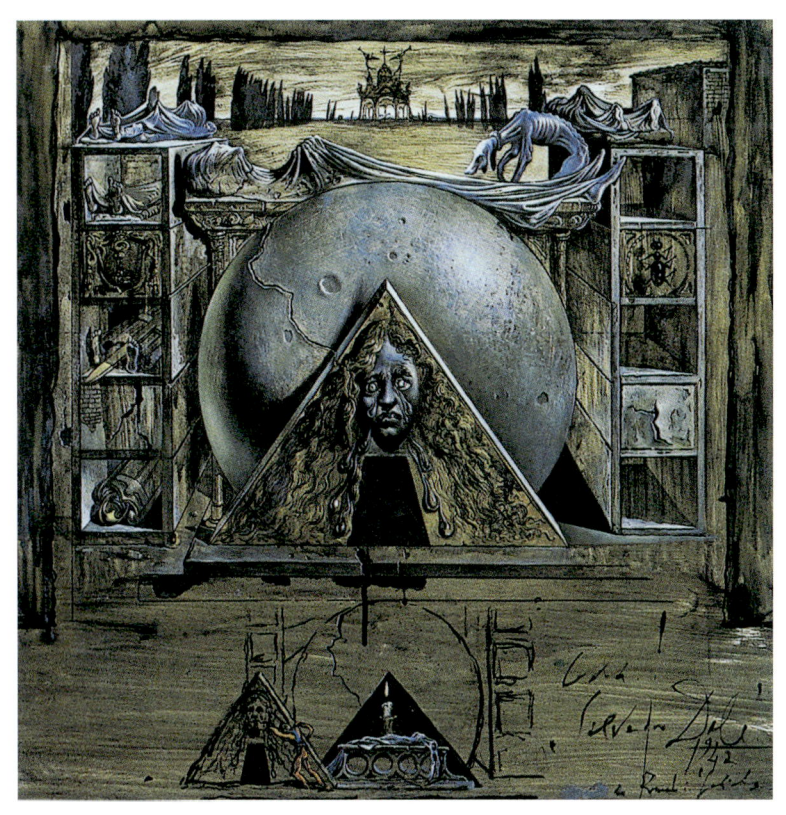

293
Project for "Romeo and Juliet"
1942
Oil on canvas, 50.7 × 50.7 cm
Private collection

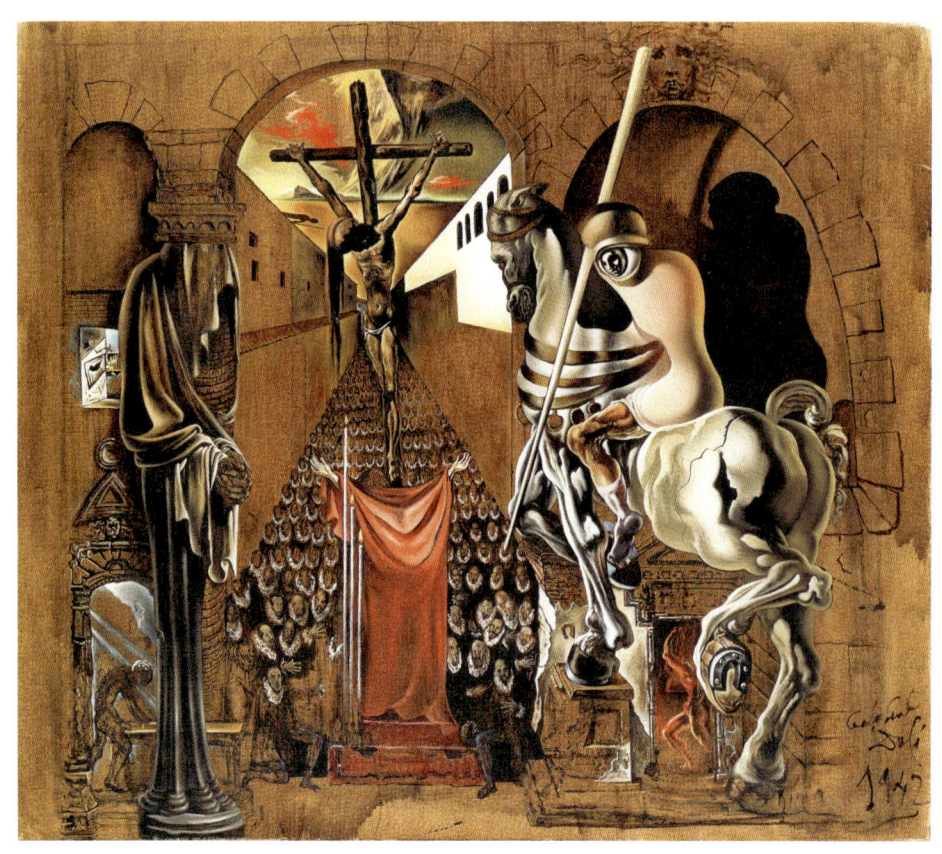

294
Project for "Romeo and Juliet"
1942
Oil on canvas, 69.4 × 79.4 cm
Pérez Simón Collection, Mexico

Dalí in America

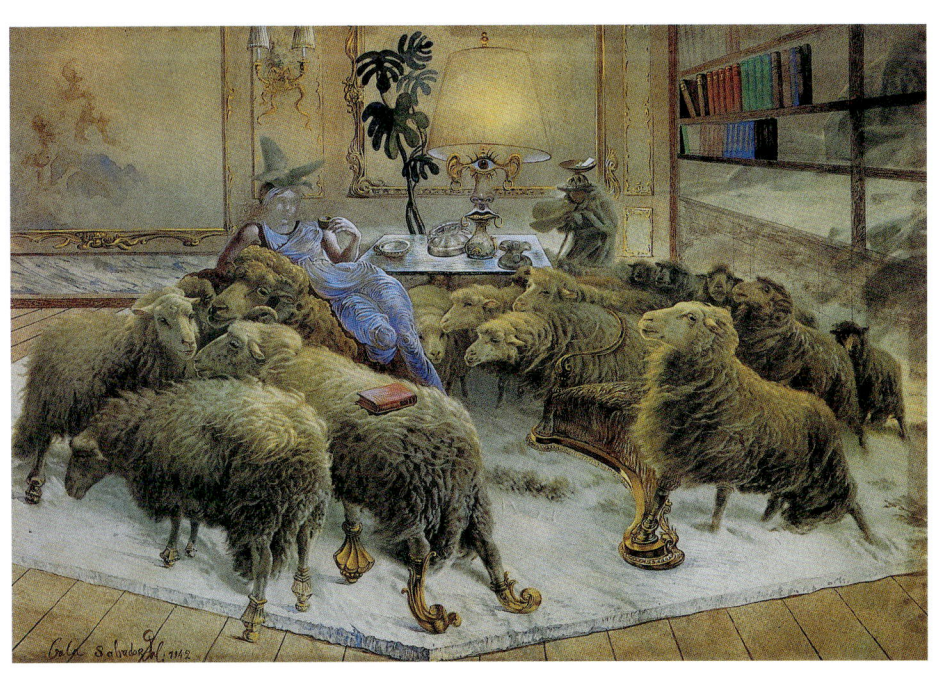

295
The Sheep (after Conversion)
1942
Watercolour and chromolithograph, 23 × 34 cm
The Dalí Museum, St. Petersburg, Florida

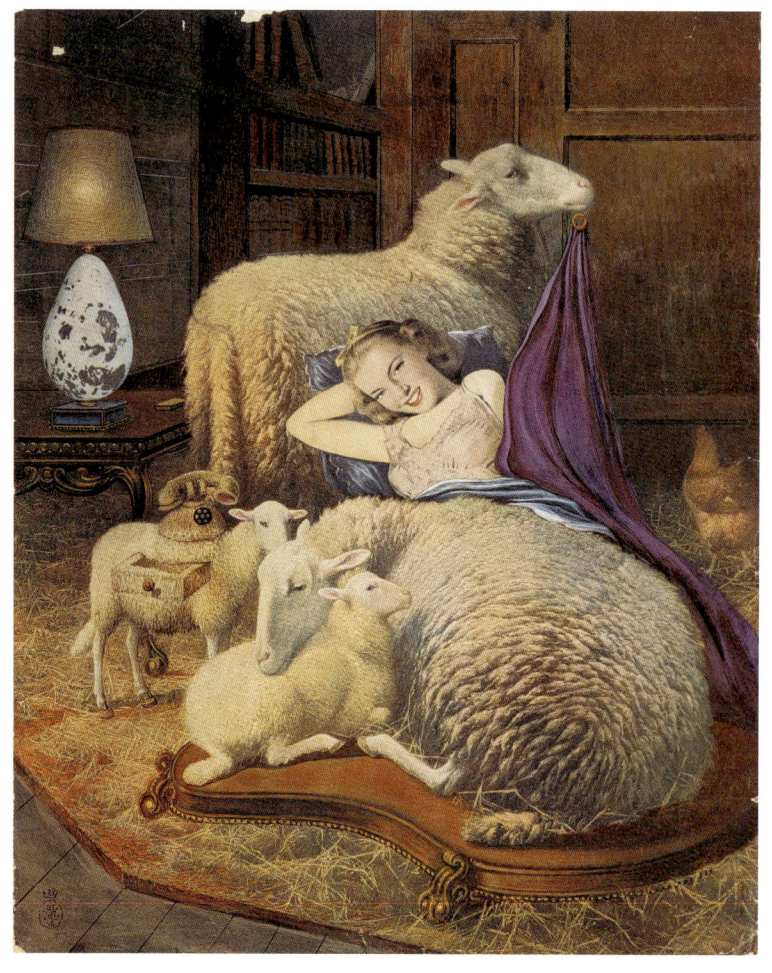

296
Design for the interior decoration of a Stable-Library
1942
Chrome overpainted with gouache and India ink, 51 × 45 cm
Fundació Gala-Salvador Dalí, Figueres

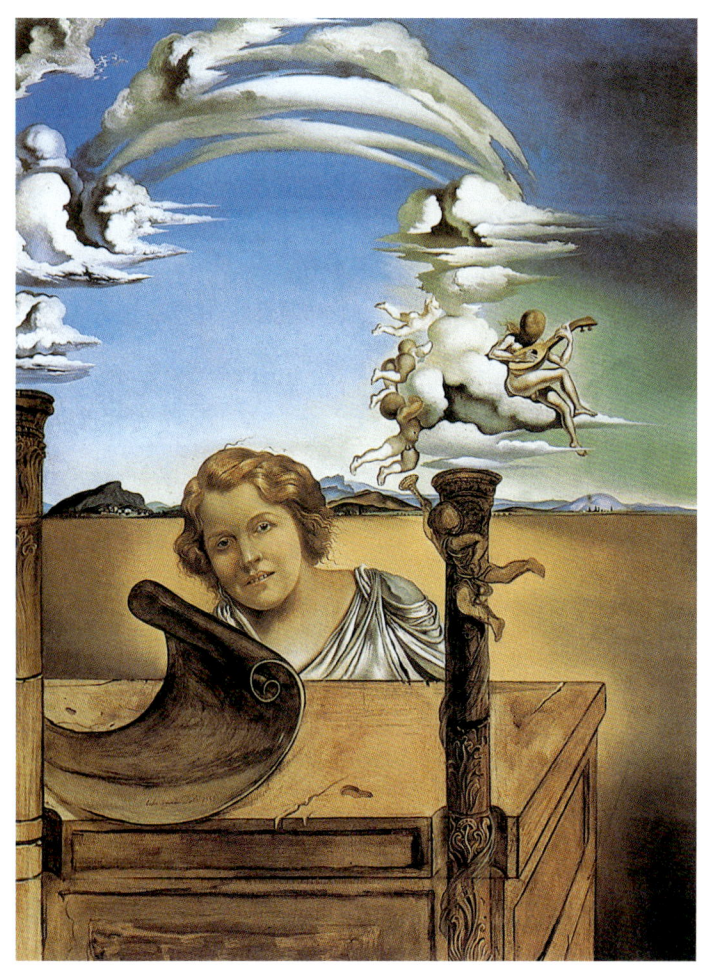

297
Mrs. Charles Swift
1942
Oil on canvas, 80 × 60 cm
Private collection

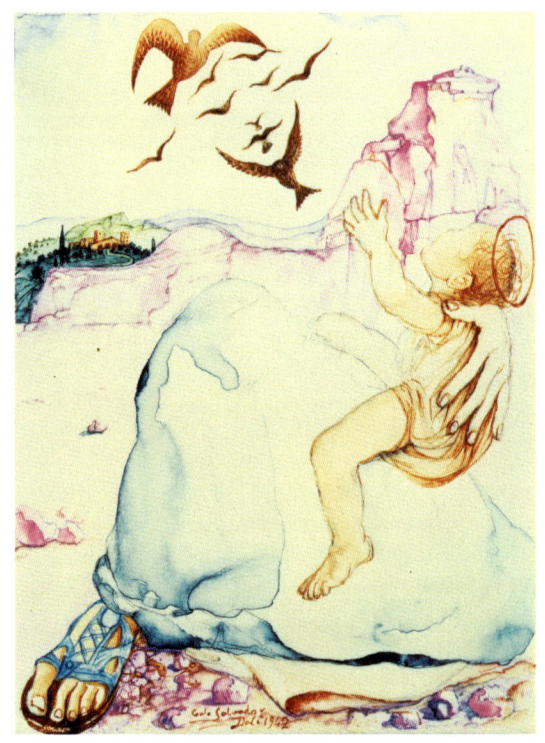

298
Virgin and child
1942
Watercolour on ivory, dimensions unknown
Private collection

Dalí in America

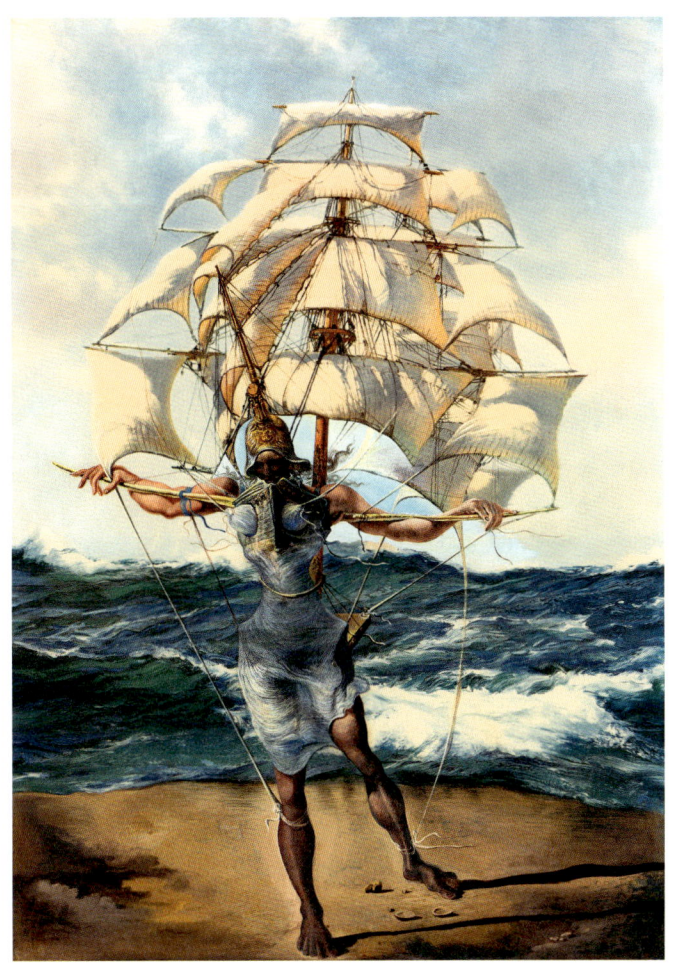

299
Costume for "Tristan Insane" – The Ship
1942–1943
Watercolour, 63 × 46 cm
The Dalí Museum, St. Petersburg, Florida

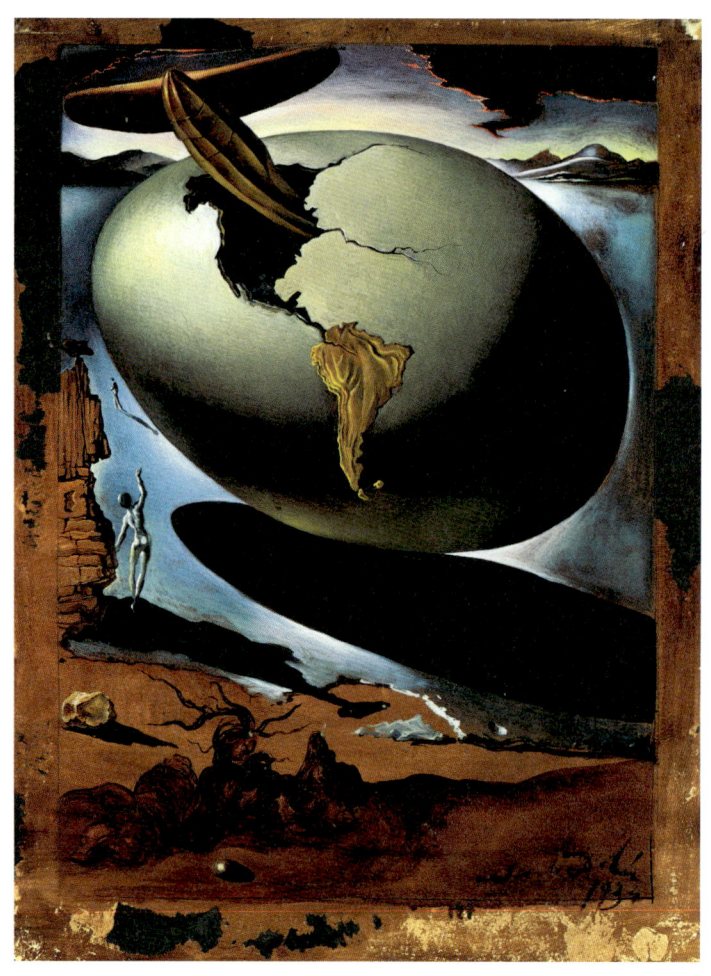

300
Allegory of an American Christmas
c. 1943 (erroneously signed 1934 by Dalí)
Oil on board, 66 × 55.5 cm
The Museum of Modern Art, Toyama Prefecture, Japan

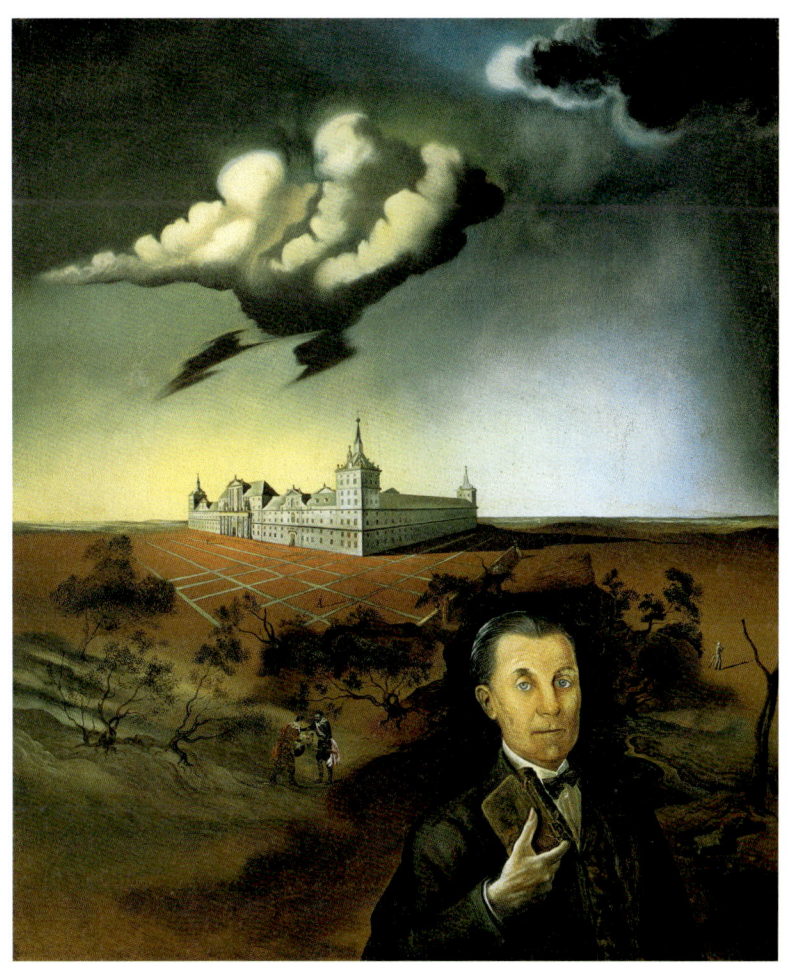

301
His Excellency Don Juan Cardenas, Spanish Ambassador
c. 1943
Oil on canvas, 61.3 × 50.8 cm
Private collection

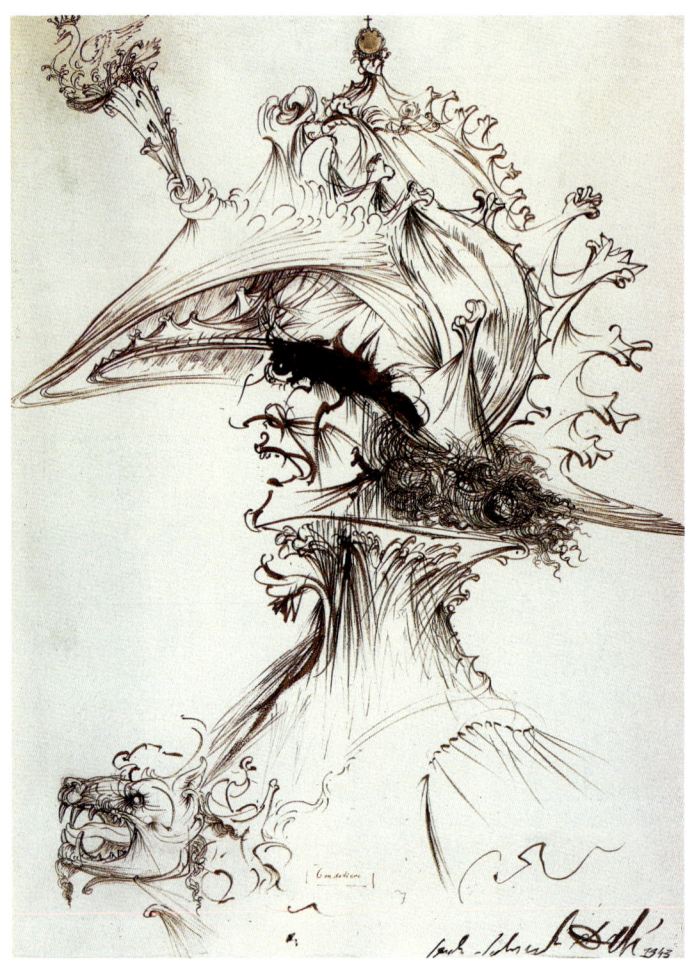

302
Condottiere (Self-Portrait as Condottiere)
1943
India ink on white paper, 76.6 × 55.8 cm
Private collection

Dalí in America

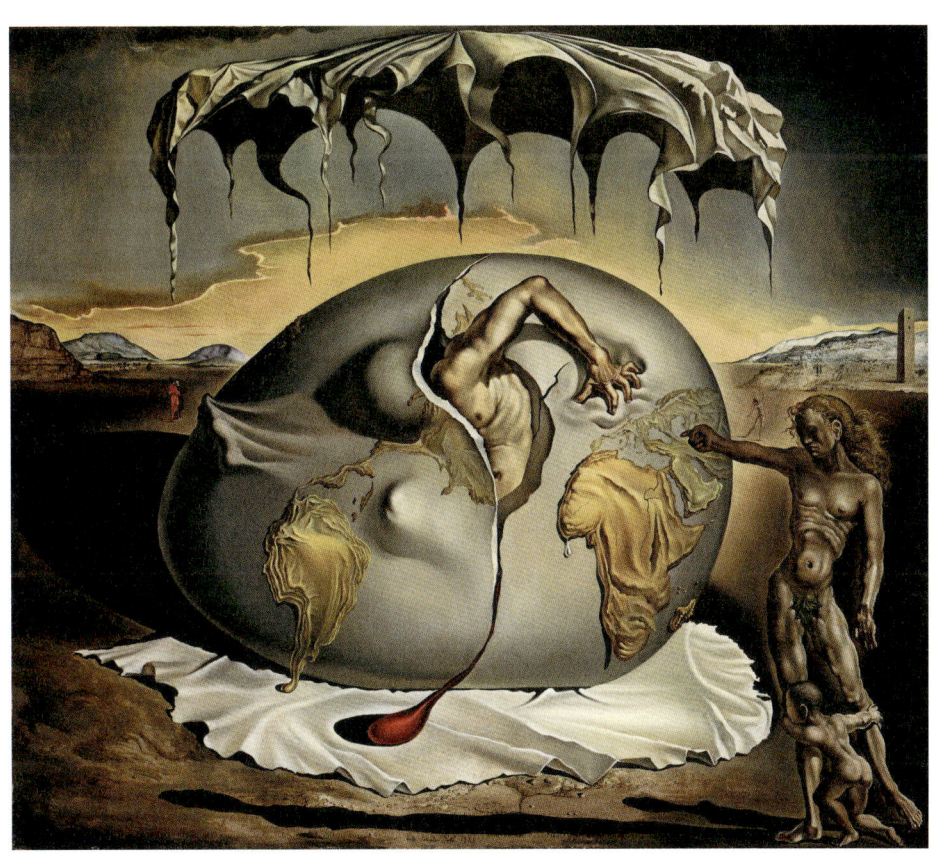

303
"Geopoliticus" child watching the birth of the new man
1943
Oil on canvas, 44.5 × 52 cm
The Dalí Museum, St. Petersburg, Florida

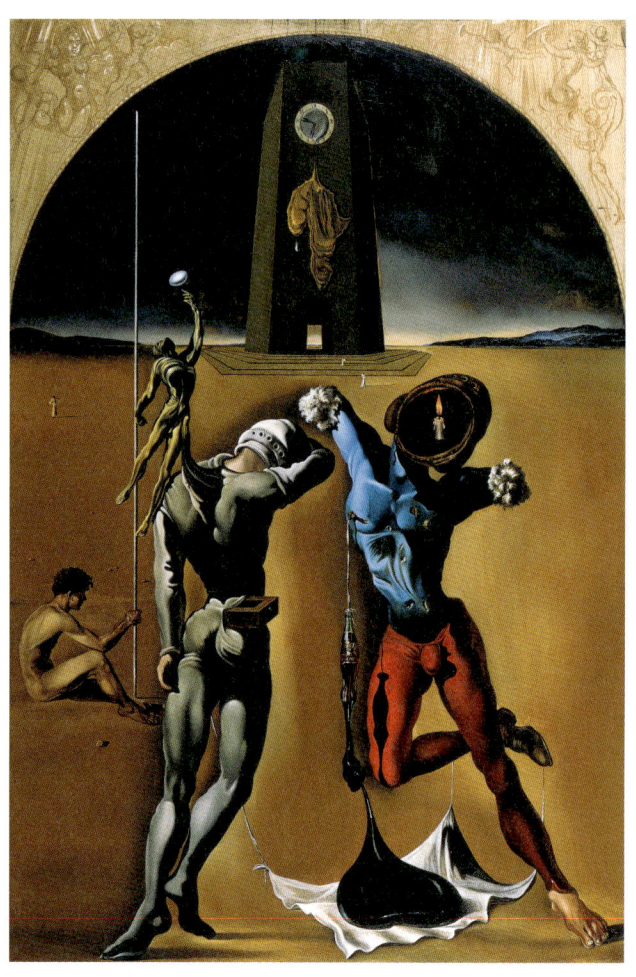

304
Poetry of America
1943
Oil on canvas, 116 × 79 cm
Town Hall of Figueres, on permanent deposit at the Fundació Gala-Salvador Dalí, Figueres

Dalí in America

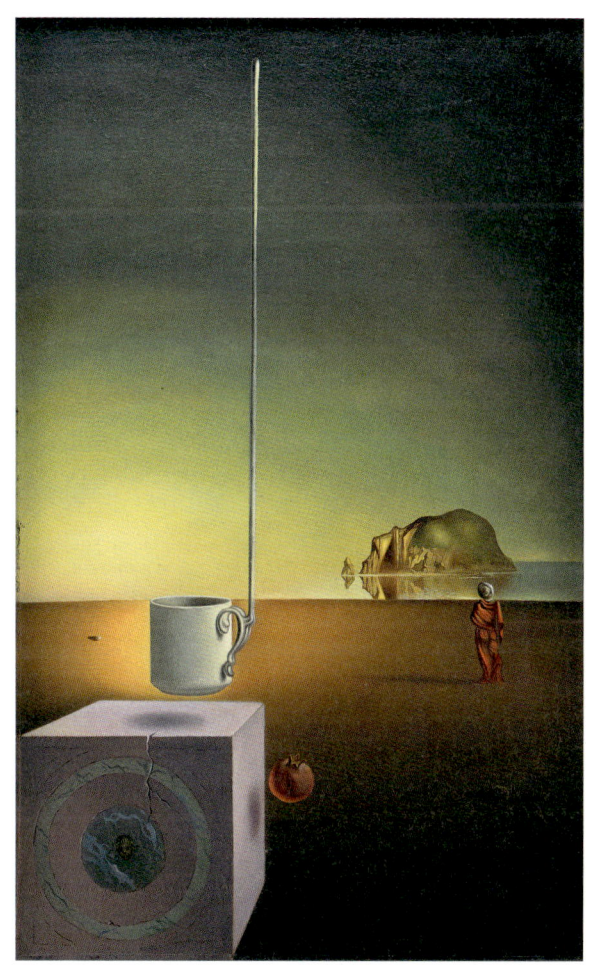

305
Flying Giant Demi-Tasse with Incomprehensible Appendage Five Metres Long
c. 1944
Oil on canvas, 50 × 31 cm
Private collection

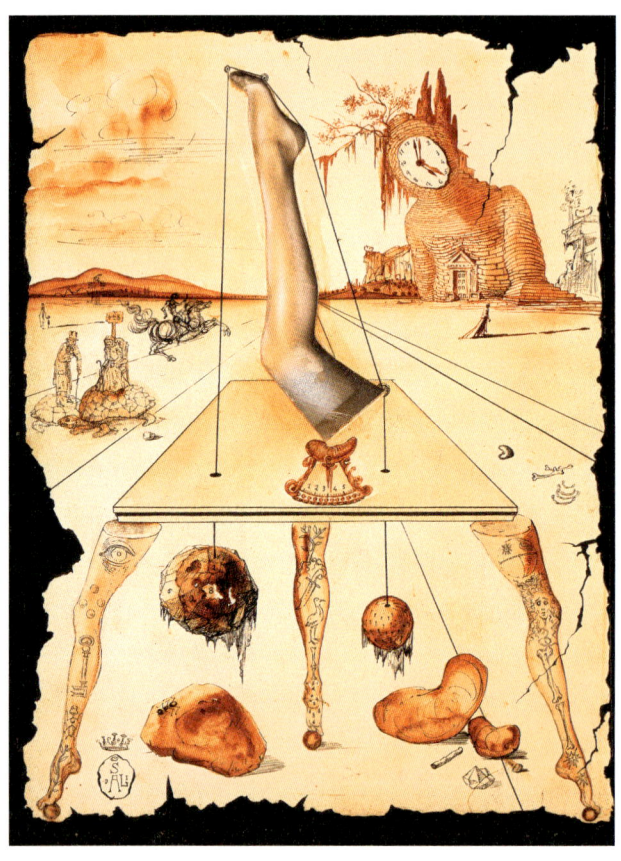

306
Leg Composition. Drawing from a series of advertisements for Bryans Hosiery
c. 1944
Watercolour and India ink, dimensions unknown
Whereabouts unknown

Dalí in America

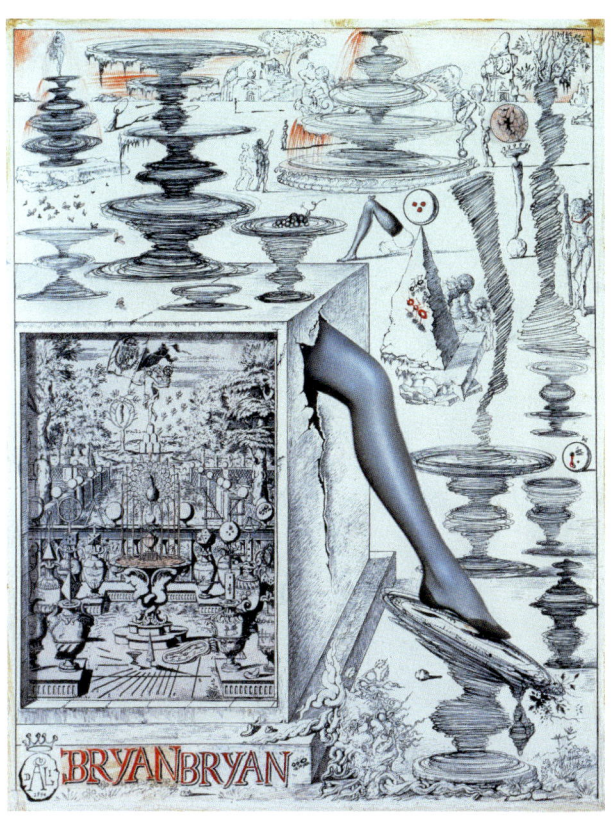

307
Leg Composition. Drawing from a series of advertisements for Bryans Hosiery
c. 1944
Watercolour and India ink, dimensions unknown
Bonhams, London

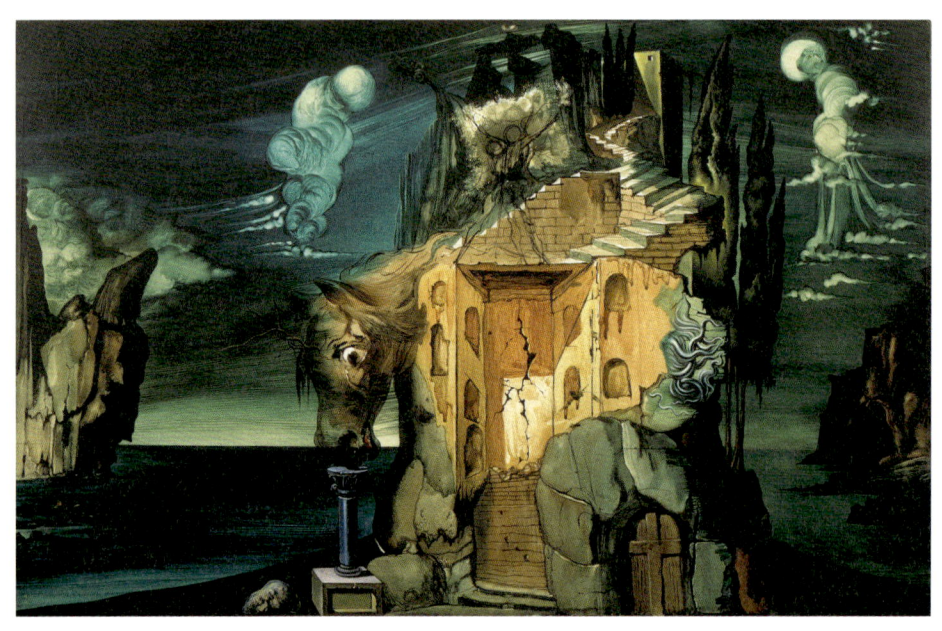

308
Study for the backdrop of the ballet "Mad Tristan" (Act III)
1944
Oil on canvas, 61 × 96.5 cm
Fundació Gala-Salvador Dalí, Figueres

Dalí in America

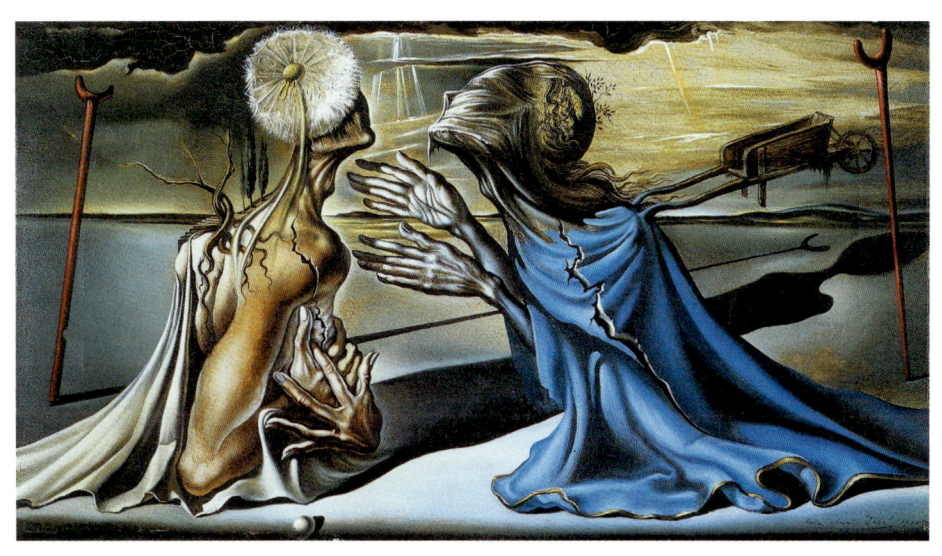

309
Project for "Mad Tristan"
c. 1944
Oil on canvas, 26.5 × 48.5 cm
Fundació Gala-Salvador Dalí, Figueres

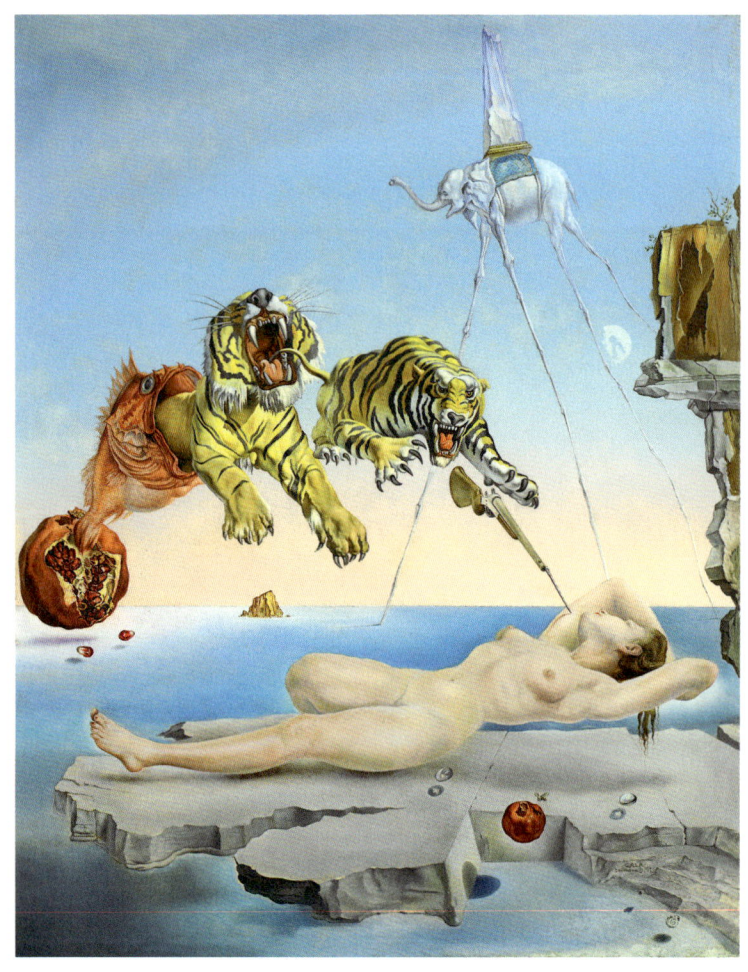

310

*One Second Before the Awakening from a Dream Provoked
by the Flight of a Bee Around a Pomegranate*

c. 1944

Oil on wood panel, 51 × 41 cm

Museo Nacional Thyssen-Bornemisza, Madrid

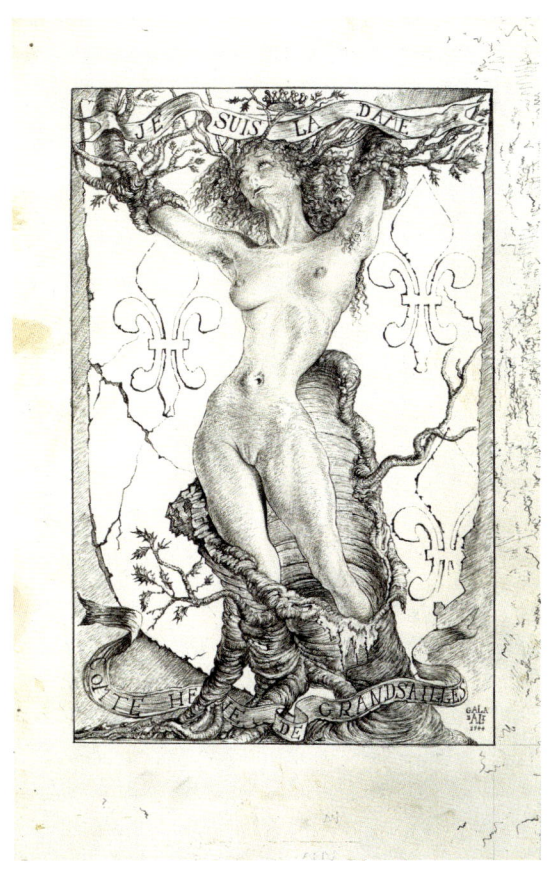

311

I am the Lady – Frontispiece for "Hidden Faces"

1944

India ink on paper, 21.5 × 14.5 cm

Gift of Dalí to the Spanish State

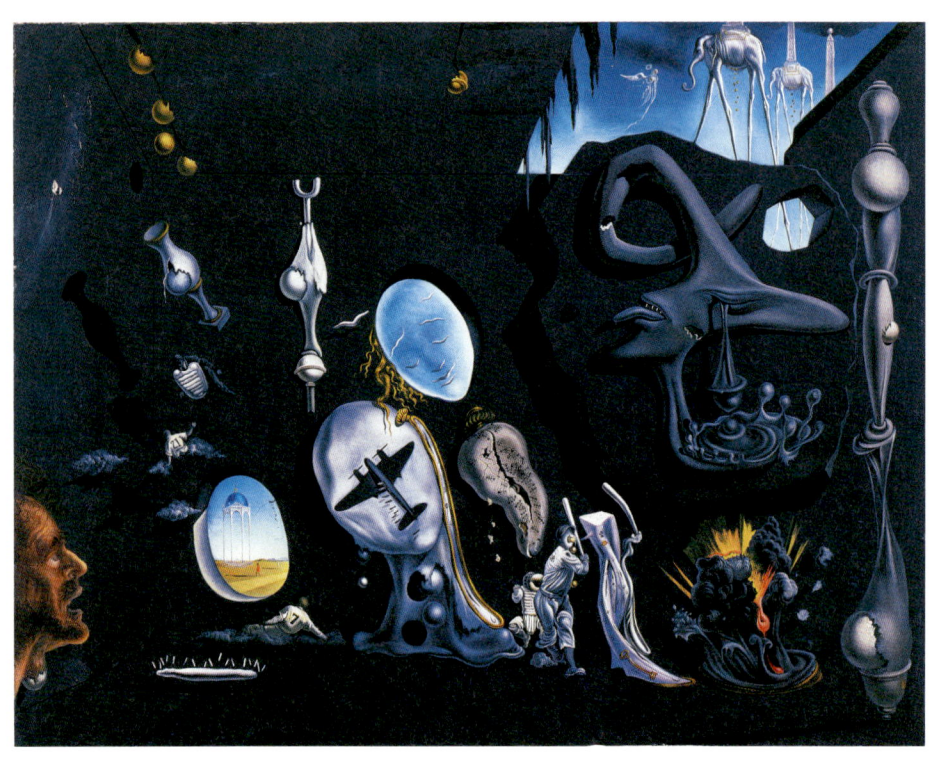

312
Uranium and Atomica Melancholica Idyll
1945
Oil on canvas, 66.5 × 86.5 cm
Museo Nacional Centro de Arte Reina Sofía, Madrid

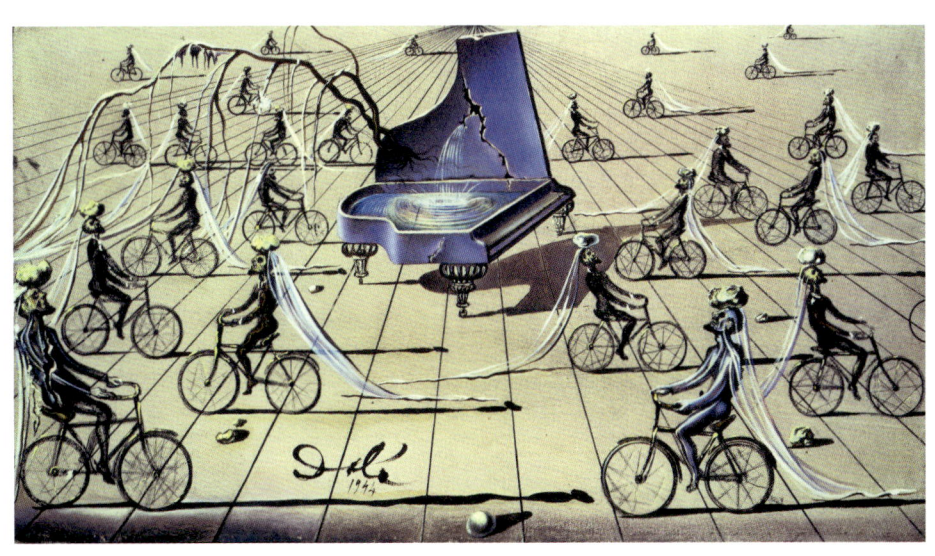

313
Project for "Sentimental Colloquy"
1944
Oil on canvas, 26 × 47 cm
The Dalí Museum, St. Petersburg, Florida

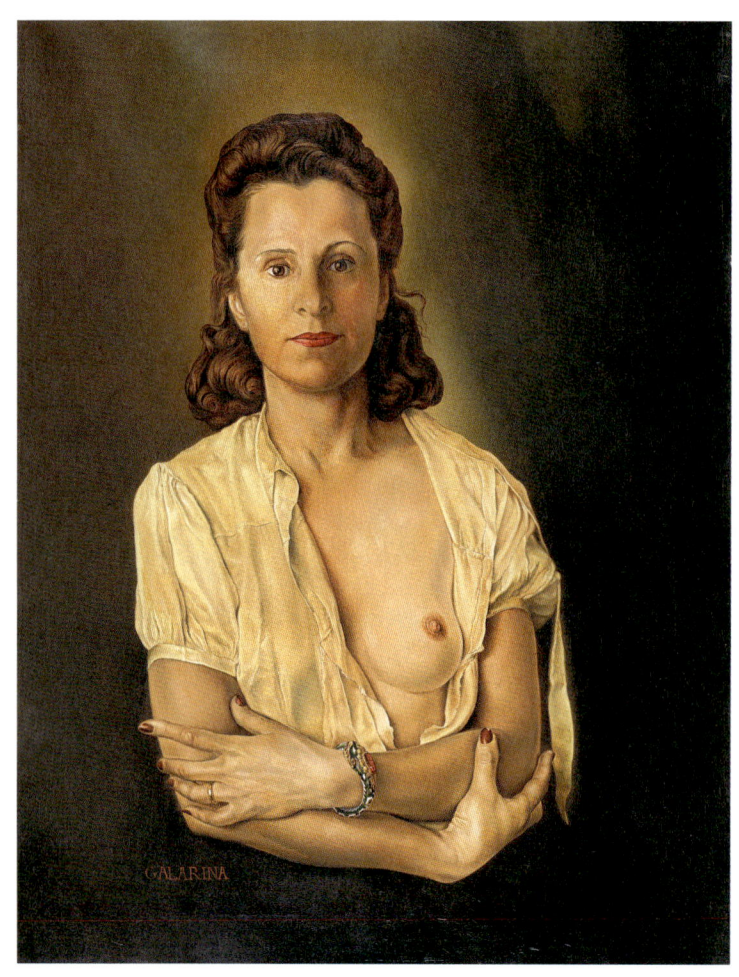

314
Galarina
1945
Oil on canvas, 64 × 50 cm
Fundació Gala-Salvador Dalí, Figueres

Dalí in America

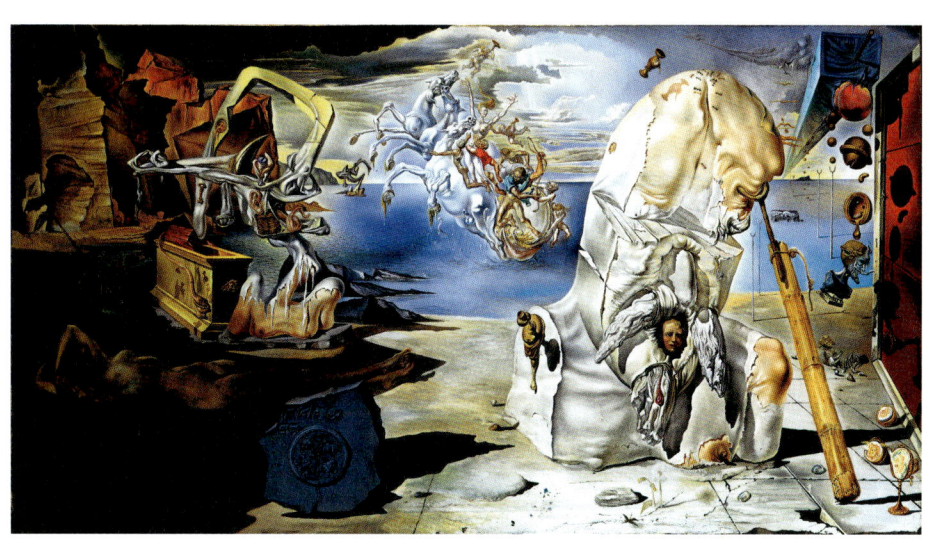

315
The Apotheosis of Homer
1944–1945
Oil on canvas, 63.7 × 116.7 cm
Bayerische Staatsgemäldesammlungen, Pinakothek der Moderne, Munich

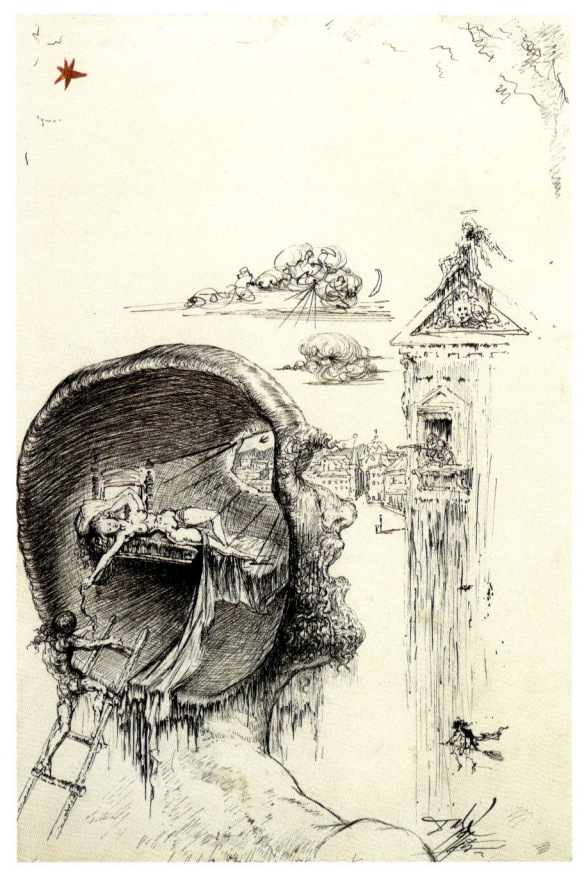

316
Illustration for "The Autobiography of Benvenuto Cellini"
1945
Pen and India ink on paper, 28 × 19 cm
Gift of Dalí to the Spanish State

Dalí in America

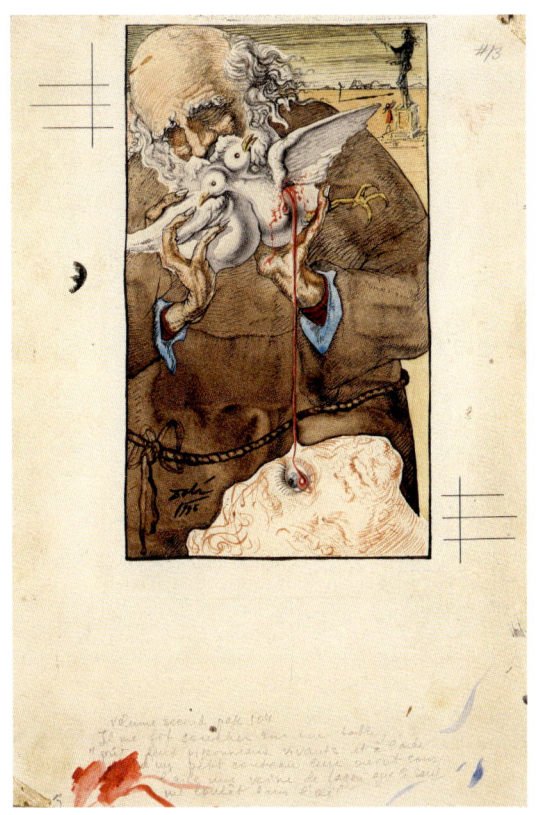

317
Illustration for "The Autobiography of Benvenuto Cellini"
1945
Pen and India ink on paper, 18 × 10.5 cm
Gift of Dalí to the Spanish State

1940–1948

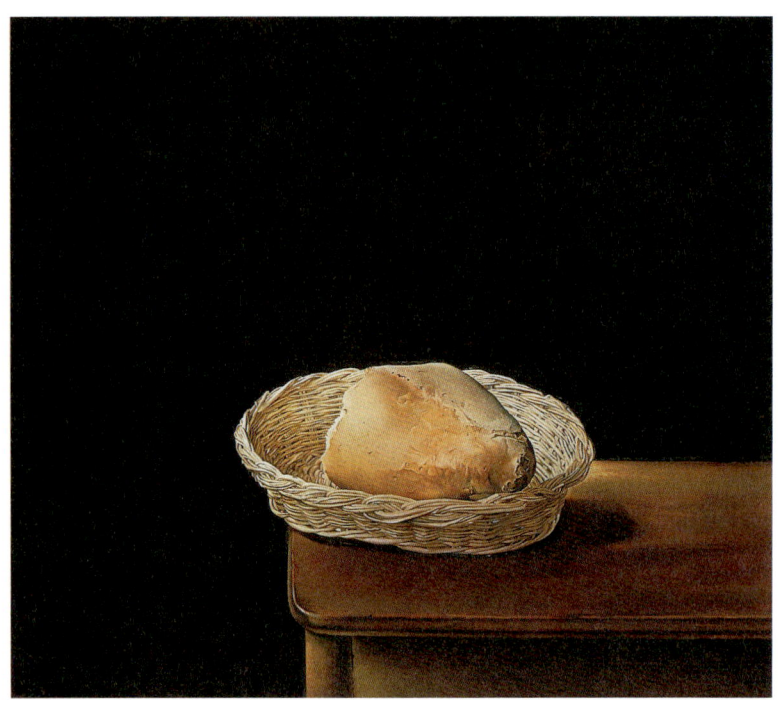

318
Basket of Bread
1945
Oil on plywood panel, 33 × 38 cm
Fundació Gala-Salvador Dalí, Figueres

Dalí in America

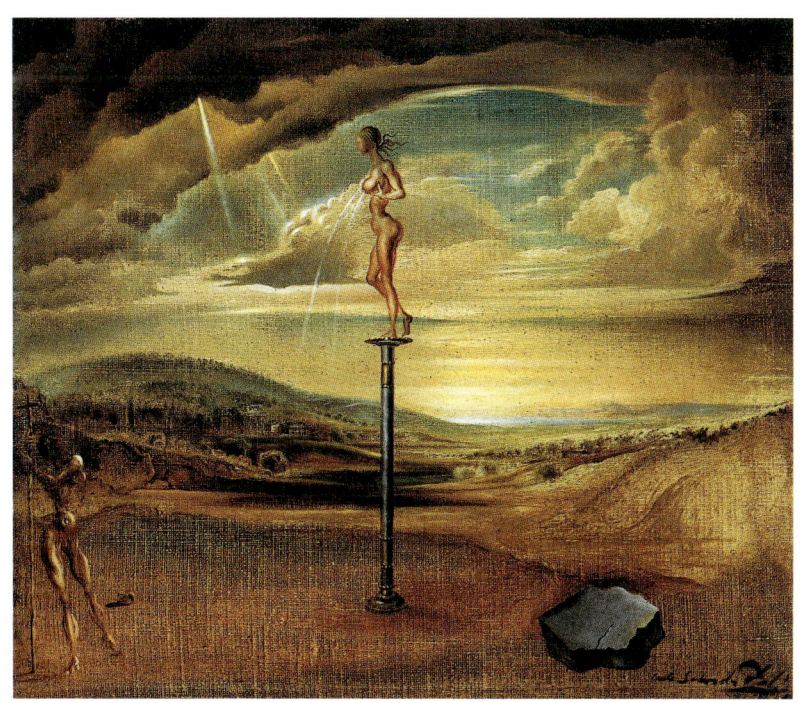

319
Fountain of Milk Spreading Itself Uselessly upon Three Shoes
1945
Oil on canvas, 18.4 × 21.6 cm
The Dalí Museum, St. Petersburg, Florida

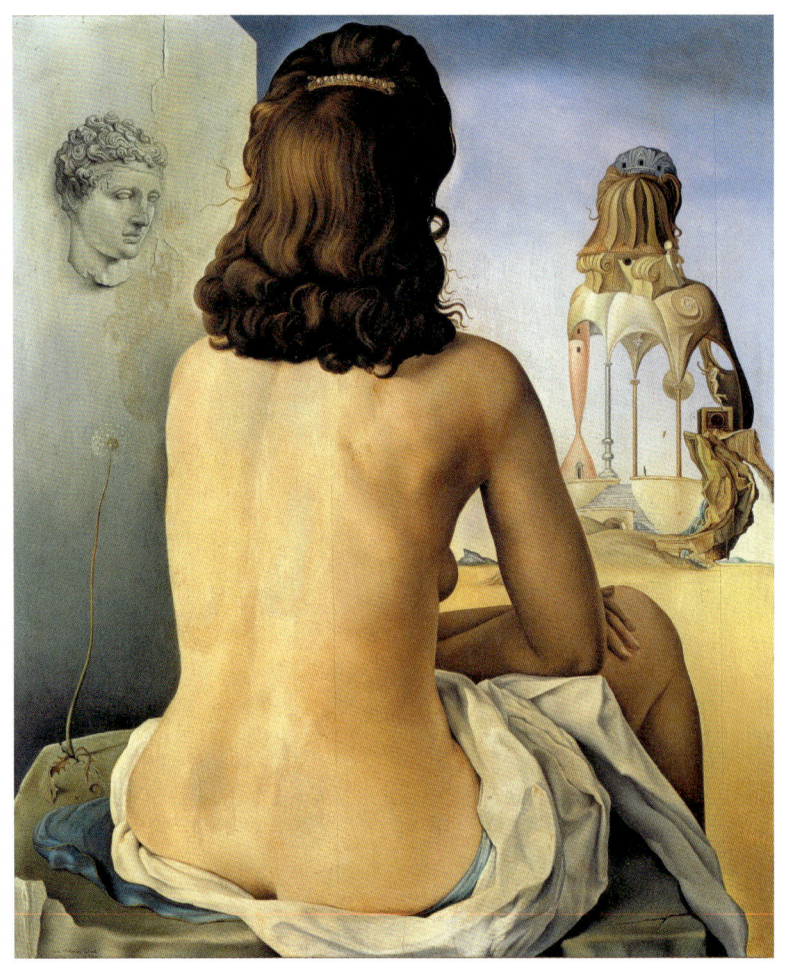

320
My Wife, Nude, Contemplating her own flesh becoming Stairs,
Three Vertebrae of a Column, Sky and Architecture
1945
Oil on wood panel, 61 × 52 cm
Private collection

Dalí in America

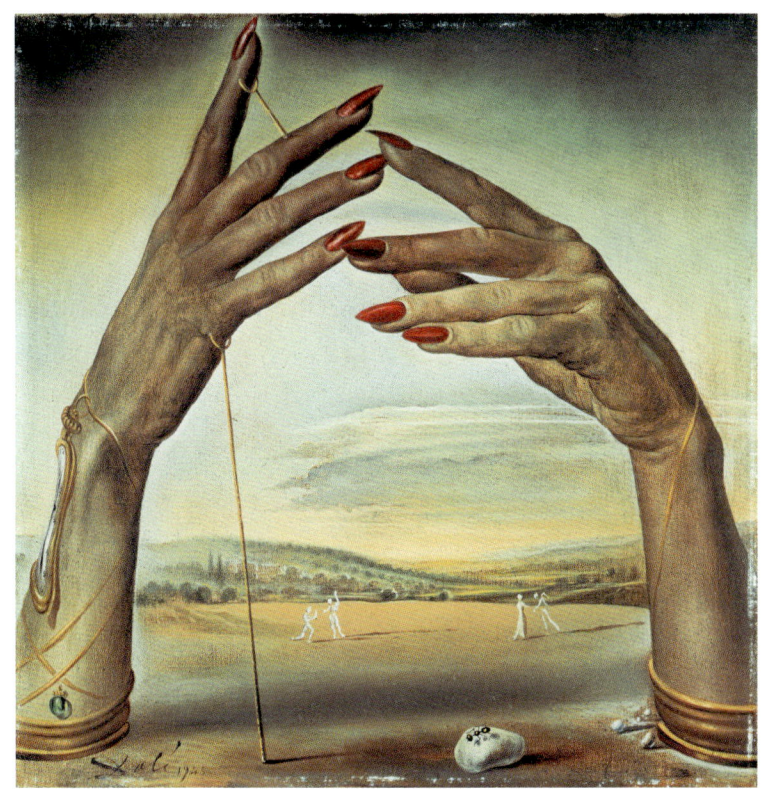

321
Portrait of a Passionate Woman (The Hands)
1945
Oil on canvas, 60 × 45 cm
Private collection

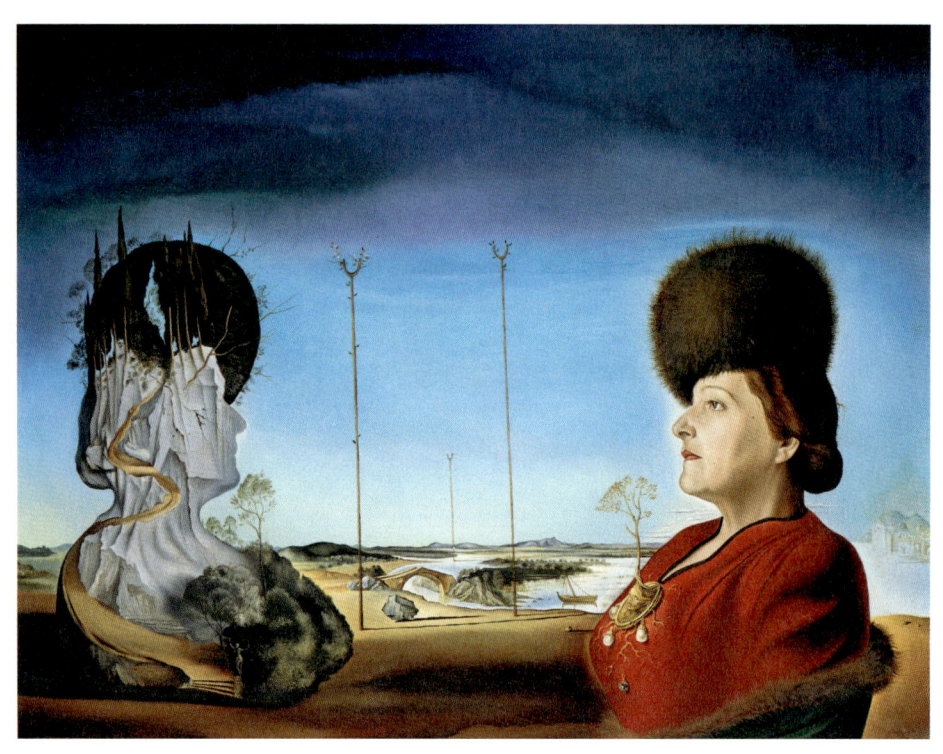

322
Portrait of Mrs. Isabel Styler-Tas (Melancholy)
1945
Oil on canvas, 65.5 × 86 cm
Staatliche Museen zu Berlin, Nationalgalerie, Berlin

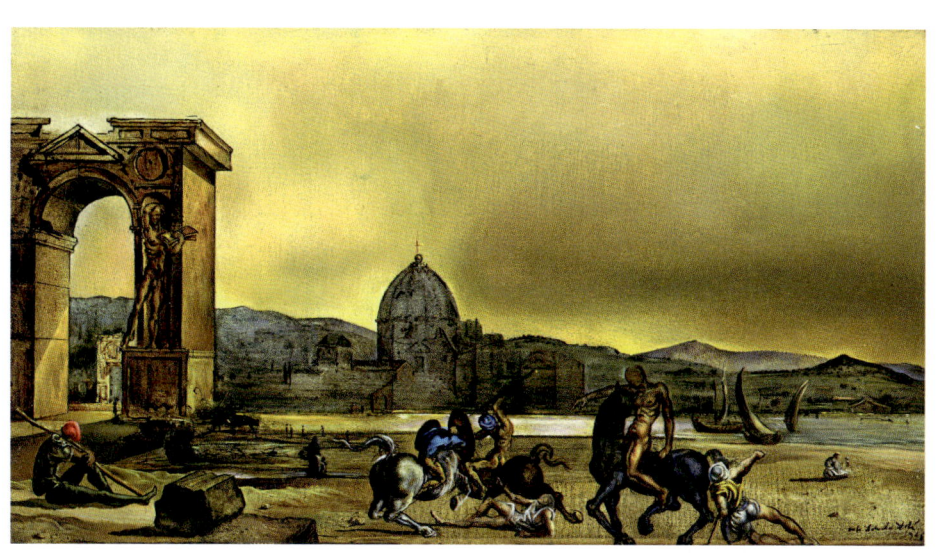

323
Autumn Sonata
1945
Oil on canvas, 16.5 × 30.5 cm
The Dalí Museum, St. Petersburg, Florida

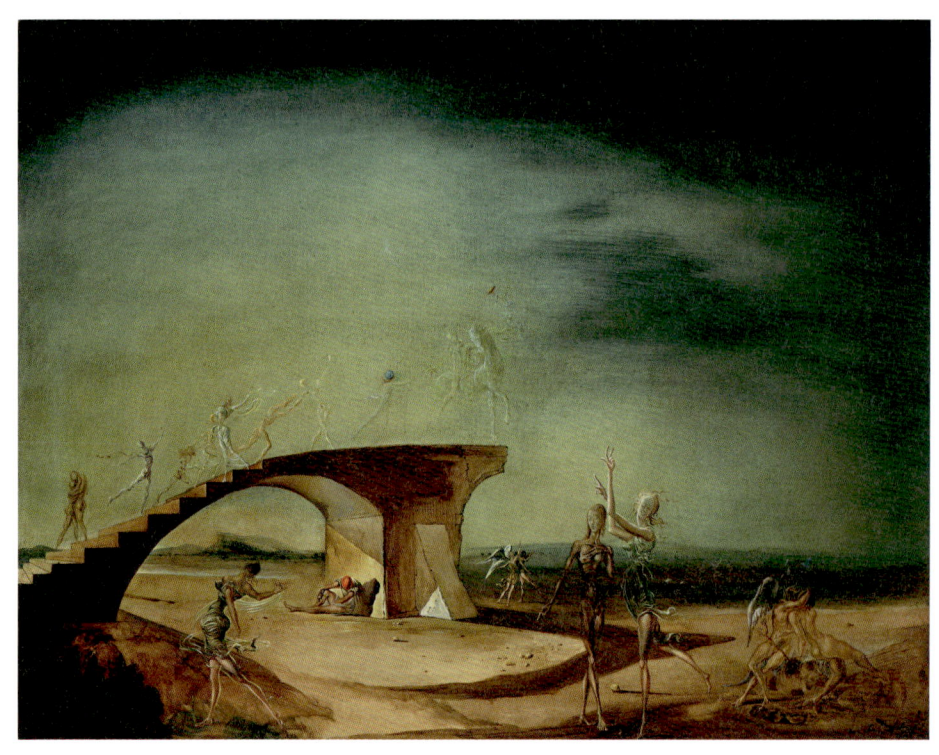

324
The Broken Bridge and the Dream
1945
Oil on canvas, 66 × 86.4 cm
The Dalí Museum, St. Petersburg, Florida

　　　　　　　　　　Dalí in America

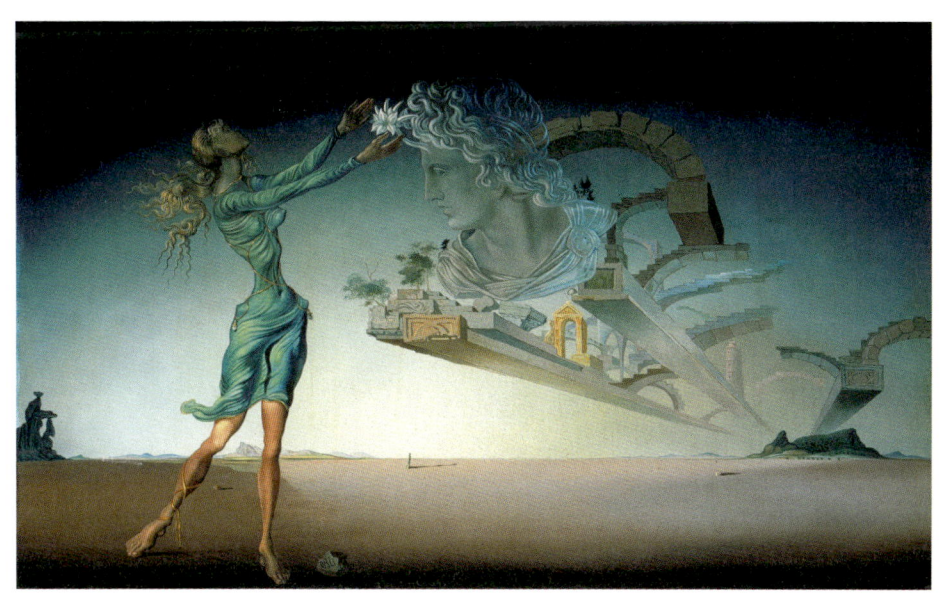

325
Trilogy of the Desert. Mirage
c. 1946
Oil on canvas, 35.6 × 60 cm
National Gallery of Victoria, Melbourne, Australia

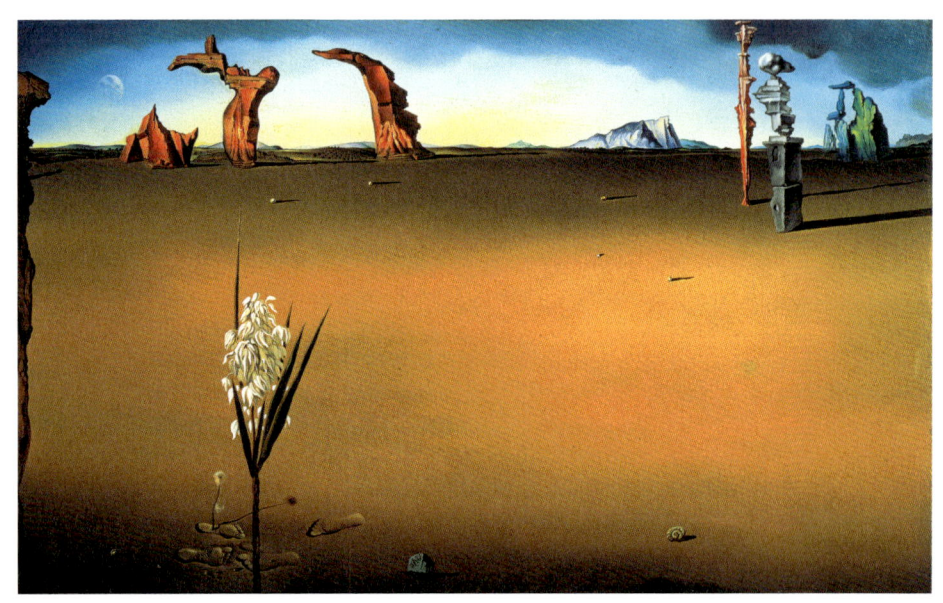

326
Trilogy of the Desert. Invisible Lovers
c. 1946
Oil on canvas, 36.5 × 60 cm
Private collection

Dalí in America

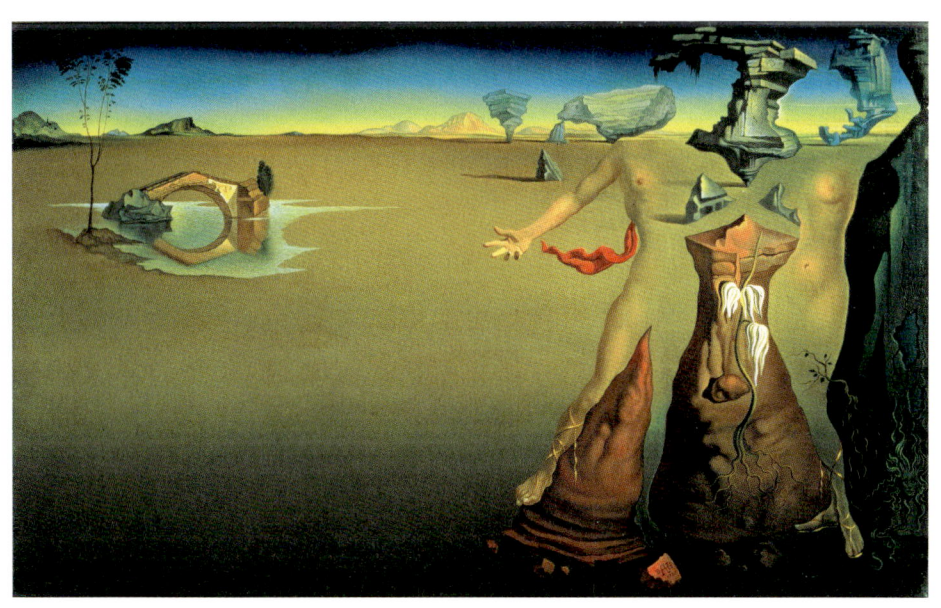

327
Trilogy of the Desert. Oasis
1946
Oil on canvas, 35.6 × 60 cm
Private collection

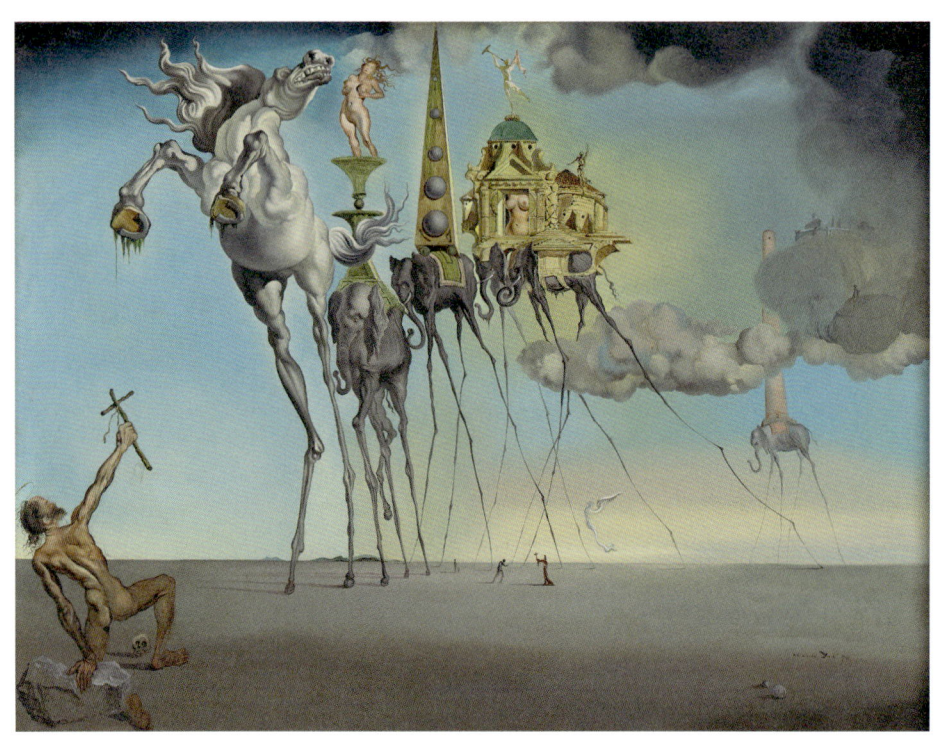

328
The Temptation of St. Anthony
1946
Oil on canvas, 89.5 × 119.5 cm
Musées Royaux des Beaux-Arts de Belgique, Brussels

Dalí in America

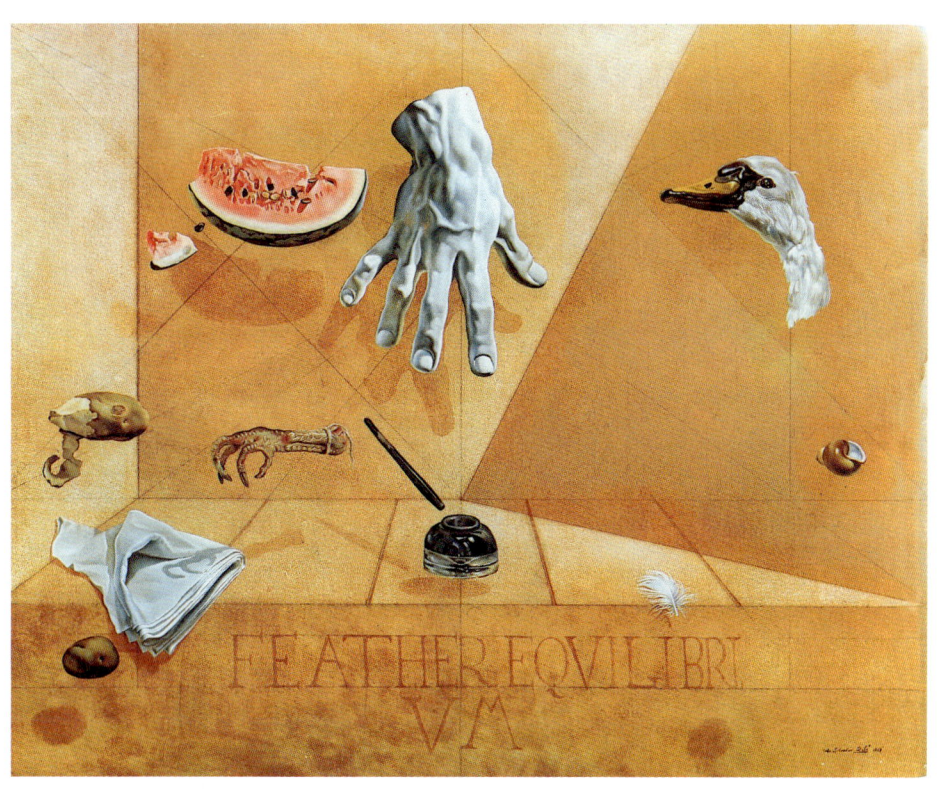

329
Intra-Atomic Equilibrium of a Swan's Feather
1947
Oil on canvas, 78 × 97 cm
Fundació Gala-Salvador Dalí, Figueres

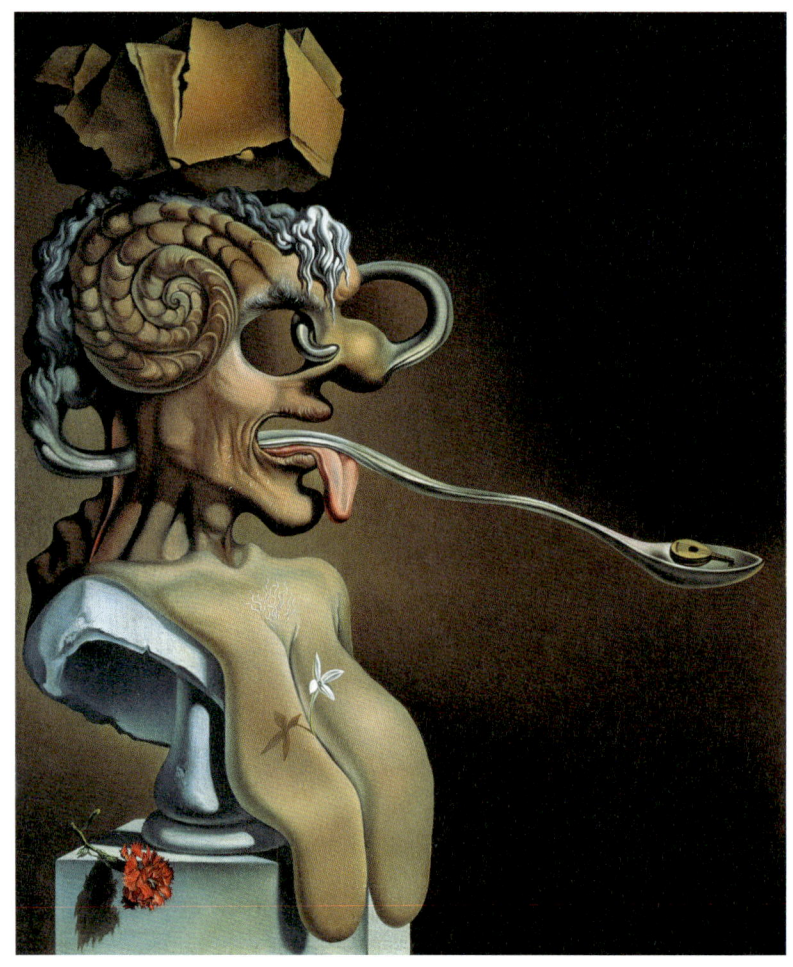

330
Portrait of Pablo Picasso in the Twenty-first Century
1947
Oil on canvas, 65.5 × 56 cm
Town Hall of Figueres, on permanent deposit at the Fundació Gala-Salvador Dalí, Figueres

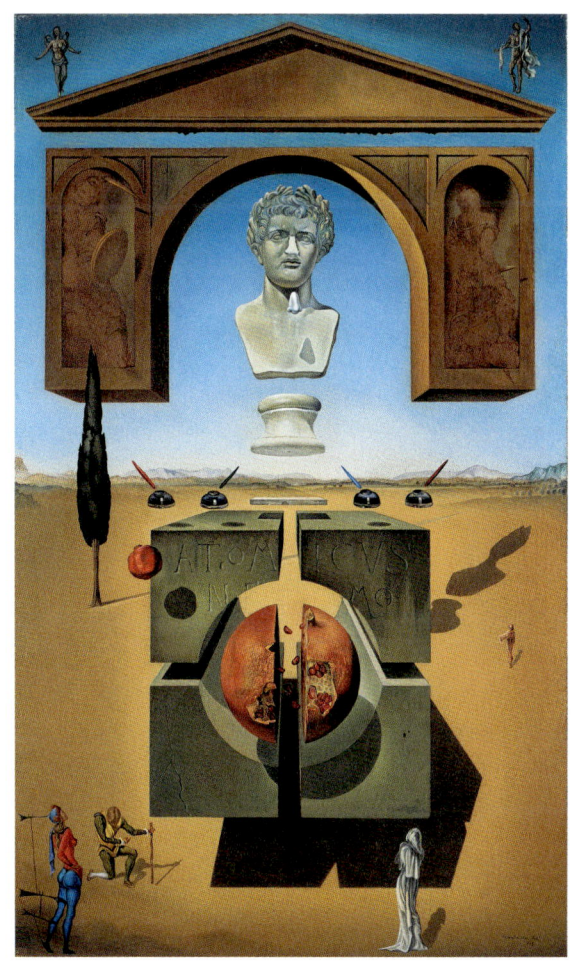

331
Dematerialization Near the Nose of Nero
1947
Oil on canvas, 76.5 × 46 cm
Fundació Gala-Salvador Dalí, Figueres

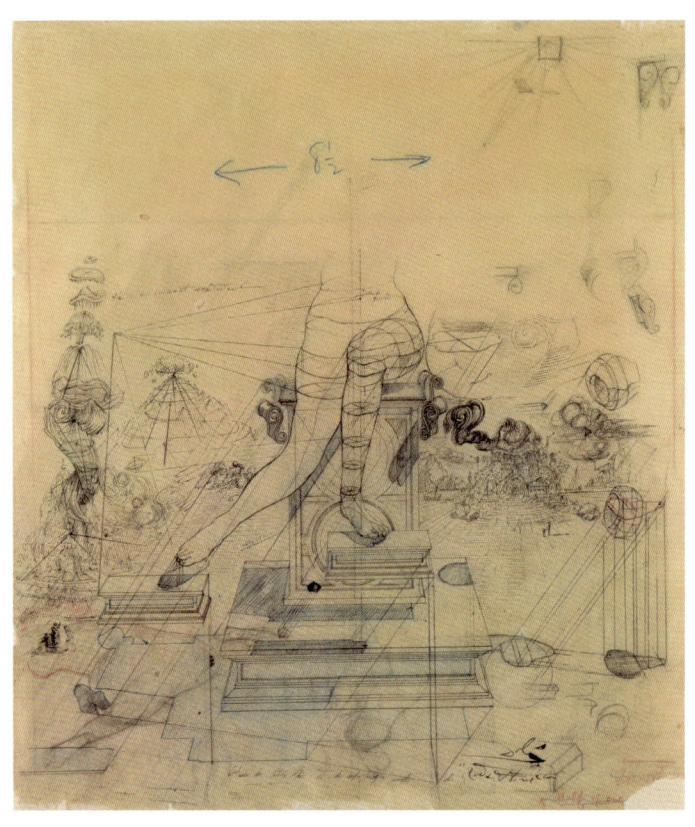

332
Studies for the Air Centers and Soft Morphologies of "Leda Atomica"
1947
Pen, India ink, pencil and coloured pencil on special paper, 54 × 48 cm
Fundació Gala-Salvador Dalí, Figueres

Dalí in America

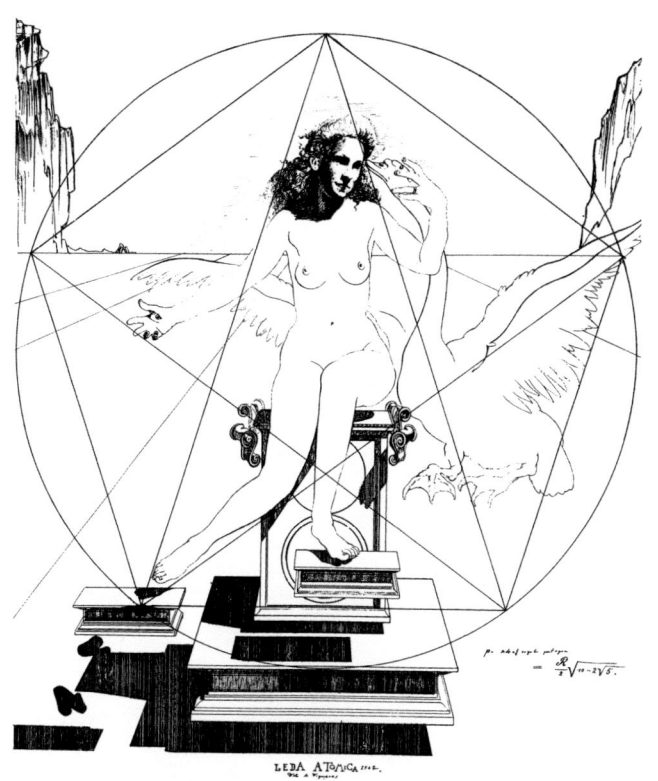

333
Study for "Leda Atomica"
1947
Pen and India ink, 60.4 × 45.3 cm
Private collection

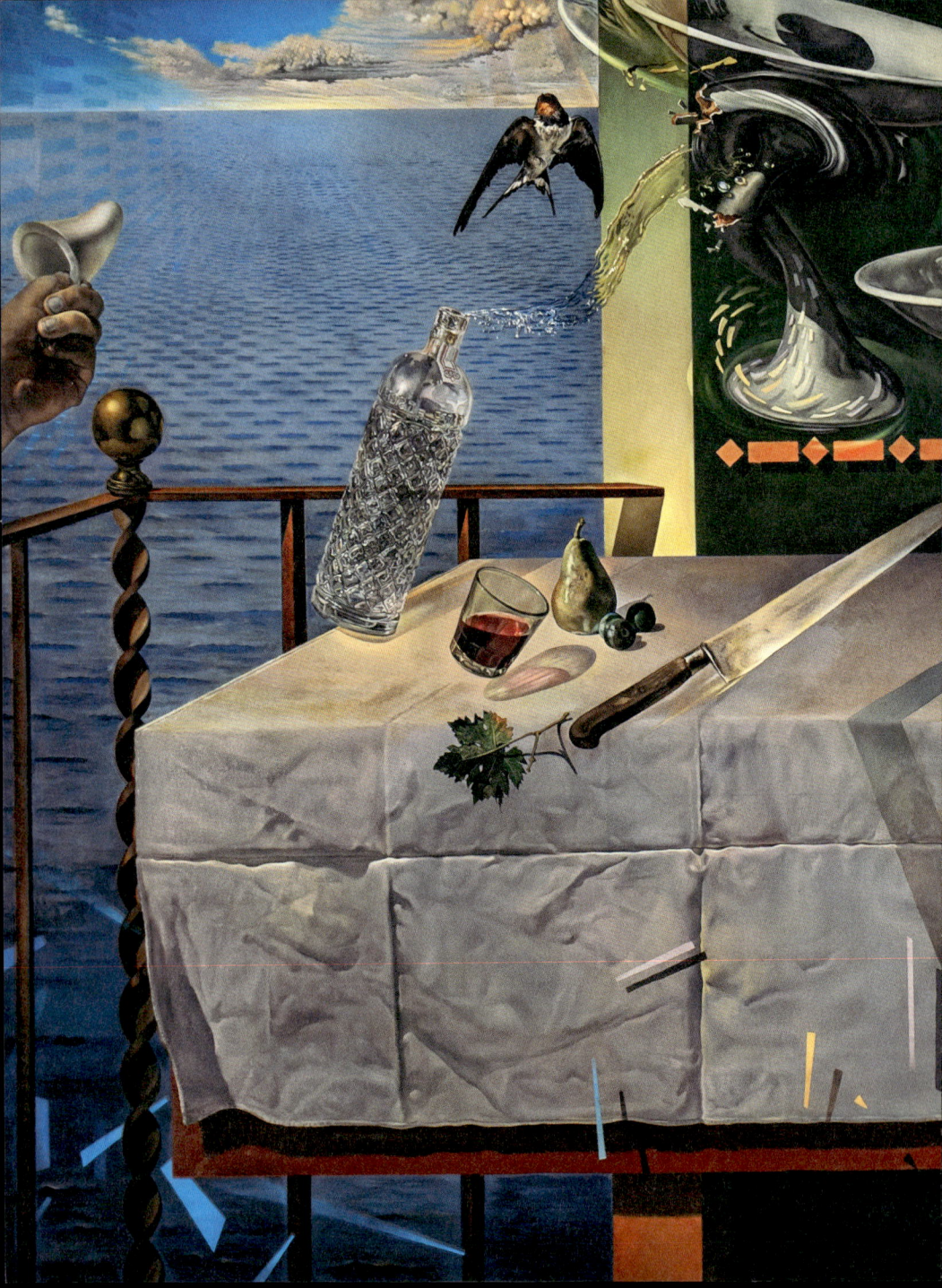

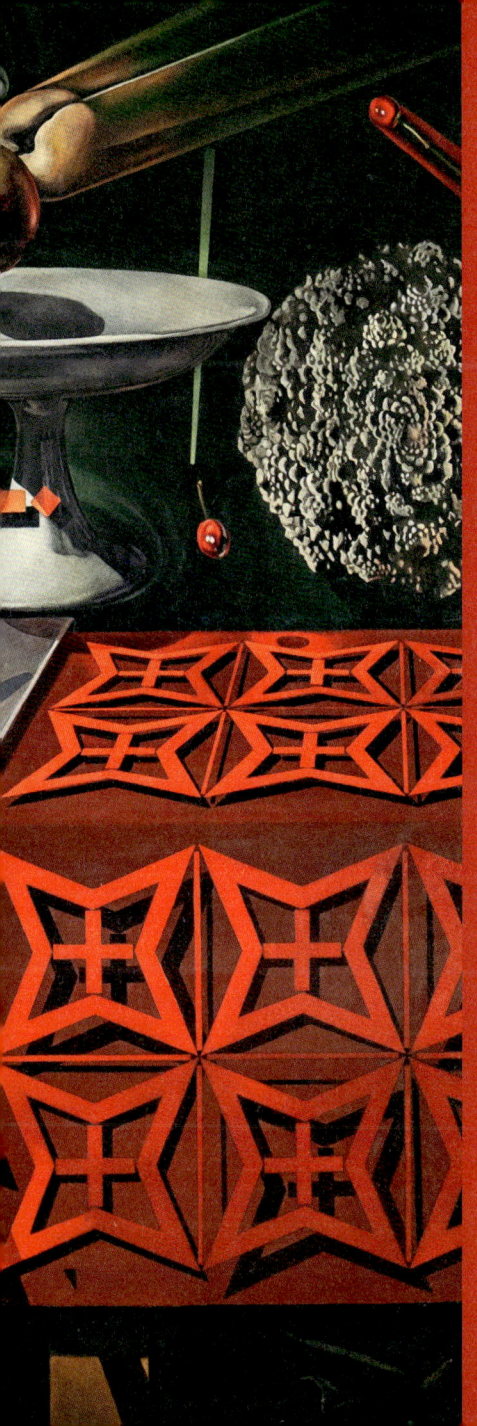

Return to Spain
and Classicism

1948–1960

Dalí and Gala returned to Spain by way of the port city Le Havre on the northern coast of France in July 1948. Their arrival in Portlligat, a small fishing village in Cadaqués, was noted by the Spanish press in August 1948. Once back, they set about extending the Portlligat house and studio.

Dalí's new turn towards Classicism prompted him to establish contact with Pope Pius XII (1876–1958), with whom he had a private audience in Rome on 23 November 1949. During this audience, Dalí presented the Pope with his painting *The Madonna of Portlligat* (1949) [335]. Dalí was seeking the Pope's acceptance of his new exploration of Catholic imagery, as well as support for him to marry Gala within the Church, an event that would eventually happen, though not until 1958, after Éluard's death in 1952.

From late November 1950 until early January 1951, Dalí exhibited *The Madonna of Portlligat* at Carstairs Gallery in New York in a presentation held in honour of the Diamond Jubilee of the Philadelphia Museum of Art. In the Carstairs catalogue, Dalí explained his intention 'to incorporate the surrealistic experiences of my life with the great classical tradition of painting.'

Dalí's new idea of fusing mysticism, classicism and modern physics was laid out in his 1951 essay *Mystical Manifesto*, which was published by Editions Robert J. Godet, Paris and launched in Paris on 19 June 1951. In his manifesto, Dalí denounced the vacuousness of much of modern abstract painting as being entirely devoid of content and stated: 'Mysticism is the paroxysm of joy in the ultra-individualist affirmation of all man's heterogeneous tendencies within the absolute unity of ecstasy. I want my next Christ to be a painting containing more beauty and joy than anything that will have been painted up to the present.' In this statement Dalí was referring to his future painting *The Christ* (1951) [339] and its preliminary drawing *Christ in Perspective* (1951) [338], which despite being a preparatory work is a highly finished drawing. During this period Dalí

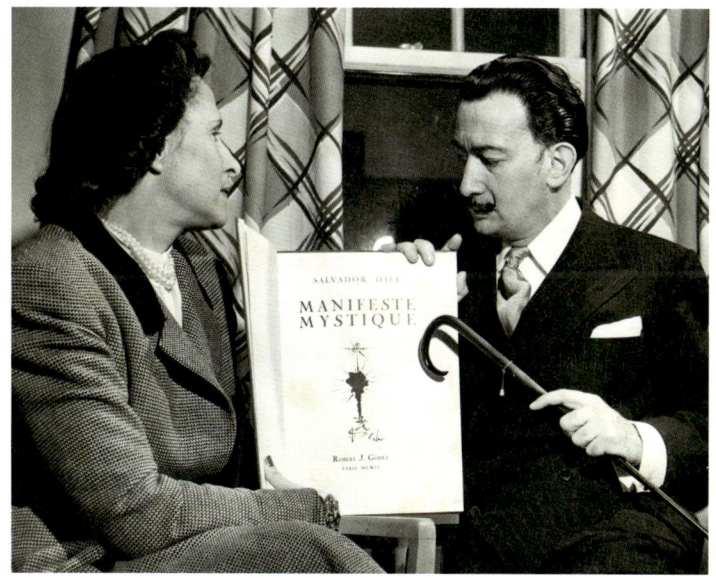

Dalí and Gala on either side of Dalí's book *Manifeste Mystique* published by Editions Robert J. Godet, February 1952. Collection of The Dalí Museum.

was deeply engaged in preparing a surprising group of highly academic paintings devoted to religious subject matter, a striking development for a former Surrealist, given the movement's pronounced anti-clericalism. In December 1951, he presented this new body of work, including the paintings *The Madonna of Portlligat* (1949), *Exploding Raphaelesque Head* (1951) [341], *Leda Atomica* (1947–49), and *The Christ* (1951) at the Lefevre Gallery in London. In addition to these paintings, the show also included a significant selection of watercolours, drawing and pastels, including the drawing *Christ in Perspective* (1950) [338] executed in sanguine (red chalk) in emulation of the Old Masters.

The London exhibition was destined for presentation in Madrid in a solo exhibition as part of the Bienal Hispanoamericana de Arte in 1951 to 1952. Dalí had already given a controversial lecture at the Teatro Maria Guerrero in

Madrid in relation to the Biennial on the 11 November 1951. Entitled 'Picasso y yo', Dalí proclaimed that, 'Mystical ecstasy is reached by ... penetrating the marrow of the spiritual castle' and that, 'As my own name, Salvador, indicates I want to save modern painting from laziness and chaos'. And he called on Picasso to join him in this mystical project. Dalí's paintings did not arrive in Madrid until early 1952, after the London exhibition closed in December. The Dalí exhibition sparked numerous articles in the Spanish press and announced Dalí's official return to Franco's Spain.

In around August 1951, as evidenced by a photograph of the three men together, the Spanish writer Rafael Santos Torroella (1914–2002) and the French art collector René Metras (1926–1986) visited Dalí in Portlligat. The following year, Santos Torroella published a monograph, *Salvador Dalí* (1952), which covered the artist's life during the 1951 to 1952 Bienal and the publication of the *Mystical Manifesto*. Santos Torroella concluded that for Dalí, 'What has changed are the ideas, the spiritual attitude of the painter.' Perhaps this was true, but Dalí was also seeking to establish an official and public presence in Spain. In 1962 Metras would open an art gallery in Barcelona focused on the international avant-garde and in 1969 presented a solo exhibition of Dalí's work.

From December 1952 until January 1953, Dalí presented his latest works once more at Carstairs Gallery in New York. The exhibition included six highly-finished paintings, including *Assumpta Corpuscularia Lapislazulina* (1952) [343], *Evangelical Still Life* (1952) [347] and *The Corpuscular Persistence of Memory* (1952–54), the latter now known as *The Disintegration of the Persistence of Memory* [349]. In the preface to the Carstairs catalogue Dalí explained that avant-garde experimentation was 'decorative art' lacking in 'theological and philosophical meaning' and concluded that it was theology and physics that address this problem, '*the great, immeasurable and categorical innovation of our time – a new conception of matter*, that of NUCLEAR PHYSICS.'

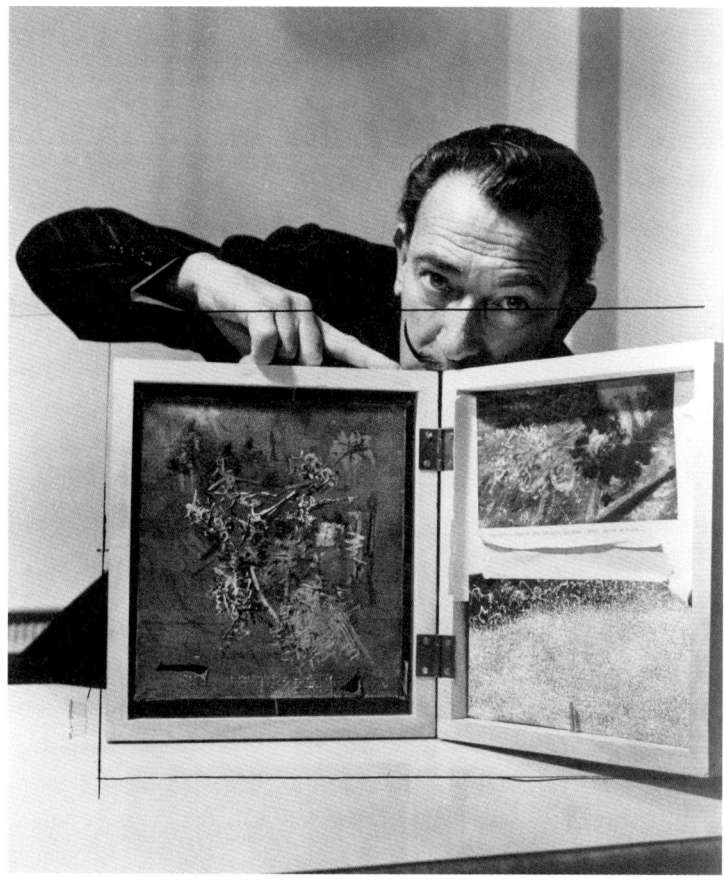

Martha Holmes (photographer), Dalí posing with *Christ at Emmaus* at Carstairs Gallery, New York, c. 1956–58. Collection of The Dalí Museum.

In his next exhibition at Carstairs Gallery, held in December 1954 to January 1955, Dalí showed *The Disintegration of the Persistence of Memory* again, along with fifteen other paintings, including *Corpus hipercubus* (c. 1954) [351], *Maximum speed of Raphael's Madonna* (c. 1954) and the flower painting *A Shower of Jasmine* (c. 1954) [357]. In these works, Dalí was fusing his earlier Surrealism with both Classicism and modern physics. In the preface he wrote of 'the new thirst and starvation of the people for ultra concrete images. Abstract art will have only served to awaken anew this thirst and hunger. May God reward it!'

One of Dalí's most ambitious paintings of 1956 was *Fast-Moving Still Life* (c. 1956) [363], which featured in his next Carstairs Gallery exhibition, held in December 1956 until January 1957. There it was shown alongside thirteen other paintings, including *Crâne de Zurbarán* (1956), *Anti-protonic Assumpta* (1956) and *Saint Helena in Portlligat* (c. 1956) [364]. The catalogue included a text by the French art critic Alain Jouffroy (1928–2015) provocatively titled, 'Will Dalí Assassinate Modern Art?' in which Jouffroy wrote in reference to Dalí, 'He attacks all modern prejudices, which consist of despising Beauty, preferring it to an "expressive" and "tragic ugliness" and confounding, in general, creation and deformation, power and vulgarity.' The catalogue article also elaborated on ideas that Dalí had put forward in his recently published book *Les Cocus du vieil art moderne* (1956).

During the 1950s, Dalí made a series of large-format canvases, at least one a year, which explored both religious and historical subjects. These were highly-finished works that evoked the academic values of the religious and history painting genres. Emblematic of this evolution were the following canvases: *Quasi-grey picture, which, closely seen, is an abstract one; seen from two metres is the Sistine Madonna of Raphael; and from fifteen metres is the ear of an angel measuring one metre and a half; which is painted with anti-matter; therefore with pure energy* [also known as *The Sistine Madonna*] (1958) and *Velázquez painting the Infanta with the lights*

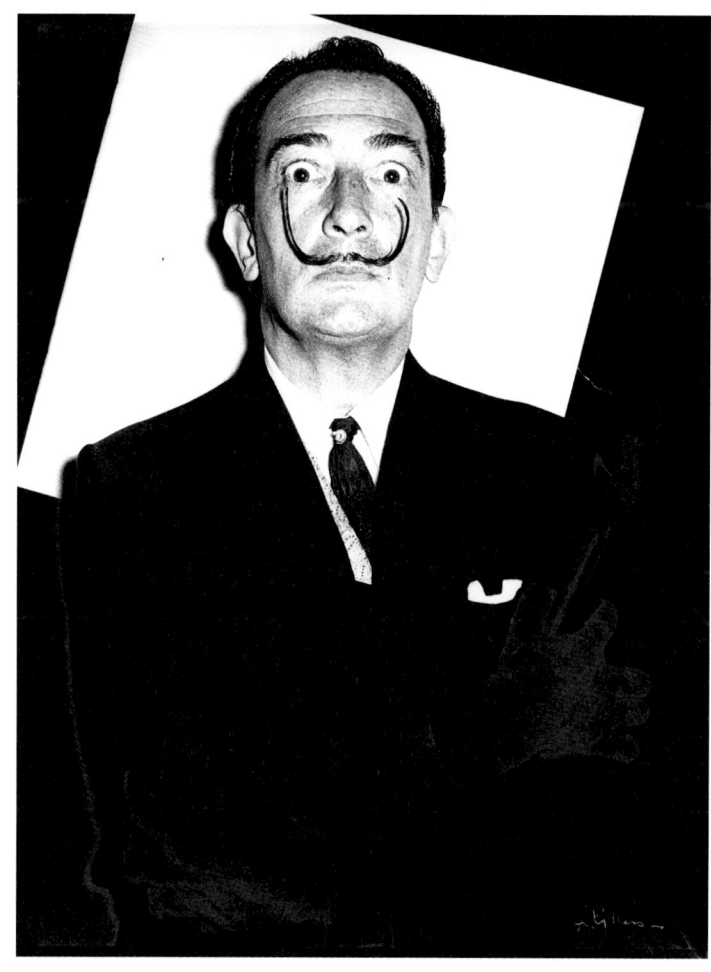

André Villers (photographer), *Portrait of Salvador Dalí*, 1956.
Collection of The Dalí Museum.

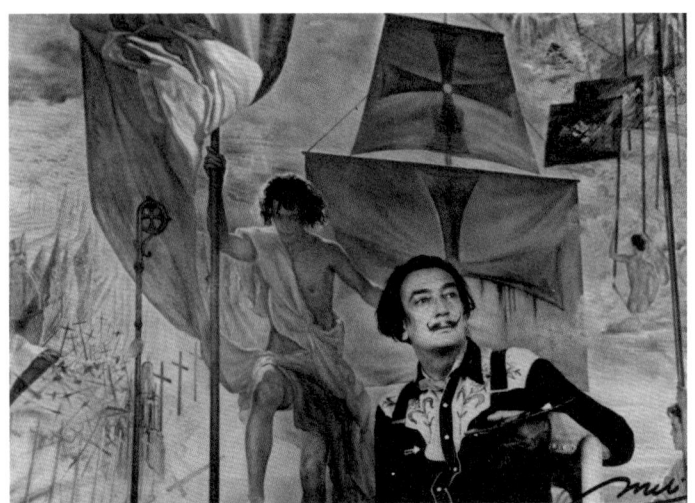

Meliton Casals (photographer), Dalí posing in front of his painting *Discovery of America by Christopher Columbus*, c. 1958. Collection of The Dalí Museum.

and shadows of his proper glory (1958) [369]. These were among thirteen paintings included in his December 1958 to January 1959 exhibition at Carstairs Gallery, which was accompanied by a catalogue in which Dalí published his 'Anti-Matter Manifesto'. In this text he expressed his view of the painterly brushstroke as akin to subatomic particles and proclaimed, 'My ambition, still and always, is to integrate the experiments of modern art with the great classical tradition.' In short, for Dalí, Heisenberg and modern physics had 'transcended' Freud's subjective psychology.

Dalí's next large-format painting was *Discovery of America by Christopher Columbus*, which he began in 1958, but completed in 1959 [370]. Though this work would not be exhibited until Dalí's 1965 New York retrospective, his 1960 painting *The Ecumenical Council* [375], was exhibited in the Carstairs Gallery show held in December 1960 to January 1961. While most of the works in the exhibition, such as *The Battle of Tetuán* (1962), had been recently made, Dalí also included his largest painting from his earlier

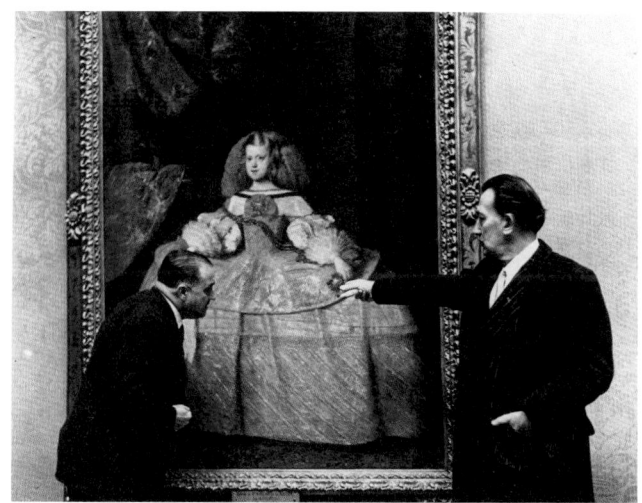

Oriol Maspons (photographer), Dalí pointing out a detail of the *Infanta* at the Museo Nacional del Prado, Madrid, 1958. Collection of The Dalí Museum.

surrealist period, *The Enigma of William Tell* (c. 1933) [178]. By presenting these works from two contrasting periods of his career, especially *The Enigma of William Tell* and *The Ecumenical Council*, Dalí, as he explained in the exhibition catalogue, set up a symmetrical relationship between these two periods of his work. Of the latter canvas, Dalí announced, 'the Ecumenical Council, which I consider the greatest historical event of our time and which, prudently, I have painted before it has met.' In this text he also introduced a term to describe his new direction, 'Quantified Realism,' by which arguably he meant that he was putting the painterly marks of abstract painting at the service of both 'tradition' and realism.

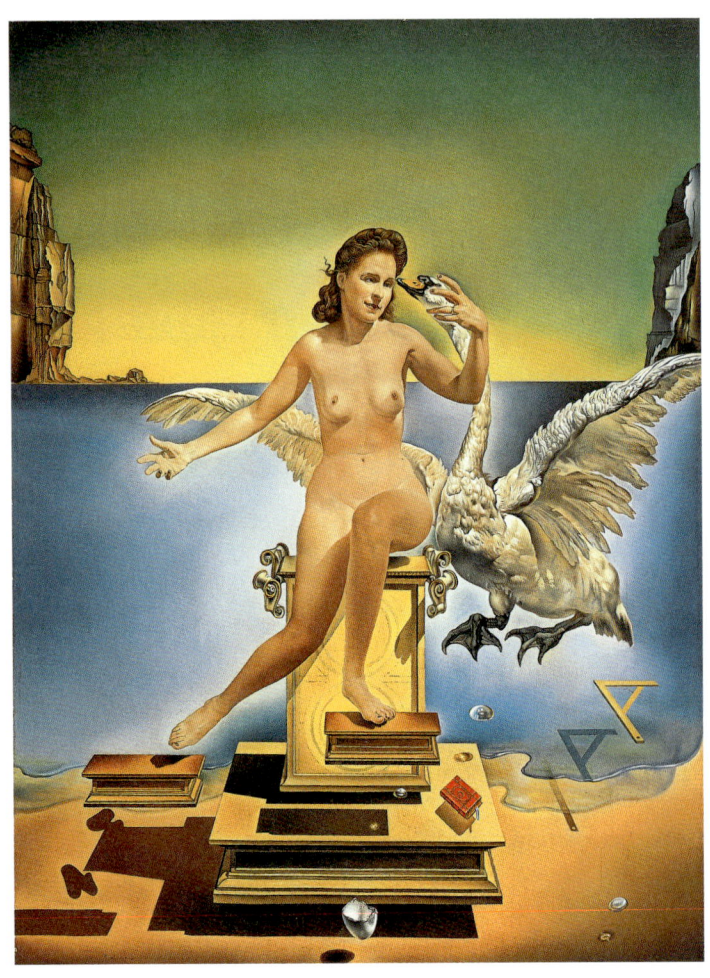

334
Leda Atomica
1947–1949
Oil on canvas, 61 × 46 cm
Fundació Gala-Salvador Dalí, Figueres

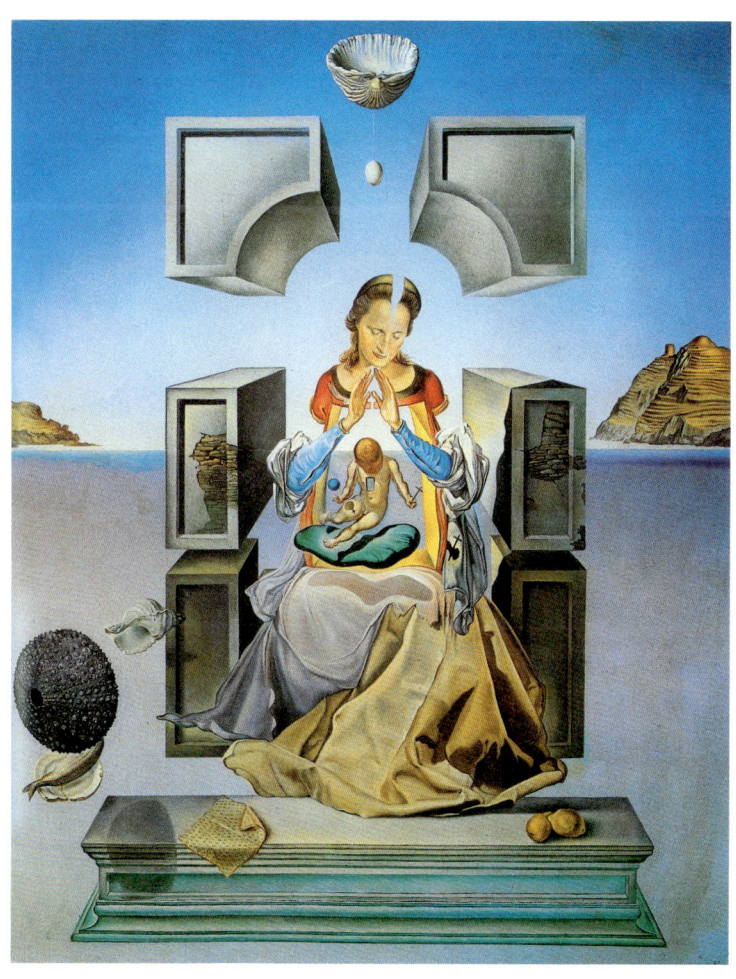

335
The Madonna of Portlligat (first version)
1949
Oil on canvas, 49.5 × 38.3 cm
Haggerty Museum of Art, Marquette University, Milwaukee, Wisconsin

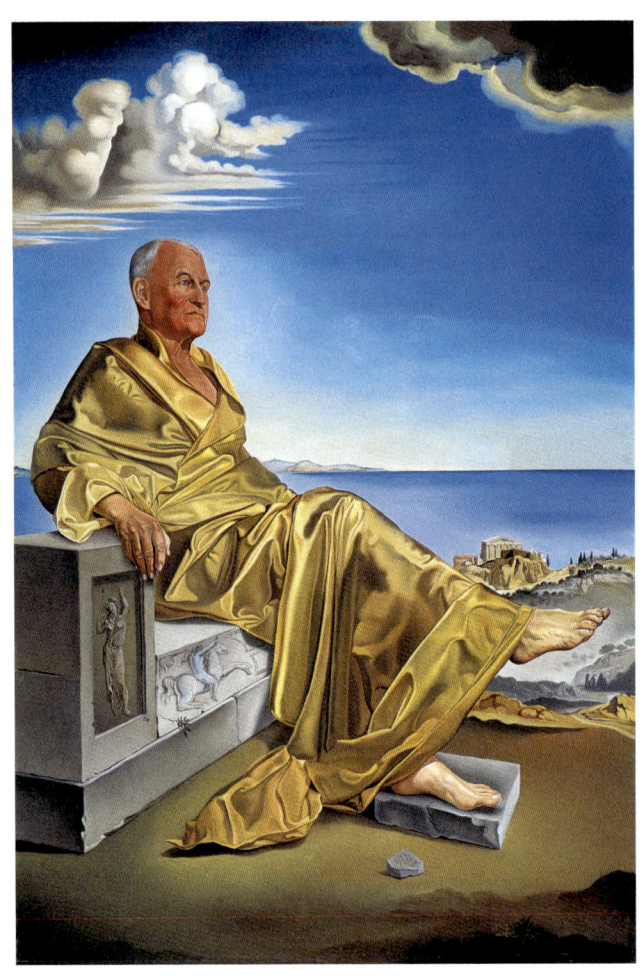

336
Portrait of Sir James Dunn
1949
Oil on canvas, 132.7 × 90.5 cm
Beaverbrook Art Gallery, Beaverbrook Canadian Foundation, Fredericton, New Brunswick, Canada

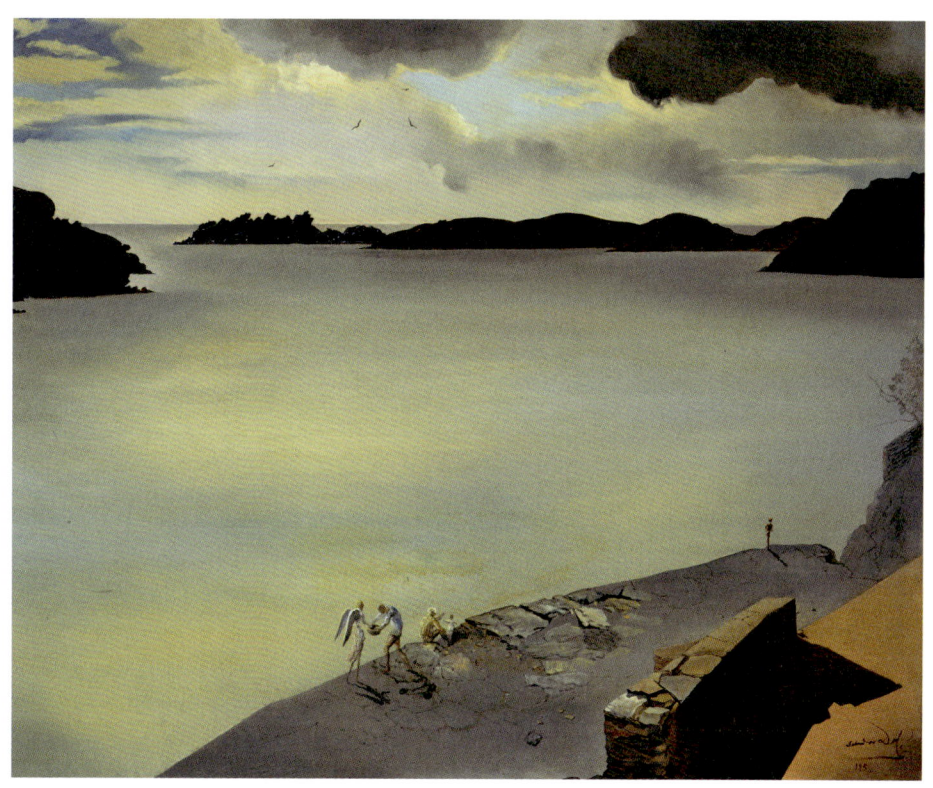

337
Landscape of Portlligat
1950
Oil on canvas, 59.5 × 78.5 cm
The Dalí Museum, St. Petersburg, Florida

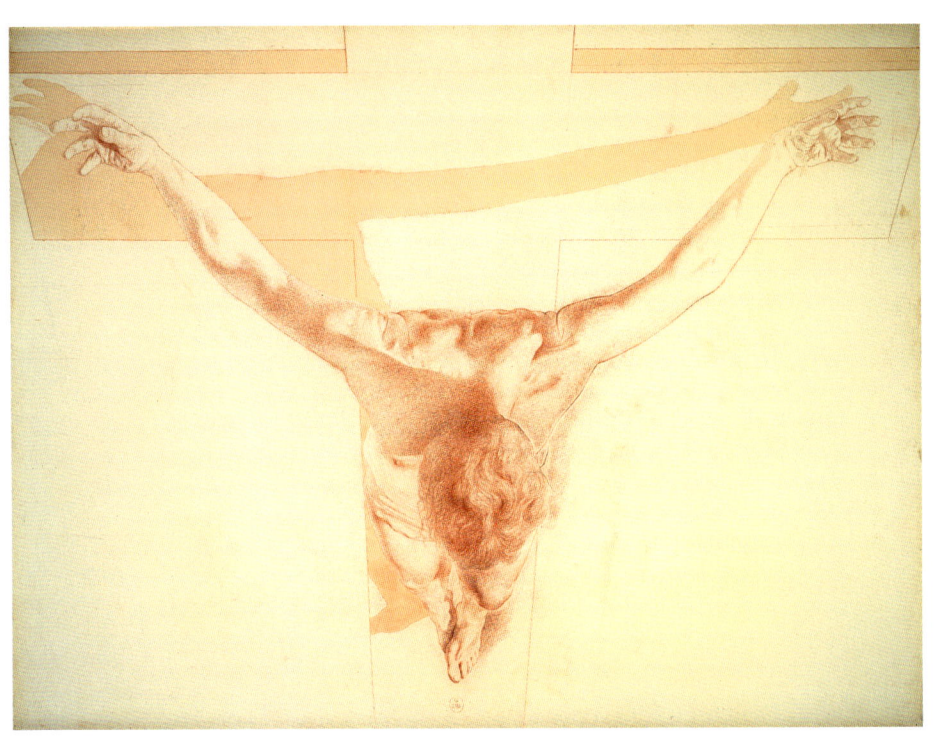

338
Christ in Perspective. Study for "Christ of St. John of the Cross"
1950
Red chalk on paper, 75.7 × 101.7 cm
The Dalí Museum, St. Petersburg, Florida

Return to Spain and Classicism

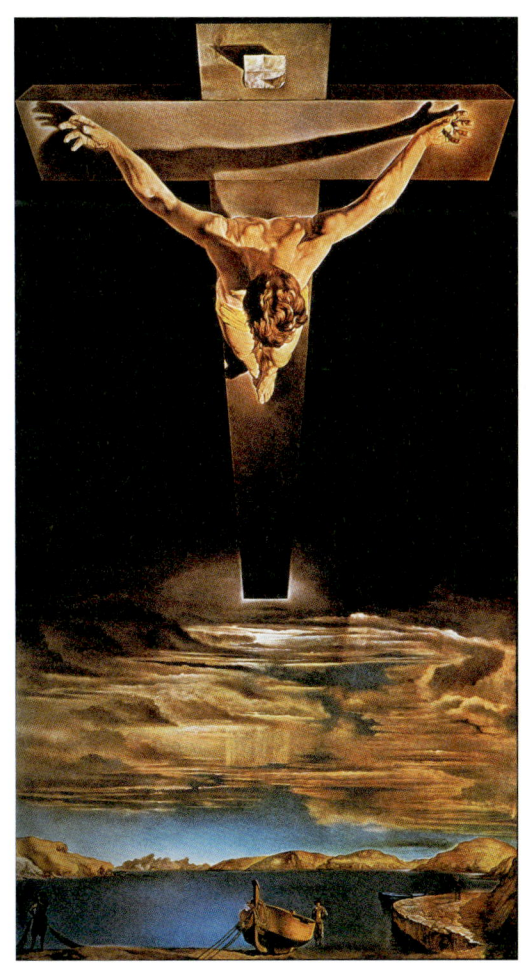

339
The Christ
1951
Oil on canvas, 204.8 × 115.9 cm
Kelvingrove Art Gallery and Museum, Glasgow

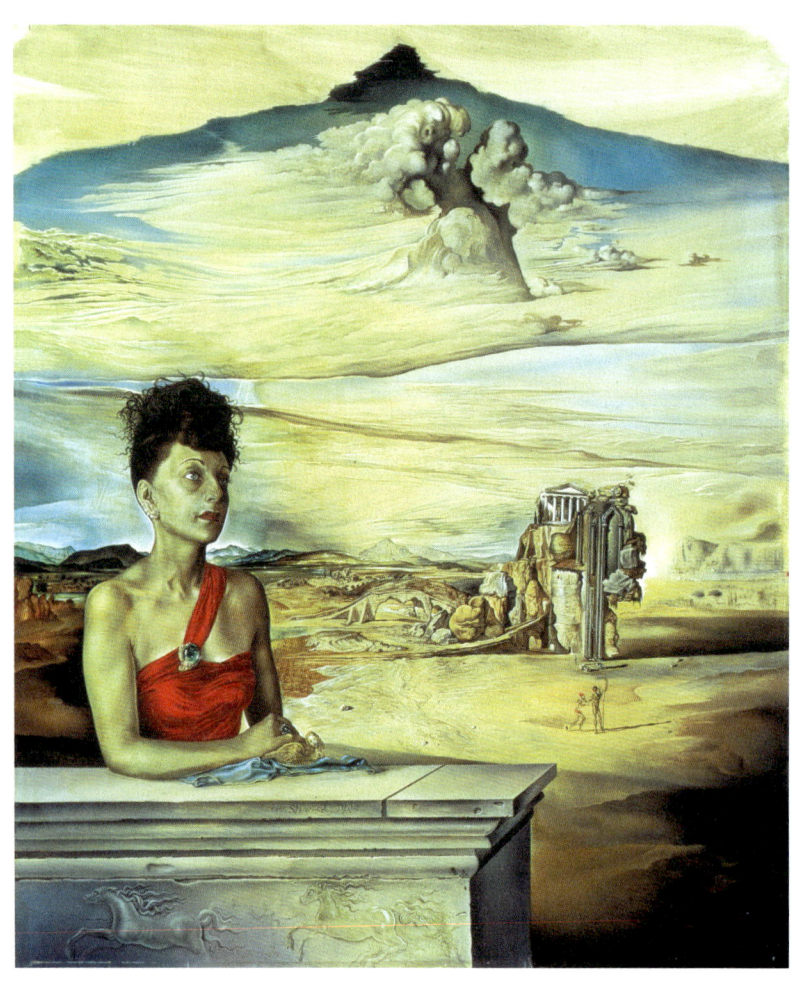

340
Portrait of Mrs. Jack Warner
c. 1944
Oil on canvas, 111.1 × 94.6 cm
Morohashi Museum of Modern Art, Kitashiobara, Fukushima Prefecture, Japan

Return to Spain and Classicism

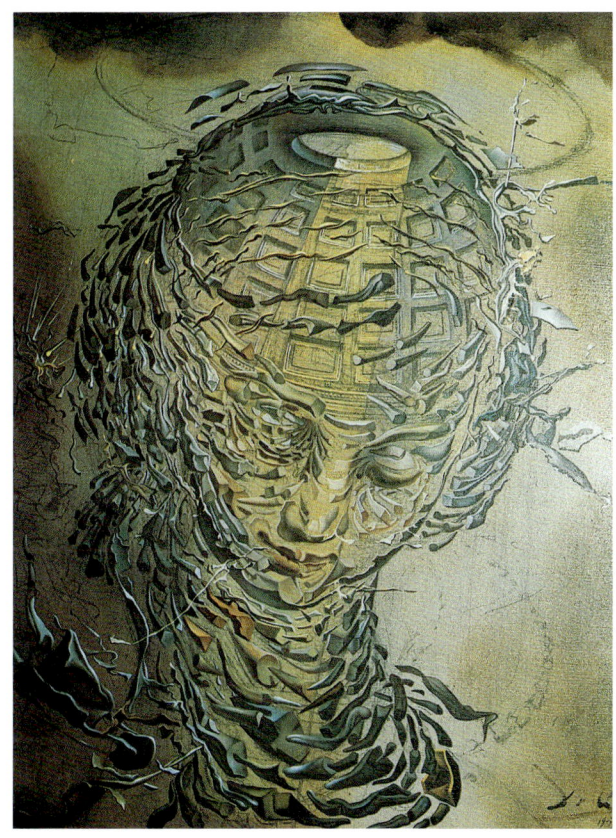

341
Exploding Raphaelesque Head
1951
Oil on canvas, 43.2 × 33.1 cm
Scottish National Gallery, Edinburgh

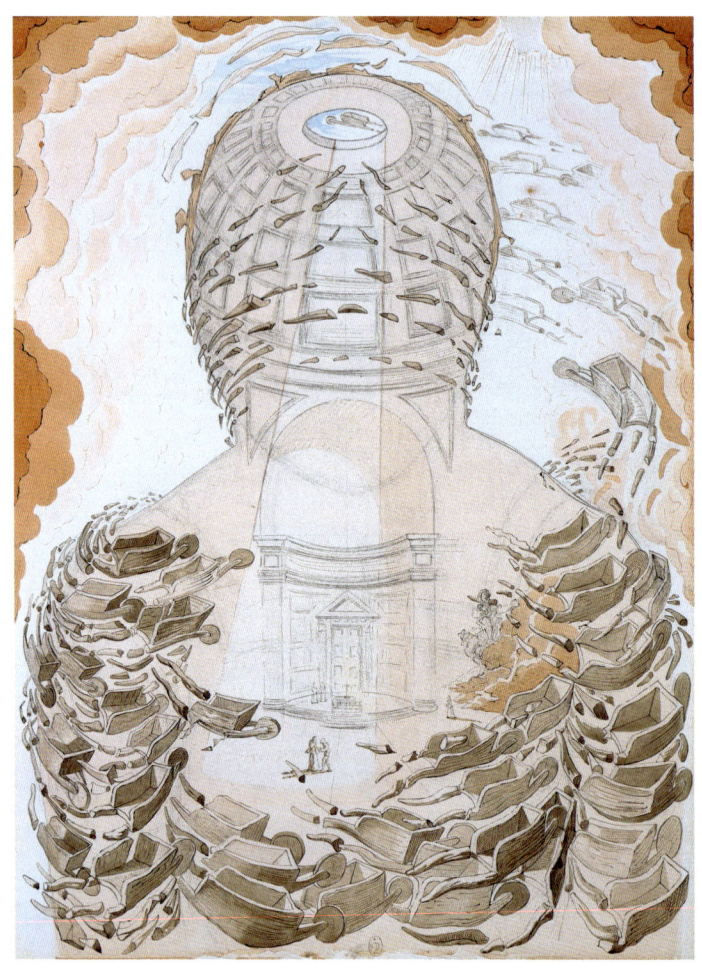

342
The Wheelbarrows (Cupola Consisting of Twisted Carts)
1951
Watercolour and ink on paper, 101.5 × 76.2 cm
The Dalí Museum, St. Petersburg, Florida

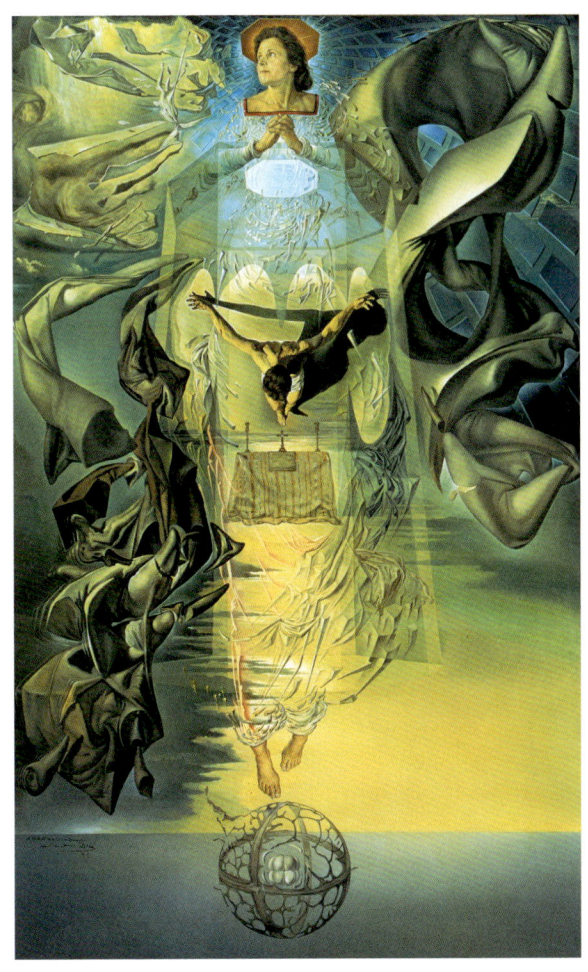

343
Assumpta corpuscularia lapislazulina
1952
Oil on canvas, 229.9 × 144.2 cm
Masaveu collection, Oviedo

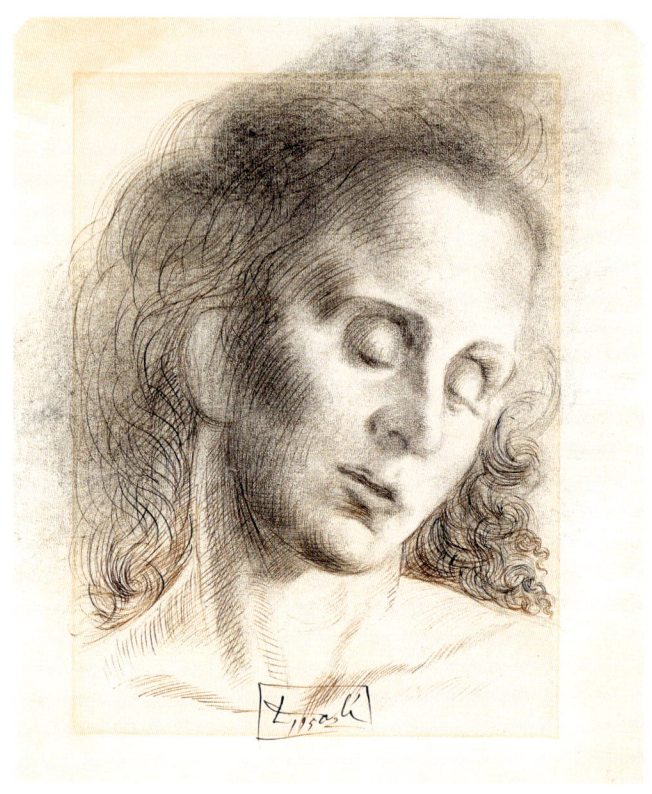

344
Gala Placidia
1952
Ink and pastel on paper, 45.7 × 34.6 cm
University of Arizona Museum of Art, The Edward Joseph Gallagher III Memorial Collection, Tucson, Arizona

Return to Spain and Classicism

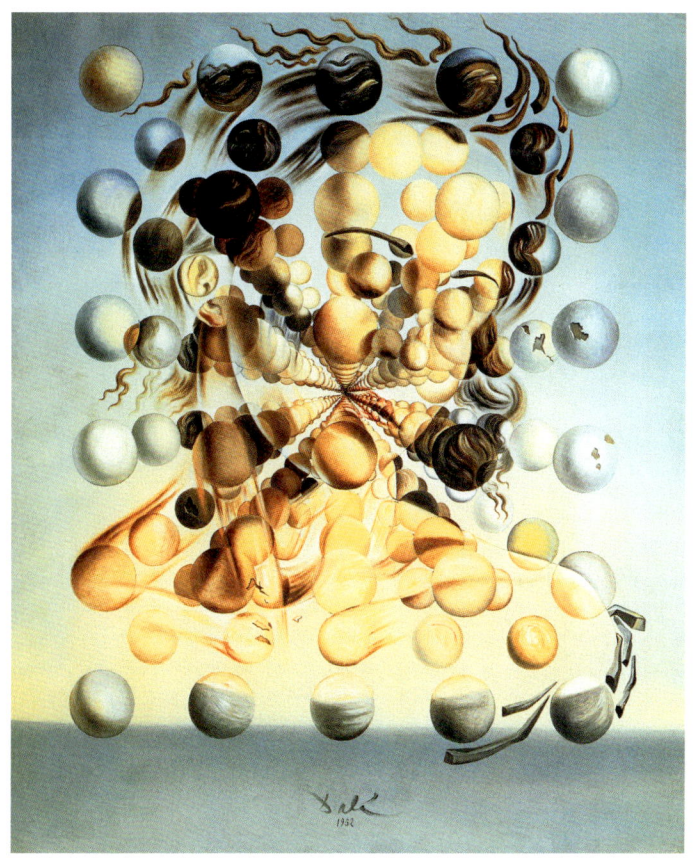

345
Gala Placidia
1952
Oil on canvas, 65 × 54 cm
Fundació Gala-Salvador Dalí, Figueres

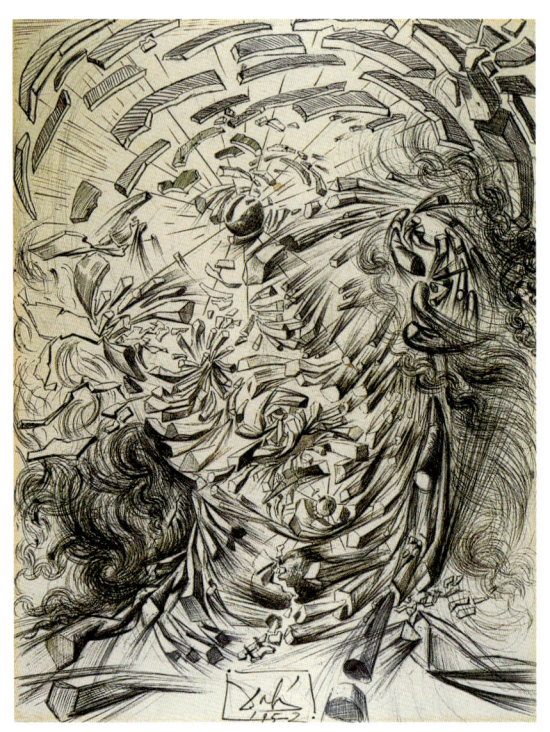

346
Nuclear Head of an Angel
1952
Black ink, sepia and pencil on paper, 56 × 43 cm
Private collection

Return to Spain and Classicism

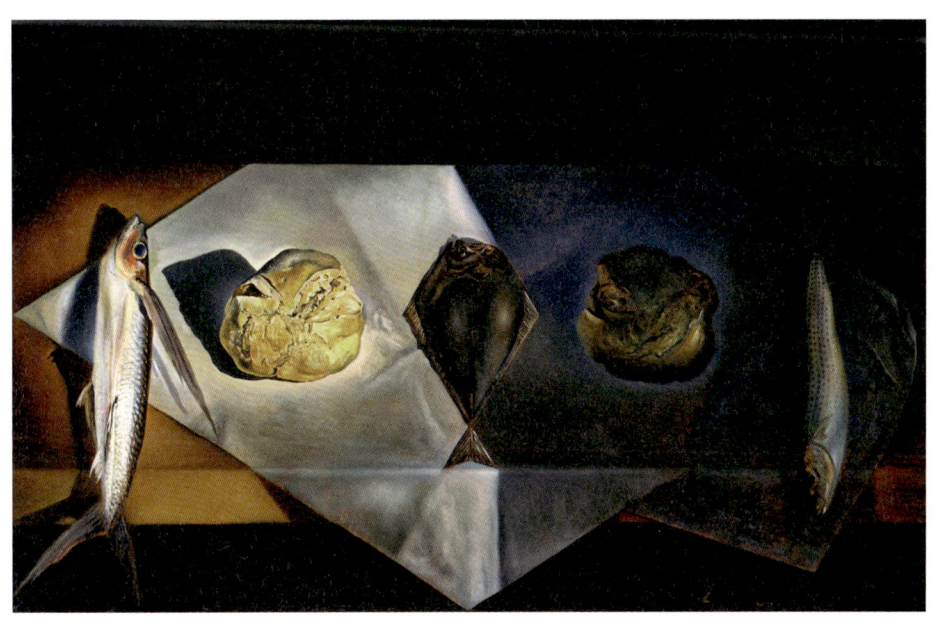

347
Evangelical Still Life
1952
Oil on canvas, 54.6 × 87 cm
The Dalí Museum, St. Petersburg, Florida

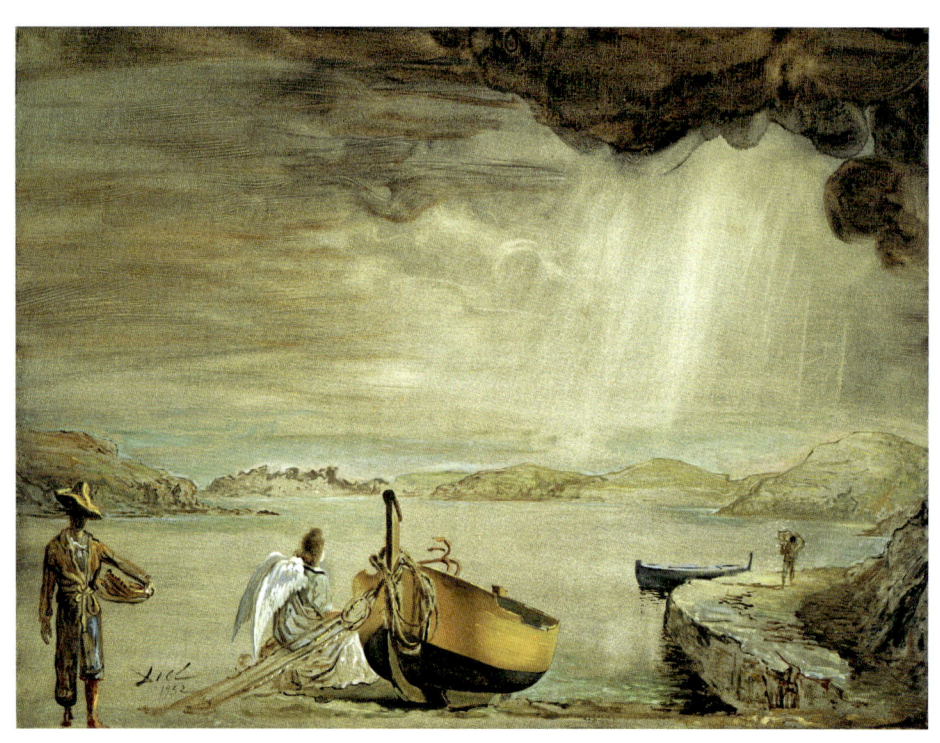

348
The Angel of Portlligat
1952
Oil on canvas, 59.8 × 78 cm
The Dalí Museum, St. Petersburg, Florida

Return to Spain and Classicism

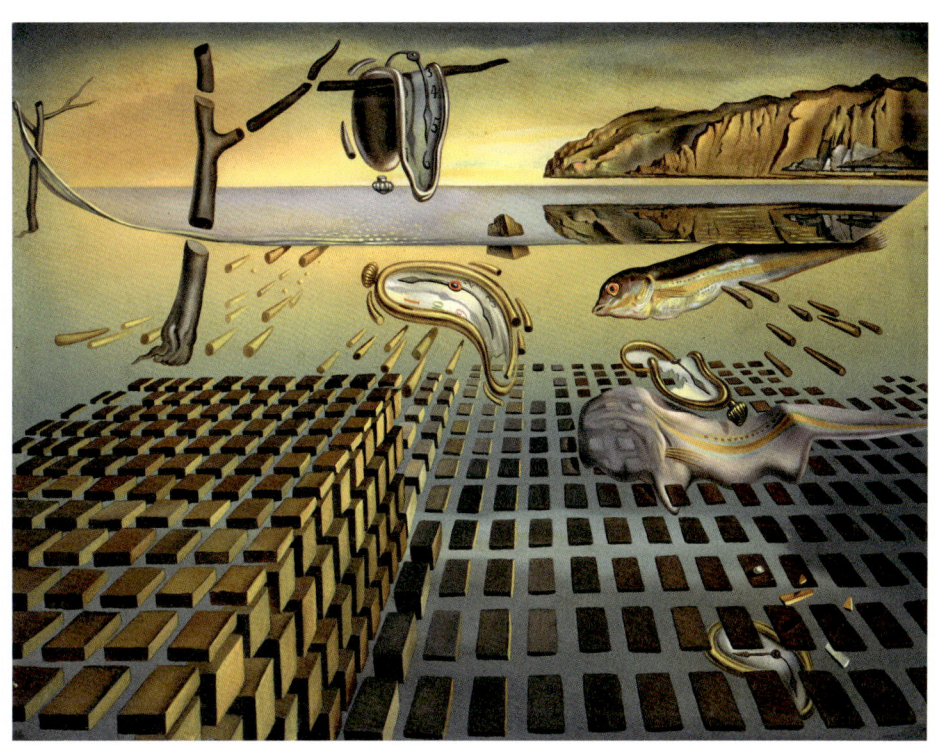

349
The Corpuscular Persistence of Memory
1952–1954
Oil on canvas, 25.4 × 33 cm
The Dalí Museum, St. Petersburg, Florida

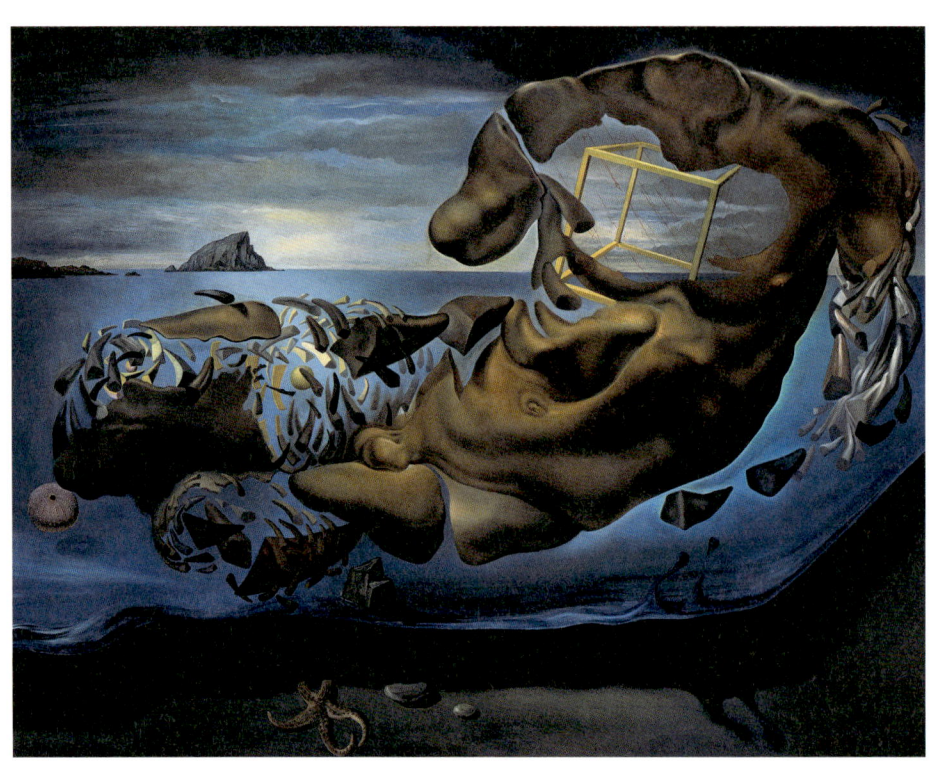

350
Creation of man
c. 1954
Oil on canvas, 101.5 × 131 cm
Fundació Gala-Salvador Dalí, Figueres

Return to Spain and Classicism

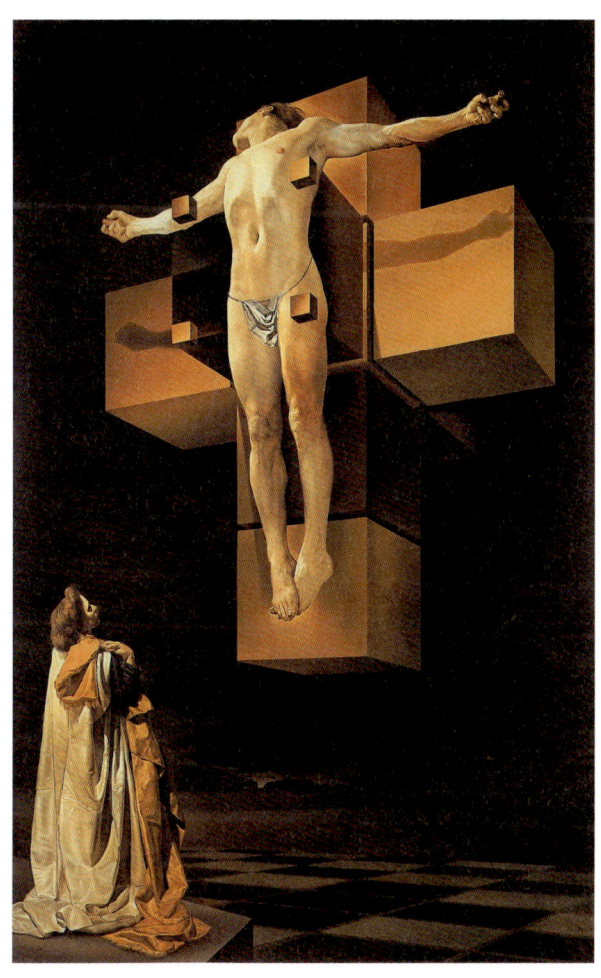

351
Corpus hipercubus
c. 1954
Oil on canvas, 194.4 × 123.9 cm
The Metropolitan Museum of Art, New York

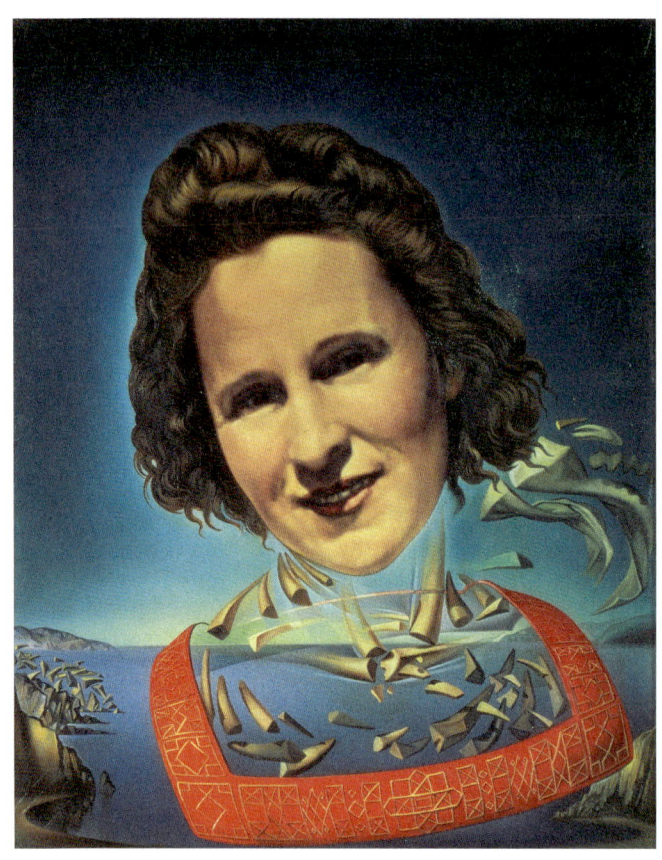

352
The Flesh of the Décolleté of My Wife, Clothed, Outstripping Light at Full Speed
c. 1954
Oil on canvas, 39 × 31.5 cm
Fundació Gala-Salvador Dalí, Figueres

Return to Spain and Classicism

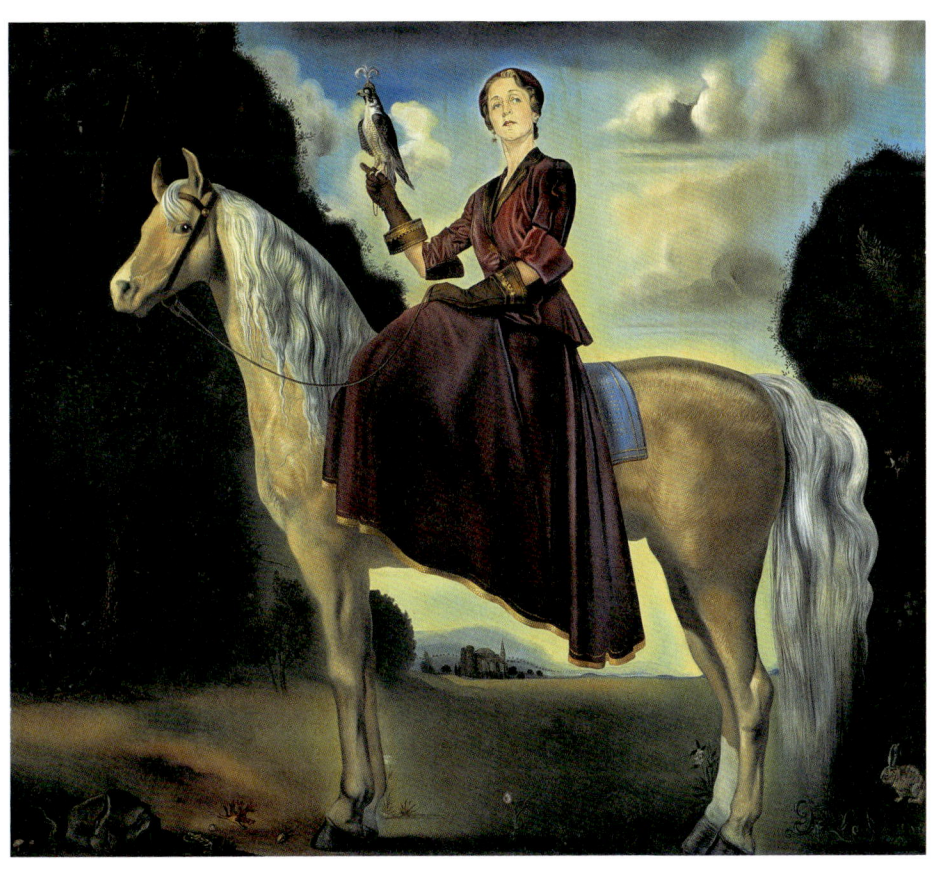

353
Equestrian Fantasy
1954
Oil on canvas, 119.7 × 134.6 cm
Beaverbrook Art Gallery, Beaverbrook Canadian Foundation, Fredericton, New Brunswick, Canada

1948–1960

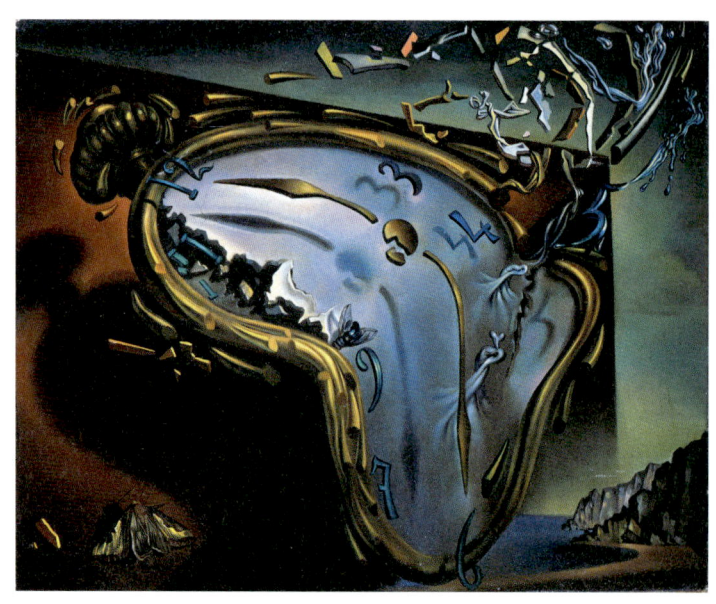

354
Soft Watch Exploding in 888 Particles after Twenty Years of Total Immobility
c. 1954
Oil on canvas, 20.5 × 25.7 cm
Private collection

Return to Spain and Classicism

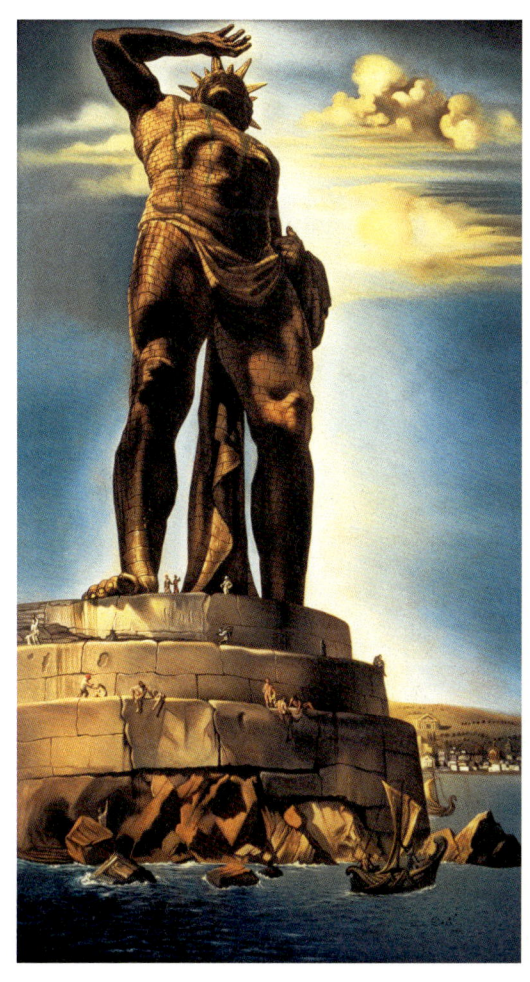

355
The Colossus of Rhodes
1954
Oil on canvas, 68.8 × 39 cm
Kunstmuseum Bern, Bern

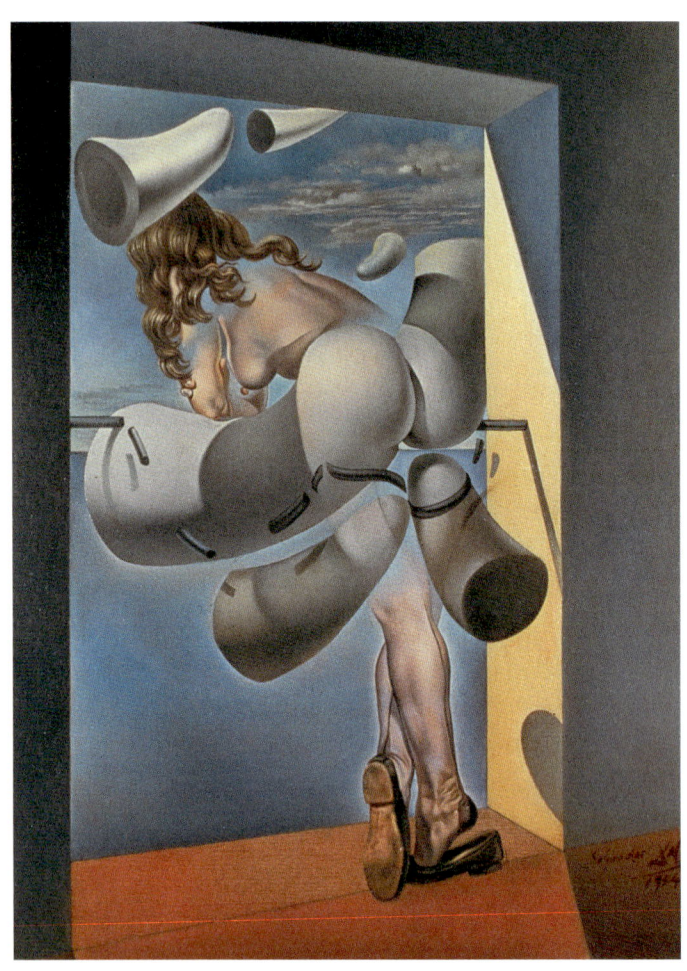

356
Young Virgin Auto-Sodomized by Her Own Chastity
1954
Oil on canvas, 40 × 30 cm
Private collection

Return to Spain and Classicism

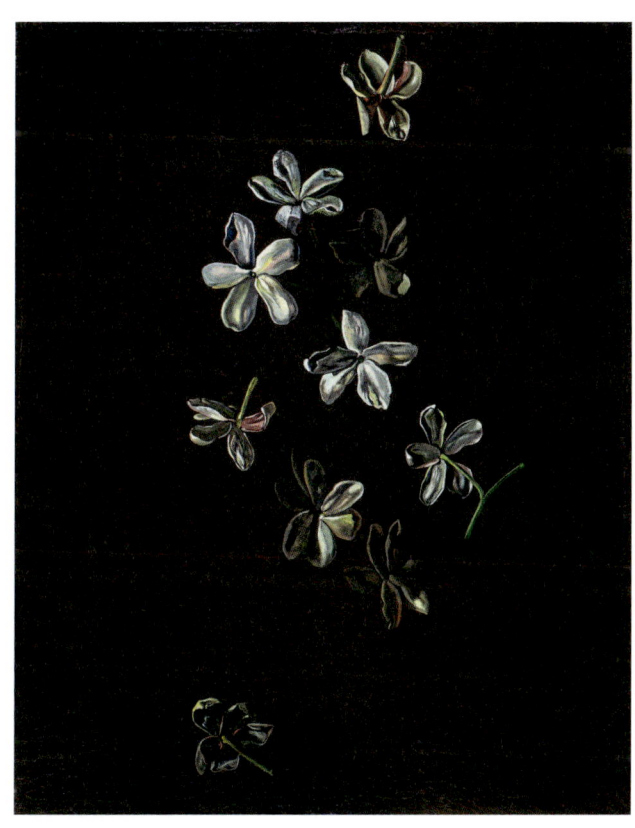

357
A Shower of Jasmine
c. 1954
Oil on canvas, 25.9 × 20.3 cm
Private collection

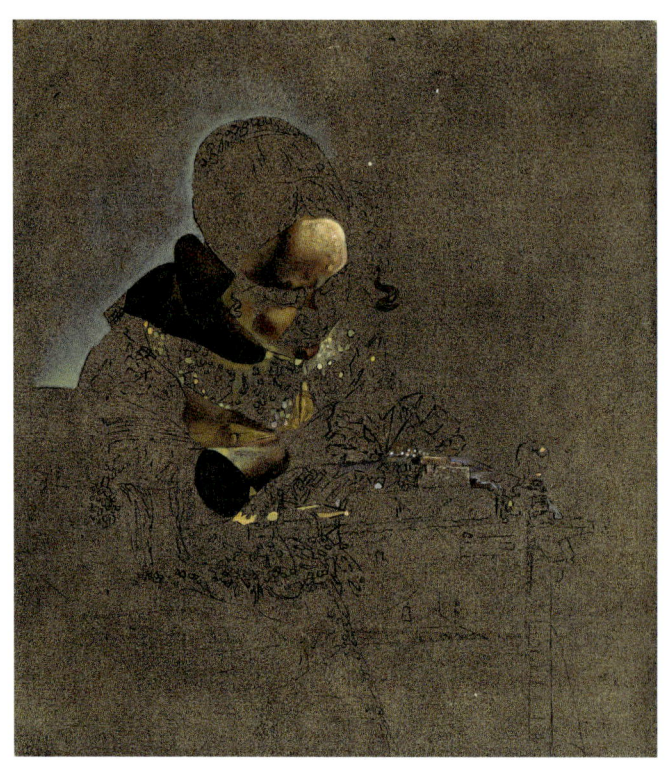

358
Study for the "Paranoiac-critical Study of Vermeer's 'The Lacemaker'"
c. 1955
Oil on canvas, 25 × 22.5 cm
Fundació Gala-Salvador Dalí, Figueres

Return to Spain and Classicism

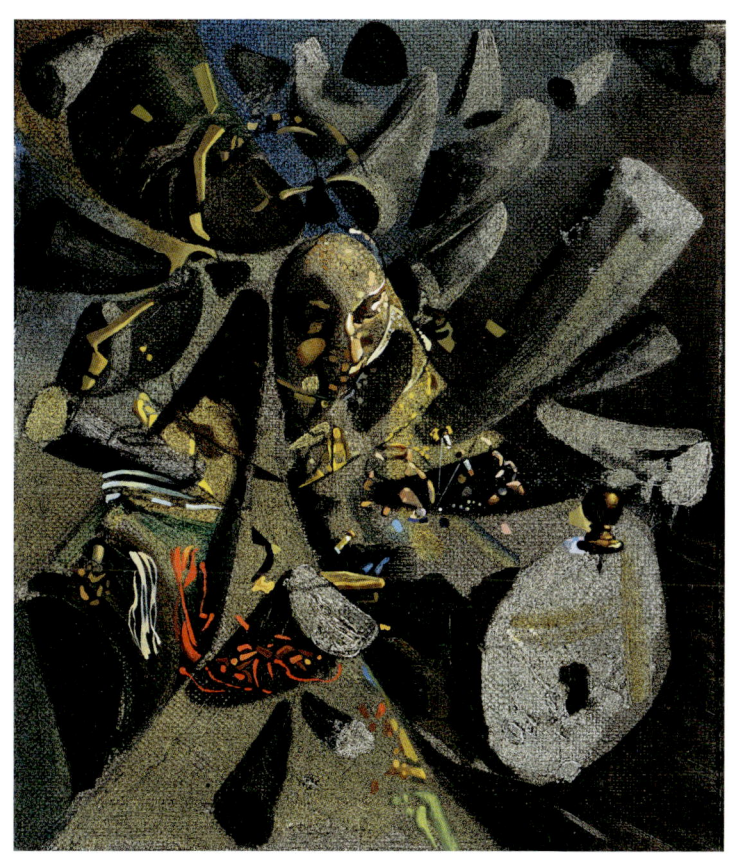

359
Paranoiac-critical Study of Vermeer's "The Lacemaker"
c. 1955
Oil on canvas, 27.1 × 22.1 cm
Solomon R. Guggenheim Museum, New York

1948–1960

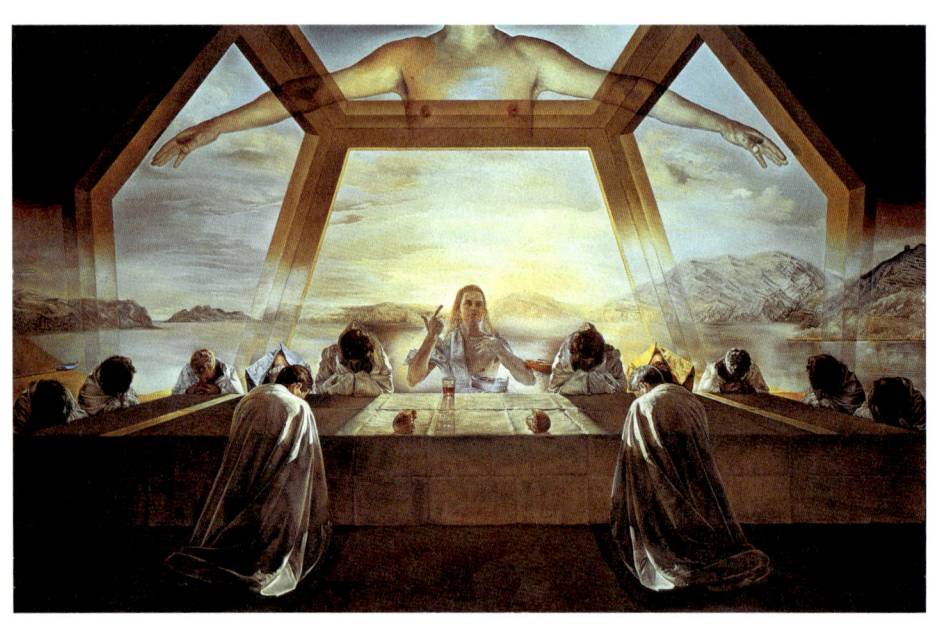

360
The Sacrament of the Last Supper
1955
Oil on canvas, 166.7 × 267 cm
Chester Dale Collection, National Gallery of Art, Washington, D.C.

Return to Spain and Classicism

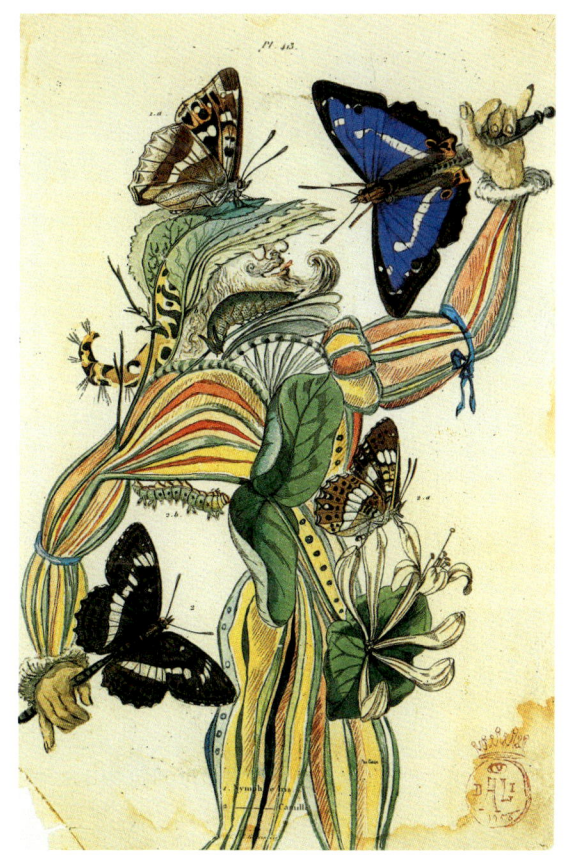

361
Illustration for "Trois papillons"
1955
Watercolour and ink on print, 26 × 18 cm
The Dalí Museum, St. Petersburg, Florida

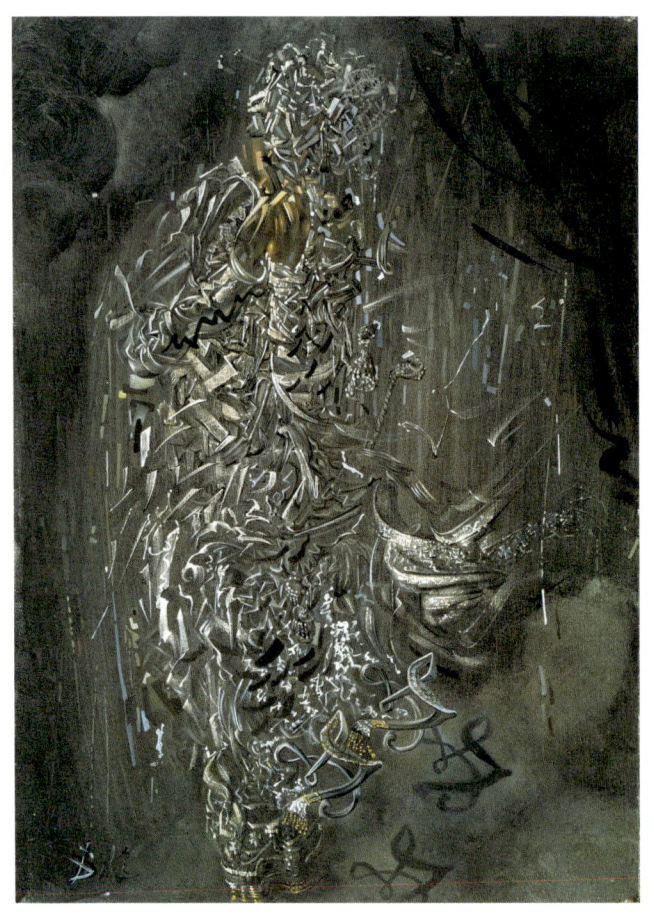

362
Saint Surrounded by Three Pi Mesons
1956
Oil on canvas, 42.5 × 31 cm
Fundació Gala-Salvador Dalí, Figueres

Return to Spain and Classicism

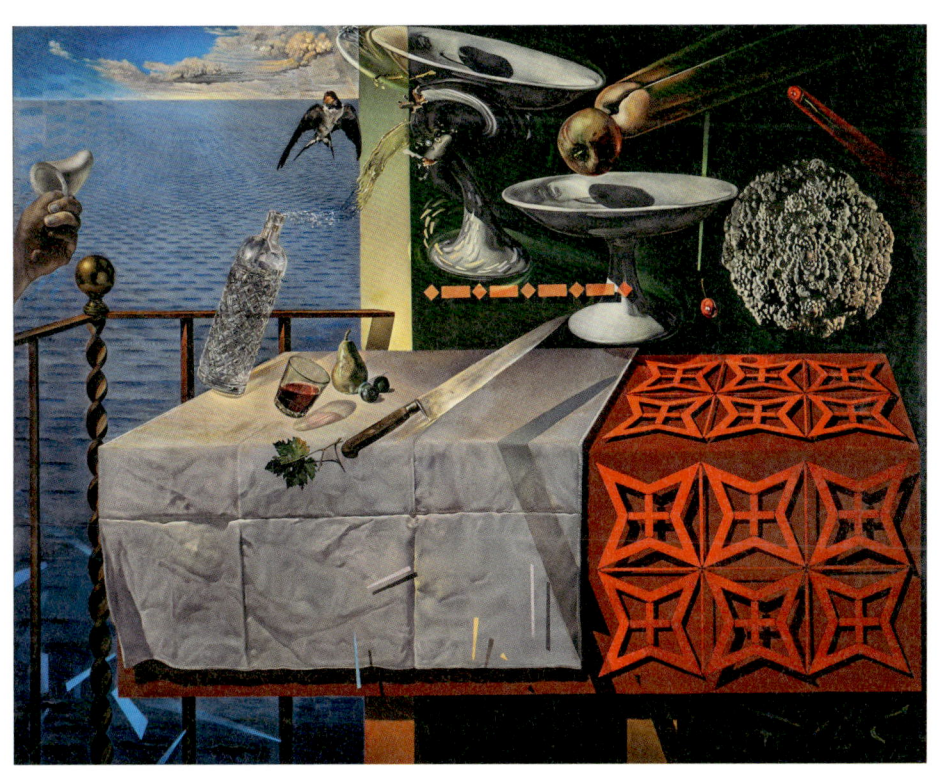

363
Fast-Moving Still Life
c. 1956
Oil on canvas, 125 × 160 cm
The Dalí Museum, St. Petersburg, Florida

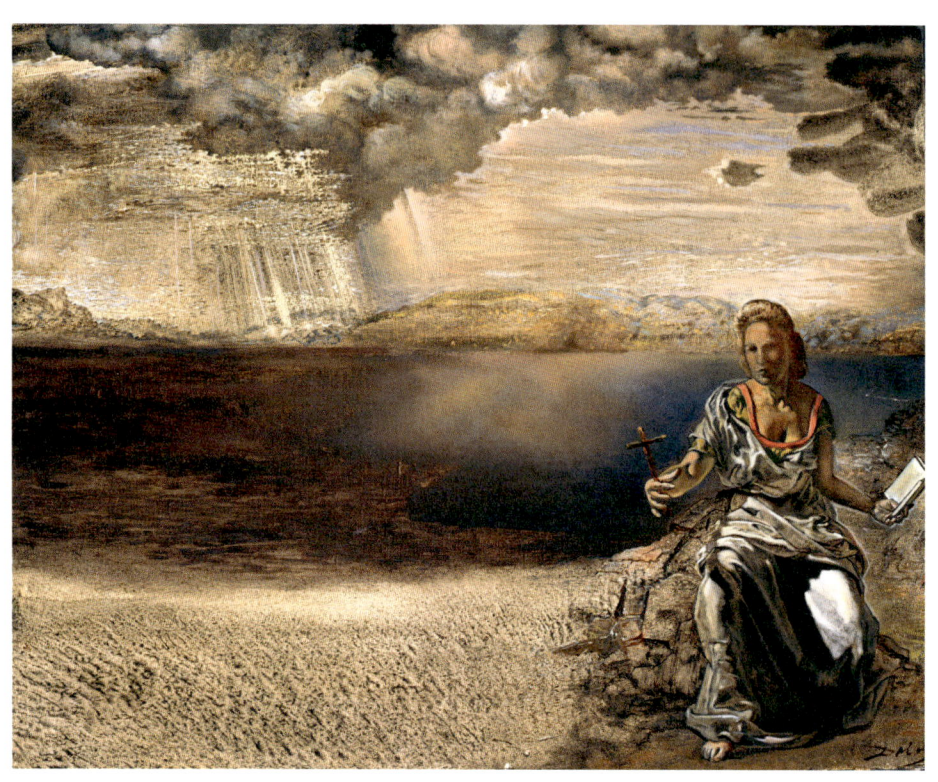

364
Saint Helena at Portlligat
c. 1956
Oil on canvas, 31 × 42 cm
The Dalí Museum, St. Petersburg, Florida

Return to Spain and Classicism

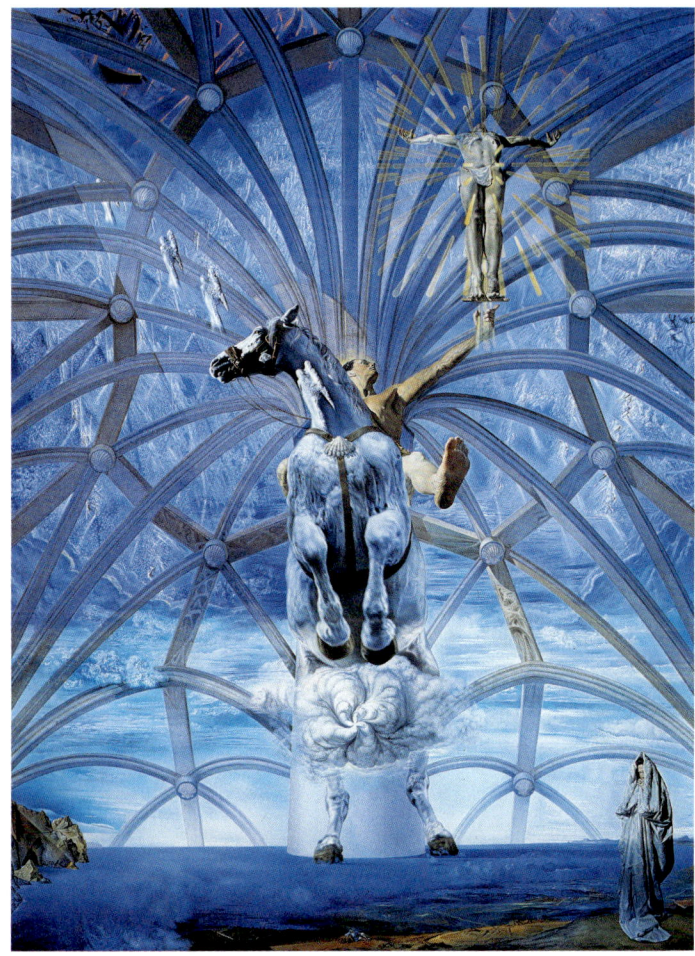

365
Saint James the Great
c. 1957
Oil on canvas, 407.7 × 304.8 cm
Beaverbrook Art Gallery, Beaverbrook Canadian Foundation, Fredericton, New Brunswick, Canada

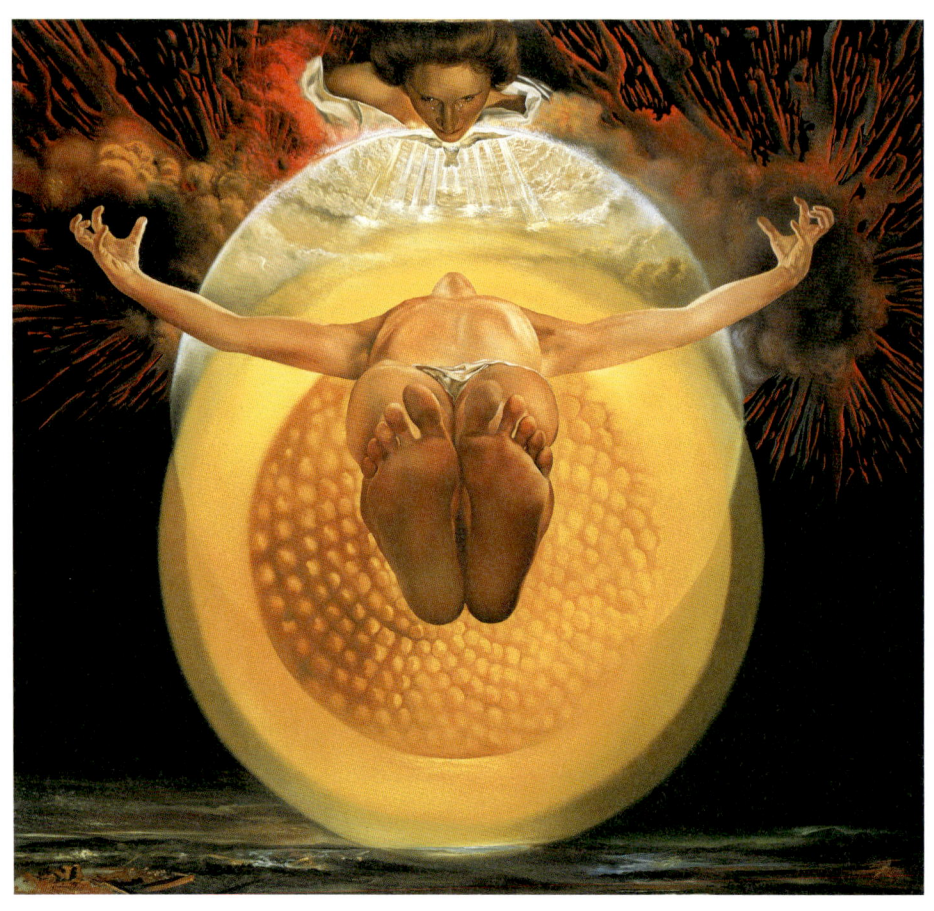

366
Pieta
1958
Oil on canvas, 115 × 123 cm
Pérez Simón Collection, Mexico

Return to Spain and Classicism

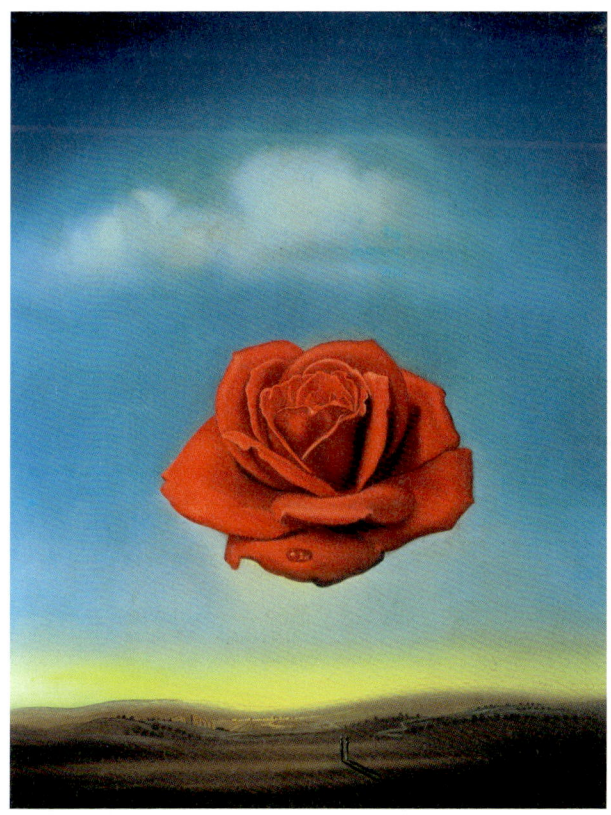

367
The Rose
1958
Oil on canvas, 36 × 28 cm
Private collection

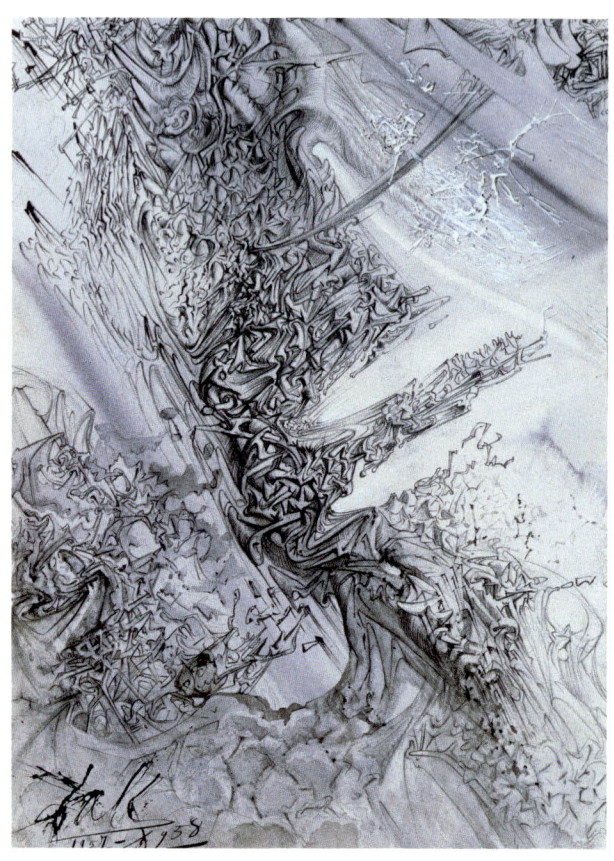

368
Pi-Mesonic Angel
1958
Watercolour on paper, 40.6 × 30.5 cm
The Dalí Museum, St. Petersburg, Florida

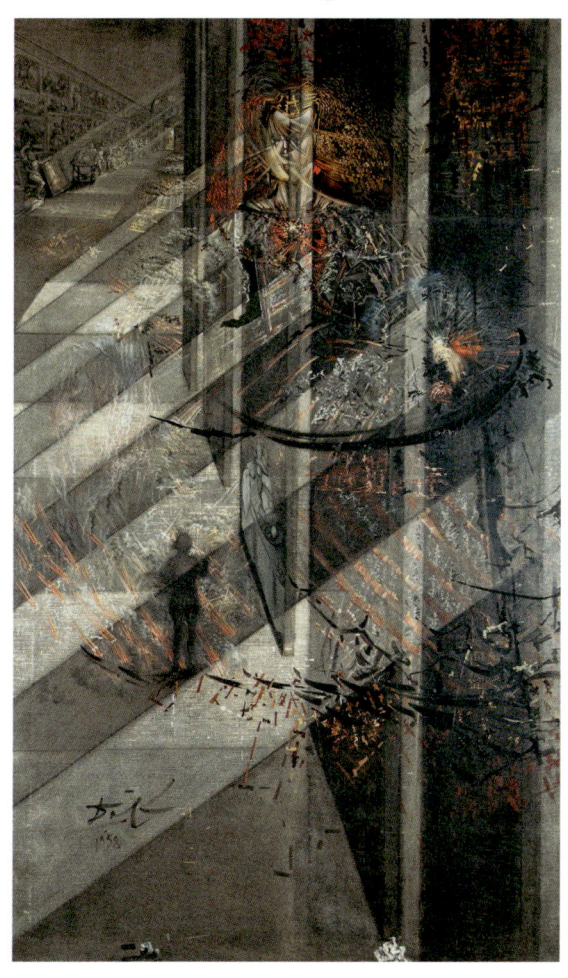

369
Velázquez painting the Infanta with the lights and shadows of his proper glory
1958
Oil on canvas, 156.1 × 92.2 cm
The Dalí Museum, St. Petersburg, Florida

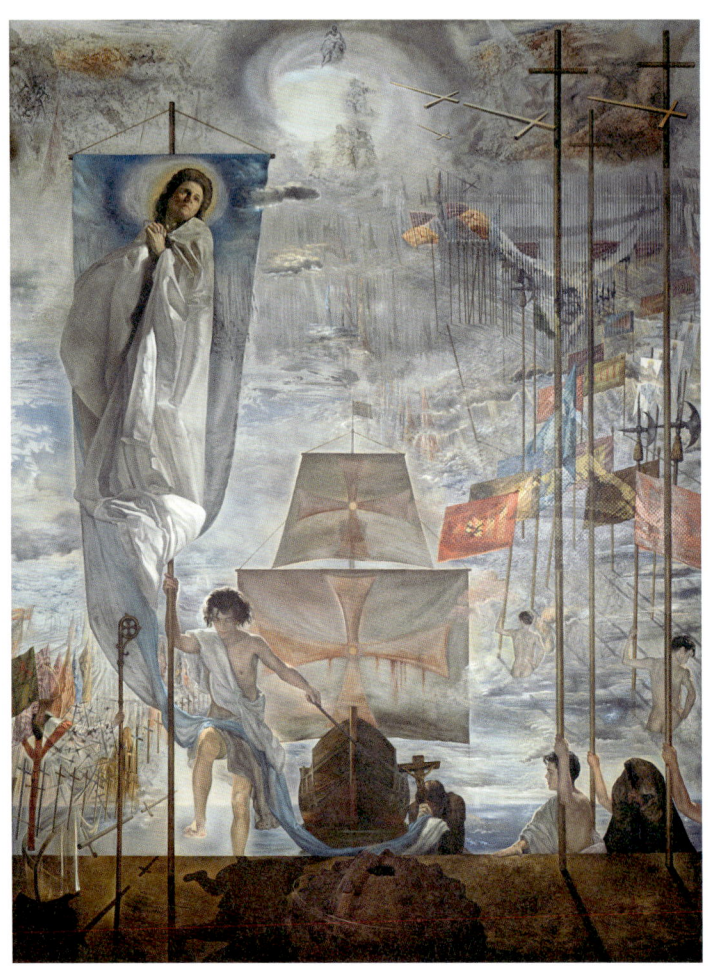

370
Christopher Columbus or *Discovery of America by Christopher Columbus*
1958
Oil on canvas, 410.2 × 310.1 cm
The Dalí Museum, St. Petersburg, Florida

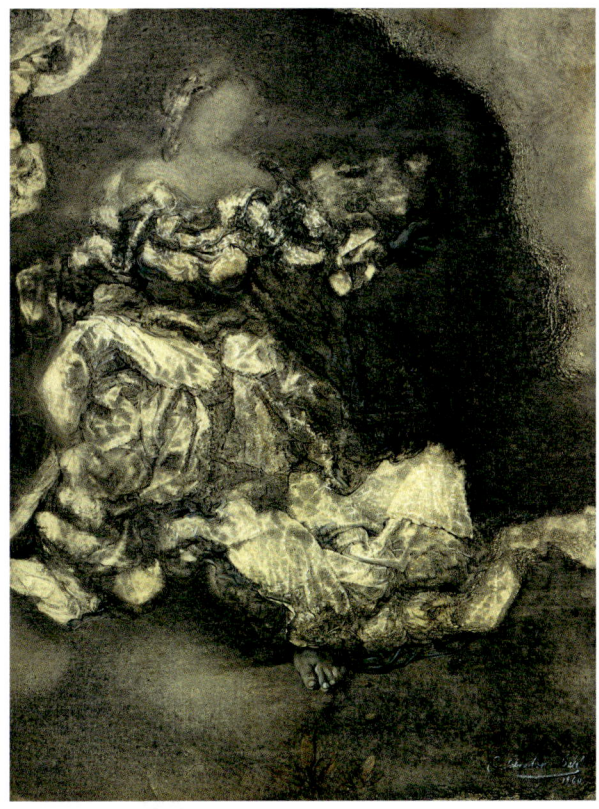

371
Beatrice
1958–1960
Oil on canvas, 39.5 × 29.6 cm
The Dalí Museum, St. Petersburg, Florida

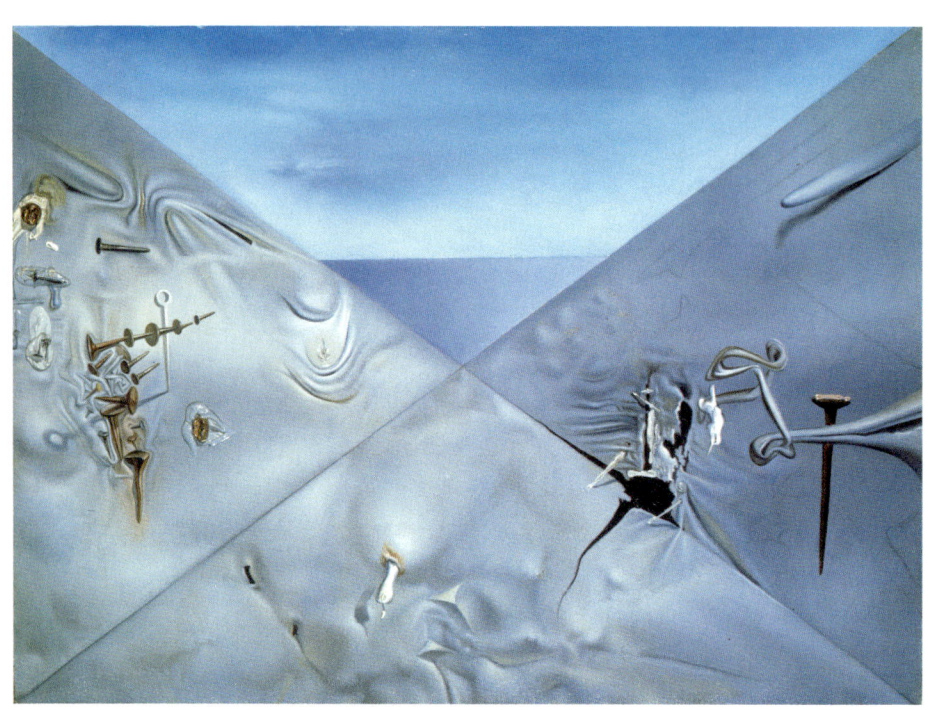

372
Hyper-xiological Sky
c. 1960
Oil, nails and teeth on canvas, 31.2 × 43 cm
Private collection

Return to Spain and Classicism

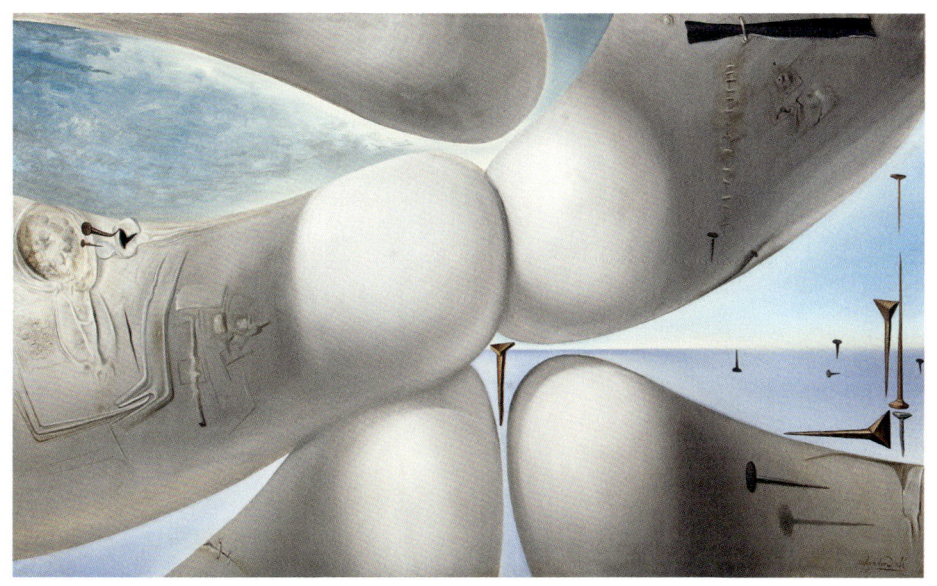

373
Goddess Leaning on her Elbow
c. 1960
Oil on canvas, 92.5 × 153 cm
Departament de la Presidència de la Generalitat de Catalunya, Barcelona

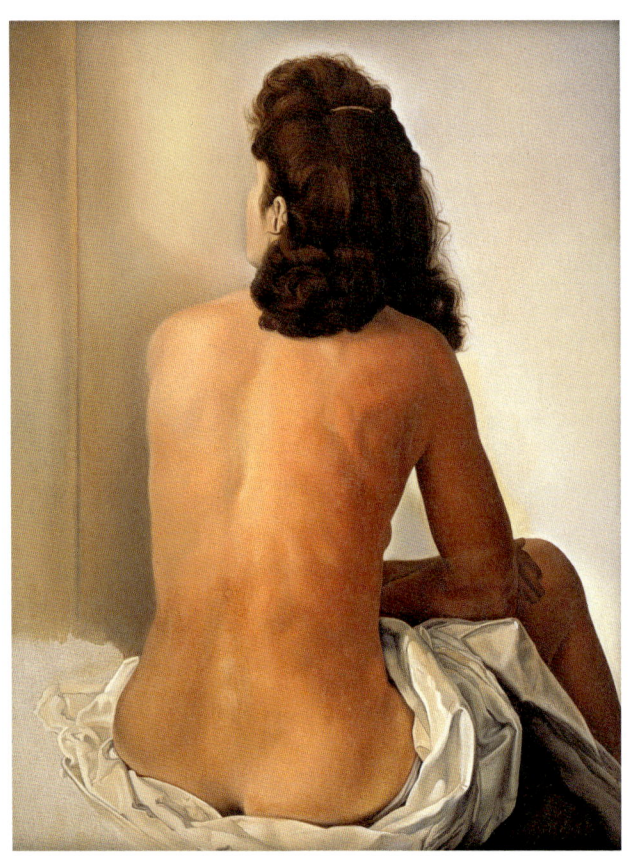

374
Gala Nude from Behind
c. 1960
Oil on canvas, 41 × 31.5 cm
Fundació Gala-Salvador Dalí, Figueres

Return to Spain and Classicism

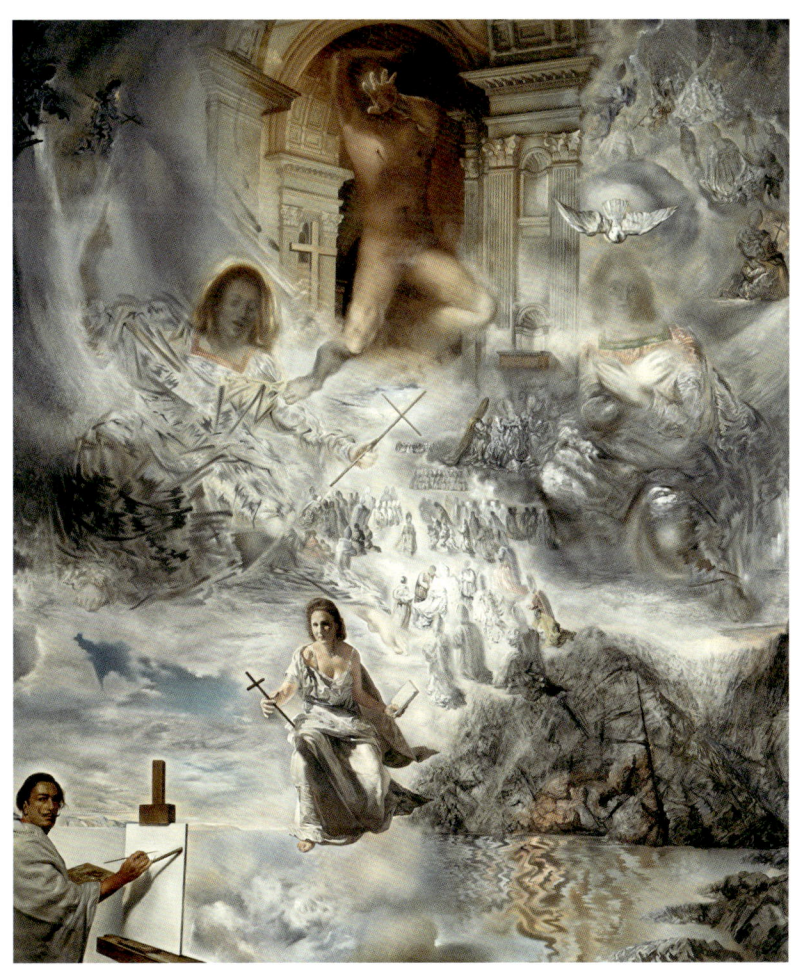

375
The Ecumenical Council
c. 1960
Oil on canvas, 300 × 254 cm
The Dalí Museum, St. Petersburg, Florida

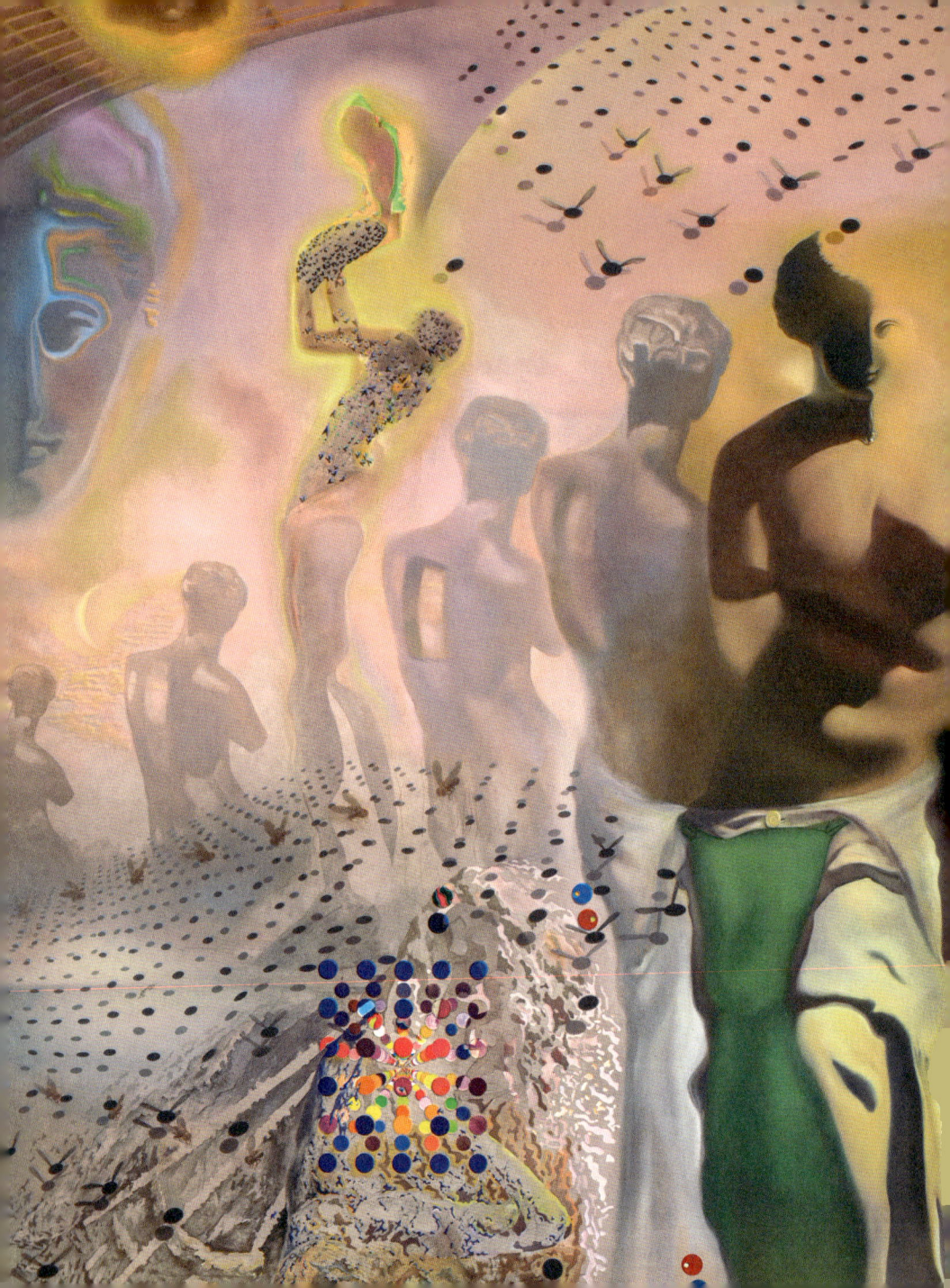

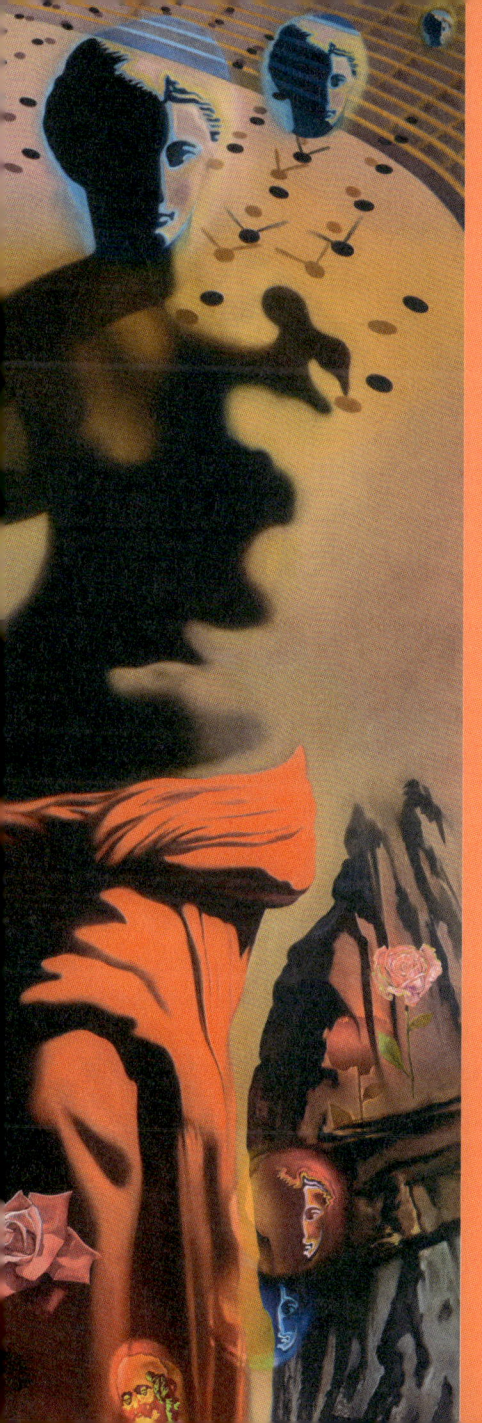

Avant-garde Experimentation

1960 onwards

During the 1960s, Dalí reaffirmed his engagement with the idea of Classicism and positioned his new work within the history of the Old Masters, while at the same time engaging with select elements of avant-garde experimentation. Specifically, he positioned himself within the tradition of Spanish painting, referring with greater frequency to the paradigmatic example of Diego Velázquez (1599–1660). Thus Dalí constructed his own historical and artistic lineage that originated with Velázquez, continued with Picasso, Juan Gris (1887–1927), Miró and culminated in Dalí himself, along with the contemporary 'Informalist' painters Antoni Tàpies (1923–2012) and Manolo Millares (1926–1972). Informalism referred to the new school of European gestural painting promoted by the French critic Michel Tapié (1909–1987). Dalí's battle was to claim for painting an intellectual function that he thought had been lost in the work of painters like Piet Mondrian (1872–1944) who he had previously challenged in his book *Les Cocus du vieil art moderne* (1956).

Dalí remained a controversial figure for the Surrealists, who considered him reactionary in both political and aesthetic terms. When the International Surrealist Exhibition was staged in late November 1960 until January 1961, the inclusion of Dalí, who had long been excluded from the movement, was controversial. It was not only the presence of Dalí (who had of course been a Surrealist for a decade) that irritated the group, but also his contribution of a painting with an overt religious subject. This exhibition, staged with the subtitle *Surrealist intrusion in the enchanters' domain*, was presented at the D'Arcy Galleries in New York. The exhibition was managed by the French poet and critic Édouard Jaguer (1924–2006) and the French author José Pierre (1927–1999), both Surrealists, under the direction of Breton and French artist Marcel Duchamp (1887–1968). The organisers clearly intended to include Dalí, but Breton remained in France and Duchamp, who was close to Dalí, took the lead in selecting many of the works. The painting in question was *The Sistine Madonna* (1958), which Duchamp added to the selection at the last minute. It was presented with the French title

L'oreille anti-matière (Antimatter Ear), a title that omitted any mention of the Madonna. Once on display in the exhibition, a number of the Surrealists were of course outraged and rapidly published the tract 'We Don't Ear it that Way,' which denounced Dalí as a reactionary and was signed by various members of the group including Breton and Jaguer. Dalí clearly remained a controversial figure within the circle of Surrealism.

On 4 March 1960, in collaboration with the American photographer Philippe Halsman (1906–1979), Dalí staged a happening, which was filmed on videotape at a New York television studio (Videotape Productions Inc.). Titled *Chaos and Creation*, this performance consisted of a model, whose body had been covered in paint rolling around on a canvas to create a chance-derived image. This extraordinary event anticipated and paralleled the emergence of similar actions by younger European artists like the French artist Yves Klein (1928–1962), the French sculptor César (1921–1998), the French artist Niki de Saint Phalle (1930–2002) and the Swiss sculptor Jean Tinguely (1925–1991).

For several years Dalí had also dreamt of staging a surreal bullfight. He had mentioned it in several interviews, as well as in conversation with the celebrated Spanish matador de toros Luis Miguel Dominguín (1926–1996), who was a close friend of Picasso's. Dalí's first iteration of the idea went back to his earlier project of March 1954 for Las Fallas, the traditional celebration held annually to commemorate San José, in Valencia. In this festival, specialist artisans construct elaborate models in papier-mâché according to an artist's design, which are then presented in the streets of Valencia before being burned. The sculpture that Dalí presented at Las Fallas depicted a moment at the conclusion of a bullfight in which Dalí imagined a helicopter would lift the dead body of the bull into the air. The model consisted of a reconstruction of a bullring set against the Montserrat mountain range near Barcelona and the giant faces of both Dalí and Picasso.

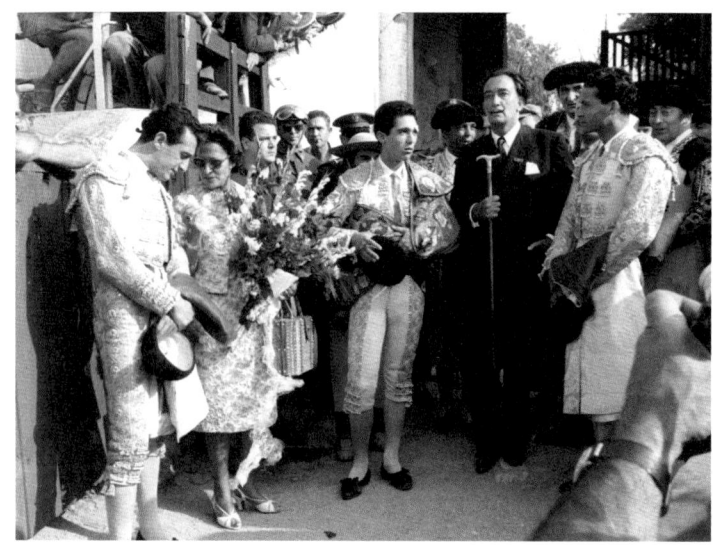

Robert Descharnes (photographer), Dalí and Gala visiting the bullfights put on in homage to Dalí, pictured here with bullfighters Fermín Murillo, Paco Camino and Curro Girón, 1961. Collection of The Dalí Museum.

Dalí finally realised his dream on 12 August 1961, when a real bullfight was staged in his honour in the arena at Figueres. Dalí also had designed the poster announcing the fight. Dalí had convinced the Mayor of Figueres to facilitate the happening, and a helicopter had been arranged for the conclusion. With the help of Duchamp and the collaboration of the younger artists Saint Phalle and Tinguely, the bullfight was preceded by a self-destructing work of art, a kind of happening. Both Saint Phalle and Tinguely were in attendance, along with Dalí and Duchamp. A construction in the form of a fighting bull was filled with fireworks and set to explode in the centre of the arena prior to the bullfight. After this performance, three celebrated bullfighters – Curro Girón (1938–1988), Fermín Murillo (1934–2003) and Paco Camino (1940–2024) – were presented with real bulls provided by the *ganadería* (cattle ranch) Molero Hermanos. At the conclusion of the fight, Dalí's intentions were thwarted, as the wind increased, and the helicopter was unable to fly.

Dalí continued to situate himself in reference both to tradition and to the present. In May 1962 he published a text titled 'Tàpies, Tàpies, classic, classic' in *Art News*, in which he defended the younger painter Tàpies, likening him to Velázquez and noting that, 'Tàpies paints the accidents of desoxyribonucleic [sic] acid, which is nothing but the central factor of Life and the Persistence of Memory.' These were not frivolous comments, as is revealed when considering the works included in in Dalí's autumn exhibition at the Saló del Tinell, Barcelona, which opened on 15 October 1962. The exhibition included six new ambitious and complex paintings, all from 1962, including *The Battle of Tetuán (Homage to Marià Fortuny)*. These works were set alongside the Catalan painter Mariano Fortuny's (1838–1874) monumental history painting *The Battle of Tetuán* (1862–66) and *The Court of the Alhambra* (1871), the latter lent from Gala's collection. In the catalogue, entitled *Fortuny, Dalí y sus Batallas de Tetuán*, Dalí wrote 'My homage to Fortuny is a spiritual battle and, this battle, can be no other than the Battle of Tetuán, since it is more metaphysical and transcendental than all those that have existed.'

In Dalí's solo show at Knoedler Gallery in New York in 1963, he continued to pursue many of these concerns and showed a smaller version of the painting *The Battle of Tetuán* with the title *Small Battle of Tetuán*. The show consisted of ten works, most of them recently completed, and was accompanied by a catalogue with the subtitle 'Hommage à Crick et Watson' and a title page that announced that 'George Keller presents Salvador Dalí.' Keller had run the Carstairs Gallery for many years, and was now planning to retire to his native Switzerland, so he placed Dalí at Knoedler. One of the largest paintings in the exhibition *GALACIDALACIDESOXIRIBUNUCLEICACID (Homage to Crick and Watson)* (1963) made reference to the double helix – a form that describes the physical structure of DNA – and melded it with other, more mystical symbols suggesting the trinity. In a more subjective, personal tone was *Portrait of my dead brother* (c. 1963) [377]. The catalogue included long analytic commentaries by Dalí explaining the symbolism of the works on show, which were already evident in the titles of the works.

During the 1960s, Dalí had a number of important solo exhibitions. He was substantially represented in the Galerie Charpentier's Surrealism exhibition in Paris in 1964. In this exhibition he presented mainly paintings from the 1930s alongside his recently completed cast of the bronze version of his *Venus de Milo with Drawers* [242]; he had created a plaster version in 1936. Rapidly, this sculpture became an icon of Dalí's late 'Surrealist' works, though it had been much less well known in the 1930s, and as we have seen, by this point, he was no longer officially a member of the group.

Dalí's retrospective at the Gallery of Modern Art in New York in 1965 was his biggest show since his exhibition at The Museum of Modern Art in New York in 1941 and attracted much attention, aided by the documentary film simultaneously produced by the British filmmaker Jack Bond (1937–2024). Though the exhibition was plagued by administrative problems, forcing some of the works to be removed before the official closing date, it provided the public with a comprehensive overview of Dalí's work from the very beginning right up to *The Battle of Tetuán* in 1962. Perhaps the largest work that Dalí had produced by that point was *Gala looking at Dalí in a state of anti-gravitation in his work of art "Pop-Op-Yes-Yes-Pompier" in which one can contemplate the two anguishing characters from Millet's Angelus in the state of atavic hibernation standing out of a sky which can suddenly burst into a gigantic Maltese cross right in the heart of the Perpignan railway station where the whole universe must converge* (c. 1965) [381] also known as *Perpignan Railway Station*, which was also featured in the Knoedler Gallery's *Exhibition of Dali's Best Paintings To-Date*, held at the end of 1965.

The following year, Dalí began working on another highly ambitious, complex, large-format work, which he finished only a year later. Titled *Tuna Fishing* (1966–67) [382], this canvas represented the 'Almadraba', a traditional and ancient technique for the fishing wild tuna using nets and

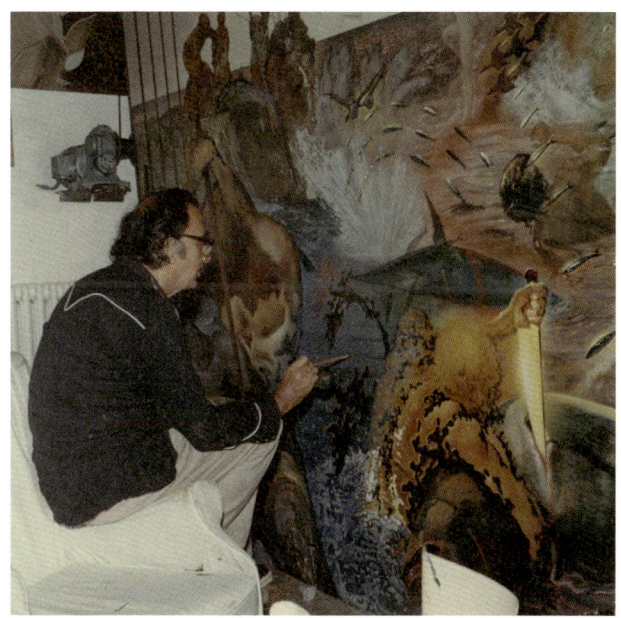

Meliton Casals (photographer), Dalí at work on his painting *Tuna Fishing*, 1967. Collection of The Dalí Museum.

harpoons. This extraordinary painting was almost immediately acquired by the French entrepreneur Paul Ricard (1909–1997). Dalí would soon exhibit it again in his 1967 exhibition titled *Hommage à Meissonier* held at the hotel Le Meurice, Paris, and again in his 1968 solo exhibition in the Palais des Beaux-Arts, Charleroi. In the 1967 exhibition catalogue, Dalí situates himself in relation to the tradition of French academic painters, such as William-Adolphe Bouguereau (1825–1905), Fortuny, Ernest Meissonier (1815–1891) and Gustave Moreau (1826–1898) among others. As he explained in the exhibition's luxurious publication, 'My metamorphosis is tradition, because tradition is precisely change and reinvention of another skin.'

Dalí's last important large-scale work of the 1960s was *The Hallucinogenic Toreador* (1970) [383], one of his most complex compositions. Beginning from a reproduction of the *Venus de Milo* that he found on a box of pencils, Dalí wove a complex set of double and multiple images set in a bullfighting arena. These included an image of the death of a bullfighter, which is likely to be an evocation of the Spanish matador Manuel Rodríguez Sánchez (1917–1947), known as Manolete and, going further back into the past, a recollection of Dalí's friend from the 1920s Ignacio Sánchez Mejías (1891–1934), who was immortalised in a poem by Lorca; both Manolete and Sánchez Mejías had died in the arena. The painting also includes a representation of a dying bull based on a photograph of Islero, the bull that had killed Manolete in 1947, as recorded in Barnaby Conrad, Jr.'s (1922–2013) book *The Death of Manolete* (1958). As well as numerous studies required to achieve this painting's ambitious composition, Dalí also made preliminary drawings alongside the photographs published in his copy of this book. At this point, Dalí was now thinking of his own youth, his dead brother and his own mortality, a subject that is revealed in this work, not only in the images of Dalí as a child, but in the importance given to the bullfighter.

Dalí featured the partially finished *The Hallucinogenic Toreador* at Knoedler Gallery in an exhibition titled *Dalí: Paintings and Drawings 1965–1970*, where it featured alongside *Tuna Fishing* (1966–67), lent by Ricard and *Apotheosis of the dollar* (1965) [380]. In the exhibition catalogue, in an article titled 'Art History's Debt to Dalí', the American art critic and editor of *Artnews*, Thomas B. Hess (1920–1978) extolled Dalí's contribution to art history, concluding that Dalí 'has discovered a powerfully original iconology in those areas traditionally dismissed as mere architectural decoration or dry classical allusion… he reanimates for our fragmented, dark time some of the radiant light and unity of the High Renaissance.'

Perhaps Dalí's most important work of the 1970s was not a painting, but the creation of his Teatre-Museu Dalí in Figueres, inaugurated on 28 September 1974. This project might be considered a carefully constructed installation akin to the Surrealists' earlier, provocative exhibition presentations. Dalí's museum is much more than a container for his own works, as the frame of the building, and the way Dalí designed its interior, is equally important. The museum also holds works by numerous other artists, including many of those mentioned above, and Dalí's selection can be seen as central to an understanding of his artistic vision. Of particular note are works by the American sculptor John De Andrea (b. 1941), Bouguereau, the seventeenth-century Dutch painter Gerrit Dou (1613–1675), Duchamp, Fortuny, the Greek artist of the Spanish Renaissance, El Greco (1541–1614) and Meissonier. The inclusion of each of these artists offers insight into Dalí's complex rethinking of both art history and the definition of art itself.

Dalí's final large-format painting was *Painting of Gala looking onto the Mediterranean sea which from a distance of 20 meters is transformed into a portrait of Abraham Lincoln (Homage to Rothko) (second version)* (1976) [391]. Dalí was inspired by the image of the US President Abraham Lincoln (1809–1865) derived from the American researcher Leon D. Harmon's article devoted to 'The Recognition of Faces', which was published in the magazine *Scientific American* in November 1973. Dalí's painting covers the gamut between the painterly fields suggested by the reference to the American painter Mark Rothko (1903–1970), who had died only three years before, the face of President Lincoln, which was instantly recognisable from the American five-dollar bill, and Dalí's own family of personal symbols including his wife Gala, the figure of Christ (recalling his 1951 painting, *The Christ*) and the subject of the Mediterranean sea of Portlligat. Harmon's article asked at what point did the fragmentation of images become impossible to read, while considering our capacity to mentally construct images from partial information. Significantly younger artists, in particular the American painter Chuck Close (1940–2021), were engaged with the implications of Harmon's research for their own painting. Dalí's painting also points towards his interest in the intersection of science and mysticism.

During the 1970s, Dalí remained curious about contemporary developments in art and science. In April 1972 he presented twenty-three paintings in an exhibition at the Knoedler Gallery, New York, along with the addition of new works at the cutting edge of technology employing the new medium of holography, in which light is used to create the appearance of three-dimensional images. The paintings were mainly recent works, though he included the earlier *Portrait of my dead brother* (c. 1963) [377]. Of the several holograms on view, *Holos! Holos! Velàzquez! Gabor!* (1972) – part of the permanent installation at the Teatre-Museu – pays homage to Dennis Gabor (1900–1979), the Hungarian-British physicist and inventor of holography, and to Velázquez, the Painter to the King, who embodies the great tradition of Spanish Old Master painting and was famous for his highly painterly realism. As Dalí explained in the pages of *Art News* in 1972, in an article bearing the same title as this hologram, 'the painting *Las Meninas* [Velázquez's 1656 painting], seen in the light of the scientific genius of my friend Dennis Gabor, is the aesthetic anticipation of holography.'

The artist's concern for tradition, mysticism and modern science persisted to the very end of his life. Velázquez's compositions were also a source that Dalí returned to repeatedly in his last years of painting. He was also increasingly interested in advanced mathematics and was in contact with the French mathematician René Thom (1923–2002). Dalí found solace in the proof of mysticism and spirituality found in geometry. Thom was known especially for 'catastrophe theory,' a special case within what is known as 'singularity theory.' Thom expressed variations of the mathematical formulas in terms of graphs, that is he translated mathematical formulas into visual representations suggesting three dimensions. We know that Dalí owned and read Thom's 1983 book *Paraboles et catastrophes* and what are considered Dalí's last paintings are known as the *Catastrophes Series* (c. 1983), including what was probably his very last canvas *Untitled (Swallow's Tail and Cellos) (Catastrophes Series)* (c. 1983) [400], a work that pays homage to Thom's famous swallowtail catastrophe equation. In Dalí's painting, apart from drawing on the shape of Thom's swallowtail graph, he also evokes

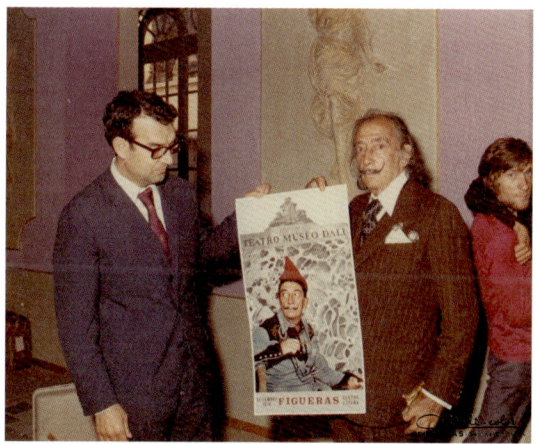

Meliton Casals (photographer), Dalí and Pere Giró, Mayor of Figueres, hold a flyer for the Teatro Museo, Figueres, Spain, c. 1974. Collection of The Dalí Museum.

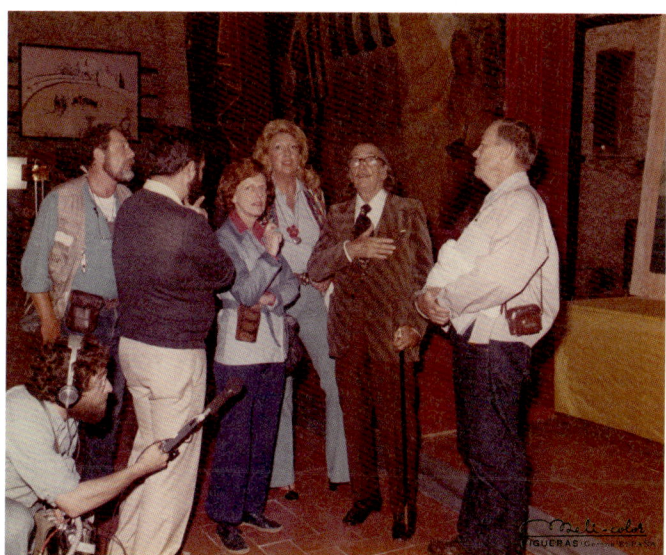

Meliton Casals (photographer), Dalí and the Morses being interviewed in front of Dalí's painting *Apotheosis of the Dollar* at the Teatro Museo, Figueres, Spain, c. 1974. Collection of The Dalí Museum.

music, with the inclusion of the form of the cello and its sound holes, as a means of suggesting a dimension beyond our conventional understanding of space and also as a representation of a divine transcendence only available though both music and mathematics.

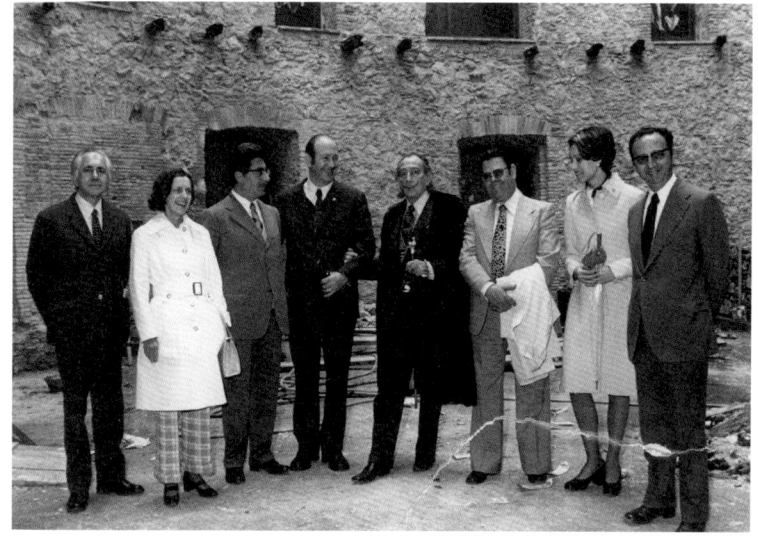

Meliton Casals (photographer), Dalí, the Morses, Guardiola (the former Mayor of Figueres) and a number of other unknown individuals in Figueres, Spain, 3 May 1974. Collection of The Dalí Museum.

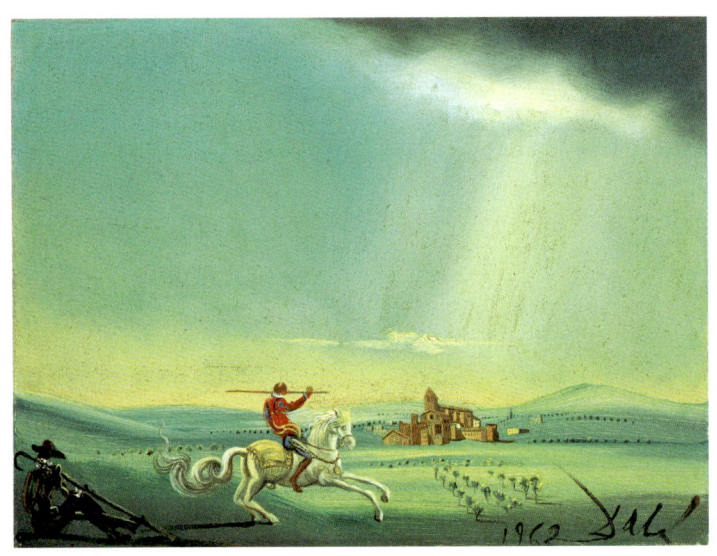

376
Saint Georges
1962
Oil on canvas, 22.9 × 30.5 cm
Private collection

Avant-garde Experimentation

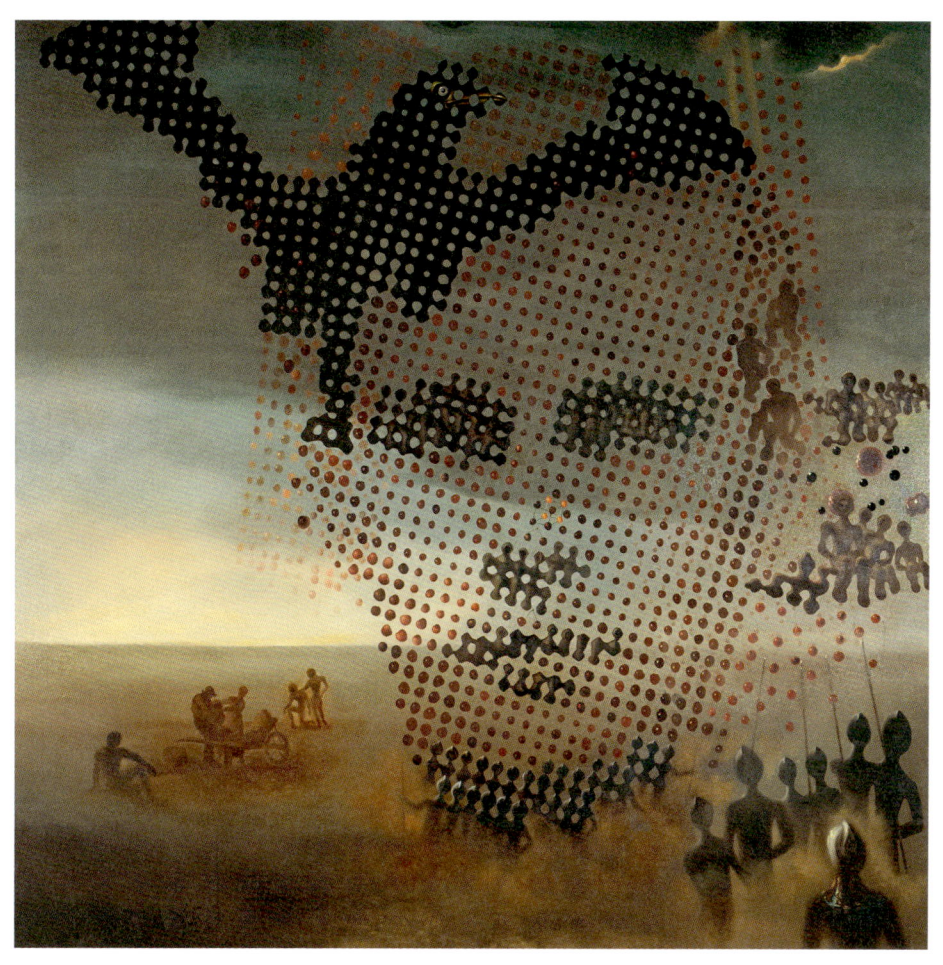

377
Portrait of my dead brother
c. 1963
Oil on canvas, 175.3 × 175.3 cm
The Dalí Museum, St. Petersburg, Florida

1960 onwards

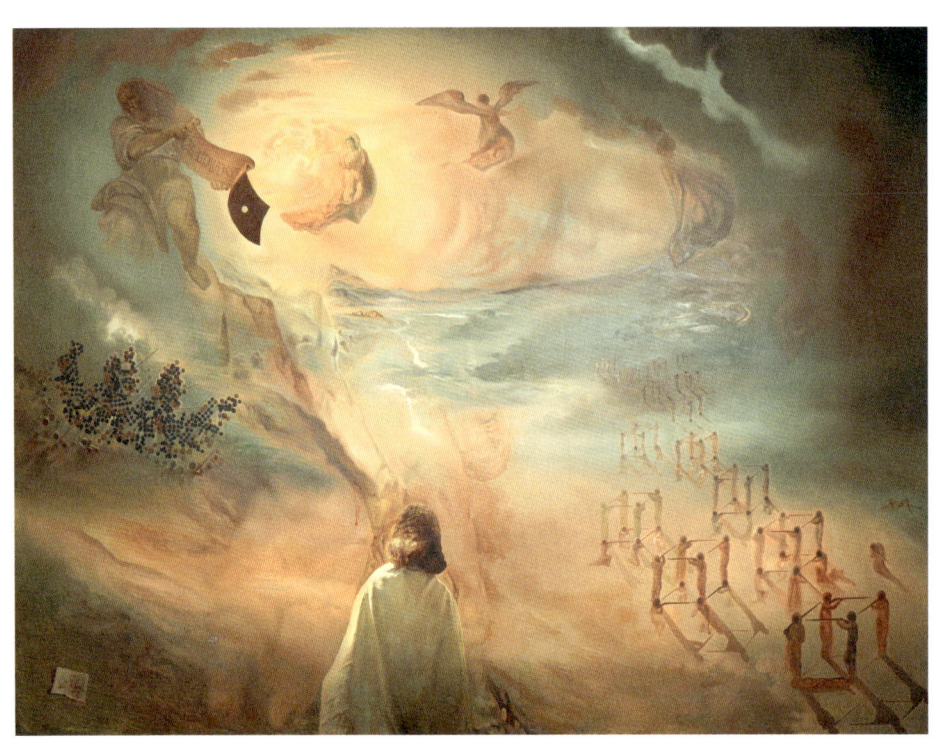

378
GALACIDALACIDESOXIRIBUNUCLEICACID (Homage to Crick and Watson)
1963
Oil on canvas, 305 × 410 cm
The Dalí Museum, St. Petersburg, Florida

Avant-garde Experimentation

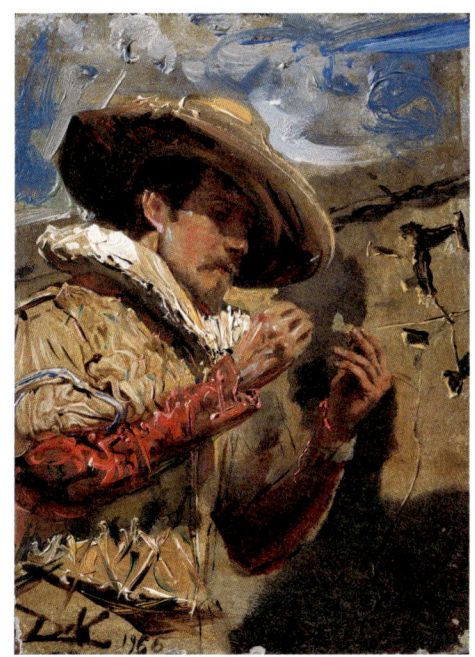

379
Character Masquerading in Pinning up a Butterfly
1965
Oil on wood panel, 12 × 9 cm
Fundació Gala-Salvador Dalí, Figueres

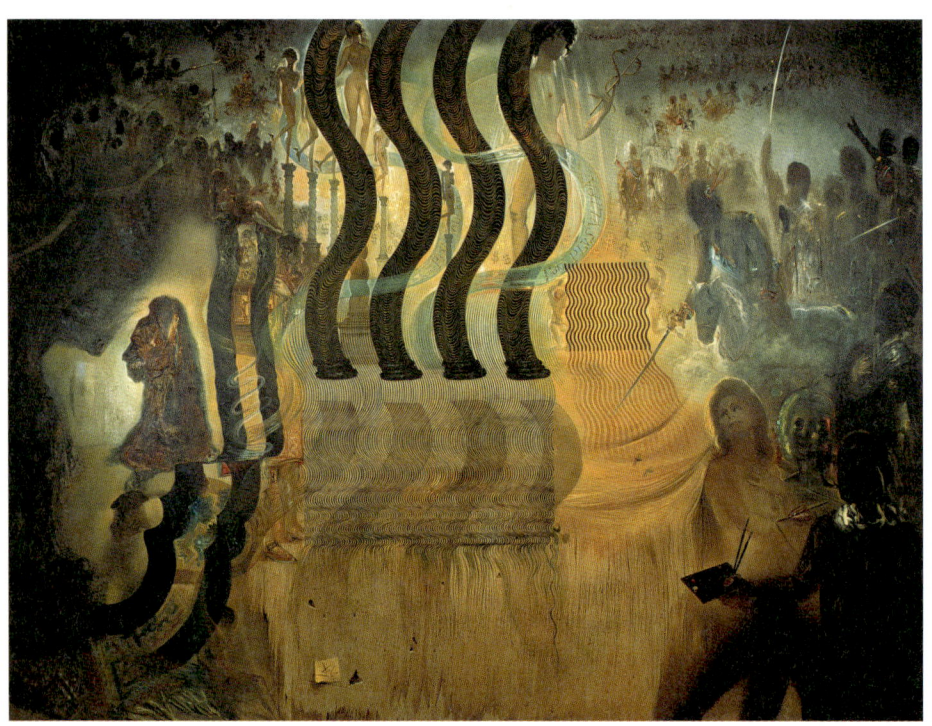

380
Salvador Dalí in the Act of Painting Gala in the "Apotheosis of the Dollar",
on the Left of Whom One Can See Marcel Duchamp Disguised as Louis XIV
behind a Vermeerian Curtain, Which Is Not a Curtain but the Invisible yet
Monumental Face of "Hermes" by Praxiteles
1965
Oil on canvas, 400 × 498 cm
Fundació Gala-Salvador Dalí, Figueres

Avant-garde Experimentation

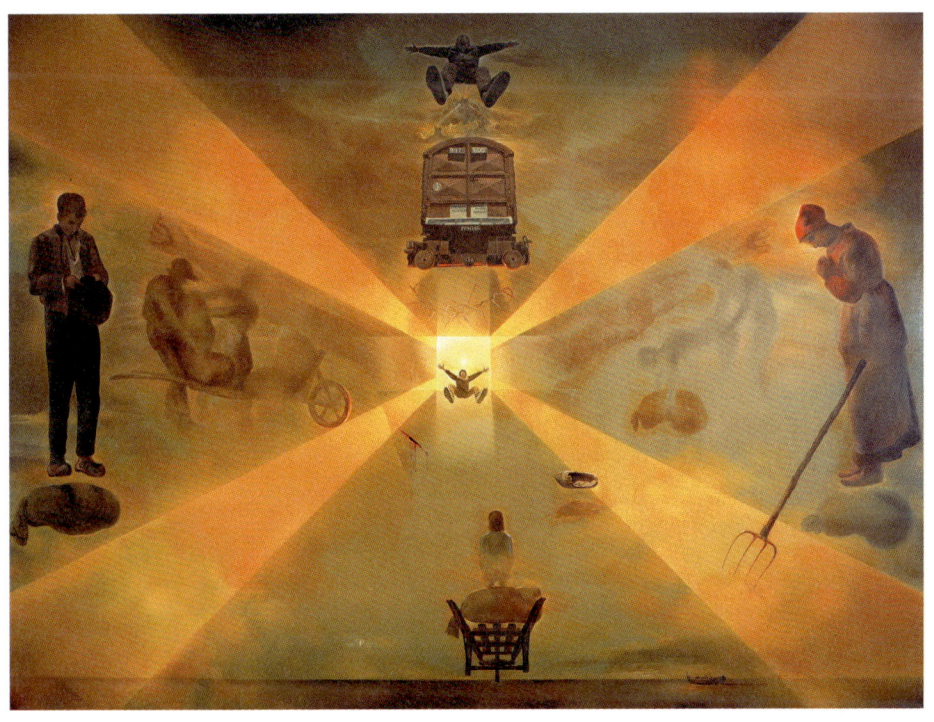

381
Gala looking at Dalí in a state of anti-gravitation in his work of art "Pop-Op-Yes-Yes-Pompier" in which one can contemplate the two languishing characters from Millet's Angelus in the state of atavic hibernation standing out of a sky which can suddenly burst into a gigantic Maltese cross right in the heart of the Perpignan railway station where the whole universe must converge
c. 1965
Oil on canvas, 295 × 406 cm
Museum Ludwig, Cologne

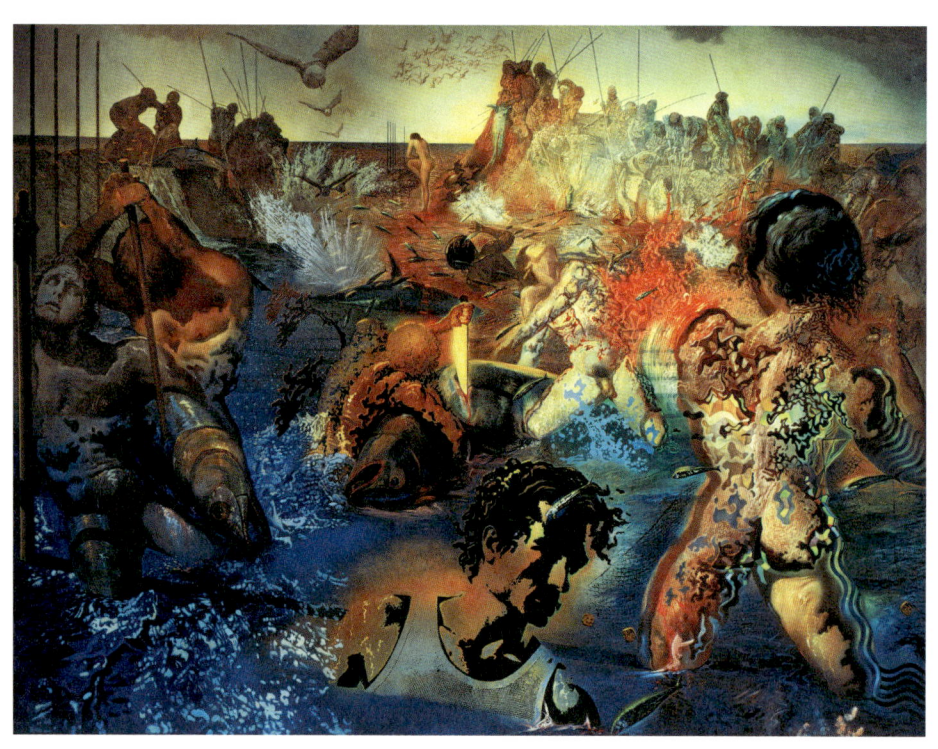

382
Tuna Fishing
1966–1967
Oil on canvas, 304 × 404 cm
Fondation Paul Ricard, Isle of Bendor

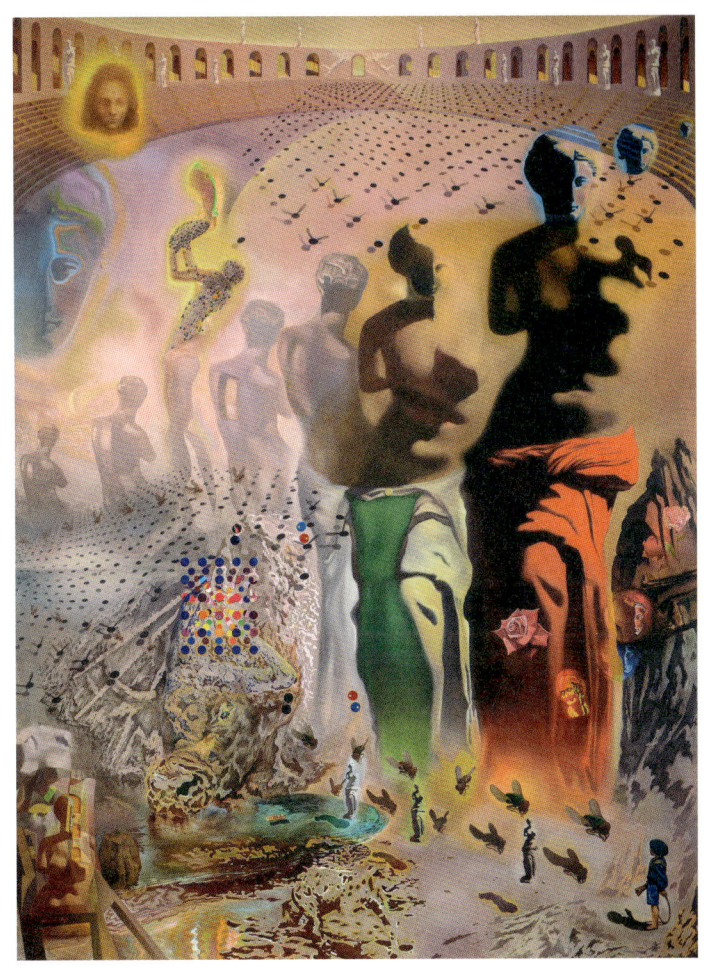

383
The Hallucinogenic Toreador
1970
Oil on canvas, 398.8 × 299.7 cm
The Dalí Museum, St. Petersburg, Florida

1960 onwards

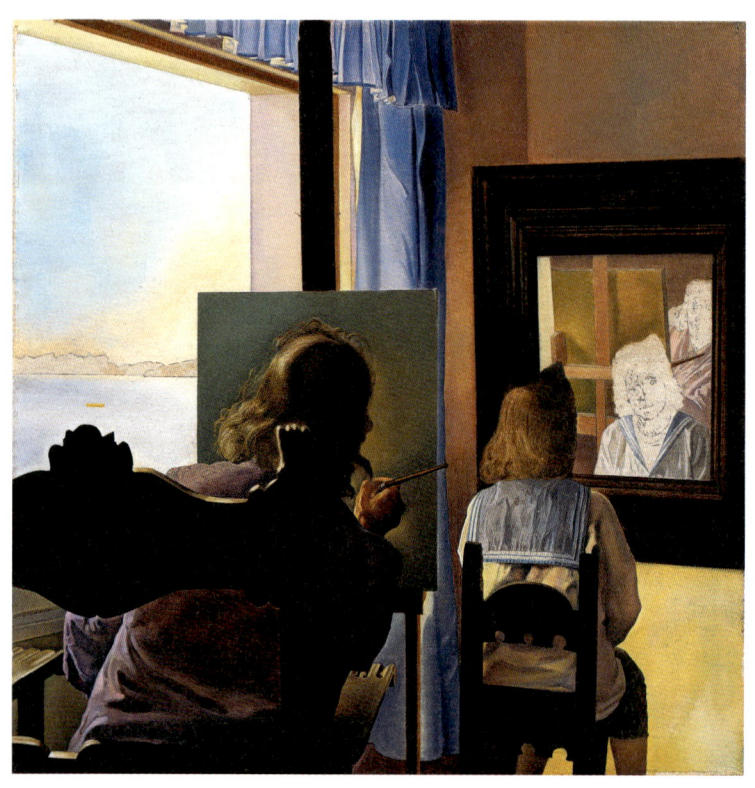

384–385

Dalí Seen from the Back Painting Gala from the Back Eternalized by Six Virtual Corneas Provisionally Reflected by Six Real Mirrors. Stereoscopic work
1972–1973

Oil on canvas, 60 × 60 cm (each)

Town Hall of Figueres, on permanent deposit at the Fundació Gala-Salvador Dalí, Figueres

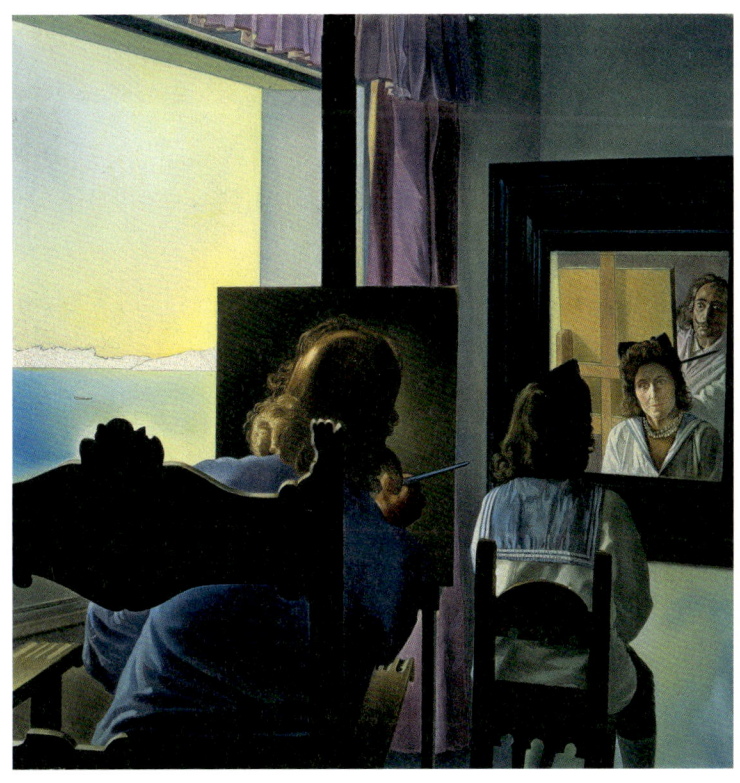

1960 onwards

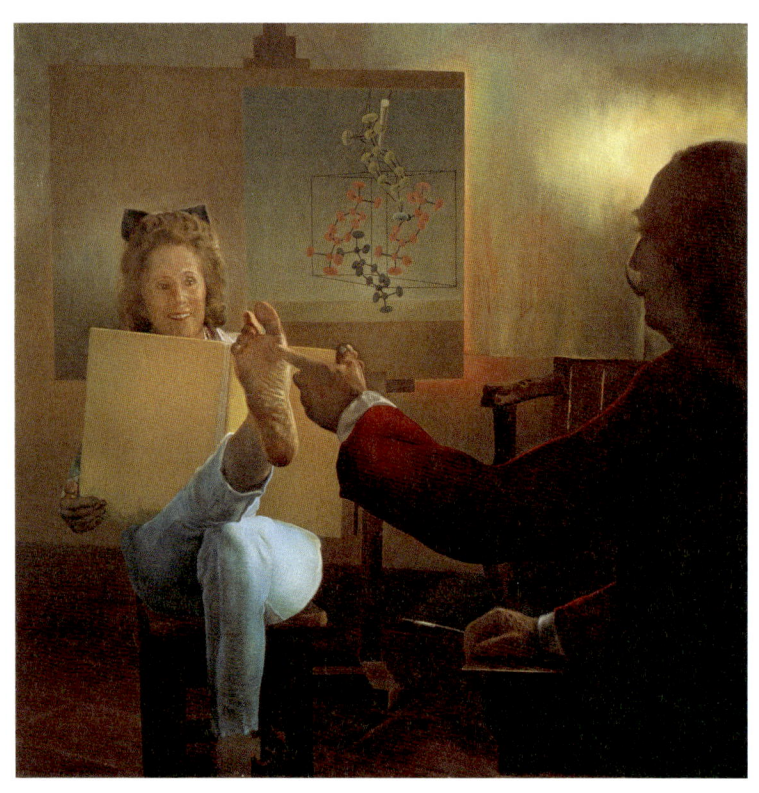

386–387
Gala's Foot. Stereoscopic work
c. 1974
Oil on canvas, 60 × 60 cm (each)
Fundació Gala-Salvador Dalí, Figueres

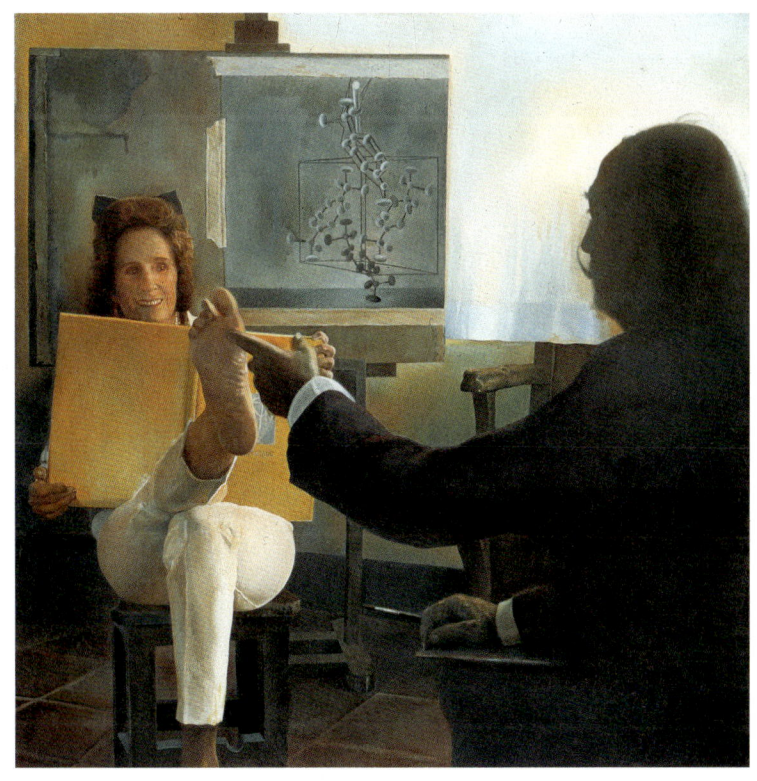

1960 onwards

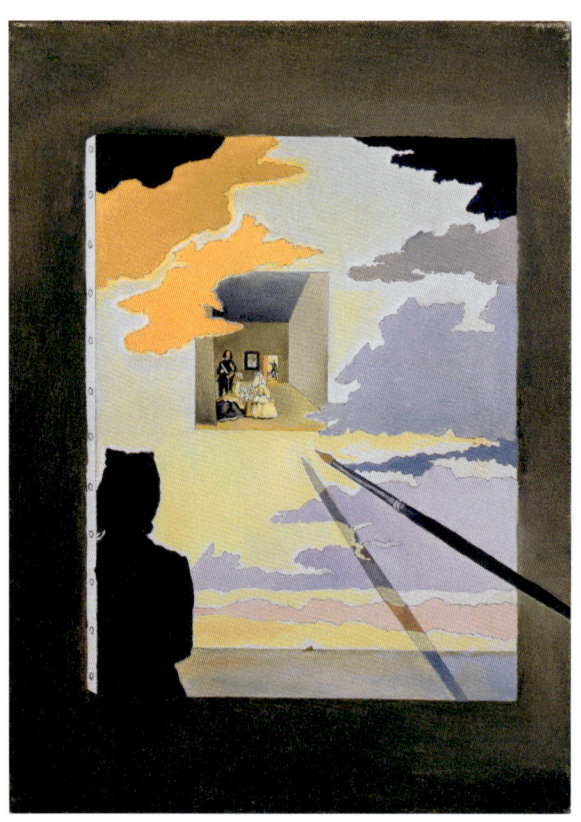

388–389
Las Meninas. Stereoscopic work
1975–1976
Oil on canvas, 35.5 × 25 cm (each)
Museo Nacional Centro de Arte Reina Sofía, Madrid

Avant-garde Experimentation

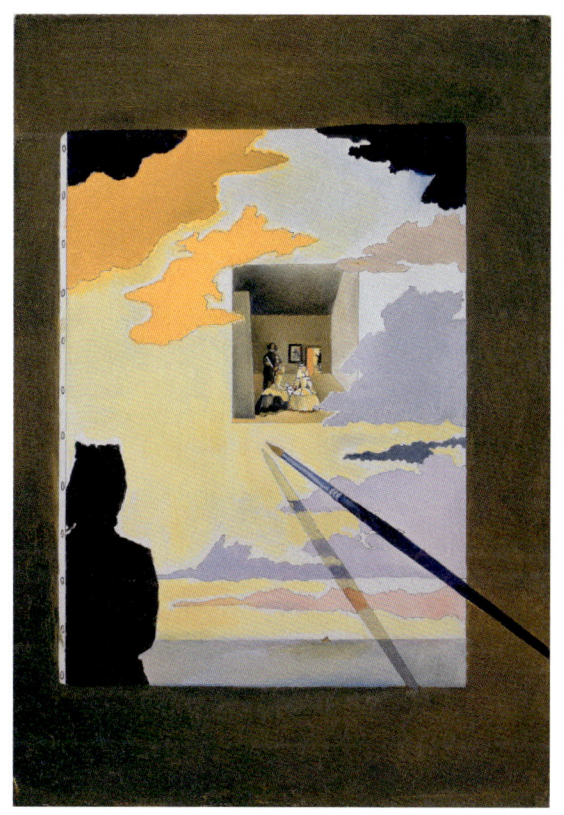

1960 onwards

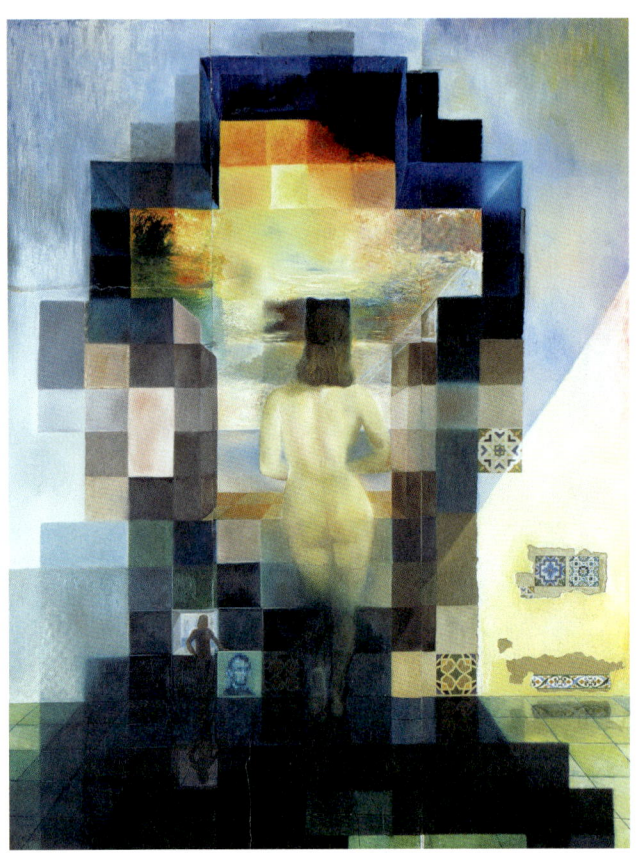

390

Painting of Gala looking at the Mediterranean sea which from a distance of 20 meters is transformed into a portrait of Abraham Lincoln (Homage to Rothko) (first version)

1974–1975

Oil on photographic paper, 445 × 350 cm

Fundació Gala-Salvador Dalí, Figueres

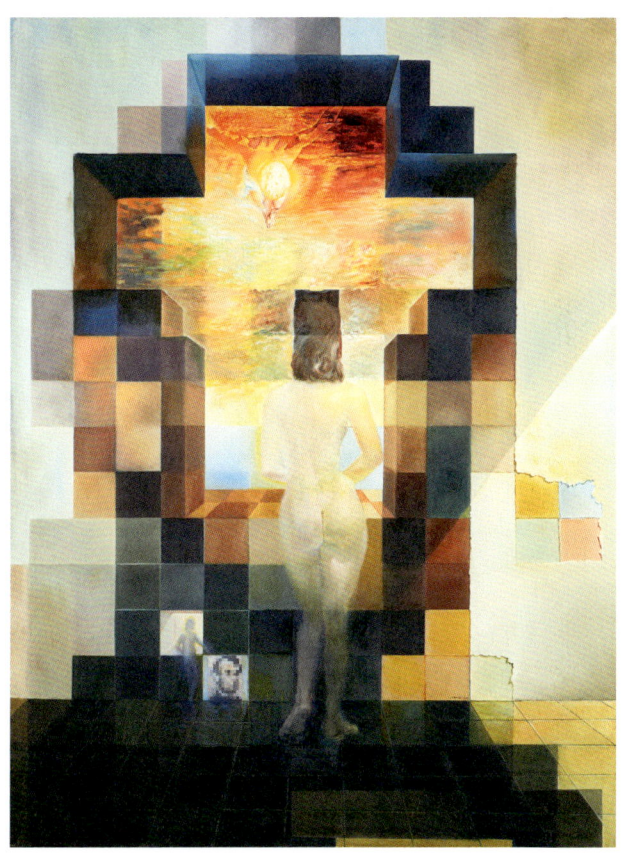

391

Painting of Gala looking at the Mediterranean sea which from a distance of 20 meters is transformed into a portrait of Abraham Lincoln (Homage to Rothko) (second version)

c. 1976

Oil on canvas, 252.2 × 191.9 cm

The Dalí Museum, St. Petersburg, Florida

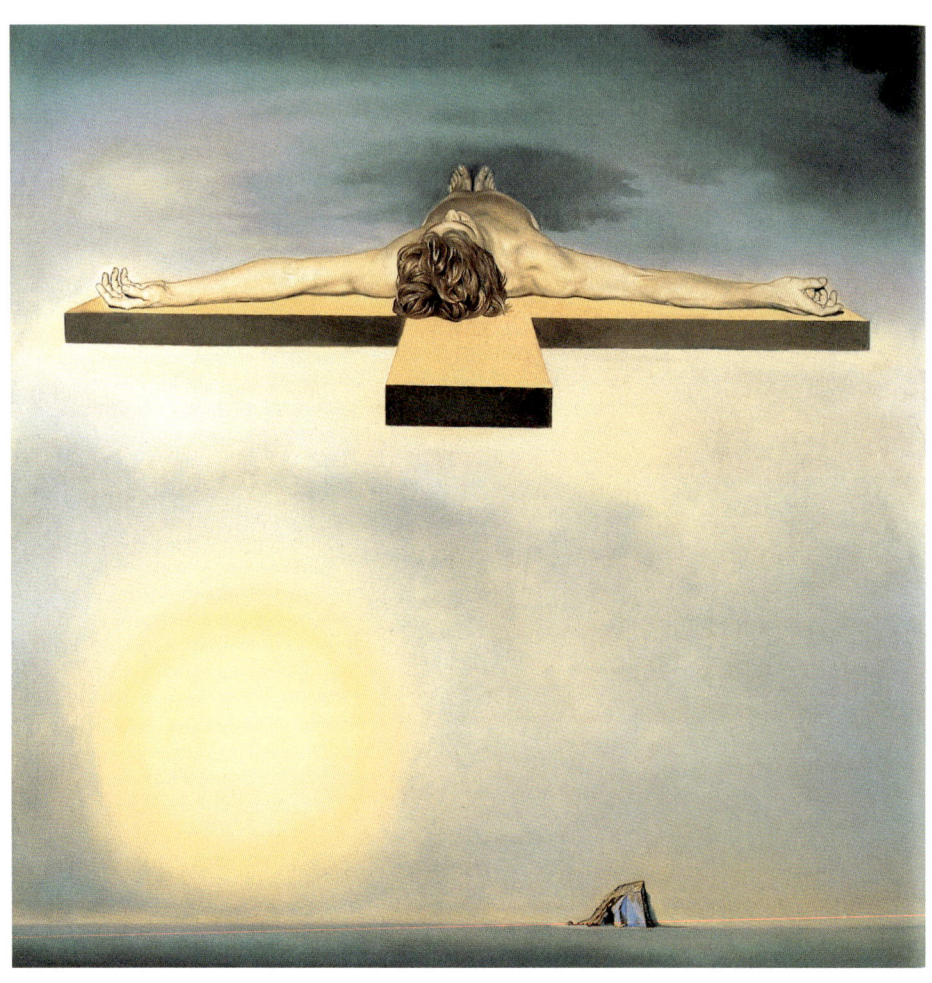

392–393
The Christ of Gala
c. 1978
Oil on canvas, 100 × 100 cm (each)
Pérez Simón Collection, Mexico

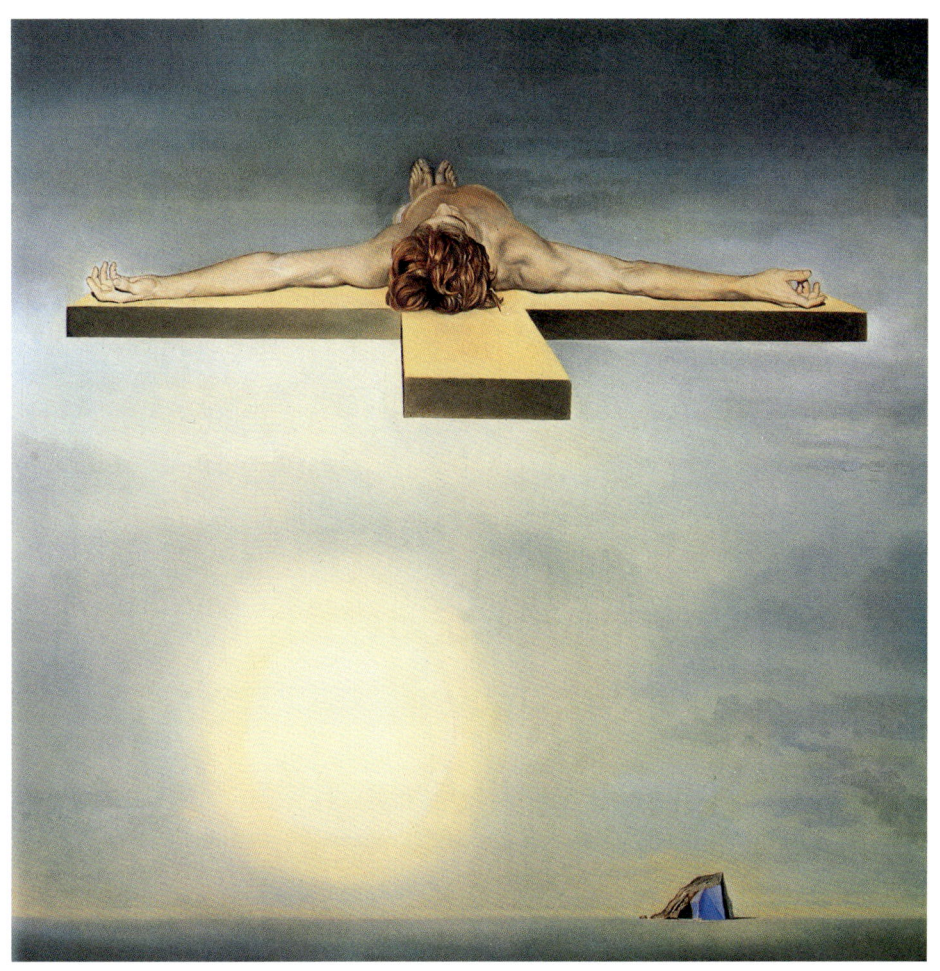

1960 onwards

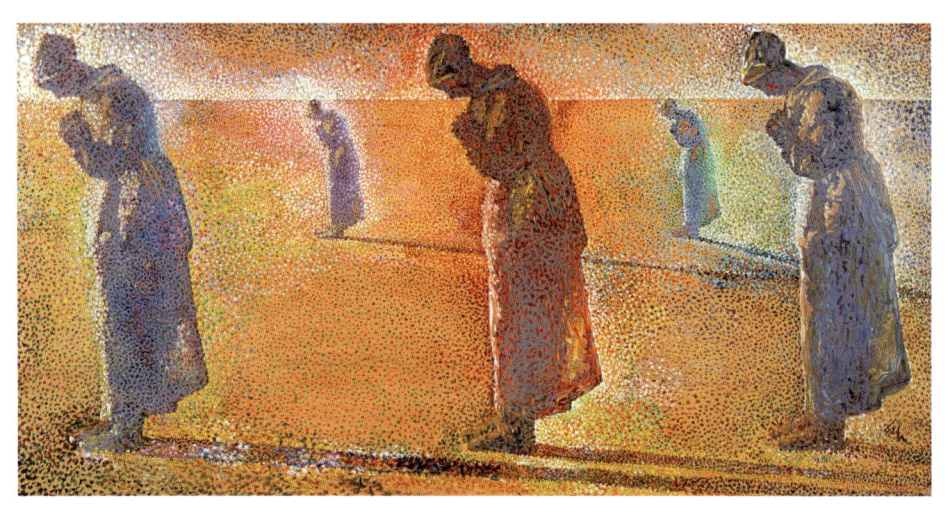

394
Dawn, Noon, Afternoon and Twilight
1979
Oil on plywood panel, 122 × 244 cm
Fundació Gala-Salvador Dalí, Figueres

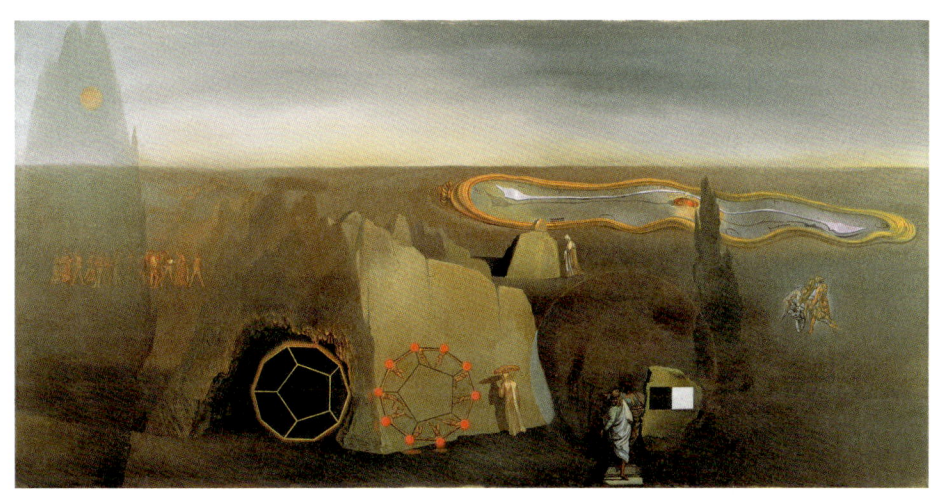

395

In Search of the Fourth Dimension

c. 1979

Oil on canvas, 122.5 × 246 cm

Fundació Gala-Salvador Dalí, Figueres

Avant-garde Experimentation

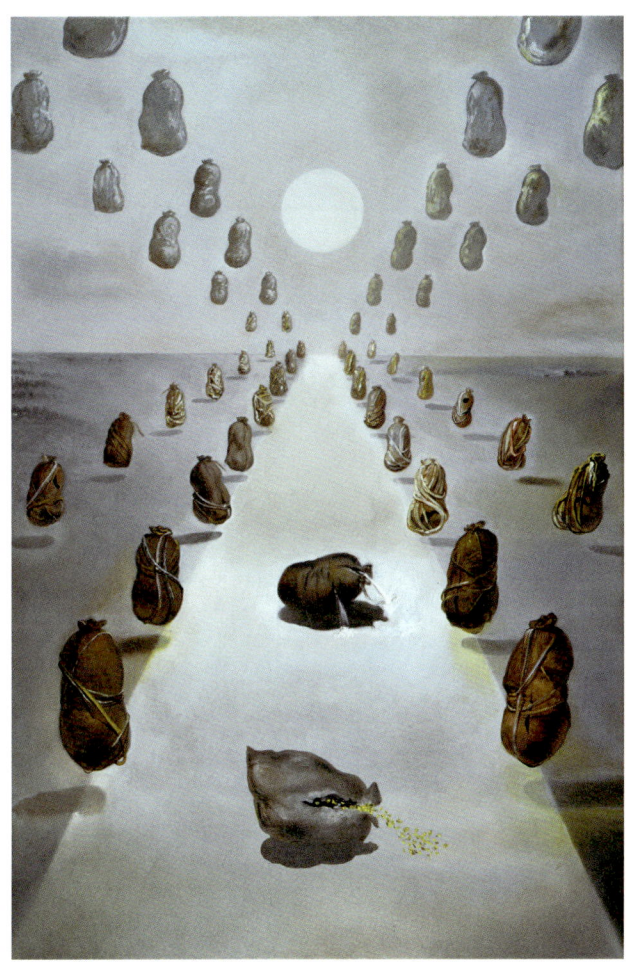

396
El camino del enigma (The Path of the Enigma)
c. 1981
Oil on canvas, 139 × 94 cm
Fundació Gala-Salvador Dalí, Figueres

1960 onwards

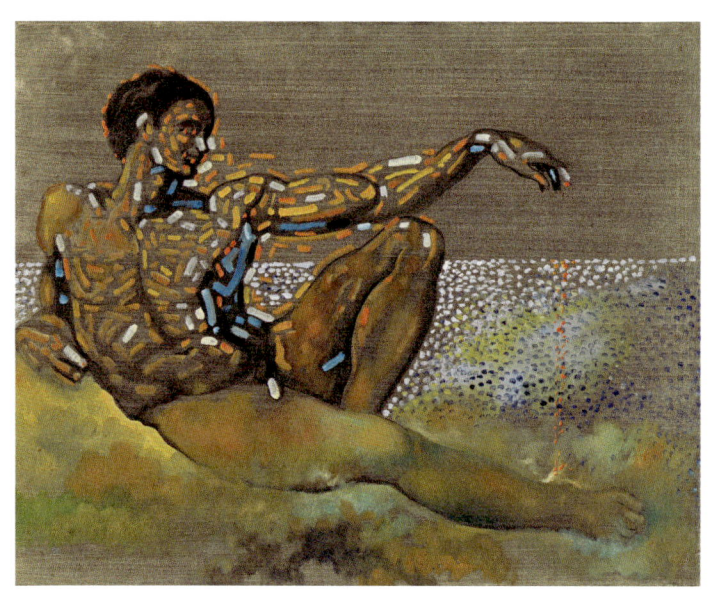

397
Untitled (Adam after "The Creation of Adam" in the Sistine Chapel by Michelangelo)
c. 1982
Oil on canvas, 60 × 75 cm
Fundació Gala-Salvador Dalí, Figueres

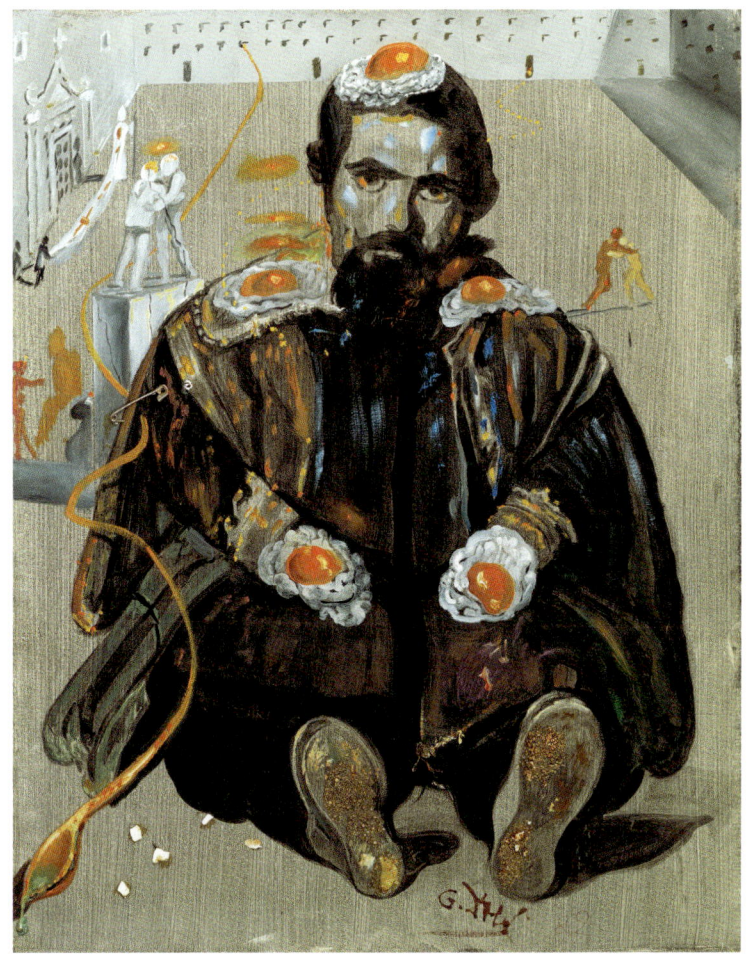

398
Velázquez Dying behind the Window on the Left Side out of Which a Spoon Projects
1982
Oil and collage on canvas, 75 × 58.5 cm
Fundació Gala-Salvador Dalí, Figueres

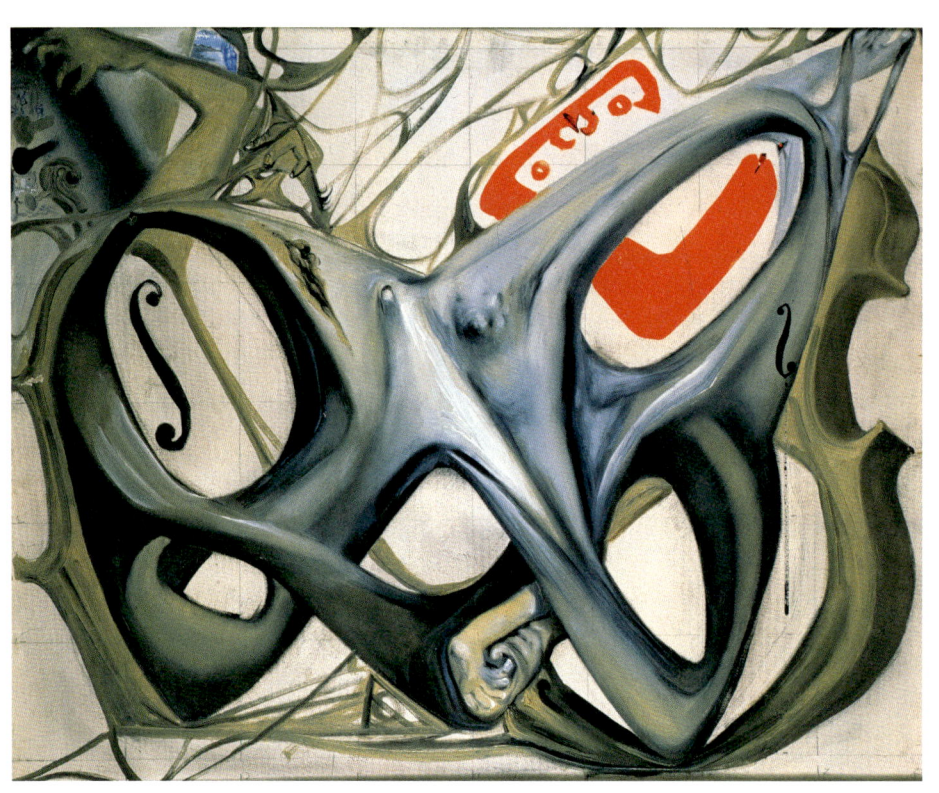

399
Untitled (Topological Contortion of a Female Figure Becoming a Cello)
c. 1983
Oil on canvas, 60 × 63.5 cm
Museo Nacional Centre de Arte Reine Sofía, Madrid

Avant-garde Experimentation

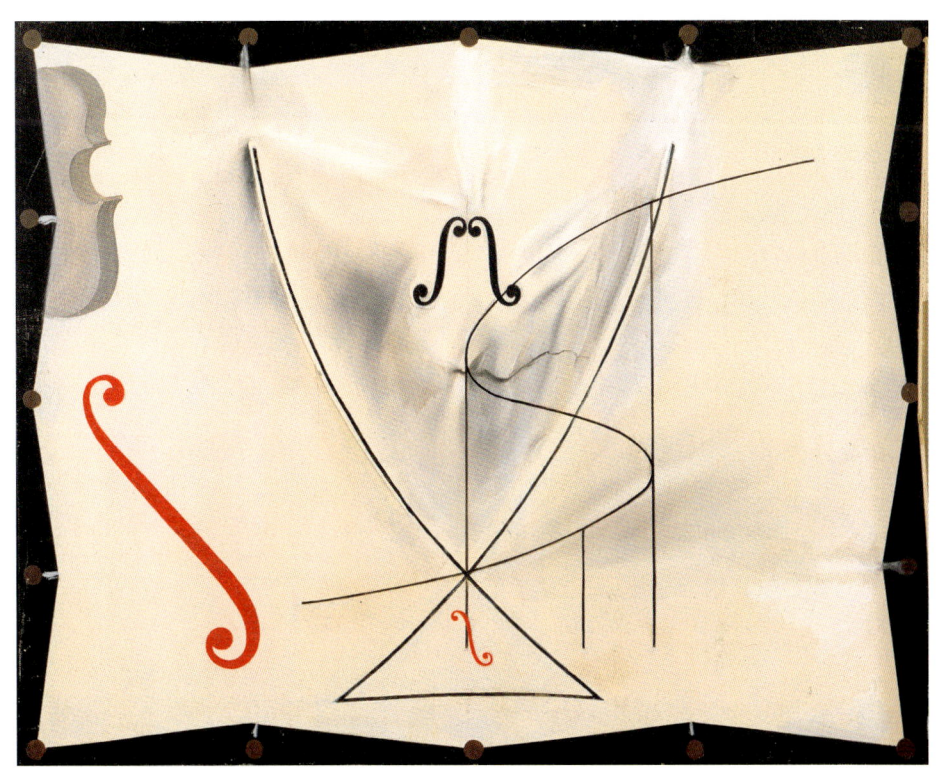

400
Untitled (Swallow's Tail and Cello) (The Catastrophes Series)
c. 1983
Oil on canvas, 73 × 92 cm
Fundació Gala-Salvador Dalí, Figueres

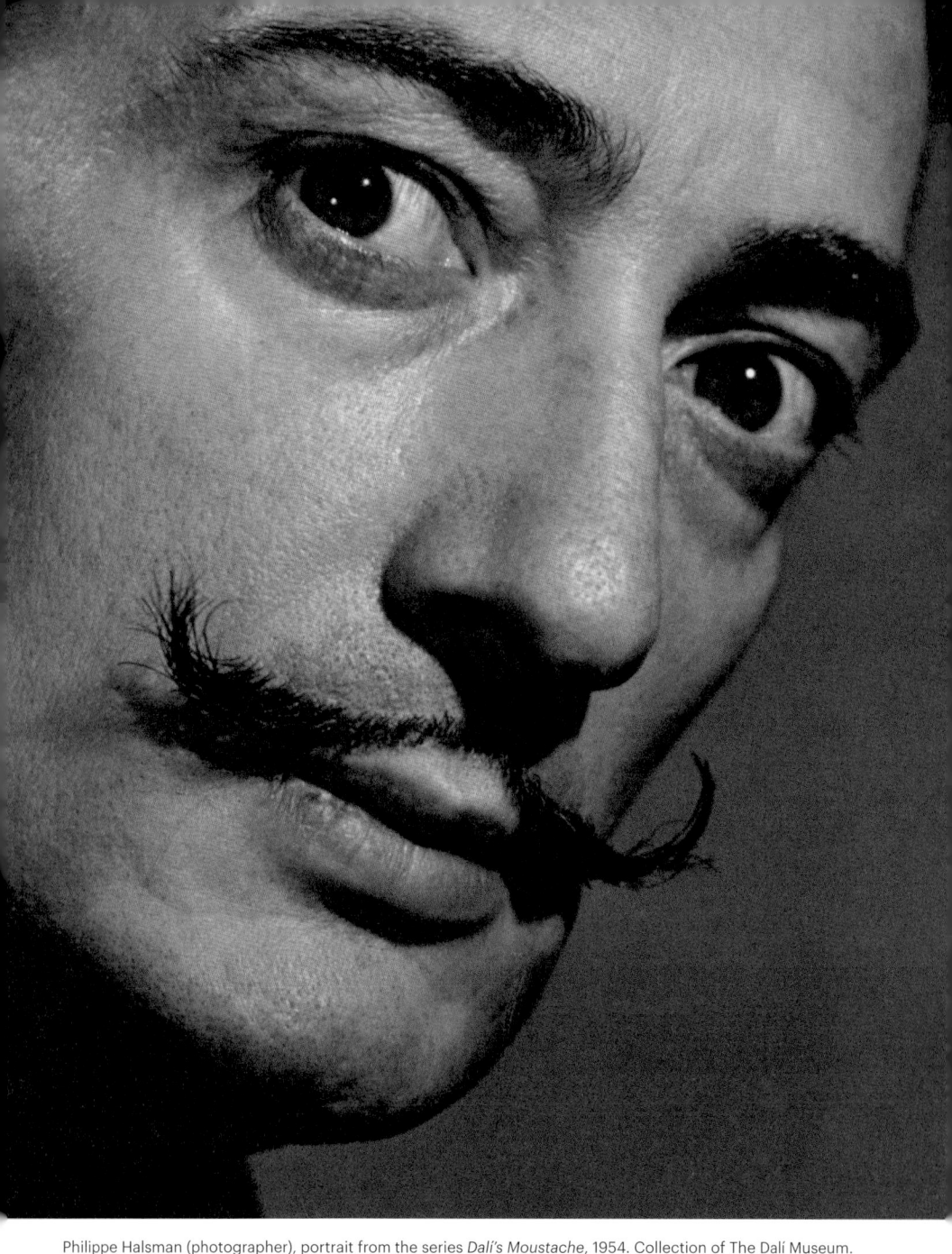

Philippe Halsman (photographer), portrait from the series *Dalí's Moustache*, 1954. Collection of The Dalí Museum.

Biography

1904
11 May: Salvador Dalí is born in Figueres, Spain.

c. 1910–1914
Begins painting. His earliest known paintings are landscapes painted on postcards. They are not dated.

1916
Stays at painter Ramon Pichot's home, Molí de la Torre (located in El Far d'Empordà in the Spanish countryside near Figueres) and is inspired by Impressionism.

c. 1918
Begins painting in a Post-impressionist style.

1920
Keeps a detailed diary, where he writes enthusiastically about the French Impressionists. He is especially interested in the work of Degas, Monet, Manet, Renoir and Cézanne.

1923–1924
Begins to paint in a Cubist style.

1924
Writer André Breton publishes the *Manifeste du surréalisme*.

1925
May: Participates in the *Primera Exposición de la Sociedad de Artistas* in Madrid.
November: First solo exhibition in Barcelona at Galeries Dalmau.

1926
April: First brief trip to Paris where he visits Pablo Picasso's studio and the Musée du Louvre.

December–January: Second solo exhibition in Barcelona at Galeries Dalmau.

1927–1928
Develops a form of anti-painting in reaction to Cubism.
Begins introducing sand and pebbles into his paintings and explores erotic subjects close to Surrealism. These works are exhibited and published and are considered provocative.

1929
Spring: Travels to Paris to work with filmmaker Luis Buñuel on the film *Un Chien Andalou*, which premiers in June. Makes contact with Breton and other Surrealist writers and artists.
Summer: Several of his Paris friends visit him in Cadaqués for the summer. Meets poet Paul Éluard's wife Gala. Dalí and Gala begin a romance and never separate.
September: His works are published in writer Georges Bataille's review *Documents*.
November: First solo exhibition at the Galerie Goemans in Paris. Breton writes the preface for the catalogue.
December: The final issue of Breton's review *La Révolution surréaliste* includes reproductions of his paintings *The Accommodations of Desire* [107] and *Illuminated Pleasures* [108] – both from his Goemans exhibition – and the screenplay for *Un Chien Andalou*. It also includes Breton's *Second manifeste du surréalisme*, which excludes several 'dissident' members of the group, including Bataille. Dalí rejects Bataille's request to reproduce his painting *The Lugubrious Game* [115], another painting included in the Goemans show, alongside the writer's article on the painting in *Documents*. Instead, Bataille publishes a diagram alongside the article.

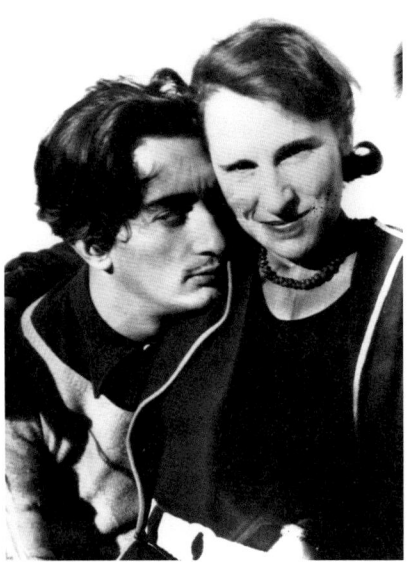

Dalí and Gala soon after they first met, c. 1930.
Collection of The Dalí Museum.

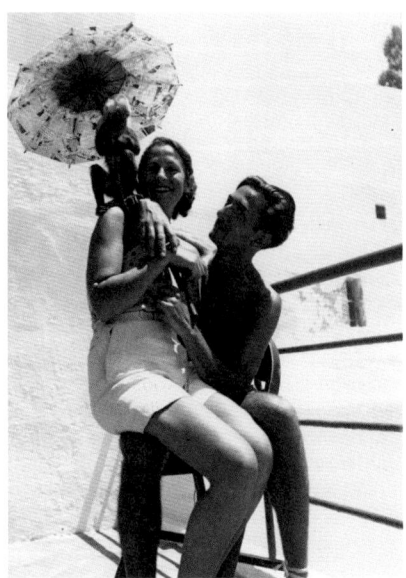

Dalí and Gala at Mas Juny, Spain, 1934.
Collection of The Dalí Museum.

1930

March: He is included in *La peinture au défi*, poet Louis Aragon's group exhibition of artists working with collage at the Galerie Goemans in Paris.

His second film collaboration with Buñuel, *L'âge d'Or,* is presented in Paris.

1931

June: Solo exhibition with Pierre Colle Gallery in Paris.

Develops the concept of 'Objects Functioning Symbolically' in response to Alberto Giacometti's sculpture *Suspended Ball* (1930).

December: Publishes a text on this subject titled 'Objets surréalistes' in the Surrealist movement's review *Le Surréalisme au service de la Révolution*.

1932

May–June: Solo exhibition with Galerie Pierre Colle in Paris.

1933

Early June: Solo exhibition at Galerie Pierre Colle in Paris.

Late June: Participates in the Galerie Colle's *Exposition surréaliste* in Paris.

October–November: Participates in the Surrealist section at the Salon des Surindépendants in Paris.

November–December: Solo exhibition at Julien Levy Gallery in New York.

December: Solo exhibition at Galeria d'Art Catalònia in Barcelona.

The first issue of the Surrealist-inclined review *Minotaure* is published and will continue to appear until 1939. Dalí's work and writing is frequently featured in this luxuriously printed publication.

1934

January: Dalí and Gala are married in a civil ceremony.

February: He is nearly expelled from the Surrealist group.

June–July: Solo exhibition at Galerie Jacques Bonjean in Paris.

November: Dalí travels to the US for the first time.

November–December: Solo exhibition at Julien Levy Gallery in New York.

1935

January: Participates in the *Exposition internationale Kubisme=Surrealisme* in Copenhagen in Denmark.

May: Participates in the Surrealist Exhibition in Santa Cruz de Tenerife in Spain.

1936

May: Participates in the *Exhibition of Surrealist Objects* at the Galerie Charles Ratton in Paris.

June–July: Participates in *The International Exhibition of Surrealism* in London and has a solo exhibition at Alex Reid & Lefevre Gallery in London.

November–January: He is included in The Museum of Modern Art's *Fantastic Art, Dada and Surrealism* exhibition in New York.

Dalí is featured on the cover of *Time Magazine.*

December–January: Solo exhibition at Julien Levy Gallery in New York.

1937

June: Participates in the *International Exhibition of Surrealism* in Tokyo, Japan.

December–January: Participates in the group exhibition *L'Art cruel* at the Galerie Billiet-Pierre Vorms in Paris curated by Jean Cassou.

1938

January–February: Participates in the

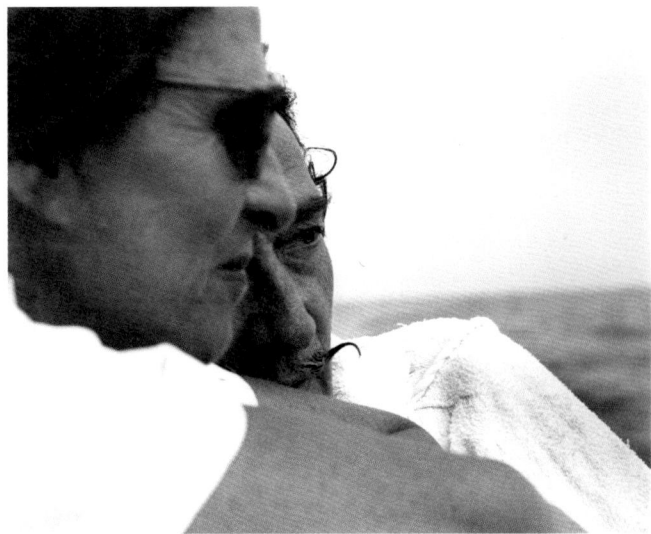

Robert Descharnes (photographer), Dalí and Gala in their boat, 1959.
Collection of The Dalí Museum.

International Exhibition of Surrealism held at the Galerie des Beaux-Arts in Paris.

1939
Spring: Definitive rupture with Breton and Surrealism, which coincides with an article by Breton published in *Minotaure*.
March–April: Solo exhibition at Julien Levy Gallery in New York.
Summer: His work is included in the 1939 New York World's Fair exhibition in New York with his *Dream of Venus* pavilion.

1940
8 August: Leaves France by ship for the US, where he arrives on 16 August and will stay until 1948.
26 August: Visits writer and patron Caresse Crosby's home Hampton Manor in Virginia for a prolonged stay, where he paints and begins writing his autobiography.

1941
April: Solo exhibition at Julien Levy Gallery in New York that travels to Chicago and Los Angeles.
November: Monographic exhibition at The Museum of Modern Art in New York in parallel with a monographic exhibition of Joan Miró's work.

1942
Publishes his autobiography *The Secret Life of Salvador Dalí*.

1943
April–May: Solo exhibition at the Knoedler Gallery in New York.
Spring: Philanthropists Eleanor and Reynolds Morse purchase *Daddy Longlegs of the Evening – Hope!* [279] from Georges Keller at the Bignou Gallery in New York. They become Dalí's most important American collectors and establish a friendship with the artist.

1944
His novel *Hidden Faces* is published.

1945
November–December: Solo exhibition at Bignou Gallery in New York.

1947
November–January: Solo exhibition at Bignou Gallery in New York.

1948
His book *50 Secrets of Magic Craftsmanship* is published.

1949
November: Has an audience with Pope Pius XII in Rome.

1950
November–January: Solo exhibition at Carstairs Gallery in New York featuring his painting *The Madonna of Portlligat* [335].

1951
June: Presents his *Manifeste mystique* in Paris.
November: Gives a controversial lecture 'Picasso y yo' at the Teatre María Guerrero in Madrid on the occasion of the Bienal Hispanoamericana de Arte.
December: Solo exhibition at The Lefevre Gallery in London featuring his new religious paintings.

1952
His religious paintings are shown in Madrid within the context of the Bienal Hispanoamericana de Arte.
December–January: Solo exhibition at Carstairs Gallery in New York.

1954
December–January: Solo exhibition at Carstairs Gallery in New York.

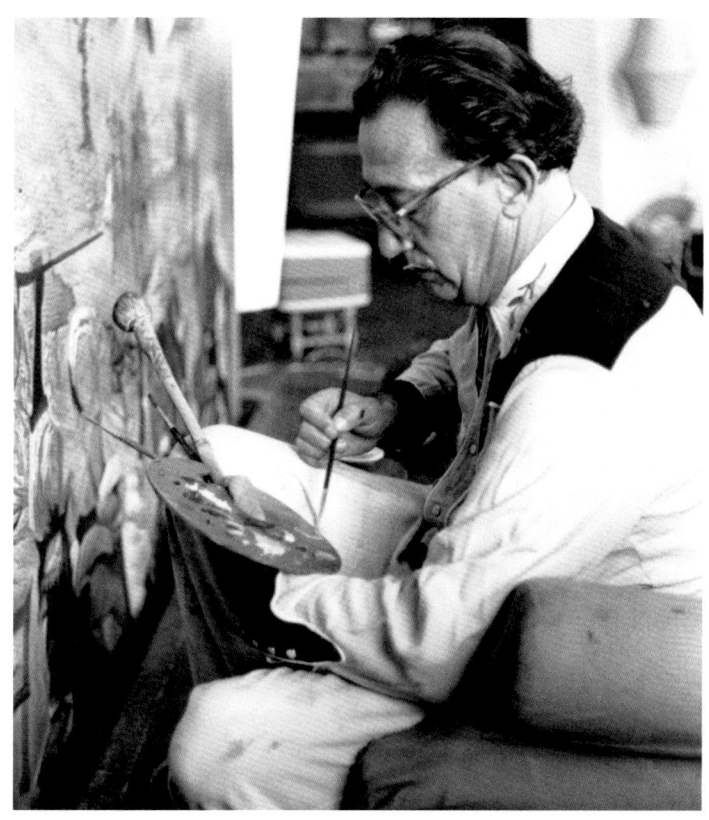

Lies Wiegman (photographer), Dalí, 1961. Collection of The Dalí Museum.

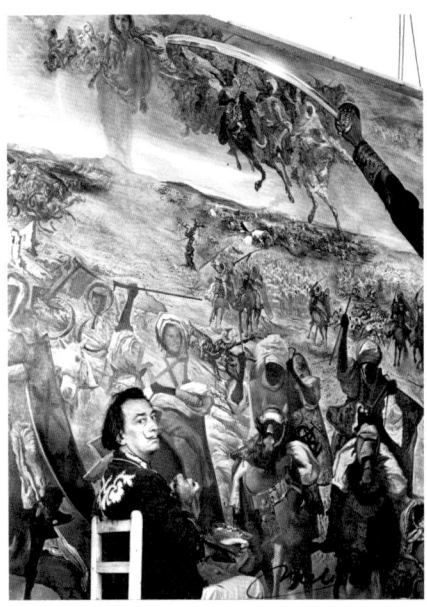

Meliton Casals (photographer), Dalí in front of his work *The Battle of Tetuán*. Collection of The Dalí Museum.

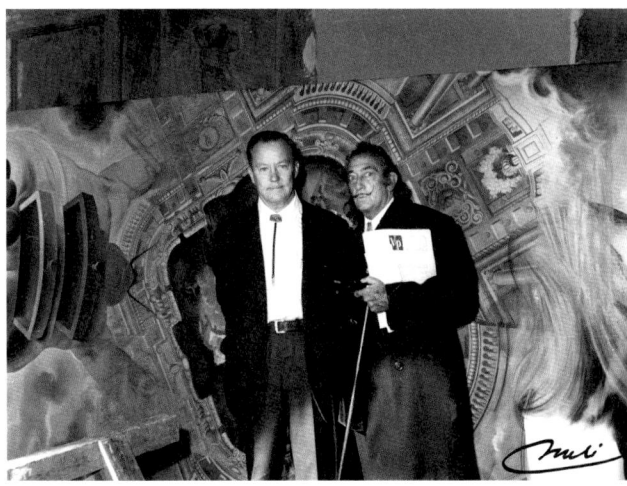

Meliton Casals (photographer), Dalí and philanthropist Albert Reynolds Morse in front of the ceiling mural for the Teatro Museo, Figueres, Spain, 1970. Collection of The Dalí Museum.

1956

December–January: Solo exhibition at Carstairs Gallery in New York.

1958

December–January: Solo exhibition at Carstairs Gallery in New York.
Dalí and Gala marry in the Church. The ceremony takes place at the sanctuary Els Àngels located in Sant Martí Vell, Girona, Spain.

1960

November–January: His work is included in *Surrealist Intrusion in the Enchanters' Domain* in New York, a Surrealist group exhibition, which causes a scandal within Surrealism. In response, the Surrealists publish the tract 'We Don't Ear it that Way' in protest against Dalí.
December–January: Solo exhibition at Carstairs Gallery in New York.

1963

November–December: Solo exhibition at Knoedler Gallery in New York.

1964

April: Participates in the Galerie Charpentier's *Le Surrealism: Sources, Histoire, Affinities* exhibition in Paris.

1965

November–February: Solo exhibition at Huntington Hartford's Gallery of Modern Art in New York, the largest since The Museum of Modern Art's 1941 exhibition.
December: Solo exhibition at Knoedler Gallery in New York.

1967

November: His exhibition *Hommage à Meissonier* features his painting *Tuna Fishing* [382] at the hotel Le Meurice in Paris.

1969

January: Solo exhibition with Galería René Metras in Barcelona.

1970

March–April: He has an important solo exhibition covering his last five years of work at the Knoedler Gallery in New York.

1972

April–May: Solo exhibition at Knoedler Gallery in New York, which includes his new works in holography.

1974

28 September: Inaugurates his Teatre-Museu Dalí in Figueres, Spain.

1979

December–April: Significant retrospective exhibition at the Centre Pompidou in Paris for which Dalí designs many elements of the exhibition installation.

1982

7 March: The Salvador Dalí Museum opens in St. Petersburg, Florida, US.
10 June: Dalí's wife Gala dies.

1983

Paints his last works. Thereafter, Parkinson's disease prevents him from painting.

1989

23 January: Dalí dies and is buried a few days later in the Teatre-Museu in Figueres, Spain.

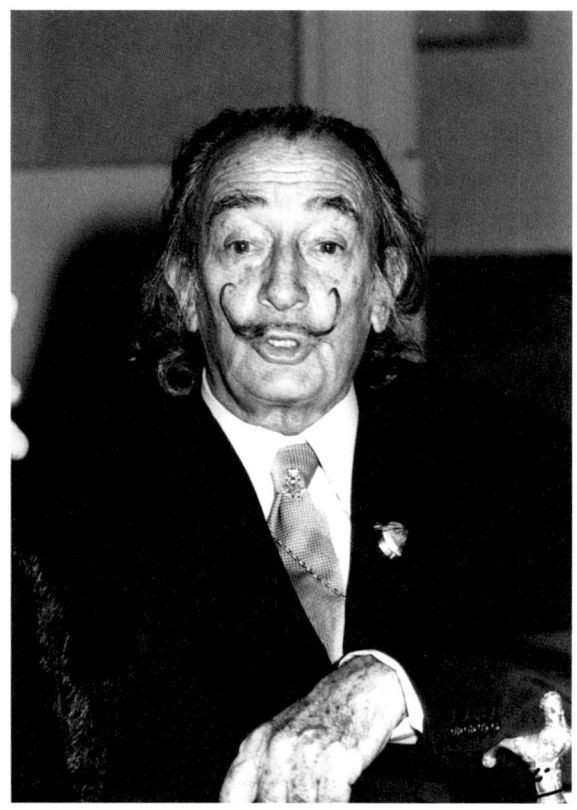

Meliton Casals (photographer), Dalí at a press conference, n.d.
Collection of The Dalí Museum.

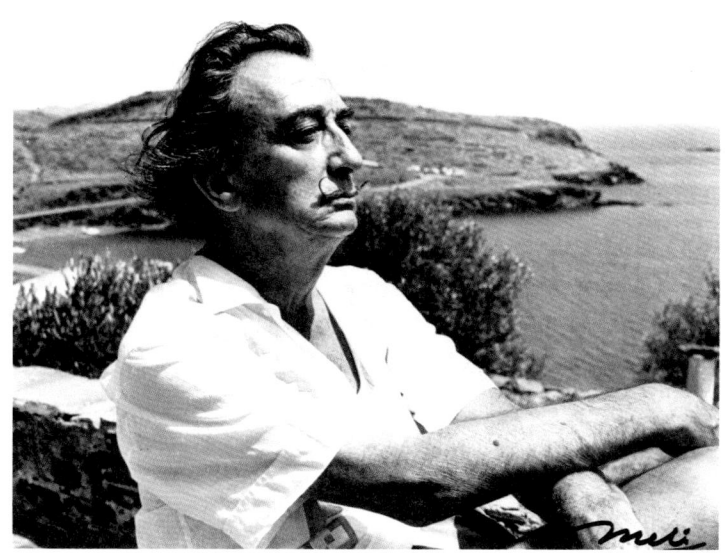

Meliton Casals (photographer), Dalí in Portlligat, Spain. Collection of The Dalí Museum.

List of Works

Colophon

Text and image selection
William Jeffett

Editing
Sarah Auld

Coordination and image research
Ruth Ruyffelaere

Graphic design
Dylan Van Elewyck

Printing
Graphius

D/2025/6328/1
ISBN 978-94-6478-114-4

Cover: *The Persistence of Memory*, 1931 [142] (detail)

Photography
© the photographers
p. 65 © Bridgeman Images
p. 323 © Pictorial Press Ltd/Alamy Stock Photo
pp. 442 and 481 © Descharnes & Descharnes sarl 2025
p. 478 © Philippe Halsman Estate 2025

First published in 2025.

The publisher wishes to thank The Dalí Museum in St. Petersburg for its support in the realisation of this publication.

Also available in the same series:

Magritte in 400 Images
Text by Julie Waseige
ISBN 978-94-9303-916-2

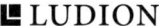

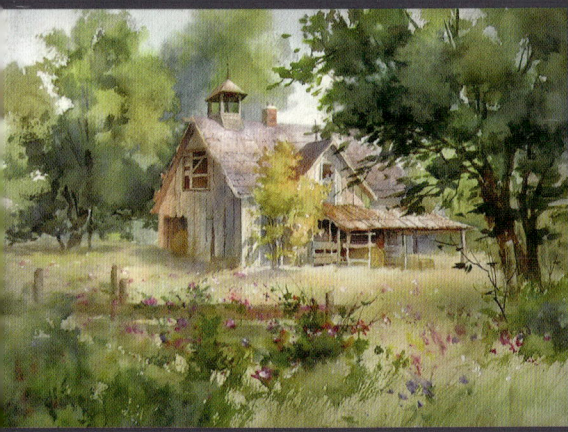

WATERCOLOR ARTIST'S INDEX

Natural
Landscape

A Field Trip of Features
and How to Paint Them

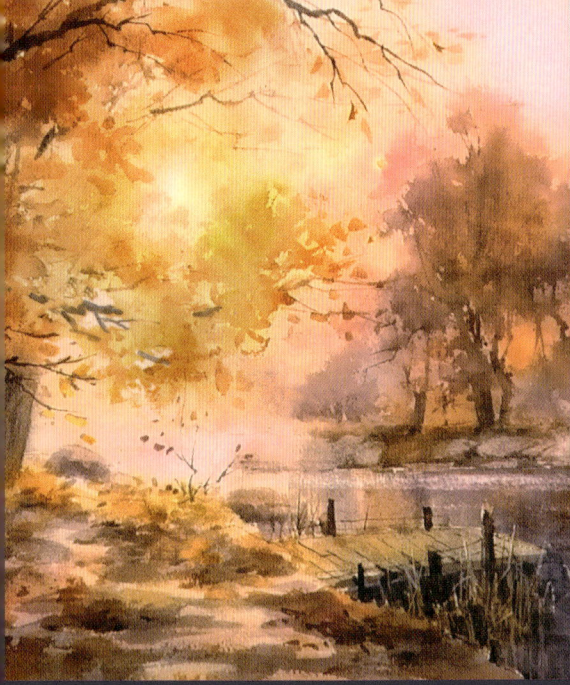

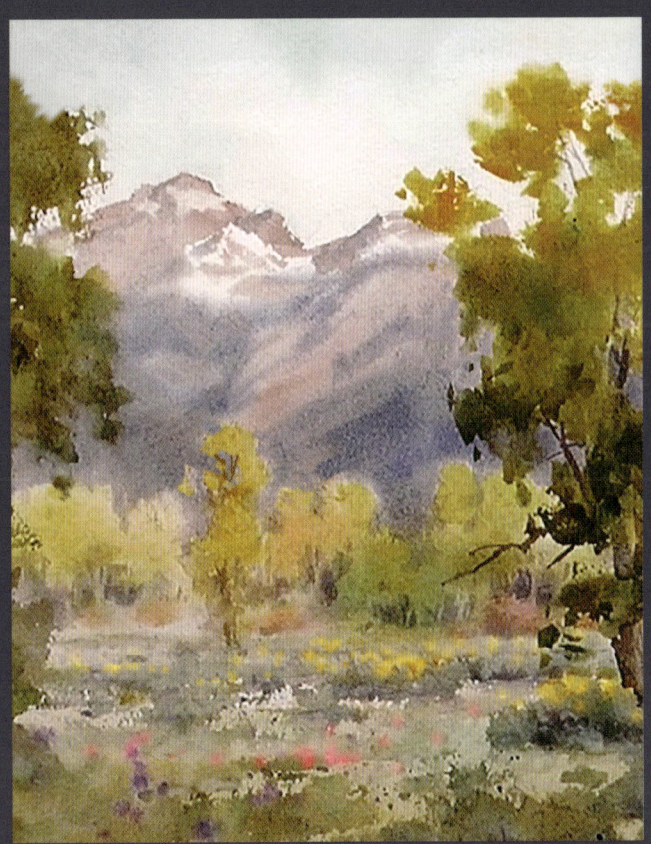

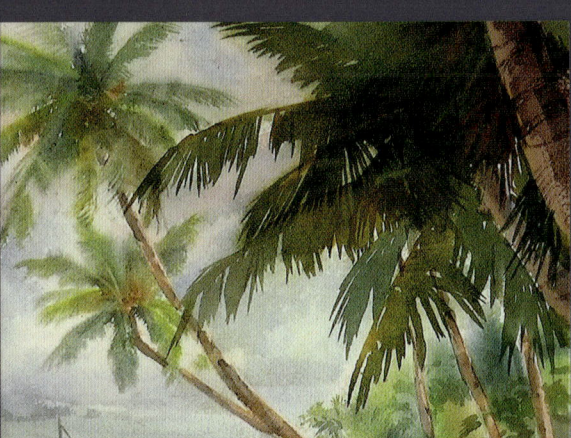

JOHANNES VLOOTHUIS